A Companion to Hume

Blackwell Companions to Philosophy

This outstanding student reference series offers a comprehensive and authoritative survey of philosophy as a whole. Written by today's leading philosophers, each volume provides lucid and engaging coverage of the key figures, terms, topics, and problems of the field. Taken together, the volumes provide the ideal basis for course use, representing an unparalleled work of reference for students and specialists alike.

A Companion
to Hume

Edited by
Elizabeth S. Radcliffe

© 2008 by Blackwell Publishing Ltd

BLACKWELL PUBLISHING
350 Main Street, Malden, MA 02148-5020, USA
9600 Garsington Road, Oxford OX4 2DQ, UK
550 Swanston Street, Carlton, Victoria 3053, Australia

The right of Elizabeth S. Radcliffe to be identified as the author of the editorial material in this Work has been asserted in accordance with the UK Copyright, Designs, and Patents Act 1988.

First published 2008 by Blackwell Publishing Ltd

1   2008

Library of Congress Cataloging-in-Publication Data

A companion to Hume / edited by Elizabeth S. Radcliffe.
      p. cm. — (Blackwell companions to philosophy)
   Includes bibliographical references and index.
   ISBN-13: 978-1-4051-1455-4 (hardcover : alk. paper)   1. Hume, David, 1711-1776.
I. Radcliffe, Elizabeth Schmidt, 1955–

   B1498.C66 2007
   192—dc22

                                                                            2007038434

A catalogue record for this title is available from the British Library.

Set in 10/12.5pt Photina
by Graphicraft Limited, Hong Kong
Printed and bound in Singapore by C.O.S. Printers Pte Ltd

The publisher's policy is to use permanent paper from mills that operate a sustainable forestry policy, and which has been manufactured from pulp processed using acid-free and elementary chlorine-free practices. Furthermore, the publisher ensures that the text paper and cover board used have met acceptable environmental accreditation standards.

For further information on
Blackwell Publishing, visit our website:
www.blackwellpublishing.com

Contents

Notes on Contributors

Kate Abramson specializes in contemporary ethics and early modern philosophy, with a particular focus on Hume's ethics. Her articles have appeared in various collections and journals. She was a 2003–4 recipient of an ACLS sabbatical grant, and a fellowship from the Rockefeller Center for Human Values at Princeton University, and thanks both organizations for support in completing her contribution to this volume. At the time this volume was being sent to press, she was working on completion of a book on the evolution of Hume's philosophical ethics over the course of his lifetime, *The Artifice of Nature in Hume's Moral Theory: From Philosopher to Reflective Man*.

Donald C. Ainslie is Associate Professor and Chair in the Department of Philosophy at the University of Toronto. He has written on Hume's conception of the self as it relates to his skepticism and to his moral philosophy. He is currently finishing a book project entitled, *Hume's Bundle: Scepticism and Self-consciousness in the "Treatise"*. He has also published widely in bioethics.

Annette C. Baier was educated at the universities of Otago and Oxford. She writes on Hume, and on trust-centered ethics. She taught at the Universities of Aberdeen, Auckland, Sydney, and Pittsburgh. In retirement she lives in her native New Zealand.

Tom L. Beauchamp is Professor of Philosophy at Georgetown University. He is one of three editors of the Clarendon Hume, a critical edition of the works of David Hume being published by Clarendon Press, Oxford. He has himself issued three volumes in the series. He also publishes in the field of biomedical ethics.

Martin Bell is Professor of History of Philosophy at Manchester Metropolitan University. He has published a number of book chapters and journal articles on Hume's philosophy, and edited Hume's *Dialogues concerning Natural Religion* for Penguin Classics.

John Bricke, Professor of Philosophy at the University of Kansas, has published essays and reviews on topics in eighteenth-century British philosophy, especially Hume, in philosophy of mind, and in moral philosophy. He is author of *Hume's Philosophy of Mind* (1980) and of *Mind and Morality: An Examination of Hume's Moral Psychology* (1996).

Janet Broughton is Professor of Philosophy at the University of California, Berkeley. Her main research interests lie in the history of seventeenth- and eighteenth-century philosophy; her book *Descartes's Method of Doubt* was published in 2002.

Charlotte R. Brown is Associate Professor of Philosophy, Illinois Wesleyan University. She is the author of articles on Hume's moral theory and theory of the passions and on the British moralists.

Stephen Buckle is Senior Lecturer in Philosophy at Australian Catholic University, Sydney. He has previously held positions at the University of Sydney, Monash, and La Trobe Universities (Melbourne), and the University of Essex. He is the author of *Natural Law and the Theory of Property: Grotius to Hume* (1991) and *Hume's Enlightenment Tract* (2001).

Rachel Cohon is Associate Professor of Philosophy at the University at Albany, State University of New York. She is the author of numerous articles about Hume's moral and political philosophy and also articles about reasons for action. She is the editor of *Hume: Moral and Political Philosophy* (2001). Her new book is *Hume's Morality: Feeling and Fabrication*.

Francis Watanabe Dauer received his AB from Dartmouth College (majoring both in philosophy and mathematics) and MA and PhD in philosophy from Harvard University. He has been a member of the Philosophy Department at UCSB since 1967 (Professor Emeritus since 2002). He has written in a number of areas and his publications on Hume include articles in *Noûs* (on causation), *The Philosophical Review* (on induction), *Hume Studies* (on skepticism with regard to reason, and on force and vivacity), and *Ratio* (on induction).

Richard H. Dees is Associate Professor of Philosophy at the University of Rochester. His Hume scholarship has focused on the relationship of the *History* to Hume's social, political, moral, and religious philosophy. He is also author of numerous articles on the philosophical foundations of toleration, including one book, *Trust and Toleration* (2004).

Don Garrett is Professor of Philosophy at New York University. He is the author of *Cognition and Commitment in Hume's Philosophy* (1997) and the editor of *The Cambridge Companion to Spinoza* (1996). He has also served as co-editor of *Hume Studies* and as North American editor of *Archiv für Geschichte der Philosophie*.

P. J. E. Kail was British Academy Post-doctoral Research Fellow with the Faculty of Philosophy, Cambridge, and then Lecturer in Philosophy at the University of Edinburgh. He is now a Fellow of St. Peter's College, Oxford, and a University Lecturer. His research interests included the notion of projection, Hume's causal realism, Berkeley, and Nietzsche.

Eugenio Lecaldano is Professor of Moral Philosophy in the Faculty of Philosophy at the University of Rome, La Sapienza, and Director of their Master of Practical Ethics and Bioethics program. He is author of several books, including *Hume e la nascita dell'etica contemporanea* (1991, 1998, 2003). He did the first Italian translations of Hume's *Treatise* (Bari, 1972) and the Italian edition of *David Hume, Collected Philosophical Works* in 2 volumes (1972), in addition to translations and Italian editions of the work of Smith, Bentham, and Mill.

Michael P. Levine is Professor of Philosophy at the University of Western Australia. Recent publications include *Integrity and the Fragile Self* (co-authored); *The Analytic Freud* (editor); *Racism in Mind* (co-editor) and articles on moral psychology, social and political philosophy, metaphysics, and film. He is currently writing on architecture and ethics and on religion and violence.

Louis E. Loeb is Professor of Philosophy at the University of Michigan, Ann Arbor. He is the author of *Stability and Justification in Hume's "Treatise"* and *From Descartes to Hume: Continental Metaphysics and the Development of Modern Philosophy*. His articles explore Hume's second thoughts about personal identity, his treatment of necessary connection, and the doctrine of the narrow circle in Hume's moral philosophy. Professor Loeb's work on Descartes focuses on the problem of the Cartesian circle, dissimulation in the *Meditations*, and mind–body interaction.

Tito Magri is Full Professor of Philosophy at the University of Rome, La Sapienza. His work on Hume has focused on the theory of motivation and of reasons for acting, on the theory of justice, and on the evolutionary aspects of Hume's philosophy. He is currently preparing a study of the role of imagination in Hume's philosophy of mind.

Michel Malherbe is Professor Emeritus of Philosophy at the University of Nantes. He has published books on Hume, Hobbes, d'Alembert, and editions of d'Alembert, Condillac, and Hume, whose works he has translated into French.

William Edward Morris is Chair of the Philosophy Department and Director of the Program in Cognitive Science at Illinois Wesleyan University. He was an editor of *Hume Studies* from 1993 to 2000, and publishes frequently on topics in Hume's epistemology.

Terence Penelhum is Professor Emeritus of Religious Studies at the University of Calgary, Canada. He and his wife, whom he wants to thank for collaboration in his essay here, were fellow-students at Edinburgh many years before it erected a statue to Hume. His writings include *Religion and Rationality* (1971), *God and Skepticism* (1983), and *Themes in Hume* (2000).

Mark Salber Phillips is Professor of History at Carleton University. He is the author of numerous books and articles on the historical thought of both the Renaissance and the Enlightenment, including *Society and Sentiment: Genres of Historical Writing in Britain, 1740–1820* (2000). He is currently completing a study of the problem of "distance" in historical writing.

Elizabeth S. Radcliffe is Professor of Philosophy at Santa Clara University. She has published on the British Moralists and on Hume's metaethics and motivational psychology. She was co-editor of the journal *Hume Studies*, with Kenneth Winkler, from 2000 until 2005. She is currently working on issues surrounding the contemporary Humean theory of motivation and its connection to Hume.

Tatsuya Sakamoto is Professor of History of Social Thought at Keio University, Tokyo, Japan. His Hume studies have focused on the place of Hume in the Scottish Enlightenment with an emphasis on his contribution to the making of modern social sciences and in particular to the rise of political economy. Besides numerous articles both in Japanese and English, his publications include two books, *David Hume's*

Civilized Society (in Japanese, 1995) and *The Rise of Political Economy in the Scottish Enlightenment*, edited with H. Tanaka (2003).

Nicholas L. Sturgeon is Professor of Philosophy at Cornell University. Besides writing on Hume and on Joseph Butler, he has published on issues in contemporary metaethics.

Jacqueline Taylor teaches in the Philosophy Department at the University of San Francisco. She has written numerous articles on Hume's moral psychology and moral philosophy. She has also written on contemporary Humean ethics.

Saul Traiger is Professor of Philosophy at Occidental College in Los Angeles, California. He is the past president of the Hume Society and has published numerous articles and reviews on Hume's metaphysics and epistemology, as well as articles in contemporary epistemology, philosophy of mind, and the foundations of cognitive science. He is the editor of *The Blackwell Guide to Hume's "Treatise."*

Wayne Waxman is an independent scholar who has taught at the New School for Social Research, Princeton, Yale, and NYU. He is the author of *Kant's Model of the Mind* (1991), *Hume's Theory of Consciousness* (1994), and *Kant and the Empiricists* (2005).

Acknowledgments

I extend thanks to M. A. Stewart and, especially, to Tom Beauchamp, for correspondence and advice in the early stages of assembling this volume. I am indebted to Jeff Dean, Danielle Descoteaux, and Jamie Harlan of Blackwell Publishing, for their encouragement and support during production. They are a fantastically efficient and pleasant team to work with. I also thank Graeme Leonard for his expert manuscript editing. I want to acknowledge the Office of the Provost at Santa Clara University for financial assistance in the creation of the index. Finally, I am very grateful to Richard McCarty for his editing help and his support in very many important ways during the years in which this book was in process.

Note on Citations

Since references to Hume's *A Treatise of Human Nature, An Enquiry concerning Human Understanding*, and *An Enquiry concerning the Principles of Morals* are used in almost every article in this volume, these works do not appear in the bibliographies of the individual articles. Authors are citing the Oxford editions of the *Treatise* and the *Enquiries* in the body of their essays. These works are cited according to the now-standard referencing system, explained below. Any other abbreviations to historical works used in the body of these essays are explained in the bibliographies of the individual chapters in which the abbreviations are used. The use of italics in quoted texts occurs in the originals unless otherwise noted.

Hume David (1739–40). *A Treatise of Human Nature*, ed. David Fate Norton and Mary J. Norton (New York: Oxford University Press, 2000).

* Cited as T by Book, part, section, and paragraph numbers.
* Introduction cited as "T Introduction" or "T Intro." by paragraph number.
* Appendix cited as "T App." by paragraph number.
* Abstract cited as "T Abstract" or "T Abs." by paragraph number.

Hume, David (1748). *An Enquiry concerning Human Understanding*, ed. Tom Beauchamp (Oxford: Clarendon Press, 2000).

* Cited as EHU by section and paragraph number.

Hume, David (1751). *An Enquiry concerning the Principles of Morals*, ed. Tom Beauchamp (Oxford: Clarendon Press, 1998).

* Cited as EPM by section and paragraph number.
* Appendices cited as "EPM App." by appendix number and paragraph number.
* "A Dialogue" (Hume's essay at the end of EPM) cited by paragraph number.

Introduction

ELIZABETH S. RADCLIFFE

David Hume's public life as a philosopher and an intellectual began with the publication of the first two books of *A Treatise of Human Nature* in 1739 when he was only 28 years old. The third book appeared a year later. Although scarce notice was taken of his work at the time, Hume's approach to philosophy was revolutionary. In his Introduction to the *Treatise* and in the abstract of that work, Hume compares his investigations to that of some recent writers who had been applying the new methods of the seventeenth-century natural philosopher, Francis Bacon, to "the science of man." Bacon recognized the proper roles of observation and reason in the study of natural phenomena, and he was among the first to formulate a method of inquiry designed to guard against fallacious reasoning due to social and personal biases. Bacon is regarded as one of the important contributors to the development of the modern scientific method. Likewise, Hume adopts an empirical approach to his study of human nature – but with results dramatically different from those near-contemporaries, John Locke and Francis Hutcheson, whom he cites as allies in this method.

In his lifetime, Hume went on to publish works that received more attention than the *Treatise*: political essays, social commentaries, a history of England, and a reformulation of his theories from the *Treatise* in his two famous books, *An Essay concerning Human Understanding* and *An Essay concerning the Principles of Morals*. As a consequence of his arguments, Hume was accused of skepticism, atheism, and moral corruption – positions whose attribution to Hume is largely due to oversimplifications and misunderstandings of his views. His *Dialogues concerning Natural Religion*, begun around 1751 and revised up until his death in 1776, was thought too controversial to publish in his lifetime. However, from the perspective of almost three centuries later, even Hume's staunchest critics admit that the breadth of Hume's thought is only matched by the genius of his arguments. Twenty-first-century scholars who study Hume's ideas are interested in his theories for much more than the significant role they played in Enlightenment thinking. Contemporary philosophers are also interested in the lasting impact of Hume's thought on philosophy of mind, knowledge, religion, action, morality, economics, and politics.

This volume is an attempt to represent the range of Hume's ideas and the ongoing debates to which his arguments have given rise. It is an attempt at the same time to show how recent close and thoughtful readings of Hume's work lead to very different

1

conclusions about the goals and results of his projects from some readings earlier considered standard. I will say more about the debates in Hume interpretation and the contents of this volume later. I begin with a bit about the philosopher himself and his writings. The following is drawn from two well-known Hume biographies, J. Y. T. Greig's *David Hume* and E. C. Mossner's *The Life of David Hume*, plus recent essays by M. A. Stewart and Roger Emerson. The biographers' accounts of Hume's life reveal a man who in his younger years was intense about his beliefs and rigorous in his thinking; and who cared about his literary reputation, but not at the cost of his commitment to reasoned inquiry and intellectual honesty. He was a man with many friends who regarded him with great affection, and he repaid them with deep loyalty. He was passionately opposed to the atrocities committed in the name of institutional religion. He understood the sometimes-odd tension between philosophy and ordinary life, and expressed in his writing the need to emerge from the abstruse thinking of the study to become involved in the social affairs of common life.

Hume's Life

David Hume was born in Edinburgh, Scotland, on April 26, 1711 to the lawyer Joseph Home and his wife Katherine Falconer, the daughter of Joseph's stepmother by a previous marriage. Joseph died only two years later, and Katherine raised David and his older brother and sister on the family estate at Ninewells and at their Edinburgh townhouse. The family was not wealthy, but they were moderately comfortable. The children were raised as Scottish Presbyterians and subjected to the rigors of all-day Sunday rituals. As a boy, David took religion very seriously and extracted a list of vices from the seventeenth-century devotional book, *The Whole Duty of Man*, with which he challenged himself. Among the vices noted there were: "not arranging any solemn time for humiliation and confession," "making pleasure, not health, the end of eating," and "wasting the time or estate in good fellowship."

Hume (still "Home" at the time) undertook four years of study at what was then Edinburgh College, starting at age 10 (some biographies say he was 12, but see Stewart 2005: 17). As was common then, he completed the course but did not take a degree. Some years later he could not see the benefits of a college education and expressed the view that college professors had nothing to offer that could not be found in books (Stewart 2005: 25). David's family expected him to be a lawyer, but his later attempt to study law floundered because he had no interest in it. He writes, "The Law, which was the Business I design'd to follow, appear'd nauseous to me, & I could think of no other way of pushing my Fortune in the World, but that of a Scholar & Philosopher" (Hume's Letters, Greig 1932: i. 13). From the years 1725–9, David is said to have spent his time in solemn reflection and independent study, reading philosophers like Clarke, Locke, Butler, and Berkeley, at which time he seems to have reasoned himself out of religious belief (Mossner 1980: 51, 64; Greig 1931: 72). It also is during this time that he developed some of the philosophical views identified with the empiricism for which he was to become famous. In 1729, he was taken ill by a depression that would linger for four years. He was said to become "lean and raw-boned" and was diagnosed by a doctor, probably facetiously, as having "the disease of the learned." The doctor prescribed anti-hysteric pills and bitters, a daily pint of English claret, exercise on horseback and warned him against isolation. Stewart conjectures that this period was one of religious crisis for Hume and that while he attempted to put his philosophical deliberations in a theistic framework, it was impossible for him to succeed (pp. 30–1).

In 1734, at age 23, David broke from his family home at last and went to France, settling in a country retreat at LaFleche. It is at this time, speculates J. Y. T. Greig, that David changed his name to "Hume" (which matched its pronunciation), possibly to signal a break with his past (p. 90). He regularly visited the Jesuit College at LaFleche and engaged some of the Jesuits in conversations. It was during his three years in LaFleche that Hume wrote the manuscript of *A Treatise of Human Nature*, regarded now by some contemporary scholars – although not by Hume himself – as his richest work. *A Treatise of Human Nature* divides into three books; Book 1, "Of the Understanding," and Book 2, "Of the Passions," were published together in 1739. Book 3, "Of Morals," appeared in 1740. The three books were published anonymously. Hume later writes of the unenthusiastic public reception of the *Treatise*, "It fell *dead-born from the Press*" (Hume 1777). It did not sell well, but a few people read it and often misunderstood it. In later years, Hume tried to disown it, leading critics to speculate why – a genuine change of views or wounded pride at being associated with a public failure? Stewart argues:

> If there was a humiliation [in the reaction to the *Treatise*] . . . his [Hume's] own judgement appears to concur with the predominant view of posterity, that it was literary rather than philosophical. He has not overtly retracted any significant body of his philosophy. (Stewart 2005: 54)

This does not entail that there was no modification or maturing of views. Little did Hume know that this work would have a place in history as the most systematic presentation of philosophical empiricism and one of the most prominent works in the whole canon of western philosophy. Despite his disappointment, Hume persisted, and in 1741–2, he published, anonymously again, two volumes of essays, *Essays Moral and Political*, which got a much warmer reaction.

When Hume applied two years later for the vacant chair in Moral Philosophy at the University of Edinburgh, his authorship of the *Treatise* and the views he expressed were now more widely known. Political, ideological and philosophical factors undermined Hume's appointment (Emerson 1995: 4). Hume complained of accusations of "Heresy, Deism, Scepticism, Atheism, etc." (Hume in Greig 1932: i. 57). Popular opinion and much of the professoriate were against Hume's appointment. Francis Hutcheson, a Presbyterian minister who occupied the Glasgow Chair of Moral Philosophy from 1730 until his death in 1746, had corresponded civilly with Hume, but even he recommended seven other men he thought more suitable (Emerson 1995: 10). Ironically, the Town Council elected Hutcheson himself to the Edinburgh Chair, but Hutcheson declined it.

At some point in the interval up to 1748, Hume rewrote the first book of his *Treatise*, making it into a work more accessible to the public, which he called *Philosophical Essays concerning Human Understanding* and published in 1748. He included with it his religiously inflammatory essays "Of Miracles" and "Of a Particular Providence and of a Future State." The title of the book was changed ten years later to *An Enquiry Concerning Human Understanding*. His rewriting of *Treatise* Book 3, *An Enquiry Concerning the Principles of Morals*, came in 1751, and critics still consider whether the differences between it and the *Treatise* signal any changes in Hume's moral philosophy (see more on this below).

Hume left Ninewells permanently in 1751, moving to Edinburgh, where he resided for seven years. Hume was once again denied a university post, this time at Glasgow University, in 1752. He was, however, appointed Keeper of the Advocates' Library, Edinburgh, and published *The History of England* in six volumes, from 1754 to 1762. The appearance of the first volume was greeted with harsh criticism, and Hume writes of his disappointment:

> I thought, I was the only Historian, that had at once neglected present Power, Interest, and Authority, and the Cry of Popular Prejudices; and as the Subject was suited to every Capacity, I expected proportional Applause: But miserable was my Disappointment: I was assailed by one Cry of Reproach, Disapprobation, and even Detestation . . .
>
> I was . . . I confess, discouraged; and had not the War been at that time breaking out between France and England, I had certainly retired to some provincial Town of the former Kingdom, have changed my Name, and never more have returned to my native Country. (Hume 1777)

However, within ten years of publication, Hume's *History* became very popular. For about ten years from 1752, Hume served as co-secretary of Edinburgh's Philosophical Society.

Hume's essays on suicide and the immortality of the soul were completed around 1755, and they were printed with three other essays as part of a book called *Five Dissertations*. The collection included "The Natural History of Religion," which traced the psychological origins of religious belief. After printing, some advance copies were circulated before the book was officially to appear, and the outrage on the part of some clerics and politicians at Hume's critique of theological arguments against suicide, of belief in immortality, and of other religious beliefs caused a change of publication plans. Hume, perhaps partly coerced by his publisher, agreed to excise the two essays, physically, from the copies already in print. They were replaced with the essay, "Of the Standard of Taste," and the book appeared in 1757 as *Four Dissertations*. Secret copies of the two withdrawn essays appeared anonymously in French (1770) and later, after Hume's death, in English.

At age 50, Hume resolved to stay in Scotland and pursue his career as writer and philosopher, but in 1763, an appointment to the position of Secretary to the Embassy in Paris lured him away. The French greatly admired David, and he remained in Paris until 1766. An interlude in Hume's life that has proven the subject of much discussion among historians is his brief and tumultuous relationship with French writer and political theorist Jean-Jacques Rousseau. Rousseau was living in France under persecution and in poverty because of harsh criticisms of the imprudent views expressed in his writings. Rousseau had a reputation for being demanding, and he was unduly suspicious of his benefactors. However, Hume, in sympathy with Rousseau's situation, offered to settle him in the English countryside outside of London and give him financial help. Rousseau eventually took the offer, and Hume was pleased to accompany him to England. Within months of their arrival in January 1766, the irrational Rousseau concluded that Hume brought him to England in order to carry out an international conspiracy against him, a charge with which he went public. Hume felt eventually pushed to defend himself and published first in Paris in October, and then in London in the next month, his narrative, *A Concise and Genuine Account of the Dispute between Mr. Hume and Mr. Rousseau; with the Letters that Passed between Them during their Controversy.* All evidence points to the conclusion that Hume was innocent of Rousseau's accusations and that Rousseau suffered from deep paranoia.

In 1767, Hume accepted an invitation to become under-secretary of state in London. However, because he had sympathies with the American colonies, it was not an ideal appointment for him. He wrote: "I am an American in my Principles, and wish we would let them alone to govern or misgovern themselves as they think proper" (Hume in Greig 1932: ii. 303–6). Still he kept the post for a year and then retired to Edinburgh and built a house in St. Andrews Square, where Ben Franklin was among his first house guests.

Beginning around 1772, Hume's health started slowly to decline. Within a few years he showed symptoms of an intestinal disorder, perhaps the same from which his mother died, and doctors debated whether his malady was of the colon or the liver. One of Hume's concerns was to insure that his *Dialogues concerning Natural Religion*, which he had written twenty-five years earlier, revised twice, and to which he added a paragraph in his last few weeks, be published after his death. Hume thought that by willing all of his manuscripts to his good friend, Adam Smith, author of *The Wealth of Nations*, the *Dialogues* would be published. Because of the provocative nature of the book, which criticizes the foundations of some traditional religious beliefs, Smith was indecisive. Hume contemplated a private printing of the book before he died, but his deteriorating health prevented him. So, he added a codicil to his will, specifying that his publisher should bring out the *Dialogues* within two years of his death; furthermore, if the *Dialogues* were not published within two-and-a-half years, they should pass to his nephew, David, who would arrange for their publication.

Biographers write that Hume's last days were serene ones. He invited friends to a farewell dinner on July 4, 1776. Hume was unaware that this was also the day on which the American Declaration of Independence was being signed in Philadelphia. Mossner remarks that, unlike most of his friends, Hume would have been pleased to hear the news when it reached Edinburgh a few days before his death (p. 596). Hume also had visits from acquaintances who tried to convert him to some form of religious belief or another. One notable visitor was James Boswell, who grilled Hume about possible covert hopes for an afterlife. Hume, however, stood on his philosophical convictions and claimed to be no more distressed at the thought of his passing out of existence than he would be at the thought that he had never existed at all. Boswell writes, "The truth is that Mr. Hume's pleasantry was such that there was no solemnity in the scene; and Death for the time did not seem dismal. It surprised me to find him talking of different matters with a tranquility of mind and a clearness of head, which few men possess at any time" (Boswell 1928–34: xii, 227–32).

5

David Hume died on August 25, 1776. In 1779, David's nephew saw to the publication of *The Dialogues concerning Natural Religion*. In 1783 the two suppressed essays were published with Hume's name attached. Along with the two essays, the anonymous editor of the 1783 edition included his own critical notes to Hume's two pieces, and excerpts from Rousseau's *La Nouvelle Heloise*, on the subject of suicide. The title page read,

> ESSAYS ON SUICIDE, AND THE IMMORTALITY OF THE SOUL, ASCRIBED TO THE LATE DAVID HUME, Esq. Never before published. With REMARKS, intended as an Antidote to the Poison contained in these Performances, BY THE EDITOR. TO WHICH IS ADDED, TWO LETTERS ON SUICIDE, From Rousseau's Eloisa. (Fieser 1995)

The event of this publication, however, was hardly the last time readers would pay attention to the writings of David Hume.

A Chronology of Hume's Significant Published Writings

1739   Books 1 and 2 of *A Treatise of Human Nature*

1740   Book 3 of *A Treatise of Human Nature*

1740   An *Abstract* of a Book Lately Published (abstract of the *Treatise*)

1741–2   *Essays Moral and Political* (in 2 volumes)

Volume 1 contains: (1) Of the Delicacy of Taste and Passion; (2) Of the Liberty of the Press; (3) Of Impudence and Modesty; (4) That Politicks may be Reduce'd to a Science; (5) Of the First Principles of Government; (6) Of Love and Marriage; (7) Of the Study of History; (8) Of the Independency of Parliament; (9) Whether the British Government inclines more to Absolute Monarchy, or to a Republick; (10) Of Parties in General; (11) Of the Parties of Great Britain; (12) Of Superstition and Enthusiasm; (13) Of Avarice; (14) Of the Dignity of Human Nature; (15) Of Liberty and Despotism. Volume 2 contains: (1) Of Essay-writing; (2) Of Eloquence; (3) of Moral Prejudices; (4) Of the Middle Station of Life; (5) Of the Rise and Progress of the Arts and Sciences; (6) The Epicurean; (7) The Stoic; (8) The Platonist; (9) The Sceptic; (10) Of Polygamy and Divorces; (11) Of Simplicity and Refinement; (12) A Character of Sir Robert Walpole. Added in 1748 edition: "Of National Characters."

1748   *An Enquiry concerning Human Understanding*

First published as *Philosophical Essays concerning Human Understanding*

1751   *An Enquiry concerning the Principles of Morals*

1752   *Political Discourses*

Contains: (1) Of Commerce, (2) Of Luxury, (3) Of Money, (4) Of Interest, (5) Of the Balance of Trade, (6) Of the Balance of Power, (7) Of Taxes, (8) Of Public Credit, (9) Of Some Remarkable Customs, (10) Of the Populousness of Antient Nations, (11) Of the Protestant Succession, (12) Idea of a Perfect Commonwealth.

1753   *Essays and Treatises on Several Subjects*

Brings together previously published works: (1) *Essays Moral and Political*, (2) *Philosophical Essays concerning Human Understanding*, (3) *An Enquiry concerning the Principles of Morals*, and (4) *Political Discourses*.

1754–62   *History of England* (in 6 volumes)

1757   *Four Dissertations*

The original collection, usually called *Five Dissertations*, contained these five pieces: (1) The Natural History of Religion, (2) Of the Passions, (3) Of Tragedy, (4) Of Suicide, (5) Of the Immortality of the Soul. When the last two essays were physically removed from the printed versions, Hume added "Of the Standard of Taste," and the book was then titled *Four Dissertations*.

1758   *Essays Moral, Political and Literary*

Essays Moral and Political combined with *Political Discourses*. Essays added in 1758 edition: "Of the Original Contract" and "Of Passive Obedience" (taken from *Three Essays*, 1748). Essays added in 1760 edition: "Of Jealousy of Trade" and "Of the Coalition of Parties" (also published as *Two Additional Essays*, 1758). Added in 1777 edition: "Of the Origin of Government."

1777   "My Own Life"

Hume's brief autobiography written in 1776, shortly before his death in August of 1776.

1779   *Dialogues concerning Natural Religion*

Hume began working on the *Dialogues concerning Natural Religion* around 1751. The main revisions of the work occurred between then and around 1757. He did some further revisions in 1761 and one significant paragraph was altered two or three weeks before his death.

1783   *Essays on Suicide and Immortality*

These essays were removed from *Five Dissertations*. A manuscript copy of the essays circulated. A somewhat corrupted version of the two essays appeared in 1777; this was more widely reprinted in 1783 with critical commentary.

The Themes and Authors in this Volume

This volume is organized topically, rather than by work, to reflect the array of topics on which Hume wrote and to explore each one individually. The emphasis is on Hume's philosophy, although his work as a historian is represented as well. The first three parts of the volume roughly follow the organization of *A Treatise of Human Nature* and its three books, on knowledge, the passions, and morality. Hume returned to some of these themes later in his two *Enquiries*, so the discussions in many of the essays here contain references to both the *Treatise* and the *Enquiries*. The fourth part is devoted to Hume's views on religious belief, a theme in many of his works, but most prominent in the *Dialogues concerning Natural Religion*. The fifth part, on Hume's economics, politics, and historical writings, draws from many of his works, but notably from his *Essays Moral and Political*, his *Political Discourses*, and the *History of England*. This volume also includes as its sixth part some critical discussions centered on specific issues of interpretation done in a contemporary vernacular, including essays that show the influence of Hume's theories on contemporary philosophy.

Many of the essays contained here, all original, are written by an emerging generation of Hume scholars, who are now shaping and will continue to influence the understanding of Hume's thought for many years to come. (By no means does it contain essays by all who fit under this description.) At the same time, this book has contributions from a sprinkling of renowned, established scholars whose work has founded a framework for many discussions of Hume in print today. This mix was deliberate. There are also many venerated scholars of Hume whose contributions to the field are beyond estimation and for whose research and expertise we are all in great debt. Their many essays and studies can be found in various prominent volumes that have been published over the years. The influence of scholars such as David Fate Norton and M. A. Stewart (to name just two, at the risk of offending others not named here) has an abiding presence in this volume in both the discussions that depend on their interpretations and in the repeated citations to their published works in the bibliographies found here. I might mention that while I cannot do justice in the short space of this introduction to all of the themes in Hume's writings, David Fate Norton's introduction to his and Mary Norton's Oxford Philosophical Texts edition of Hume's *Treatise* has an excellent overview of Hume's philosophical theories, and Tom Beauchamp's introductions to the Oxford Clarendon Editions of each *Enquiry* offer invaluable background. The Oxford Clarendon Edition (critical edition) of the *Treatise*, edited by the Nortons (2007), has only just appeared at the time of this writing, and it promises to be an essential enduring resource for the scholar.

This *Companion to Hume* opens with Stephen Buckle's essay (ch. 1) situating Hume in the tradition of Enlightenment thinking. The Enlightenment was an era of increasing confidence in the human mind and in the experimental method, an era in which secular values based on nature and notions of social reform were gaining currency. Buckle explains that on stereotypical views of both the Enlightenment and Hume, Hume's theories are only coincident with the period, and he has no essential connection with the trends that were created by the social critics and reformers in France who defined the era. This is because Hume's interests have often been narrowly defined in terms of epistemology and more specifically in terms of epistemological skepticism. Buckle's essay is an excellent starting point for this collection because it corrects this mistaken branding of Hume as a destructive philosopher and opens up discussion to the ways in which Hume held constructive views in many areas – not only in epistemology, but in psychology, ethics, and politics. The theme of Hume as a naturalist, as a philosopher who, Buckle writes, proposes to replace "old metaphysical dreams with a new system of empirical studies which aim at usefulness for human lives" is prominent throughout the papers in this volume.

Mind and Knowledge

The first part, on Mind and Knowledge, starts with a discussion of Hume's theory of ideas, which is the foundation for Hume's philosophical views in almost all arenas

– not only knowledge, but psychology, ethics, and religious belief. Hume calls any content of the mind a "perception." To understand Hume's project is to understand why he distinguishes the contents of the mind on the grounds of their phenomenal "feel," how they feel to us, rather than by the supposed mental processes or external objects that might be the causes of the perceptions: We are immediately aware of the quality of an experience, but not of its cause, whether mental or extramental. So, to begin with something *not* inferred, as an empirical inquiry should, we must start by studying the perceptions themselves.

Don Garrett's essay (ch. 2) examines in detail the most basic distinctions Hume draws among kinds of perceptions and the fundamental principles he identifies describing their operations. Hume divides perceptions into the classes of impressions and ideas. Impressions are the vivid and forceful experiences we have when we see, hear, taste, smell, or touch (impressions of sensation) or when we feel passions such as love, pride, envy, or desire (impressions of reflection, the products of reflecting on the sources of pleasure and pain). Ideas, on the other hand, are the less vivid and less lively mental states we have when we think about the original ones. Garrett's chapter investigates the distinction Hume draws between mental states that are representations of something outside themselves and those that are not, a difference which, Garrett suggests, does not correspond to Hume's basic distinction between ideas and impressions, as some critics have thought. All agree that our ideas represent the objects they are about, but so can sense impressions represent the objects that cause them, Garrett argues, and he explains many senses of representation that can be culled from Hume's discussions. Furthermore, just as physicists can formulate laws of physics to describe the regularities we find in nature, Hume offers principles of the mind to capture all the features of human cognition. Garrett identifies and explains several. These fundamental distinctions and principles articulated in Hume's philosophy of mind have numerous critical implications for the whole of his philosophical system, which are explored in the essays that follow Garrett's.

For instance, impressions return to the mind as ideas, but how we distinguish ideas of memory from those of imagination is an intriguing question in Hume's philosophy, which Saul Traiger (ch. 3) takes up. One way to make the distinction is to say that memory preserves the order of ideas as they came in experience, while imagination does not; however, we have no way of applying such a criterion to make the distinction, since we cannot conjure up the past impressions and compare their order to our present ideas. Instead, Hume says, an idea of memory "retains a considerable degree of its first vivacity, and is somewhat intermediate betwixt an impression and an idea"; an idea of imagination "entirely loses that vivacity, and is a perfect idea" (T 1.1.3). Traiger investigates the quandaries to which Hume's characterization gives rise. Another crucial question is how Hume's principles can account for our acquisition of the ideas of space and time. Wayne Waxman (ch. 4) argues for understanding Hume as employing all three of the natural relations that derive from the three principles of association in his explanation how the ideas of space and time originate in experience.

Hume's system, of course, goes beyond an account of idea acquisition to an analysis of belief formation. Since, as he argues, all beliefs in facts about the world are based on the relation of cause and effect, he offers an analysis of the how the mind originates the causal connection. That analysis, discussed here in Francis Dauer's essay (ch. 5), was one that dramatically changed the way philosophers viewed causality, and those who could not accept Hume's theory were compelled to respond to it (most notably, the German philosopher, Kant). On Hume's theory, one component in our idea of causality is necessary connection, but, Hume shows, the idea of necessity cannot be traced to any impression. Rather, Hume describes the psychological process that produces belief in causal connections this way: The constant conjunction of perceived events produces in us an association of the two perceptions, until the association becomes so strong that we feel a "determination of the mind" to pass from the perception of the first to a thought of the second (an effect of custom and habit). When we reach this point, we posit a necessary connection between the events. Our imagination fills in the gaps in our experience by supplying the notion that the two events are necessarily bound to each other, even though they are experienced distinctly. Dauer considers three interpretations of Hume's analysis that commit him to theses of various strengths about the status and existence of necessity in the world and in laws of nature.

Louis Loeb's essay on induction (ch. 6) continues the discussion of Hume's study of belief: How do we *ever* arrive at beliefs concerning causes and effects, which are supposed to take us beyond present experience, when such beliefs have to be based on present experience? If I can add to my present experience and my memory of past experience a belief that the future will be like the past, then I could formulate an argument with a conclusion about the future. It would go like this: (1) in the past, my experience of fire has been conjoined with the experience of heat; (2) the future will resemble the past; (3) therefore, my experiences of fire and heat will be conjoined in the future. The conclusion gets us to the future, as causal connections should; so it is indicative for us of causality. But, as Hume points out, the second premise is itself based on experience, namely, on experience of past pasts and past futures, and so its justification is circular. This leads to what Loeb labels the traditional interpretation of Hume as an inductive skeptic. Loeb's essay highlights the reasons to doubt this interpretation and offers in its place evidence that Hume thought inductive inference justified.

So far, then, we have Hume's account of how we attribute qualities to objects; but we have no account of how we come to believe that objects exist outside the mind. Causal reasoning can only make correlations between perceptions, and never between external objects and perceptions, so we cannot make an inference to the existence of objects in that way. And this issue is connected with another vexing question: How do I arrive at the idea of myself, or of my mind, as the subject, or possessor, of these perceptions, when all the perceptions in my mind, on which my ideas must be based, are presumably of other objects? These discussions are taken up, respectively, by Michel Malherbe (ch. 7) and Donald Ainslie (ch. 8).

In his analyses, Hume concludes that we have ideas of external objects and of the self (and of other selves), but that these ideas have a special status like that of necessity. The mind does not derive these ideas directly from experience, but by operating on the ideas that do come directly from experience; they are "fictions" the mind creates for the sake of coherence and consistency. As Malherbe points out, Hume's theory of how we come to believe in the existence of bodies (objects) makes for an interesting mix of naturalism and skepticism. Ainslie's article on the self focuses on the interpretative problem Hume's account of personal identity poses. Hume explains in Book 1 of the *Treatise* that our notion of self is a product of our bundling our individual perceptions into a whole because we feel they are unified. However, in a puzzling passage in his Appendix, published a year or so later with Book 3, Hume contends that his own account is mistaken. In what way Hume thinks it is misguided has been the subject of much debate, which Ainslie explores. Ainslie argues for a reading of Hume that retains the bundle theory and instead interprets Hume's concern as one over the explanation of a belief about consciousness: Hume's worry is how we can explain our belief that the ideas in virtue of which we are aware of our own perceptions are themselves part of the same mind as the perceptions we observe within us.

Passions and Action

In his psychology of the passions, Hume distinguishes the direct from the indirect passions. The direct passions are those which arise immediately from reflection on pleasures and pains, without the need to call upon other perceptions. (What this means is more easily explained after we have before us an account of the opposite set, the indirect passions.) The indirect passions are those which are caused in us by reflection on pleasure and pain, but in cooperation with other perceptions.

Hume explains the production of the indirect passions in terms of what he calls a double relation of impressions and ideas. His analysis is explored in careful detail here in an essay by Rachel Cohon (ch. 9). Among the indirect passions are pride, humility, ambition, vanity, love, hatred, envy, pity, malice, and generosity. For instance, when I think of my beautiful pottery, the idea of myself, which I associate with the pottery, transports my mind to the idea of the self that is the object of the passion of pride (an association of ideas); likewise, the pleasure I take in the beautiful quality of the pottery moves my mind along to the similar sensation of pleasure that is essential to pride (an association of impressions). The cause is doubly related to the effect, and both lines of mental association contribute to the generation of the passion of pride. Cohon argues that there is ample evidence to think that Hume's moral sentiments are among the indirect passions as well, even though he never explicitly says so.

The direct passions, on the other hand, occur with no introduction of an idea of self or others; we simply feel a certain way about an object that causes us pleasure or about one that causes us pain. Among the direct passions Hume lists desire, aversion, grief, joy, hope, despair, security, and volition. There are also, however, a few passions that Hume discusses as direct passions that do not arise from perceptions of pleasure and pain. These he identifies as natural impulses or instincts. Among the natural impulses or instincts Hume at one point includes "benevolence and resentment, the love of life, and kindness to children" (T 2.3.3.8) and at another "desire of punishment to our enemies, and of happiness to our friends; hunger, lust, and a few other bodily appetites" (T 2.3.9.8). Some of the passions serve as motives or potential causes to action and some do not.

Tito Magri's essay (ch. 10) develops a reading of Hume's arguments concerning the direct passions in which he uncovers two different theories of motivation in Hume. One depends on the "noncognitive" characterization of the direct passions as feelings that are caused directly by impressions of pleasure and pain, and are themselves causes of

11

action. However, this theory, Magri argues, does not account for the common sense view of conduct and of agency that Hume himself seems to share – one that includes the idea that beliefs motivate action, that agents control their conduct, and that agents consider and choose intrinsic values. Magri shows that Hume suggests another theory of motivation in which our original propensities to certain objects interact with beliefs to produce motives, and argues that in this sense, beliefs motivate. Magri also finds in Hume the materials for an account of practical choice and control over action by appealing to Hume's characterization of the "calm" passions. The calm passions are the reactions we experience when we take a more distant view of things and respond to the greatest possible good or to the general and stable features of objects that make them intrinsically desirable.

The third essay in this part, by John Bricke (ch. 11), takes up Hume's views on determinism and responsibility for action. On Hume's view (and others' as well), if our actions were not necessitated, they would be uncaused, and to be uncaused is to be random and left to chance. So, if we are to be held responsible for our actions, they must be caused, and Hume thinks they are caused by our motives. However, our motives are caused as well. Bricke explores the question how Hume attempts to combine his naturalistic view of a human being as subject to causal laws with the notion of moral responsibility.

Morality and Beauty

Moral philosophers in the seventeenth and eighteenth centuries were engaged in debates over how we derive our moral distinctions: Do we make them by the rational part of our nature or by the sensitive part? Hume's way of putting this question was: "Do we make the distinction between virtue and vice by means of our ideas or by means of our impressions?" Hume thinks our moral evaluations are ultimately about character, even though we can only observe the actions of others, which we then take as signs of their motivations, and motivations comprise character. Now, when Hume asks whether we distinguish virtue from vice by means of ideas or by means of impressions, he is not asking whether the idea of virtue or the idea of vice derives from experience; we already know that all legitimate ideas (non-fictions) originate in experience and are copies of impressions. He is asking instead whether, after we have acquired the ideas involved, our regarding, for instance, malice as vicious and kindness as virtuous, is something we do merely by the use of reason, or whether it requires experience. He offers the following argument: (1) Reason alone never motivates. (2) Morals excite passions and produce or prevent actions; that is, they motivate. (3) Therefore, morality cannot be derived from reason alone (T 3.1.1).

The part opens with Charlotte Brown's careful account of Hume's ethics (ch. 12). She begins with a discussion of the views of Hume's rationalist opponents and then explains the arguments Hume offers against the view that morality cannot be based on reason by itself. Her essay explores Hume's positive views on sentiment, sympathy, and judgment of character. Hume's own account says that we derive our moral distinctions from our sentiments. In the attempt to explain our mental life in terms of a few natural principles, Hume finds that a fundamental human principle, sympathy, underlies our moral judgments. Why do we feel pleasure at the thought of some actions or characters, and pain at the thought of others? Hume's answer is that it is natural for us to sympathize with the feelings of others. In so doing, we consider the effects of an action or character in isolation from our personal connections to the actor. More specifically, the general point of view from which we make moral distinctions is the viewpoint of one who sympathizes with the circle of people most directly affected by the agent's actions. Kate Abramson's chapter (13) then focuses on a distinctive feature of Hume's ethics, namely, its spectator-based account of virtue. What traits are virtuous or vicious is determined by the reactions of approval and disapproval of a judicious spectator to the actions others perform. Hume's view makes explanations of phenomena, like the motivating effect of moral distinctions and the action-guiding or normative force of moral judgments on actors, trickier. Various commentators have raised difficult questions about the implications of moral judgment's originating in this third-person perspective, and Abramson responds to three of them: (1) that such sentiments are inappropriate as that through which we hold one another accountable; (2) that Humean sentiments of moral disapproval lead to exclusion of those we condemn and destroy Hume's otherwise "gentle" morality, and (3) that the standard of virtue in Hume's spectatorial account of moral evaluation allows practically any trait to qualify as a virtue.

Eugenio Lecaldano's essay (ch. 14) continues the discussion of Hume's ethics by exploring his theory of justice, or artificial virtue. The notions of the just and the unjust are different from those who exemplify natural virtue because acts of justice are ones we approve, not because they are the immediate sources of pleasure to those directly affected by the actor, but because we derive a kind of pleasure from the system in which they play a part. If Hume's account of justice works, then sympathy must be transformed beyond the capacity to take on the pleasures and pains of the agent's close circle into the capacity to feel approval at actions that serve the long-term good of all persons in society. Commentators have spent much effort working out Hume's answer to two key questions: (1) From what motive are the rules of justice established? (2) Why do we consider observance of these rules virtuous, and violation of them vicious? Lecaldano argues that Hume's theory of justice is a form of sentimental conventionalism, distinct from contractarian, natural law and utilitarian accounts.

Jacqueline Taylor's contribution (ch. 15) treats questions surrounding Hume's theory of beauty, which is in many ways analogous to his spectator theory of morality. After tracing the sentimentalist tradition out of which Hume's aesthetic theory arises, Taylor shows first how the *Treatise* account of beauty and morality appeals to sympathy as the basis of evaluation, offering a causal account of the origin of our sentiments. She then argues that Hume, in his later *Enquiry concerning the Principles of Morals* (often called "the second *Enquiry*") and his essay "Of the Standard of Taste," alters his views, giving more emphasis to reflection and to delicacy of taste in moral and artistic discrimination and showing an appreciation of the historical and cultural diversity in moral and aesthetic values.

Finally, Annette Baier (ch. 16) also discusses the issue that has long fascinated Hume commentators: Just how is the *Enquiry concerning the Principles of Morals* account of ethics different from that of the *Treatise*, and why did Hume himself write that the second *Enquiry* was his best book published to that point? Baier herself is not sure who should judge whether Hume's assessment was correct, but she explains her

13

admiration for the *Enquiry*, due to several pleasing features, including its "intellectual acuteness," "gentle morality," "literary craft," "lightness of touch," and "playful wit." Baier explores in great depth the ideas of the second *Enquiry*, the thinkers who influenced Hume in its writing, and why Hume might have been so pleased by it.

Religion

Scholars debate the question whether Hume was an atheist, an agnostic, or perhaps even a deist. Hume's perspective on religion is introduced here with Terence Penelhum's essay (ch. 17) on the intellectual and cultural factors that set the backdrop against which Hume's own views on religion were developed. Penelhum identifies four influences on Hume: (1) his own experience with Scottish Presbyterianism and its doctrines of predestination and original sin; (2) the skepticism of the ancient philosopher, Cicero; (3) the writings of Pierre Bayle, who attempted to undermine the notion that atheism entailed moral depravity; and (4) the debate between the deists and Joseph Butler, over whether God intervenes in the natural order. Penelhum shows how certain views in Hume's writings on religion are in interesting ways either responses to or developments of the influences he identifies.

Martin Bell's essay (ch. 18) focuses on Hume's treatment of beliefs about the nature and existence of God. His discussion draws from a section of Hume's first *Enquiry* (section 11), where Hume argues that natural religion (religious beliefs based on reasoning) can have no practical consequences, and thus no implications for the moral life. Bell's discussion, however, highlights Hume's *Dialogues concerning Natural Religion*, examining the debate among the characters in the dialogues over arguments for God's existence. The *Dialogues* have been the source of endless interpretive debates, key among them which character actually represents Hume's views, and Bell addresses some of these interesting questions. The final essay of the part, by Michael Levine (ch. 19), analyzes Hume's arguments concerning belief in miracles and in immortality. Levine shows how Hume's discussion of miracles is based on his theory of ideas and his analysis of causation, which do not warrant the positing of supernatural causes. He also examines the details of Hume's several arguments against belief in immortality, a belief that Hume attributes ultimately to the work of the passions of hope and fear over reason.

Economics, Politics, and History

Hume occupies a prominent place in the history of classical economic theory. He is best known for his anti-mercantilist arguments; that is, for arguments against the view that a country's wealth was determined by the amount of money (gold) it held and that it should sell and export more than it imports. Hume held, instead, in a country taking in increasingly large amounts of money, the price of goods there would increase, thus forcing a demand for imported items. Thus, exports are susceptible to an economic limiting mechanism, which became known as the price – specie – flow mechanism. It was Hume's view that all nations were wealthier as a result of mutual foreign trade. Tatsuya Sakamoto here (ch. 20) explains the sometimes-paradoxical content of Hume's economic theory, developed mostly in Hume's *Political Discourses*. Sakamoto offers insights not only into the content of Hume's views on topics like luxury, money, and foreign trade, but also into the reasons why Hume's writings have received great and lasting acclaim in the history of economics, despite the fact that some of his predecessors had attempted to promote similar ideas.

Richard Dees suggests in his chapter (21) on Hume's politics that Hume's theory of the origin and justification of government has been appropriated by conservatives and liberals alike, and many factions in between. Hume was liberal in his valuing of liberties, like freedom of the press, and conservative in his discouraging reforms that departed from well-entrenched customs. On the other hand, he did believe in a right to revolution under circumstances in which the abuse of authority undermined the security that governments exist in order to guarantee. He refused to affiliate with either of Britain's two political parties, the Whigs and the Tories. As Dees shows, drawing from Hume's *Treatise*, *Essays* and the *History of England*, Hume's theory of government is very subtle and complex, perhaps best thought of as a form of pragmatism, a theory in which government exists to solve certain problems whose solutions require familiarity with local details and specific circumstances.

Mark Phillips remarks in his piece (ch. 22) on Hume's *History of England* that "by the time he died in 1776, Hume was better known to British readers as a historian than as a philosopher." Because of its style and national narrative, the *History* finally brought Hume the literary fame he claimed to crave; and yet it is much less known to Hume's present-day readers than his philosophical writings. Phillips's essay offers insights into several facets of Hume's *History*: the events preceding the "moment" in which Hume wrote the *History*; Hume's development of a new historiographic style with government, manners, finances, arms, trade, learning as central themes; the maxims to which Hume adhered in his historical interpretations; and Hume's own recasting of British history and characters.

Contemporary Themes

The final part of this volume presents some critical discussions framed in contemporary terms. Admittedly, such a characterization of essays is somewhat arbitrary, given that many of the other chapters here also introduce contemporary debates in Hume scholarship and all cite recent literature. Nonetheless, these particular essays ask questions about Hume that come from our twenty-first-century perspective, using concepts that philosophers have developed since Hume as tools of critical discussion.

Janet Broughton (ch. 23) confronts directly the question broached in several previous essays, whether Hume is a skeptic or a philosophical naturalist. That is, is Hume's philosophy meant to undermine our beliefs in causality, the self, and the external world, showing them philosophical or rationally unjustified? Or is his aim to reveal how the mind arrives naturally at certain beliefs that employ fictions, with the purpose of developing standards of belief-acquisition for these beliefs, knowing they are useful in ordinary life and that we cannot get along without them? Peter Kail (ch. 24) addresses a related interpretive question, one also suggested in Dauer's essay on causality: Does Hume think that talk of causality, external objects, and the self reduces to (is nothing more than) talk of perceptions experienced in certain patterns (the "Old Hume" interpretation), or is there something else, something extra-mental that these claims are about, even though we cannot access that something else (the "New Hume" interpretation, prominent in the last century)? Kail's essay shows that what constitutes the realist, New Hume interpretation is intricate, and the answer to the question posed is even more so.

William E. Morris (ch. 25) continues part VI with his discussion of Hume's influence in contemporary epistemology. Morris shows how Hume's thought has informed current debates over the problems of induction and causation, and how his views have affinities with contemporary naturalized epistemology and cognitive science. Morris claims that Hume's most significant and underappreciated contribution to epistemology is his firm refusal to do metaphysics. Many critics either consciously or unwittingly commit Hume to metaphysical positions, when, in fact, Morris argues, Hume's rejection of traditional approaches to philosophy partly "consists in shifting the ground of discussion from what he regards as incoherent metaphysics to the only area where he believes we can have a fruitful discussion – where we have a clear understanding of the cognitive contents of the central ideas involved."

Elizabeth Radcliffe then explains the roots in Hume of the contemporary Humean theory of motivation, the "belief/desire" model, which has become the standard theory of motivation for naturalists. One is said to have a reason for action when one has a desire for something and a belief about how to attain it. This theory of reasons for action has set up one side of an ongoing philosophical debate between the present-day Humeans and present-day rationalists, with the latter claiming that reasons for action need not always depend on desires and that they can even have authority over one's desires. This live debate in motivational psychology is an impressive illustration of Hume's enduring impact on central philosophical concerns.

This volume concludes with two essays on major contemporary interpretive questions arising out of the study of Hume's moral theory. First, Tom Beauchamp (ch. 27) addresses a deep concern of moralists: does Hume have a theory of normativity whereby he prescribes a certain moral system for human beings, or is his project meant to be only descriptive of the moral practices to which we adhere? Many scholars understand it in the latter way, and Beauchamp corrects this perception by arguing that Hume's whole philosophical system offers norms for developing both causal judgments about the world and moral judgments about character. Second, because of Hume's emphasis on sentiment as the origin of morality, readers often ask the question whether Hume intended to identify moral judgments with feelings, a view which implies that our claims about morality do not describe anything real; instead, they are just expressions of the feelings we have toward actions and characters. This reading makes Hume's ethics a version of what contemporary philosophers have called moral noncognitivism, and some critics have taken for granted that this is the view with which Hume would identify. Nicholas Sturgeon (ch. 28) concludes the volume by addressing this interpretation of Hume and asking about its ties to twentieth-century emotivism. He shows that an interpretation of Hume on this score relies on answers to complex questions – on interpreting Hume's theses that morality is not a matter of fact discovered by reason but rather by sentiment, that an "ought" conclusion cannot be deduced from an "is" premise, and that moral judgments affect motives and actions. In the end, as one might expect from a philosopher as nuanced as Hume, his moral theory defies clear categorization.

16

References

Allestree, Richard (1677). *The Whole Duty of Man* (London: printed by R. Norton for Robert Pawlet).

Boswell, James (1928–34). *Private Papers of James Boswell from Malahide Castle*, ed. G. Scott and F. A. Pottle, 18 vols. (New York). (Quoted in Mossner.)

Emerson, Roger (1995). "The 'Affair' at Edinburgh and the 'Project' at Glasgow: The Politics of Hume's Attempts to Become a Professor," in M. A. Stewart and John P. Wright (eds.), *Hume and Hume's Connexions* (University Park, PA: Pennsylvania State University Press), pp. 1–22.

Fieser, James (1995). "Introduction to the Essays on Suicide and the Immortality of the Soul" (1783 edn.), in James Fieser (ed.), *The Writings of David Hume* (internet publication).

—— (2003). *A Bibliography of Hume's Writings and Early Responses* (Bristol, England: Thoemmes Press, internet publication).

Greig, J. Y. T (1931). *David Hume* (New York: Oxford University Press).

Hume, David (1932). *The Letters of David Hume*, ed. J. Y. T. Greig, 2 vols. (Oxford: Clarendon Press).

—— (1777). "My Own Life," in J. Y. T. Greig (ed.), *The Letters of David Hume*, 2 vols. (Oxford: Clarendon Press, 1932), vol. 1, pp. 1–7.

Mossner, E. C. (1980). *The Life of David Hume*, 2nd edn. (Oxford: Clarendon Press).

Stewart, M. A. (2005). "Hume's Intellectual Development," in M. Frasca-Spada and P. J. E. Kail (eds.), *Impressions of Hume* (Oxford: Oxford University Press), pp. 11–58.

Further Reading

Beebee, Helen (2006). *Hume on Causation* (London: Routledge).

Frasca-Spada, Marina (1998). *Space and the Self in Hume's Treatise* (Cambridge: Cambridge University Press).

Harris, James A. (2005). *Of Liberty and Necessity: The Free Will Debate in Eighteenth-century British Philosophy* (Oxford: Clarendon Press).

Herdt, Jennifer A. (1997). *Religion and Faction in Hume's Moral Philosophy* (Cambridge: Cambridge University Press).

Jones, Peter (ed.) (2005). *The Reception of David Hume in Europe* (London and New York: Continuum).

Mazza, Emilio and Ronchetti, Emanuele (eds.) (2007). *New Essays on David Hume* (Milan: FrancoAngeli).

Stewart, M. A. (2000). "The Dating of Hume's Manuscripts," in Paul Wood (ed.), *The Scottish Enlightenment: Essays in Reinterpretation* (Rochester, NY: University of Rochester Press), pp. 267–314.

—— (2002). "Two Species of Philosophy: The Historical Significance of the First *Enquiry*," in Peter Millican (ed.), *Reading Hume on Human Understanding: Essays on the First Enquiry* (Oxford: Clarendon Press), pp. 67–95.

Hume's Context

1

Hume in the Enlightenment Tradition

STEPHEN BUCKLE

David Hume was the outstanding philosopher of the Scottish Enlightenment, so his place in the Enlightenment tradition might seem to be secure. But things are not so simple. One problem is uncertainty concerning the connection between the Scottish Enlightenment and what is normally designated more simply and authoritatively as *the* Enlightenment – the Enlightenment of the French *philosophes*. The latter is commonly recognized as the chief formative influence on the modern world, even to the extent of defining the meaning of modernity as the progressive unfolding of "the Enlightenment project." The former, in contrast, has often been cast as a mere fringe phenomenon, the appropriate preserve only of dedicated Scotticists, such that to connect it to Hume is to dignify a merely provincial intellectual movement.

The Scottish Enlightenment is no longer dismissed, but the long neglect from which it suffered has not been without effect. That it was a major intellectual phenomenon, a significant component of the wider eighteenth-century European Enlightenment – and recognized as such at the time – is no longer seriously doubted. That Hume was its outstanding philosopher is likewise accepted. But that the interpretation of Hume's philosophy suffers when not conducted with an eye to this background is not similarly accepted. The problem does not lie with specialists in Hume's philosophy, most of whom are well acquainted with the context in which Hume worked. It lies, rather, with the everyday practice of average modern philosophy departments. In the everyday setting, Hume's philosophy is standardly tied to a limited array of contemporary philosophical problems. These problems – essentially epistemological and metaphysical – are treated in abstraction from any sense either of their place in Hume's overall philosophy, or of the philosophy's place in the wider intellectual movements of his day. Moreover, in the same corridors, the Enlightenment is typically judged to be essentially concerned with critical social theory and social improvement rather than with "the problems of philosophy." The result is that Hume the philosopher and the Enlightenment seem to be connected only by an accident of history.

Plainly, this view depends on certain stereotypes. The first, philosophical, stereotype is that philosophy is essentially epistemology and metaphysics; its history, their history. The originators of modern philosophy thus divide into rationalists and empiricists, competing schools of thought divided on the question of the sources, nature, and extent of our knowledge. Hume belongs in the latter camp, but as a purely destructive thinker who even destroyed empiricism itself. The most influential source of this opinion is Bertrand Russell's *History of Western Philosophy*. We read there that "Hume . . . developed to its logical conclusion the empirical philosophy of Locke and Berkeley, and by making it self-consistent made it incredible." In the history of modern philosophy, then, Hume is a philosopher who "represents, in a certain sense, a dead end" (Russell 1995: 634).

The second, historical, stereotype portrays the Enlightenment as a constructive movement, a beginning, the well-spring of almost everything that we think of as modern: scientifically minded secular society, democratic in form, and committed to the idea of social progress through technological innovation, the progress measured by reference to a foundation of natural values. So it is a beginning with respect to principles of social and political organization, and of the good life. Its central figures – the French *philosophes* Voltaire, Condillac, Montesquieu, Diderot, d'Alembert, and (somewhat problematically) Rousseau – were thus social critics and reformers rather than epistemologists, and so not *properly* philosophers at all. (Hence the enduring popularity of identifying them by the French term "*philosophe*": the Anglophone reader knows to interpret the term to mean, not "philosopher" – its literal meaning – but "socially critical public intellectual.")

These two stereotypes jointly imply that Hume's philosophy and the Enlightenment, although roughly concurrent, are essentially distinct. The former is a destructive demolition of epistemological and metaphysical orthodoxies, the latter an optimistic, progressive, social reform movement; the one is politically neutral intellectual endeavour of high seriousness, the other politically engaged social activism. Thus the one is studied in departments of philosophy, the other in departments of history and cultural studies. Students of the latter may come across occasional references to something called "Hume's philosophy," but students of the real thing will not allow mere social history to distract them from the logic of Hume's central arguments. In short, those inducted into these stereotypes will recognize that Hume's philosophy and the Enlightenment are "distinct existences."

The stereotypes are, however, misleading on both fronts: the former relies on a selective and contentious handling of Hume's work, the latter on ignoring the philosophical origins of canonical Enlightenment views. To begin with Hume. To recognize in his work a powerful concern with epistemological questions is to state the obvious; but to think of it as *essentially* epistemology and metaphysics is something else altogether. It depends on a dubious understanding of the relation between these two concerns, and so fails to see what Hume's examination of our rational powers is meant to open up. As a result, it requires ignoring (or demoting) most of what he actually wrote. Hume's philosophical corpus is effectively reduced to his first work, *A Treatise of Human Nature*, written in his early twenties – and, indeed, only to the first of its three books. Bertrand Russell again: "What is important and novel in his doctrines is in the first book, to which I shall confine myself" (Russell 1995: 635). Following Russell's lead, "properly philosophical" attention confines itself to the first book and its themes, consulting Hume's later productions only in so far as they help to clarify the arguments developed there. This means, in practice, consulting them only rarely, because they are lesser achievements. Russell again: "He shortened the *Treatise* by leaving out the best parts and most of the reasons for his conclusions; the result was the *Inquiry into*

Human Understanding" (Russell 1995: 634). Russell's judgment is extreme; but in the force of its opinion, not in its basic perspective. It remains the case that, for most modern analytic philosophers, the "distinctively Humean" contributions to philosophy are found in the *Treatise*, and mainly in Book 1. The mature works play, at best, supporting roles.

Hume and his contemporaries would have been astonished by this radical narrowing of focus. But, for Russell as for others, the justification for this selectivity is taken to have been given by Hume himself. This is because in his short autobiography, "My Own Life," written shortly before his death in 1776, Hume describes his later decision to rework the *Treatise* as proceeding from his belief that the public dissatisfaction with the work stemmed "more from the manner than the matter" (*Essays*, p. xxxv). This comment has been taken to mean that the views expressed in the later reworkings of the *Treatise* contain nothing new. Hume's further comment that his "love of literary fame" was his "ruling passion" is then invoked to explain why the various reworkings were written at all (*Essays*, p. xl). The *Treatise*, as he put it, "fell *dead-born from the press*" (*Essays*, p. xxxiv), so, the story goes, the young man anxious for literary fame rewrote them in more popular style – and content. He thus gained the fame he craved by diluting the strong liquor of the *Treatise*, and serious philosophers must now charitably ignore his weakness of character and return to the pure source of his original philosophical opinions and arguments.

This is a pretty tale, no doubt – it just isn't true. In the first place, it is inconsistent: it begins from the premise that the later reworkings differ only in manner, but ends up affirming that there are differences in content after all. The "love of literary fame" is then invoked to explain away this awkwardness – despite it nowhere being explained why this ruling passion does not similarly infect the *Treatise*! Secondly, it depends on an arbitrary use of sources: it requires taking "My Own Life" at its word, while ignoring Hume's explicit "disowning" of the *Treatise* in the "Advertisement" he appended to the final edition of his philosophical works (containing the *Enquiries* but not the *Treatise*) – despite the fact that both were written at roughly the same time, shortly before his death. Thirdly, it depends on a naïve approach to "My Own Life," simply ignoring the real possibility that it was intended, not as a kind of "death bed" confession, but as a deliberate provocation – as his own way of not apologizing for his life and opinions, and of announcing the absence of any fear of death. Fourthly, it depends on completely misconstruing Hume's reference to "literary fame," taking it to mean *merely* literary (and thus non-philosophical) ambition, when Hume's point is simply that he wanted to be *esteemed for his writings*, whether those writings were philosophical, historical – or "literary." Finally, it completely ignores the fact that most of the philosophical opinions *least* digestible to Hume's contemporaries appear in the later works! This popular interpretation is, in short, a shambles.

Once this interpretative picture is undone, there no longer remains any justification for taking Hume's writings so selectively. The full range of his concerns – epistemology, psychology, moral, political and economic theory, religious criticism, and politically charged history – can be reinstated without prejudice. To do so immediately reveals that Hume's concerns and tendencies are much like those of any of the French *philosophes*. No wonder, then, that he was often their welcome dinner-guest! If, then, we set aside (for the time being) the allegedly destructive character of his philosophy, focusing instead on the spread of his interests and the decidedly secular, empirical, and sociological air of his social and political essays, it is clear that he at least breathes the same air as the major French Enlightenment figures.

The other obstacle to placing Hume in the Enlightenment context is the failure to identify the French Enlightenment's own intellectual origins. The fact is, however, that its most distinctive figures understood themselves to be applying to the social world the intellectual breakthroughs – epistemological breakthroughs included – of the modern natural philosophers. They saw themselves as social critics who were *extending* the revolution in scientific doctrine and method. The truly great men of this development were English, so their heroes were, by and large, English scientists and philosophers: Bacon, Newton, and Locke.

The acknowledgment was first made by Voltaire, in his early *Letters on England* (first published in 1733), a work inspired by his British exile in the late 1720s. Voltaire there contrasts the freedom and enlightenment of English life with the oppressive feudal situation in France. The specifically intellectual case is made in chapters on Bacon and Locke, and by a comparison between the careers and achievements of Descartes and of Newton (Voltaire 1733: chs. 12–14). Although brief, these chapters exercised a significant effect on the imagination of the *philosophes*, and, by extension, on the self-image of the Enlightenment. Most importantly, they provided the template for d'Alembert's "Preliminary Discourse" to the *Encyclopedia* (1751) – the *locus classicus* for the French Enlightenment's self-understanding. The "Preliminary Discourse" is an introduction to the themes and motivations of the *Encyclopedia*. Its central part is a potted history of intellectual progress since the Renaissance, and it is in this section that English scientists and philosophers loom large. The story there has the familiar ring of Enlightenment history: of great men who rescued intellectual endeavour from the darkness and superstition imposed on it by ignorance and priestcraft.

Of these great men, "the immortal Chancellor of England, Francis Bacon, ought to be placed at the head" (d'Alembert 1751: 74). He is commended, first, for making known "the necessity of experimental physics, of which no one was yet aware," and secondly, for his resolutely humanistic focus: "Hostile to systems, he conceives of philosophy as being only that part of our knowledge which should contribute to making us better or happier, thus apparently confining it within the limits of the science of useful things, and everywhere he recommends the study of nature" (d'Alembert 1751: 75). The key was his anti-metaphysical temper, from which flowed both his experimentalism and his concern with practical human benefits. Newton's greatness, in contrast, lay in his actual scientific achievement: he "gave philosophy a form which apparently it is to keep." No less than Bacon, he also resisted metaphysical speculation, and insisted on the limits of human knowledge:

> That great genius saw that it was time to banish conjectures and vague hypotheses from physics, or at least to present them only for what they were worth . . . But perhaps he has done more by teaching philosophy to be judicious and to restrict [it] within reasonable limits. (d'Alembert 1751: 81)

Locke then provided Newton's system with its necessary foundations:

he undertook and successfully carried through what Newton had not dared to do, or perhaps would have found impossible. It can be said that he created metaphysics, almost as Newton had created physics . . . In order to know our soul, its ideas, and its affections, he did not study books, because they would only have instructed him badly; he was content with probing deeply into himself . . . [thereby presenting] mankind with the mirror with which he had looked at himself. In a word, he reduced metaphysics to what it really ought to be: the experimental physics of the soul. (d'Alembert 1751: 83–4)

So, for d'Alembert, the legacy of the English philosophers is, first, the knowledge of the basic workings of the natural world; secondly, the recognition that the sure path to what can be known lies in the empirical methods shared by the learned and the common people alike; and, thirdly, the conviction that the proper yardstick of intellectual progress is human benefit. This is the explicit message of both Bacon and Locke. Scientific revolution thus holds out the prospect of moral and political reformation. Moreover – as Voltaire's *Letters* shows – these benefits are not merely speculative: they can be directly observed by comparing liberal, enlightened England with illiberal, anti-intellectual France. In short, French Enlightenment critique is founded on English natural science.

Nevertheless, d'Alembert does not neglect one famous compatriot. Descartes, he says, by applying algebra to geometry – "one of the grandest and most fortunate ideas that the human mind has ever had" – proved himself a great geometer. As a philosopher, however, "he was perhaps equally great, but not so fortunate" (d'Alembert 1751: 78). He made many errors, but nonetheless deserves special praise for his method of doubt, by which he made himself the destroyer of old myths and prejudices. "Descartes," d'Alembert observes,

dared at least to show intelligent minds how to throw off the yoke of scholasticism, of opinion, of authority – in a word, of prejudices and barbarism. And by that revolt whose fruits we are reaping today, he rendered a service to philosophy perhaps more difficult to perform than all those contributed thereafter by his illustrious successors.

Moreover, he adds, even Descartes' errors were useful, because they undermined philosophers' dogmatic convictions, teaching them "to distrust their intelligence," and creating in them "that frame of mind that is the first step towards truth." (d'Alembert 1751: 80)

Descartes' method of doubt is thus the means by which all the inherited institutions and mores of French society can be called into question: it removes all appeal to traditional authority, and thereby places all contending explanations – whether scientific, moral, political, or religious – on an equal footing. It says: all views must confront the tribunal of doubt, and allegiance is owed only to those views that can survive the test. Thus construed, the method of doubt is a call to radical social reevaluation and reform. Descartes thereby becomes an *ally* of the highly praised Englishmen. His errors require that praise for him must be qualified, but his truly great achievement is that, more sharply than the Englishmen, he has drawn out the radical potential of the new science. The upshot is that scientific revolution and social reform can be seen as enterprises linked by a common method, and (adding the English component) by a common measure, the benefit of human society. Metaphysics

25

is the first casualty. "Philosophy," d'Alembert concludes, has learnt that "it is designed principally to instruct. For that reason the taste for systems – more suited to flatter the imagination than to enlighten reason – is today almost entirely banished from works of merit" (d'Alembert 1751: 94).

The message is plain. The reforming project of the *philosophes* is the continuation of the intellectual revolution begun in the natural sciences. That revolution had emphasized the need for a critical method; it had returned human knowledge from the clouds of metaphysical speculation to the solid ground of empirical observation; and it had established that the proper aim of intellectual endeavor is the improvement of human life. English scientists and philosophers best developed this viewpoint, and in England the fruit of their efforts is visible. The task, then, is to extend this revolution, geographically, by realizing it across the Channel, and intellectually, by applying it to the assessment of human institutions. The starting-point for this enterprise – the French contribution – is the Cartesian method of doubt, which shows that, contrary to traditional views, all social institutions are not inheritances from an antique divine endowment, but human creations – and as such subject to all the frailty and foolishness of the human frame. Social radicalism is the consequence of the modern empirical temper fortified by the method of doubt.

Unfortunately, the *philosophes* themselves erected an obstacle to this conception of their activity. Their recurring appeal to "Reason" has made their revolution appear to be embedded in French rationalist doctrines, and so to belong to a thought-world alien to the English world of ideas. Some distinctively rationalist themes did play a role in their thinking; nevertheless, the best conclusion is that their appeal to "Reason" was not essentially rationalist, but an appeal to what is *rationally justifiable*. "Reason" is thus, first and foremost, a short-hand way of referring to the new scientific outlook itself; and, given their attachment to English experimentalism, it can even be a term for broadly empiricist philosophy (Diderot 1754: 44–5). So "Reason" itself can be thought of as the philosophy of Locke sharpened up by the method of doubt: the sensual origin of all ideas, and so the non-existence of any innate source of intellectual authority; the limitation of rational powers to experience; the improvement of our practical condition as the goal of intellectual endeavor; the limitation of religion in this spirit; the separation of morals and politics from theology, and the emphasis on thinking for oneself and on political freedom. To this should be added a further element of Locke's philosophy, passed over in silence by d'Alembert, but made much of by Voltaire in the *Letters*: his proposal that matter might think (Locke 1690: 4.3.6). Locke's account of the workings of the mind amounted to "sensualizing" the intellect – explaining its workings in terms borrowed from the description of sensory processes – and so providing a starting-point for a materialist theory of mind. Thus the radical materialist theories of Diderot, d'Holbach and La Mettrie all acknowledged Lockean debts. French Enlightened "Reason" is shorthand, then, for a philosophy based on experimental principles, sympathetic to materialism, and opposed to all entrenched authority. These themes are all present in Locke, so in this sense French Enlightened "Reason" is continuous with the best of English "experimental" philosophy.

This brings us back to Hume. If we turn to his earliest attempts to explain the inspiration and general thrust of his philosophy – in the opening pages of the *Treatise* – it is apparent that he is presenting himself in recognizably similar terms. The famous

26

subtitle, "An Attempt to Introduce the Experimental Method of Reasoning into Moral Subjects," announces its continuity with the experimental natural philosophy, and its aim to develop the experimental account of human functioning begun by Locke. In the Introduction, these connections, and their specifically *English* character, are made explicit. Hume observes that, in the modern world just as in the ancient, breakthroughs in moral philosophy have followed those in natural philosophy after a lapse of around a hundred years. Just as Thales preceded Socrates by a full century, so there is a full century between Bacon and "some late philosophers in *England*, who have begun to put the science of man on a new footing, and have engaged the attention, and excited the curiosity of the public." These "late philosophers" – Locke and a selection of intellectual inheritors, Shaftesbury, Mandeville, Hutcheson, and Butler – are united in contributing to the development of a new moral science in the spirit of the new natural science (T Introduction 7). By placing himself in this tradition, Hume places himself in precisely the position endorsed by the *philosophes*: an inheritor of the revolution in natural science engaged in completing that revolution by the creation of a new science of the human. In this light, the *Treatise*'s epigraph falls into place: "Rare the happy times when we can think what we like, and are allowed to say what we think." If this epigraph graced the title-page of a work by Voltaire, its pronounced Enlightenment air would be obvious: it rejects authoritarian control of opinion and affirms toleration of diverse views. Not only, then, does Hume place himself in the Enlightened tradition of English "experimental" social thought, he also affirms the anti-authoritarian, tolerant attitude so much emphasized by the *philosophes* themselves. Plainly, then, the *Treatise* presents itself as a contribution to Enlightenment. Why then has it not generally been recognized as such?

Two, related, factors have already been mentioned: the very selective reception by modern philosophers, and the tendency to interpret Hume's arguments as uncompromisingly destructive. A third cause, however – all the more striking given its context – has been the artificially narrow interpretation of what Hume means by his subtitle. His "attempt to introduce the experimental method of reasoning into moral subjects" has commonly been understood to mean that it is nothing more than the introduction of the experimental *method* (e.g. Passmore 1980: ch. 3). To see the problem here, consider how we would respond if we came across a new book subtitled "a scientific approach." We would expect that the author would indeed attempt to follow an appropriately scientific method – but we would also expect more than that. We would expect the author to endorse, by and large, what science had *achieved* by following it. (Why else adopt the approach?) On reflection, we would also expect that the author accepted the necessity of the method because the truth about the natural world is *difficult to achieve*. The disciplined methods of science are to be followed because the meaning of the world does not lie open to casual survey; progress in knowledge requires disciplined methods that restrain flights of fancy. To adopt a scientific approach is thus, typically, also the adoption – even if the provisional or qualified adoption – of science's achievements and background assumptions.

Hume emerges as a true son of the Enlightenment when it is recognized that he does endorse these views. First, the *Treatise*'s Introduction explicitly affirms that nature's secrets are difficult to discover. He takes up the prominent Newtonian theme that the philosopher must eschew "hypotheses" (dogmatic first principles) and the search for "occult qualities" (hidden powers or essences that explain the *why* of things), and must instead stay within the bounds of what is observed, appealing only to "manifest qualities" and to general descriptions of observed regularities – "laws of nature." The improvement of philosophy depends on being experimental in this sense, and does so because the hidden properties of things can never be known. All these themes had been endorsed by both Newton and Locke; in fact, in the *Essay concerning Human Understanding*, Locke even insists that experimentalism's limits must be observed because the alternative – the attempt to discover the essences of natural bodies – is simply "lost labour" (Locke 1690: 4.3.29).

Hume accepts all of this. He even repeats Locke's phrase, observing in the Introduction that we have often "lost our labour" in the pursuit of metaphysical certainties. The central passage, however, endorses the Newtonian denial of knowledge of hidden essences, in a passage that seems to be a rewriting of Newton's remarks in the *Opticks*:

> For to me it seems evident, that the essence of mind being equally unknown to us with that of external bodies, it must be equally impossible to form any notion of its powers and qualities otherwise than from careful and exact experiments, and the observation of those particular effects, which result from its different circumstances and situations. And tho' we must endeavour to render all our principles as universal as possible, by tracing up our experiments to the utmost, and explaining all effects from the simplest and fewest causes, 'tis still certain we can never go beyond experience; and any hypothesis, that pretends to discover the ultimate original principles of human nature, ought at first to be rejected as presumptuous and chimerical. (T Introduction 8; cf. Newton 1730: 401–2)

Here we see experimental method and the unknowability of the essences of objects treated as two sides of the same coin. Experimental method is necessary because nature has hidden secrets that will *remain* secrets because human capacities cannot penetrate beyond experience – that is, beyond appearances. The enemy of experimentalism is thus "hypothesis, that pretends to discover . . . ultimate original principles." It is *because* nature's secrets lie beyond human experiential powers that the experimental method is necessary. Hume's chosen method thus reflects his acceptance of experimental natural philosophy's starting-point: that nature's essences and powers lie beyond our capacity to know.

What then of experimental *moral* enquiry? Its subject matter is the human being: specifically, the workings of the human mind. Since the essence of that mind is hidden, all forms of armchair theorizing must give way to an examination of the human being in action: the mind can be studied only by studying its observable effects. Hume sums up the point in the Introduction's concluding remarks:

> We must therefore glean up our experiments in this science from a cautious observation of human life, and take them as they appear in the common course of the world, by men's behaviour in company, in affairs, and in their pleasures. Where experiments of this kind are judiciously collected and compared, we may hope to establish on them a science, which will not be inferior in certainty, and will be much superior in utility to any other of human comprehension. (T Introduction 10)

The science will be of superior utility simply because it treats of us ourselves. It will not be inferior in certainty for several reasons. In the first place, because it will respect the limits imposed by experimentalism, and not pretend to discover "ultimate original principles." It will explain the mind's workings only in the sense of "explaining all effects from the simplest and fewest causes" in the manner of Newton's laws of motion: it will be a science composed wholly of "manifest principles." Secondly, it will not be inferior in certainty simply because it *cannot* be: *all* sciences are built on this foundation. "Even *Mathematics, Natural Philosophy, and Natural Religion,* are in some measure dependent on the science of MAN; since they lie under the cognizance of men, and are judged of by their powers and faculties"(T Introduction 4).

This is a striking claim, and not to be misunderstood. Hume is not saying that the "science of man" provides the logical foundations of the other sciences, but that it reveals the *limits* to other forms of enquiry. As such, the claim hints at the wider implications of the experimentalists' denial of access to essences, and thus at conclusions to be reached in the body of the work itself. It is implicitly to acknowledge that experimentalism denies that human beings possess any mental faculty capable of knowledge of essences, and therefore that the human being is not, in the sense intended by Aristotle, the "rational animal." Experimentalism denies that human beings are distinguished from animals by their possession of Reason, in the metaphysical tradition's sense of a faculty that orients them towards the truth about reality, by enabling them to grasp real essences of things and therefore ultimate principles that explain the *why* of the world. Experimentalism thus also denies that tradition's conception of the human being as the half-animal, half-divine "glory, jest, and riddle of the world" (Pope 1966: 251). In its place it erects a sober, unheroic naturalism in which truth-discerning metaphysical Reason is replaced by the limited capacity of reason*ing* in the service of the everyday utility of a naturally active being.

The implication – fully recognized in the Introduction – is that, if all the sciences are grounded in the powers and faculties of human beings, then they can no longer be thought simply to aim at truth. They must instead reflect the vagaries of human psychology: logic will not explain the steps to knowledge of the world, but simply "the principles and operations of our reasoning faculty"; moral philosophy will not discover real, objective goodness but "our tastes and sentiments"; political theory, in like manner, will limit itself to the practical study of "men as united in society, and dependent on each other." The value of these enquiries is that they "tend either to the improvement or ornament of the human mind" (to the "useful and agreeable," as he will later put it). In the end, then, Hume's proposal for "a compleat system of the sciences, built on a foundation almost entirely new" is a proposal to replace the impossible pursuit of ultimate truths with a system of *useful* principles – their usefulness deriving from their foundation in the (manifest) principles of human nature.

The Introduction thus aligns the *Treatise* with social critics and reformers who apply the new physical science to the human condition; colludes with them in rejecting the metaphysical tradition's conception of Reason; and therefore also rejects everything built upon that foundation: all traditional authorities, religious authority not least. Finally, it proposes to replace those old metaphysical dreams with a new system of empirical studies which aim at usefulness for human lives. These are precisely the themes emphasized by the *philosophes*. The conclusion must be that the *Treatise*'s Introduction has all the air of an Enlightenment manifesto.

Presumably, Hume knows what he is doing; so the content of the *Treatise* must justify its manifesto. So what doctrines does it affirm – explicitly or implicitly – to justify its publicity? At this point we need a brief synopsis of the *Treatise* as a whole, to bring out the radical nature of its central themes.

Book 1 opens with a very brief, but very bold, set of claims about the contents and functioning of the mind. Ideas are pale copies of vivid impressions. (Vivacity is not clarity and distinctness – the modern criterion of truth – but attributable to bodily processes: cf. Descartes 1641: II, 37ff., 52; Locke 1690: 2.29.) Ideas are thus limited by their origin in impressions, and this limits the kinds of theories we can accept. Our ideas of space and time provide an illustration. They remain image dependent, and so we must rule out theories and ideas which violate the limits thus imposed: such as theories of infinite divisibility, and the idea of a vacuum. Whatever the ultimate nature of reality, the mind has limits which theories cannot escape. Ideas are naturally connected by associations, which are processes of the imagination rather than rational connections, and this explains our vulnerability to errors in conceiving and in reasoning. Associations themselves may be supposed to be deviant motions in the brain (T 1.2.5.20). Beliefs are vivid conceptions, not rational conclusions. Beliefs about the future arise from transferring past experiences to the future. Where past experience has been uniform, the future will be believed to be likewise uniform, and conforming events will therefore be thought to arise necessarily. The idea of causation, so central to philosophical (scientific) explanation, thus arises instinctively, and depends on no insight into why things happen. Where uniformity in experience is lacking, the relative frequencies of contrary experiences will determine expectations (through a Newtonian opposition of forces), and these we express as probabilities. Reason has nothing to do with these processes: any attempt to show that it does depends on a circular argument. So "reasoning" in this sense (making inferences from experience) is really a kind of instinct. It is possessed by animals no less than by humans. The traditional powers of Reason are entirely resolvable into either sense-perceptions or (inertial) habits – and so into non-intellectual powers (T 1.3.7.5n, 1.3.14).

Furthermore, reason undermines all our beliefs because relying on it generates an infinite regress, but we escape total skepticism because human nature opposes reason's tendencies. Our belief in the reality of the external world is due to inertial tendencies ("smooth transitions") of the imagination, which connect up all fleeting but resembling impressions to create the belief in enduring objects; but the modern scientific explanation of them depends on an unstable compromise between imagination and reason. Ancient science went astray by reading into nature the emotions we observe in ourselves. The problem for modern science is that (given empiricism's implication that ideas are images) the primary–secondary qualities distinction on which it is built is incoherent. Disputes between dualists and materialists about the nature of thought show dualism to become enmired in paradoxes, so the materialist alternative – that thought is matter in motion – is the more plausible of the two (T 1.4.5.32–3). Our idea of the self, which may seem an obstacle to materialism, is nothing more than a construct of experience, put together by associative processes. So the human condition seems to be an unhappy one, since reason and the other processes of human nature tend frequently to conflict. In particular, the life of the rational enquirer seems doomed to misery: reason is a very leaky vessel, ill-fitted to resist the storms and shoals of life. Nevertheless, the philosophical life, if pursued with the diffident spirit of the true skeptic, is to be preferred to superstition and its attendant vices.

Thus Book 1's sometimes dramatically skeptical conclusions emphasize the limits and uncertainty of all that we claim to know. This means its purposes are essentially epistemological and psychological. It is an extended attack on the rationality of human functioning. Hume's aim is not, however, simply destructive, because he denies that we either are or ought to be rational animals in the traditional sense, and so lost if Reason should be undermined. His aim is, rather, to shift our conception of ourselves: in modern terms, to naturalize human nature by showing it to fit patterns of explanation consistent with a scientific materialism. His method reflects early modern orthodoxies: he dethrones the old emperor, Reason, and places us under "the empire of the imagination" (T Abstract 35). In the early modern context, the meaning of this is plain, since it was widely accepted that the imagination is the faculty – shared by animals and humans alike – that unites the disparate deliverances of the different senses. According to a then-standard definition, its operations depend on brain processes (Chambers 1728: II, 375); and most philosophers of the period understood it in the same terms (Descartes 1641: II, 19, 22, 51, 59; Hobbes 1641: 20; Malebranche 1674–5: 3; and (implicitly) Leibniz 1714: 271–2).

The imagination is thus understood to be the mental activity produced by bodily processes, in contrast to the pure mental activity of the faculty of Reason or Intellect. So Hume's claim that we are under "the empire of the imagination" is equivalent to claiming that our mental life is fully explicable according to the effects of bodily processes, as conceived by modern science. It is equivalent to claiming that materialism might be true, because materialist explanations leave nothing unexplained. They leave nothing for an immaterial soul to do, and so leave no explanatory gap that requires appeal to such an entity. (Hume argues exactly this in his posthumously published essay, "Of the Immortality of the Soul" [*Essays*, pp. 590–8].) Hume's explanations effectively reduce our rational powers to just one more consequence of bodily processes, and therefore to no more than one among several kinds of natural *force* to which the human mind is subject (T 1.4.1.1, 12). Hence his conclusion that, "where reason is lively, and mixes itself with some propensity, it ought to be assented to. Where it does not, it never can have any title to operate upon us" (T 1.4.7.11). This is to deny reason both autonomy and status. It is therefore to deny that it is a *distinct faculty* of the mind, and so necessarily to reject its traditional status as the ruling faculty in the human being. So, whereas Locke had sought to show the possibility of materialism by "sensualizing" the intellect, Hume goes further and seeks to abolish it. This is the rational kernel in the view that his purposes are destructive; but it needs to be set in the context of his materialism-friendly rejection of any privileged or even independent role for rational activity.

Books 2 and 3 work out the implications of this naturalizing project. In Book 2 our reasoning capacity is subordinated to the internal mechanical responses to external stimuli: the passions. The passions are internal reflections of external perceptions, mediated by ideas, and give rise to further ideas and impressions. Through these processes, the vivacity of images can vary: ideas can mutate into impressions and back again. So ideas do not stand apart in some separate domain. These changes are initiated by associations, so the account is once again consistent with materialism. Where does reason come into the picture? Hume's famous conclusion is that reason "is, and ought only to be the slave of the passions" (T 2.3.3.4). Philosophical attempts to govern the passions by reason – in metaphysically influenced religious morals, for instance – are thus doomed. The passions are natural responses to stimuli that shape both our immediate actions, and, by directing our interests, human understanding itself. So they produce in us a natural outlook that directs reason according to the general features of human experience.

The task of Book 3 is to explain the process by which this occurs. Hume gives a historical account of the development of the human mind proceeding hand in hand with the development of necessary social institutions. In contrast to Hobbes's twin arguments that self-interest renders the natural state of human beings dangerous, and that the solution to these dangers is to contract into an authoritarian political order, Hume argues, first, that we possess a capacity for sympathetic identification with the interests of others (a "moral sense") as a counter to our self-interest. Moral values are natural to us, but arise from perceptual, rather than intellectual, capacities. Only morality thus construed can explain the transition from fact to obligation – from "is" to "ought." The circumstances that govern the human situation require forging this moral raw material into new forms: "artificial virtues" such as systems of justice. Justice cannot arise from promises, because its value must be discovered rather than deduced – and in any case reason remains at the mercy of the violent passions that violate just principles for short-term goals. So useful moral institutions like promising and justice systems can develop only by the steady recognition over time that they are useful for all, and so justifiably authoritative for all. The natural virtues reflect the immediate facts of human psychology, but the artificial virtue of justice arises only because historical experience teaches us its utility. Legal rules are, in short, created rather than discovered; and, in line with Enlightenment orthodoxies, the rules themselves are measured according to their *usefulness* for human society. Usefulness is, however, always for some end; and these ends derive not from theology or metaphysics, but from the natural sympathetic regard for the general good.

This rather opinionated summary of the argument of the *Treatise* has picked out materialist tendencies at the heart of its explanations for mental phenomena, and so has brought out important continuities with the more radical of the French *philosophes*. However, it also shows other features that seem to push in different directions: the *Treatise* makes no commitment to materialist dogma; it offers no support for a radical political program; and it presents a moral theory explicitly opposed to the central dogma of materialist ethics, that the origin of ethics is to be found in self-interest. If Hume's project in the *Treatise* is to be fitted into the Enlightenment tradition, then, these apparent problems need to be resolved.

Perhaps the best way to approach the issue is to reconsider Hume's philosophical problematic. The familiar epistemological triad Locke–Berkeley–Hume gets one thing right: Hume's work does reflect Berkeley's critical examination of some of Locke's central doctrines. It is mistaken, however, in limiting Hume's concerns to the issues Berkeley brought to center-stage, and so ignores Hume's engagement with the Cartesians, Bayle, Shaftesbury, Hutcheson, and of course Cicero. Moreover, it assumes that Hume's project is simply the extension of the Berkeleian critique, such that Hume's philosophy is, as Russell thought it to be, wholly negative – simply the further erosion of the Lockean project. This latter assumption is the more potent, so it will be helpful if fresh light can be thrown on Hume's project.

Hume's debts to Locke, and to Berkeley's criticisms of Locke, are profound, but it does not follow from these facts that he was merely extending the Berkeleian critique. The Introduction suggests a positive program, and the *Treatise*'s title indicates that the program involves broadening the focus from human understanding to human nature. The specific arguments of the book show that the former is to be subordinated to the latter. How then are we to place Hume against his British forebears? The clue is provided by his later remark that Berkeley's arguments *"admit of no answer and produce no conviction"* (EHU 12.15n). Berkeley's criticisms of Locke cannot be faulted on rational grounds, but cannot persuade us. This shows that human nature is too strong for reason. What it doesn't show is: how is that possible? It is *this* question that Berkeley's arguments raise for Hume. Berkeley's critique of Locke did present him with a road that he then traveled to its (dead) end. But he saw that it was a dead end, and also saw that it raised the question of (causal) *psychology*. What are the principles that explain the functioning of the human mind, including why it should go its own way in the face of effective rational critique? What is the nature of human nature?

If one is to be faithful to Lockean experimentalism, the question can be answered only by finding the most satisfactory set of manifest principles. But any philosophy, no matter how dogmatic, can be mined to provide manifest explanatory principles. The philosophy Hume finds most adequate to the task is materialist. And, although he may have made use of other works in the materialist tradition – and certainly found negative inspiration in Malebranche's defense of Cartesianism – it seems to me undeniable that central features of his account of mental functioning derive from Hobbes's materialist psychology. The resemblances are so striking that it seems possible to describe the *Treatise* as a skeptical rewriting of the core Hobbesian project: to found moral and political conclusions on a materialist account of human nature. Hume takes over both Hobbesian doctrines and even order of exposition. This can be brought out by a thumbnail sketch of the opening chapters of *Leviathan*.

Hobbes limits mental contents to what comes through the senses. Sense-perceptions cause motions in the body which are, for us, feelings and ideas. Ideas are internal motions caused by external motions, and so are quite distinct from the objects or motions that cause them. Bodily motions make us attribute our ideas to an external source. The imagination is the repository of images that linger in the body: "decaying" sense. So its contents are pale copies of sense-perceptions. What is called "the understanding" is not a distinct faculty of reason, but simply those *imaginings* due to words. It is common to man and beast. Thought is connected imaginings. Transitions of thoughts reflect past sequences of sensations (past experience): the same initial sensation prompts the imagination to call up the *whole string* of sensations that followed it. This generates expectations about the future. "Trains of thought" even when unguided are not "wild ranging of the mind," but connected by associations. Guided thoughts are governed not by reason but by desires, and concern causes and effects. When concerned with the future, they depend on the thought that like events will follow like actions – they are suppositions about the future based on experience of the past. Reasoning is just a calculative power; it is not a special faculty that equips us for discovering hidden truths, but a fallible human skill developed through experience. Human actions begin in passions, internal motions in the body caused by internal or external motions, which therefore display predictable patterns. Reason is a "scout" for passion – its eyes and ears – and so its servant.

Hume's theory of basic human function is a refinement of this Hobbesian picture. He adopts nearly all the main themes of Hobbesian psychology, even to the extent of building his account of our inductive practices and our conceptions of cause and probability out of Hobbes's account of the origin of expectations from the tendency to transfer past experience to the future. Moreover, Hobbes defends a psychological (non-rational) source of our belief in enduring external objects, and similarly subordinates reason to passion. In short, Hume's displacement of reason in favor of the non-rational processes of the imagination has its roots in Hobbesian materialist psychology.

In a further respect, however, Hobbes and Hume are sharply at odds. For Hobbes, the passions that drive the material being we are aim at self-preservation; reason its servant, therefore, does the same. The natural condition of human beings thus reflects the logic of self-interest. It is the all-too-miserable condition of permanent possibility of conflict. Escaping it depends on working out the means to *mutual* preservation, the "laws of nature." These laws can only be made effective by instituting strong central government, and so it is only thereby that human life becomes tolerable. Religion is a threat to this security and so must be subordinated to government. Only when all individuals and institutions are subordinated to absolute political authority can human life flourish.

Locke had rejected this dismal conclusion by insisting that reason does rule in the natural condition. Hume, however, is not tempted by that course. Instead he preserves the passionate psychology but cuts its links with self-interest. For Hobbes this had been a datum, because, although he denied the ancient and established view that Reason should rule in the soul, he accepted its most influential (Stoic) account of the material part of our nature as aimed only at self-preservation. So he accepted, as did almost everyone, that materialism and egoism were natural bedfellows – but he also accepted that they were both true. For Hume, however, a new interpretation of materialism was suggested by Newton's physics. Since the physical world followed laws of motion based on principles of inertia and gravitation, why could not the mental world be construed in a similar spirit? Shaftesbury and Hutcheson had shown, against Hobbes, that human psychology is not simply self-interested, but includes impartial affections. Hume took over their conclusions, adapted them to Newtonian principles, and so produced a theory in which sympathetic "moral sense" and customary connection – gravitational and inertial psychological principles – underpin an evolutionary account of the development of human laws and institutions. He thereby avoided Hobbes's authoritarian conclusion while remaining more faithful to their shared commitment to reason's limited powers. Moreover, since it is Hobbes's authoritarianism that most separates him from the outlook of the *philosophes*, Hume's revisions are most congenial to Enlightenment orthodoxies. In short, Hume rewrites Hobbesian philosophy for Enlightened ends.

Of course, Hume differs from Hobbes on another crucial point: he rejects Hobbes's dogmatism. Explaining why enables us to tie up several loose threads. The important point here is that Hume's skepticism is not to be opposed to his materialist sympathies, but flows naturally from them. In fact, the necessity for a skeptical outlook can be read directly out of Hobbes's own arguments. Hobbes had insisted that, because there is no distinct faculty of Reason oriented to discovering hidden truths or essences, the traditional idea of "right reason" must be discarded: there is no "right reason," only your reasonings and mine. However, he simultaneously presents his own theory as if it simply *is* right reason. He does not face the implication of his own position: that his own arguments, no matter how cogent they seem to him, cannot claim to possess some final authority. So a sympathizer with Hobbesian views alert to this problem can be expected to rewrite Hobbes's theory by purging it of its dogmatism – by accepting, indeed, that by the theory's own lights, the truth simply cannot be *known* to be true.

One way of doing this would be to show, by example, the *adequacy* of Hobbes's materialistic styles of explanation, all the while avoiding appeal to any explicitly materialist premises. This would generate a non-rationalist account of human psychology applied to a range of theoretical and practical issues: in short, a new *treatise of human nature*. The "anxiety of influence" might limit the number of explicit references to Hobbes's work – most notably, the omission from the *Treatise*'s list of "late philosophers" (T Introduction 7) – but later in life the author might acknowledge that the main problem with Hobbes's philosophy was his inconsistent attitude to reason. So it harmonizes nicely with this suggestion that, in the final volume of his *History of England*, Hume assesses Hobbes's achievement in just these terms. Hobbes's philosophy, he observes, "partakes nothing of the spirit of scepticism; but is as positive and dogmatical as if human reason, and his reason in particular, could attain a thorough conviction in these subjects" (*History*, 1754–78; 6, p. 153). If there is no special faculty of Reason that orients us to truth, then ultimate truths cannot be known. If materialism is true, there is no such faculty – so materialism cannot be known to be true. The best case for materialism is therefore an experimental philosophy that shows the adequacy of materialist styles of explanation. Hume's skeptical philosophy is designed to satisfy just this requirement.

Finally, Hume's skepticism has a political consequence: it rules out the dogmatic radicalism of the *philosophes*, recommending instead a more thorough-going commitment to experimental methods and values. The experimental philosopher must remain, as the *Treatise*'s Introduction affirms, within the constraints imposed by a *cautious* examination of human life, and by the *judicious* collection and comparison of experiments; and the consistently skeptical spirit requires us to be diffident of our solutions no less than of our criticisms. The genuinely skeptical spirit is therefore not to be confused with the non-reflexive skepticism of the professional doubter, and for this reason he later provides an explicit rejection of the Cartesian radical doubt. Such forms of doubt, he says, being "*antecedent* to all study and philosophy," are "entirely incurable": they demolish even the foundations on which they hope later to build. So Hume distances himself from the radical critique derived from the Cartesian method. Nevertheless, he does not reject its critical employment altogether. He adds that this method, "when more moderate," can serve to wean us from "all those prejudices, which we may have imbibed from education or rash opinion" (EHU 12.3–4).

It is therefore reasonable to conclude that the difference between Hume and his French contemporaries is a matter of degree rather than of kind, the difference deriving from Hume's more qualified attitude towards the method of doubt. This is not, however, the whole story, since Hume's anti-radicalism can easily be overplayed. After all, his experimental principles justify committing to the flames all the sophistry and illusion of works in divinity and school metaphysics. But they do not justify comparable incendiarism in practical affairs. Hume's experimentalism pronounces radically on theology and other speculative enterprises; but on the established practices of common life, Hume's evolutionary theory of social development implies that, on the whole, utility *has* been the actual standard of our practices, whatever the flights of fancy offered as explanations for them (EPM 3.29). This is particularly evident in his account of the origins of the system of justice, but it is also implied by his more general account of the customary foundations of social order. In the end, then, it is Hume's more sanguine interpretation of everyday human history – that in this domain nature has always been too strong for metaphysical beliefs, that the "useful and agreeable" have always been socially efficacious – that separates him from his more radical French contemporaries.

References

d'Alembert, J. Le R. (1751). *Preliminary Discourse to the Encyclopedia of Diderot*, trans. R. N. Schwab (Chicago: University of Chicago Press, 1995).

Broadie, A. (ed.) (2003). *The Cambridge Companion to the Scottish Enlightenment* (Cambridge: Cambridge University Press).

Chambers, E. (1728). *Cyclopaedia: Or, An Universal Dictionary of Arts and Sciences* (London: James and John Knapton, John Darby, Daniel Midwinter, Arthur Bettesworth, John Senex [and 13 others]).

Descartes, R. (1641). *Meditations on First Philosophy*, in *The Philosophical Writings of Descartes*, trans. J. Cottingham, R. Stoothoff, and D. Murdoch (Cambridge: Cambridge University Press, 1985).

Diderot, D. (1754). *Thoughts on the Interpretation of Nature and Other Philosophical Works*, ed. D. Adams (Manchester: Clinamen Press, 1999).

Hobbes, T. (1641). *Leviathan*, ed. R. Tuck (Cambridge: Cambridge University Press, 1991).

Hume, David (1741–77). *Essays Moral, Political and Literary*, ed. F. Eugene Miller (Indianapolis, IN: Liberty Fund, 1987). (Cited as *Essays*.)

—— (1754–78). *The History of England* (Indianapolis, IN: Liberty Fund, 1983). (Cited as *History*.)

Leibniz, G. W. (1704). *New Essays on Human Understanding*, ed. P. Remnant and J. Bennett (Cambridge: Cambridge University Press, 1996).

—— (1714). *Monadology*, in *Philosophical Texts*, trans. R. Francks and R. S. Woolhouse (Oxford: Oxford University Press, 1998).

Locke, John (1690). *Essay concerning Human Understanding*, ed. P. H. Nidditch (Oxford: Clarendon Press, 1975). (Cited by book, chapter, paragraph.)

Malebranche, N. (1674–5). *The Search after Truth*, ed. T. M. Lennon and P. J. Olscamp (Cambridge: Cambridge University Press, 1997).

Newton, I. (1687). *Sir Isaac Newton's Mathematical Principles of Natural Philosophy and His System of the World*, trans. A. Motte and F. Cajori (Berkeley: University of California Press, 1934).

—— (1730). *Opticks, or a Treatise of the Reflections, Refractions, Inflections, & Colours of Light*, 4th edn. (New York: Dover, 1979).

Passmore, J. (1980). *Hume's Intentions*, 3rd edn. (London: Duckworth).

Pope, A. (1966). *Poetical Works*, ed. H. Davis (Oxford: Oxford University Press).

Russell, B. (1995). *History of Western Philosophy* (London: Routledge).

Voltaire, F.-M. A. (1733). *Letters on England*, trans. L. Tancock (Harmondsworth: Penguin Books, 1980).

Further Reading

Buckle, S. (1991). *Natural Law and the Theory of Property: Grotius to Hume* (Oxford: Clarendon Press).

—— (2001). *Hume's Enlightenment Tract: The Unity and Purpose of "An Enquiry concerning Human Understanding"* (Oxford: Clarendon Press).

Craig, E. (1987). *The Mind of God and the Works of Man* (Oxford: Clarendon Press).

Forbes, D. (1975). *Hume's Philosophical Politics* (Cambridge: Cambridge University Press).

Force, J. E. (1987). "Hume's Interest in Newton and Science," *Hume Studies*, 13, pp. 166–216.

Habermas, J. (1987). *The Philosophical Discourse of Modernity*, trans. F. G. Lawrence (Cambridge, MA: MIT Press).

Jones, P. (1982). *Hume's Sentiments: Their Ciceronian and French Context* (Edinburgh: Edinburgh University Press).

Livingston, D. W. (1984). *Hume's Philosophy of Common Life* (Chicago: University of Chicago Press).

—— (1998). *Philosophical Melancholy and Delirium: Hume's Pathology of Philosophy* (Chicago: University of Chicago Press).

Owen, D. (1999). *Hume's Reason* (Oxford: Clarendon Press).

Porter, R. (2000). *Enlightenment: Britain and the Creation of the Modern World* (Harmondsworth: Penguin Books).

Rivers, I. (2000). *Reason, Grace, and Sentiment: A Study of the Language of Religion and Ethics in England, 1660–1780*, vol. 2 (Cambridge: Cambridge University Press).

Russell, P. (1985). "Hume's *Treatise* and Hobbes's *The Elements of Law*," *Journal of the History of Ideas*, 46, pp. 51–64.

Stewart, J. B. (1992). *Opinion and Reform in Hume's Political Philosophy* (Princeton, NJ: Princeton University Press).

Stewart, M. A. (ed.) (1990). *Studies in the Philosophy of the Scottish Enlightenment* (Oxford: Clarendon Press).

Wood, P. B. (1989). "The Natural History of Man in the Scottish Enlightenment," *History of Science*, 27, pp. 89–123.

Wright, J. P. (1983). *The Sceptical Realism of David Hume* (Manchester: Manchester University Press).

Yolton, J. (1983). *Thinking Matter: Materialism in Eighteenth-century Britain* (Oxford: Basil Blackwell).

—— (1991). *Locke and French Materialism* (Oxford: Clarendon Press).

Part I

Mind and Knowledge

2

Hume's Theory of Ideas

DON GARRETT

Thomas Reid, David Hume's philosophical contemporary and fellow Scot, character-ized many early modern philosophers, from Descartes to Hume, as holding "the com-mon theory of ideas." By this he meant that they regarded the mind as *immediately* perceiving only certain mental entities, usually called *ideas*. Although Hume differed from most of his early-modern predecessors in using the term "perception" for these mental entities, reserving the term "idea" for the proper subset of them experienced in thought as opposed to feeling, Reid was clearly right to classify Hume as part of this tradition; for Hume confidently asserts, "'twill readily be allow'd that . . . nothing is ever really present to the mind, besides its own perceptions" (T 1.4.2.21). Yet the label Reid helped to popularize can easily obscure many important differences among the philosophers to whom he applied it, and this is nowhere truer than in the case of Hume.

Hume's philosophical ambition, as expressed in the Introduction to *A Treatise of Human Nature*, was to establish a "science of man" that, by explaining the operations of the human mind, would provide a foundation "almost entirely new" for all of the sciences. The primary objects of that foundational science are the mental entities that he calls perceptions, and especially those perceptions that he classifies as ideas. There is a way, then, in which most of his philosophy is a "theory of ideas" even in his narrower sense of the term "idea," and a fortiori in Reid's broader sense. This essay, however, will be limited to considering (1) the most basic distinctions he draws among kinds of perceptions and (2) the most basic principles that he propounds concerning their operations. As one would expect, grasping these is essential to understanding Hume's philosophy as a whole. In examining these distinctions and principles, we will have occasion to note some of the uses to which he puts them, some of the objections that have been raised against them, and some of the important ways in which Hume's version of "the com-mon theory of ideas" differs from those of his predecessors.

Basic Distinctions

Although Hume briefly recapitulates many basic aspects of his theory of ideas in *An Enquiry concerning Human Understanding*, his fullest account of it by far is to be found in *A Treatise of Human Nature* – primarily, although not exclusively, in Book 1, part 1

41

("Of ideas, their origin, composition, connexion, abstraction, &c."). He begins that work by drawing two basic distinctions between kinds of perceptions generally. He then goes on to draw several basic distinctions within the domain of those perceptions he calls *impressions* and several basic distinctions within the domain of those perceptions he calls *ideas*. A final important distinction between kinds of perceptions is not drawn as explicitly but emerges gradually in the course of the text.

Distinctions between kinds of perceptions

The opening paragraph of the main body of the *Treatise* is devoted to the distinction between *impressions* and *ideas* itself: "The difference betwixt these consists in the degrees of force and liveliness, with which they strike upon the mind, and make their way into our thought or consciousness" (T 1.1.1.1). Impressions include "all our sensations, passions and emotions, as they make their first appearance in the soul"; ideas include "the faint images of these in thinking and reasoning," such as "all the perceptions excited by the present discourse, excepting only, those which arise from the sight and touch, and excepting the immediate pleasure or uneasiness it may occasion." The difference between having impressions and having ideas is thus that "between feeling and thinking."

In addition to "force and liveliness," Hume frequently uses the term "force and vivacity," or simply "liveliness" or "vivacity," to designate the difference between impressions and ideas. The term "force" suggests a degree of causal efficacy, while the terms "liveliness" and "vivacity" suggest a more purely phenomenal difference. Since it proves to be a central tenet of Hume's philosophy that the causal efficacy of a quality can never be phenomenally present in the quality itself, these characterizations are not obviously equivalent. Evidently, Hume's view is that impressions and ideas differ in their degrees of a particular phenomenal quality, degrees that are reliably correlated with differences in causal efficacy. The terms "liveliness" and "vivacity" naturally suggest degrees of an ordinary kind of perceptible character, such as visual brightness or auditory loudness, and Hume himself suggests degrees of brightness (which can vary while the shade of color remains the same) as an analogy (T 1.3.7.5); but the analogy can mislead. For he requires that degrees of liveliness or vivacity (which apply to all perceptions and not merely to those of one sense modality) be degrees of a distinctive kind of phenomenal "manner" that does not alter the qualitative character of the perception itself, so that an impression and an idea can be identical in qualitative character even in such respects as brightness or loudness while differing *only* in this one further dimension.

Hume concludes the first paragraph of the *Treatise* by remarking that, despite the ease with which the distinction can usually be drawn, "our ideas may approach to our impressions" in sleep, fever, or madness, and that, on the other hand, our impressions "can become so faint and low, that we cannot distinguish them from our ideas." This concluding remark has seemed to many readers to be incompatible with the opening of the paragraph, for it seems to imply that some impressions and ideas do *not* differ in force and vivacity. Closer examination reveals that the remark does not quite entail that conclusion; for ideas may "approach" impressions in vivacity without ever reaching them, and a difference may exist that the mind cannot reliably distinguish (since distinguishing can also require accurate memory and skill at fine comparison). Still, it is clear that Hume is supposing that impressions and ideas typically have different kinds of causes as well as different kinds of effects, and he is at least as concerned with these as he is with their intrinsic phenomenal character.

The second basic distinction that Hume draws between kinds of perceptions is that between *simple* and *complex* perceptions:

> There is another division of our perceptions, which it will be convenient to observe, and which extends itself both to our impressions and ideas. This division is into SIMPLE and COMPLEX. Simple perceptions or impressions and ideas are such as admit of no distinction nor separation. The complex are the contrary to these, and may be distinguished into parts. Tho' a particular colour, taste, and smell are qualities all united together in this apple, 'tis easy to perceive they are not the same, but are at least distinguishable from each other. (T 1.1.1.2)

It has often been assumed that Hume's distinction between simple and complex perceptions corresponds exactly to John Locke's distinction between simple and complex ideas. In *An Essay concerning Human Understanding* (Locke 1690), Locke identifies as simple the ideas of particular colors, sounds, tastes, and smells, as well as heat and cold; solidity, extension (i.e., the having of extent in spatial dimensions), figure, space, motion, and rest; volition and perception; and pleasure, pain, unity, succession, power, and existence. In some cases, he holds, there are necessary connections among such simple ideas, and these can provide an important source of knowledge. Hume, however, regards many of these ideas as complex – including those of space, extension, figure, motion, and succession – because he regards the spatial or temporal complexity of an idea as incompatible with its simplicity. (The reference to the color of the apple in his example concerns a *type* of simple idea, since on his view a perception of an apple must be composed, in part, of a large number of colored but spatially indivisible *minima*, and each of these is a perception of color in its own right.) Furthermore, he denies that there is any separate or distinct simple perception of unity or existence. Hume's way of drawing the simple/complex distinction, together with his theory of abstract ideas, allows him to deny that there are any necessary connections between different simple ideas.

Distinctions between kinds of impressions

Every impression, Hume holds, is either an *impression of sensation* or an *impression of reflection*. The former, he writes, arise "in the soul originally, from unknown causes," while the latter arise "in great measure" from ideas that have been copied in memory or imagination from impressions of sensation (T 1.1.2.1). Impressions of reflection thus include all of the passions, such as love, hatred, pride, humility, anger, benevolence, hope, fear, and desire. They also include sentiments, such as those of approbation and disapprobation, that are more delicate than the passions, as well as other feelings that arise in the mind in the course of its operations with ideas, such as impressions of "determination" or "necessity" and "facility" or "ease." Hume's claim that impressions of sensation "arise . . . from unknown causes" should not be taken as an expression of total skepticism about the existence of external objects of sense perception. One reason for caution on this score is that he may be intending only to express ignorance of the particular means by which external objects, operating though complex sense organs, nerves, and brain structures, produce impressions in the mind. But even if his denial of knowledge is meant to extend to the very existence of external objects as the causes of impressions of sensation, his official standards for *knowledge* are extremely high, encompassing mathematics and a few other intuitive or demonstrable truths but no causal relations, so that to say that one lacks "knowledge" of something in this sense is not to deny that one can have a strongly warranted belief about it. On the contrary, he has already indicated with a high degree of confidence, just a few paragraphs earlier, that we typically have sensory impressions as the result of the stimulation of sense organs by external objects. Later in the *Treatise*, he states without hesitation that impressions of sensation arise "from the constitution of the body, from the animal spirits, or from the application of objects to the external organs" (T 2.1.1.1).

Within the domain of impressions of sensation, Hume acknowledges the common distinction between those of *primary qualities* (such as solidity, extension, shape, size, and motion) and *secondary qualities* (such as colors, sounds, tastes, smells, heat, and cold) of bodies. This distinction is of course derived from Locke, who defines *qualities* of bodies as "powers to produce ideas" in minds and asserts that the primary qualities do, while the secondary qualities do not, *resemble* the ideas (i.e., Humean impressions) that they produce there (*Essay* II.viii). Hume does not unambiguously endorse this doctrine of what he calls "the modern philosophy" concerning secondary qualities, but he does allow that the modern philosophers have one "satisfactory" causal argument for it (T 1.4.4, "Of the Modern Philosophy"), derived from the relativity of their perception (see chapter 7).

The manner in which qualities of bodies *can* resemble impressions is quite different, however, in Hume from what it is in Locke. For Locke – as for Descartes and indeed nearly all of the early modern philosophers except Spinoza and Malebranche – the human mind is a substance, of which ideas are mere qualities or *modes*. Thus, Locke specifically compares the relation in which minds stand to their ideas with the relation in which bodies stand to their motions. As mere modes of a substance that, on Locke's view, is probably immaterial and unextended, "ideas" of primary qualities are not literally extended, solid, figured, or sized. So how can he suppose that they *resemble* these qualities of body? Presumably, Locke is thinking of the ideas *of* primary qualities as containing those qualities through an intrinsic representational capacity – containing them *objectively*, as Descartes puts it, rather than *formally*. Descartes' use of the term "objective" in connection with this intrinsic representational capacity derives from the notion of the *objective being* of a thing, originally conceived by Descartes' scholastic forebears as one of two ways of being that a thing could have; thus, a thing could have formal being in reality, objective being in an idea in the mind, or both.

Hume, in contrast, recognizes no such distinction between formal and objective being, even implicitly. On the contrary, he insists that there is only one kind of existence (T 1.2.6, "Of the idea of existence and of external existence"). For him, perceptions of *extension* are literally extended (and hence complex rather than simple, as we have already noted); perceptions of *squares* are literally square; and perceptions of *red* are literally red. The question of whether the objects causing these impressions *have qualities that resemble them* is therefore a quite straightforward one, even if it is difficult in some cases to establish the correct answer. At the same time, however, this Humean literalism about the qualities of perceptions makes it correspondingly more difficult to think of perceptions as *modes of a thinking substance*, and indeed Hume denies that they are; instead, he holds, the mind is a collection or "bundle" of causally interrelated mental particulars, some extended and others (such as smells and passions) unextended:

> the true idea of the human mind is to consider it as a system of different perceptions or different existences, which are linked together by the relation of cause and effect, and mutually produce, destroy, influence, and modify each other. (T 1.4.6.19; see ch. 8)

Distinctions between kinds of ideas

Because ideas share the qualitative characters of impressions while differing in force and vivacity, any distinction originally drawn within the domain of impressions can readily be matched by a corresponding distinction within the domain of ideas (e.g., between ideas of impressions of sensation and ideas of impressions of reflection, or between ideas of primary qualities and ideas of secondary qualities). However, Hume's most general distinction specifically within the domain of ideas is that between ideas of *memory* and ideas of *the imagination*. These differ in two main respects. First, ideas of memory have more force and liveliness than ideas of the imagination, although not as much force and liveliness as impressions. Second, while the mind may voluntarily alter the order or arrangement of ideas of imagination, ideas of memory preserve a certain fixed order that is not subject to voluntary control. (The distinction between memory and imagination is explored extensively in chapter 3.)

Within the domain of ideas of imagination, Hume draws a number of further distinctions. One of these is the distinction between *beliefs* and *mere ideas* (i.e., those that are not beliefs) – which is again a distinction of degrees of force and liveliness, with beliefs having less force and liveliness than memories but more than is possessed by those ideas that are not beliefs. The processes by which ideas acquire the force-and-liveliness that makes them beliefs is a topic explored at length in chapter 6; but it is worth emphasizing that for Hume belief in its most basic form is not an act of judgment that employs concepts, but is rather the having of a particular mental image – i.e., a mental map or model – that, in virtue of its liveliness, is able to motivate and guide behavior.

Although Humean belief need not involve concepts, many of them nonetheless do. What we would call *concepts*, Hume calls *abstract ideas*. For Locke, abstract ideas achieve generality through intrinsic indeterminacy. The abstract idea of a man, for example, would simply be inherently indeterminate with respect to height or color, while the abstract idea of a triangle would be inherently determinate with respect to the number of angles but inherently indeterminate with respect to their size; similarly, the idea of unity would represent oneness that was not the oneness of any particular thing. Because Hume implicitly but firmly rejects the notion of ideas representing through their containing "objectively" that which they represent, he cannot accept the Lockean account of generality; an inherently indeterminate idea would have to be literally (i.e., "formally") indeterminate, and that would be no more possible than the existence of an indeterminate object. Instead, he agrees with George Berkeley that all

45

ideas are fully determinate in their own nature and achieve generality only through their use. On Hume's account, an idea becomes an abstract idea when it is associated with a "general term" of a language in such a way that the particular idea (which we may call the *exemplar*) is disposed to call up other resembling ideas (which we may call the *revival set*) as needed in thinking or reasoning (T 1.1.7, "Of abstract ideas"). Thus the abstract idea (i.e., the exemplar) of TRIANGLE will be the idea of a triangle determinate in angles, size, and color; it may be red and equilateral, for example. Yet if a claim is made that "all triangles are equilateral," an idea of a right triangle or of an obtuse triangle will come readily to mind, leading to the denial of the claim. To form the conceptual judgment that something exists as a triangle is presumably to include a lively idea of it within the revival set of the abstract idea of TRIANGLE.

It is sometimes objected to Hume's theory of abstract ideas that the activity of coming to associate a variety of resembling particulars with an exemplar under a common term requires that one *already* possess the concept of the respect in which they resemble one another (e.g., Kemp Smith 1941: 257; Mounce 1999: 27–8; Johnson 1995: 73–5). This objection, however, misses the point of his naturalistic theory of concept acquisition, which requires only that similar instances be able to produce similar *effects* in the mind, including the idea of a similar word. For Hume, similar causes can often produce similar effects, whether outside the mind or inside it, prior to the existence of any *concept* of the respect of similarity.

Humean abstract ideas thus differ from ideas of particulars not through their intrinsic character but through their causal and functional relations. The distinction between ideas of *substances* and ideas of *modes* is another distinction of this kind. Ideas of both kinds are complex ideas composed of ideas of particular qualities and designated by a single term. In the case of ideas of substances, however, additional ideas may be added to the complex without changing the term, whereas any addition to the complex idea of a mode requires a new term (T 1.1.6, "Of modes and substances").

For Hume, thinking about something requires having an idea of it. As is therefore implied by his discussion in the *Treatise* of external objects ("bodies"), impressions, and ideas, he recognizes ideas (of memory and imagination) of external objects, of impressions, and of ideas themselves. Indeed, since he also discusses ideas of ideas, it follows that he even recognizes ideas of ideas of ideas. Yet how can qualitatively similar ideas represent such different things? The answer must lie in his theory of representation.

Representation: a final distinction between kinds of perceptions

All ideas are *representations*, according to Hume, for he remarks that "ideas always represent their objects or impressions" (T 1.3.14.6; see also T 1.2.3.11). In contrast, it is often supposed that, on his view, impressions cannot represent anything at all (see, for example, Owen and Cohon 1997). In fact, however, while he straightforwardly denies that the passions "contain any representative quality" or have any "reference to any other object" (T 2.3.3.5), he never denies that impressions of sensation do. On the contrary, he regularly writes of impressions "of" various external objects. He also claims explicitly that some impressions of sensation "represent" extension or "represent" large external objects as being minute (T 1.2.1.5 and T 1.2.3.15). And in *An Enquiry concerning Human Understanding*, he remarks concerning impressions of sensation:

[N]o man, who reflects, ever doubted, that the existences, which we consider, when we say, this house and that tree, are nothing but perceptions in the mind, and fleeting copies or *representations* of other existences, which remain uniform and independent. (EHU 12.9, emphasis added)

The interpretation of Hume as denying that impressions of sensation can represent rests largely on the following remark from the *Treatise*:

Now since nothing is ever present to the mind but perceptions, and since all idea are deriv'd from something antecedently present to the mind; it follows, that 'tis impossible for us so much as to conceive or form an idea of any thing specifically different from ideas and impressions. (T 1.2.6.8)

If impressions of sensation represent anything, it seems, they represent bodies and their qualities; but it also seems that whatever is inconceivable cannot be represented by perceptions in the mind. Hence, if the mind cannot conceive anything "specifically different" from perceptions, one might reason, impressions of sensation cannot represent bodies or their qualities, and so cannot represent at all.

This interpretation, however, depends on a misunderstanding of what Hume means by "specifically different from ideas and impressions." He is not denying that we can conceive of bodies, understood as objects having what he calls a "continu'd and distinct existence" – that is, as (1) continuing to exist when not perceived by the mind and (2) having an existence that is distinct from the mind in having an external location and causally independent existence and operation. Indeed, a later section of the *Treatise* (T 1.4.2, "Of skepticism with regard to the senses") is largely devoted to explaining how we *do* conceive objects in this way. Rather, he is denying only that we can conceive of such bodies either as having a *separate species of existence* (e.g., Lockean "real existence" understood as just one kind of existence in contrast with ideal or "objective" existence) or as having specific, conceivable intrinsic qualities (e.g., color, sound, taste, smell, heat, cold, shape, motion) different from those of perceptions. Hume immediately goes on to explain our only recourse for conceiving of bodies as having intrinsic qualities different from these:

The farthest we can go towards a conception of external objects, when suppos'd *specifically* different from our perceptions, is to form a relative idea of them, without pretending to comprehend the related objects. (T 1.2.6.9)

That is, we can conceive of the qualities of bodies in a relative way merely as *whatever is the cause of the qualities of our perceptions*. This is in no way incoherent – Hume recognizes the conceptual legitimacy of "relative ideas" by which one conceives of an unknown relatum by conceiving it *as* what stands in a known relation to a known relatum – but it does not capture any "specific" difference, since the unknown qualities of bodies that would cause the qualities of perceptions are left unspecified. "Generally speaking" however, he continues, "we do *not* suppose them [i.e., bodies] specifically different [even in this way]; but *only* attribute to them different relations, connexions, and durations" (emphasis added) – referring the reader in a footnote to *Treatise* 1.4.2, where the conception of bodies as continued and distinct existences

47

through the attribution of such different "relations, connexions, and durations" is fully explained.

Thus, Hume does not deny that impressions of sensation represent. Indeed, more broadly, he nowhere denies that impressions of reflection *other than the passions* represent. On the contrary, he seems to think of moral and aesthetic sentiments as representing the moral and aesthetic qualities or persons or objects (virtue and vice, beauty and deformity, respectively) for which they constitute a kind of "sense." Similarly, when he writes of impressions "of" mental determination or "of" facility in mental transition, he seems to think of these impressions as representing the features of the mind's operations that they reliably serve to indicate.

Exactly why some but not all perceptions represent is something that Hume does not explicitly explain. However, he does provide enough clues to allow readers to come to a reasonable conclusion about the answer. First, he makes it clear that no perceptions – not even ideas – are *inherently* representational; rather, "the reference of the idea to an object [is] an extraneous denomination, of which in itself it bears no mark or character" (T 1.1.7.6). In adopting this doctrine, he is departing considerably and crucially from his most influential predecessors in "the common way of ideas" who, as we have seen, regard at least many ideas as representing what they do in virtue of an intrinsic representational property by which they contain the objective reality of that which they represent. Second, he makes it clear early in the *Treatise* that the resemblance of ideas to the impressions from which they are causally derived, in a way that amounts to *copying*, plays a fundamental role in their ability to represent them. Yet ideas can represent without *entirely* resembling what they represent, on Hume's view, for his definition of "falsehood" (T 3.1.1.9; see also T 2.3.10.2) requires that false ideas represent things as having qualities or relations that they do not have. More importantly, resemblance and causal derivation, even when together constituting a kind of copying, are not *in general* sufficient for representation (for example, decorative motifs in a building's architecture may be copied from those of another building without representing them), and he could reasonably be expected to recognize that fact. Third, Hume gives a number of examples of *non-mental* representation throughout his works: words can represent "objects and facts" and "sentiments and impressions"; the space of a theater can represent the place where a play is set; children can represent their parent's family (in the eliciting of passions); money can represent the beautiful and agreeable objects that it affords the power of obtaining; the giving of "stone and earth" can represent the conveyance of a manor in property law; and a "taper, habit, or grimace" may represent a religious mystery. In each of these cases, he writes of *representation* precisely because the representing item or event is taking on a significant part of the causal and/or functional role of what is said to be represented, and it is doing so through its production of mental effects such as ideas, beliefs, sentiments, passions, and volitions – or at least dispositions to them. In some cases, the representation plays the *causal* role of the represented object by reliably producing its typical mental effects and dispositions as a causal intermediary. Such representation occurs, for example, when a word is used to indicate the presence of the thing named – or when an impression of sensation indicates the presence of a body, which in turn produces effects in the mind through the mediation of that impression. This is representation through *indication*. In some cases, the representation plays the *functional* role of the represented object by producing mental effects and dispositions that *replicate* or *parallel* effects and dispositions typically produced by the represented object itself in similar or parallel circumstances. This occurs, for example, when the space of a theatrical stage contributes to the production in the minds of audience members of the same mental effects or dispositions that would be produced in the minds of auditors of the events represented – or when a *belief* in the existence of some object produces mental effects and dispositions parallel to those that would be produced in the external world and/or the mind by the presence of the object itself. Similarly, even a *mere idea* of an object will typically give rise at least to *ideas of* its typical mental effects. This is representation through *modeling.* Both kinds of representation – indication and modeling – may be combined in a single case, as when an object causes an impression of sensation that thereby indicates the object causing it, while also giving rise to beliefs about the object's causal consequences that parallel the actual consequences of that object in the external world, thereby modeling it as well.

If this is indeed Hume's understanding of representation in general, it would explain why he regards both resemblance and causal derivation as particularly *conducive* to representation, even if (as is evident from some of his examples of non-mental representation) they are not always required. For resembling objects are *more likely* to have resembling effects, particularly on the mind. And causal derivation, in addition to being essential to *indication* (i.e., playing the causal role of something else as an intermediary), also often serves to determine more precisely *what* object's functional role is being played in the production of mental effects and dispositions. *Mental representation* – that is, representation by perceptions – would then be a special case of representation in general for Hume: specifically, it would be the special case in which not only the effects and dispositions produced but also the representations themselves were mental entities. Representation *by ideas* would then be a yet further special case. Because ideas have the causal roles they do almost exclusively through their phenomenal properties, causal roles that naturally mimic those of the perceptions that they resemble and from which they are causally derived, it is understandable that copying should be essential or nearly essential to representation, as Hume indicates it is, in the special case of ideas.

That this is Hume's general understanding of mental representation is confirmed by the fact that differences in the representational capacities of individual ideas that are identical in phenomenal character – such differences, for example as representing all members of a general class as opposed to just a particular, or representing a substance as opposed to a mode – are determined by the causal and functional role of the ideas in question. At the same time, a causal/function understanding of representation would serve to explain how one idea represents only an impression, while another idea identical in phenomenal character represents a body, or even another idea. Thus, an idea will represent an *impression* by mediately producing some of the effects of that impression and also by modeling it, producing mental effects and dispositions that parallel the effects that the impression itself produces. An idea will represent a *body* when it also produces *additional* effects and dispositions – namely, effects and dispositions parallel to those that the impression would have produced if it had been present at a time at which it was not actually perceived. For in this way, the idea represents its object as having a continued and distinct existence. Ideas *of ideas* will differ from ideas of impressions or bodies in two respects. First, they will tend to produce only *ideas of*

49

passions, sentiments, and volitions. Second, and more importantly, they will be accompanied by an idea *of* the distinctive feeling of the mind that, according to Hume, always accompanies ideas:

> [W]e need not be surprized to hear of the remembrance of an idea; that is, of the idea of an idea, and of its force and vivacity superior to the loose conceptions of the imagination. In thinking of our past thoughts we not only delineate out the objects of which we were thinking, but also conceive the action of the mind in the meditation, that certain *je-ne-scai-quoi*, of which it is impossible to give any definition or description, but which every one sufficiently understands. (T 1.3.8.16)

Ideas *of ideas of ideas*, we may suppose, will tend to generate *ideas of ideas* of sentiments, passions, and volitions, and will be associated with a *pair* of ideas of the distinctive feeling of mind that always accompanies ideas: one corresponding to the occurrence of the original idea and one corresponding to the occurrence of the idea of the idea. (For further discussion of Hume's theory of representation, see Garrett 2006.)

Basic Principles

One notable distinction common to many early modern philosophers that is *not* to be found in Hume is the distinction between *ideas of the intellect* and *ideas of the imagination*. Descartes, Spinoza, and Leibniz all recognize two classes of ideas: (1) radically non-imagistic ideas whose content is innate and (2) imagistic ideas (understanding the term "imagistic" broadly enough to include auditory, gustatory, olfactory, and even emotional images) whose content is derived from experience. Hume, however, like Locke and Berkeley before him, recognizes no ideas of the former, intellectual, kind. In effect, then, he aims to explain all human cognition with only the two representational faculties of imagination and memory, both understood as providing imagistic representations whose content is derived from experience. He invokes four basic principles in the course of his efforts to do so.

The Copy Principle

Standing in a particularly intimate relation to Hume's endeavor to avoid ideas of Cartesian intellect is the most basic and best-known principle of his science of man, which has come to be called the *Copy Principle*: "That all our simple ideas in their first appearance, are derived from simple impressions, which are correspondent to them, and which they exactly represent" (T 1.1.1.7). These simple ideas may then be used to construct new complex ideas – for example, of a unicorn or the New Jerusalem – to which no previous complex impression need have corresponded.

Critics have sometimes accused Hume of treating the Copy Principle as a priori (see, for example, Flew 1961: 22–3; Bennett 1971: 226–7). This would be an inconsistency on his part since, as a principle about causal dependence (specifically, of ideas on prior impressions), it is a proposition of the kind that he repeatedly insists can be established only by experience. In Hume's defense, however, it may be observed that he tries to establish the principle with two appropriately empirical arguments: first, when one has had both a simple idea and a simple impression with the same character, one finds that the simple impression has always preceded the first appearance of the idea in one's experience; and, second, when one is unable to have a particular simple impression, either through a defect in a sense organ or some other lack of opportunity, one also lacks the corresponding simple idea. Hume characterizes the Copy Principle as a clearer and more precise version of Locke's famous denial of innate ideas, a denial that Locke aims to confirm by giving experiential derivations for all of the crucial intellectual ideas that Descartes had characterized as innate; and, indeed, Hume could cite any of the Lockean attempts to provide such derivations that he regards as successful as partial additional confirmations of the Copy Principle.

One common source of consternation with Hume's treatment of the Copy Principle is his seemingly cavalier dismissal of the notorious "missing shade of blue." As he describes the case, a series of closely resembling shades of blue are arranged from lightest to darkest, with one shade removed from the series. Even without conducting the experiment, he readily grants – as he expects his readers will also – that an observer would be able to imagine an idea of the missing shade without having had an impression of that particular shade before. While admitting that such an occurrence would be an "exception" to his principle, he concludes that "the instance is so particular and singular, that it is scarce worth our observing, and does not merit that, for it alone, we should alter our general maxim" (T 1.1.10).

Although strictly speaking the instance is not entirely singular – similar examples could be constructed with missing tones, or even missing degrees of heat – such counter-examples would (even if they were actually to occur) constitute "near misses" for the Copy Principle, inasmuch as the character of the idea of the missing shade of blue (and its analogs in the other cases) is clearly very closely derived, if not quite precisely copied, from the impressions presented. For this reason, the instances do not constitute serious impediments to the two uses to which Hume actually puts the Copy Principle. First, it underwrites a methodological directive: where one is uncertain of the nature of an idea, try to trace it to the impression from which it is copied, because the impression will have additional force and liveliness, making it less subject to obscurity and confusion. This directive is invoked most explicitly in the case of the idea of necessary connection. Second, the principle provides confirmatory evidence against the existence of purported ideas whose existence is already questionable on other grounds:

> When we entertain, therefore, any suspicion, that a philosophical term is employed without any meaning or idea (as is but too frequent), we need but enquire, *from what impression is that supposed idea derived?* And if it be impossible to assign any, this will serve to confirm our suspicion. (EHU 2.9)

The suspect terms to which Hume applies this principle are relatively few: "substance" (as intended to designate a subject in which modes, qualities, or perceptions inhere), "vacuum" (intended as existing space that is empty), "eventless time" – and "power" and "necessary connexion" when these two latter term are intended to designate a genuinely necessitating capacity intrinsic to some cause or a genuinely necessitating relation located in the cause and effect themselves. But in each of these cases, he also has antecedent grounds to be suspicious of the meaningfulness of the term in question. In the case of "substance," for example, the idea of substance would have to be of something that could bestow simplicity at a time and lack of change through time on things that are already seen to be complex and changing. Similarly, the perception of a necessary connection in nature would "amount to a demonstration" of the inseparability of two distinct events, the separation of which can already be seen to be possible. In no case is the Copy Principle his sole reason for pronouncing a philosophical term meaningless; the sense that Hume's uses of the Copy Principle treat it as a priori derives in part from failure to appreciate this point.

Some critics (e.g., Kemp Smith 1941: ch. 14; Johnson 1995: 90–3) have argued that the missing shade of blue is not the only exception that Hume allows to the Copy Principle, for he allows that we have ideas of space, time, and existence even while denying that we have any "separate," "distinguishable," or "particular" impression of them. It would be odd indeed if the idea of space were a counterexample to the Copy Principle, for he emphasizes the importance of the principle in the midst of his explanation of the nature of that idea (T 1.2.3.1). But in fact, his account of abstract ideas makes it clear why the Copy Principle does not require an impression of space, time, or existence that is separable from the impressions of the things that are in space, time, or existence. For the ideas of space, time, and existence, as abstract ideas, each consists of a particular idea, serving as an exemplar, associated with a general term in such a way as to be disposed to elicit ideas of a revival set. The exemplar of the abstract idea of space must be a complex idea whose parts are in a spatial arrangement, and so must each of the ideas in its revival set. Similarly, the exemplar of the abstract idea of time must be a complex idea whose parts are in a temporal arrangement, and so must each of the ideas in its revival set. The exemplar of the idea of existence must be an idea of something taken to exist, as must each of the ideas in its revival set. In every case, however, these ideas will either be copied from an impression or composed of simpler ideas each of which has been copied from an impression, in accordance with the Copy Principle. Because each impression has multiple aspects of resemblance and can serve either as the exemplar or a member of the revival set of many different abstract ideas, a single simple or complex impression may be "of" many things: of Lassie, of collie, of dog, of brown, of space, of time, and of existence, for example, or of a flute, of a tune, of time, and of existence. There is no need for a separate impression "of" space or time that is distinct from the impressions of the things that appear in spatial or temporal arrangements, and no need for an impression "of" existence that is distinct from the impressions of the things that are perceived to exist.

The Separability Principle

Hume's second basic principle is sometimes called the *Separability Principle*: "Whatever objects are different are distinguishable, and . . . whatever objects are distinguishable are separable by the thought and imagination" (T 1.1.7.3). He uses this principle at several key points in the *Treatise* – for example, in arguing against the infinite divisibility of space, in arguing that there is no perception of time different from the perceptions of things in temporal succession, in arguing against the demonstrability of the principle that there is a cause for every beginning of existence, in arguing that there is no perceived "necessary connexion in nature" between causes and effects, and in arguing that perceptions do not inhere in a mental substance. Although he refers to experience in remarking on how very readily the imagination can usually distinguish and separate, in idea, whatever things it finds to be different (T 1.1.3.4), the Separability Principle itself is evidently a direct consequence of his definition of the simple/complex distinction. For simple perceptions, as we have seen, are "such as admit of no distinction nor separation," while the complex – that is, those that have parts that are different from one another – "are the contrary to these." In offering this definition and the principle that is derived from it, Hume is of course assuming that things are separable if and only if they are distinguishable. This assumption is defensible, however, if the imagination can distinguish two things only by separating them in idea.

Despite the ultimate grounding of the Separability Principle in the definitions of "simple" and "complex," it has often been objected (e.g., Kemp Smith 1941: 266; Mandelbaum 1974; Bricke 1980: 71) that Hume himself violates it in the discussion of *distinctions of reason* with which he concludes the section of the *Treatise* "Of abstract ideas" (T 1.1.7). He offers three examples of such distinctions: that between "figure [i.e., shape] and the body figur'd," that between "motion and the body mov'd," and that between "the figure and color" of a body. As he remarks,

> the difficulty of explaining this distinction arises from the principle above explained, *that all ideas which are different are separable*. For it follows from thence, that if the figure be different from the body, their ideas must be separable as well as distinguishable; if they be not different, their ideas can neither be separable nor distinguishable. What then is meant by a distinction of reason, since it implies neither a difference nor separation? (1.1.7.17)

For Hume's critics, the "difficulty" of reconciling these distinctions with the Separability Principle is an evident impossibility.

Hume, however, remarks that the difficulty can be resolved by appeal to the theory of abstract ideas that he has just explained:

> It is certain that the mind would never have dreamed of distinguishing a figure from the body figured, as being in reality neither distinguishable, nor different, nor separable, did it not observe, that even in this simplicity there might be contained many different resemblances and relations. Thus, when a globe of white marble is presented, we receive only the impression of a white colour disposed in a certain form, nor are we able to separate and distinguish the colour from the form. But observing afterwards a globe of black marble and a cube of white, and comparing them with our former object, we find two separate resemblances, in what formerly seemed, and really is, perfectly inseparable. After a little more practice of this kind, we begin to distinguish the figure from the colour by a distinction of reason; that is, we consider the figure and colour together, since they are, in effect, the same and undistinguishable; but still view them in different aspects, according to the resemblances of which they are susceptible. (T 1.1.7.18)

The impression of the color of the entire globe of white marble is a complex impression composed of all of the spatially simple white impressions arrayed in certain shape. The impression of the figure of the globe is precisely the same complex impression composed of precisely the same components. This complex idea is neither different, nor distinguishable, nor separable from itself. The distinction is instead between two aspects in which the white globe may resemble other objects; but these "aspects" are not *objects* in the sense of the Separability Principle ("whatever *objects* are different"). We recognize these aspects by means of two different abstract ideas: an abstract idea of white color, and an abstract idea of spherical shape. These abstract ideas *are* objects that are distinguishable and separable from one another – but they are also different, involving different revival sets, different token exemplars, and different terms. (For further discussion of the Copy Principle and the Separability Principle, see Garrett 1997: chs. 2 and 3.)

The Conceivability Principle

A third principle of ideas, which may be called the Conceivability Principle, provides a criterion of possibility: "[N]*othing we imagine is absolutely impossible*" (T 1.2.2.8; see also T Abstract [Hume 1741], 11: "Whatever we conceive is possible, at least in a metaphysical sense"). Hume employs this principle in arguing that space and time can conform to our ideas of them, in arguing that any event may occur without a cause or without its usual effect, and in arguing that the annihilation of the soul is possible. He does not accept the unqualified converse of the principle – i.e., that what is inconceivable is impossible – since inconceivability may simply be the result of lacking the appropriate ideas, as will occur when one lacks the appropriate impressions. However, an inability to conceive, due to contradiction, something for which one has the appropriate ideas is a mark of impossibility.

While Hume characterizes the Principle of Conceivability as "an establish'd maxim in metaphysics," it may also be derived from his account of necessity. For he holds that, in general, the application of the term "necessity" describes the mind's determination to conceive things in a certain way – i.e., its inability to conceive and affirm otherwise – whether the necessity in question is that of "relations of ideas" (which are always either self-evident or demonstrable) or that of causes. Thus he writes:

> As the necessity, which makes two times two equal to four, or three angles of a triangle equal to two right ones, lies only in the act of the understanding, by which we consider and compare these ideas; in like manner the necessity or power, which unites causes and effects, lies in the determination of the mind to pass from the one to the other. (T 1.3.14.23)

In the "absolute" necessity of relations of ideas, the inconceivability of the opposite is a function of the intrinsic character of the ideas themselves. Causal necessity is often conflated with absolute necessity in Hume's view, but it is in fact a weaker kind of necessity, amounting not to the *absolute* unthinkability of the cause without its effect but rather in the psychological *difficulty* of separating their ideas following experience of their constant conjunction, together with a psychological *inability to believe* them to be separated. Given this understanding of necessity, the conceivability of something indeed entails its absolute possibility – subject only to the caveat that the mind must indeed conceive the very thing in question. To establish the possibility of squaring the circle, for example, it is not sufficient to imagine feeling pleased with oneself for having done so – one must imagine in detail how the procedure actually works.

The Principle of Association

One of Hume's primary aims is to explain, as far as possible, why we have the complex ideas we do – both why simple ideas are combined into particular complex ideas at a single time and also why they compose the temporally complex trains of ideas that they do. In both cases, he invokes the *Principle of Association*: that ideas tend to occur in complexes when their objects are related by resemblance, contiguity, or cause-and-effect. (Employing the term "principle" in the somewhat different sense of "basic causal forces," he also calls the three relations themselves "principles of association.")

As one can infer from the parallels Hume offers in the Introduction to the *Treatise* concerning central figures in the development of the natural and the moral (i.e., human) sciences (T Introduction 7), it was his ambition to be the Newton of the moral sciences. The Principle of Association contributes to that aim particularly because, on analogy with gravitation, it provides

> a kind of ATTRACTION, which in the mental world will be found to have as extraordinary effects as in the natural, and to shew itself in as many and as various forms. (T.1.1.4.6)

The Principle of Association explains why similar ideas are regularly combined into similar ideas of substances and modes by very different cultures, and why some particular ideas so often succeed other particular ideas in chains of thoughts, even the loosest reveries. Hume even invokes it to explain the requirements for "unity of action" in literary performances such as epic and dramatic poetry (EHU 1.3, "Of the Association of Ideas"). Most importantly, however, it proves to be of crucial importance in explaining probable reasoning, which is, on his view, by far the most frequent kind of reasoning. For all causal reasoning, he argues, depends on the relation of cause and effect. When ideas are related as ideas of causes and effects, the occurrence of one idea will immediately bring to mind the other; furthermore, if the first has the force and vivacity of a memory or belief, a share of that force and vivacity will be communicated to the idea of other, rendering it a belief as well. (This will also occur when the first perception is an impression.) Resemblance and contiguity may also contribute to the enlivening of one idea by another and hence contribute to the strength of a belief.

Hume was not the first to assign a role to the association of ideas in the explanation of human cognitive performance; Locke devotes a full chapter of his *Essay* (*Essay* II.33, "Of the Association of Ideas") to the topic. But Locke appeals to the association of ideas exclusively to explain defective reasoning and madness: when ideas become associated together by "custom," he holds, they become difficult to separate, and the tendency of one to draw the other with it leads to non sequiturs and fallacies. Proper reasoning for Locke, in contrast, depends on "perception of the agreement or disagreement" of ideas in the case of demonstrative reasoning; and in the case of probable reasoning, it depends on perception of the seeming or probable agreement or disagreement of ideas, mediated by the "grounds of probability" (which he identifies as "testimony" and "conformity to past experience"). Hume, in contrast, argues in effect that *all* probable reasoning is a kind of association of ideas produced by custom or habit. The perception of relations of agreement or disagreement among ideas is limited to the case of demonstrative reasoning.

It is because of this extensive use of the Principle of Association that Hume writes in his own anonymous review of the *Treatise*:

> Thro' this whole book, there are great pretensions to new discoveries in philosophy; but if any thing can entitle the author to so glorious a name as that of an inventor, 'tis the use he makes of the principle of the association of ideas, which enters into most of his philosophy. (T Abstract 35)

In this respect, as in so many others, Hume's theory of ideas begins from a Lockean inspiration but transforms it radically so as to produce a foundation for his own philosophical "science of man."

See also 3 "Hume on Memory and Imagination"; 4 "Hume and the Origin of Our Ideas of Space and Time"

References

Bennett, Jonathan (1971). *Locke, Berkeley, Hume: Central Themes* (Oxford: Oxford University Press).

Bricke, John (1980). *Hume's Philosophy of Mind* (Princeton, NJ: Princeton University Press).

Flew, Antony (1961). *Hume's Philosophy of Belief* (London: Routledge and Kegan Paul).

Garrett, Don (1997). *Cognition and Commitment in Hume's Philosophy* (New York: Oxford University Press).

—— (2006). "Hume's Naturalistic Theory of Representation," *Synthese*, 152, pp. 301–19.

Hume, David (1741). *An Abstract of a Book Lately Published: Entituled a Treatise of Human Nature* (London: C. Corbet). Included in Hume, David (1739–40), *A Treatise of Human Nature*, ed. David Fate Norton and Mary J. Norton (Oxford: Oxford University Press, 2000). (Cited by paragraph number.)

Johnson, Oliver A. (1995). *The Mind of David Hume* (Urbana-Champaign, IL: University of Illinois Press).

Kemp Smith, Norman (1941). *The Philosophy of David Hume* (London: Macmillan).

Locke, John (1690). *An Essay concerning Human Understanding*, ed. Peter H. Nidditch (Oxford: Clarendon Press, 1979). (Cited by book, chapter.)

Mandelbaum, Maurice (1974). "The Distinguishable and the Separable: A Note on Hume and Causation," *Journal of the History of Philosophy*, 12, pp. 242–7.

Mounce, H. O. (1999). *Hume's Naturalism* (New York: Routledge).

Owen, David and Cohon, Rachel (1997). "Representation, Reason, and Motivation," *Manuscrito*, 20, pp. 47–76.

Further Reading

Bennett, Jonathan (2001). *Learning from Six Philosophers*, vol. 2 (Oxford: Clarendon Press).

Broughton, Janet (2006). "Impressions and Ideas," in Saul Traiger (ed.), *The Blackwell Guide to Hume's "Treatise"* (Malden, MA: Blackwell Publishing), pp. 43–58.

Fodor, Jerry A. (2003). *Hume Variations* (Oxford: Clarendon Press).

Fogelin, Robert (1984). "Hume and the Missing Shade of Blue," *Philosophy and Phenomenological Research*, 45, pp. 263–72.

Noonan, Harold W. (1999). *Hume on Knowledge* (London: Routledge).

Owen, David (1999). *Hume's Reason* (New York: Oxford University Press).

Passmore, John A. (1952). *Hume's Intentions* (Cambridge: Cambridge University Press).

Strawson, Galen (1989). *The Secret Connexion* (Oxford: Clarendon Press).

Stroud, Barry (1997). *Hume* (London: Routledge and Kegan Paul).

Waxman, Wayne (2005). *Kant and the Empiricists: Understanding Understanding* (New York: Oxford University Press).

Wright, John P. (1983). *The Sceptical Realism of David Hume* (Manchester: Manchester University Press).

3

Hume on Memory and Imagination

SAUL TRAIGER

The distinction between memory and imagination is among the first and most important applications of Hume's theory of impressions and ideas. Hume's accounts of causal inference, belief, and personal identity are couched in terms of it. Yet, like so many distinctions in Hume, attempts at careful explication lead to fascinating questions of analysis and interpretation. We will set out a number of these questions as we explore Hume's treatment of memory and imagination and we'll discuss some of the attempts to answer them in the recent literature. Hume introduces us to the faculties of memory and imagination very early in *A Treatise of Human Nature*. Our topic will bring us face to face with some of the most fundamental concerns of Hume's science of human nature.

Although we will survey Hume's treatment of memory and imagination, it will not be possible to cover everything Hume has to say about these two aspects of the human mind. Specifically, we will have less to say about imagination than we will about memory. The main reason for this has to do with the very wide usage of the term "imagination" in Hume's texts. Often Hume uses the term "imagination" to encompass the entirety of the understanding. He says, for example, that the "understanding or imagination can draw inferences from past experience" (T 1.3.8.13). We will limit our treatment of the imagination to those passages where it is contrasted with the faculty of memory.

In the very first paragraph of the *Treatise* Hume divides the perceptions of the mind into impressions, our original sensations and feelings, and ideas, which are "faint images of these in thinking and reasoning" (T 1.1.1.1). Using the example of a survey of his chamber, Hume describes ideas as the reflection of our impressions. As Hume looks at his chamber, he forms impressions, and then shuts his eyes. With eyes shut, he thinks of his chamber, forming ideas which are "exact representations of the impressions" (T 1.1.1.3). This suggests that "all the perceptions of the mind are double" (T 1.1.1.3), and while he has yet to introduce memory officially, it also suggests that all our ideas are memories of antecedent impressions.

Hume quickly retracts the claimed doubling of perceptions, and in so doing, paves the way for a distinction between memory and imagination. There are impressions for which there are no exactly corresponding complex ideas. Hume poses the rhetorical question, "I have seen *Paris*; but shall I affirm I can form such an idea of that city, as will perfectly represent all its streets and houses in their real and just proportions"

(1.1.1.4)? The implied observation, that one cannot form an idea that will perfectly represent all the streets and houses, is a bit puzzling. Hume's point seems to be that some of the details of perception are lost when we form the corresponding ideas. But the idea that he claims he can't form isn't an idea that matches his impression of some *part* of Paris in all its detail; rather it's an idea of the *entirety* of Paris. Surely, no one has a single complex idea, or even a set of complex ideas encompassing all the streets and houses and everything else that makes up Paris at a time, or over time. So why would Hume care about whether he has such an idea? One way to make sense of this is as follows: Hume reminds us of the complexity of Paris (the city) in order to emphasize that even one's ordinary impressions of some portion of that city will have more complexity than is typically present in the corresponding ideas. Thus there are impressions which are not "reflected" exactly in ideas. On this interpretation, the reference to "all" the streets and houses is a bit hyperbolic.

Hume's point here is of particular significance for what he will say about memory. If our ideas are often not as detailed as our initial impressions, then we can't treat memory ideas as those ideas which in all instances exactly copy prior complex impressions. I may see streets in Paris on a particular occasion, and remember them, even if I don't form ideas of all the houses I saw on that occasion. Hume's treatment of memory will have to accommodate this fact. We will see that at first blush it appears that it does not.

The distinction between simple and complex perceptions is also needed to account for the fact that "many of our complex ideas never had impressions, that corresponded to them" (T 1.1.1.4). This is the second way in which the purported doubling of perceptions fails. Hume reports that he can imagine a city he has never seen, a New Jerusalem, "whose pavement is gold and walls are rubies" (T 1.1.1.4). This is his first *Treatise* example of the activity and output of the faculty of imagination. It is a faculty that forms complex ideas without regard to the order of the complex impressions which precede them. Simple perceptions, considered as such and not as constituents of complex perceptions, appear not to be products of the faculties Hume will refer to as memory and imagination.

Hume officially introduces the topics of memory and imagination in Book 1, part 1, section 3, "Of the ideas of the memory and imagination" (T 1.1.3). As we explore Hume's distinctions and explanations, we should be aware of an interpretive issue that faces us at the outset: Does Hume think of memory and imagination primarily as faculties of the mind, or is he just describing two kinds of ideas, without buying into the tradition of faculty psychology? There's evidence for both answers, and thus it's not surprising that it is an issue in recent Hume scholarship (Garrett 1997). The section title suggests that Hume is interested in the *ideas* rather than the faculties. But in the immediately previous section Hume says that our impressions of reflection, like our impressions of sense, are "copied by the memory and imagination, and become ideas" (T 1.1.2.1). In this context, memory and imagination are not types of ideas, but faculties which copy ideas. Clearly Hume can have it both ways: the faculty of memory produces memories, and the faculty of imagination can produce imaginings. The interpretive question still remains: When we look for Hume's account of the distinction between memory and imagination, is it a distinction among types of faculties or a distinction among types of ideas? We will return to this question below.

59

A second, related, and perhaps more basic interpretive issue is the question of what Hume is trying to accomplish. Does Hume intend to set out an analysis, a set of necessary and sufficient conditions for memory ideas, as opposed to ideas of the imagination, or is the plan to introduce some general features of memory and imagination? To what purpose will the analyses, theories, or distinctions be put? Is this part of Hume's descriptive empirical cognitive psychology or an element in a normative epistemology? If we find both descriptive and normative projects, how are they related? We will touch on all these questions, and others, as we explore the text.

Memory in *Treatise* 1.1

The title of section 1.1.3, "Of the ideas of the memory and imagination" suggests that the perceptions of memory and imagination are ideas, and we've already seen that Hume may intend to restrict these species of perceptions further to complex ideas. In 1.3.5, however, Hume appears to allow that memories can be impressions, when he writes: "All our arguments concerning causes and effects consist both of an impression of the memory or senses, and of the idea of that existence, which produces the object of the impression, or is produc'd by it" (T 1.3.5.1). Another terminological worry is generated from Hume's description of the missing shade of blue. Hume famously allows that a person who has seen every shade of blue except one, when prompted with the visual stimulus of the spectrum of all the colors except the shade never experienced, will, "from his own imagination," supply the missing shade (T 1.1.1.10). The difficulty is that if color ideas are simple, Hume is having the imagination supply simple ideas as well as complex ideas (Russow 1980). Hume likely would have dismissed this unusual role for the imagination along with the missing shade, as a singular exception to a general maxim. At any rate, as we investigate Hume's views on memory and imagination, or indeed on any topic, we need to note the terminological variations in the text, and take account of them in our overall interpretation.

Once we have had an impression, say of a blue cube, the appearance of the perception "as an idea" is either as an idea with "a considerable degree of its first vivacity" or as an idea which "entirely loses that vivacity" (T 1.1.3.1). Memory, Hume says, is that faculty which produces high-vivacity ideas. Imagination is the faculty which produces non-lively ideas, or what Hume calls "perfect ideas." So all our ideas are the products of either memory or imagination, and they are either very lively, as memory ideas, or not lively, as ideas of the imagination. Although it appears that Hume has described a property possessed by ideas of one faculty but not that of another, he has not described the faculties themselves. Hume does, however, refer to the manner in which memory ideas enter the mind, and he distinguishes that manner from the way ideas of the imagination enter the mind. He says: "When we remember any past event, the idea of it flows in upon the mind in a forcible manner; whereas in the imagination the perception is faint and languid, and cannot without difficulty be preserv'd by the mind steady and uniform for any considerable time" (T 1.1.3.1). Although this is suggestive at best, Hume seems to be saying that there is a difference in how ideas of memory and imagination are infixed. Memory strongly infixes ideas in the mind, while imagination loosely attaches ideas in the mind, and such ideas can easily fail to be retained by that faculty. This bifurcation may seem to leave no place for belief. If all ideas are either memories or ideas of the imagination, how will Hume classify beliefs? We'll return to this question when we come to the role of memory in causal inference.

Vivacity figures prominently in Hume's treatment of memory, and we will soon see that it is even more central in the account of memory presented in *Treatise* 1.3.5. Hume's appeal to vivacity raises important questions. What does Hume mean by vivacity? Is vivacity a phenomenal characteristic, accessible only by introspection? Are "liveliness" and "strength," two other terms Hume introduces to characterize memory ideas, equivalent to vivacity, or are they other, perhaps related properties? Hume says that memory "paints its objects in more distinct colours" than does the imagination (T 1.1.3.1). Is the distinctness of perceptions a separate feature from vivacity, or is vivacity a cause or an effect of distinctness?

There are surprisingly few detailed interpretations of Hume's notion of vivacity. Govier (1972) argues that Hume's notions of force and vivacity are unclear, yet they appear to do a lot of work. She notes that Hume admits in the appendix to the *Treatise* that he did not provide a completely satisfying account of vivacity in connection with belief, and that he was hinting at difficulties with a reliance on the phenomenal character of vivacity. Anticipating the work of Loeb (2002), Govier suggests that vivacity is understood by Hume to include the role that perceptions characterized as lively or forceful play in one's epistemic life. Rather than just looking at the phenomenal/affective properties of perceptions, how the perception "feels," Govier argues that the most important thing is the role a perception plays in inference. When we turn to Hume's treatment of memory in part 3 of Book 1, we'll see that there's strong evidence that Hume emphasized the inferential role of memory ideas.

Memory ideas contrast with what Hume calls "perfect ideas." Perfect ideas are present to the mind without having any vivacity at all. Since every idea is a copy of an antecedent impression, and all impressions have a high degree of vivacity, perfect ideas have lost the vivacity of the original impressions. Kemp Smith suggests that Hume calls such ideas "perfect" because they are freely available to the imagination for concatenation with other ideas; they are not "tied down by any act of assent or belief" (Kemp Smith 1941: 234). It is by no means obvious, however, that when such ideas are actually entertained in the imagination, they can retain their "perfect" status. Ideas typically acquire vivacity in virtue of their relations to other perceptions.

Two other aspects of memory ideas are described as pertaining to the liveliness of memory in contrast to imagination. We have already noted that complex ideas do not always retain all the detail of our original impressions. Hume suggests that memory presents more detail than does the imagination. " 'Tis evident at first sight, that the ideas of the memory are much more lively and strong than those of the imagination, and that the former faculty paints its objects in more distinct colours, than any which are employ'd by the latter" (T 1.1.3.1). Hume's reference to "painting in distinct colours" is clearly metaphorical. His point is that memory ideas have more specificity than ideas of the imagination. We noted above Hume's reference to another feature, which he adds to this one, namely that we preserve memory ideas as "steady and uniform" over time, while ideas of the imagination are continually changing. Although Hume doesn't say so directly, these two features, the persistence of memories, and the specificity of memory, appear to be effects of the high vivacity of memory ideas. High-vivacity ideas

61

persist. The more ideas persist at a time, the higher the specificity of the complex ideas in the mind. However powerful the persistence of memories, we have already seen from the "streets and houses of *Paris*" example that complex ideas do not always retain the full specificity of the impressions from which they are derived.

The specificity of memory may be a cause of the high vivacity of memories as well as an effect. Later in the *Treatise* Hume reiterates the point that the ideas we assent to are "more strong, firm and vivid than the loose reveries of a castle-builder" (T 1.3.7.8). The same text, taken as a romance or as a work of history produces different effects, Hume claims. We enter into the events described in a historical text more strongly than we do when the same described events are taken as a work of fiction. Hume's explanation of this difference is that when we take something as fact, when we assent to it, we "enter deeper into the concerns" of those represented in the text than we do in the case of a work of fiction. Our ideas of the events described have greater detail than they do when we take the text to be a work of fiction. Such detail results in higher vivacity for the component ideas.

The apparent oddness of Hume's claim that history has a stronger claim on us than fiction has not gone unnoticed in the secondary literature. Noxon (1976) calls this "Hume's eccentric verdict." Traiger (1994) argues that Hume's empirical claim is plausible if one appreciates that he emphasizes that one can take a text *as* a history or *as* a romance, and that these different "takings" have different cognitive consequences. Assenting to something, taking it as fact, leads to greater specificity in our ideas. The same is true for memory. We can take ideas that we have *as* memories or *as* ideas of the imagination. When we take them as memories, associative relations lead to other ideas which increase the vivacity of the original ideas. This "taking as" memory or imagination is an important piece of Hume's account of memory, a piece often underappreciated by commentators.

Ideas of memory may be distinguished from those of the imagination not only by the respective difference in vivacity, but by differences in "order and form." Ideas of the imagination are not "restrain'd to the same order and form with the original impressions." Memory ideas are so restrained, "without any power of variation" (T 1.1.3.2). Commentators often refer to this as Hume's second criterion for distinguishing memory from imagination, where vivacity is the first criterion. However, such an appellation raises a host of difficult questions. If this is a second criterion, what is its relation to the first? Are both criteria necessary? Are they jointly sufficient? Can they conflict? It is important to note these questions only arise if Hume is taken as intending to introduce both vivacity and order and form as joint criteria for distinguishing memory from imagination. While Hume clearly introduces "order and form" as "another difference," it doesn't follow that he is offering a second criterion in an analysis of memory and imagination. This will become particularly clear when we look at what Hume says about memory in part 3 of Book 1.

What does Hume mean when he says that memory ideas are "ty'd down" with respect to the "order and form" of the original impressions? Are there two distinct ways memory ideas are "ty'd down," one of order and another of form? In the paragraph following immediately on the introduction of "order and form" Hume indeed describes two ways in which memories mirror the original impressions. The first is that memories retain the temporal order of the original impressions. When historians deviate from the precise temporal order of past events, this "proceeds from some defect or imperfection" in the faculty of memory (T 1.1.3.3). Hume uses the terms "form" and "position" to refer to this temporal structure. In this same paragraph Hume claims that it is "the same case in our recollection of those places and persons which we were formerly acquainted." What is the same is that memory retains what he now refers to as "order and position." The examples of places and persons are non-temporal. While Hume uses the term "position" to refer to both temporal order and such non-temporal order as spatial order, he uses "form" in connection with the temporal sequence and "order" for spatial order. Regardless of whether Hume is terminologically consistent here, it is clear that he is saying that memory ideas must retain both the temporal and non-temporal structure of their original impressions. It is also clear that memory ideas are typically complex ideas, particularly with respect to what we're here calling (non-temporal) "order." Ideas of the imagination are ideas which are not "ty'd down" to the form and order of any original impressions, though of course any component simple idea in a complex idea of the imagination derives from some antecedent simple impression.

How "ty'd down" are memories to the original impressions? Any departure from the form and order of the original impressions is the result of "some defect or imperfection" of the faculty of memory (T 1.1.3.3). If we take Hume to be saying that strict adherence to the form and order of the original impressions is required for memory, then in light of our earlier observation that, for Hume, complex ideas rarely retain all the detail of the impressions from which they are copied, it would follow that very few of our complex ideas would count as memories. But Hume doesn't draw this conclusion, and he suggests that historical narrations which get the temporal order right are ideas of memory. We'll return to historical belief and its relation to memory below.

This is the account of memory and imagination in the context of Hume's theory of impressions and ideas in the earliest sections of the *Treatise*. We can summarize the account as follows: The faculty of memory produces ideas of memories and the faculty of imagination produces the ideas of the imagination. Memory ideas have a high degree of force and vivacity. Ideas of the imagination are faint and languid. Indeed they are often "perfect ideas," having no vivacity at all. Memory ideas are those which have the same form and order as antecedent original impressions. Ideas of the imagination need not retain the form and order of any prior complex impressions.

Memory in *Treatise* 1.3

If Hume's account of memory and imagination were limited to what he says in *Treatise* 1.1.3, many of our initial questions would remain unanswerable. Fortunately, he returns to the topic in *Treatise* 1.3.5. Of course the section introduces new interpretative difficulties as well. We'll begin by seeing how this section sheds light on the criteria of memory introduced in 1.1.3 and then we'll turn to problems frequently noted by commentators.

Section 5 of part 3 is entitled "Of the impressions of sense and memory." It sets the stage for Hume's treatment of causal inference. In the immediately prior section Hume argued that causal inferences are founded on impressions or memories. When we infer that Caesar was killed on the ides of March, we draw our inference from our impressions or memory of "characters or letters" (T 1.3.4.2). That is, we infer the fact of Caesar's death from seeing, hearing or remembering reports of his death by historians. When one infers that fire is hot, one draws that inference from either a present impression of fire, or from a memory of fire. The present impression or memory is just one element of the inference, but is an essential element. In this part of the *Treatise* Hume is interested in memory insofar as it plays a role in causal inference. Memories can occupy the same role as impressions of sense in causal inference.

To establish that impressions of sense and memories are the starting points for our inferences Hume argues that we can't trace our inferences back any further than sense or memory. The matter of the origins of our impressions of sense, Hume claims, is "perfectly inexplicable by human reason" (T 1.3.5.2). But what about memory? We know from 1.1.3 that ideas of memory retain the order and form of original impressions. So can't we trace back the inference from memories to the original impressions? Hume's often noted answer here is that we can't trace back memories to original impressions, since it is "impossible to recal the past impressions, in order to compare them with our present ideas, and see whether their arrangement be exactly similar" (1.3.5.3). The distinction here is between what makes something a memory idea and what counts as evidence that some complex idea is an idea of memory. Hume's claim parallels what he has just said about impressions, though the reasons are different. Just as we can't provide evidence that something is an impression, since the causes of our impressions are inexplicable to human reason, we can't provide evidence that something is a memory, that it has the exact form and order of the original impressions, because we could never be in a position to compare present ideas with those original impressions.

On what basis then can we be sure that the ideas on which we found our causal inferences are memories rather than ideas of the imagination? It's the same basis we have for holding that we found causal inferences on impressions of sense rather than ideas derived from them, namely the vivacity of the perceptions. It is the force and vivacity of memory ideas which distinguishes them from ideas of the imagination, and renders them appropriate as inferential starting points for causal inference, along with impressions of sensation. Hume could have raised a skeptical worry about our reliance on vivacity, but it is important to note that he does not pursue the issue of skepticism about the faculty of memory, though, as we'll emphasize below, he was well aware of the fact that purported memories are not always accurate.

Critiques of Hume's Account

Many commentators share the view that Hume's treatment of memory in the passages just reviewed is flawed. Some of these criticisms start with the point that memory is an epistemic concept, and that an account of memory must be able to both distinguish memories from non-memories and explain how memories count as justified beliefs. Pears (1990) holds that Hume does not, and cannot, distinguish the idea formation aspect of memory from the epistemic aspect as evidence. If the criterion for memory is ultimately just vivacity, then Hume can't distinguish actual recollection from one's merely seeming to remember something. The ideas can have the same vivacity. But only actual memory can serve as proper evidence in a knowledge claim. Johnson (1987) raises the same problem, suggesting that Hume can't distinguish a low-vivacity memory from an idea of the imagination. Kemp Smith (1941) suggests that this line of criticism was originally raised by Thomas Reid (1849).

While Pears and Johnson take vivacity to be the criterion for distinguishing memory from imagination, Noxon (1976) takes Hume to be offering two competing and incompatible criteria, namely vivacity and form and order. A high-vivacity idea counts as a memory idea on the vivacity criterion, but if it doesn't have the form and order of the original impressions, then it isn't a memory on the second criterion. Alternatively, a low-vivacity complex idea with the form and order of original impressions counts as a memory idea on the second criterion, but not on the first. A similar complaint is raised by Urmson (1967).

Still other commentators emphasize the form and order criterion, even though Hume seems to put it aside in T 1.3.5. Daniel Flage (1985) acknowledges the difficulties noted above with the vivacity criterion, and argues that for Hume, a memory idea is a complex idea which is caused by antecedent complex impression. This is Flage's reading of "form and order," which captures just the non-temporal aspect, and ignores what Hume refers to as the temporal order of memories as components of sequences of ideas. A difficulty for this interpretation is that it does not allow for the possibility that we can remember our ideas, a possibility Hume explicitly acknowledges at T 1.3.8.16 (Traiger 1985).

It has also been suggested that Hume isn't sensitive to the difference between memories and historical belief. I may remember falling off my bicycle, but it would be odd to say that I remember Caesar being killed on the ides of March, since I didn't witness Caesar's death. I might, however, remember *that* Caesar was killed on the ides of March, where I am issuing a first person recollection of acquisition of the *de dicto* belief. While one might think that Hume's account of memory is restricted to first person recollection, we've already seen that the text suggests otherwise. We noted earlier that Hume cites historical narration as retaining the form and order of original impressions in T 1.1.3, that is, as paradigmatic cases of memory. The examples of memory presented in 1.3.5, in contrast, are all first person recollections. So what are we to make of this? Does Hume lump together memory with belief about the past more generally? While it may not be possible to answer this question by looking at these passages on memory, Hume has a great deal to say about historical belief and beliefs about the impersonal past generally in part 3 of Book 1, where they are clearly treated as products of causal reasoning rather than as memories.

The most persistent charge against Hume's account of memory in the literature is that Hume can't distinguish between real memories, merely apparent memories, and ideas of the imagination more generally. Again, it's important to be clear about the charge: Is the charge that Hume's *analysis* of memory can't make the distinctions, or is the charge that in the context of justification, an epistemic agent can't tell whether an idea is a real idea of memory, an apparent memory, or some other idea of the imagination? McDonough (2002) calls the first question the "constitutive question," and he suggests that where Hume contrasts accurate memories with both inaccurate memories and imagination he is concerned with the constitutive question. Where Hume

65

contrasts both accurate and inaccurate memories with ideas of the imagination he is concerned with the question of how we distinguish memories from imagination in practice.

Hume tries to answer the constitutive question in 1.1.3 and the epistemic question in T 1.3.5. As we have seen, in 1.1.3 Hume characterizes memories as ideas which retain the form and order of original impressions. So real memory fully retains that form and order. Putative memories which are inaccurate do not. Vivacity, while introduced here as well, does not serve as the constitutive basis of memory. Both accurate and inaccurate memories, however, the ideas we *take* to be memories, whether rightly or wrongly, have high vivacity, and that distinguishes them from the mere offspring of the imagination. But this takes us back to the concern first introduced by Reid: Can Hume tell us how we can distinguish the real memories from the apparent ones, since both kinds of ideas can have high vivacity?

Some of Hume's critics charge that Hume was unaware of this issue, that he simply lumped inaccurate memories with ideas of the imagination as low-vivacity ideas. Even a cursory glance at T 1.3.5.4–7, however, reveals that this is not the case. In these paragraphs Hume discusses a range of examples, from partial recollection, to decayed memory, to ideas of the imagination which pass for real memories. The first of these examples is a case where someone has an idea with the form and order of the original impressions, since the "scene of action" in question is being described to him by a friend who also experienced it. The individual fails to remember the friend until "at last he hits on some lucky circumstance, that revives the whole, and gives his friend a perfect memory of every thing" (T 1.3.5.4). Until his friend hits on the "lucky circumstance," the individual will not take the ideas recalled as memories, and will not use them as the basis of causal inference, even though, from a constitutive perspective, they count as memories.

While memories can be revived, as in this last example, in such a way that "perfect memory" is restored, Hume notes that memories are often uncertain, that the passage of time often obscures memory. Hume's example is that of a painter who relies on his memory of an observed emotion in another in order to represent it in a painting. The high vivacity of a memory of a recently observed emotion will serve the painter better than would a later memory of the same observation. Often we cannot tell whether an idea is an idea of memory or "the pure offspring of my fancy" (T 1.3.5.5, SNB 628). The reason we can't tell that the later memory is a memory has to do with the loss of vivacity. In such cases, Hume says, one may qualify the claim to remembering by saying that one thinks one remembers.

One may claim to be certain that one remembers something which is in fact an invention of the imagination. Liars come to believe and "remember as realities" what they profess by repetition of their lies (T 1.3.5.6). That is, they take some of their ideas of the imagination as memories. But lies are not mere ideas of the imagination; they are ideas with a particular importance for the liar, and their repetition in the mental history of the liar increases their vivacity to a level equal with that of actual memories.

Thus Hume is fully aware that vivacity, as the feature we use to take our ideas as memories, will lead to the full variety of epistemic errors. We will fail to recognize some ideas as memories. We take non-memories to be memories, and sometimes we are uncertain whether an idea is a memory or the offspring of the imagination. Hume's observations about memory include descriptions of memory at work in actual human reasoning. So his treatment of memory is broader in scope than accounting for justification for knowledge claims. Hume takes there to be canonical cases of accurate memory, and canonical cases of misremembering. Broughton (1992) suggests Hume's account of memory is a helpful case study of Hume's proposed observational methodology in his science of man. Hume's observations of the phenomena of memory show that his project was not an examination of skepticism about memory. Hume presupposes that there are canonical cases of remembering.

Let's return to the question of how, on a particular occasion, one can tell whether one has a genuine idea of memory. Hume's examples suggest that one can't always tell, and this is a fact of our cognitive organization. But this should not be surprising, since Hume introduced memory as playing the same epistemic role as our impressions, and he does not think that we can give an account of the epistemic credentials of our original impressions. Of our impressions Hume writes, "We may draw inferences from the coherence of our perceptions, whether they be true or false; whether they represent nature justly, or be mere illusions of the senses" (T 1.3.5.3). Hume says this while explaining the epistemic context of ideas of memory, and thus it applies to memory ideas as well as to impressions of sense. Indeed throughout the *Treatise* and first *Enquiry* Hume almost always conjoins a reference to impressions with a reference to memory, typically referring to the "memory and senses" or "memory or senses" (T 1.3.6.4 and 7, T 1.3.7.6, T 1.3.9.2, T 1.3.13.1, T 1.3.16.6, T 1.4.1.9, EHU 4, part 1; EHU 5, parts 1 and 2; EHU 7, part 2; EHU 8, part 1; EHU 12, part 2). Again this suggests that the roles the senses play in inference, can be played as well by memory. Hume is strikingly consistent on this matter.

We noted earlier that Hume sometimes appears to characterize memories as impressions. Section 5 of part 3 is entitled "Of the impressions of the senses and memory." This instance may just be a scope ambiguity. Elsewhere there is no doubt that Hume explicitly refers to "impressions of the memory." He does so five times in the *Treatise*. For example, Hume writes "The impressions of the memory never change in any considerable degree" (T 1.3.9.7). Hume says that the imagination sometimes produces ideas with such high vivacity that they have "the same influence as the impressions of the memory" (T 1.3.10.9). As he describes the role of memory in our propensity to feign the continued existence of objects, Hume says that it is a propensity which "arises from some lively impressions of the memory" (T 1.4.2.42). The same propensity causes belief "by means of the present impressions of the memory, since, without the remembrance of former sensations, it is plain we never should have any belief of the continued existence of body" (T 1.4.2.43). Finally, in his wonderful example of the prisoner who discovers that the will of the jailer is as much a cause of his continued imprisonment as are "the walls and bars with which he is surrounded" Hume says of these two types of causes, natural and voluntary, that "the mind feels no difference betwixt them in passing from one link to another; nor is less certain of the future event than if it were connected with the present impressions of the memory and senses by a train of causes cemented together by what we are pleased to call a *physical necessity*" (T 2.3.1.17).

Passmore argues that the reference to impressions of memory is consistent with Hume's theory of ideas but that it is a position that Hume finds himself forced to adopt (Passmore 1980: 94ff.). It is inconsistent with the theory of ideas because

67

memories are ideas, derived from original impressions. Memories cannot be impressions, since a perception can't be both an impression and idea. That Hume is forced into this position, Passmore argues, is the result of Hume's concession that we can't compare memories with original impressions to establish the accuracy of memories as memories. Instead, Hume must take them to be impressions, with the epistemic credentials enjoyed by impressions.

Passmore's criticism presupposes that Hume intended to offer criteria for distinguishing real from apparent memories, and that the admission that we can't compare our ideas to the original impressions amounts to skepticism about memory. Yet Hume's reference to impressions of memory can hardly be the crude error Passmore takes it to be. Rather, as we noted above, Hume often groups memory and sense together because what we take to be memories, whether they are accurate or not, form the basis of our causal inferences, both our good inferences and our bad inferences. When in summer one draws the inference that avalanches are more likely on wind-loaded slopes of greater than 35 degrees than on slopes of less than 35 degrees, one need not have a present impression of deep snow in the mountains. One relies on memory, or more accurately, what one takes to be memory, which plays the same inferential role as impressions of sense would play were one on a snow covered mountain.

Memory, Belief, and Causal Inference

The early sections of part 3 of Book 1 spell out the central role of memory as providing the starting point in causal inference. How does memory function in belief formation beyond supplying the initial "impressions of sense and memory" from which we derive a related high-vivacity idea? In the canonical case of belief formation we infer effects when we are both supplied with an impression of sense or memory and we have experienced a constant conjunction of impressions of the cause followed by impressions of the effect. Is our experience, our stored experience of the constant conjunctions, a form of memory? Does Hume assign the task of remembering the perceptual pairings he refers to as constant conjunctions to the faculty of memory? Hume's description of experience makes explicit reference to memory. He says: "We remember to have had frequent instances of the existence of one species of objects; and also remember, that the individuals of another species of objects have always attended them, and have existed in a regular order of contiguity and succession with regard to them" (T 1.3.6.2). Hume clearly has an account of how our memories of constant conjunctions are structured. We have two complex memories: We remember the set of instances of one species of objects, and we remember another set of instances as being in regular contiguity and succession with members of the first. Hume doesn't say that we remember three things, namely the first set of instances, the second set, and the fact of the relation between members of the first set and members of the second set.

Can the account of memory Hume provides in 1.1.3 and 1.3.5 accommodate such complex memorial processes? In particular, can Hume make sense of remembering that the instances of a species bear some relation or relations to instances of some other species? This question introduces a fundamental issue in Hume's philosophy, namely the issue of whether there is a place for ideas of relations in Hume's theory of impressions and ideas. If we can't have ideas of relations, it's not clear how we could remember relations in the way Hume describes in 1.3.6. One way of making sense of such complex acts of memory is to treat them as dispositions (Costa 1998). Regardless of what account of memory we attribute to Hume in connection with causal inference, it is clear that memory has a central role in all stages of such inferences.

Are memories, as Hume characterizes them in 1.1.3 and 1.3.5, beliefs? That is, once we have Hume's theory of belief in place, should we count memories as beliefs? Would Hume say that if someone remembers something, that they believe it? And are some of the beliefs, beliefs about the past, memories?

We've already seen that Hume isn't always careful about distinguishing first person memories from impersonal beliefs about the past. Some commentators think the distinction is blurred. Loeb, for example, refers to beliefs about the past as "memory beliefs," a term Hume himself never employs (Loeb 2002). Treating some beliefs as memories is unobjectionable, as long as one notes that the route by which vivacity is acquired in belief is different from the way paradigmatic memories obtain their vivacity. Were all memories simply beliefs, Hume would not be able to classify memories with impressions as the starting point for causal inference. Hume's interest in memory as a faculty is largely restricted to the sections of the *Treatise* which occur before the introduction of his theory of belief. Perhaps this is why there are many phenomena associated with memory which Hume doesn't address at all, such as remembering how to do something, and the distinction between remembering something from a year ago and remembering it from yesterday, or a week ago (Martin and Deutscher 1966).

The Creation and Discovery of Personal Identity

Hume returns to the topic of memory at the end of T 1.4.6, in the positive phase of his account of the idea of the self. His view is that reflection on our past train of perceptions gives rise to the idea of the self when we notice that those perceptions are primarily related by resemblance and causation. Reflection on the past train of a person's perceptions will reveal resembling perceptions because the faculty of memory produces ideas which resemble the original impressions. So memory, Hume says, works by "producing the relation of resemblance among the perceptions" (T 1.4.6.18). Memory produces the memory ideas, and so produces the resemblance to original impressions, and our memory of such memories. In the reflective mental act of remembering our memories we encounter the resemblance relations "produced" by memory.

This reflection on memory also makes possible our comprehension of the relation of cause and effect. "Had we no memory, we never shou'd have any notion of causation, nor consequently of that chain of causes and effects, which constitute our self or person" (T 1.4.6.20). In order to have a notion of causation, we need to remember at least some constant conjunction pairs, present impressions, and ideas of effects. Hume does not claim here that memory is required for causal inference itself, though in light of our discussion in the last section, it is clear that he would endorse that claim too. The concept of causation, to which Hume appeals in characterizing the "true idea of the human mind," can't be had without our reflection on the memory's function of producing resemblance among perceptions (T 1.4.6.19).

The combination of memory and causation makes it possible to extend our understanding of our mental histories beyond our own memories. Just as we can go "beyond our senses" and infer the existence of Caesar, we can infer beyond our memories that we existed during periods of time for which we do not have direct memories. Hume describes this as the "discovery" of personal identity by memory. He writes: "In this view, therefore, memory does not so much *produce* as *discover* personal identity, by showing us the relation of cause and effect among our different perceptions" (T 1.4.6.20). It might appear that Hume is taking back the claim about the production of memory made just a few paragraphs earlier, but he is not. He is merely emphasizing that memory has this second role as well in personal identity. Memory both produces and discovers personal identity.

In the appendix to the *Treatise* Hume famously raised doubts about his Book 1 account of personal identity. Some commentators have sought to find the locus of that doubt in the role of memory in Hume's treatment of personal identity. Waxman (1992) argues that "retentive memory" is Hume's problem with personal identity. Hume can't explain our memory of our perceptual successions without presupposing that identity. On Baxter's (1998) interpretation, we get the idea of personal identity by misrepresenting the multiplicity of past perceptions as a single thing. If memory preserves form and order of our past perceptions, Baxter argues, it can't do the misrepresenting job required by the account of personal identity.

Memory and Imagination in Other Hume Texts

Book 1 of the *Treatise* is the only text where Hume explicitly treats the distinction between memory and imagination. In section 2 of the first *Enquiry* Hume describes ideas of the imagination, which can "form monsters, and join incongruous shapes and appearances" as easily as it can "conceive the most natural and familiar objects" (EHU 2.4). Here the contrast is between two kinds of ideas the imagination can form, the unbounded ideas of the imagination, or the ordinary ideas of natural and familiar objects. When Hume does refer to memory in the first *Enquiry*, he almost always conjoins memory with sense, as we noted above. While this is consistent with the views expressed in the *Treatise*, it also reflects Hume's attempt to clear away much of the complexity of his epistemology in the later work. The topic of memory, like that of continued and distinct existence and the self, does not make an appearance. Fortunately, we still have much with which to occupy ourselves in the rich and complex account of imagination and memory present in Hume's first published work.

See also 2 "Hume's Theory of Ideas"

References

Baxter, Donald L. M. (1998). "Hume's Labyrinth concerning the Idea of Personal Identity," *Hume Studies*, 24, pp. 203–34.

Broughton, Janet (1992). "What Does the Scientist of Man Observe?" *Hume Studies*, 28, pp. 155–68.

Costa, Michael (1998). "Hume on the Very Idea of a Relation," *Hume Studies*, 24, pp. 71–94.

Flage, Daniel (1985). "Hume on Memory and Causation," *Hume Studies*, 10th anniversary issue, pp. 168–88.

Garrett, Don (1997). *Cognition and Commitment in Hume's Philosophy* (Oxford: Oxford University Press).

Govier, Trudy (1972). "Variations on Force and Vivacity in Hume," *Philosophical Quarterly*, 86, pp. 44–52.

Hansen, Stacey J. (1988). "Hume's Impressions of Belief," *Hume Studies*, 14, pp. 277–304.

Johnson, Oliver (1987). " 'Lively' Memory and 'Past' Memory," *Hume Studies*, 13, pp. 343–59.

Kemp Smith, Norman (1941). *The Philosophy of David Hume* (London: Macmillan).

Loeb, Louis E. (2002). *Stability and Justification in Hume's Treatise* (Oxford: Oxford University Press).

Mackay, D. S. (1945). "The Illusion of Memory," *Philosophical Review*, 54, pp. 297–320.

Martin, C. B. and Deutscher, Max (1966). "Remembering," *Philosophical Review*, 75, pp. 161–96.

McDonough, Jeffrey K. (2002). "Hume's Account of Memory," *British Journal for the History of Philosophy*, 10, pp. 71–87.

Noxon, James (1976). "Remembering and Imagining the Past," in Donald W. Livingston and James T. King (eds.), *David Hume: A Re-evaluation* (New York: Fordham University Press).

Owen, David (1999). *Hume's Reason* (Oxford: Oxford University Press).

Passmore, John (1980). *Hume's Intentions*, 3rd edn. (London: Duckworth).

Pears, David (1990). *Hume's System: An Examination of the First Book of His "Treatise"* (Oxford: Oxford University Press).

Reid, Thomas (1849). *The Works of Thomas Reid*, ed. William Hamilton (Edinburgh: Maclachlan, Stewart, and Co.).

Russow, Lilly-Marlene (1980). "Simple Ideas and Resemblance," *The Philosophical Quarterly*, 30, pp. 342–50.

Traiger, Saul (1985). "Flage on Hume's Account of Memory," *Hume Studies*, 12, pp. 166–72.

—— (1994). "Beyond Our Senses: Recasting Book I, Part III of Hume's *Treatise*," *Hume Studies*, 20, pp. 241–59.

Urmson, John (1967). "Memory and Imagination," *Mind*, 76, pp. 83–91.

Waxman, Wayne (1992). "Hume's Quandary concerning Personal Identity," *Hume Studies*, 18, pp. 233–54.

Further Reading

Baier, Annette C. (1991). *A Progress of Sentiments: Reflections on Hume's "Treatise"* (Cambridge, MA: Harvard University Press).

Bricke, John (1980). *Hume's Philosophy of Mind* (Princeton, NJ: Princeton University Press).

Hendel, Charles (1963). *Studies in the Philosophy of David Hume* (Indianapolis, IN: Bobbs-Merrill).

Waxman, Wayne (1994). *Hume's Theory of Consciousness* (Cambridge: Cambridge University Press).

4

Hume and the Origin of Our Ideas of Space and Time

WAYNE WAXMAN

Together with relations of resemblance and cause and effect, relations of contiguity in time or place are the fundamental principles of the associationism at the core of Hume's theory of human understanding. Like resemblances, but in contrast to causal relations, contiguity operates on the associative imagination prior to and independently of customs of thought inculcated in us by previous experience. Nevertheless, their psychological efficacy (again like that of resemblances) depends, in several regards, on the underpinning of custom. For example, contiguity presupposes custom in the form of cause and effect relations in order to extend its influence beyond the scope of objects immediately present to the senses (T 1.3.2.3), since its capacity to generate belief is otherwise extremely limited (T 1.3.9.6). But, most importantly, contiguity association is actuated by customs of thought rooted in our lifelong experience as creatures existing in a spatio-temporal world:

> 'Tis likewise evident, that as the senses, in changing their objects, are necessitated to change them regularly, and take them as they lie *contiguous* to each other, the imagination must by long custom acquire the same method of thinking, and run along the parts of space and time in conceiving its objects. (T 1.1.4.2; also 2.3.7.5 and 2.3.8.8)

Our bodily movements always proceed from one place to the adjacent place. The objects that come into our tangible reach with each new step are those contiguous to those which were in our reach before, and something analogous occurs with motion through visible space. And not only our bodily actions but our mental ones as well unfold from one time to the next. So used do we become to these constant patterns of change that we form a custom of associating objects according to this sensible framework. But how do we arrive at the idea of this framework in the first place? Or, in other words, how do our minds form ideas of space and time?

We shall see in what follows that, in the case of space and time, Hume did what he did in the cases of causal connection, identity, and other ideas for which he could find no originating impression of the senses: he traced it to a source in the psychological action and affect distinctive of operations of customary association. In sections 1 and 2, we shall see that in their most elementary incarnation, space and time are instances of the kinds of association whereby abstract general ideas are produced:

customary resemblance relations. However, since contiguity together with resemblance prove inadequate to yield the ideas of space and time we implicitly affirm in all our reasoning regarding matters of fact and real consequence, Hume found it necessary to incorporate causal association into the mix. Thus, in sections 3 and 4, we shall see how Hume employed causal association to account for: (1) how we come to accord a reality to space and time that extends their bounds beyond the purview of the senses, at every scale and distance, without limit; (2) the general points of view whereby, for example, we "see" an unchanging object even though at different distances it fills more or less of the visual field; and (3) the integration of visible and tangible space into a single space common to both senses, wherein we can see and touch the very same objects (i.e., sense-divide transcendent objects).

First Origins: Visual Space

Since Hume's account of the nature and origin of the idea of time is modeled on that of space (sometimes termed 'extension'), let us start with the latter. "The idea of space is convey'd to the mind by two senses, sight and touch; nor does anything ever appear extended, that is not either visible or tangible" (T 1.2.3.15). This is not because Hume supposed spatial perceptions – extension, shape, place, distance, etc. – to be *contents* common to vision and touch. Quite the contrary, at the level of sensory inputs (impressions of sensation), he deemed the appearances of vision – arrays of color and light – to be as fully incommensurate with the appearances of touch – qualities of soft/hard, wet/dry, warm/cold, sharp/blunt, etc., as well as proprioception – as they are with the qualities of olfactory, gustatory, and auditory sensory inputs. Indeed, he took this so far as to reject the view (favored by Locke and other philosophers) that the mind has the power to distinguish the spatial aspects common to vision and touch from the contents of visual and tactual sensation that are unique to each sense. Such "distinctions of reason," or "partial considerations," run foul of Hume anti-abstractionism (T 1.1.7): his denial that our minds are endowed with a capacity to distinguish in sensory appearances items that cannot each be perceived in the absence of the other. Applied to the case of space (as Hume did: T 1.2.4.12), it follows from the impossibility of either seeing shape and other spatial features in the absence of all color and light, or feeling them in the absence of all distinctively tactual qualities (softness et al.), that the perceived contents of their appearances cannot be the reason both senses qualify as sources of ideas of space and extension.

Rather than in the sensible qualities of the parts themselves, Hume located the resemblance between visual and tangible objects in "the disposition of their parts" (T 1.2.3.5). What did he mean by this? How, without re-introducing abstract distinctions through the back door, do our minds recognize a resemblance in respect of a disposition of parts? And to what extent does its recognition suffice to explain the origin of the idea of space? To answer these questions, we need to start with what, for Hume, is the first inception of the idea:

> This table before me is alone sufficient by its view to give me the idea of extension. This
> idea, then, is borrow'd from, and represents some impression, which this moment appears

> to the senses. But my senses convey to me only the impressions of colour'd points, dispos'd in a certain manner. If the eye is sensible of any thing farther, I desire it may be pointed out to me. But if it be impossible to shew any thing farther, we may conclude with certainty, that the idea of extension is nothing but a copy of these colour'd points, and of the manner of their appearance. (T 1.2.3.4)

Because the distinction between colored points and the manner of their appearance is one between items that cannot be perceived independently of one another, it fails to satisfy the separability criterion (T 1.1.7.3) that Hume used to differentiate items genuinely distinguishable by the human mind from ones that are distinct only in language (as signs signifying different items by virtue of the different customary associations capable of being triggered by the same idea: T 1.1.7.9). Hume consequently proceeded to resolve it as he did all purportedly abstract differences (aspects, distinctions of reason):

> Suppose that in the extended object, or composition of colour'd points, from which we first receiv'd the idea of extension, the points were of a purple colour; it follows, that in every repetition of that idea we wou'd not only place the points in the same order with respect to each other, but also bestow on them that precise colour, with which alone we are acquainted. But afterwards having experience of the other colours of violet, green, red, white, black, and of all the different compositions of these, and finding a resemblance in the disposition of colour'd points, of which they are compos'd, we omit the peculiarities of colour, as far as possible, and found an abstract idea merely on that disposition of points, or manner of appearance, in which they agree. (T 1.2.3.5)

How far Hume deemed it possible to "omit the peculiarities of colour" he made clear in his analysis of abstract ideas in T 1.1.7: "the mind wou'd never have dream'd of distinguishing a figure from the body figur'd, as being in reality neither distinguishable, nor different, nor separable; did it not observe, that even in this simplicity there might be contain'd many different resemblances and relations" (T 1.1.7.18). Similarly, while the disposition of visible points is one and indistinguishable from their color, we can form distinct "abstract" general ideas of them thanks to the different resemblances and relations of which they admit. In particular, when we compare a purple table with a purple flower we associate them in a relation of resemblance which can thereafter be extended to other things; if this procedure is repeated often enough, a custom of thought will be instilled which lies in readiness to be triggered by any appropriate stimulus (i.e., all the things we term "purple"). But when the same impression of a purple table is compared to that of a red table, these too are apt to be found resembling in a different way that thereafter may be extended to encompass quite different things, eventually instilling in us a new custom of thought susceptible of being triggered by different stimuli than the first (i.e., tables of whatever color). Similar such comparisons can lead to innumerably many other customary associations of resemblance (graininess, smoothness, rectangularity, pieces of furniture, wooden artifacts, four-legged things, etc.); and among these is the one that lies in readiness to be triggered specifically by any and all dispositions of colored points, that is, the visual idea of space. Thus, on Hume's account, we separate out the visual idea of space not by exercising any special capacity to discern abstract differences of aspect in a single, isolated perception, but by performing innumerable comparisons between distinct perceptions, associating them in accordance with a certain resemblance relation, and doing so with sufficient frequency and regularity as to instill a custom of thought: *an idea that therefore owes its origin as much to the impression of reflexion contributed by associative imagination as it does to impressions of sensation contributed by the sense of sight.*

Here, one may well wonder why Hume opted to describe the associative custom in which the idea of visual space has its origin in terms of indivisible colored points rather than regions or figures. What kind of points did he have in mind? Not the kind of minimal unit that "is merely a fictitious denomination, which the mind may apply to any quantity of objects it collects together," such that, by the mere stipulation of a rule of numeration, twenty men, the "whole globe of the earth, nay the whole universe *may be consider'd as an unite*" (T 1.2.2.3). The units of multiplicity concerned in the idea of visual space are present to our consciousness prior to and independently of any denomination (general term) we may care to apply, and are in effect built into each and every visual perception (impression or idea) itself. To discern any such *minimum visibile*, simply "Put a spot of ink upon paper, fix your eye upon that spot, and retire to such a distance, that at last you lose sight of it; 'tis plain, that the moment before it vanish'd the image or impression was perfectly indivisible" (T 1.2.2.4). The multiplicity of a visual impression, then, corresponds to the actual number of colored points that appear in it.

This should not be thought to mean that Hume was under the delusion that we see the world pointillistically, even indeed when no variation of light or color is apparent. But there is another sense, grounded on past experience rather than immediate perception, in which his pointillistic characterization seems warranted. From the beginning of our visual lives, we are all experienced in comparing our present visual impression to that of an instant previous and finding that they differ in these ways: the appearance or disappearance of a single colored point (as when a distant bird comes into or passes out of view); the replacement of a point of one color with a point of another color (as when the bird's wings catch the light of the sun and suddenly flash brightly); the changing location of a single colored point (a fly zigzagging against a white background just near enough to see); a point that before was indivisible expands to a divisible size, or vice versa; as a multitude of separated points (sand grains, stars in the night sky); and so on. After we have had enough experience of paying heed to visible points and marking their situations and relations with respect to other points, they become as deeply ingrained in our habits of visual reckoning as distinguishable visible figures or regions.

Why then does Hume's account of the origin of the idea of space/extension focus on points rather than regions or the wholes they compose? Surely, part of the answer is that a sense able to resolve detail all the way down to, and permits us to maintain a focus on, indivisible points is one that permits the very finest discriminations to be made (albeit subject to the infirmity described in T 1.2.4.7). If our vision consisted instead of only blurred patches (as is the case with eyes without lenses), so that no points ("what has neither length, breadth nor depth"), linear contours ("length without breadth or depth"), or surfaces ("length and breadth without depth," T 1.2.4.9) could become visible to us, then the formal multiplicity of vision – the fineness and range of detail it enables us to discriminate – would be no greater than that of smell or taste. And smell and taste are senses that, precisely because of their deficiency in this respect, are incapable of furnishing us with an idea of space ("nor is there any thing, but what is colour'd or tangible, that has parts dispos'd after such a manner, as to convey that idea," T 1.4.5.9). The focus on points in Hume's account thus has the effect of stressing the centrality of a *suitably rich and varied formal multiplicity* to the status of vision, or any other sense, as a source of the idea of space/extension.

In addition, this focus enabled Hume to emphasize another element, lacking from an account of the origin of space such as that offered by Locke, which considers space only as an indeterminate extension and distance (Locke 1690: 2.13.3): *determinability*. For while a visual impression consisting of a wash of blurs or invariable in lighting and color is certainly indeterminate enough to satisfy Locke's description of the idea, it falls well short of visible space/extension properly so called, as the idea of something in which visible objects appear and disappear, change their color and contour, grow, shrink, and alter their relative positions and situations inside, outside, alongside, adjacent to, separated from, above, below, right of, left of, in front of, or behind one another. The idea of such limitless determinability is impossible except when visual perceptions are conceived as "a composition of visible . . . points dispos'd in a certain order" (T 1.2.5.21): an *ordered* manifold, or *nexus* of positions, formed of coexistent loci (points) which preserve their situation and relations to one another through any and all changes in respect of light and color ("co-existent parts dispos'd in a certain order, and capable of being at once present to the sight," T 2.3.7.5).

Notions like "discrimin*ability*" and "determin*ability*" imply powers, which, on Hume's view, resolve into customs of thought. (He used "power" to denote customary resemblance association at T 1.1.7.7 and 12.) In the present context, this is just to say that the idea of visible space/extension is the outcome of comparing visual perceptions, associating them according to their various resemblances, and forming habits when these associations are strongly reinforced, whether by frequent recurrence or some other cause. The key, as with aspects and distinctions of reason generally, is that visible space is never anything present to our eyes, prior to and independent of experience and habit, but rather something that exists only in and through the actions and affects of associative imagination as directed upon visual objects (impressions and ideas). Even while seeming not to take place at all (EHU 4.8), the customary association in which the idea of the determinable ordered manifold of space has its origin confers on immediately perceived sensations of light and color determinate spatial form, so that the two seem to be as inseparably one as the motion we are accustomed to seeing communicated from one object converging upon another, stationary object seems to us a single continuous motion. (Hume says, "the relation . . . binds the objects in the closest and most intimate manner to each other, so as to make us imagine them to be absolutely inseparable," T 1.3.9.10). Yet, no matter how immediate and primitive a datum visible space may *seem* to us to be, for Hume the fact remains that, without comparison, association and custom grounded on experienced repetition, we could no more form an idea of the formal multiplicity and determinability distinctive of visible space than we could form an idea of necessary connections between distinct existents. The distinctive phenomenology of visual space – the characteristic "look" of flat, concave, and convex surfaces, interposed forms, foreshortening, etc. – is thus as much an amalgam of sensory inputs and associative imagination as the distinctive facial physiognomy of embarrassment or agonizing pain.

76

The Space Common to Vision and Touch, the Time Common to All the Senses

The existence of a formal multiplicity in tactual sensation comparable to that of visual accounts for the ability to form an abstract idea of an *ordered manifold* of tangible points, with a *determinability* comparable to that found in visible space. The challenge facing Hume was to explain how the complete qualitative incommensurateness between visual and tactual sensation is overcome by an associative relation of resemblance of sufficient strength to fuse them into a single, still more general idea of space/extension, whereof each is thereafter regarded as an instantiation. (Even so, how the two ideas become integrated into a single external sense of objects that transcend the divide between vision and touch cannot be understood until we shift our focus from customary association in relations of contiguity to those of causation in the next section.)

The key to confronting this challenge is the recognition that the principle of resemblance is not dependent, as philosophers previous to Hume tended to suppose, upon the sensible appearances of things:

> Resembling ideas are not only related together, but the actions of the mind, which we employ in considering them, are so little different, that we are not able to distinguish them. This last circumstance is of great consequence; and we may in general observe, that wherever the actions of the mind in forming any two ideas are the same or resembling, we are very apt to confound these ideas, and take the one for the other. (T 1.2.5.21)

This principle would prove indispensable to Hume's account of identity according to which resembling actions of the mind lead us to conceive, and believe in the existence of, identities between distinct objects notwithstanding their lack of resemblance in appearance (T 1.4.2.32–6 and n; and 1.4.6.5–6). Although not explicitly invoked in his account of the origin of an idea of space common to both vision and touch, this principle seems indispensable to understanding how, notwithstanding the qualitative disparity of their objects, both alike give rise to ideas of extension, figure, place, motion, etc. For the actions of associative imagination, first in constituting, then in continually operating with the equally determinable ordered manifolds of vision and touch, are so closely resembling that the imagination is induced to disregard the qualitative incommensurateness of the objects – visible and tangible *appearances* – and treats these too as resembling.

The application of Hume's principle to the case of time is, if anything, even more unavoidable than that of space. Time differs from space in two principal regards: (1) whereas ideas of spatial features originate only in vision and touch, temporal ideas can be "deriv'd from the succession of our perceptions of every kind, ideas as well as impressions, and impressions of reflection as well as of sensation" (T 1.2.3.7), and (2) whereas the manner of appearance of the spatial is defined by "that quality of the co-existence of parts," the temporal "is compos'd of parts that are not co-existent . . . and consequently that idea must be deriv'd from a succession of changeable objects" (T 1.2.3.8). Yet, these differences notwithstanding, the psychological processes whereby ideas of the temporal are acquired are identical to those which give rise to ideas of the spatial. From an unchanging object no idea of time can be derived "since it produces none but co-existent impressions"; only "a succession of changeable objects" (T 1.2.3.8) can yield the idea of something composed of non-coexistent parts. But since the successiveness of, say, five notes played on the flute cannot be perceived or conceived independently of the sounds – "The ideas of some objects it [the mind] certainly must have, nor is it possible for it without these ideas ever to arrive at any conception of time" (T 1.2.3.10) – any supposition that the former, as the *manner* of appearance of these auditory objects, is something really distinct from these auditory objects themselves falls foul of Hume's anti-abstractionism. So in order to distinguish the former and "conjoin it with any other objects" (T 1.2.3.10), we must undertake comparisons between distinct perceptions, associate them in resemblance relations, and, among the habits of mind that result, acquire one that remains in readiness to be triggered by all and only those stimuli to which temporal predicates are applied. Thus, time, understood as an ordered manifold of determinable positions composed of indivisible, non-coexistent instants, is, on Hume's account, as much an amalgam of the senses and associative imagination as space.

The significance of this dual origin, in the case of space/extension no less than that of time/duration, is that while, on the one hand, these abstract general ideas suffice for us to *talk* of things succeeding or enduring without reference (even implicitly) to the perceptions continually coursing through our minds, or to *talk* of the extension, figure, etc., of objects without reference to their colors and/or feel, on the other hand, we can neither perceive nor conceive individual things that instantiate these general ideas other than these perceptions. For since abstract ideas are "in themselves individual" (T 1.1.7.6) and " 'tis only by custom they can become general in their representation" (T 1.1.7.16), we cannot detach temporal or spatial predicates from the individual objects from which they can be acquired and employ them to represent unchangeable objects or invisible, intangible extended objects:

> I know there are some who pretend, that the idea of duration is applicable in a proper sense to objects, which are perfectly unchangeable; and this I take to be the common opinion of philosophers as well as the vulgar. But to be convinc'd of its falshood we need but reflect on the foregoing conclusion, that the idea of duration is always deriv'd from a succession of changeable objects, and can never be convey'd to the mind by any thing stedfast and unchangeable. For it inevitably follows from thence, that since the idea of duration cannot be *deriv'd* from such an object, it can never in any propriety or exactness be *apply'd* to it, nor can any thing unchangeable be ever said to have duration. Ideas always represent the objects or impressions, from which they are deriv'd, and can never without a fiction represent or be apply'd to any other. (T 1.2.3.11, emphasis added)

Hume's anti-abstractionist, associationalist account of the origin of our ideas of space and time so restricts their scope of application that, *talk* though we may of the contrary, they afford human understanding the means to perceive or conceive (become conscious of) nothing enduring save non-coexistent complexes of instantaneously existing sensations, emotions, and thoughts, and nothing extended save for co-existent complexes of colored or felt points. In other words, Hume's account of the origin of space and time, and the consequences he drew from it, is as thoroughly Berkeleyan as the analysis of abstract ideas it exemplifies (T 1.1.7.17 and n), and so carries with it a similarly extreme idealist implication: unchangeable things, and extended things that are neither visible (colored) nor tangible (soft, dry, smooth, etc.) are, in a strict ideational sense (as distinct from the looser linguistic sense), utterly unintelligible to us, and only by means of certain fictions of the imagination can we ever, *per impossibile*, be induced to suppose the contrary.

Association by Cause and Effect: A World in Mind

Abstract ideas of space and time are all that is requisite to begin associating perceptions by contiguity in conformity with the myriadly determinable, super-rich formal multiplicity of these ordered manifolds. Thereafter, despite the fact that the human "body is confined to one planet, along which it creeps with pain and difficulty; the thought can in an instant transport us into the most distant regions of the universe; or even beyond the universe, into the unbounded chaos, where nature is supposed to lie in total confusion" (EHU 2.4). Yet, our adherence in thought to the same order of space and time to which the human body is subject results from the fact that contiguity is an *associative* relation, with just enough force to prod the imagination out of its native situation of indifference into one in which transitions in thought to contiguous places are easier and more natural than others:

> in the conception of those objects, which we regard as real and existent, we take them in their proper order and situation, and never leap from one object to another, which is distant from it, without running over, at least in a cursory manner, all those objects, which are interpos'd betwixt them. (T 2.3.7.2)

We "trace the succession of time by a similar succession of ideas," except for one difference arising from the fact that instants, unlike points, are never coexistent: the association is strengthened by transitions of thought that proceed in the same direction as time (from past to future), and decreased when proceeding the opposite way, with the consequence that "A small degree of distance in the past has . . . a greater effect, in interrupting and weakening the conception, than a much greater in the future" (T 2.3.7.8).

Yet, the easy transitions effected by contiguity association are still "very feeble and uncertain" (T 1.3.9.6) in themselves, and such poor transferors of vivacity from impressions to associated spatially and/or temporally contiguous ideas, that they would not figure prominently in Hume's associationalist account of human understanding were it not for the foundation provided them by causal association:

> As the relation of cause and effect is requisite to persuade us of any real existence, so is this persuasion requisite to give force to these other relations . . . There is no manner of necessity for the mind to feign any resembling and contiguous objects; and if it feigns such, there is as little necessity for it always to confine itself to the same, without any difference or variation . . . The mind forsees and anticipates the change; and even from the very first instant feels the looseness of its actions, and the weak hold it has of its objects. And as this imperfection is very sensible in every single instance, it still encreases by experience and observation, when we compare the several instances we may remember, and form a *general rule* against the reposing any assurance in those momentary glimpses of light, which arise in the imagination from a feign'd resemblance and contiguity. (T 1.3.9.6)

Although it may be easier for the imagination to conceive of two contiguous objects together after a first encounter, the association is too weak to create an expectation that they will be similarly related at the next encounter. Only if some cause of their proximity (or distance) is discovered, or a cause which enables us to predict how their relative relations will change over time, will the relation acquire a fixity in imagination (T 1.3.2.2), and become, as it were, a new reference point on the mental maps we continually draw up of our world. In this way, I take for granted a cause that keeps my feet on the earth when I walk; a cause which makes my next step take me into the contiguous place rather than one a continent away, and the contiguous time rather than one a million years hence; causes that constitute and maintain the structure of my body; causes that explain the mountain range that exists between China and India, and why the continents are in their present positions; causes of the existence, situation, and actions of the moon, the solar system, the galaxy, and galaxy clusters; and everything else that enters into the conceptions which give contiguity its special role in constituting the fixity and order of the world and my place within it.

Yet, this only scratches the surface of the role causal association plays in our consciousness of a world of objects integrated in a single natural order extending to the farthest reaches of space and time. When a custom of thought, triggered by the sight and smell of smoke coming in through the transom, induces me to imagine a fire in the hall outside, I do not simply make a facile transition in thought to the idea of the fire, I conceive the fire in the forceful, lively manner Hume equated with *belief in its real existence*. And it is owing entirely to the vivacity with which I conceive what is after all merely an object of my thought (and, in that regard, no different from a fire in a daydream) that I take precautions not only against asphyxiation, but against being incinerated as well. Similarly, if I hear familiar voices outside, I imagine the people with whom I associate these voices, and do so with the same belief (degree of vivacity feeling) in their presence as I confer on the sound (auditory impression) itself. In these, and countless other instances, causal association prompts us to attribute real existence to things present to our consciousness only in thought (idea), not in sensation or reflexion (impression).

Nor is this all. At the same time we attribute real existence to objects by means of causal inference, we do so to the places and times they occupy as well, and thereby extend the bounds of existent (non-fictive) space beyond the immediate confines of vision and touch, and time beyond the range of present perception and memory. This effect is multiplied by the fact that all causes are themselves deemed the effects of other causes: the fire in the hall was caused, say, by an electrical short, this by a frayed wire, the fraying by the nibblings of mice, the presence of mice in the building an effect of their being driven out of the next building by construction taking place there, the construction resulting from the renovation plans of the new owner, who got the money for it from an inheritance which came about when his father was murdered by a junky seeking money for his next fix, and so on and on and on. Since similar causal chains, with fewer or more of the blanks filled in, are taken for granted in respect of every event to which I am witness, or which I hear or read others attesting to, the space and time of real things demarcated by the purview of the senses and memory is easily dwarfed by the sphere comprised of the realities we infer to exist by means of customary association in relations of cause and effect:

'Tis this latter principle, which peoples the world, and brings us acquainted with such existences, as by their removal in time and place, lie beyond the reach of the senses and memory. By means of it I paint the universe in my imagination, and fix my attention on any part of it I please. I form an idea of *Rome*, which I neither see nor remember; but which is connected with such impressions as I remember to have received from the conversation and books of travelers and historians. This idea of *Rome* I place in a certain situation on the idea of an object, which I call the globe. I join to it the conception of a particular government, and religion, and manners. I look backward and consider its first foundation; its several revolutions, successes, and misfortunes. All this, and every thing else, which I believe, are nothing but ideas; tho' by their force and settled order, arising from custom and the relation of cause and effect, they distinguish themselves from the other ideas, which are merely the offspring of the imagination. (T 1.3.9.4)

These dimensions are further expanded by the progress of science: the very large, the very small, the very remote in time, additional dimensions, repeating Big Bang universes, universes within universes, etc. Even if scientists were to conclude that they had discovered the farthest limit of the humanly knowable universe, we would still not treat these bounds as absolute, if only on account of our unshakeable conviction in the truth of the general causal maxim (T 1.3.3 and *Letter from a Gentleman to his Friend in Edinburgh* II), which allows us to infer for each existence (things, their states, their actions) some cause prior to it in the order of time without which it would not have existed.

Causal association is also indispensable to our ability to construct general points of view independent of our particular viewpoint at any instant. With each movement of the eyes or hand, each shift of the head, each movement of the body, the appearances of visible objects change: in size, shape, and/or tint; from horizontal to vertical, top to bottom, inside to outside, and/or front to back; in their proximity or remoteness from other objects; in their being at rest or in motion, fast or slow, accelerating or decelerating, constant or erratic; etc. How then is it possible to form a stable point of view, from which the objects are not only *understood* not to change with our continuously changing points of view, but even *seem* (phenomenologically) not to change? Hume's answer lies in the capacity of the imagination to develop habits of adapting the causal information it gradually accumulates to compensate for the peculiarities of each point of view, thereby circumventing the need for deliberative reflection:

The judgment here corrects the inequalities of our internal emotions and perceptions; in like manner, as it preserves us from error, in the several variations of images, present to our external senses. The same object, at a double distance, really throws on the eye a picture of but half the bulk; yet we imagine that it appears of the same size in both situations; because we know, that, on our approach to it, its image would expand on the eye, and that the difference consists not in the object itself, but in our position with regard to it. And, indeed, without such a correction of appearances, both in internal and external sentiment, men could never think or talk steadily on any subject; while their fluctuating situations produce a continual variation on objects, and throw them into such different and contrary lights and positions. (EPM 5.41; also T 3.3.1.30 and 3.3.3.2)

The imagination, operating in accordance with *general rules* founded on experience-bred causal associations, quite literally alters the "look" of things:

> 'Tis universally allow'd by the writers on optics, that the eye at all times sees an equal number of physical points, and that a man on the top of a mountain has no larger an image presented to his senses, than when he is cooped up in the narrowest court or chamber. 'Tis only by experience that he infers the greatness of the object from some peculiar qualities of the image; and this inference of the judgment he confounds with sensation, as is common on other occasions. (T 1.3.9.11)

Why does a great mountain, formerly seen only in the distance, strike us as huge on nearer approach even though we can blot it out, and much else beside, by holding a hand in front of our eyes? Clearly, the point of view of the imagination is not that of the senses. From infancy, we assemble a body of general rules whereby to accommodate our viewpoint to the causal profile of each species of object, as well as to the order, circumstances, and other factors distinctive of their efficacy, whether in exercising their powers on other objects or on our sense organs. This "reflexion on general rules" becomes so ingrained and automatic that, as with all customary acts of mind, it pre-empts the need for comparison and reckoning, and is inevitably mistaken for "immediate" perception. Objects then come to seem as fixed and unalterable in their sensible qualities as we imagine them to be, notwithstanding the fact that these qualities are actually in a continual flux and movement:

> Where an opinion admits of no doubt, or opposite probability . . . the understanding corrects the appearances of the senses, and makes us imagine, that an object at twenty foot distance seems even to the eye as large as one of the same dimensions at ten. (T 1.3.10.12)

Just as it is rule-governed imagination, rather than the senses, to which the posture of a human face seems happy, so too the world, both within and without, takes on its stable, orderly phenomenology only when the point of view of the imagination has become seamlessly amalgamated into that of the senses.

Whether because Locke, in his treatment of three-dimensional seeing (Locke 1690: 2.9.8–10), and, still more so, Berkeley, in his writings on vision, had already so extensively worked this vein, or for other reasons, Hume did not enter into detail as to how imagination transforms the phenomenology of visual experience so profoundly that what we take ourselves to be directly sensing is in fact the product of its rule-governed synthesis. Nevertheless, the cases of magnitude and distance, as well as similar examples (T 1.3.12.24, 1.3.13.14, 2.2.5.18, 2.3.8.8, and 3.3.1.15), make clear that he was no less cognizant than his predecessors that the world constituted (and inhabited) by imagination has a markedly different "look" than the one our senses actually present to us. If the contribution of the former could be stripped out, the scene we would find before us would be "a perpetual flux and movement":

> Our eyes cannot turn in their sockets without varying our perceptions. Our thought is still more variable than our sight; and all our other senses and faculties contribute to this change. (T 1.4.6.4)

And:

Nay farther, even with relation to that succession, we cou'd only admit of those per-ceptions, which are immediately present to our consciousness, nor cou'd those lively imagines, with which the memory presents us, be ever receiv'd as true pictures of past perceptions. (T 1.4.7.3)

Before we are even out of our cradles, however, we accumulate sufficient causal inform-ation to become firm believers in the uniformity of nature (EHU 4.23 and 5.22), and to devise general rules to correct for our fluctuating points of view, so that, before long, the kaleidoscopically shifting scene our senses actually present to consciousness becomes as strange and attentively inaccessible as the blindspot at the center of the visual field or the continuous ribbon of sound conveying (discretely articulated) speech in our native tongue. For by then customary association has so indelibly affixed the lens of "common" (T 3.3.1.30), "steady and general points of view" (T 3.3.1.15), formed in accordance with "some general inalterable standard" (T 3.3.3.2), that, very early in life, we lose the ability to view the world in any other way.

Yet, the general point of view fashioned in the imagination has an importance in Hume's system that goes far beyond the phenomenology of experience. Even when we compensate for our fluctuating points of view from moment to moment, there is still a natural tendency to consider the world from the point of view focused on the enduring self. For "our consciousness gives us so lively a conception of our own person, that 'tis not possible to imagine that any thing can in this particular go beyond it" (T 2.1.11.4). "This lively idea changes by degrees into a real impression . . . and conveys a sensible degree of vivacity to the idea of any other object, to which we are related" (T 2.2.4.7), space and time not excepted:

There is an easy reason, why every thing contiguous to us, either in space or time, shou'd be conceiv'd with a peculiar force and vivacity, and excel every other object, in its influence on the imagination. Ourself is intimately present to us, and whatever is related to self must partake of that quality. But where an object is so far remov'd as to have lost the advantage of this relation, [and], as it is farther remov'd, its idea becomes still fainter and more obscure.

'Tis obvious, that the imagination can never totally forget the points of space and time, in which we are existent; but receives such frequent advertisements of them from the pas-sions and senses, that however it may turn its attention to foreign and remote objects, it is necessitated every moment to reflect on the present . . . When we reflect, therefore, on any object distant from ourselves, we are oblig'd not only to reach it at first by passing thro' all the intermediate space betwixt ourselves and the object, but also to renew our progress every moment; being every moment recall'd to the consideration of ourselves and our present situation. The *fewer* steps we make to arrive at the object, and the *smoother* the road is, this diminution of vivacity is less sensibly felt, but still may be observ'd more or less in proportion to the degrees of distance and difficulty. (T 2.3.7.1–2)

From this *subjective* point of view, imagination situates and relates objects not accord-ing to their own *objective* situation and relations in space and time but according to their spatial and temporal orientation relative to oneself. Objects are near or far according to their distance from oneself; so too they are right and left, above and below, in front and behind, at rest and in motion, even earlier and later (present, future, and past) in relation to oneself. Moreover, the vivacity of the idea of the self is extended to objects and makes them more vivid, so they weigh more in our thought and action, in proportion to their temporal and spatial proximity to the self. So, objects the imagination can reach only by a complicated, difficult path suffer a sensible loss of vivacity, and our belief in their real existence diminishes and may even disappear altogether. In principle, this effect should extend to other facets of their spatial and temporal situation and relations as well. For example, because it is more difficult to imagine the setting sun as vastly larger and more distant than the huge mountain behind which it is about to disappear than to consider it to be just as it appears to us (since "the present situation of the person is always that of the imagination," T 2.3.7.8), this lesser facility should translate into a lesser degree of belief. Why then does it not? Why, that is, does the objective state of affairs prevail in our reasoning over the subjective disposition of the imagination in shaping our belief here as well as in countless other cases?

Although Hume did not address this issue specifically, he provided us with the means to do so when he made clear that customary association in relations of cause and effect has the power to facilitate transitions of thought, and thereby to transfer force and vivacity (belief) from impressions to ideas without sensible diminution. We have then only to connect this with the features essential to all causal relations to understand how the subjective point of view, together with the space and time defined conformably to it, can be integrated into, and subordinated to, an *objective point of view*, with its own distinctive *objective* space and time, constituted conformably with general rules of causal relation. The features in question are these: (1) causal connections are never immediately perceptible, but always depend, either directly or indirectly, on experience to be discovered (T 1.3.8.14, 1.3.12.3, 1.3.15.1, and 1.4.2.42); (2) although distinct (distinguishable, separable) from one another, all causes are immediately contiguous to their effects in the order both of time (T 1.3.2.7) and (when all the relata are spatial) of space ("nothing can operate in a time or place, which is ever so little remov'd from its existence," T 1.3.2.6); and (3) all objects joined in causal relations, whether internal or external, are beneficiaries of the projective illusion that places the efficacy in them rather than in the mind that considers them (T 1.3.14.25 and EHU 7.29n). Because we situate powers in the objects to which we attribute them, we cannot help believing that the cause is immediately antecedent to and contiguous to its effect, and consequently cannot help using these relations as "general unalterable standards" to correct for appearances to the contrary. For example, if I smell smoke before I feel the heat of the fire, the custom of regarding the latter as the cause of the former leads me, without pausing to reflect, to reverse their order in imagination and regard the fire as earlier in *objective* time despite the fact that *subjectively*, in relation to *me*, both my thought of the fire and my sensation of it occurred after my sensing the smoke. Similarly, although I can never see all the sides of a building simultaneously, the causal associations that enter into my belief that the parts of the building maintain a constant relation in space and time induces me to treat them as *objectively* coexistent, despite the subjective successiveness (T 1.3.2.2). Or, again, although an object such as a rock ten miles into the interior of the earth beneath my present position or the non-facing hemisphere of the moon have only the most "philosophical" of relations to my subjective point of view, they nevertheless are regarded as no less really existent objectively than objects within arm's reach. For, as each is an extension of a causal chain firmly rooted in natural relations and associated with a present impression, the imagination will apply a general rule to enhance the vivacity of any idea I should chance to form of them to a degree equal to that of the floor I feel beneath my feet or the casement through which I see the moon. It should thus be clear that it is well within the capacity of Hume's system to explain how we integrate the ego-centric order of space and time befitting our subjective point of view into the inferred objective space and time synthesized in imagination in accordance with general rules founded on causal association.

Sense-Divide Transcendent Space and Time

A topic given still sketchier treatment by Hume is the role of causal association in uniting the spaces of vision and touch to yield what is, for all intents and purposes, a single, integrated external sense, with its own sense-divide transcending objects. That he was familiar with, and endorsed, at least the part of Berkeley's theory of vision that deals with the role of customary association in integrating the formal multiplicities of vision and touch, is suggested by his allusion to one of its most novel and important tenets: the role of eyeball motion in judging the distance between visible objects ("the motion that is requir'd in the eye, in its passage from one to another," T 1.2.5.12). Since eyeball movements are sensed by feeling rather than by vision, this amounts to an implicit endorsement of the emphasis placed on them by Berkeley in integrating what we see with the haptic spatial axes centered on one's own body (Berkeley 1732: ss. 16, 97–8, and 145). Although Hume was not explicit about the role of causal association in this connection, it is difficult to see how else to cash out his claim that our visual judgments depend as much on (empirical) reason as on the eyes themselves except in terms of customary association in relations of cause and effect:

> I need not insist upon the more trite topics, employ'd by the sceptics in all ages, against the evidence of *sense*; such as those which are derived from the imperfection and falla-ciousness of our organs, on numberless occasions; the crooked appearance of an oar in water; the various aspects of objects, according to their different distances; the double images that arise from the pressing of one eye; with many other appearances of a like nature. These sceptical topics, indeed, are only sufficient to prove, that the senses alone are not impli-citly to be depended on; but that we must correct their evidence by reason, and by considerations, derived from the nature of the medium, the distance of the object, and the disposition of the organ, in order to render them, within their sphere, the proper *criteria* of truth and falsehood. (EHU 12.6; also T 1.4.2.9 and 45)

The corrections of the evidence of the senses by reason Hume mentions are all *causal* in nature: the effect of different media on our organs, the effects of affection at differ-ent distances, the effects of being directly impinged on, etc. Since none of the unusual examples offered here would be in the least puzzling in the absence of habitual expecta-tions about how things seen will feel and vice versa, Hume may reasonably be credited with a recognition that we depend on these and other causal considerations in order to integrate vision with touch in the first place. After all, what other explanatory option

85

was there for a post-Berkeleyan empiricist? For Hume, no less than for Berkeley before him, the objects of vision and touch are not only qualitatively incommensurate but distinct in existence as well (by the separability criterion of T 1.1.7.3). Although their similar formal multiplicities are enough to give rise to a resemblance founded on the disposition of associative imagination in operating with their data, this suffices only to make visible and tangible space instances of a single *kind*, but not to integrate them to the point where they become in effect the one space of a single external sense. Hence, without causal connections to overcome their reciprocal isolation, how else could they be unified, or indeed integrated in any way? Among other things, causal connections between visible and tangible objects must figure as an essential element in the ability of the imagination to construct the general points of view that, according to Hume, are the only means whereby we can transcend the limitations inherent in any particular sensory viewpoint. And how else could the mind effect such connections except in associative imagination? For if the visible world is not to have the continually shifting, often jerky aspect it would have if vision were left entirely to the mercies of the movements of our eyes, head, and body, then we need some way to integrate the stability distinctive to tangible space directly into the phenomenology of visual experience. Since deliberative reasoning is obviously incapable of supplementing sight in so immediate a way, Hume can have had no option but to credit the integration of vision with touch to causal relations founded on customary association, which "operates immediately, without allowing any time for reflection" (T 1.3.12.7; also T 1.3.6.14, 1.3.8.10, 1.3.8.13, and 1.3.13.8).

This conclusion is confirmed by the role Hume assigned to causal association in the constitution of sense-divide transcending objects. Because there is no impression from which to copy the idea of a substrate which supports the existence of sensible qualities, "our idea of any body, a peach, for instance, is only that of a particular taste, colour, figure, size consistence, & c." (T Abstract 28); that is, these qualities resolve into so many distinct simple ideas in the sense proper to the separability criterion (T 1.4.3.7, 1.4.5.6, and 1.4.5.24). To unite any such "collection of simple ideas" into the idea of a single multi-sensory object, associative "relations of contiguity and causation" must supply the "principle of union" (T 1.1.6.2). For a cause must be inferred here, just as in all cases where distinct existents maintain a constant spatial and temporal relation (T 1.3.2.2), because the qualities are not only "always co-existent" but also "co-temporary in their appearance in the mind" (T 1.4.5.12). Since constant conjunctions yield the strongest causal associations, such collections of qualities become so "closely and inseparably connected" (T 1.1.6.2) in the imagination that they cease to be thought of as a collection at all, and are instead regarded as something simple and individual. This Hume explained as an associative fiction resulting from the same kind of confusion that takes place in cases of identity:

> The imagination conceives the simple object at once, with facility, by a single effort of thought, without change or variation. The connexion of parts in the compound object has almost the same effect, and so unites the object within itself, that the fancy feels not the transition in passing from one part to another. Hence the colour, taste, figure solidity, and other qualities, combin'd in a peach or melon, are conceiv'd to form *one thing*; and that on account of their close relation, which makes them affect the thought in the same manner, as if perfectly uncompounded. (T 1.4.3.5)

The case exactly parallels that of identity, where a close resemblance in the affective disposition of the imagination can induce us to overlook the manifest difference in appearance between an object that preserves a genuine identity over time and something variable or interrupted and attribute identity to the latter as well. Here the feeling of conceiving something genuinely simple by a single effort of thought and the effort of conceiving a coexistent manifold so closely interrelated that its conception feels indistinguishable from a single effort of thought leads the imagination to disregard the manifest complexity of the latter and consider it as simple and individual.

Now, if this is the case with qualities that are merely "co-existent in general" and "co-temporary in their appearance in the mind," how much more so must it be when the purview of the imagination is restricted to the qualities of "colour and tangibility" which, in addition, admit of "a conjunction in place" (T 1.4.5.12)? Certainly, if the projective illusion is to operate on those qualities which exist "without any place or extension" as Hume prescribes, it presupposes that those constantly conjoined qualities which really do have extension and exist in a place have *already* been confounded with something simple and indivisible. But how could this occur so long as the extension of vision and the extension of touch continued to be considered generically but not numerically the same? Clearly, the only way the constantly coexistent, co-occurrently appearing spatial objects of vision and touch can be "conceiv'd to form one thing" is by uniting them in a relation of "*conjunction in place.*" So, notwithstanding their qualitative incommensurability, the imagination indulges its affective disposition to consider their objects simple and individual by conjoining them in place. It presumably was thus that Hume explicated the inception of the fiction of a sense-divide transcending object. When supplemented by the illusion whereby the objects of the senses besides vision and touch are regarded as conjoined in the same places their common objects are, the fiction is expanded to incorporate all the senses into what is, for all intents and purposes, a single, integrated *external sense* with its own simple and individual sense-divide transcending objects. And the collective result of positing such objects must inevitably be the conflating of visible and tangible extension themselves in the fiction of a single, individual space, common to all our senses, with a single, sense-divide transcending ordered manifold of positions (points).

Because of the dearth of textual evidence in this matter, the most that can be claimed for the proceeding is that such an account is implicit in Hume's associationism. Even so, given that he unquestionably regarded visible objects as distinct from tangible objects in the sense of the separability principle, the only way he *could* have accounted for our seeming possession of a single, integrated external sense would have been by means of the fiction resulting from a confusion of the affective disposition in considering something genuinely simple and individual with the feeling incident to conceiving a coexistent complex united by the closest bonds of association and custom. For, as remarked earlier, customary association by resemblance and contiguity by itself can only explain how visible and tangible extension come to be regarded as instances of the same kind, but not why we take visible and tangible objects to be conjoined in *numerically* the same place. For this, only customary association in relations of cause and effect can suffice, since only they can create a strong enough affective disposition in imagination to induce it to regard as simple and individual visual and tactual appearances that are manifestly distinct, both qualitatively and numerically. Thus, our extrapolation from Hume's account of the fiction of simple and individual objects to our account of sense-divide transcending objects situated in a single, individual space common to all the senses at least has this much to be said for it: it meets a genuine Humean need by genuinely Humean means.

See also 2 "Hume's Theory of Ideas"

References

Berkeley, George (1732). *An Essay towards a New Theory of Vision*, in Michael R. Ayers (ed.), *Philosophical Works, Including the Works on Vision/George Berkeley* (London: J. M. Dent, 1975).

—— (1732). *Alciphron, or, the Minute Philosopher in Focus/George Berkeley*, ed. David Berman (London: Routledge, 1993).

Hume, David (1745). *A Letter from a Gentleman to His Friend in Edinburgh containing Some Observations on a Specimen of the Principles concerning Religion and Morality, Said to be Maintain'd in a Book Lately Publish'd Intituled a "Treatise of Human Nature,"* ed. Ernest Campbell Mossner and J. V. Price (Edinburgh: Edinburgh University Press, 1967).

Locke John (1690). *Essay concerning Human Understanding*, ed. Peter H. Nidditch (Oxford: Clarendon Press, 1975).

Further Reading

Costa, Michael (1990). "Hume, Strict Identity, and Time's Vacuum," *Hume Studies*, 16, pp. 1–16.

Fogelin, Robert (1985). *Hume's Skepticism in the "Treatise of Human Nature"* (London: Routledge).

Holden, Thomas (2002). "Infinite Divisibility and Actual Parts in Hume's *Treatise*," *Hume Studies*, 28, pp. 3–26.

Jacquette, Dale (2001). *David Hume's Critique of Infinity* (Leiden: Brill Academic Publishers).

Waxman, Wayne (1996). "The Psychologistic Foundations of Hume's Critique of Mathematics," *Hume Studies*, 22, pp. 123–69.

—— (2004). *Kant and the Empiricists: Understanding Understanding* (New York: Oxford University Press).

5

Hume on the Relation of Cause and Effect

FRANCIS WATANABE DAUER

Relying on earlier results, T 1.3.14 climaxes Hume's discussion of causation, a climax that is celebrated but internally problematic, intrinsically implausible yet suggestive.

Looking at the Text (T 1.3.14)

The first third of T 1.3.14 mainly surveys views of metaphysicians. He prefaces this survey by noting that members of the family of expressions (which I shall call the necessity family) "efficacy, agency, power, force, energy, necessity, connexion, and productive quality" are nearly synonymous and it would be "an absurdity to employ any of them in defining the rest." Hume tends to switch back and forth between members of the family and I follow this loose practice hoping nothing of substance is affected. (By "necessity" I shall mean *natural* necessity, something that "must" be true in our world but isn't true in all conceivable or even possible worlds.) Eschewing useless inter-definitions, he urges we "must look for [the idea of necessity] in the impressions, from which it is originally derived." This point is central and follows from his Copy Principle in T 1.1.1: "*all our simple ideas in their first appearance are deriv'd from simple impressions, which are correspondent to them, and which they exactly represent.*" All ideas are complexes of simple ideas and the idea of necessity is relatively simple; so, we need one or more impressions, which the idea of necessity represents, and from which the idea derives. Hume throughout assumes the genetic question ("What gives rise to the idea?") and the representation question ("What does the idea represent?") have the same answer in impressions. He criticizes metaphysicians of falsely imagining that they possess an idea in using the necessity family. If we use these terms as they do, "we have really no distinct meaning, and make use only of common words, without any clear and determinate idea." He immediately adds: "as 'tis more probable, that these expressions lose their true meaning by being *wrong apply'd*, than that they never have any meaning; 'twill be proper to bestow another consideration." This launches Hume's positive discussion, which consists of two arguments for his account (which I call the main and mini arguments), a defense and discussion of this account, and two definitions of cause.

The main and mini arguments

The main argument (occurring in T 1.3.14.15–20) starts with

1   Given a single instance of a cause C and an effect E, "from the simple consideration of one, or both these objects we never shall perceive the tie, by which they are united."

Some background is useful and provides the overarching structure of T 1.3. Distingui-shing *a priori* from *a posteriori* relational claims in T 1.3.1, T 1.3.2 first notes that, among the latter, inferring (e.g., Mary's presence from Tom's) differs from perceiving (them together). For Hume, *a posteriori* inferences involve inferring the unobserved from the observed. He then urges a "conclusion beyond the impressions of our senses can be founded only on the connexion of *cause and effect*" (T 74). This is not a normative but descriptive point: We infer unobserved events from observed events only when we believe some connection binds them. Identifying it as a causal connection, he asks from what impressions the idea of causation arises. Quickly noting temporal priority and spatial contiguity, he adds, "There is a NECESSARY CONNEXION to be taken into consideration; and that relation is of much greater importance, than any of the other two above mention'd." Yet however closely we look at C and E, none of the observable qualities or relations can be identified with necessary connection, i.e., (1). Rather than aban-doning the Copy Principle, he proposes beating around the bush (up to T 1.3.14) by inquiring into the nature of causal inferences.

(1) is followed by:

2   If we observe several instances in which C-like events and E-like events "are always conjoin'd together, we immediately conceive a connexion betwixt them, and begin to draw an inference from one to another."

3   "This multiplicity of resembling instances, therefore, constitutes the very essence of power or connexion, and is the source, from which the idea of it arises. To under-stand the idea of power, we must consider that multiplicity."

T 1.3.6 discovered that once we recall observed constant conjunction, "Without any farther ceremony, we call the one *cause* and the other *effect*, and infer the existence of the one from the other," i.e., (2). Given (1) and (2), (3) is plausible provided it is taken as an hyperbole for the observed regularity being the critical (essential) factor in mak-ing a causal inference, an inference which *pari passu* involves conceiving the items to be causally related. How then can observed regularity engender the idea of necessity? This leads to:

4   "The repetition of perfectly similar instances can never *alone* give rise to an original idea, different from what is to be found in any particular instance."

5   Therefore, the repetition "must either discover or produce something new, which is the source of that idea [of power]," and "wherever we find any [such new] thing, there we must place the power."

(4) basically stipulates what "repetition *alone*" can engender: it is limited to what can be found in any particular instance. Even the idea of repetition cannot be engendered

by repetition alone since that idea is absent in a single instance. So understood, (4) is unproblematic and gives a wide enough range for what a repetition can "discover" to make (5) a plausible consequence of (3).

The next three steps are:

6   "The repetition of like objects in like relation of succession and contiguity discovers nothing new in any one of them."
7   "This repetition of similar objects in similar situations produces nothing new either in the objects, or in any external body."
8   "There is, then, nothing new either discover'd or produc'd in any objects by their constant conjunction."

(6) and (7) need to yield (8): repetition can produce nothing new in, or reveal something new about, the repeated objects. Granting the fairly obvious (7), isn't constant conjunction something new discovered by the repetition? A parallel puzzle occurred in T 1.3.6: Joy that "We have insensibly discover'd a new relation between cause and effect, [the] relation [of] their CONSTANT CONJUNCTION," quickly turns to despair: "From the mere repetition of any past impression, even to infinity, there never will arise any new original idea, such as that of a necessary connexion." But why couldn't the *complex* idea of constant conjunction, rather than some new original idea, be the idea of necessity?

Hume's argument for (6) isn't clear but contains a clue: "repetition *discovers* nothing new since we can draw no inference from it." The idea of constant conjunction won't do for that of necessity because of the latter's role in inferring the unobserved. *Observed* constant conjunctions (conjunctions true in all observed cases) don't persuade us of anything about the next instance unless we take it to be evidence for a connection, the very idea in question. As for *eternal* constant conjunctions (conjunctions true in all cases whatsoever) or anything science may discover, our access to them is through a projection from the observed, a projection which presupposes, or has as its part and parcel, our taking observed conjunctions to be instances of causal necessity. So, the idea of eternal conjunctions also cannot play the role of inferring the unobserved. Thus, the idea of necessity cannot be identified with any idea of constant conjunction. This will do as well as (8) for the next step of the argument, which was anticipated in T 1.3.6: "Perhaps 'twill appear in the end, that the necessary connexion depends on the inference, instead of the inference's depending on the necessary connection."

The anticipated climax is:

9   "the *observation* of [constant conjunction] produces a new impression *in the mind*, which is [the] real model [of the idea of power]. We feel a determination of the mind to pass from one object to its usual attendant."

T 1.3.6 argued observed constant conjunctions produce inferences by the association of ideas: The inference "is not determin'd by reason, but by certain principles, which associate together the idea of those objects and unite them in the imagination." We can read (9)'s "determination of mind" in two ways: (a) Feelings (impressions) indicated by such words as "felt compulsion" or "a sense of having no choice but to believe E." (b) Dispositions, e.g., to infer Es from Cs, i.e., the ideas of C and E being associated.

Dispositions aren't felt but I can empirically access my current disposition to infer being burned from placing one's hand in fire by answering counterfactuals like, "Would I now infer Descartes was burned in 1621 if I were to believe his hand was placed in fire in 1621?" This is not an inference about how I would infer tomorrow, but an unmediated (albeit fallible) access to how I am *now* disposed to infer. We can, if we wish, add feelings of compulsion to actual and counterfactual inferences. (b) is the happier reading, and I shall hereafter adopt it, since Hume often drops "the feeling of" and simply speaks of determination of mind and his second definition of "cause" is clearly in terms of our inferences.

We now reach Hume's conclusion:

10 "This determination is the only effect of the resemblance; and therefore must be the same with power or efficacy. Necessity is the effect [of observing constant conjunctions], and is nothing but an internal impression of the mind, or a determination [of the mind]."

This conclusion depends on two highly plausible claims: (a) [Lacking innate ideas,] our idea of power or necessary connection is an effect of observing constant conjunctions. (b) The *only* effect of observing constant conjunctions (relevant to inferring the unobserved) is the determination of the mind. Given (a) and (b), the Copy Principle (an idea represents what gives rise to it) makes it *inevitable* that the idea of necessity represents the determination of the mind.

He immediately adds the mini-argument:

[1] The necessary connexion betwixt causes and effects is the foundation of our inference from one to the other. [2] The foundation of our inference is the transition arising from the accustom'd union. [3] These are, therefore, the same. (T 1.3.14.21)

Because of possible slippage between reality and our take on it, [1] can't be quite right; the "foundation" of our inference must be our *belief* in necessity. So, [3] can at best claim this belief and the transition are the same. Still, one might complain of an equivocation: belief in necessity is the "foundation" of an epistemologically "justified" inference while the transition arising from the accustomed union is the "foundation" by being the psychological condition of the inference. But, this complaint is misguided: as already urged, [1] (derived from T 1.3.2) merely describes without raising normative issues. Still, while a functional equivalence between a belief in C and E's necessary connection and the corresponding inferential disposition is plausible, an outright identification is problematic: the intentional object of the belief is hard to locate in the disposition whose only intentional objects are those of C and E.

Defense and discussion (T 1.3.14.22–30)

The main argument ends by adding: without considering necessity as the mind's determination, "we can never arrive at the most distant notion of it, or be able to attribute it either to external or internal objects." But if necessity is the mind's determination, can he have recaptured the meaning of common words that allows attributing necessity to objects? He recognizes the problem: He soon announces this is "the most violent paradox" he has occasion to advance, and later considers the objection: "What! the efficacy of causes lies in the determination of the mind! Thought may well depend on causes but not causes on thought." His main response repeats the unassailability of his main argument, once before and twice after announcing the paradox.

Before proclaiming the paradox, he claims:

> as the necessity, which makes two times two equal to four lies only in the act of the understanding; in a like manner the necessity or power lies in the determination of the mind [and] belongs entirely to the soul, which considers the union of two or more objects in all past instances.

Wittgenstein urged against Russell that logical necessities don't correspond to logical facts but lie in the methods of representation. Hume might be read to claim: though I can observe that doubling my two pigs results in four, I can't observe its *logical necessity*; that is due to relations among ideas we have formed. Similarly, though we can observe constant conjunctions, we cannot observe their natural necessity; that is due to the associative union the ideas acquire. Just as the relation between the ideas we formed engenders (recognition of) logical necessity, the association of ideas engenders (belief in) natural necessity. While Hume may intend this analogy, there is a disanalogy: while the parenthetical "recognition of" could perhaps be dropped for logical necessity, the parenthetical "belief in" seems ineliminable for natural necessity.

Two points of Hume's defense are noteworthy: (a) Bias against his view is explained by "the mind ['s] propensity to spread itself on external objects, and to conjoin with them any internal impression, which they occasion," e.g., we falsely locate sounds and smells in things occasioning them. This thought presumably underlies his claim:

> When we make the terms of power and efficacy signify something, of which we have a clear idea [viz., the mind's determination], and which is incompatible with those objects, to which we apply it [mindless external objects occasioning the determination], obscurity and error begin to take place, and we are led astray by a false philosophy [that necessity is in the objects]. (T 1.3.14.26)

(EHU 7.29n supports the reading in brackets.) External objects clearly don't infer, but Hume must allow ascribing necessity to objects in order to recapture the meaning of common words. (b) To his opponents, he says:

> If we have really no idea of a power or efficacy, 'twill be to little purpose to prove that an efficacy is necessary in all operations. We do not understand our own meaning in talking so.

His attitude that the necessity family has no meaning unless one accepts his account isn't consistent with his own words two paragraphs later: "The uniting principle among our internal perceptions is as unintelligible as that among external objects." Does he think the subject of this sentence is without meaning?

The two definitions (T 1.3.14.30–1)

Hume prefaces his definitions of cause, a pre-analytic notion he has used throughout, by noting "we have been oblig'd to advance in this seemingly preposterous manner, and make use of the term before we were able exactly to define them." The first definition defines cause as a philosophical relation or a comparison of two ideas: "An object precedent and contiguous to another, where all objects resembling the former are plac'd in like relation of precedency and contiguity to those objects, that resemble the latter." His usual talk of *observed* constant conjunctions is here replaced by *eternal* conjunctions (presumably because the former can subsequently fail). Since necessity is far more important than contiguity and priority, let us concentrate on the last clause and take it to define necessary connection. Let us also think in terms of species causation (fire causes heat) rather than this causing that. This is substantive by bypassing issues of singular causation but perhaps not too damaging since Hume repeatedly talks of constant conjunction, a notion applicable only to species. The first definition then becomes: C is necessarily connected with E just in case C and E are eternally (constantly) conjoined.

The second definition defines cause as a natural relation or an association of ideas:

> An object precedent and contiguous to another, and so united with it, that the idea of the one determined the mind to form the idea of the other, and the impression of the one to form a more lively idea of the other.

Given our simplifications, C is necessarily connected with E just in case we are disposed to infer E from C or the ideas of C and E are associated. This is one clear instance where Hume allows necessity to be ascribed to objects since it is the objects that are so united that their ideas are associated.

Postponing a discussion of these definitions, two points may now be made: (a) J. A. Robinson (1962) pointed out the obvious *prima facie* problem: these definitions can't define the same thing since they are not materially, let alone logically, equivalent. (b) Hume expresses unease about these definitions and says of the first,

> If this definition be esteem'd defective, because drawn from objects foreign to the cause, we may substitute [the second definition]. Shou'd this definition also be rejected for the same reason, I know of no other remedy.

The obvious reading is that since he is defining singular causation, both definitions import things foreign to it. One could read in a deeper unease.

Three Readings

The attempts to make satisfactory sense of Hume's undoubtedly problematic account in T 1.3.14 are too numerous to canvass. I shall limit myself to three readings that are in play in recent discussions. In each case I offer a few less than decisive criticisms.

Reductionist readings

The standard reading of Hume is that the first definition is *the* definition of causation. Despite various nuanced versions, for our purposes a sketch of the underlying idea may suffice: Since the determination of the mind cannot be part of the truth condition for causation, the idea of the former cannot represent causation. From what impressions, then, could the idea of causation be derived if it isn't observed constant conjunctions, which are eternalized to give us that idea? Yearning for a "thicker" connection violates the Copy Principle and causation is thus "reduced" to eternal conjunctions. A twentieth-century logical positivist replaces the Copy Principle by a verification principle whereby (a) the truth and falsity of a meaningful contingent claim must be observationally disclosable, and (b) the meaning of such a claim is the class of observation sentences each of which confirms the claim if true and falsifies it if false. "C causes E" means the class sentences of the form "c is conjoined with e," i.e., Cs and Es are eternally conjoined; by providing neither confirming nor falsifying conditions, the second definition is dismissed. For anyone with strong empiricist inclinations, a reductionist reading makes best sense of Hume. But Hume did say necessary connection is the most important part of causation, dismissed constant conjunction even unto infinity as giving us the idea of necessity, and the core of T 1.3.14 claims that necessity is the determination of the mind. To dismiss the second definition dismisses the overall structure of T 1.3 and its culmination in the core of T 1.3.14. This surely dismisses too much of the text. (The best reductionist option may deny Hume's claim that necessity is a component of causation and take T 1.3.14 to deal with the independent idea of necessity (see Beauchamp and Rosenberg 1981). This *is* an option and may be close to the revisionary reductionist discussed in the third reading below.)

A realist reading

Against the reductionist, a realist urges that even for Hume observed regularities are due to event binding real necessary connections. Taking Galen Strawson (Strawson 1989) as my sample realist reading, he relies on our pre-analytic notion of necessity, much as Hume was obliged to proceed in a "preposterous manner." His Hume is a non-committal skeptic insisting, "we know nothing about the true nature of causal power" (p. 3). But then Hume cannot claim, "causation in the objects was definitely (knowably) nothing but regular succession" (p. 12). Besides, since regular succession is knowable and causation isn't, causation cannot be regularity (cf., p. 86). Though we cannot *know* there are real connections,

> The belief that there is such a thing as natural necessity or causal power is not ruled out. Strictly non-committal skepticism can acknowledge the naturalness and overall theoretical plausibility of this belief. (p. 13)

Belief in real connections (causation) is natural because for Hume we cannot but believe it. As for theoretical plausibility, Strawson imagines a universe where some random generator produces a sequence of observable events that is "in respect to its perfect regularity, *just like* our universe. And so according to the Regularity-theory, it is, in respect to *causation*, just like our universe" (p. 25). Strawson urges it is wildly implausible for most of us (Hume included) that the regularity we observe is a fluke, and thus plausible that Causation underlies it (cf. p. 95).

Much of what Hume says suggests that the necessity family has no meaning except the one he provides. But for Strawson this is misleading:

> There is a familiar ambiguity in the word "mean." On the one hand, "mean" means "positively-contentfully" mean (and this is how Hume standardly uses the word "mean"): a term can [so] mean something only [if] it has impression-derived content. On the other hand "mean" means "refer to." And so long as we have a way of picking out something X by reference to some relation to us, we can have a relative idea of it even though we may be unable to "positively-contentfully mean" it. (p. 122)

By one fell swoop of inserting "contentful" Strawson can disarm any possible counter-evidence, and there is one (but, I think, only one) passage where Hume allows a relative idea:

> The farthest we can go towards a conception of external objects, when suppos'd *specifically* different from our perceptions, is to form a relative idea of them, without pretending to comprehend the related objects. (T 1.2.6.9)

How *might* Hume refer to Causation by a relative idea? Strawson says:

> The central observable effect that Causation has on us is the regular character of our experience of object. Of course its having this effect on us is itself a Causal matter. But there is nothing problematic about the reference to an effect in an account of how we can come to acquire a ("relative") idea of Causation. (p. 123)

If we rely on our pre-analytic notion of causation, the reference succeeds (if there is Causation). But if we don't, the attempt seems no better than: "Rathation" refers to that which raths dogs. I am uneasy about Hume proceeding to the very end in the "preposterous manner" of using a term without defining it.

Strawson's account has other problems: (a) How can constant conjunction or the mind's determination be a (contentful) conception of Causation? The conception of a footprint includes a conception of a man whose walk on the ground caused it. But the concept of a depression on the ground differs from that of a footprint, which imports the idea of what caused the depression. Strawson's very argument against reductionism claims the concepts of regularity and Causation are disparate. The conception of regularity is as little a conception of Causation as that of a depression is that of what caused it. Again, if a relative conception of an external object X is a conception of something specifically different from perceptions, no conception of perceptions (e.g., shape) is a conception of X (contentful or otherwise). The same applies to conceptions of constant conjunctions and the mind's determination. Yet for Hume these *are* conceptions of necessary connection. (b) Since "power" (or "necessity") can't refer both to the mind's determination and Causation, Strawson urges Hume

> needs to differentiate *necessity*, understood as something that is "only in the mind," from the "ultimate connexion." If one accepts to call this something "necessity," and thinks of

all necessity in the extreme subjectivist way, one risks losing one's grip on this point. Hume is pulled in this direction. But he continues to recognize and appeal to the distinction between causal power and necessity just outlined. (p. 158)

To support the last sentence he claims Hume "never actually uses the term 'necessity' in the referring expressions which he uses to refer to Causation. Instead he uses expressions like 'power,' 'ultimate force and efficacy,' [etc.]." I find this unpersuasive. "Necessity," "power," and "efficacy" belong to Hume's nearly synonymous necessity family and his main argument claimed, "This determination is the only effect of the resemblance; and therefore must be the same with power or efficacy."

An intermediate reading

Those who eschew real connections which can't be contentfully conceived and yet have the intuition that causation can't be mere regularity hope to find a non-reductive, anti-realist account in Hume, a hope encouraged by Hume having provided *two* definitions. Simon Blackburn's reading outlined in Blackburn (2003: 269–71) is an example. He claims Hume's two definitions provide

> the contribution of the world and the non-representative, functional difference in the mind that apprehends the regularity. [When the latter] takes place we think of the events as thickly connected; we talk of causation.

Against reductionists, Blackburn claims his reading

> happily predicts the "intuitions" that lead people to detest the positivistic "regularity" theory. Someone talking of cause is voicing a distinct mental set: he is by no means in the same state as someone merely describing regular sequences. The difference in this case is in the fixity the sequence of events takes in our thinking.

This difference may be true of someone describing *observed* constant conjunctions but is less clear of someone who, by an inductive inference, believes an eternal con-junction, which is what the reductionist takes causation to be.

As for Blackburn's anti-realism, consider first a contradiction he claims any reading of Hume faces: (a) The Copy Principle, (b) the lack of an impression of necessity to be copied, and (c) having the idea of necessity (p. 260). Hume denies (b) but Blackburn is dismissive: "Hume shows little interest in such questions [of representation] and can point only in misleading directions: He says, for example, by a necessary connexion we 'mean' a connection in the mind." Blackburn's solution denies (c) "by distinguishing a representative idea of connexion, which we do not have, from a capacity to make legitimate use of a term whose function is given non-representatively, which we can have." Clearly if there is no representative idea of necessity, we have no idea represent-ing the realist's causation. But how can Blackburn's anti-realist "think of events as thickly connected" if there is no representational idea of thick connections? He thinks prospects of an answer "must be quite bright" and gestures towards the plausibility "of explaining the apparently objective content of moral judgments given their source in the passions."

In another essay Blackburn gives a fuller outline of the kind of (quasi-) realism he accepts:

> The stage (which I called quasi-realism) explains on this basis [mental states, habits, dispositions, etc.] the *propositional behavior* of the commitments [which are verbal expressions of mental states, habits, dispositions, etc.]. The aim is to see these propositions as constructions that stand at a needed point in our cognitive lives – they are the objects to be discussed, rejected, or improved upon, when the habits [and] dispositions need discussion, rejection or improvement. *Their truth corresponds to correctness in these mental states, by whichever standard they have to meet.* (Blackburn 1993: 55, my italics)

The idea seems to be: Utterances of "C causes E" initially express (are projections of) our disposition to infer E from C. They acquire an objective dimension by being used to discuss, reject or improve the inferential disposition and are true when the inferential disposition is correct.

Two things need to be noted: (a) Only by relying heavily on linguistic behavior can utterances merely expressive of non-representational inferential dispositions dance the dance of objectivity and be true. Beliefs calling for believed ideas are bypassed. While Hume allows words can substitute for ideas, never in T 1 does he suggest ideas can be completely bypassed. (b) The truth of "C causes E" is aligned to the correctness of the disposition to infer Es from Cs, and the latter is surely never being led from truth to falsity, i.e., C and E being eternally conjoined. Simplicity considerations can "correct" inferential dispositions but the truth of "C causes E" remains eternal conjunctions elegantly inferred. Since Blackburn takes moral judgments to be supervenient on natural facts and structurally like causal judgments, causal talk is supervenient on eternal conjunctions (elegantly inferred). Because the supervenient can differ only through a difference in the subvenient, in the end causal judgments involve gilding or staining constant conjunctions by our inferential dispositions just as moral judgments involve "gilding or staining all natural objects with colours, borrowed from internal sentiment" (EPM App. 1.21). In describing his projectivism Blackburn approvingly quoted this second *Enquiry* passage in Blackburn (1984: 171).

Even if the reductionist grants that our concept of causation injects something not given by eternal conjunctions, if it is just gilding or staining, he can become revisionary and urge dispensing with the concept of cause in favor of that of cause*, viz., eternal conjunction. What real gain is there in causal talk? Blackburn urges the main gain "is that we 'make no longer any scruple of foretelling' [the future]. We may [also] become willing, to hold the sequence constant as we think about [counterfactual conditionals]" (Blackburn 2002: 271). But couldn't causal* talk achieve the same? Once we predict eternal conjunctions, we make no scruple of foretelling the future. To accommodate counterfactuals, the revisionary reductionist can appeal to Goodman type considerations (Goodman 1955) whereby inferential dispositions are corrected so that by projecting only "projectible conjunctions," they project "law-like" generalizations that sustain counterfactuals. To distance his quasi-*realism* from reductionism, Blackburn has to show that the gilding or staining does real work.

Reconstructions and Speculations

All three readings considered dismiss Hume's identification of necessity with the mind's determination despite the Copy Principle making it the inevitable result of the main argument. The intrinsic implausibility of the identification dictates its rejection by suspending the Copy Principle for the idea of necessity since genetic and representational issues diverge here. Except for that, let's see what the text yields and where the three readings would stand. Call this the modest reconstruction or R1. Since R1 (and later R2) *are* reconstructions, what follows are text based "Humean" views rather than straightforward textual interpretations.

Reconstruction R1

Our pre-analytic notion of necessary connection isn't completely opaque. C and E are not so connected if there is a C without E. T 1.3.2 also indicates we infer the unobserved precisely when we believe there is a necessarily connection. Since Hume thinks inferential confidence has degrees, let's align maximal confidence with what he calls "proofs" in T 1.3.11, the confidence we have in inferring we are mortal. That we have maximal confidence precisely when we believe there is a necessary connection is not normative but descriptive and, I suggest, descriptive of our use of the concept of necessity. For animals and young children lacking that concept, the inferential confidence is caused by the association of ideas but isn't matched by a belief in necessity. Even for those having the concept of necessity, though the inferential confidence is aligned with a belief in necessity, the causal basis of the confidence is not the belief but the association of ideas. We might then glean from Hume's view something like a conceptual claim concerning our use of the concept of necessity:

1   If one has the concept of necessary connection, one believes C and E are necessarily connected if and only if one places maximal confidence in the inference from C to E.

Though (1) is silent on what engenders the confidence, it accords with my suggestion (in discussing the mini-argument) that a belief in necessity is functionally equivalent to an inferential disposition.

Fused with (1) is Hume's causal account:

2   One places maximal confidence in an inference from C to E if and only if one has observed a constant conjunction between Cs and Es.

This is rough. (2) must exclude the mentally incapacitated. Also, in T 1.3.12–13 Hume distinguishes the wise and the vulgar by the kind of general rules governing their inferences. The wise discount certain failures in conjunctions by empirically inferring undetected interfering factors. Extensive constant conjunctions whose instances are terminated may be discounted if they suspect "essential and efficacious" factors were lacking. The wise adjust their inferential confidence to the data that are not discounted. However, let's avoid epicycles and simply work with (1) and (2), which give us:

3 If one has the concept of necessary connection, one believes C and E are necessarily connected if and only if one has observed a constant conjunction between C and E.

Given the conceptual (1) and causal (2), (3) can yield the counterfactual: If our belief in a necessary connection and our observation of constant conjunction were not attuned (through our inferential disposition), we would lack the concept of necessary connection. This gives the condition for our possessing the concept of necessity, which approximates Hume's view with alterations suggested in braces:

> The several instances [of an observed constant conjunction] lead us into the notion of power and necessity. These instances have no union but in the mind. {Belief in} Necessity, then, is the effect of this observation, and is nothing but {i.e., is functionally equivalent to} a determination to [mind]. Without considering it in this view, we can never arrive at the most distant notion of it. (T 1.3.14.20)

Turning to Hume's two definitions, we find a temporal mismatch: one is in terms of eternal conjunctions, the other in terms of current associations. One way to correct this eternalizes the second definition: C and E are connected just in case some actual or counterfactually possible observations would result in, and none would thwart, associating the ideas of C and E. Material equivalence is now plausible but logical equivalence still fails: we can conceive the associative mechanisms being different or absent while events are eternally conjoined. Don Garrett (Garrett 1997: 110–11) urges our concept of cause couldn't reach such worlds. For all possible worlds accessible by our concept, the definitions are coextensive. I find this counterintuitive and shall allow causal relations in possible worlds lacking our presence. This rules out the semantic adequacy of the second definition and any definition that has it as a conjunct (since the conjunction inherits the defect of any conjunct). The first definition fares no better. Someone's inferential capacities could be damaged so that observing constant conjunctions fails to engender inferential confidence and thereby beliefs in necessary connections. He lacks the concept of necessity by (3) but he could surely conceive (though not believe) that leap year marriages are eternally conjoined with divorce. But, lacking the concept, he doesn't conceive a causal connection. Since semantic adequacy should allow interchange in propositional attitude contexts, the first definition isn't semantically adequate and the reductionist reading fails. Both definitions of necessity are semantically inadequate and this could account for Hume's unease with them.

What then do the two definitions provide? To match them temporally by de-eternalizing the first may be preferable to eternalizing the second. For Hume the definitions present necessity as a philosophical or natural relation but in the eternalized second definition, associability isn't a natural relation. Craig urged the definitions are "best understood as presenting two descriptions of the circumstances under which belief in a causal connection arises" (Craig 2002: 227). Though the first doesn't state belief conditions, Craig suggests since Hume talks of how we may view the relation, "the thought of the observer is not too far away" (Craig 2002: 225). The second aligns belief in necessity with the inferential disposition and is our (1). If the observer is close at hand, the first becomes a variant of (3):

3* If one has the concept of necessary connection, one believes that C and E are necessarily connected if and only if one believes that C and E are eternally conjoined.

Since necessarily connections entail eternal conjunctions, one direction is obvious. Conversely, believing an eternal conjunction involves inferring from the observed, and by (1) we confidently infer precisely when we believe there is a necessary connection (provided we have the concept). (3*) and (1) rightly align the two definitions: Beliefs in necessity are related by (3*) to beliefs in philosophical relations and by (1) to inferential dispositions or natural relations. The two definitions then provide belief conditions for necessity, which can be variously stated: observed constant conjunction, maximal inferential confidence, or believed eternal conjunction. The key is Hume's associative mechanism: because of it observed constant conjunctions result in maximal inferential confidence and thereby beliefs in necessity and eternal conjunctions. Belief conditions are in the region of assertability conditions (*sans* normativity) and this is all R1 can glean from the *Treatise* for the concept of necessity. The content of the concept in terms of truth conditions remains elusive.

R1 rejects reductionism and is consistent with Blackburn's and Strawson's readings without endorsing either. R1 joins Blackburn in urging the concept of necessity emerges from inferential dispositions but Strawson needn't deny this. R1 is silent on (a) Blackburn's reliance on linguistic practice to imbue objectivity and representational capacity to utterances merely expressive of non-representational inferential dispositions and (b) Strawson's use of pre-analytic notions to secure reference for Causation. In taking causal talk to supervene on observations and inferential dispositions, Blackburn urges the standard anti-realist conversion of assertability or belief conditions ("at the ideal" of eternal conjunctions) into truth conditions. R1 is silent on this conversion as well as Strawson's standard realist resistance to it and insistence that real connections are the truth conditions of causal claims. In the end, I think one's realist or anti-realist commitments are the engines driving one's interpretation of the *Treatise*, a work which makes no such commitments (once the Copy Principle is suspended for the idea of necessity). Hume may have been pulled in both directions without taking a stand in the *Treatise*.

The reductionist will feel short changed. Against Strawson he will insist one can't forgo the Copy Principle without a substitute like the verification principle. A realist has responses: (a) Hume is a term-by-term empiricist and could allow a compositionality principle whereby compounds have meaning through their components. Since ordinary, finite dreams have empirical meaning, Hume need not reject as meaningless the Cartesian eternal dream hypothesis. Since (the "wise" recognize) "accidental finite constant conjunctions" can have empirical meaning, Strawson's thought experiment isn't meaningless. (b) Plausibly, we can attach meaning to terms applying to our world only if empirical evidence is assigned for and against their application. But one can resist the need for *decisive* evidence (at the ideal). Observed conjunctions are evidence for necessity and failure of conjunction (and evidence for accidental finite constant conjunctions) are evidence against necessity. Against Blackburn, the reductionist will become revisionary, and this move affects R1 as well. Real workload for the concept of necessity must be found. To investigate this, we need a more speculative reconstruction R2 that goes beyond the *Treatise*.

Reconstruction R2

We cannot foretell the future well without the aid of science. Medical newsletters report finding correlations, say, between drinking red wine and reduced cardio-vascular problems, but warn a causal connection hasn't been shown. An explanation of the correlation enhances confidence in the wine's preventive virtues and the isolated critical ingredient allows finding it elsewhere and producing pills. Roughly, science seeks deep structure explanations with two components: (a) claims of relations between theoretical entities, and (b) claims that macro-objects are constituted by theoretical entities, which along with (a) predict the observational properties of macro-objects. While the acceptability of scientific claims is gauged by observational evidence, these claims cannot be *replaced* by talk about observational data. We cannot locate relevant regularities and their epicycles at the observational level (data without theory is useless) and science enables the production of rockets and nuclear plants creating new regularities. Since we take scientific claims to claim natural necessities, the workload of the concept of necessity must lie here, and this idea R2 attempts to exploit.

While the *Treatise* is silent on scientific explanations, in *Enquiry* (EHU 4.12) Hume talks of the effort of human reason to "reduce the principles, *productive* of natural phenomena, to a greater simplicity" (my italics), and claims

> Elasticity, cohesion of parts, communication of motion by impulse; these are probably the ultimate causes and principles which we shall ever discover in nature; and we may esteem ourselves sufficiently happy, if, by accurate enquiry and reasoning, we can trace up the particular phenomena to, or near to, these general principles.

(There are surrounding skeptical remarks which I shall discuss later.) Since Hume took claims of science to be claims of necessities or productive principles, R2 will have some basis in Hume.

Because observable objects are identified independently of each other, though we believe observed conjunctions are necessary, there is the possibility of accidental conjunctions even unto eternity. We take a theoretical explanation of the correlation to "confirm" our surmise that the conjunction wasn't accidental and to "show" drinking red wine to be a causal factor for health. This suggests the truth of a belief that a correlation is necessary lies in there being a true theoretical explanation of the correlation. These intuitive considerations suggest R2's characterization:

4   (a) The possibility of conceiving an eternal conjunction between C and E to be accidental depends on the possibility of independently accessing C and E. (b) If we can conceive the conjunction to be accidental, it is necessary just in case a true explanation explains it.

Though R1 provides belief conditions for necessary connections among observable objects, since the truth of necessity claims lies in there being deep structure explanations, the concept of necessity drives us towards these explanations. Since we cannot "get along just as well" with observational regularities, the concept of necessity is indispensable and revisionary reductionism is wrong. As for Blackburn and Strawson, (4) is again consistent with both.

For an "intermediate position" the key is that being inter-defined, theoretical entities can't be accessed independently of each other. (4a), then, rules out the possibility of accidental relations between theoretical entities and, by default, the relations become necessary unless the theory is false. This has some intuitive basis. The idea of correlation has a firm foothold at the observational level precisely because we can independently access items and observe them to be correlated or not. The idea of finding genuinely theoretical entities to be correlated or not gains no foothold since they cannot be identified independently of the relational and constitutive roles the theory claims. We gauge the truth of theoretical claims by the success or failure of observational predictions the theory as a whole more or less deductively entails, not by finding correlations between theoretical entities. We might understand "genuinely theoretical entities" along the lines Quine suggests:

> Reference and ontology recede to the status of mere auxiliaries. True sentences, observational and theoretical, are the alpha and omega of the scientific enterprise. They are related by structure, and objects figure as mere nodes of the structure. What particular object there may be is indifferent to the truth of observation sentences, indifferent to the support they lend to the theoretical sentences, indifferent to the success of the theory in its prediction. (Quine 1992: 31)

Since theoretical statements are false or truths of natural necessity, content of beliefs in necessities become content of beliefs in theoretical claims. Since Hume allowed (in T 1.1.7.12 and 14) that words could substitute for ideas of government and large numbers, the object of a belief in a theoretical claim could just be a sentence. While Hume perhaps thought words could *in principle* be replaced by ideas, a sentence being a part of a web of sentences that relates holistically to positive and negative empirical evidence may have to suffice. (I depart here from Blackburn's "expressive" theory.) A theory's possible under-determination even at the ideal is problematic and would undercut supervenience. But there may be ways of dealing with this (cf., Quine 1992: 95–101), and if we can, (in an anti-realist Hegelian serpentine manner) a constant conjunction at the observational level acquires its necessity through theoretical claims whose truth lie, not in the initial constant conjunction, but in the totality of observational truths that makes the indispensable, holistically conceived scientific superstructure true.

R2 can also accommodate a realist who rejects anti-realist accounts of science. Even if theoretical entities are inter-defined, the claims of science as a whole can be taken to fix (rigidly) the reference of theoretical terms. Theoretical entities conceived *de re* allow for conjunctions or correlations, albeit of a massively complex sort, and (4a) engenders the possibility of the correlation being accidental. By (4b), if a believed explanation of a correlation is true, the correlation is necessary, and if we are right in thinking there is no true explanation of a correlation (such as an astrological one), the correlation is accidental. But there are no available explanations for the ultimate explanations available at any given moment. This not just a human limitation: unless there is an unending series of deeper explanations, there is going to be an ultimate explanation having no explanation. At the ultimate level of massively complex correlations of theoretical entities, there are no further explanations. But if the ultimate correlations were accidental, this would transmit to observed correlations. Since we believe many of the latter are necessary, we must believe the ultimate correlations are also necessary. Evidently we must believe there is some bond in *rerum natura* binding theoretical entities, and that surely is Strawson's Causation.

R2 is again neutral between the realist and anti-realist outlooks. But Hume accepts the realist conception of science. The *Enquiry* passage is surrounded by skeptical remarks: "as to the causes of these general causes [cohesion, gravity, etc.], we should in vain attempt their discovery," and "The most perfect philosophy of the natural kind only staves off our ignorance a little longer." These aren't passing remarks but steps in arguing, "the observation of human blindness and weakness is the result of all philosophy, and meets us at every turn, in spite of our endeavor to elude or avoid it." Even if one invokes science, the causes of general causes must remain inexplicable. Since this *Enquiry* argument is so obvious, one *could* urge the *Treatise* simply collapsed the argument and claimed the uniting principles between observed events to be unintelligible.

R2 attempted to lend substance to the concept of necessity (which was thin and potentially dispensable under R1), and if not the *Treatise* at least the *Enquiry* suggests the *Humean* view is the realist option under R2. However this realism differs from Strawson's. His approach is "top down" from the unknowable, and his appeal to Causation as that which Causes regularity is unhelpfully circular. My approach is "bottom up" and ties the necessity of correlations to their explanations. However, this account *tends* to lead the concept of necessity towards an antinomy: To save the necessity of observational regularities, theoretical entities must be necessarily connected, not just correlated. Yet necessary connections between the ultimate theoretical entities would be precluded since ultimate explanations have no further explanations. We could plead an unending series of deeper explanations so that there is no ultimate explanation beyond what is ultimate for us at any given moment. But would an infinite regress of explanations be an explanation? Alternatively, we could plead that the relations between the ultimate entities are self-explanatory. But what could this mean to us except that the ultimate laws of nature are true *a priori*, something that seems utterly implausible and un-Humean? In claiming the ultimate uniting principle to be unintelligible perhaps Hume was pointing to these conceptual difficulties rather than relying on the Copy Principle (or its variants) or the possibility of there being things in the universe we are unacquainted with. But where does this leave us? We *do* have a partial, incomplete understanding of the concept of necessity in terms of deeper structure explanations. But we cannot complete this understanding without facing insuperable conceptual difficulties, a sign that a full or complete conception of necessity (contentful or otherwise) is beyond the limits of our understanding. The anti-realist option under R2 would be more in keeping with streamlined empiricism, but it does not seem to be Hume's perspective.

See also 2 "Hume's Theory of Ideas"; 6 "Inductive Inference in Hume's Philosophy"; 23 "Hume's Naturalism and His Skepticism"; 24 "Is Hume a Realist or an Anti-realist?"

References

Beauchamp, Tom L. and Rosenberg, Alexander (1981). *Hume and the Problem of Causation* (New York: Oxford University Press).

Blackburn, Simon (1984). *Spreading the World* (New York: Oxford University Press).

—— (1993). *Essays in Quasi-realism* (New York: Oxford University Press).

—— (2002). "Hume and Thick Connexions," in Peter Millican (ed.), *Reading Hume on Human Understanding* (New York: Oxford University Press), pp. 259–76.

Craig, Edward (2002). "The Idea of Necessary Connexion," in Peter Millican (ed.), *Reading Hume on Human Understanding* (New York: Oxford University Press), pp. 211–29.

Garrett, Don (1997). *Cognition and Commitment in Hume's Philosophy* (New York: Oxford University Press).

Goodman, Nelson (1955). *Fact, Fiction, & Forecast* (Cambridge, MA: Harvard University Press).

Quine, W. V. (1992). *Pursuit of Truth* (Cambridge, MA: Harvard University Press).

Robinson, J. A. (1962). "Hume's Two Definitions of 'Cause'," *Philosophical Quarterly*, 12, pp. 162–71.

Strawson, Galen (1989). *The Secret Connexion* (New York: Oxford University Press).

Further Reading

Ayer, A. J. (1936). *Language, Truth and Logic* (London: Gollancz).

Baier, Annette C. (1991). *A Progress of Sentiments: Reflections on Hume's "Treatise"* (Cambridge: Harvard University Press).

Craig, Edward (1987). *The Mind of God and the Works of Man* (Oxford: Clarendon Press).

Dauer, Francis W. (1975). "Towards a Copernican Reading of Hume," *Noûs*, 9, pp. 269–93.

Kemp Smith, Norman (1941). *The Philosophy of David Hume* (London: Macmillan).

Mackie, J. L. (1974). *The Cement of the Universe: A Study of Causation* (Oxford: Clarendon Press).

Millican, Peter (2002). *Reading Hume on Human Understanding* (Oxford: Oxford University Press).

Owen, David (ed.) (2000). *Hume: General Philosophy* (Aldershot and Burlington, VT: Ashgate).

Pears, David (1990). *Hume's System* (Oxford: Oxford University Press).

Read, Rupert and Richman, Kenneth A. (eds.) (2000). *The New Hume Debate* (London: Routledge).

Robison, Wade (1982). "One Consequence of Hume's Nominalism," *Hume Studies*, 8, pp. 102–18.

Stroud, Barry (1977). *Hume* (London: Routledge and Kegan Paul).

Wright, John P. (1983). *The Sceptical Realism of David Hume* (Minneapolis, MN: University of Minnesota Press).

6

Inductive Inference in Hume's Philosophy

LOUIS E. LOEB

Hume's discussions of non-demonstrative or inductive inference may be grouped under a number of headings. First, the development of a general theory of simple or enumerative induction occupies the bulk of *A Treatise of Human Nature* 1.3 and sections 4–6 and 9 of *An Enquiry concerning Human Understanding* (hereinafter, "the *Enquiry*"). Second, there are applications of the theory: to inference to the existence of external objects, in *Treatise* 1.4.2 and *Enquiry* 12; and to inference to the existence of God, in *Enquiry* 11 and *Dialogues concerning Natural Religion* 2. Third, *Treatise* 1.4.2 also introduces a complication in regard to the underlying treatment of induction.

Some Context

Fundamental aspects of Hume's conception of epistemology must be gleaned from scattered remarks. To spot them, it is helpful to have in view a contrast with Descartes, though not a standard distinction between "empiricism" and "rationalism." Descartes seeks to explain how knowledge is possible for idealized cognizers for whom the search for truth is an overriding objective, and who fully and conscientiously employ their cognitive faculties under the most favorable conditions (Williams 1978). Descartes maintains that such cognizers can achieve *scientia*, "scientific knowledge" that meets exacting standards. Where, in Descartes' view, does this leave everyday epistemic agents? Evidently, any knowledge they possess is relegated to a second-rate status.

For Hume, if knowledge is possible, it is possible for the common person – and not just as a consolation prize. This formulation needs some explanation. There is in Hume a strict sense of "knowledge" in which the term is reserved for "assurance arising from the comparison of ideas" (T 1.3.11.2 – cf. 1.3.1), intuitive and demonstrative knowledge. At the same time, Hume recognizes other epistemic achievements. Some inductive inferences (for example, inferences to the conclusion that "the sun will rise to-morrow, or that all men must dye") constitute "proofs" (T 1.3.11.2, EHU 6n.10 – cf. 10.6). Hume even links such proofs to "knowledge," now more liberally construed: "No matter of fact can be proved but from its cause or its effect. Nothing can be known to be the cause of another but by experience" (T Abs. 21). Similarly, Hume writes that a person who stops his journey at a river "foresees the consequences of his proceeding forward; and his *knowledge* of these consequences is convey'd to him by past experience" (T 1.3.8.13, emphasis added – cf. 1.3.8.14, 1.3.13.10).

In Hume's view, philosophy should account for the knowledge – the epistemic accomplishments – of everyday persons who are not especially reflective. In the *Natural History of Religion* 6, Hume's observation that "the vulgar . . . are never led into [theism] by any process of argument, but by a certain train of thinking, more suitable to their genius and capacity" (Gaskin 1998: 154) generates constraints on an explanation of religious belief; these are a constant refrain in this work. Although Hume casts this point in terms of belief, a component of knowledge, issues about the reasonableness of the belief in God stand in the background (cf. Gaskin 1978: ch. 8). In *Treatise* 1.4.2.14, Hume writes in regard to another fundamental belief:

> [W]hatever convincing arguments philosophers may fancy they can produce to establish the belief of objects independent of the mind, 'tis obvious these arguments are known but to very few, and that 'tis not by them, that children, peasants, and the greatest part of mankind are induc'd to attribute objects to some impressions.

This passage carries an epistemic resonance.

Hume also thinks that epistemology must account for the knowledge of non-human animals. In "Of the reason of animals," he writes:

> When any hypothesis . . . is advanc'd to explain a mental operation, which is common to men and beasts, we must apply the same hypothesis to both . . . The common defect of those systems, which philosophers have employ'd to account for the actions of the mind, is, that they suppose such a subtility and refinement of thought, as not only exceeds the capacity of mere animals, but even of children and the common people in our own species. (T 1.3.16.3; cf. EHU 9.5)

Hume again has knowledge, as well as belief, in view: "the most ignorant and stupid peasants, nay infants, nay even brute beasts, improve by experience, and *learn* the qualities of natural objects, by observing the effects, which result from them" (EHU 4.23, emphasis added). Some commentators highlight Hume's treating animal and human mental capacities alike as parts of the natural world (Huxley 1909; Bennett 2001; Millican 2002a). It is crucial that Hume includes knowledge within the purview of this naturalism. The principles that explain "the operations of the understanding" in humans should "explain the same phenomena in all other animals" (EHU 9.1); that "animals as well as men learn" is an example (EHU 9.2). Whereas for Descartes the proper object or chief subject matter of epistemological study is the idealized cognizer, for Hume it is the knowledge possessed by a variety of perfectly ordinary organisms.

Hume's epistemological interests are embedded in his commitment to contributing to a "science of human nature" (T Intro. 9, 1.1.1.12) by establishing an associationist psychological theory. For Hume, associationist mechanisms include one perception (conscious state) inducing the existence of a related perception and also the transfer of vivacity between related perceptions. Hume analyzes mental phenomena (such as belief) in terms of vivacity or liveliness and appeals to principles of association to explain their occurrence. Associationism permeates the structure of the *Treatise* (cf. T Abs. 35). As early as 1.1.4, Hume introduces associative principles specifically for ideas, one kind of perception. In 1.3, association by the relation of cause and effect explains causal inference; in 1.4, confusing the idea of identical objects with that of related objects explains various mistaken beliefs about mind and body; in 2.1–2, a double association of impressions and ideas explains the indirect passions; and in 3.2–3, an associationist mechanism of sympathy explains ideas of justice and morality.

The Traditional Interpretation

For Hume, basic inductive inference takes place against the background of the repeated observation of conjoined instances of two kinds of objects. (Non-basic inductive inference includes chains of basic inferences and also inferences from observing a single instance of a conjunction.) On a new occasion, one observes an object of one kind, but without observing an object of the kind with which it is usually conjoined. One then infers the existence of an unobserved instance of an object of the latter kind. Hume's associationism is at work here; the repeated, past observation of the conjunction, together with the new observation, induces a lively idea of the unobserved object. After repeatedly observing fire followed by smoke and smoke preceded by fire, on a new occasion one observes fire without observing smoke or observes smoke without observing fire, and infers the existence of the smoke or the fire. In these examples, the smoke is the unobserved cause of the fire and the fire the unobserved effect of the smoke. Hume has a pronounced tendency to assimilate all inductive inference to causal inference (Price 1940b: 25, 1969: 176–9; Passmore 1952/1968: 29–34; Pears 1990: 71–2), though this need not concern us.

According to the traditional interpretation, Hume maintains that it is in principle impossible to have any justification for beliefs about the unobserved, and does so on the basis of what has come to be known as "the (skeptical) problem of induction." This problem may be stated as follows:

1   Any argument for a belief about the unobserved depends upon a uniformity principle: that observed conjunctions (regularities, uniformities) hold also in unobserved cases.
2   No demonstrative argument can be the basis of belief in the uniformity principle by showing that it must, of necessity, be true; it is conceivable, and hence possible, that nature is not uniform.
3   No non-demonstrative (empirical, probable) argument can be the basis of belief in the uniformity principle; any such argument would extrapolate from observed to unobserved conjunctions, thus presupposing the point at issue, that the observed conjunctions hold also in unobserved cases.
4   Thus, the uniformity principle is not based on argument.
5   Thus, there can be no justification for any belief about the unobserved.

In other words, there is equal justification for every belief about the unobserved – none whatsoever. (For statements of the problem and possible solutions, see Swinburne 1974; Skyrms 1986; Howson 2000.)

108

It can seem easy enough to document that Hume subscribes to each of these steps. For step (1), see *Treatise* 1.3.6.4 and *Enquiry* 4.18–19 and 21. For (2), see *Treatise* 1.3.6.5 and *Enquiry* 4.18 and 21. (At T 1.3.6.8–10, Hume considers a possible escape route from the argument for this step.) For (3), see *Treatise* 1.3.6.6–7 and *Enquiry* 4.19 and 21. Step (4) is implicit at *Treatise* 1.3.6.12 and explicit at *Enquiry* 4.17 and 21. For (5), there are the *"no reason" passages*, statements about the inference to belief in an unobserved object: "there be no reason to determine us to that transition"; the mind makes the "transition without any reason" (T 1.3.6.12 – cf. 1.3.6.11, 1.3.12.20).

What I call "the traditional interpretation" dominated the literature for four decades beginning in the 1940s (Price 1940b, though he finds Hume "of two minds" about induction; Kemp Smith 1941: 46, 121, 374–5; Russell 1945; Popkin 1951; Stove 1965, 1973; Bennett 1971: 299–304; Penelhum 1975; Stroud 1977) and is presupposed in attempts to explain why the problem of induction emerges in Hume, but not before (Hacking 1975; Milton 1987). By the mid-1970s, the traditional interpretation was encountering systematic resistance. (This is consistent with its having staying power – Fogelin 1985; Stroud 1991; Johnson 1995; Dicker 1998.) Since 1990–2000, there has been a scholarly consensus that the traditional interpretation is mistaken. Dissenters have emerged (Penelhum 1992; Winkler 1999), but no serious historical work on Hume can ignore the case against the tradition.

All parties concede that Hume flirts with broadly skeptical or destructive conclusions. For example, Hume argues that our faculties lead to contradictory beliefs about the existence of matter (T 1.4.4.15; EHU 12.15–16). The present question, however, is whether Hume subscribed to skepticism specifically with respect to induction. Hume writes in the concluding section of Book 1: "I am ready to reject all belief and reasoning, and can look upon no opinion even as more probable or likely than another" (T 1.4.7.8). This seems to imply, as a special case, that beliefs about the unobserved are to be rejected, and rejected because they are equally probable in that they are not justified at all – the conclusion at (5). Still, Hume's finding some argumentative path to this result (for example, via the claim that our faculties are incoherent) does not show that he propounded *the problem of induction*, an argument for (5) along the lines of (1)–(4).

Indeed, in route to his 1.4.7 announcement that all beliefs are equally probable, Hume appeals to various perplexities and supplies cross-references to sections of the *Treatise*: the contradiction in our faculties uncovered in 1.4.4 (1.4.7.4); the discovery in 1.3.14 that causation involves no connection outside the mind (T 1.4.7.5); and a "dangerous dilemma" stemming from the contention in 1.4.1 that the understanding subverts itself (T 1.4.7.6–8). Hume also expresses qualms about the role of enlivening in his account of belief (T 1.4.7.3). Since this concern applies to any belief, it is too general to attribute to the problem of induction. Also, the claim that belief is a lively idea is developed in 1.3.7. Notably absent from the inventory in 1.4.7 is any reference to 1.3.6. This omission is inexplicable on the hypothesis that Hume arrives at skepticism on the basis of his main argument about induction (Arnold 1983; Broughton 1983). This should give pause with respect to the viability of the traditional interpretation, at least as regards the *Treatise*.

Disarming the Evidence for the Traditional Interpretation

Any attempt to undermine the traditional interpretation must disarm the textual evidence that Hume subscribed to (5). An important strategy is to interpret the "no reason" passages to mean that inferences to the unobserved are not the product of a faculty of reason *as conceived by other philosophers*. Commentators differ in their characterizations of the conception of reason Hume has in his sights: deductivist, syllogistic, or demonstrative (Beauchamp and Mappes 1975; Connon 1976; Winters 1979; Beauchamp and Rosenberg 1981; Broughton 1983; Baier 1991; Wolterstorff 1996); as caused by further reasoning or argument (Ferreira 1986; Garrett 1997; Noonan 1999); as due to a faculty of rational insight or rational perception (Craig 1987; Millican 2002b); or as requiring intermediate steps (Owen 1999). If, as most of these commentators maintain, Hume does not assume that his target exhausts possible conceptions of reason, the "no reason" passages do not imply that he subscribed to the claim at (5). (Millican's detailed 2002b examination of the structure of part 2 of *Enquiry* 4 illuminates the constraints on what Hume's target could be.)

The lead paragraph of the main argument about induction suggests that Hume's target is more general than particular historical models of "reason":

> [T]he next question is, whether experience produces the idea by means of the understanding or imagination; whether we are determin'd by reason to make the transition, or by a certain association and relation of perceptions? (T 1.3.6.4)

Hume identifies reason with the understanding and contrasts it with the imagination, conceived as a faculty of association. It is reason, so characterized, that must rely on the uniformity principle, by way of a demonstrative or probable argument. In either case, reason must proceed non-associatively. Hume thus concludes:

> When the mind, therefore, passes from the idea or impression of one object to the idea or belief of another, it is not determin'd by reason, but by certain principles, which associate together the ideas of these objects. (T 1.3.6.12)

Taken in context, the "no reason" claim means that the inference to belief in an unobserved object is not due to a putative non-associative faculty, without implying that inductive inference is any the worse for that (Loeb 2002). This is also the case in 1.3.12, where Hume turns his attention to inductive inferences based on observation of statistical regularities, conjunctions that are not constant. In such inferences, we often "carefully weigh the experiments, which we have on each side" (T 1.3.12.7). At 1.3.12.8–19, Hume provides an associationist explanation of these inferences. At 1.3.12.20, he recalls the result in 1.3.6:

> [T]hat even after the observation of the frequent or constant conjunction of objects, we have no reason to draw any inference concerning any object beyond those of which we have had experience . . . These principles we have found to be sufficiently convincing, even with regard to our most certain reasoning from causation . . . with regard to these conjectural or probable reasonings they still acquire a new degree of evidence.

Hume takes 1.3.12 to confirm his 1.3.6 conclusion; inductive inferences, whether based on constant or imperfect conjunctions, are not due to a non-associative faculty of reason. This reading coheres nicely with Hume's associationist ambitions.

Although the traditional interpretation has been widely applied to the *Enquiry* (Flew 1961, 1986; Penelhum 1975, 1992; Broughton 1983: 4, 15; Stroud 1991: 235–237; Fogelin 1993; Winkler 1999), its critics have focused on the *Treatise*. (Buckle 2001 and Millican 2002b are exceptions.) There is a case to be made against reading Hume as subscribing to skepticism about induction even in the *Enquiry*. Hume asks in the first paragraph of part 2 of section 4: "*What is the foundation of all conclusions from experience?*" (EHU 4.14 – cf. 4.21). We can construe him as seeking to locate a *psychological* found-ation, the faculty that gives rise to causal inference. In the next paragraph, he announces: "I shall content myself, in this section, . . . to give a negative answer . . . [O]ur conclusions from . . . experience are *not* founded on reasoning" (EHU 4.15 – cf. part 2 of section 5). He introduces his positive view at 5.5: "All inferences from experience . . . are effects of custom." In both the *Treatise* and the *Enquiry*, after arguing that the uniformity principle is not based on reason, Hume concludes that inductive inference has some other source, custom or habit. (*Enquiry* 6 extends this conclusion, in the manner of *Treatise* 1.3.12, to statistical inference.) The recurrent statements in part 2 of *Enquiry* 4 and early in part 1 of *Enquiry* 5 that inductive inference is not due to *argument*, sometimes cited to support the traditional interpretation (Fogelin 1985: 45–6, 153; 1993), are consonant with Hume's constructive theme that animals, young children, and common persons learn from experience.

Nowhere in part 2 of *Enquiry* 4 does Hume claim that there is "no reason" for inductive inference or that such inference occurs without "any reason" (though, eight sections later, there is 12.25). (I consider 12.21 and 12.22 too vague and too far removed from the earlier argument to support the skeptical reading.) Passages within *Enquiry* 4–5 that engender a skeptical interpretation include the section titles – "Sceptical Doubts concerning the Operations of the Understanding" and "Sceptical Solution of these Doubts"; and 4.21, where Hume considers an objection – "My practice, you say, refutes my doubts." A promising response is that the doubts involve *the scope* of the understanding, whether reason's operation extends to inductive inference (Beauchamp and Rosenberg 1981: 47–8).

In the *Treatise*, Hume contends early in 1.3.6 that inductive inference is due either to reason or to a faculty of association. He thus structures the dialectic so that a positive conclusion – that inductive inference is due to an associative process – follows immediately on the heels of (4). In part 2 of *Enquiry* 4, Hume is content with a stark "negative answer" and "negative argument" (EHU 4.17): that inductive inference cannot be supported by argument or reason. Against this background, as Moore observed (1909: 155–6), Hume's announcement in part 1 of *Enquiry* 5 of the constructive result that inductive inference is due to custom invites the reading that it is due *merely* to custom, a result of custom and thereby groundless. Hume's discussions of custom, however, do not carry this pejorative force.

Evidence that Hume Considers Inductive Inference Justified

The traditional interpretation tends to draw on a narrow range of texts. Commentators, especially those who have sought to disarm the evidence that Hume was a skeptic about induction, have produced wide-ranging evidence that Hume considers inductive inference justified. I arrange the points of evidence in the order they emerge in the *Treatise*. Item (g), to my knowledge, is new to the literature.

(a) The *Treatise* carries the subtitle, "BEING AN ATTEMPT TO INTRODUCE THE EXPERIMENTAL METHOD OF REASONING INTO MORAL SUBJECTS." As early as 1.1.1.8, Hume relies on inductive evidence to establish his principle that every simple idea exactly resembles a preceding impression (cf. EHU 2.6–7). Just two sections following the main argument about induction, Hume appeals to "experience" and "experiments" to confirm – indeed, "to prove" – his associationist account of belief (T 1.3.8.3, 4, 5). As in other contexts where he employs inductive inference, Hume does not pause to note some would-be epistemic difficulty.

(b) Hume writes of causal inference leading to belief in the unobserved in a way that implies epistemic success. Causation is the only relation that enables the mind to "go beyond what is immediately present to the senses, either to *discover* the real existence or the relations of objects" (T 1.3.2.2); the relation of causation "*informs us* of existences and objects, which we do not see or feel" (T 1.3.2.3). We then find 1.3.8.13, previously cited; also, the relation of cause and effect "*brings us acquainted with such existences, as* . . . lie beyond the reach of the senses and memory." We have in the *Enquiry*:

> Had not the presence of an object instantly excited the idea of those objects, commonly conjoined with it, all our *knowledge* must have been limited to the narrow sphere of our memory and senses. (EHU 5.21)

And this: "The existence . . . of any being can only be *proved* by arguments from its cause or its effect; and these arguments are founded entirely on experience" (EHU 12.29). Emphases have been added in quotations under (b).

(c) Hume writes: "cause and effect . . . 'tis the only [connexion or relation of objects], on which we can found a just inference from one object to another" (T 1.3.6.7). This endorsement occurs within Hume's main argument about induction, where the skeptical tone that pervades 1.4 is absent. At 1.3.13.3, causal inference is "just and conclusive." At 1.4.4.1, Hume writes:

> One who concludes somebody to be near him, when he hears an articulate voice in the dark, reasons justly and naturally; tho' that conclusion be deriv'd from nothing but custom.

In *Enquiry* 10: "One, who, in our climate, should expect better weather in any week of JUNE than in one of DECEMBER, would reason justly, and conformably to experience" (EHU 10.3 – cf. 10.10). *Enquiry* 11 includes numerous references to "rules of just reasoning" or to a "just reasoner" (EHU 11.13, 18, 23, 26).

(d) Hume applies "reason" and its cognates to causal inference in T 1.3.6 subsequent to the main argument about induction (T 1.3.6.15), in 1.3.7 (T 1.3.7.2, 3, 5n), and also after attributing causal inference to custom (T 1.3.8.12, 13, 15). What are we to make of these passages, in light of Hume's characterization of reason as non-associative at 1.3.6.4 and his conclusion that inductive inference is not due to reason (T 1.3.6.12, 1.3.7.6)? Hume's position is that if reason is the faculty that generates inductive inference, it is a mistake to characterize reason as non-associative. He writes at 1.3.9.19n:

> When I oppose the imagination to the memory, I mean the faculty, by which we form our fainter ideas. When I oppose it to reason, I mean the same faculty, excluding only our demonstrative and probable reasonings.

The imagination in the first, inclusive sense, is the faculty of association. Within this faculty, Hume draws a distinction between reason, which includes probable reasoning or causal inference, and the imagination in a second, narrow sense. Earlier in the section, Hume contrasts beliefs "arising from custom and the relation of cause and effect" with beliefs that "are merely the offspring of the imagination" (T 1.3.9.4), that is, that arise within the imagination in the restricted sense. Hume is here disparaging associative processes not based on custom, not custom itself. At 1.3.9.19, 1.4.2.14, and 1.4.4.15, reason is identified with causal inference.

(e) Hume recognizes gradations in inductive evidence. At 1.3.13.19–20, he provides an inventory of "degree[s] of evidence" that includes proofs and also probability, beliefs based on observation of conjunctions that are not constant or on infrequent observation of conjunctions (T 1.3.12.2–4, 25). (The term "probability" has a wider meaning at T 1.3.9.19n) Within probability, there are degrees of "force" (T 1.3.12.2) and "evidence" (T 1.3.12.2, 1.3.13.19). Hume devotes 1.3.13 to "unphilosophical probability," in contrast to "kinds of probability [that] are receiv'd by philosophers, and allow'd to be reasonable foundations of belief and opinion" (T 1.3.13.1). In the *Enquiry*, some events are "more probable" (EHU 6.4) than others; and "A wise man . . . proportions his belief to the evidence" (EHU 10.1.4 – cf. 10.16).

(f) Hume writes at 1.3.13.11: "We shall afterwards take notice of some general rules, by which we ought to regulate our judgment concerning causes and effects." Hume's footnote references 1.3.15, "Rules by which to judge of causes and effects," where he offers eight rules, "all the LOGIC I think proper to employ in my reasoning" (T 1.3.15.11). Hume writes that the fourth rule (same cause, same effect; same effect, same cause) "is the source of most of our philosophical reasonings" (T 1.3.15.6).

(g) The "philosophical system" of the double existence of perceptions and objects (indirect or representative realism) postulates extended objects as causes of perceptions. Hume writes: "[t]he relation of cause and effect can never afford us any just conclusion from the existence or qualities of our perceptions to the existence of external continu'd objects" (T 1.4.2.54 – cf. 1.4.2.14). He explains:

> The only conclusion we can draw from the existence of one thing to that of another, is by means of the relation of cause and effect . . . The idea of this relation is deriv'd from past experience . . . But as no beings are ever present to the mind but perceptions; it follows that we . . . can never observe [a conjunction] between perceptions and objects. 'Tis impossible, therefore, that from the existence or any qualities of the former, we can ever form any conclusion concerning the existence of the latter, or ever satisfy our reason in this particular. (T 1.4.2.47)

Hume reproduces the argument in the *Enquiry*:

> By what argument can it be proved, that the perceptions of the mind must be caused by external objects . . . ? . . .
>
> It is a question of fact . . . How shall this question be determined? By experience surely . . . But here experience is, and must be entirely silent. The mind has never any thing present to it but the perceptions. (EHU 12.11–12)

On the traditional interpretation, this argument would be unnecessary; if there is no justification for inductive inference based on observed conjunctions, a fortiori there is no justification for inductive inference not backed by observed conjunctions. Perhaps Hume's position is that although inference from observed conjunctions is unjustified, *even if it were justified* there would be a special difficulty for inference to extended objects. Against this suggestion, *Treatise* 1.4.2.47 and 54, and *Enquiry* 12.11–12, say or imply that inductive inference based on observed conjunctions is justified. In his contention that no inductive inference to extended objects can get off the ground, Hume does advocate skepticism about some inductive inferences, but his argument presupposes the legitimacy of inductive inference based on observed conjunctions.

Items (a–g) constitute impressive evidence that Hume endorses inductive inference. Some commentators who seek to disarm the case for the traditional interpretation want to minimize this evidence as well. They agree (against the traditional interpretation) that Hume is not a skeptic about inductive inference, but caution that Hume does not engage in epistemological or philosophical evaluation (negative or positive) of inductive inference until *Treatise* 1.4; 1.3 and perhaps much of 1.4 is purely descriptive – either of epistemic distinctions internal to a practice (Owen 1999), or of the psychology of epistemic evaluation (Garrett 1997). Focusing especially on (a), (c), (d), (e), and (f), these cautious critics of the traditional interpretation try to explain away the evidence that Hume considers causal inference justified in 1.3. (For detailed criticism, see Loeb 2006.) Since even those who favor the descriptivist reading agree that in 1.4 Hume comes around to offering a normative epistemological position intended to sustain inductive inference, I put these ongoing controversies to the side.

The Traditional Interpretation Revisited

How might proponents of the traditional interpretation respond to the evidence of Hume's favorable evaluation of inductive inference? Some charge Hume with inconsistency (Russell 1945: 672; Flew 1986: 56–7). In light of (a–g), the self-contradiction attributed to Hume is of breathtaking proportions. Fogelin tries to remove the sting: in Hume's view, we are psychologically compelled to undertake epistemic assessments (1985: 148–9). Even so, Hume was not compelled to report such evaluations, much less to do so without taking note of the inconsistency.

A more charitable response originates with Kemp Smith (1905, 1941). He and his successors (Price 1940b; Popkin 1951; Jessop 1952; Penelhum 1975; Stroud 1977; Ayer 1980; Woolhouse 1988) are traditionalists: Hume advances the problem of induction and accepts its skeptical conclusion. The Kemp Smith interpretation, however, plays up Hume's statements that "all probable reasoning is nothing but a species of sensation," a matter of "taste and sentiment" (T 1.3.8.12); and that *"belief is more properly an act of the sensitive, than of the cogitative part of our natures"* (T 1.4.1.8). Beliefs are feelings; they are not due to reason, and hence not so much irrational as arational or nonrational. Further, beliefs about the unobserved are "irresistible" and "inevitable"; the claim that such beliefs are unjustified and that we ought not to hold them is thus pointless, or even false (if ought implies can).

Although a significant advance, the Kemp Smith interpretation has difficulty accommodating the evidence of Hume's epistemic approval of inductive inference. In the Kemp Smith interpretation, inductive inference is nonrational, not due to a faculty deserving of the name "reason." The interpretation entirely overlooks the significance of the passages at (d): once his main argument about induction is complete, Hume persists in attributing causal inference to "reason," which he reconstructs as a component of the faculty of association carrying epistemic pride of place.

Hume's Epistemic Options

If Hume is not a skeptic about induction on the basis of *Treatise* 1.3.6 and part 2 of *Enquiry* 4, it remains to identify the grounds on which he considers inductive inference reasonable. The Kemp Smith interpretation invokes irresistibility to explain why skepticism does not dislodge inductive beliefs. One interpretive option is to jettison Kemp Smith's emphasis on nonrationality while retaining that on irresistibility: inductive inference is justified or reasonable because it is irresistible (Wilson 1997: 113–20). Such "justification," however, amounts to nothing more than the inescapability of beliefs; this is a rather thin sense in which beliefs about the unobserved are justified (Lenz 1958), or as at (c), "just." Similarly, the assessments at (b), cast in terms of "knowledge" and other language implying epistemic success, are more robust than the interpretation allows.

Furthermore, Hume endorses beliefs that are not justified even in the attenuated sense of accounts in terms of irresistibility. At (e), inductive evidence admits of degrees. Unlike proofs, which are conditioned by frequent observation of constant conjunctions (T 1.3.11.11, 1.3.13.8), judgments of probability are not irresistible (T 1.3.12.2–3, 25, 1.3.13, 19–20 – cf. 1.4.4.1). Nor are justified inferences based on observing a single instance of a conjunction; they arise in an *"oblique* and *artificial* manner" via the second-order belief that like objects in like circumstances produce like effects (T 1.3.8.14 – cf. 1.3.15.6). In light of these cases, perhaps Hume should take the justification of resistible beliefs to consist in their systematic interconnections or coherence with those inductive expectations that are irresistible.

Hume does allude, in the *Enquiry*, to a "methodized and corrected" (EHU 12.25) refinement of common beliefs. Hume writes in the *Dialogues* that "[W]e always render our principles the more general and comprehensive," and calls attention to "a more regular and methodical operation of the same kind" (DNR 1; Kemp Smith 1947: 134). These remarks, applied to inductive inference, encourage a coherentist interpretation in which reasonableness is a matter of codification and systematization (Noxon 1973: 8–16, 81–90; cf. Passmore 1952/1968: 53–63). The rules at (f) are an element of such a system. The theory attributed to Hume has affinities with that of Goodman (1955: ch. 3.2): justification consists in coherence, where particular instances of inductive inference conform to beliefs about general canons of induction, and vice versa. In Hume, there is the twist that the irresistible beliefs, which cannot be sacrificed, provide constraints on such codification (Strawson 1958, 1985: 10–14; Penelhum 1992; Millican 2002b).

An initial worry is this. In the *Enquiry* and the *Dialogues* passages, Hume is characterizing "philosophical decisions" and "*philosophy*." He is discussing a distinctive, reflective activity, not providing a general account of reasonableness. This is a symptom of a large problem: a justification for induction in terms of systematization is incompatible with Hume's anti-Cartesian epistemological project. Animals, young children, and ordinary adult humans have knowledge, for example, about their immediate and prospective physical environment. In the *Enquiry*, Hume introduces this theme in the concluding paragraph of part 2 of section 4. In the *Treatise*, it is deferred to 1.3.16, where the "reason" of animals confirms Hume's account of inductive inference:

> Beasts . . . can never by any arguments form a general conclusion, that those objects, of which they have had no experience, resemble those of which they have. 'Tis therefore by means of custom alone, that experience operates upon them. All this was sufficiently evident with respect to man. But with respect to beasts there cannot be the least suspicion of mistake. (T 1.3.16.8)

These observations apply to codification: much as nonreflective creatures possess knowledge, but lack the ability to support beliefs with arguments, their belief systems seem insufficiently sophisticated to meet the required threshold of systematization. They might, for example, lack sufficiently "general and comprehensive" beliefs. A coherentist epistemology threatens to deprive many organisms of routine knowledge. Interpretations that stress reflective approval, locating justification in the successful application of (higher-order) induction to inductive methods themselves (Baier 1991; Winkler 1999 – cf. Korsgaard 1996: 49–66), also founder on this objection.

What sorts of epistemological theories might license attributions of knowledge to animals and children, as well as to adult humans, however reflective? Externalism is the obvious possibility. (Another possibility is a "negative" coherence theory. See Loeb 2001.) According to externalism, the epistemic status of a belief depends, at least in part, upon naturalistic facts about the mechanisms that produce it. Hume was a forerunner of externalism, at least in sharing one of the motivations of its recent proponents: to account for the knowledge of infants and non-human animals (Goldman 1975; Dretske 1991; Kornblith 2002).

Externalism represents a class of theories. One prominent option is reliabilism; true beliefs constitute knowledge if they result from belief-forming mechanisms that tend to produce a sufficiently high proportion of true beliefs. A related theory identifies knowledge with true beliefs that result from mechanisms that are adaptive; another, with true beliefs that result from the proper functioning of cognitive faculties. Some see Hume as a reliabilist (Dauer 1980; Costa 1981; Schmitt 1992, who also considers an adaptivist alternative). Others attribute a proper functioning account to Hume (Craig 1987: 81; Wolterstorff 1996: 166, n.6). Another interpretation focuses on mechanisms that tend to produce psychologically stable sets of beliefs (MacNabb 1951/1966: 94–100; Loeb 2002). Each of these externalist theories has the potential to explain the epistemic accomplishments of the common person, young children, and animals.

Hume's conclusions at *Treatise* 1.3.6–7 and part 2 of *Enquiry* 4 and part 1 of *Enquiry* 5 that inductive inference is due to an associative faculty and to custom in particular, and the arguments that support them, have no tendency to show that custom is unreliable, or not adaptive, or not conducive to stability in belief. They thus have no tendency to establish skepticism about induction, by externalist standards. Much to the contrary. In the *Enquiry*, Hume finds "a kind of pre-established harmony between the course of nature and the succession of our ideas" (EHU 5.21). He elaborates:

> [T]his operation of the mind, by which we infer like effects from like causes, and *vice versa*, is so essential to the subsistence of all human creatures, it is not probable, that it could be trusted to the fallacious deductions of our reason, which is slow in its operation; appears not, in any degree, during the first years of infancy; and at best is, in every age and period of human life, extremely liable to error and mistake. It is more conformable to the ordinary wisdom of nature to secure so necessary an act of the mind, by some instinct or mechanical tendency, which may be infallible in its operations, may discover itself at the first appearance of life and thought, and may be independent of all the laboured deductions of the understanding. . . . [N]ature has . . . implanted in us an instinct, which carries forward the thought in a correspondent course to that which she has established among external objects. (EHU 5.22)

In attributing inductive inference to custom, Hume sees himself putting it on a firm epistemic footing (Monteiro 1976; Dauer 1980 – but see Passmore 1952/1968: 146–7; Stroud 1991). The final paragraph of *Treatise* 1.3.16 has a similar character. These and related passages, especially 1.3.10.2–3 and 1.4.4.1–2, bring to light externalist strands in Hume's thinking that begin to explain how he could assign inductive inference a positive epistemic status: *because* it results from custom.

Although we cannot attribute a coherentist theory to Hume, we can accommodate his remarks about systematization within an externalist interpretation. At the *Enquiry* 12.25 and *Dialogues* 1 passages that stress methodical procedures, Hume sees philosophy as supplementing, and continuous with, "the reflections" or "principles" of "common life". In the *Dialogues*, common life has its roots in "our earliest infancy." Against the background of the anti-Cartesian project, this suggests relying on externalism to subsume and explain the importance of codification. Beliefs that arise from custom filtered by codification and systematization will be more reliable, more adaptive, more stable, and the like, than beliefs that arise from custom in a purely unreflective way. Young children and animals can secure genuine knowledge without employing such filters. Since codification and systematization are available to reflective adults, their beliefs count as knowledge only if they would result from custom that is suitably filtered. Creatures differ in the belief-forming mechanisms available to them, but the underlying epistemology is externalist in all these cases. This is the point of *Enquiry* 9.5n, where Hume explains why "men so much surpass animals in reasoning, and one man so much surpasses another," even though "all reasoning concerning facts or causes is derived merely from custom."

Applications to Extended Objects and Belief in God

At (g), Hume insists that inductive inference cannot justify belief in extended objects: induction depends upon the observed conjunction of "two beings [that] are constantly conjoin'd" (T 1.4.2.47). In the *Enquiry*, Hume marshals a parallel case against the argument from design:

> It is only when two *species* of objects are found to be constantly conjoined, that we can infer the one from the other . . . If experience and observation and analogy be, indeed, the only guides which we can reasonably follow in inference of this nature; both the effect and cause must bear a similarity and resemblance to other effects and causes . . . which we have found, in many instances, to be conjoined with another . . . [T]o pursue the consequences of this principle, I shall just observe, that . . . the antagonists of EPICURUS always suppose the universe, an effect quite singular and unparalleled, to be the proof of a Deity, a cause no less singular and unparalleled. (EHU 11.30)

Earlier, "The Deity . . . is a single being . . . not comprehended under any species or genus" (EHU 11.26). In *Dialogues* 2, Hume reiterates the argument with respect to the singularity of the universe (Kemp Smith 1947: 149–51).

We observe internal perceptions, but not extended objects, and hence no conjunction between them; we observe neither God nor other universes, and hence no conjunction involving them. There is no observed conjunction to ground an inference either to extended objects or to God, as unobserved causes (Mounce 1999: 115). In this respect, these inferences are in the same boat. Here we have an important pattern of argument – the *no new kinds* argument – to the conclusion that there is no justification for inductive inference to the existence of kinds of objects that have not been observed. Whereas Hume regards inference to unobserved instances of kinds of objects that have been observed as unproblematic, he is a genuine skeptic about inductive inferences to "new kinds" of objects. Let us evaluate his grounds for this.

Within Hume's theoretical framework, it is difficult to locate a principled basis for applying the no new kinds argument to belief in God. Legitimate inductive inference depends upon an observed conjunction between two "species" (T 1.3.6.2, 14; EHU 7.27 – cf. *Dialogues* 2; Kemp Smith 1947: 144, 149) or "kinds" (EHU 5.8). A difference "of kind" is a difference in "resemblance" (T 1.1.5.10). Although "An experiment loses of its force, when transferr'd to instances, which are not exactly resembling," Hume allows "it may still retain as much as may be the foundation of probability, as long as there is any resemblance remaining" (T 1.3.12.25 – cf. EHU 9.1); "any traces of . . . resemblance" (T 1.3.13.8) ground probability.

The strategy of the design argument is to claim that observed conjunctions between ordered, complex objects (such as clocks) preceded by intelligent (human) design ground the inference to an intelligent designer of the universe. The argument meets the test of resemblance: the order and complexity of the universe is similar to that of machines; similarly, God belongs to the species of intelligent beings. God may be singular in the sense of possessing a specific property to an unparalleled degree or possessing a unique set of properties; however, from the existence of an enormous cloud of smoke we might properly infer the existence of a fire that is unparalleled in its extent or that has a unique combination of properties. Hume's restrictions on inductive inference are too strong (Plantinga 1967: 98–101; Pike 1970: 149–54; Swinburne 1979/1991: 117–18). (Commentators who seek to defend Hume include Flew 1961: 227–33, 1986: 64–7; Hurlbutt 1965: 153–4; Gaskin 1978: 20–2, 2002: 363–5; Buckle 2001: 288–92; O'Connor 2001: 71–5.)

Related difficulties beset Hume's application of the no new kinds argument to belief in extended objects (Moore 1909: 161–3). In considering the argument from design, Hume assumes the existence of the material world – the cosmos, machines. In considering indirect realism, the existence of extended objects is the point at issue. Indirect realists postulate "another existence, resembling these perceptions" (T 1.4.2.48 – cf. 1.4.2.54, EHU 12.11). Hume's point is that indirect realists hold that perceptions resemble at least the primary qualities (size, shape, etc.) of external objects. Extended objects bear some resemblance to perceptions, much as an intelligent God bears some resemblance to intelligent human designers. The "new kinds" of entities meet the requirement that the inferred bears traces of resemblance to the observed.

It is helpful to consider the distinction between enumerative induction, inferences to objects of the same kind that have been observed, and theoretical induction, inference to kinds of entities that have not been observed. It is natural to classify the inferences from order to God (Flew 1961: 225–6) and from perceptions to extended objects as paradigmatically theoretical. In subjecting these inferences to the no new kinds argument, Hume assimilates them to enumerative induction. (Harman 1965 and, in the Hume literature, Mounce 1999: 111–12, suggest just the opposite: that enumerative induction is a form of inference to the best explanation.) Hume thus evaluates inferences we regard as theoretical within an enumerative framework. This opens the door to bringing similarities to observed objects to bear, undermining his no new kinds argument.

Perhaps the thought behind the no new kinds argument is that the offending inferences are to entities that are *in principle unobservable* (Flew 1961: 246; Noxon 1973: 161). Theoretical inference is thus to be eschewed, at least in metaphysics. This interpretation has some plausibility in the case of extended objects, since Hume maintains that we are directly aware only of perceptions (T 1.2.6.7–8, 1.4.2.9, 14, 1.4.5.15, EHU 12.9). Hume's posture toward the inference to God is more difficult to explain along these lines. Granted, Hume claims that an immaterial soul or spirit is unobservable (Hurlbutt 1965: 155), even that we have no idea of such an entity (T 1.4.5.2–5, 1.4.6.2). If, however, we put aside theological obstacles (DNR 4; Kemp Smith 1947: 158–60), we may think of the mind of God as metaphysically like any other – a bundle or collection of perceptions (T 1.4.2.39, 1.4.6.4). If God, understood in this way, is unobservable in principle, so too is the mind of any other person. Yet, Hume raises no reservations in regard to beliefs about the mental states of others, beliefs required for the operation of sympathy (T 2.1.11.4–7, 2.2.9.13).

Mounce (1999: 18–21, 108–11) suggests that Hume simply assumes that all inductive inference is enumerative. Perhaps there is more to say. Hume absorbed a Newtonian caution with respect to "hypotheses" (T Intro. 8, 1.1.4.6; Abs. 2; EHU 4.12

– see Passmore 1952/1968: 42–9; Noxon 1973). There is an additional factor. Theoretical inference is a species of inference to the best explanation. Berkeley, in the *Principles of Human Knowledge* I, 19, recognized the possibility that it is "easier to conceive and explain [sensations'] production, by supposing external bodies in their likeness," so that "it might be at least probable there are such things as bodies" (Ayers 1993: 96). He nevertheless rejected indirect realism as an explanatory hypothesis, on the ground that even its proponents, such as Locke, deem body–mind interaction incomprehensible. Berkeley's preferred hypothesis, that God's volitions cause perceptions, involves no such dualistic interaction. Berkeley thus appeals to differences in the intelligibility of various causal relations to adjudicate between competing explanations of perceptions. Such considerations are not available to Hume; one of his central claims is that for all we know a priori, "any thing may produce any thing" (T 1.3.15.1, 1.4.5.30 – cf. 1.4.5.32, EHU 12.29). Perhaps he can fall back on considerations of "simplicity" (Wright 1983: 194–5), but Hume's views about causation are an obstacle to his formulating criteria for discriminating among explanations (Passmore 1952/1968: 49–51).

Can Hume salvage the no new kinds arguments within the confines of his theory of enumerative induction? The fundamental difficulty is to explain why some resemblances, but not others, are legitimate foundations for inference to the unobserved (Plantinga 1967: 101–7). Since Goodman (1955: ch. 3, 4), this has been a well-known problem within the theory of inductive inference. In discussing the fourth kind of unphilosophical probability, Hume considers rash generalizations based on irrelevant similarities (cf. T 1.3.13.7, 9). Hume's "general rules" at 1.3.13.7–18, in their "second influence" (T 1.3.12), are best construed as higher-order generalizations about the success of lower-order extrapolations that rely on particular kinds and degrees of similarity (Falkenstein 1997; Loeb 2002: 105–11). (General rules are among the filters that reflective humans can apply to custom.) Anticipating Goodman (1955: ch. 4) and Quine (1969), standards of similarity can be refined. In order to sustain his no new kinds argument, Hume needs to show that enumerative arguments for the religious hypothesis and for indirect realism rely on kinds of similarities that would not themselves be inductively ratified.

What is more, an embarrassing enumerative inference is waiting in the wings. As Berkeley maintained at *Principles* I, 28 (Ayers 1993: 99), we can excite faint perceptions, as in day-dreams, at will. Also, at *De Motu* 25 and *Philosophical Commentaries* 548 (Ayers 1993: 261, 371), our volitions to move a particular limb are followed by vivid visual and tactile perceptions of the limb moving. (For Berkeley, a "limb" consists in a set of perceptions.) We have observed that many of our perceptions are preceded by our own volitions. Consider perceptions that we receive passively, that are not within our voluntary control. Since passive perceptions resemble those that are preceded by our volitions, probably these passive perceptions are preceded by volitions, volitions of some other being (putting aside, as these figures would, the possibility of unconscious volitions of our own). Hume is mistaken in his claim that "experience is, and must be entirely silent" on the question of the external causes of perceptions. Experience supports a Berkelian world-view, where the volitions of some other spirit are the direct causes of sensory experiences!

Limitations on Enumerative Induction

In *Treatise* 1.3, Hume writes as if there are numerous cases of the frequent observation of constant conjunctions. In 1.4.2.20–22, more careful consideration shows that the earlier model is highly idealized; observation is haphazard and fragmentary. Hume here discovers a difficulty for enumerative induction that is prima facie distinct from both the problem of characterizing relevant similarities and the skeptical problem of induction. Although Hume focuses on observed conjunctions between sense-impressions (e.g., visual and auditory experiences), the point that emerges about induction is independent of the ontology on offer. In what follows, I apply Hume's discussion to observed conjunctions between material objects.

Adapting one of his examples, when Hume hears "a noise as of a door turning," he infers a prior "motion of a door" (T 1.4.2.20) as its cause. Even on previous occasions, however, Hume has not observed a constant conjunction between the noise and a prior motion. We can suppose that he is typically asleep or engrossed in thought, so that his seeing the door move prior to hearing the noise is an exception. In these circumstances, how is habit to account for the inference to the existence of the moving door?

The difficulty is not that the observed conjunction is statistical rather than constant. Hume allows inductive inferences based on observed statistical regularities and provides an associationist explanation of why we assign a probability equal to the ratio in the observed sample (T 1.3.12.22, 1.3.13.20). If 30 percent of smokers develop lung cancer, we infer (other things equal) a 30 percent probability that this smoker will develop lung cancer. If the observed correlation between the noise and a prior motion is 30 percent, we nevertheless think it overwhelmingly probable, not 30 percent likely, that the door moved. Hume's 1.3.12 treatment of statistical inference does not explain this judgment.

Hume's response is to appeal to a supplementary psychological principle. The mind, "like a galley put in motion by the oars, carries on its course without any new impulse" (T 1.4.2.22). There is a propensity to enhance observed statistical regularities, treating them (insofar as doing so is not inconsistent with observation) as if they were non-statistical. The mind proceeds as if the moving door had been observed on the occasions that we were asleep or preoccupied. Hume recognizes that invoking the regularity-enhancing principle might seem ad hoc and tries to defend himself against this criticism (T 1.4.2.22). That is as far as he took the discussion (Price 1940a: 50–9).

There are deeper difficulties for the psychological galley (Williams 1977: 137–44; Pears 1990: ch. 11). We might fail to see the door, even though we hear the noise, because we are asleep, day-dreaming, or looking the other way, and hence not positioned to observe it. Alternatively, we might fail to see the door because it has been removed for repair and the porter simulated a turning noise, or because doors intermittently pop in and out of existence. We should not want to rely on the regularity-enhancing propensity in these latter cases, where we do not see the door because it is not present. Reliance on the propensity must therefore be constrained or mediated by beliefs about the sources of failures to observe the door, explanations

121

that presuppose an elaborate theory about the world. The lesson seems to be that enumerative induction can itself take place only against a background theory. Hume did not draw this moral, but he recognized the difficulty that exerts pressure in its direction.

See also 2 "Hume's Theory of Ideas"; 5 "Hume on the Relation of Cause and Effect"; 7 "Hume on Belief in the External World"; 18 "Hume on the Nature and Existence of God"; 23 "Hume's Naturalism and His Skepticism"

Acknowledgments

I am indebted to Peter Millican for a series of extensive comments (over the course of six months) that helped me to clarify both my understanding of the literature and my own views, and to James Joyce for reading a draft and providing valuable suggestions. I am also grateful to Lawrence Sklar for helpful discussion and to Hilary Kornblith for bibliographical references.

References

Arnold, N. Scott (1983). "Hume's Skepticism about Inductive Inference," *Journal of the History of Philosophy*, 21, pp. 31–55.

Ayer, A. J. (1980). *Hume* (New York: Hill and Wang).

Ayers, Michael (ed.) (1993). *Philosophical Works: Including the Works on Vision / George Berkeley* (London: J. M. Dent).

Baier, Annette C. (1991). *A Progress of Sentiments: Reflections on Hume's "Treatise"* (Cambridge, MA: Harvard University Press).

Beauchamp, Tom L. and Mappes, Thomas A. (1975). "Is Hume Really a Sceptic about Induction?" *American Philosophical Quarterly*, 12, pp. 119–29.

Beauchamp, Tom L. and Rosenberg, Alexander (1981). *Hume and the Problem of Causation* (New York: Oxford University Press).

Bennett, Jonathan (1971). *Locke, Berkeley, Hume: Central Themes* (Oxford: Clarendon Press).

—— (2001). *Learning from Six Philosophers: Descartes, Spinoza, Leibniz, Locke, Berkeley, Hume*, vol. 2 (Oxford: Clarendon Press).

Broughton, Janet (1983). "Hume's Skepticism about Causal Inferences," *Pacific Philosophical Quarterly*, 64, pp. 3–18.

Buckle, Stephen (2001). *Hume's Enlightenment Tract: The Unity and Purpose of "An Enquiry concerning Human Understanding"* (Oxford: Clarendon Press).

Connon, R. W. (1976). "The Naturalism of Hume Revisited," in David Fate Norton, Nicholas Capaldi and Wade L. Robison (eds.), *McGill Hume Studies*, vol. 1: *Studies in Hume and Scottish Philosophy* (San Diego, CA: Austin Hill Press), pp. 121–45.

Costa, Michael A. (1981). "Hume and Justified Belief," *Canadian Journal of Philosophy*, 11, pp. 219–28.

Craig, Edward (1987). *The Mind of God and the Works of Man* (Oxford: Clarendon Press).

Dauer, Francis W. (1980). "Hume's Skeptical Solution and the Causal Theory of Knowledge," *Philosophical Review*, 89, pp. 357–78.

Dicker, Georges (1998). *Hume's Epistemology and Metaphysics: An Introduction* (London: Routledge and Kegan Paul).

Dretske, Fred I. (1991). "Two Conceptions of Knowledge: Rational vs. Reliable," *Grazer Philosophiche Studien*, 4, pp. 15–30, reprinted in Fred I. Dretske, *Perception, Knowledge, and Belief: Selected Essays* (Cambridge: Cambridge University Press, 2000), pp. 80–93.

Falkenstein, Lorne (1997). "Naturalism, Normativity, and Scepticism in Hume's Account of Belief," *Hume Studies*, 23, pp. 29–72.

Ferreira, M. Jamie (1986). *Scepticism and Reasonable Doubt: The British Naturalist Tradition in Wilkins, Hume, Reid and Newman* (Oxford: Clarendon Press).

Flew, Antony (1961). *Hume's Philosophy of Belief: A Study of His First Inquiry* (London: Routledge and Kegan Paul).

—— (1986). *David Hume, Philosopher of Moral Science* (Oxford: Basil Blackwell).

Fogelin, Robert J. (1985). *Hume's Skepticism in the "Treatise of Human Nature"* (London: Routledge and Kegan Paul).

—— (1993). "Hume's Scepticism," in David Fate Norton (ed.), *The Cambridge Companion to Hume* (Cambridge: Cambridge University Press), pp. 90–116.

Garrett, Don (1997). *Cognition and Commitment in Hume's Philosophy* (New York: Oxford University Press).

Gaskin, J. C. A. (1978). *Hume's Philosophy of Religion* (London: Macmillan).

—— (ed.) (1998). *Principal Writings on Religion: Including "Dialogues concerning Natural Religion" and "The Natural History of Religion"* (Oxford: Oxford University Press).

—— (2002). "Religion: The Useless Hypothesis," in Peter Millican (ed.), *Reading Hume on Human Understanding* (Oxford: Oxford University Press), pp. 349–69.

Goldman, Alvin (1975). "Innate Knowledge," in Stephen Stich (ed.), *Innate Ideas* (Berkeley, CA: University of California Press), pp. 111–20.

Goodman, Nelson (1955). *Fact, Fiction, and Forecast* (Cambridge, MA: Harvard University Press).

Hacking, Ian (1975). *The Emergence of Probability: A Philosophical Study of Early Ideas about Probability, Induction, and Statistical Inference* (Cambridge: Cambridge University Press).

Harman, Gilbert (1965). "Inference to the Best Explanation," *Philosophical Review*, 74, pp. 88–95.

Howson, Colin (2000). *Hume's Problem: Induction and the Justification of Belief* (Oxford: Clarendon Press).

Hurlbutt, Robert H., III (1965). *Hume, Newton, and the Design Argument* (Lincoln, NE: University of Nebraska Press).

Huxley, T. H. (1909). *Hume* (London: Macmillan).

Jessop, T. E. (1952). "Some Misunderstandings of Hume," *Revue Internationale de Philosophie*, 20, pp. 155–67, reprinted in Vere Chappell (ed.), *Hume: A Collection of Critical Essays* (Garden City, NY: Doubleday, 1966), pp. 35–52.

Johnson, Oliver A. (1995). *The Mind of David Hume: A Companion to Book I of "A Treatise of Human Nature"* (Urbana, IL: University of Illinois Press).

Kemp Smith, Norman (1905). "The Naturalism of Hume (I)," *Mind*, 14, pp. 149–73.

—— (1941). *The Philosophy of David Hume: A Critical Study of Its Origins and Central Doctrines* (London: Macmillan) (reprinted New York: St. Martin's Press, 1966).

—— (ed.) (1947). *Hume's Dialogues concerning Natural Religion* (Edinburgh: Thomas Nelson).

Kornblith, Hilary (2002). *Knowledge and Its Place in Nature* (Oxford: Clarendon Press).

Korsgaard, Christine M. (1996). *The Sources of Normativity*, ed. Onora O'Neill (Cambridge: Cambridge University Press).

Lenz, John W. (1958). "Hume's Defense of Causal Inference," *Journal of the History of Ideas*, 19, pp. 559–67, reprinted in Vere Chappell (ed.), *Hume: A Collection of Critical Essays* (Garden City, NY: Doubleday, 1966), pp. 169–86.

Loeb, Louis E. (2001). "Integrating Hume's Accounts of Belief and Justification," *Philosophy and Phenomenological Research*, 63, pp. 279–303.

—— (2002). *Stability and Justification in Hume's "Treatise"* (New York: Oxford University Press).

—— (2006). "Psychology, Epistemology, and Skepticism in Hume's Argument about Induction," *Synthese*, 152, pp. 321–38.

MacNabb, D. G. C. (1951/1966). *David Hume: His Theory of Knowledge and Morality* (Oxford: Basil Blackwell).

Millican, Peter (2002a). "The Context, Aims, and Structure of Hume's First *Enquiry*," in Peter Millican (ed.), *Reading Hume on Human Understanding* (Oxford: Oxford University Press), pp. 27–65.

—— (2002b). "Hume's Sceptical Doubts concerning Induction," in Peter Millican (ed.), *Reading Hume on Human Understanding* (Oxford: Oxford University Press), pp. 107–73.

Milton, J. R. (1987). "Induction before Hume," *British Journal for the Philosophy of Science*, 38, pp. 49–74.

Monteiro, J. P. (1976). "Hume, Induction, and Natural Selection," in David Fate Norton, Nicholas Capaldi, and Wade L. Robison (eds.), *McGill Hume Studies*, vol. 1: *Studies in Hume and Scottish Philosophy* (San Diego, CA: Austin Hill Press), pp. 291–308.

Moore, G. E. (1909). "Hume's Philosophy," *New Quarterly*, 2, pp. 545–65.

Mounce, H. O. (1999). *Hume's Naturalism* (London: Routledge and Kegan Paul).

Noonan, Harold W. (1999). *Hume on Knowledge* (London: Routledge and Kegan Paul).

Noxon, James (1973). *Hume's Philosophical Development: A Study of His Methods* (Oxford: Clarendon Press).

O'Connor, David (2001). *Hume on Religion* (London: Routledge & Kegan Paul).

Owen, David (1999). *Hume's Reason* (Oxford: Oxford University Press).

Passmore, John (1952/1968). *Hume's Intentions* (London: Gerald Duckworth).

Pears, David (1990). *Hume's System: An Examination of the First Book of his "Treatise"* (Oxford: Oxford University Press).

Penelhum, Terence (1975). *Hume* (London: Macmillan).

—— (1992). *David Hume: An Introduction to His Philosophical System* (West Lafayette, IN: Purdue University Press).

Pike, Nelson (ed.) (1970). *Dialogues concerning Natural Religion* (Indianapolis, IN: Bobbs-Merrill).

Plantinga, Alvin (1967). *God and Other Minds* (Ithaca, NY: Cornell University Press).

Popkin, Richard H. (1951). "David Hume: His Pyrrhonism and His Critique of Pyrrhonism," *Philosophical Quarterly*, 1, pp. 385–407, reprinted in Vere Chappell (ed.) (Garden City, NY: Doubleday, 1966), pp. 53–98.

Price, H. H. (1940a). *Hume's Theory of the External World* (Oxford: Clarendon Press).

—— (1940b). "The Permanent Significance of Hume's Philosophy," *Philosophy*, 15, pp. 7–37, reprinted in Alexander Sesonske and Noel Fleming (eds.), *Human Understanding: Studies in the Philosophy of David Hume* (Belmont, CA: Wadsworth, 1965), pp. 5–33.

—— (1969). *Belief* (London: George Allen & Unwin).

Quine, W. V. (1969). *Ontological Relativity and Other Essays* (New York: Columbia University Press).

Russell, Bertrand (1945). *A History of Western Philosophy* (New York: Simon and Schuster).

Schmitt, Frederick F. (1992). *Knowledge and Belief* (London: Routledge & Kegan Paul).

Skyrms, Brian (1986). *Choice and Chance: An Introduction to Inductive Logic* (Belmont, CA: Wadsworth Publishing).

Stove, D. C. (1965). "Hume, Probability, and Induction," *Philosophical Review*, 74, pp. 160–77, reprinted in Vere Chappell (ed.), *Hume: A Collection of Critical Essays* (Garden City, NY: Doubleday, 1966), pp. 187–212.

—— (1973). *Probability and Hume's Inductive Scepticism* (Oxford: Clarendon Press).

Strawson, P. F. (1958). "On Justifying Induction," *Philosophical Studies*, 9, pp. 20–1.

—— (1985). *Skepticism and Naturalism: Some Varieties* (New York: Columbia University Press).

Stroud, Barry (1977). *Hume* (London: Routledge & Kegan Paul).

—— (1991). "Hume's Scepticism: Natural Instincts and Philosophical Reflection," *Philosophical Topics*, 19, pp. 271–91, reprinted in Margaret Atherton (ed.), *The Empiricists: Critical Essays on Locke, Berkeley and Hume* (Lanham, MD: Rowman & Littlefield, 1999), pp. 229–52.

Swinburne, Richard (1974). *The Justification of Induction* (London: Oxford University Press).

—— (1979/1991). *The Existence of God* (Oxford: Clarendon Press).

Williams, Bernard (1978). *Descartes: The Project of Pure Enquiry* (Harmondsworth: Penguin).

Williams, Michael (1977). *Groundless Belief: An Essay on the Possibility of Epistemology* (New Haven, CT: Yale University Press).

Wilson, Fred (1997). *Hume's Defence of Causal Inference* (Toronto: University of Toronto Press).

Winkler, Kenneth (1999). "Hume's Inductive Skepticism," in Margaret Atherton (ed.), *The Empiricists: Critical Essays on Locke, Berkeley, and Hume* (Lanham, MD: Rowman & Littlefield), pp. 183–212.

Winters, Barbara (1979). "Hume on Reason," *Hume Studies*, 5, pp. 20–35.

Woolhouse, R. S. (1988). *The Empiricists* (Oxford: Oxford University Press).

Wolterstorff, Nicholas (1996). *John Locke and the Ethics of Belief* (Cambridge: Cambridge University Press).

Wright, John P. (1983). *The Sceptical Realism of David Hume* (Minneapolis, MN: University of Minnesota Press).

7

Hume on Belief in the External World

MICHEL MALHERBE

We believe that there exists an external world where there are flowers in their first bloom, high green trees and steep mountains, beautiful women too, political societies and the working class, bad and good actions and even ugliness. We can pick up flowers, climb trees and mountains, meet the woman of our life, improve the condition of our nation and become better in our behavior and conduct. This belief is so universal, steady, and essential to our practice that there is no way to discuss it or even to put it in a hyperbolic suspense. In this respect, Cartesian doubt is a metaphysical vagary or an epistemological joke, since there are certainties which are merely indisputable. Therefore, we do not have to prove the existence of the external world: it does exist. And the Skeptic does not have to prove that the existence of the external world cannot be proved: it would be useless.

This is why Hume directly asks the question: how do we come to believe in the existence of bodies? Whereas, when he was dealing with causality, he had first skeptically argued that there could be no rational or experimental foundation for causal relation, and then had proceeded to the study of how we make inferences from causes to effects or from effects to causes.

So plain as this question might appear, yet we must consider it with some care. And first of all, is this question relevant? Thomas Reid and others think that it is not, because this belief, being indisputable, is natural: everybody knows not only that the external world exists, but also that he unquestionably knows that. Since we do not have to prove the existence of the external world, we do not have to explain how we would come to this belief. It is a first principle of the human mind that can only be described. Of course, such a naïveté is not quite innocent, since it entails that, wherever the *why* question is irrelevant, so is the *how* question; or, in other words, that there can be no good explanation but rational and only when it is possible. Reid's commonsense argument still pertains to a disillusioned foundationalism; and one might suspect that to dismiss the *how* question and to consider the belief in the external world as an original fact is a byroad to push aside the skeptical import of any questioning of such a fact. On the contrary, in Hume's philosophy, a fact is to be taken as an effect and every effect may have a cause; it being known that to give a cause of a fact never means to give its reason.

Second, let us consider the terms of the question. Hume does not ask *what causes induce us to believe in the existence of the external world*, but *what causes induce us to believe in the existence of body.* For, there are several objections to the first question. Firstly, strictly speaking, we never have an experience of the world, but only of objects in the world. If every object is in the world, the world is not an object. In the *Dialogues on Natural Religion* (part 2) Philo will argue that we cannot take the part for the whole nor the whole on the model of any of its parts; the world is the elaborate system of objects that we have experienced in the past or will experience in the future, by making causal inferences. Secondly, assuming this, we might say that, when we speak of the existence of the external world, we mean that every object which is in the world has an existence external to the mind and that the world is, in some way, an original principle of being (either it has been created by God or has been existing for ever or is the result of the Big Bang, etc.). The existence of the external world would signify that our perceptions are caused in our minds by some matter which is independent from them. Now, Hume is not the first philosopher to say that such an "externality" is quite obscure: we do not perceive anything external to our perceptions and certainly not externality itself (T 1.2.6.7–9).

But, let us be immaterialists with Berkeley and come back to Descartes' hyperbolic doubt; and let us suppose that delusions and dreams would be good reasons for doubting the existence of the external world in such a way that we could not be totally certain that high trees and steep mountains do exist. But, whether there is or not an external world, we still have the ideas of these high trees and steep mountains; they are *cogitata* of our *cogitationes*. Thus, *externality* appears to imply not only the idea of independent causes of our perceptions, but also the notion of determined objects (whether they exist or not) that are distinct from their perceiving. For, I may doubt the actual existence of something, I will still have the idea of this thing as an intentional object of my thinking and, therefore, as an object distinct from my perception, my imagination or my thought. *Distinct* from the mind and *external* to the mind are two different statuses, even if, of course, there is nothing external to the mind which would not be distinct from it. The School in the middle ages and more recently Austrian and Phenomenological philosophies at length discussed whether this distinction of the intentional object could mean some kind of independence and in which sense. But Hume has cut the Gordian knot, at the start, in *Treatise* 1.2.6. By what may appear as a puzzling confusion between what Descartes, after the Schoolmen, called the formal reality and the objective reality of ideas, he claims that "there is no impression nor idea of any kind, of which we have any consciousness or memory, that is not conceiv'd as existent; and 'tis evident that from this consciousness the most perfect idea and assurance of *being* is deriv'd" (T 1.2.6.2). Everything perceived or conceived is an existence. Even the difference between impressions and ideas does not alter this quite strange statement, from which several consequences follow: (1) "the idea of existence is the very same with the idea of what we conceive to be existent" (T 1.2.6.4) and to think of something and to think of it as existent are the same thing; (2) since any idea corresponds to an impression and is an existence so far as it is the copy of an impression, every impression must be in itself an existence, and there are as many existences as impressions; (3) impressions and existing objects are the same: there is no reason to distinguish between perception and object; and the same can be said about ideas: although an idea is a copy of an impression, an idea is not in itself a representation of an external body or an intentional object; (4) existence not being a distinct idea or impression, is not a quality that could be a part of a complex idea or even some feature of simple impressions, nor could it be obtained by a distinction of reason (T 1.2.6.6; cf. T 1.1.7.17–18).

Therefore *existence, being, perception, object*, mean the same thing. And yet, we see high trees, we climb steep mountains, we meet beautiful women in the external world; and we can also, during winter, think of spring, or dream of climbing rocky mountains, or idealize female beauty. We do have the ideas of things existing in the external world. How do we acquire such ideas?

But, beforehand, a point must be clarified: is the existence in the external world an idea? We just have said that the idea of existence adds nothing to the idea of what is conceived as existent; that is to say, does not extend the determined content or meaning of this idea. But there are things which exist and others which do not. To exist in the external world makes a difference. Consequently, in order to correct a rather loose vocabulary from Hume, let us use the words *being* or *entity* to denote any perception or object and save the word *existence* to designate such a difference. A perception or an object *is*, but it may *exist* or not. Existence will be taken here as a modality. It is meaningless to ask whether beings or entities are external to the mind, since perception and object are the same thing, but it is very useful to ask whether this thing exists or not in the external world. There is nothing to say about the being of perceptions/objects, but there is much to say about their existence, since modalities can only be posited in belief. Now, there are two main beliefs: the belief in necessary existence, supported by causal inferences, and the belief in external existence, supported by sensible perception. Consequently, there are two main modalities: to be necessarily existent and to exist in the external world. And we could argue analogically. Whatever we may think about the psychological explanation of the idea of necessity as corresponding to the feeling of the transition of the imagination in causal inferences, let us retain that there is an "idea" of necessary existence, that this idea has something to do with the association of ideas and impressions, and that it arises in causal belief. In the same way, let us say that there can be an "idea" of external existence, this idea having something to do with the association of ideas and impressions, and arising in sensible belief. We will find out up to which point this analogy can stand.

Now, let us try to describe the sensible existence of things or bodies in the external world. It cannot mean that an object would be external to its perception, since we know that objects and perceptions are the same thing. And they will never become two different things, except among philosophers. A high tree is an impression if I am seeing it; an idea if I am thinking of it. A high tree is what it is. Neither impressions nor ideas are representative in themselves of something external; nor are they given as effects, symptoms, or signs of external causes. When we say that bodies exist outside ourselves, we say that they are outside our own body. But to say so, we must consider our own organic body as a body in space, situated relatively to others, and we have to deal with things located in space and having parts. Now, all objects are not in space (for instance, smells, tastes, which are said in space only by being assimilated to tactile or visible objects) (T 1.4.5.10). Thus we must be careful not to employ the spatial metaphor for any kinds of objects, but to refer their alleged externality to their independence from the mind, so far as this one cannot be the cause of their existence and operation. But Hume makes a further move. This independent or distinct existence itself is to be referred to continued existence, because bodies in the external world exist independently of the mind if they enjoy a continued existence, at the very time the mind does not perceive them. Even if Hume claims that this reasoning is reciprocal, the fact that he starts with considering the continued existence of things in the world is of first importance. Many entities (or perceptions or objects) appear in spatial order (juxtaposition), all of them in temporal order (succession). In spatial order, things can be contiguously conjoined; in temporal order, they appear the one after the other. All of them are perishable beings. In order to keep them together, memory and imagination are required. This observation is the more crucial that various entities, taken one by one, cannot give the idea of time: a single entity *is*, it has no duration, since to be able to perceive its duration we should have the idea of time; but time cannot be perceived in itself, since it is perceived so far as a succession of entities is perceived. But a mere succession without duration does make up time: how are we able to join the ideas of succession and duration together and to be conscious of time?

Another problem is to be emphasized. Each entity appears and disappears successively. Each one can be said to be *one*; but none can be said to *be the same*, since, even if the following one is similar to the preceding one, they are two and the preceding one has disappeared. From the succession of two or more perceptions or objects, we cannot derive the idea of the same perception or object continuing to exist in two or more moments of time. And Hume is not Kant. An entity cannot be identified as a limit by the moment it occupies in any sensible a priori form, since there is no original perception of time: "As 'tis from the disposition of visible and tangible objects we receive the idea of space, so from the succession of ideas and impressions we form the idea of time, nor is it possible for time alone ever to make its appearance, or to be taken notice of by the mind" (T 1.2.3.7). Time is the appearance or the sensible phenomenon of successive perceptions. Thus the question of the continued existence of entities is also the question of their own identity, since, when we believe in the existence of things in the world, we believe that they remain the same when we do not perceive them, at least during some period of time. Thus, we have this alternative: either we perceive only one perception, and that does make *one*, but the idea of unity cannot be taken for the idea of identity; or we successively perceive two (or more) perceptions, but that will make *two*, even if these two perceptions are alike. "Betwixt unity and number there can be no medium" (T 1.4.2.28). The identity of things cannot be more easily perceived than their permanence or their externality, as Barry Stroud has rightly observed (1977: ch. 5).

This identity is all the more a problem, when we consider that, strictly speaking, we do not perceive a tree, but a color, a figure, a volume, a smell, etc. Of course, we say that we see a tree, *this* tree. But how does it happen that so various and different impressions or ideas are taken together as qualities or attributes belonging to this determinate tree, taken as a singular and identical existence? Locke already claimed that things which we are said to see, to touch, to hear, etc. are only collections of ideas or perceptions united by the imagination, under a single name (*Essay* II, 23, 1ff.). But Hume goes further than Locke: it is not only substantial identity that makes a problem, but as well and potentially objective or transcendental identity.

Let us now explain how the mind can acquire the notion of the continued and distinct existence of external objects. Hume successively considers whether it is the senses, reason or the imagination, that produce such an opinion. It cannot be the senses, since they cannot make the mind perceive anything beyond what immediately appears to it: "All sensations are felt by the mind, such as they really are" (T 1.4.2.5). And they could not be presented to the mind as external to or independent of us, except by some kind of fundamental delusion which from one single sensation would derive both the external object and its subjective image; but a sensation is not representative. Not to mention that we should be ourselves obvious to our senses; which is to add one difficulty to another. And what is said about external and independent existence can be said about continued existence, since sensation should give us the perception of an existence of which there is no present sensation. Nor can it be our reason which makes us attribute distinct and continued existence to objects: in this case, only philosophers would entertain such a belief. There remains the imagination.

It is well known that in Hume's philosophy the imagination joins several perceptions together by associating them, that is to say, by moving swiftly from one to another, and that it is actuated by a constant tendency to easiness, to smoothness, as if its liveliness was to help to the restlessness of our life. For it is hard to live when the train of things is interrupted and the soul split into pieces. But the flowing of the imagination, through different and perishing instants of time, would be also a source of uneasiness, if, with the help of the memory, it did not operate mainly as a regular transition between perceptions, connecting the like with the like, suggesting inferences, modeling systems. Indeed, time itself is a principle of association, since it connects one perception to another, but the weakest one (weaker than space) since it is mere succession, and consequently a kind of temporal scattering. In the opposite, the imagination is the pacified flood of our ideas and it runs continuously and regularly. This observation may appear somewhat naïve, but one must remember that not only do we believe in the existence of the external word, but also that we live in this same external world. Anyway, at the core of this belief, there is our consciousness of time and our fragile power to get hold of it.

Hume's doctrine of time can be compared to Kant's one, in several respects. It is the sensible form of appearances, but an a posteriori form. "Five notes play'd on a flute give us the impression and idea of time; tho' time be not a sixth impression, which presents itself to the hearing or any other of the senses" (T 1.2.3.10). Time cannot be separated from perceptions or objects appearing in it. Now, in common experience, these objects are used to appear in the same order or in a constant order, even if we lose sight of them for a moment. This constancy will give philosophers a seeming good reason of distinguishing between perceptions and objects, since if objects are used to appear in a constant order, the contingent succession of their appearances, so they say, must be attributed to the mind. But, at the start, constancy happens when any similar series of entities appear in certain analogous spatial and temporal connections, that is to say, when resemblance between series of entities introduces a kind of repetition and acquaintance in the disorder of time. On the other hand, it may also happen that there is some change from one series to another, but this change is itself regular or at least coherent with the remainder of our experience. Thus, constancy and coherence are the main attributes of the world, when it is taken in a temporal prospect.

Hume begins with the study of coherence. The world, whether it exists externally or not, this point being not yet settled, is essentially a more or less ordered framework in which things happen. For what do we do when we say that a body is in the world, but express the idea that, even if this body appears for the first time, it must take place in the network of the numerous and crossed sequences of phenomena with which we are acquainted by experience and knowledge? Nothing can be added to the world without being incorporated in it. Of course, we may have some quite new experiences, but if they do not fit in, to some degree, with the common or scientific world, they are a threat for life and a problem for science. The famous example given by Hume shows how the imagination can overcome the incoherencies of our experience of the world. Hume is seated in his chamber, in front of his fire. He is seeing flames playing in the chimney, he feels warm, etc. And *then* he hears a noise behind him, sees a man who gives him a letter, recognizes the hand-writing and remembers a friend who is far away. Here we have a series of perceptions and, if some of them can be connected together with the help of the memory (for instance, seeing the hand-writing and remembering the friend who is the author of the letter) others cannot (there is no immediate link between feeling warm and hearing a noise behind one's back). His present series of perceptions disagree with the other ones which make up his experience of the world; if this disagreement was not to fade away, this very quiet scene of Hume getting warm would change into a bewildering disorder. Thus, the world is a general principle of organization for any new experience. Now, an agreement can be reached and a happy life preserved only if Hume supposes that there is a door behind his back, continuing to exist whereas he is looking at the fire; that the porter opened it, crossed the room, before giving him the letter; that the friend who is far away wrote the letter, committed it to a postal service, etc. The world can keep coherent if it is supposed enjoying a continued existence. "Here then I am naturally led to regard the world, as something real and durable, and as preserving its existence, even when it is no longer present to my perception" (T 1.4.2.20).

This conclusion from the coherence of several appearances, Hume says, leads to the same effect as conclusions drawn from our causal inferences and makes the world more uniform and harmonious; but he adds that there is a great difference, so far as, in causal inferences, from similar series of phenomena, the necessary existence of an absent object is posited – an absent object that existed in the past as an impression – whereas, in the present argument, the principle of coherence has the mind compare an irregular series with other series which are regular, but made up with objects enjoying a continued and independent existence – an existence of which we have no experience at all. In Berkeley's words, we cannot compare our interrupted perceptions with objects that would exist permanently and independently in the world, since the only content of our mind is our own perceptions. The idea of a coherent world is a fiction contrived by the imagination in order to soothe the disorder of our own experience.

This first argument is too weak to support the whole frame of a permanent and independent world. Besides the coherence of the appearances of mundane objects, we must consider their constancy. I look around at my room, I shut my eyes and when I open them again, my room, with all its furniture, looks the same, that is to say, the new set of perceptions in my mind perfectly resembles the previous one; and I say that I am staying in the same room which continued to exist when my eyes were shut. To explain how the mind can draw such a conclusion, Hume builds up a remarkable

131

argument which comes again several times (it is summed up in 1.4.2.35–6 and note) and is still at work, in a way, in the chapter devoted to personal identity. First, let us present it and then fix its successive stages.

We know that all perceptions or objects are in themselves different, distinguishable and separable entities or existences. We also know that the imagination is a tendency to a smooth and easy transition and feels uncomfortable when its ideas or principles contradict one another; and that it obtains more regularity or uniformity by the means of association. Now there are two kinds of association: the association of ideas and the association of passions or tendencies, both proceeding here by resemblance. At last, the imagination creates fictions; and all the successive fictions it invents ends at a philosophical one: our perceptions *represent* objects which are identical with themselves and exist permanently and independently in the external word.

Consider a perception or an object. It is a determined being, an entity or an appearance (take the word you like). If you say that it is lasting some time, you say more, since you suggest that it is still the same in two different instants of time. You cannot confer duration to it without giving it an identity. But you cannot derive this identity from its original being. "One single object conveys the idea of unity, not that of identity" (T 1.4.2.26). Nor can you obtain it by considering two moments of time, since, in this case, you have two distinct and separable ideas or two different beings, even if the imagination can proceed from one to the other upon the account of the most exact resemblance. Thus, either you consider one perception and you have no consciousness of time; and having no consciousness of time, you do not have any idea of duration nor any means to confer a temporal identity to the considered entity; or you consider several instants of time and, indeed, you have the idea of succession, but not of duration; you have the ideas of two different perceptions or objects, but not of an identical and permanent one. How can one single entity be the same with itself in a certain elapsing period of time, that is to say, under two or more appearances (or beings)? To overcome this formal contradiction, the imagination seeks for some way between unity and number – precisely, the possibility for an entity to keep the same in time. And, while considering only one perception, it supposes a succession of time. Now, this first fiction is the result of the bringing together of two dispositions of the imagination (T 1.4.2.29). Let us consider any two moments of time. We may survey them at the very same instant and they give us the idea of number: we perceive that they are two and accordingly the given object must be multiplied by two, in order to be conceived at once as existent in these two different points of time. There are two views compared to each other in a single instant. We may also conceive the first moment, with its object, and then, without interrupting our surveying the object, we imagine afterwards a supposed change of time. The idea of identity arises from these two points of view taken together: the object is two and one or, rather, less than two and more than one; and time is both succession and duration. By this very simple but also quite astonishing argument (as it happens very often in Hume's philosophy), the imagination is installed at the core of our consciousness of time and our perception of objects. Thus, by a kind of reciprocation, several objects give the impression of time; the mere idea (or fiction) of time gives the idea of a single object keeping identical.

Nevertheless, in our sensible belief in the existence of bodies in the external word, we begin with two or more perceptions or appearances which, however similar, are different in number and occupy several instants of time: they are "broken and inter-rupted." In the preceding fiction, one object appears to be the same in a supposed variation of time; the imagination deals with a difference that must be inserted into pure unity; here, the problem is inverse: how out of two to make one? The difference of the perceived objects is real; it is the unity or the identity of the object that will be fictitious. The imagination is the easy transition from one perception to another and the more these perceptions are similar, the more the transition is easier, but not so easy that the real difference could be forgotten (in this case, we would have an internal relation from one term to the other). In a word, any relation is external and this externality cannot be overcome. But, what the imagination cannot do by converting two objects into one, it can do by changing its own disposition. A series of resembling objects puts the mind in the same condition as it is when considering an invariable object in a supposed variation of time. And the same attracts the same. "We may establish it for a general rule, that whatever ideas place the mind in the same disposition or in similar tones, are very apt to be confounded" (T 1.4.2.32). It is easy to confound an easy disposition with another one.

Let us observe where we are at this point, since, in these rather meandering details, Hume is aiming at explaining how the mind comes to believe in the continued and, consequently, external existence of things in the world. Previously, identity was only invariableness in a supposed variation of time; now, it is the numerical identity (assimilated to the precedent one) of two or more appearances or objects. And this last one is more than a fiction; it is an illusion, that is to say, an incipient belief. The imagination operates to its own profit, though it is a manifest contradiction to say that two are only one and the same and what is perishing keeps identical. This con-tradiction is an objection for philosophers who will solve it by saying that there are two (or more) *perceptions* for one identical *object*; but it can be endured and managed by common belief which has nothing to do with logical coherence, without such a philosophical device. However, the practical rule of the imagination being easiness, a contradiction, so far it is perceived, can make life uneasy and unpleasant. And this is the case, since there is a contrariety between what the imagination perceives (several perceptions/objects) and what it does, while muddling up these several entities into one. It cannot yield up the opinion of identity since it would be to sacrifice its own tendency and it is like a river: you can throw obstacles in its way and divert it, but you will never stop its flow. But it can work out as many suppositions as are needed: succession being contrary to identity, it can trump up the idea of a con-tinued existence. We will accordingly allow that a perception can be absent without being annihilated and then come back to the mind, without being different. Thus, the only way out is to attribute a continued existence to our elapsing perceptions and to invest them with the modality of a permanent identity. We believe that perceptions or objects (still the same thing at the present stage of the argument) continue to exist even if we do not perceive them, and that all of them taken together make up the constant world where we are living.

A supposition is a supposition, not a belief, all the more, in the present case, that the fictitious aspect of this new fiction cannot be deleted. This fiction is added to the two previous ones; and the more the imagination invents new solutions, the more these solutions are philosophically untenable. But common sense does not go so far and feels more comfortable with steady and reliable beliefs than with skeptical doubts. Belief consists in nothing but the vivacity of an idea, and we know that an idea is used to acquire this vivacity by its relation to some present impression. This relation causes a smooth passage from the impression to the connected idea. And one might conclude that in the present case resemblance has the same influence as causation. But we cannot be as confident as Hume, even if he introduces the operation of the memory. For, though our memory presents us with a vast number of similar instances and gives us a propensity to consider these interrupted perceptions as the same and fictitiously to take them as an identical object, the further step, from numerical identity to continued existence, cannot be so easily explained. This is so, even though the first one entails the second: indeed, sensible belief goes beyond relation. Resemblance, in itself, carries the mind from the similar to the similar, that is to say from one term to another one, connected by their similarity; let us allow that it also has the power to carry the mind from the same to the same; but in the belief in the continued existence of identical objects, it carries it from one modality of existing to another one or, in our own words, from being as an entity to existing as an object. Now, firstly, a modality is just a modality, not a thing; secondly, a continued existence cannot be given nor tested nor settled in any way. Sensible belief is, so to speak, a totally blind belief, a point emphasized by J. M. Costa (1988) who gives a solution, drawn from abstract ideas, which is more ingenious than perfectly convincing.

The last step is easily taken. Since objects enjoy a continued existence, whereas perceptions are broken and interrupted, they are distinct from these perceptions and independent of the mind; and thus they belong to the external world, taken as a distinct principle of being, whereas perceptions belong to the internal world. Or, to speak more exactly concerning common belief, the same entities are taken at one time as permanent objects, at another time as perishing perceptions. Besides, in our idea of the world, causal belief and sensible belief are coordinated, since an object cannot be independent from the mind if it is not apt to take place into the causal network which makes the substance of the world.

This quite singular doctrine might appear extravagant. Two of its features should be underlined. At first, its logical frame: each further step is the logical condition of the preceding one, as if human nature, though naturally prompted, followed a rational regress. In other words, this "natural history" of sensible belief is somewhat analytical, the progress in the successive effects being a regress in the formal conditions of the problem. You may feel indignant with such an outrageous proceeding and object that it is unworthy of an honest philosopher. But the reason would be that you do not take the second feature into account. This natural history is the history of imagination, not of reason; Hume does not try to justify our belief, but explain how it arises. If you are angry with him, I suspect that you secretly entertain the idea that human nature is essentially rational. Is it? "'Tis certain that almost all mankind, and even philosophers themselves, for the greatest part of their lives, take their perceptions to be their only objects, and suppose that the very being, which is intimately present to the mind, is the real body or material existence. 'Tis also certain, that this very perception or object is suppos'd to have a continued uninterrupted being, and neither to be annihilated by our absence, nor to be brought into existence by our presence" (T 1.4.2.38). I look out of the window; I see a couple of hopping blackbirds on the grass; I shut my eyes

134

and open them again; I see a couple of hopping blackbirds and I say: "Hey, there is a couple of hopping blackbirds!" You may object that a blackbird as a perception is not the same thing as a blackbird as a winged creature existing in the world and you may add that the blackbird as a perception represents the blackbird as a real being. But the common sense will stand firm in maintaining that there is only one couple of blackbirds. And you certainly agree with your fellow-creatures, at least if you are monist and not dualist (see Flage 1990: ch. VI).

Of course, Hume, as much as any philosopher, readily observes that "a very little reflection and philosophy is sufficient to make us perceive the fallacy of that opinion" (T 1.4.2.44). This opinion of a continued existence entailing the opinion of an independent existence, our perceptions must be considered as independent, and this is a contradiction that a philosopher as shrewd as Berkeley cannot overcome (it is not contradictory only if, the continued existence being taken as *granted*, one examines whether independent objects can momentarily appear to the mind: see Cook 1968). Philosophers follow the profession of solving contradictions. And their usual device is to introduce some distinction or to make clear and precise what is obscure and confused. Human nature, they say, is mistaken when it surrenders to imagination; or, rather, since it will not be easily allowed that nature is really mistaken, they tell that common sense frames its beliefs in an erroneous way that can be corrected by giving the true philosophical explanation. Nature is potentially, if not actually, rational and philosophy will only straighten up what, given to itself, is a mere and somewhat erroneous tendency. Since the same entities cannot at the same time enjoy a perishing or interrupted existence and a continued one, to be both dependent and independent, the easiest thing to do is to stick to the distinction between perceptions and objects and, instead of upholding a double existence for the same thing, argue that the two existences imply that there are two kinds of things, internal and external, each of them having an existence of their own. Philosophers' specific discovery is the distinction between being and appearing: things existing in the external world produce perceptions of the mind, where they appear in an interrupted way, without losing their permanent identity. To exist means to exist in an external world. The external world, taken as an ontological principle, is philosophers' great argument.

In the last paragraphs of section 2 and in section 3 and 4 of this fourth part of *Treatise* 1, where he enquires into the metaphysical foundation of this argument, Hume both refutes the idea that the contradiction would be solved by the theory of representation and shows that this system, having no rational strength, is only one more belief, not a common but a philosophical belief where the imagination is triumphant. "However philosophical this new system may be esteem'd, I assert that 'tis only a palliative remedy, and that it contains all the difficulties of the vulgar system, with some others, that are peculiar to itself" (T 1.4.2.46). Thus the natural history of sensible belief goes further than the producing of natural belief, up to philosophical belief. Of course, the lesson is hard to take: what philosophers call *reason* is, concerning this question, only an unnecessary belief.

It would be too long to enter into a detailed analysis, but let us characterize the basic argument and suggest the general import of this damaging doctrine.

Our experience gives us only our perceptions-objects and does not acquaint us with anything such as the double existence of perceptions *and* objects. And it is impossible to infer the existence of bodies from their appearances to the mind, since any causal inference can carry us from one thing to another one inside the system of our experience, but not from a perception to an object or from the whole system to the external world. Therefore, the double existence doctrine is merely speculative, although it can operate in a philosophical mind as an undeniable belief. And every belief, even those of the philosophical kind, must and can be explained. Now, reason cannot produce this belief, since (to say it in these words) Berkeley has shown that it cannot be proved by any argument (not to mention Descartes, who has no other argument than God's veracity). Thus, the philosophical system "must derive all its authority from the vulgar system; since it has no original authority of its own" (T 1.4.2.49). If philosophers were thoroughly rational, they should conclude that the belief in an external and independent existence and, consequently, in a continuous existence, is contradictory, and suspend it; but, no Skeptic being so foolish as to take such a step, they fall under a new contradiction between common belief (our perceptions are our objects) and a critical reflection which easily proves that the same entity cannot be both a perception and an object. And the same spring as previously, the same tendency to easiness, operates in philosophers' minds: the formal distinction between perception and object, between appearance and existence, pleases both their reason, in allowing that our perceptions are interrupted, and their imagination, in saving the common belief in objects endowed with continuous existence. And they hasten to add that the objects resemble the perceptions. But it is easy to notice that they do nothing but use their favorite device, i.e., change a contradiction into a distinction. It would not be a pitiful trick, if they were able to determine the relation between perceptions and objects and lay the foundation of the existence of the external world.

Here, it should be noticed that Hume, while skeptically chasing after any pretended solution, is gradually sketching a general history of philosophical systems, as if he could under this question sum up past, present, and, we may add, future philosophy. And he does this by complicating the initial problem. Till now, we have talked about perceptions and objects rather loosely, for we do not have to pay attention to the difference between simple and complex impressions (or ideas) and we have ignored the fact that the original content of perception is not *the* tree or *the* mountain, but a color, a figure, a smell, a certain hardness, etc., that is to say, various qualities. And it is a question how we can say that we see *the* tree or climb *the* mountain, by joining these qualities together. This way, the question of identity can be more exactly settled and we will observe that, being determined in their degrees of quality and quantity, each of the various entities (qualities) is numerically one but not identical to itself and that objects alone are supposed to be identical to themselves, in the stream of their different qualities, and to enjoy a continued and external existence.

The simplest and the grossest way to deal with this brain-racking problem is provided by ancient philosophy, which gives a metaphysical answer going from externality to identity. The external world exists; it is the general set of all things that have the principle of their being in themselves, i.e., that are substances. By definition, substances enjoy a permanent existence and, so far, are identical to themselves. Concerning their qualities, one must distinguish between their essence, by which they are what they are, and their accidents, which can be destroyed without entailing their own destruction. As to perception, these substances send forth species which are like their predicates and impress the human mind. Of course, there are many problems at stake and the most important was already at the core of Aristotle's ontology (*Metaphysics*, book Z). Substance (at least sensible substance) is both matter and form, the undetermined (and nevertheless simple) substrate and the determining and general essence. How can a determining essence qualify an undetermined subject, so that an individual being can be accounted for? What is inhesion? By pushing forwards this problem, one easily comes to the idea that, when trying to solve the substrate question, Aristotle went the wrong way and that, contrary to his metaphysical naïveté, we should go from identity to externality. And Hume, on the same ground as previously, explains how metaphysicians have been able to reach such an assumption and entertain a belief that, in this regard, is not naïve at all. Indeed, Locke had made a part of the job in his critique of the idea of substance (*Essay* II, 23): the human mind has no idea of substance except as a collection of various ideas, the two difficulties being how to change a collection into one and simple being and to determine it by such or such predicates. But, concerning the first question, Locke rather awkwardly stands in midstream: he takes a step towards the Kantian notion of transcendental objectivity and nevertheless claims that substance is a fiction, relying upon language. Concerning the second question, he makes the most of the well-known distinction between the primary and the secondary qualities, in harmony with the requirements of modern science, but, obviously, still in the trouble of justifying such a distinction. Hume rushes into this breach: the imagination, running fast from one idea to another, when they are regularly conjoined, piles and mixes them up, takes one for another and arrives at the belief that two (or more), however dissimilar, are one, which is the definition of identity. The resulting identical object is supposed to survive the flow of ideas or predicates thanks to the philosophical fiction of substance. Thus, philosophical belief is obtained in the same way as common belief and rests on it. "The imagination is apt to feign something unknown and invisible, which it supposes to continue the same under all these variations; and this unintelligible something it calls a *substance*, or *original and first matter*" (T 1.4.3.4).

A substance subsisting in itself, that is to say by being such or such, this metaphysical belief adds to the identity problem the simplicity problem: not only two must become one, but also the compound must become simple; and this is another contradiction. Ancient philosophy, in a way, operated like common sense, by confusing different and various perceptions. Modern philosophy sagaciously draws back from this embarrassment, claims that phenomena, internal appearances, and external beings must be distinguished, adds that phenomena are perceptions and external beings are objects continuing to exist and that perceptions are various and different and objects alone identical. And it comes to this problem: how is the understanding able to determine objects not only by their formal identity (the reason why they can be distinguished from perceptions), but also by real attributes? Locke's philosophy tries to find out an answer by analyzing phenomena: there are perceptions that are essentially variable, produced in the mind by some unknown quality in the object, and others that are permanent (all the attributes required by modern science) and which can be taken as determinations of an object, since not only they are produced in the mind by the external thing, but they are (or supposed to be) the internal image of one of its attributes. Obviously the basic problem is still the same and Hume only needs to prove

137

that the distinction between secondary and primary qualities does not stand up. A mechanical explanation of the external world needs the ideas of motion and body; but what is a body? How are we to determine a body? By its extension in space, but extension requires solidity. What is solidity? Two bodies are solid when they cannot penetrate each other. But it is a vicious circle, since the definition of solidity requires the idea of body. In a word, the idea of body (that is to say, the metaphysical remainder essential to modern science) is a mere fiction. Newtonian science has taken a great step towards the knowledge of the external world by rising up to general principles and using mathematics, but at a very high cost: its basic concepts are mere fictions. Modern science requires modern philosophy, but modern philosophy does nothing more than common belief, plus several philosophical problems.

The following moment of the story would be the Kantian philosophy: it is impossible to attribute to any object a metaphysical or even a physical determination; any object is a transcendental object (= X) and the only question is to explain how the understanding can synthesize various perceptions under the unity of a priori concepts (categories) the correlate of which is the transcendental object. Externality (understood in an empirical realism) derives from identity and identity from objectivity (understood in a transcendental idealism), and objectivity proceeds from the synthetical function of concept. One might guess Hume's answer: "This is an excellent way of putting the matter philosophically." Kant is much more lucid than Locke. But to characterize the problem is not to solve it: what is a transcendental object?

Hume's positive doctrine of common belief in the existence of objects and of the external world might itself appear fictitious; but it depends on the science of human nature to prove that it is experimentally false and to correct it. His naturalistic doctrine of philosophical belief in the double existence of perceptions and ideas might appear unacceptable to philosophers: so much the worse for philosophers! It is obvious that his skeptical critique is formidable: it is for the best of philosophy! His whole analysis appears quite uncommon by this strange mixture of naturalism and skepticism and, accordingly, uneasy for our common way of thinking. This might be the reason why Hume dropped it in the *Enquiry concerning Human Understanding*, only alluding to it, in section 12, part 1, by recalling the basic contradiction between nature and reason, belief and logic: nature knows how to curve philosophy into a mitigated and amiable skepticism.

See also 4 "Hume and the Origin of Our Ideas of Space and Time"; 5 "Hume on the Relation of Cause and Effect"; 6 "Inductive Inference in Hume's Philosophy"

References

Cook, J. W. (1968). "Hume's Scepticism with Regard to the Senses," *American Philosophical Quarterly*, 5, in Stanley Tweyman (ed.), *David Hume: Critical Assessments*, vol. 3 (London: Routledge, 1995), pp. 567–96.

Costa, J. L. (1988). "Hume and the Existence of an External World," *Philosophical Studies*, (1988–90), from Stanley Tweyman, (ed.), *David Hume: Critical Assessments*, vol. 3 (London: Routledge, 1995), pp. 555–66.

Flage, Daniel (1990). *David Hume's Theory of Mind* (London: Routledge).

Fogelin, Robert J. (1985). *Hume's Scepticism in the "Treatise of Human Nature"* (London: Routledge and Kegan Paul).

Locke, John (1690). *Essay concerning Human Understanding*, ed. Peter H. Nidditch (Oxford: Clarendon Press, 1975). (Cited as *Essay*, with book, chapter, paragraph.)

Tweyman, Stanley (ed.) (1995). *David Hume: Critical Assessments*, vol. 3 (London: Routledge).

Further Reading

Malherbe, Michel (2002). "David Hume: système sceptique et autres systèmes" (*Traité* I, 4). [David Hume: "Of the Sceptical and Other Systems" (*Treatise* I, 4)] (Paris: le Seuil).

O'Connor, D. (1981). "Hume's Scepticism with Regard to the Senses," *Philosophical Studies*, 28, from Stanley Tweyman (ed.), *David Hume: Critical Assessments*, vol. 3 (London: Routledge, 1995), pp. 597–612.

Price, H. H. (1940). *Hume's Theory of the External World* (Oxford: Clarendon Press).

Stroud, Barry (1977). *Hume* (London: Routledge and Kegan Paul).

8

Hume on Personal Identity

DONALD C. AINSLIE

Introduction

Perhaps no aspect of Hume's philosophy has been the source of more interpretive disagreement than his discussion of personal identity. He addresses the topic only in the *Treatise*, where "Of Personal Identity" (T 1.4.6) is the penultimate section of Book 1. A relatively short and seemingly self-contained discussion, it starts off by considering a view that Hume attributes to some unnamed philosophers according to whom we are constantly aware of ourselves as the same unified thinker throughout our many and diverse experiences. Hume quickly rejects this view for failing to comport with our experience of ourselves. Instead, our minds are merely a "bundle or collection" of perceptions, with nothing tying these perceptions together except for our tendency to *feel* as if they are unified at a time and across time. There is no metaphysical foundation for our sense that we are the same persons throughout our lives. This is perhaps a shocking conclusion, though Hume – in keeping with his commitment throughout the *Treatise* to a philosophy that "suits with common practice and experience" (T 1.4.7.14) – sees it as insulated from our concerns in everyday life. He leaves his investigation of our everyday sense of ourselves for his discussion of the "indirect" person-oriented passions of pride, humility, love, and hatred in Book 2 (T 1.4.6.5).

The interpretive controversy arises because Hume rejects his initial account of personal identity in the Appendix to the *Treatise*, published along with Book 3 of the *Treatise* in 1740, almost two years after the original appearance of Books 1 and 2. The Appendix lists numerous minor corrections and additions to the text, and contains several pages explaining that his original treatment of the vivacity of perceptions had been oversimplified. But he also uses the Appendix to describe his discussion of personal identity as containing what he takes to be his one "very considerable mistake" (T App. 1) in all of Books 1 and 2:

> [U]pon a more strict review of the section . . . I find myself involv'd in such a labyrinth, that, I must confess, I neither know how to correct my former opinions, nor how to render them consistent. (T App. 10)

Hume elaborates that the source of his problem is a commitment to two inconsistent principles, neither of which he can afford to give up. Interpreters have struggled with the Appendix because these two principles are clearly not inconsistent, nor are they obviously linked to the discussion of personal identity.

I review some of the main families of interpretations below, and then offer a defense of my favored reading of the Appendix. But before I examine the Appendix, I first sketch Hume's argument in "Of personal identity." I start with an overview of the background to Hume's discussion and the target for his criticisms in its early paragraphs – Locke's iconoclastic treatment of the same topic.

Locke on Personal Identity

Throughout most of the pre-modern philosophical tradition, human beings were recognized to have distinctive characteristics – rationality, a grasp of the divine, and the like – but they were nonetheless thought of as substances, and thus open to the same metaphysical account as other substances. In particular, an object that undergoes change can nonetheless count as the same object if it is a persisting substance. The seedling that grows into the tree counts as one entity despite its massive changes of appearance because it remains the same substance throughout. So also the identity of a human being as it grows from a helpless infant into a rambunctious boy, into a rebellious adolescent, into a mature adult man, into an elderly gentleman is guaranteed by its being a persisting human substance.

Locke revolutionized philosophical thinking about persons by suggesting that accounts of substance fail to do justice to the metaphysics of persons. The problem was that his empiricist commitment to grounding all ideas in the senses left him unable to give a robust account of substances. Consider my thought of an apple. I sense its shape, color, and odor, but I do not similarly sense a substantial ground that unites these qualities into a unified object – the apple that *has* the shape, color, and odor. Locke thinks that we nonetheless suppose the existence of a unifying substratum in virtue of which these qualities belong together as shared features of one object. But this substratum is an "I know not what" that underlies the sensible qualities. He thus allows that there are substances, but is sceptical about our capacity to understand them (Locke 1690: II.xxiii).

This scepticism creates problems for Locke when he tries to explain our everyday thoughts about persons (Locke 1694: II.xxvii). Consider the transition from the rebellious adolescent into the mature man. Is the adolescent the same as the adult? On the traditional pre-modern view, he would be if the substance underlying the two appearances were the same. But for Locke the substance involves an "I know not what." For all we know, then, the substratum underlying the rebellious adolescent could have lasted only for a year, at which point it was replaced by another substratum that then lasted into the adult stage. In such a case the traditional view would have to say that the adult would be different from the rebellious adolescent because there were different substances at work in unifying each one's sensible qualities. Locke's scepticism means that he cannot even rule out the possibility that the substratum underlying the rebellious adolescent is the same as the substratum that had previously unified, say, an apple. And if sameness of underlying substance makes for the sameness of the object, Locke would have to countenance the possibility that the adolescent is the same as the apple!

It is not just common sense that is in jeopardy. We need a firm grasp of the identity of persons if we are to secure morality. If the adolescent had committed a murder that was not discovered until he was an adult, we want to be able to punish the adult for the adolescent's crime. We are in trouble if we need to know that the adult and the adolescent are the same substance in order to justifiably punish the adult: Locke thinks that our grasp on the identity of substances is too insecure. And if there might not be a persisting substance connecting the adolescent and the adult, punishing the adult would seem to be as plausible a practice as punishing a stranger for the adolescent's crime. For all we can know, the stranger-qua-substance might be the same as the adolescent-qua-substance (Locke 1694: II.xxvii.14).

Locke is thus forced to account for the metaphysical and moral unity of persons not by an appeal to substance, but by an appeal to something else. He focuses on the fact that the adult's experiences were continuous with those of the rebellious adolescent. The adult can remember breaking curfew, having his nose pierced, playing in a punk band, and he can remember a series of experiences between that time and the present. He remembers it from the first-person point of view: He thinks to himself, "I was on that stage; I remember what it was like to have my nose pierced." Locke suggests that this internal grasp of our continuity is what makes us the same as we move through time. Even if the adolescent might not be the same substance as the adult, he is nonetheless the same *person*, because there is a continuous *consciousness* linking up the adult and adolescent. Locke thus introduced persons as a special metaphysical kind, the identity of which is defined not by the continuity of an underlying substance, but by the continuity of consciousness (Locke 1694: II.xxvii.9). And it is the special sense of person that is relevant to morality. We punish the adult for the adolescent's crime, not because they are the same substance (for all we know, they might not be), but because the continuous consciousness that links them makes them into the same person. As Locke says, "Person is a Forensick Term" (Locke 1694: II: xxvii.26).

Locke's radical revision of the traditional metaphysics of persons did not go unchallenged. Critics were concerned that his use of continuity of consciousness as a criterion for personal identity meant that the adult is the same person as the adolescent if and only if he *remembers* the adolescent's experiences (Reid 1785: 356–62). But obviously we do not remember everything we experience. The mature adult probably remembers nothing of the infant's experiences. Does that make them different persons? If the mature man forgot that the adolescent had murdered someone, would that mean that the mature man is not the same person as the murderer, and thus not deserving of punishment? And sometimes we seem to remember things that we did not in fact do. If there had never been a murder, but the mature man somehow falsely believed that as an adolescent he had committed one, would that mean he should be punished for the non-existent murder? Surely not. But if *seeming* memories are not sufficient to make someone the same as the subject of the seeming memory – if there must be *real* memories to secure personal identity – we seem to have entered into a vicious circle

(Butler 1736: 312–20). For what makes a memory real but the fact that the one with the memory is the *same person* as the one whose experience is being remembered? That is to say that the distinction between real and seeming memories depends on a prior account of personal identity. Defining personal identity in terms of memory, as Locke's critics suppose that he has done, thus seems to run into serious difficulties.

Hume's Critique of Locke

It is not obvious that these objections actually succeed in undermining Locke's view, but they do establish the context in which Hume approaches the topic of personal identity. On the one hand, Hume agrees with Locke that the notion of substance is of no help in settling debates about identity. Indeed, Hume's radical empiricism drives him even farther than Locke in his rejection of the traditional metaphysics. There is nothing to an object other than a bundle of sensible qualities because experience gives no indication of an "I know not what" underlying the qualities (T 1.1.6.1–2; see also T 1.4.3). On the other hand, Hume rejects Locke's invocation of continuity of consciousness as an explanation of personal identity.

The problem is with Locke's model of consciousness. Locke thinks that every time we have an idea we have an internal sense that it is our *own* experience, and thus we are always aware of ourselves as the subjects of experience. In going about our business, we say to ourselves, as it were: "I am the one typing"; "I am the one gazing out the window at the tree"; "I am the one who is hungry"; "I am the one who remembers having left the stove on" (Locke 1690: IV.ix.3). This last example – a memory – is especially complex, for not only do I have a sense of myself as the one remembering, I also had a similar sense of myself when I was leaving the stove on. In remembering, I equate myself, the one who remembers, with myself-then, the one who left the stove on. The continuity of consciousness that constitutes Lockean personal identity involves the ongoing persistence of an "I" that constantly grasps itself as the one having the changing experiences.

Hume thinks that this Lockean model of consciousness is empirically false. Introspective reflection – "intimate entry into what I call *myself*" (T 1.4.6.3) – shows that our perceptions do not come always accompanied by a recognition that we are the ones having them. Perceptions typically present their objects – the words on the page, the tree outside the window, the hunger in the gut – without presenting ourselves as the ones who read, see the tree, or feel hungry. Though it is *by means of* perception that we become aware of the objects around us, most of the time these perceptions are transparent to us. We are immersed in the world, without having even an implicit grasp that we are getting only our own perspective on things (T 1.4.2.31). Accordingly, when we introspect, all we observe is "a bundle or collection of different perceptions, which succeed each other with an inconceivable rapidity, and are in a perpetual flux and movement" (T 1.4.6.4). We do not stand over the various perceptions, aware of ourselves as the same "I" having each of them; instead, we *are* the bundle of perceptions, or at least our minds are.

Hume's argument here is not the strongest. For example, Locke might reply that, in the course of arguing against his conception of consciousness as always including self-consciousness, Hume helps himself to the very thing he is trying to deny. Notice his use of first-person language:

> For my part, when *I* enter most intimately into what *I* call *myself*, *I* always stumble on some particular perception or other, of heat or cold, light or shade, love or hatred, pain or pleasure. *I* never can catch *myself* at any time without a perception, and never can observe any thing but the perception. (T 1.4.6.3; original emphasis on "myself" only)

Locke might say that his view of consciousness as self-intimating is what supports Hume's capacity to say of himself that *he* is the one entering into himself, stumbling on particular perceptions, failing to catch himself, and observing perceptions; moreover, it could be said that Hume helps himself to a grasp of himself as the *same one* who successively enters, stumbles, fails to catch, and observes. The bundle view seems only to account for that which is observed, and misses out on the one observing. We will see below that Hume's second thoughts about personal identity in the Appendix might spring from a similar concern.

Be this as it may, Hume rejects not only the conception of consciousness found in Locke's treatment of persons, he also rejects Locke's attempt to combine the metaphysical question of sameness of persons with the moral or "Forensick" question concerning how we manage to hold one another responsible for various deeds in everyday life. For Hume, the former, metaphysical question is "abstruse" (T 1.4.2.6), in that it only comes up for those people who "intimately enter" into themselves. In everyday life we do not "observe" our personal bundle of perceptions and worry over whether it is the same despite the rapidity of its changes. Hume does not, of course, deny that we are concerned about what happens to us, hold one another responsible for our good and bad behavior, and care about the kinds of persons we are. But, unlike Locke, he thinks that this topic of "personal identity as it regards . . . the concern we take in ourselves" is best treated by an investigation of the passions, not of mental unity (T 1.4.6.5; see also Penelhum 2000: 61–98; Ainslie 1999). The metaphysical issue of the unity of the bundle of perceptions, in contrast, Hume labels "personal identity as it regards our thought or imagination" (T 1.4.6.5). My discussion here is restricted to this latter issue.

The Belief in Mental Unity

Hume's introspective discovery that the mind is merely a bundle of perceptions means that it has no real unity (T 1.4.6.4). So far as we can tell, there is nothing tying the perceptions together at a single time: The mind lacks *simplicity*. And, so far as we can tell, there is nothing tying the perceptions together across time: The mind lacks *identity*. We have seen that these facts do not register with us in everyday life. But even if most of us rarely "enter most intimately" into ourselves in order to "observe" our perceptions, Humean "scientists of man" repeatedly introspect in an attempt to get clearer on the workings of the mind. For example, they notice that the repeated experience of conjoined objects causes the mind to associate the idea of one object with the idea of the other (T 1.3.8). The scientists thus *believe* that the mind experiencing the conjunctions is the *same as* the one associating the ideas. Similarly, they observe that the co-presence of several impressions each of contiguous objects constitutes a "manner of appearance" responsible for the idea of space (T 1.2.3.5); the scientists thus *believe* that it is *one* mind undergoing the several simultaneous experiences. So even if intro-specting philosophers can recognize that the bundle of perceptions they observe has no intrinsic unity at a time or across time, they nonetheless typically *believe* that it is unified. Accordingly, Hume's explanandum is not the *real* unity of the bundle of perceptions: There is none. Instead his explanandum is our tendency to *believe* that the mind is unified when it is under observation.

His strategy is to explain this tendency in the same manner as he explains our everyday tendencies to find diverse and changing objects to be simple at a time and identical across time. Where Locke thinks that persons need a special metaphysical story, Hume returns to the pre-modern outlook that assimilates the identity of persons to that of other kinds of objects. He does not, however, return to the pre-modern substance theory (T 1.1.6; 1.4.3). Instead, objects are just bundles of sensible qualities; they have no real unity in the same way that the mind as a bundle of perceptions has no real unity. But we nonetheless tend to believe that ordinary objects are simple at a time and identical across time because our ideas of their qualities are associated together, causing us to feel as though the qualities themselves belong together (T 1.4.2.31–6, 1.4.6.6–14). For example, because the different parts of my dog are contiguous with one another, resemble one another, and are causally connected to one another, my ideas of these parts are associated together. Even as she sheds hair, gets covered in mud, and grows fat, her new conditions are related to those revealed by my previous perceptions of her. These relations cause the mind to associate together my various ideas of the dog, thus leading me to overlook the diversity of the ideas at one time and the changes in these ideas through time. It feels to me as if I have been observing the same, single, unchanging dog even though in fact I have experienced many diverse perceptions. For Hume, beliefs about the identity and simplicity of objects are the result of the mind's tendency to overlook its associating ideas of the parts or qualities of the object that resemble, are causally linked, or are contiguous with one another.

Hume appeals to the very same mental mechanism to explain why scientists of man believe in the simplicity and identity of the bundle of perceptions when invest-igating the mind. Their ideas of their perceptions are associated together because a sufficient number of those perceptions resemble one another and are causally connected with one another (he denies that contiguity can apply to perceptions themselves, as opposed to their objects (T 1.4.5.9–10, 1.4.6.17). Just as the association of my *ideas* of my dog makes me believe that the *dog* is unified, so also the association of the sci-entists' *ideas* of their perceptions make them believe that the *bundle of perceptions* is unified. As Hume says:

> [I]dentity is nothing really belonging to these different perceptions, and uniting them together; but is merely a quality, which we attribute to them, because of the union of their ideas [i.e. the ideas of the perceptions] in the imagination, when we reflect upon them. (T 1.4.6.16)

Note, then, that the difference between our ordinary beliefs in the unity of everyday objects and the philosophers' beliefs in the unity of the mind is a difference in level, not in kind. The ideas that are associated in the everyday cases are ideas that are *of external objects* – of dogs, apples, tables, and the like. The ideas that are associated in the philosophers' case are ideas *of perceptions* (where the perceptions in question might be of dogs, apples, tables, and the like). The introspective reflection that the scientists of man engage in involves their making the perceptual mediation of their everyday lives explicit. They look at their perceptions by means of ideas of them, instead of looking at dogs, apples, tables, and the like by means of perceptions of them. Hume calls ideas that take other perceptions as their objects *secondary ideas* (T 1.1.1.11).

It is not just philosophers who form secondary ideas. In everyday life, for example, we occasionally remember an event not by focusing on the event itself, but by focusing on our *experiencing* of it. The memory then would take the form of a secondary idea, an idea of the *impression* of the event; an ordinary memory, in contrast, would be a more direct copy of the original impression by being an idea of the *event*, not of the impression of it (T 1.3.8.16–17). Philosophers take this ordinary capacity to focus on perceptions to an extreme. They aim to make all of their perceptions into objects of awareness, even their occurrent ones. "Intimate entry" into themselves signals their withdrawal from the everyday sense of immersion in the world, in favor of an observational stance on the mind. Hume aims throughout the *Treatise* to describe the mind's workings by observing its operations. Thus throughout the *Treatise*, he relies on secondary ideas as the vehicles by means of which be becomes aware of the mind's perceptions (T 1.1.1.11).

Just as Locke appeals to memory in his explanation of personal identity, Hume also appeals to memory in his explanation of the belief in personal identity. Scientists of man observe an experience followed by a memory of it that resembles the original experience – in Hume's taxonomy, an impression followed by a vivacious idea that copies it. Because ideas of resembling perceptions tend to be associated together and thus contribute to the belief that the bundle of perceptions is unified, Hume says that when we remember we do not simply *recognize* an identity that is secured independently of memory; rather, memory's role in supporting the resemblance-based associations between ideas of perceptions "contributes to [the] production" of the belief in the identity of the mind (T 1.4.6.18). Moreover, memory is also involved in the causation-based associations between ideas of perceptions (T 1.4.6.20). Scientists of man discover many causal connections between perceptions: impressions cause ideas (T 1.1.1), the idea of a future pleasure causes desire (T 2.3.9), the passion of love causes the passion of benevolence (T 2.2.6); and so on. But in order for scientists to *believe* that these causal connections obtain, they must *observe* the constant conjunction of the relevant perceptions in such a way that they come to associate their ideas of the perceptions. Even if they do not need *explicit* memories of, say, *this* episode of love followed by *that* episode of benevolence, they need to *retain* the impact of their observation of the conjunction. It is this retentive memory that stands behind the developing tendency to associate their ideas of love and benevolence – to believe that the passion of love causes the passion of benevolence. Because memory is involved in the production of both the resemble-based and causation-based association of ideas of perceptions, Hume sees himself here as aligned with Locke against his critics in making memory productive of the belief in personal identity.

But Hume also acknowledges the critics' point that a person can forget an experience – even irremediably forget it – and it can nonetheless be counted as one of her experiences, albeit an unremembered one. Once the scientists of man learn that the causal connections and resemblances between the perceptions that are observed in the bundle are responsible for their beliefs that their minds are unified, they can then acknowledge that, if there are causal connections between the observed perceptions and other earlier ones, those earlier ones will also be believed to be part of the same bundle. An unremembered experience, then, can be recognized as part of a person's mind if it can be causally connected to the perceptions that are observed to constitute her bundle (T 1.4.6.20).

Hume's Second Thoughts

Despite his assertion in the opening paragraph of the Appendix that his original treatment of personal identity is the "one article" in Books 1 and 2 where his "reasonings" contain a "very considerable mistake" (T App. 1), Hume spends most of that portion of the Appendix that is devoted to personal identity (T App. 10–21) reaffirming his original account. He devotes ten paragraphs to recounting his argument that there is no real unity to be found in the mind:

> When I turn my reflection on *myself*, I never can perceive this *self* without some one or more perceptions; nor can I ever perceive any thing but the perceptions. 'Tis the composition of these, therefore, which forms the self. (T App. 15)

The problem arises with his earlier attempt to explain why we believe that the mind is simple and identical. Though his original explanation of this belief in terms of the association of secondary ideas of perceptions seems "promising," his "hope vanishes," when he comes "to explain the principles, that unite our successive perceptions in our thought or consciousness" (T App. 20). Hume goes on to say:

> there are two principles, which I cannot render consistent; nor is it in my power to renounce either of them, viz. *that all our distinct perceptions are distinct existences*, and *that the mind never perceives any real connexion among distinct existences*. (T App. 21)

He offers two possible escapes from his dilemma: the inherence of perceptions in something simple and individual or the discovery of real connections between perceptions (T App. 21). In either case, there would be something unifying the perceptions other than the mind's associating ideas of them. But Hume is unwilling to countenance either option. Instead he "pleads the privilege of a sceptic," and leaves the difficulty as an open problem.

Hume's interpreters, however, have not spent time trying to find solutions to it. Instead they have wondered what exactly he thought the problem was. Most obviously, the two closely related principles that Hume says are inconsistent are in fact consistent. The first simply gives what he takes to be a fact about perceptions: Distinct perceptions exist independently of one another and thus qualify as distinct existences. In the section of the *Treatise* immediately preceding the personal identity section, Hume had even argued that, given the traditional conception of substance as that which can exist in its own right, perceptions should be counted as substances (T 1.4.5.5). The second principle's denial of perceivable real connections between distinct existences is in part an explication of what it means for something to count as a distinct existent: It must not have any perceivable connections to anything else.

Each principle is central to many of Hume's main arguments in the *Treatise*, especially in Book 1. For example, in his argument about causation, Hume relies on the fact that the idea of a cause and the idea of an effect are distinct existences, with no real connections being perceived between them, as part of his argument that the association of ideas stands behind the inference from cause to effect (T 1.3.6.1). If Hume really thought that the two principles were inconsistent, he would be rejecting significant swaths of arguments from Books 1 and 2; he would not think that the personal identity section contained his single mistake. It follows that the inconsistency that Hume identifies in the Appendix must be enthymematic. Interpreters must supply additional premises with which the two principles are inconsistent. There has been no consensus in the secondary literature about what the missing premises are.

Some Interpretations

One school of thought has it that, when Hume says in the Appendix that he cannot find the "principles that unite our successive perceptions," he is looking for something more than an explanation of his *belief* in mental unity; he is looking for an account of the mind's *real* simplicity and identity (McIntyre 1979a; McIntyre 1979b; Beauchamp 1979; Swain 1991). An advantage of this interpretation is that Hume's suggested escapes from his dilemma would obviously provide real escapes. If he could appeal to the mind's being a traditionally conceived substance in which perceptions inhere, or if there were real connections between perceptions, then he would indeed have accounted for the real unity of the mind.

There are, however, many problems with this kind of interpretation. For one thing, it leaves Hume in the Appendix as reaffirming the bundle view; then, one paragraph later, in the course of revisiting his explanation of the *belief* in mental unity, he would all of a sudden be returning to the issue of the *real* unity of the mind, worrying that he has failed to account for it. If he were truly vexed by his conclusion that the mind is not really unified, surely he would have raised that problem without bothering to return to the issue of our beliefs about that unity. Moreover, the proposed interpretation would require Hume to have succumbed to inexplicable backsliding from his empiricist commitments. Why should the lack of a real unity to the mind bother him? And if he did start to become so bothered, why would it be confined to *minds*? The unity of apples, chairs, and trees would seem to create similar difficulties. And Hume relies on the mind's being a mere bundle of perceptions, lacking intrinsic unity, elsewhere in the *Treatise* – notably at a crucial moment in his discussion of our sensory awareness of external objects (T 1.4.2.39). If the Appendix's worry is that he has not explained the real unity of the bundle, then he should have acknowledged that the problem ramifies outside of the personal identity section; he would not have said that that section contains his only mistake. A further piece of evidence against Hume having become uncomfortable with his view that the mind lacks real unity is its reappearance in his final work, the posthumously published *Dialogues concerning Natural Religion*: "[T]he soul of man . . . [is] a composition of various faculties, passions, sentiments, ideas; united, indeed, into one self or person, but still distinct from each other" (Kemp Smith 1947: 159).

For these reasons, most interpreters take Hume's concern in the Appendix to be addressed to his explanation of the *belief* in the mind's unity, allowing him to retain his commitment to the mind's in fact being a collection of distinct perceptions lacking real connections. One set of these interpreters take Hume's search for the principles that "unite our successive perceptions" to be a search for those relations that support the association of ideas involved in the belief in mental unity (see Patten 1976; Stroud 1977: 125–7; Garrett 1981: 347–50 and 1997: 172–3). Perceptions must resemble or be causally connected for the mind to associate ideas of them. But are there sufficient such relations between perceptions? For example, I might have a perception of a tree, simultaneously with an impression of hunger, followed by an idea of the Pythagorean theorem, followed by an impression of a chalkboard. How can these disparate perceptions support the associations necessary for the belief in their unity? The chalkboard does not resemble the tree, nor is either of them the cause or effect of the Pythagorean theorem or hunger.

But Hume does not need relations between the tree, the chalkboard, the Pythagorean theorem, or the hunger in his explanation of the belief in mental unity. I do not believe that these disparate items are *themselves* unified; I believe that my *perceptions* of them are. And there are many relations between the perceptions in our bundles. The impression of the tree causes and resembles the idea of it; the impression of the tree resembles the impression of the chalkboard and the perception of hunger, in that each is especially vivacious. An impression of willing might have been the cause of my no longer looking out of the window at the tree, and instead focusing on the chalkboard, thus serving as a contributing cause to the impression and idea of it. And so on. Hume need only think that the mind-bundle is a network of ideas and impressions that has lines of causal influence and resemblance running throughout it in order for his original explanation of the belief in mental unity to remain unimpugned. It does not seem unreasonable for him to think that there will be sufficient relations among the perceptions in the bundle to support the belief in mental unity. In any case, if Hume were truly worried about the presence of such relations, it is hard to see that he would express this worry by means of the two supposedly inconsistent principles.

A third school of interpreters think that Hume's second thoughts are the result of his recognition that his account of the belief in mental unity relies on *mental actions* – the association of ideas, the tendency to mistake a series of related experiences for the experience of a persisting object, and the like (see Robison 1974; Passmore 1980: 82–3). But he also says that the mind is a mere bundle of perceptions. There seems to be an inconsistency. The mind should include the bundle and in addition the various tendencies and activities that he repeatedly invokes. The problem, of course, is that Hume invokes these tendencies and activities throughout the *Treatise*. If the Appendix is meant to be a recognition that these invocations are illegitimate, he should have thought it was a wide-ranging problem indeed, not a single mistake, confined only to the personal identity section. And, again, it is hard to see that Hume is pointing to a problem with mental activities when he gives the two principles that he identifies as the source of his problem. In fact the second of these principles itself invokes a mental activity – the mind's inability to *perceive* real connections between distinct existences, such as distinct perceptions. "Perceive" here is used as a verb, indicating a mental action, as opposed to "perceptions," used here to indicate the objects of the mental action. Finally, as several interpreters have pointed out (Stroud 1977: 130–1; Garrett 1981: 344), there is no inconsistency between Hume's appeal to mental actions and his bundle theory of the mind. All mental action talk can be read as shorthand for the appearance of perceptions in the bundle. The mind's associating two ideas means that the appearance of the first idea in the bundle tends to be followed by the second (with a relevant increase in vivacity). The mind's mistaking one idea for another is the appearance of a series of ideas in a bundle that usually follow in the train of the first idea, appearing instead in the wake of the second. If verbal ideas are also involved, this becomes even clearer. Ideas that are usually associated with the idea of one word instead appear in the bundle in the wake of the appearance of the idea of a different word. Thus Hume can consistently appeal to mental activities in the *Treatise* without jeopardizing his commitment to the bundle view.

The fourth general strategy for interpreting the Appendix focuses on the issue of how perceptions end up in bundles (see Stroud 1977: 134–40; Pears 1990: 135–51; Haugeland 1998: 63–71; Garrett 1981 and 1997: 180–5). Why are perceptions organized so that one person's impression of a tree does not count as causing another person's idea of it in such a way that the two perceptions end up being bundled together? Why does the introspecting philosopher observe only a small subset of all the perceptions in the world? The problem seems to be particularly acute for those perceptions of objects that Hume says are nowhere – namely those of tastes, smells, and the like (T 1.4.5.9–10; see Garrett 1981: 350–8). For surely two people could simultaneously have qualitatively identical smell-impressions, say of a particularly strong cheese. How can we say that the one impression belongs in one bundle and the other in the other? Any resemblances that obtain in connection with one impression would also apply in connection with the other. And causal connections require only the constant conjunction of the cause and effect; as the two principles in the Appendix remind us, perceptions are distinct existences, lacking any perceivable real connections between them. But why, then, say that one of these two smell-impressions causes the one person's desire for cheese, in that, given the absence of spatial features (remember that the impression is locationless), the other is just as much conjoined to the desire? We cannot appeal to the fact that the smell-impression and the desire must appear in the *same* bundle because it is the causal connection between the impression and the desire that constitutes their being members of the same bundle. Thus this interpretation holds, that Hume recognized in the Appendix that his account had failed to explain how locationless perceptions are "united" with other perceptions into discrete mind-bundles.

Interpretations that worry about the bundling problem are nonetheless open to several objections. Like the other interpretations of the Appendix discussed above, they see Hume as discovering a problem that he should have recognized to have major ramifications for his project throughout Books 1 and 2 of the *Treatise*. He would have been unlikely to treat it as his "single considerable mistake." More significantly, the interpretations that focus on bundling attribute to Hume an implausible starting point for his discussion of personal identity: a universe of unbundled perceptions that await the operations of the imagination before being divided into bundles – as if we have to decide to which bundles perceptions belong, be they qualitatively identical or not. The only text that suggests such a picture can be found in "Of scepticism with regard to the senses" (T 1.4.2) where Hume says that

> what we call a *mind*, is nothing but a heap or collection of different perceptions, united together by certain relations, and suppos'd, tho' falsely, to be endow'd with a perfect simplicity and identity. Now as every perception is distinguishable from another, and may be consider'd as separately existent; it evidently follows, that there is no absurdity in separating any particular perception from the mind; that is, in breaking off all its relations, with that connected mass of perceptions, which constitute a thinking being. (T 1.4.2.39)

This passage is difficult to interpret, as indeed is all of "Of scepticism with regard to the senses." And it occurs at a point where Hume admits that he is working with a non-standard notion of "perception" in which it is used interchangeably with "object" (T 1.4.2.31, 46). In his more standard usage, he never suggests that scientists of man face perceptions in any other fashion than as already bundled. So reflection reveals to them a particular set of perceptions, relations between which lead them to take it to be unified. If a particular smell-impression is introspectively revealed to them, along with a desire for cheese, then – supposing they have previously experienced smell-impressions followed by desire – they can say that the observed impression causes the desire. That perceptions come in a *bundle*, that introspection does not yield awareness of all the perceptions in the universe, is a brute fact. Hume shows no inclination to shy from brute facts.

Unity in Reflection

In order to arrive at an interpretation of the Appendix that avoids the problems connected with the four approaches surveyed above, notice that Hume starts to question his original account of personal identity only after he summarizes it by saying:

> Most philosophers seem inclin'd to think, that personal identity *arises* from *consciousness*; and *consciousness* is nothing but a reflected thought or perception. The present philosophy, therefore, has so far a promising aspect. (T App. 20; original emphasis on "arises" only)

He here allies himself with Locke's treatment of persons in terms of consciousness, but at the same time he clarifies what he himself takes consciousness to be in a manner that contrasts with Locke's view. For Locke, reflection is a process of turning within ourselves to observe our mental operations, and it yields ideas of reflection with these operations as their objects. But he thinks that *all* ideas – ideas of sensation and ideas of reflection – are conscious. Lockean consciousness is thus different from Lockean reflection. In the quoted passage, however, Hume *identifies* reflection and consciousness, and he seems to identify each with his version of Lockean reflection. The belief in personal identity "arises from consciousness" because philosophers *reflect* on the mind, forming secondary ideas of perceptions that are then associated together. Hume describes his problem in the Appendix as starting when he tries to "explain the principles, that unite our successive perceptions in our thought or *consciousness*" (T App. 20; emphasis added). I take this to mean that he has now turned his attention to the unity of the *conscious* mind, the unity of the reflecting mind with that on which it is reflecting. Why do scientists of man believe that the secondary ideas, the vehicles of their introspective reflection, are unified with those perceptions that they observe within themselves (by means of the secondary ideas)? The secondary ideas are distinct existences and accordingly the mind cannot find any real connections linking them with the rest of the mind. Nor are there further ideas of them (tertiary ideas?), associations of which would bring the scientists of man to believe that the secondary ideas are unified with the other observed perceptions. My suggestion is that Hume realizes in the Appendix that he believes that secondary ideas are part of the mind and yet is unable to explain this belief.

This interpretation of the Appendix has the advantage that it can explain why Hume did not see the problem in his original treatment of personal identity. Recall that his explanandum there was philosophers' belief in the simplicity and identity of the minds that they were observing. Because secondary ideas are not themselves under observation – they are instead the vehicles of observation – Hume did not need to explain a belief that included them in their scope. Just as the vulgar take themselves to be immersed in the world, overlooking the role of perceptions in affording them their sense of immersion, so also introspecting scientists of man take themselves to be immersed *in the mind*, overlooking the role of secondary ideas in affording them their sense of immersion. Scientists of man are thus typically *vulgar with respect to the mind.*

In Hume's original treatment of personal identity, this *philosophical vulgarity* about the mind shows up in at least two places. Consider his analogy between the mind and the performance of a play, with the perceptions being compared to the actors:

> The mind is a kind of theatre, where several perceptions successively make their appearance; pass, re-pass, glide away, and mingle in an infinite variety of postures and situations. There is properly no *simplicity* in it at one time, nor *identity* in different; whatever natural propension we may have to imagine that simplicity and identity. The comparison of the theatre must not mislead us. They are the successive perceptions only, that constitute the mind; nor have we the most distant notion of the place, where these scenes are represented, or of the materials, of which it is compos'd. (T 1.4.6.5)

When Hume goes on to explain that the association of ideas of the actors/perceptions is responsible for the belief in the unity of the play/mind, he helps himself to a seat in the audience of his mind, as it were. The spectator is the one believing that the play is unified because of the association of ideas within him, just as the spectator of the mind is the one believing that the mind is unified because of the association of secondary ideas within him. Hume does not worry that the secondary ideas are themselves part of the mind that is believed to be unified, because he has restricted the scope of the belief to be explained to those perceptions in the mind that are *observed*. The fact that unobserved perceptions (the secondary ideas) are involved in his explanation does not matter so long as the explanandum remains restricted.

Similarly, Hume analogizes the scientists of man's views of their minds to the view we would have if "we cou'd see clearly into the breast of another, and observe that succession of perceptions, which constitutes his mind or thinking principle"

(T 1.4.6.18). The relations among the observed perceptions would cause our secondary ideas of the perceptions to be associated together, yielding the belief that the other person's mind is unified. Hume ends the thought experiment by saying: "The case is the same whether we consider ourselves or others" (T 1.4.6.18). Of course, the case is not the same. When investigating someone else's mind, the secondary ideas, associations of which produce the belief in mental unity, are not in the same mind as the perceptions that are believed to be unified. When investigating our own minds, the secondary ideas are in the same mind as those perceptions believed to be unified. But so long as the role of secondary ideas in producing the belief remains unthematized – so long as the introspecting philosophers remain oblivious to the perceptual mediation of their awareness of their minds – then Hume's explanation counts as a success.

In the Appendix, when reviewing the portion of his original explanation of personal identity that he takes to be "promising" (T App. 20), Hume makes a similar separation of the observing scientists of man from the bundles of perceptions that they observe, this time by considering only the scientists' retrospective beliefs about their minds:

> [T]he thought alone finds personal identity, when reflecting on the train of *past* perceptions, that compose a mind, the [secondary] ideas of them are felt to be connected together, and naturally introduce each other. (T App. 20; emphasis added)

Here the scope of the belief about the mind does not extend to the secondary ideas: They are in the present, but the belief concerns only the mind *in the past*.

Hume enters the "labyrinth" of difficulties about personal identity when he acknowledges that, by appealing to the association of secondary ideas in his explanation of the belief in mental unity, he is no longer ignorant of their occurrence in the mind. He is in a position where he *knows* that his belief in the unity of the observed perceptions is produced by the association of unobserved secondary ideas; thus he knows that his mind includes both observed and unobserved perceptions, both of which he takes to be present in the *same mind*. How can he explain this new belief in mental unity – not the belief that the observed perceptions are unified, but the belief that the secondary ideas are unified along with the observed perceptions? Bringing the secondary ideas themselves under observation, by means of tertiary ideas, would allow for a process of association that would explain the belief in the unity of the secondary ideas with the observed perceptions. But these tertiary ideas remain themselves unobserved, and any belief about their unity with the rest of the mind remains unexplained. Hume's problem in the Appendix, then, occurs when he comes to *believe* his original explanation of the belief in personal identity. He is left believing that unobserved secondary ideas are in his mind, being so associated as to produce the belief in mental unity. The scope of that belief, however, has changed, for he now believes that there are unobserved perceptions in his mind in addition to the observed ones that his reflection reveals to him. His original explanation of the belief no longer works.

It might seem that Hume could explain the unity of the secondary ideas with the rest of the mind in the same way that he extends the bundle to include unremembered past experiences (Penelhum 2000: 99–126). Secondary ideas are *caused* by the perceptions that they have as their objects (T 1.1.1.11). Perhaps then the causal relations between secondary ideas and the rest of the bundle can serve the same role as the causal relations between observed perceptions and the unremembered past experiences that bring those experiences within the boundaries of the bundle. The problem is that in order to explain the *belief* that secondary ideas are in the mind by means of their causal relations with other perceptions, there would need to be further ideas as vehicles of this belief. Hume requires that a causal belief take the form of a vivacious idea resulting from the association of the idea of the cause and the idea of the effect. So the belief that a secondary idea is caused by the perception that is its object requires an association between a tertiary idea of the original secondary idea and a secondary idea that takes the perception that is the object of the original secondary ideas as its object. Believing that secondary ideas are causally connected with the bundle thus involves the presence of further higher-order ideas, and the belief in the unity of these ideas with the rest of the mind will remain unexplained.

In fact, the same problem will re-occur for any associative mechanism that might be offered to explain the belief in the unity of the mind. For the association of ideas can explain beliefs about only the *objects* of those ideas, as happens when the association of the *idea* of fire and the *idea* of smoke causes the belief that *fire causes smoke*. In this case, someone can know that her belief about fire's causal powers is a result of the association of ideas in her mind without that knowledge undermining the belief, though, as Hume explores in the Conclusion to Book 1 of the *Treatise* (T 1.4.7), self-awareness about one's psychological propensities can induce a kind of vertigo. But the situation is different when it is a belief about the unity of the mind that is to be explained. Since an associative mechanism can explain a belief about only the *objects* of the ideas being associated, not about the *ideas* themselves (in this case the higher-level ideas of other perceptions), there will be ideas in the mind different from those believed to be unified. This would not be a problem if the person in question was ignorant of the presence of those ideas, for Hume is not trying to explain the *actual* unity of the mind, just our *beliefs* about it, even if those beliefs fail to match the real contents of our bundle of perceptions. What Hume cannot allow is for someone to believe that her mind is unified at the same time as she *believes* this belief to be the result of ideas being associated in her. For she is then aware of ideas that she takes to be part of her mind even though the associative mechanism posited to explain her beliefs about mental unity does not encompass them. Hume's problem in the Appendix arises when he takes seriously what it would be like to believe that the mind is as he describes it (Ainslie 2003).

Because no associative explanation for the belief in mental unity will succeed, Hume says that he is left with only two other possible explanations of it (T App. 21), each positing a real foundation for the unity of the mind. First, if secondary ideas were to inhere in the same substance as the observed perceptions, then their unity could be secured without reliance on further ideas, the belief in the unity of which with the others would be in need of explanation. Second, if secondary ideas were *really* connected with the other perceptions in the bundle, then belief in their unity could again be secured without needing to appeal to an associative mechanism. Hume can countenance neither substance ontology nor real connections given the fundamentals of his theory, and so he ends this portion of the Appendix "pleading the privilege of the sceptic" (T App. 21).

To conclude, the proposed interpretation of the Appendix has the following five advantages. First, it fits with Hume's suggestion that the problem arises when he tries to "explain the principles, that unite our successive perceptions in our thought or consciousness" (T App. 20). His concern, I have suggested, is not to explain the real unity of our perceptions, but the belief that the secondary ideas in virtue of which we are *conscious* – reflectively aware of our perceptions – are themselves part of the same mind as the perceptions we observe within us.

Second, Hume is left with an inconsistency related to the two principles he lists in the Appendix: Secondary ideas are distinct existences, and thus the mind never perceives a real connection between them and the rest of the mind. Only an associative explanation could explain our belief in their being unified with the rest of the mind, but if we were to believe that an associative explanation was responsible for that belief, we would be invoking further unobserved ideas, the unity of which with the rest of the mind would be in need of explanation.

Third, Hume's two proposed escape routes do indeed provide him with an escape from the problem. If the mind were really unified, he could appeal to that real unity in explaining our beliefs about our secondary ideas.

Fourth, the interpretation is charitable, in that it makes sense of both Hume's having missed the problem when he first presented the account, and his having realized his mistake in fairly short order. As I emphasized above, there is a sense in which the original explanation of the belief in mental unity is a success, so long as one does not know the source of the belief. In such a case, the association of secondary ideas happens, as it were, behind the thinker's back, producing the belief in the simplicity and identity of the observed perceptions without adverting to the presence of those secondary ideas that are responsible for the belief. Hume's problem arises only when he investigates the situation of someone who knows that secondary ideas are doing the work in causing him to believe that the mind is unified. It is understandable that Hume might not have realized the problem that knowledge of his own view creates for him when he originally presented it. Nonetheless, the problem is close enough to the surface that it is unsurprising that he found it soon after it had appeared.

Finally, the interpretation locates a problem for Hume that is quite narrow, thus making it plausible that he would regard it as his only serious mistake in Books 1 and 2. My suggestion is that he rejects only his associative account of the belief in mental unity, not the bundle theory of the mind. He can thus in the Appendix legitimately leave the bundle theory's appearance elsewhere in the *Treatise* unaddressed, and we should not be surprised to find that he later recapitulates it in the *Dialogues*. Moreover, the problem that the interpretation finds in the explanation of the belief in mental unity depends crucially on the fact that the mechanism invoked to account for it itself involves perceptions that fall within the scope of the belief. Hume can continue to rely on the very same mechanism to explain beliefs that are not self-referential in this way, and thus he need not revisit those parts of the *Treatise* that attempt to explain our beliefs in the unity of external objects (T 1.4.2, 1.4.3).

Though the interpretation I have argued for here shows why *Hume* might have regarded the problem he explores in the Appendix to be singular and self-contained, I have not argued that the problem is *in fact* inconsequential for his larger philosophical project. We have seen that, for scientists of man, the belief in the unity of the mind is a condition for the possibility of their investigation. It allows them to treat the perceptions that they observed as a single economy, governed by various principles.

Hume's incapacity to fully explain this philosophical belief in the unity of the mind is thus perhaps his Achilles heel, leaving him vulnerable to a more rationalistic philosopher's rejoinder that the mind must be recognized as something more substantial than a mere bundle of perceptions.

See also 2 "Hume's Theory of Ideas"; 23 "Hume's Naturalism and His Skepticism"

References

Ainslie, D. C. (1999). "Scepticism about Persons in Book II of Hume's *Treatise*," *Journal of the History of Philosophy*, 37, pp. 469–92.

—— (2001). "Hume's Reflections on the Identity and Simplicity of Mind," *Philosophy and Phenomenological Research*, 62, pp. 557–78.

—— (2003). "Hume, a Scottish Socrates?," *Canadian Journal of Philosophy*, 33, pp. 133–54.

Beauchamp, Tom L. (1979). "Self Inconsistency or Mere Self Perplexity," *Hume Studies*, 5, pp. 37–44.

Butler, Joseph (1736). *The Analogy of Religion to the Constitution and Course of Nature: Also Fifteen Sermons* (London: Religious Tract Society, 1881).

Garrett, Don (1981). "Hume's Self-doubts about Personal Identity," *Philosophical Review*, 90, pp. 337–58.

—— (1997). *Cognition and Commitment in Hume's Philosophy* (New York: Oxford University Press).

Haugeland, John (1998). *Having Thought: Essays in the Metaphysics of Mind* (Cambridge, MA: Harvard University Press).

Hume, David (1779). *Dialogues concerning Natural Religion*, ed. N. Kemp Smith (Indianapolis: Bobbs-Merrill, 1947).

Locke, John (1690, 1694). *An Essay concerning Human Understanding*, ed. Peter H. Nidditch (Oxford: Clarendon Press, 1975). (Cited by book, chapter, paragraph.)

McIntyre, Jane L. (1979a). "Is Hume's Self Consistent?," in D. Fate Norton, N. Capaldi, and W. L. Robison (eds.), *McGill Hume Studies* (San Diego, CA: Austin Hill), pp. 79–88.

—— (1979b). "Further Remarks on the Consistency of Hume's Account of the Self," *Hume Studies*, 5, pp. 55–61.

Passmore, John Arthur (1980). *Hume's Intentions*, 3rd edn. (London: Duckworth).

Patten, S. C. (1976). "Hume's Bundles, Self-consciousness, and Kant," *Hume Studies*, 2, pp. 59–75.

Pears, David (1990). *Hume's System* (Oxford: Oxford University Press).

Penelhum, Terence (2000). *Themes in Hume: The Self, the Will, Religion* (Oxford: Clarendon Press).

Reid, Thomas (1785). *Essays on the Intellectual Powers of Man* (Cambridge, MA: MIT Press, 1969).

Robison, Wade (1974). "Hume on Personal Identity," *Journal of the History of Philosophy*, 12, pp. 181–93.

Stroud, Barry (1977). *Hume* (London: Routledge).

Swain, Corliss (1991). "Being Sure of Oneself: Hume on Personal Identity," *Hume Studies*, 17, pp. 107–24.

Part II

Passions and Action

9

Hume's Indirect Passions

RACHEL COHON

Introduction

Hume analyzes the emotions as part of his science of man in Book 2 of *A Treatise of Human Nature* and subsequent *Dissertation of the Passions*. The emotions (as we would call them) or passions or affections (as Hume's predecessors call them) fascinate many philosophers of this period. There is, however, no single shared set of issues, no standardized terms of debate about the passions in the seventeenth and eighteenth centuries.[1] So we must ask what Hume's particular interest is in the topic. One goal is made clear in the final sentence of his *Dissertation*:

> It is sufficient for my purpose, if I have made it appear, that, in the production and conduct of the passions, there is a certain regular mechanism, which is susceptible of as accurate a disquisition, as the laws of motion, optics, hydraulics, or any part of natural philosophy. (DP, p. 181)

Thus his analysis of the passions is intended to extend the naturalistic, empiricist study of human nature that he began in Book 1 of the *Treatise* with his associationist account of the workings of the understanding. One can describe a "regular mechanism" without indicating its purpose or that of its parts, and his description of the regular production of the passions is indeed free of any reference to final causes.[2] In explaining the emotions Hume makes no fundamental appeal to any kind of good or evil distinct from pleasure and pain, which he construes simply as introspectively observable feelings or qualities of feelings. He does not presuppose any theory of the good for man, whether teleological in a naturalistic vein as in Aristotle or theological as in many of the moral rationalists. In keeping with the assumption that nature is parsimonious and the best causal explanations tend to be simple, Hume explains the production of all our varied emotions by appeal to a few associative mechanisms and other "principles" or causal factors, most of which also play other roles in the human mind.

Hume's account of the passions is indeed spare, and original. His basic taxonomy divides them into two groups, the direct and the indirect passions; this distinction dictates the structure of both *Treatise* Book 2 and the *Dissertation*. He subdivides each group into a small number of types of passions, and explains how the passions of each type are caused using a few causal factors. But these categories of direct and indirect passions and his prominent, detailed treatment of those he labels indirect present us with many unsolved puzzles. Here we take up only two of them: why Hume divides the passions into those two groups, direct and indirect, and (much more briefly) what connection there might be between his treatment of the indirect passions, particularly in the *Treatise*, and his theory of the moral sentiments.

Hume's account in both the *Treatise* and the *Dissertation* concentrates on four passions he groups together under the label "indirect": pride, humility, love, and hatred. (He mentions other indirect passions, but apparently they are all combinations or simulacra of these four.) They occupy more than two-thirds of *Treatise* Book 2 and more than half the *Dissertation*. Although there are elements of Hume's view that reflect the thought of others, he is, to my knowledge, the only philosopher to draw a distinction between direct and indirect passions and to feature these four emotions together in prominent, symmetrical roles.[3] Why does he do so? What is especially indirect about pride, humility, love, and hatred, and what sets them apart from other emotions? When we examine Hume's account of the causal mechanism that on his view generates these four sentiments, we will see that he thinks they are created by a certain complex process involving simultaneous causal inputs from different sources, while the passions he labels direct are produced much more simply. Kemp Smith (1941/1964: 166) says the indirect passions rely on Hume's associative operations of the mind for their production while the direct passions do not, which is mostly right. But before Hume identified these mechanisms, what led him to survey the whole panoply of human feelings (described so variously by his predecessors) and single out these four as different from the rest and similar to each other, and as calling out for a more complex explanation than desire, or fear, hope, or joy, all of which he calls direct passions? This is the first puzzle we shall address.

For Hume the moral sentiments – approval and disapproval experienced from a sympathetically-engaged and unbiased perspective – are the basis of all our moral evaluations. There are many straightforward individual connections between aspects of Hume's theory of the passions in Book 2 and the theory of the moral sentiments to which he devotes *Treatise* Book 3.[4] But is there a systematic connection between the lengthy description of the main *indirect* passions and Hume's account of the moral sentiments? There are two interconnected issues here. First, Hume does not say explicitly whether the moral sentiments are direct or indirect passions or neither, and interpreters disagree about it. Where do the moral sentiments fit in his careful taxonomy? Second, does Hume explain pride, humility, love, and hatred in so much detail in Book 2 in part because he thinks they assist in his explanation of moral approval and disapproval in Book 3 in some way? If so, in what way? That is the second puzzle.

Below I review the basic features Hume attributes to the four principal indirect passions and then offer my solutions to these two puzzles. I shall argue that the passions Hume calls indirect have a different kind of intentional object than those he calls direct; and as a result they are evaluative in a way in which the others are not. (This is one thing that sets them apart and unites them; there may be others.) And without decisively settling their precise classification, I shall argue that the moral sentiments are indirect in just the ways that pride, humility, love, and hatred are, with the same sort of intentional object and a very similar status as evaluations; and that consequently Hume's account of the four main indirect passions lays the groundwork for his naturalistic explanation of the moral sentiments.

These hypotheses are modest in an important respect. If they prove true, they will not rule out a number of other theses about the importance of the direct/indirect distinction and the classification of the moral sentiments. And of course they say nothing about how the theory of the passions employs and extends the associationism or enriches the concept of the self Hume articulates in Book 1, as those are topics for another occasion.

The Basic Features of the Indirect Passions

In Book 2 of the *Treatise* Hume reiterates his division of all the perceptions (that is, all the contents) of the mind into impressions and ideas, and subdivides the impressions into original and secondary, renaming his Book 1 distinction between impressions of sensation and reflection. Original impressions "are such as without any antecedent perception arise in the soul, from the constitution of the body, from the animal spirits, or from the application of objects to the external organs." Secondary impressions "proceed from some of these original ones, either immediately or by the interposition of its idea." Of this latter kind are "the passions, and other emotions resembling them" (T 2.1.1.1). He divides the secondary impressions into the calm and the violent, though it is not clear how seriously he takes this "vulgar and specious" dichotomy (T 2.1.1.3).

Hume insists that *all* passions are "simple and uniform impressions" that cannot be analyzed into component parts, and so in giving an account of passions of any sort "[t]he utmost we can pretend to is a description of them, by an enumeration of such circumstances, as attend them" (T 2.1.2.1). His descriptions consequently do not identify the passions' (nonexistent) components but instead specify their qualities and (primarily) their causes and effects. (Whether Hume can consistently treat all the passions as simple is contested; see Baier 1991: ch. 6; Bricke 1996: 21–7; Weller 2002, for opposing views.) He thinks of a passion, rightly or wrongly, as a feeling with both a distinctive phenomenological quality and an identifying or characteristic set of causes and effects, perhaps even causes and effects necessary for the feeling to qualify as that particular passion – love, say, or hope. (On this see Davidson 1976: 755; Radcliffe 2006: 364.) Note that the cause of passions is "that idea, which excites them" (T 2.1.2.4). Thus Hume considers their mental causes only (the "antecedent perception" that regularly precedes them in the mind), not physiological ones, whether usual (hormones or changes in the brain) or out of the ordinary (such as sleep deprivation, which might make me irritable and so cause my anger). Presumably physiological accounts are left to the natural philosopher. The focus on mental causes also suggests that he intends only those causes by which we identify or understand the passions, and physiological ones are not like that.

Early in *Treatise* Book 2 he distinguishes the passions into the two groups, direct and indirect, in the following vague way:

By direct passions I understand such as arise immediately from good or evil, from pain or pleasure. By indirect such as proceed from the same principles, but by the conjunction of other qualities. This distinction I cannot at present justify or explain any farther. (T 2.1.1.4)

(Note that *all* the passions arise from pain or pleasure. This is slightly revised later.) In the *Dissertation of the Passions* we fare no better. He takes up the direct passions first, and when he comes to the indirect passions says:

Besides those passions abovementioned, which arise from a direct pursuit of good and aversion to evil, there are others of a more complicated nature, and imply [*sic*] more than one view or consideration. (DP, p. 132)

In both places, though, he argues that indirect passions have (and indeed must have) a *cause distinct from their object*. The *object* of both pride and humility is always the self, Hume says, and that of love and hatred is always some other person (T 2.1.2.3; T 2.2.1.2–3). What this means, in part, is that in virtue of a "natural and original quality of the mind" these four passions always direct our attention to the self or the other person (T 2.1.3.2–4; T 2.2.1.2–3); it is of the very nature of the mind, or of these passions, that when we feel pride or humility we think of ourselves, and when we feel love or hatred we think of some other person. (We further examine the notion of the object of a passion below.) Thus all four are person-directed affections.[5] The cause of each of these passions is always (the idea of) something pleasant or painful that is closely associated with the self or with some other person. Strictly speaking, the cause is (or is the idea of) an object, such as a suit of clothes, that has a quality such as beauty, and that quality causes or has caused a separate pleasure or pain to the person who experiences the indirect passion (either first-hand or via sympathy with someone else) (T 2.1.2.6).

Hume uses his associationism to explain the generation of the indirect passions. According to Book 1, ideas can be related to one another by resemblance, contiguity, and cause and effect. Ideas so related are associated in the mind, which means, in part, that when one of two related ideas arises, the other tends to be called up next (T 1.1.4.1–2 and passim). In Book 2 Hume adds that secondary *impressions* are also subject to association as a result of their relations, though apparently the only relation that allows one impression to call up another is resemblance, and the main resemblance between secondary impressions seems to be their hedonic tone. Thus one pleasant emotion tends to be followed by other pleasant emotions, and one painful one by other psychic pains (T 2.1.4.3).[6]

Hume invokes these two kinds of association (between ideas and between impressions) to explain the causation of pride, humility, love, and hatred by a mechanism that involves a double relation of impressions and ideas. The causes of these passions are items (or the ideas of items) we think of either as part of the self or another person, or as bearing a very close relation – to self or another – of resemblance, contiguity, or cause and effect. The cause and effect relation plays a dominant role in the indirect passions, for the causes of indirect passions are often things we have produced or items that are our property (and "property may be considered a species of causation," T 2.1.10.1).

So the idea of a particular cause of pride, such as a beautiful suit of clothes, is closely associated with the idea of its creator or owner by a relation of ideas. The causes of pride, humility, love, and hatred are items with qualities that also produce a pleasure or uneasiness quite independent of the indirect passions themselves; for example, a beautiful suit of clothes produces aesthetic pleasure in an observer, and an ugly one displeasure. This pleasure or uneasiness would occur whether or not the item occasioned any pride, humility, love, or hatred, and even if it were not appropriately related to the self or any other person (as when the suit of clothes hangs in a shop). This separate pleasure or uneasiness, while independent of the indirect passions, resembles them, for pride and love are pleasant, humility and hatred painful. Thus when the item is suitably related to the observer there are two relations present among these contents of the mind, one between ideas and one between impressions. This, then, is how the four canonical indirect passions are generated. The cause of my pride – my beautiful suit of clothes – is related to me because I own it, and so its idea calls up in my mind the idea of myself (thought of as the owner of the clothes), the very object that nature has allocated to the passion of pride. At the same time the sensation of aesthetic pleasure from looking at the beautiful suit resembles the pleasant feeling of pride. These two relations (between the ideas of the clothes and myself, and between the impressions of aesthetic pleasure and pride) make it easy for the first idea and sensation in each pair to be converted into the second: the idea of the suit of clothes is converted into or calls up an idea of myself, and the feeling of aesthetic pleasure is converted into or calls up the feeling of pride (see especially T 2.1.5.5; for the application to all four indirect passions, T 2.2.1–2, e.g. 2.2.2.28). Hume adds some needed qualifications: for something that causes an independent pleasure to produce pride, for example, it must be very closely related to the self and more so than to other people, it must be shared with no more than a few others, it must be "very discernible and obvious" both to ourselves and others (T 2.1.6.6; DP, p. 152, is similar), and its relation to us must be of reasonably long duration. Furthermore, the production of the indirect passions is regularized by custom or general rules, so that, for example, someone may be proud of his wealth or high social standing even if it fails to give him pleasure, because such things so commonly do give pleasure.[7]

Turning to the direct passions, in both *Treatise* Book 2 and the *Dissertation* Hume characterizes them quite briefly. All affections arise from pleasure and pain (T 2.3.9.1), whether it is presently felt or (more often) thought of in prospect (and so makes its appearance in the mind as a believed idea, T 1.1.2.1, 1.3.10.2). He explicitly calls pleasure and pain in this context "good and evil." Those passions "which arise from good and evil most naturally, and with the least preparation are the direct passions of desire and aversion, grief and joy, hope and fear, along with volition" (T 2.3.9.2). Good and evil that are thought certain to occur cause joy and grief respectively; good and evil that are uncertain cause hope and fear; and "[d]esire arises from good considered simply, and aversion is deriv'd from evil" (T 2.3.9.7, DP, p. 122). In the *Treatise* (though this discussion is omitted from the *Dissertation*), in addition to these direct passions Hume also describes under that heading a separate category of passions, the natural impulses or instincts, which do *not* arise from pleasure or pain. These are hunger, lust, and some other bodily appetites, desire of good to friends and harm to enemies (T 2.3.9.8), and perhaps also the love of life and kindness to children (T 2.3.3.8). The two instincts

163

of anger (also called resentment) and benevolence ("desire of punishment to our enemies, and of happiness to our friends," T 2.3.9.8) are consistently produced by hatred and love respectively, and directly move us to aid or harm those we love or hate, without the help of any expectation of pleasure or pain for ourselves. They do *result* in pleasure and pain for the agent, but "proceed not from them, like the other affections" (T 2.3.9.8). Although one might read Hume in T 2.3.9 ("Of the direct passions") as saying that these instincts are themselves distinct direct passions, what he literally says is that the very same direct passions he has already listed there (joy, grief, hope, fear, desire, and aversion), besides arising from the consideration of pain and pleasure, "frequently arise from a natural impulse or instinct, which is perfectly unaccountable" (T 2.3.9.8; SBN 439) – that is, for which we cannot give any causal explanation. So desire, for example, might arise either from pleasure "consider'd simply" (T 2.3.9.7) or from the instinct of hunger or anger/resentment. Presumably this means that I might desire to eat a certain delicacy because I think it will be pleasant (good considered simply), or because I am hungry, or because I wish to pain my enemy (another instinct) by showily indulging when he cannot.

Why These Four Emotions? The Foundations of the Distinction between Direct and Indirect Passions

Now we turn to the first puzzle, why Hume finds, on surveying the variety of human emotions, that pride, humility, love, and hatred have something in common with one another and differ from other passions, and why he consequently characterizes them as indirect. I will argue that one important reason is that these emotions have a different kind of object than those he calls direct, one that requires a shift in our attention.

Objects of passions

We should clarify what Hume means by the object of a passion and how those of the indirect passions differ from their causes. His language suggests that he is talking about what today we would call the intentional objects of the passions. There is controversy over what, exactly, the intentionality of a mental state consists of, but "[a]ll writers agree that intentionality is the directedness of the mind upon something, or the about-ness of mental states" (Crane 1998). An intentional object, then, is that to which a mental state is directed, or what the mental state is about. (The metaphysical status of intentional objects is controversial, but does not matter here.) It might easily be assumed that Hume does not think the direct passions have objects at all, but he never says this. In fact, it is fairly clear that Hume takes both direct and indirect passions to have intentional objects in this general sense. One enjoys or fears something, hopes for something, desires or is averse to something; the direct passions are about or direct the mind to particular items. (Hume does not discuss the possibility that one might have "free-floating" fear, for example, not directed to anything in particular, but clearly he does not think this sort of phenomenon typical.) The "objects" of the indirect passions that Hume distinguishes from their causes seem to be intentional objects as well: one is proud or ashamed of oneself, and one loves or hates another person. (There are other indirect passions, but they are parallel in this respect to pride, humility, love, or hatred, which are the main types.) There are difficult textual issues about whether Hume countenances any intentionality of original impressions such as sense perceptions, but no such problem arises here. He says explicitly that the indirect passions have objects, and his description of this passion-to-object relation fulfills the very general characterization above of what it is for a mental state to have an intentional object, so he plainly thinks passions have them.[8]

For our purposes we do not have to give a precise account of what Hume means by an intentional object, but we can say a little. The object of indirect passions is "that to which they direct their view when excited. Pride and humility, being once raised, immediately turn our attention to ourself, and regard that as their ultimate and final object." The cause of pride or humility "excites the passion connected with it; and that passion, when excited, turns our view to another idea, which is that of self" (T 2.1.2.4). "Here at last the view always rests, when we are actuated by either of these passions" (T 2.1.5.3). The passion causes our attention to turn to something and rest there; that on which it focuses our attention is the passion's object. Note that he speaks indifferently of the passion itself directing *its* view or attention to its object and the passion directing *our* view to its object. (Since the passion is simple, it is hard, though not impossible, to see how *it* could have a direction or a view. The claim that the passion causes the mind to attend to something is less problematic.) Similarly, love and hatred are described as "directed to" a greater rather than a lesser object, such as a master rather than his servant, and this easily produces "anger or good-will to the servant" who is related to him (T 2.2.2.24). (Here we see both an indirect and a direct passion having an intentional object.) The passion of hunger or lust (each of which is a direct instinctive passion) "turns the view to a certain object," food or sex (T 2.2.11.6). The intentional object of a passion seems then to be what the passion causes us to think of or attend to. Hume slides easily between talk of things and talk of the ideas of things in discussing the intentional objects of a passion, as we see from the passages just quoted, e.g. "the passion . . . turns our view to another *idea*, which is that of self," and "pride and humility . . . turn our attention to *ourself*" (emphasis added). From his perspective it does not much matter, since to focus attention on something (oneself, food, or whatever it may be) just is to attend to a perception, in these cases an idea.

Only the indirect passions have intentional objects distinct from their causes; so we may infer that, by contrast, for direct passions these two are identical. In the case of an indirect passion, as we have seen, the cause (the idea of a possession or accomplishment, for example) "excites the passion, connected with it; and that passion, when excited, turns our view to another idea, which is that of self" for pride or humility, or another person, for love or hatred. "Here then is a passion plac'd betwixt two ideas, of which the one produces it, and the other is produc'd by it" (T 2.1.2.4). This shows the added complexity of indirect passions, the "more than one view or consideration" involved in their occurrence, that Hume notices even before he explains them in terms of the double relation of ideas and impressions. The direct passions, by contrast, arise directly from believed sources of pleasure or pain (good or evil) either considered simply or thought of as having a certain likelihood of occurrence. Hume does not say whether direct passions also "turn our view" to the idea of their objects. But since the cause of a direct passion is the same as its object, what he seems to think is that there is no need for any turning; in coming to have the direct passion our view is already on its object. If I fear a snarling dog, the idea or impression of the dog causes my fear, and my attention is on the dog. There is no shift of focus; the passion is about the dangerous dog and directs my attention there alone. But if I am proud of my beautiful house, the idea of my beautiful house causes a feeling of pride which turns my attention from the house and onto myself. Indirectness, then, involves at least a shifting of focus or attention from one item (the cause) to another (the object distinct from the cause).[9]

This shift in attention, in fact, apparently creates the need for a more complicated causal mechanism for the generation of indirect passions than is needed for a direct passion. "In order to excite pride, there are always two objects we must contemplate, *viz.* the *cause* or that object which produces pleasure, and the self ... But joy has only one object necessary to its production, viz. that which gives pleasure" (T 2.1.6.5). Since in pride we contemplate two objects, its origin must be traced to both, and their relations to one another in the causal process must be ascertained.

Intuitive grounds for the distinction

Now that we know what it is, according to Hume, for a passion's object to be identical to or distinct from its cause, why might he think pride, humility, love, and hatred have objects distinct from their causes? Some insight comes from first considering pride and humility alone. Hume rightly observes that "Pride is a certain satisfaction in ourselves, on account of some accomplishment or possession, which we enjoy" (DP, p. 132). Usually, when I feel pride, I am proud of something in particular: my work, my looks, my child, even something I said. But the attitude of pride is a pleasure or satisfaction not merely in that particular accomplishment or possession, but in myself in my entirety – in me as a person, albeit insofar as I have that accomplishment or possession. It is even more striking with humility, which today, in many contexts (though not all), we would more naturally call shame. I feel humble or ashamed because of something in particular as well: my errors, my appearance, or something disreputable I did. But my displeasure is not merely directed at the item in question. When I am ashamed, I am displeased with *myself*. It is one thing to dislike the fact that I have ragged clothes or acted badly; it is something further to be *ashamed*. "I am ashamed of myself," we sometimes say, but it is clearly redundant. To be ashamed is not only to feel displeased about the particular, but to feel displeased with oneself, though often on account of the particular. Even to be ashamed of someone else (such as one's child or parent) is to take an attitude of displeasure toward oneself. I can be displeased with other people in many other ways, but I can only be ashamed of another person if I regard that person's defect as reflecting badly upon *me*.

Hume recognizes this (far more clearly than Hobbes does, for example), and apparently draws two morals from it. First, pride and humility involve both an awareness of a particular item that is related to the self and an attitude toward the self as a whole. Since he thinks the feelings themselves are simple, their causation must then be complex. Second, they are invariably attitudes toward a person, and in this they differ from attitudes that can be directed toward inanimate objects. One can equally fear a mugger (a person) or a storm at sea, but one can only be proud or ashamed of oneself, a thinking and feeling person. So it appears that the causes of these emotions (our houses, clothes, deeds, and so forth) are indeed distinct from that to which they ultimately direct our attention.

In these respects pride and shame actually do differ from desire and aversion, joy and grief, hope and fear. If I think of something pleasant, such as eating raspberry sorbet, I may consequently come to desire it. This is a simple process: I think of some good and I am drawn to it. (The process may not be as simple as Hume supposes, but he is on the right track.) Perhaps I next remember that there is some raspberry sorbet left in the freezer downstairs. Then I feel joy. Or perhaps I am not sure, but think it very probable that there is some left; then I feel hope. Each of these passions directs my attention to the pleasure of eating some sorbet. In this respect these emotions resemble appetites. This is not limited to desires for bodily pleasure, either. If I think of reading another clever science fiction story, I will feel the same emotions: a desire to read one, joy that there is still one in the anthology on my bedside table that I haven't yet read, or hope that there may be one. These feelings are ways in which I relate to objects in the world. I take no attitude to myself in this process. My attention is squarely on the prospect of pleasure.

Emotions of this kind are not only produced by the prospect of pleasure or pain but are directed toward (or direct our attention toward) the pleasant or painful object. Not only does my idea of pain from a dog's bite cause my fear, but it is the object of my fear: it is that to which my fear is directed. Whereas in the case of pride, I think of a fine suit of clothes and then my attention, and indeed my feeling, is directed somehow to myself. Thinking about my beautiful clothes gives me a good feeling about myself. It seems important that pride and humility are not appetites or desires. Though they are caused by items that we think good or bad, they are not directed to or focused on *obtaining* the good or avoiding the bad. To be proud or ashamed of something is not to think "what will it do for me?" It is to assess myself in some respect.[10]

Thus when it comes to pride and humility Hume seems to be onto something (though I do not mean to endorse all he says on this). Specifically, first, pride and humility do have intentional objects distinct from their causes; they do involve a direction of attention to something else, a person. Secondly, they are not desire-like passions: unlike desire, hope, or fear, their intentional object is not something that we want to obtain, produce, or avoid.

A concern about love and hatred, and its resolution

So far so good with regard to pride and humility. However, Hume's parallel claims about love and hatred are initially less plausible. Hume tells us he means to use the terms 'love' and 'hatred' broadly, to include esteem, admiration, friendship, and affection between family members on the one hand, and dislike, enmity, and contempt on the other.[11] But if we are very loose in the way we use the terms, then it seems hard for Hume to defend his claim that "the *object* of love and hatred is some other person, of whose thoughts, actions and sensations we are not conscious" (T 2.2.1.2). Are love and hatred really directed "always" to "some other person" (T 2.2.1.3)? Can't someone love her dog, her job, a piece of music, life, or honor? Such uses were common long before Hume's day, as in "I could not love thee (Deare) so much, Lov'd I not Honour

167

more" (Lovelace, 1649). (See *The Oxford English Dictionary*, "love, v.4" for earlier examples). Hobbes actually says that "desire and love are the same thing" (Hobbes 1651: 38), so of course on his view one can love power, money, food, and drink. Even Hume himself uses the terms this way at times, saying that people hate pain and love fame (EPM App. 1.18; T 2.1.11). Presumably this is not the sense of "love" and "hatred" Hume has in mind in his theory of the indirect passions. He apparently thinks there is a type of love (and esteem, friendship, and so on) and hatred (and the like) that is readily distinguishable from the other feelings we call by that name and is directed exclusively to other persons by a natural and original quality of the mind. Is there really such a feeling or cluster of feelings (or at least a characteristic attitude)? It is possible that Hume is right about pride and humility, but is overly enamored with the parallel he thinks he sees with other-regarding feelings, and tries to make the emotions much more symmetrical than they are. But I shall suggest that there is indeed a similarity between pride and humility and certain other-regarding emotions that we call love and hatred, starting from the common-sense thought that while I can love a friend for his wit and I can love a stew for its flavor, the love in the two cases is not the same sort of emotion.[12]

We should first clarify the conception of love and hatred Hume has in mind. Hutcheson's remarks about this matter in another context shed some light. Natural goods, for Hutcheson, are "all objects which are apt to excite pleasure" (1725/1994: 70), such as "houses, lands . . . strength, sagacity" (p. 69), and natural evils those apt to excite pain. He says:

> Our senses of natural good and evil would make us receive, with equal serenity and composure, an assault . . . from a neighbour, a cheat from a partner, or trustee, as we would an equal damage from the fall of a beam, a tile, or a tempest. (p. 71).

We would no more hate the cause of the one than of the other. He uses this point to argue for the existence of a moral sense.

> Had we no sense of good distinct from the advantage or interest arising from the external senses . . . the sensations and affections toward a fruitful field, or commodious habitation, would be much the same with what we have toward a generous friend, or any noble character . . . and we should no more admire any action, or *love any person* in a distant country, or age, whose influence could not extend to us, than we love the mountains of Peru, while we are unconcerned in the Spanish trade. We should have the same sentiments and affections toward inanimate beings, which we have toward rational agents, which yet everyone knows to be false. (p. 70, emphasis added).

For Hutcheson the feelings of love and hatred, as well as the moral sense, are responsive specifically to the *intentions* of the person loved or approved, and do not depend for their responses on the advantage or harm that may accrue to the one who feels them.

This thought appears to have influenced Hume in his discussion of love and hatred even where moral evaluation is not at issue. Hume apparently agrees that the feeling of love or hatred toward a man or woman is different from our feelings toward a tempest or the fall of a beam. But he explains the source of the difference in another way. On Hume's account, the generous or hostile intentions of another person are among the possible sources of the independent pleasure or pain that gives rise to love or hatred, but they are not the only such sources. "There are some," says Hume, perhaps meaning Hutcheson, "who . . . require not only that the pain and pleasure arise from the person, but likewise that it arise knowingly, with a particular design and intention" (T 2.2.3.2). This, according to Hume, is too narrow a requirement.

> If that quality in another, which pleases or displeases, be constant and inherent in his person and character, it will cause love or hatred independent of the intention; But otherwise a knowledge and design is requisite, in order to give rise to these passions. (T 2.2.3.4)

Actions are fleeting and so not readily connected in our minds with their agents, unless they are "deriv'd from a particular fore-thought and design" (T 2.2.3.4) that reveals qualities that remain in the agent long after the action is over. Actions must be the product of their agent's feeling and/or thinking part, something durable enough to facilitate the transition of the observer's mind from the action to the person who performed it, if we are to love or hate people for their actions. But many things other than intentions are sufficiently durable to produce love and hatred of this kind, such as a person's "deformity or folly" (T 2.2.3.4), wealth or poverty, power, or familial relation to ourselves. Lasting features are always needed, because they must be closely associated with the person loved or hated so they can call up our idea of him or her and shift our attention to it.

The need for a cause of love and hatred that bears a persistent relationship to a person reveals that the kind of love and hatred Hume has in mind is a kind that is directed toward a person as a whole, a kind that would be parallel to pride and humility in this respect.

Is Hume right that there are such feelings? Clearly there are some; we admire some people from afar for achievements that will never benefit us, for example. But one may wonder whether the various emotions Hume groups under these headings all qualify as attitudes toward a person as a whole. He does after all include under love and hatred some fairly mundane feelings toward people, such as liking them because they are familiar or disliking them (perhaps without realizing it) because they are ugly. These may not seem to be fundamentally person-directed feelings. Isn't their object really just the trait and not the person? Yet on closer scrutiny we see that there *are* feelings of this sort that are directed toward persons as whole beings in the way that other feelings are not. Although what causes me to like my aunt may only be her familiarity, I like my aunt herself and not only her familiarity. Although what makes me feel uneasy with a certain man may be his habit of talking too loudly, if I dislike him as a result, I dislike *him* and not merely his trait. (If I merely dislike the *trait* then I might not dislike him at all; I might find it a foible I can overlook. That is not the same as disliking *him* as a result of the trait, which is, I think, a different but also common attitude.) Even if Anne Gregory's suitor in Yeats's poem does not love her for herself alone but only for her yellow hair, he nonetheless loves *her*; it is not the case that he loves only her yellow hair. (It would not alleviate his despair if she were to cut off her hair and give it to him, or give him a lovely painting of herself but never see him again.) If he stops loving her when she dyes her hair, that shows him to be a shallow man who did not love her as she wished to be loved, but does not show that he never loved her at all. People's traits can and often do lead us to have feelings for them that take the person as intentional object, even when these feelings are neither exalted nor ideal. It is a bit misleading to say they take the person "as a whole" as their intentional object, because this suggests that we love the person *for* her whole self, which may not be so. But they are directed at the person and not just her feature.

There are other feelings we naturally call love and hatred, of course: I love Thai food and hate grading papers. But those are of a different kind. What we call love and hatred in those latter cases are more like habitual appetites, focused on what an item in the environment can do for me, viewing the world as something that satisfies or thwarts my desires. And this self-centered liking or dislike can apply to people's traits as well, whether temporary or enduring, without generating the sort of emotion Hume calls indirect. A student can like her professor's lenient way of grading without liking the professor; what she likes (that is, what she desires and enjoys) is the trait that serves her own advantage. In fact, she thinks of the trait only as a means to her advantage; the ultimate object of the joy occasioned by the professor's trait is simply her own pleasure in getting a good grade. (For this it does not matter whether the professor's trait endures into next year, provided the student has completed the course.) The love and hatred that interest Hume in his discussion of the indirect passions is not mere joy or grief caused by a trait. The object to which it directs our attention is not the lover's or hater's own advantage or disadvantage, but rather the loved or hated person. This is so even when it is occasioned by the most mundane accomplishments or possessions that can be linked enduringly to the person in question, including mere familiarity and yellow hair. (See Korsgaard 1999, for very similar points that form part of a rather different view.)

One way to understand this re-orientation toward the person is to consider the role of pleasure or advantage in the persistence of the passion. If Thai food ceases to give me pleasure, I can no longer say that I like or love it. But as Hutcheson says, we can love people in distant countries and even eras, people who cannot feed or frustrate our appetites or serve our interests in any way. Some perceived good quality is indeed necessary to trigger the love, and in the case of distant people this may result from sympathy with those I read about in a history or travelogue; but I can persist in my love or hatred even though I have nothing to gain or lose from them.

So while not everything that Hume says about love and hatred is convincing, there is a kind of love and hatred that is fundamentally person-directed.

Two kinds of valuing

One way to describe what Hume has in mind here is to say that pride, humility, love, and hatred are person-*valuing* passions – they are *assessments* of oneself and others. This is clearly true of pride and humility: to feel proud or ashamed is to feel oneself to be good or bad. Love and hatred of the particular kind Hume has in mind are similarly assessments of others as good or bad. (This may be moral goodness or badness, but it is very likely to be goodness or badness of another kind, including whatever kind of goodness we attribute to familiar people.) It is not new to suggest that the four major indirect passions are person-evaluative emotions (see Árdal 1977: 408), but we must ask what that means for Hume. Aren't all the passions evaluative, and aren't the direct passions the most fundamental sorts of evaluation? If I desire some raspberry sorbet, in a way that too is an evaluation: I expect it to be pleasurable – that is, *good*. Every desire is a response to "good consider'd simply" (T 2.3.9.7). Are pride, humility, love, and hatred evaluative in a way in which desire is not? For Hume, I suggest, they are.

A remark in the *Dissertation on the Passions* may shed light here: he describes the direct passions as those that "arise from a direct *pursuit* of good and aversion to evil" (DP, p. 132, emphasis added). Similarly in the *Treatise* in discussing direct passions as motives to action he says "[b]oth these kinds of passions [the calm and the violent direct passions] pursue good, and avoid evil" (T 2.3.4.1). What is it that we desire, fear, and so on when we feel the direct passions? To what are these passions directed? Earlier we had the example of a snarling dog, and I said we fear the dog. But Hume's considered view seems to be that while the dog is called (an) evil and our thought of it elicits fear, the ultimate intentional object of our fear is not the dog but the pain it is likely to cause us if it attacks. Thus the example of fearing a mugger is not faithful to Hume's considered position: we talk about fearing a mugger (and so fear seems to take persons as its object at times), but the mugger is only an intermediate object of our attention when we feel this fear; the ultimate object is not the person but what he is likely to do to us. It is natural to say that when I go to the freezer what I want is the raspberry sorbet, but Hume's view may well be that what I ultimately attend to, the true intentional object of my desire, is the (characteristic) pleasure I expect to get by eating it. This makes sense of the thesis that the object of a direct passion is identical with its cause. The cause of my desire or aversion, Hume makes very clear, is the prospect of pleasure or pain. If the cause is to be the same as the object of the passion, then the true or ultimate object of my desire or aversion must be that pleasure or pain. With regard to the direct passions, then, he seems to have stayed close to Hobbes, who sees pleasure and the avoidance of pain as the true objects of desire and aversion (1650: 4). The direct passions can be thought of as evaluations in the following sense: they track pleasure and pain, i.e. natural good and evil, and it is only when we think something (naturally) good or evil that we feel them. (The natural instincts described in the *Treatise* constitute an exception. They are grouped with the direct passions but are not evaluative in the way the others are, since they are not responses to the idea of pleasure or pain, and also they are not directed at getting pleasure or avoiding pain.)

The indirect passions, by contrast, are evaluative in a very different way. They do not track pleasure or pain; they do not "arise from the direct pursuit of good or aversion to evil" for the one who feels them. They are triggered, in part, by pleasurable and unpleasant features of persons, but once we have them they do not take pleasure or pain as their intentional objects – they are not directed to the idea of the (expected) pleasure or uneasiness of the person who feels them. In wanting sorbet I seek my own pleasure and my attention is focused on that prospective pleasure; in wanting to avoid a vicious dog I seek to avoid my own pain and my attention is

171

focused on that prospective pain. But being ashamed or proud, loving or hating someone, is not a state of craving or seeking to obtain or avoid my own pleasure or pain, nor is my attention focused on those possible experiences. My feeling has to do with what is good or bad, but it is directed to persons, and those persons are found *by this feeling* to be good or bad. In taking pleasure or displeasure in the person as a whole, I value or disvalue him or her. In a way, the indirect passions are more autonomous with respect to value than the direct ones; they do not so much track value as impart it.

A consequence: why the indirect passions are not motives

If this hypothesis about Hume's thinking is correct, it solves a further mystery about the indirect passions: why does Hume deny that they themselves are motives to the will? In common speech we talk of people being moved to act by each of these feelings, for example being moved by love to make a sacrifice or by hatred to do violence. Hume accommodates our observation that love and hatred lead to characteristic actions (benefiting those we love and harming those we hate) by arguing that "by the original constitution of the mind" there is a causal connection between love and a direct (and instinctive) passion, benevolence, and the same sort of connection between hatred and another direct, instinctive passion, anger or resentment (T 2.2.6.6). Benevolence and anger *are* motives, and this is why we act as we do toward those we love or hate. But pride and humility, which we might have expected to move us to boast or to grovel (for example), he claims are "pure emotions in the soul, unattended with any desire, and not immediately exciting us to action" (T 2.2.6.3). Why? For Hume the will is an "immediate effect of pain and pleasure" (T 2.3.1.2) which "exerts itself, when either the good or the absence of the evil may be attain'd by any action of the mind or body" (T 2.3.9.7). Although it is not a passion, it is sufficiently like the direct passions to be classed and explained with them, and arises as they do from the consideration of the prospect of some pleasure or pain for the agent. Action, for Hume, and hence the will, aims at getting pleasure and avoiding pain. (The instincts provide a set of exceptions to this, but it does not affect the general point.) But pride and humility are not expectations of pain or pleasure and do not aim at their production or avoidance for the proud or humble person. Nor are they instinctive drives. They are instead evaluative responses to persons and they rest with their intentional objects. They can strengthen passions of the other sort that aim at outcomes for an agent (T 2.3.9.4), but they are not themselves of that sort. The same is true of love and hatred. The indirect passions do not actuate the will because they do not focus the agent's attention on her own pleasure or pain, and the will is only actuated when the agent realizes that "either the good or the absence of the evil may be attain'd by any action of the mind or body." If we are not attending to any good or evil for ourselves, our will is not activated. (This does not tell us how Hume would explain the expressive behavior that characteristically accompanies pride and humility, such as bragging or hiding one's face, but that is an instance of a broader problem that we cannot address here of how to explain expressive behavior in Humean terms – jumping for joy is another kind of example.)

Does this mean that Hume is a motivational egoistic hedonist, contrary to what many commentators, going back to Kemp Smith (1941: 140–1, 164), have thought? Does he trace all human action to the pursuit of one's own pleasure and avoidance of one's own pain? No. He makes extensive use of the instinctual passions, especially benevolence and anger, to account for many of our actions. And he does not analyze these instincts as arising from the prospect of one's own pleasure or pain.[13] So on many occasions we help and harm others with an eye to *their* pleasure or pain rather than our own. He is committed to thinking the will can be actuated by these (inexplicable) motives as well. All the other passions that qualify as motives, however, engage the will only by means of the prospect of pleasure and pain.[14] This is his position in the *Treatise* and *Dissertation*. He does make Butlerian arguments in the moral *Enquiry* against the claim that all benevolence is a species of self-love (EPM App. 2.12–13), and in support of the claim that we must have some original outward-directed impulses "to give a relish" (that is, impart pleasure) to the objects of self-love (EPM 9.20), arguments that led Kemp Smith to say that for Hume "desire is not desire for pleasure" (1941: 169); but really Hume's position in that later work is not substantially different from what we have seen in the *Treatise*. Apart from our instincts (which are more numerous in the moral *Enquiry*), only the prospect of pleasure or pain for ourselves moves us to act.

A unique account of valuing

A perennial issue in moral philosophy is whether a thing is good because we (human beings) value it or we value it because it is good. Philosophers who regard either The Good, or goodness for human beings, as independent of people's psychological reactions will naturally understand valuing as a recognition of and response to this independent feature that resides in such things as characters or actions. Samuel Clarke, for example, says "the mind of man unavoidably acknowledges a natural and necessary difference between good and evil" (1705: 204). This is not, of course, Hume's approach. His view is that things are good because we value them. For that approach to succeed in an empiricist and naturalistic philosophy, valuing itself must be explained in empirical and natural terms, without smuggling in presuppositions about what is antecedently good. One does not first assume that there is such a thing as goodness and explain valuing as a response to it; rather, one observes the phenomenon of valuing, and then either builds up an account of goodness as that which people value, or at least grants that what people *call* "good" is that toward which they have the attitude of valuing.

A frequent starting point for this latter type of analysis is the psychological state of desire, which looks to be empirically observable and understandable by science. Thus some adopt the position that valuing is some sort of desiring. Hobbes tries this in a very simple way in *Leviathan*: "whatsoever is the object of any man's appetite or desire; that is it which he for his part calleth *good*; and the object of his hate, and aversion, is *evil* . . ." (1651: 39). (Spinoza's position, at least initially, is similar: "we do not desire a thing because we judge it to be good; on the contrary, we call the object of our desire good" [1677: 126–7].) But this is too simple; not all desiring is valuing, and not all aversion is disvaluing. Sometimes we want what we regard as

173

bad. In recent years David Lewis and others have proposed to analyze valuing in terms of desire by explaining the valuing of something, whether an action or a character trait, as the more complex psychological state of desiring to desire (Lewis 1989; the notion of second-order desire on which he draws is developed earlier in another context by Frankfurt 1971).

Hume likewise wishes to give a naturalistic and empiricist account of valuing, in particular valuing of persons, and one that does not presuppose any independent conception of the good beyond natural good (pleasure). Interestingly, though he shares with Hobbes and with present-day naturalists the goal of psychologizing evaluation, he does not try to analyze it in terms of desires, perhaps because of the lesson he learns from Hutcheson that at least some of our evaluative attitudes to people differ fundamentally from our pleasure-seeking and pain-avoiding sentiments, which is what Hume thinks desires fundamentally are.[15] He sees desire (and aversion, hope, fear, and the other passions he classes as direct) as different in kind from the sort of evaluative feelings involved in admiration or respect for persons. We neither desire ourselves nor (literally) others; instead we value ourselves and others – we are proud of ourselves and love others. In valuing or disvaluing a person we do not ask "what will she do for me?" even though pleasure or pain of our own may have been involved in the genesis of our attitudes. Valuing and disvaluing of persons is part of what occurs in pride and humility and in the specially person-directed forms of love and hatred that Hume discusses. So at least part of the answer to the question why Hume selects these four passions from among the great variety of human emotions is that they have this in common: they are person-*evaluating* attitudes. Hume thinks that valuing of persons can indeed be explained within the science of the mind, using only familiar materials, efficient causation, and no prior conception of goodness beyond pleasure; but it is best done without relying on desire. For Hume valuing of persons is not desiring to desire; it is the having of indirect passions.

The Moral Sentiments

Now we can fairly quickly solve (or partly solve) the second puzzle, whether there is a fundamental connection between the indirect passions and the moral sentiments, and whether we can classify the moral sentiments as either direct or indirect passions.

Parallels between the moral sentiments and the indirect passions

For Hume moral evaluations arise from sentiments of a certain kind, ones he explains using the same associative mechanisms engaged in non-moral aspects of human experience, so that he need not invoke any uniquely moral faculties. For Hume moral assessment is fundamentally evaluation of "characters." This term often means individual character *traits* but sometimes means complete persons, those of whom we "draw a character" (as in "A Character of Sir Robert Walpole," *Essays*, pp. 574–6). The moral sentiments also evaluate actions, but derivatively, based on the traits or settled motives of which we take the actions to be signs (T 3.2.1.2).

Given this approach, it is not surprising that before he takes up the topic of morals Hume first offers a careful analysis of some *other* sentiments (probably) distinct from the moral ones that are also, like them, evaluative and directed to persons as their intentional objects. By giving the causal explanation of these four evaluative passions in a way that distinguishes them from desire-like sentiments, Hume demystifies one kind of evaluation; explaining moral sentiments in a similar way demystifies another kind.

According to Hume, in nearly all cases the moral sentiments arise as a result of the working of sympathy which is adjusted by imagining oneself to occupy a common point of view. Moral approval and disapproval are triggered by reflection on or "survey" of someone's quality of mind, action, or "character." Approval is a kind of pleasure, or a feeling with a pleasant hedonic tone, and disapproval an uneasy feeling. But how does contemplation of a trait or person generate pleasure or uneasiness? That trait or person is beneficial or agreeable to particular individuals or to society as a whole, and sympathy "takes us so far out of ourselves, as to give us the same pleasure or uneasiness in characters which are useful or pernicious to society, as if they had a tendency to our own advantage or loss" (T. 3.3.1.11). (This is what he says about the artificial virtues; contemplation of the natural virtues and vices gives us the pleasure or uneasiness in characters that is felt by those individuals who have direct interactions with the person judged – call them that person's *associates* – rather than all of society.) Sympathy is a psychological mechanism whereby the feelings of one person are communicated to another, so that the observer comes to feel the same feelings or types of feelings as the person she surveys. In the generation of moral approval or disapproval of a person or his trait, we sympathize with those on whom he or his trait has its impact, coming to feel their pleasure or uneasiness; and this feeling, adjusted by adopting the common point of view, becomes the moral approval or disapproval of him or his trait.

Here we find an interesting gap in Hume's account of the generation of moral sentiments. I can sympathize with a poor man who struggles to survive – I can share in his suffering – without making any moral evaluation. (My sympathetic uneasiness, under the right circumstances, will lead me to feel pity or compassion for the poor man, a feeling that closely resembles benevolence and leads to love, but that in itself is not a moral sentiment [see T 2.2.7; DP, pp. 160–1].) But if I learn that he suffers as he does because of the choices and attitudes of a grasping, insensitive sweatshop owner, then I experience moral disapproval – of her. My sympathetically derived uneasiness is the same: an idea of his distress enlivened to become my own distress, whether his suffering is caused by some natural disaster or by the owner's character. But in the former case my feeling is not a moral evaluation while in the latter it is or becomes one, and in the former case my feeling does not have the sweatshop owner as its intentional object while in the latter it does. Somehow this uneasy feeling is redirected or transformed into moral disapprobation *of* the sweatshop owner, a different person entirely from the one with whom I sympathize. Hume does not offer any explanation of how this occurs. This is a significant gap in his otherwise meticulous explanation of the generation of the moral sentiments.

This redirection occurs whenever we feel the moral sentiments. The intentional object of moral approval is the character thought to be good or bad, not the people affected by that character. Yet sympathy produces in us only the pleasure or pain of those beneficiaries or victims. This transition from sympathy to evaluation of character goes unexplained. Hume does identify a number of conditions that must be met if a genuinely moral sentiment is to be felt. In making moral evaluations we (as observers) disregard our own advantage, and we reflect on the person's character from the common point of view, which means that we imagine and sympathize with the impact of a character on those beneficiaries or victims most directly affected by it (its possessor's associates, for the natural virtues and vices, and all members of society, for artificial virtues and vices such as justice and injustice). It also means that we sympathize with the *usual* impact of such a trait rather than the anomalous effect it may happen to have on a given occasion (T 3.3.1.15–17; T 3.3.1.20). All of these constraints on the formation of the moral sentiments, though, are constraints on our sympathy with the victims or beneficiaries of the character under evaluation. They do not explain how this sympathetic pleasure or pain comes to have the *possessor* of the character as its intentional object.

The gap is concealed in certain kinds of cases. Hume thinks we approve of traits that are either advantageous or immediately agreeable to the person who possesses them or to others (T 3.3.1.30; EPM 9.1). For certain virtues, such as frugality and cheerfulness, which are (respectively) advantageous and immediately agreeable to their possessor, the person we evaluate happens to be the same as the beneficiary of the trait. I receive via sympathy the pleasure a man gains from the financial security afforded by his frugality, for example; this pleasure, adjusted from the common point of view, becomes or gives rise to my approval of the man's character. My attention is on him all along, so it is hard to see that there has been any shift in attention. In fact there has been, for I first think of him as a beneficiary of the trait, but rather than merely rejoicing with him in his benefits, I approve the trait and perhaps approve him insofar as he has it. But since the same person is involved it is difficult to see the shift. However, it is obvious in cases where the trait is beneficial or agreeable to others. A woman's honesty contributes to the wellbeing of society as a whole but may not profit her – suppose it does not. By means of sympathy I share in the general pleasure of secure ownership to which her trait contributes (as I perceive it from the common point of view), but I do not merely enjoy the pleasure of her fellow citizens; as a result of sympathetically acquiring their pleasure, I approve her character. Their pleasure, transferred to me, becomes my approval of her. There the shift of focus is evident. It may be less obvious in another kind of case as well, where the sweatshop worker hates the owner and we also acquire that hatred by sympathy, for that hatred is already directed at the owner and so draws our attention to her. But the worker might not know that the owner or anyone is responsible for his suffering, and so might have no owner-directed sentiment with which we could sympathize; yet according to Hume's account, if we observers know the owner is the cause of the worker's suffering, that gives us what we need for moral disapproval of her. Here the shift of focus (from the worker's or observer's suffering to the owner) is again made plain.

Hume does say quite explicitly that moral approval and disapproval will result from sympathy with a victim or beneficiary of an *action* only if the action arises from some enduring feature of its agent, and not if it is inadvertent or "casual" (T 2.3.2.6; T 3.2.1.2–3).[16] So in order to disapprove of the sweatshop owner for her treatment of the worker I must associate that behavior with a durable feature of the owner, so that my thought can be directed to my idea of *her*. This obviously parallels Hume's remarks about love and hatred arising only from a person's enduring features. In that case, only such features are sufficiently related to the person to engender love or hatred; and similarly, unless enduring features enable us to associate actions closely with the persisting agent, they "infix not themselves upon him" (T 2.3.2.6) and cannot give rise to a moral evaluation of him. This shows that experiencing a moral sentiment, like experiencing an indirect passion, requires a shift of attention that depends upon a marked association with a person.

Indeed, we can see now that the moral sentiments resemble the four principal indirect passions in being indirect in just the same ways. First, they take as their intentional object something distinct from their cause. What causes me to approve Mother Theresa's character is the feelings of relief and joy experienced by the poor of Calcutta as a result of her compassion, transmitted to me via corrected sympathy; but the intentional object of my feeling of approval is not the poor of Calcutta or their feelings, but Mother Theresa's character. Because this particular human being is associated in my mind with the reactions of the poor by the relation of cause and effect, the sentiment I feel is re-oriented or perhaps transformed in such a way that it directs my attention to Mother Theresa. The moral sentiment is thus an impression "plac'd betwixt two ideas, of which the one produces it, and the other is produc'd by it," just as Hume says of pride and humility. The feeling of approval is caused by the feelings (or idea-copies of the feelings) I receive from the poor, and calls up the idea of Mother Theresa. Second, the moral sentiments are not desire-like: they do not pursue pleasure or pain-avoidance for the person who feels them nor turn her attention to her own prospective pleasure or pain. They are psychological states with a different kind of intentional object from that of direct passions such as desires and aversions: they fix upon and rest with the person evaluated. This makes it possible for the moral sentiment to be a feeling of assessment that in the relevant way "takes us out of ourselves."

In fact, the moral sentiments are indirect in an even more pronounced fashion than the four main indirect passions. Where love, for example, is caused in me by some pleasing trait or possession of another person but is redirected onto that very person who possesses it, moral approval is caused by a pleasure I get from sympathizing with one person but very often is redirected onto some other person whose character caused the pleasure. As we have seen, sometimes we morally approve a trait useful or agreeable to its possessor, so the beneficiary and the evaluated person are the same, but often they are distinct. Thus while pride typically involves one person (oneself), and love typically involves two people (the lover and the beloved), moral approval in many cases requires three: the observer, the person whose trait is evaluated, and the beneficiary of that trait. Not only is the observer's attitude to the evaluated person caused indirectly by some independent pleasure (as are pride and love), but that pleasure is the pleasure of a different individual both from the observer who feels the resulting sentiment and from the one who is its object. Now this phenomenon also occurs in love sometimes: A can love B because of the pleasure B causes to C, which A acquires by means of sympathy with C. In fact, pride can involve two people if the independent pleasure I get, e.g. from my beautiful clothes, comes to me from sympathy with the enjoyment of another, so I am proud of the clothes because of the pleasure they give him. So pride can involve two and love can involve three. But nearly *all* instances of the moral sentiments are produced by sympathy, so they involve this sort of indirection in its fullest form. This makes the moral sentiments indirect emotions *par excellence*.

Granted, Hume does not explicitly invoke the double relation of impressions and ideas in order to explain the causation of the moral sentiments.[17] This leads some to think the moral sentiments are not indirect. But in fact that explanation would fit fairly smoothly into his account of the generation of moral sentiments. Here is one way it might work. Sympathy brings to the observer the suffering of the sweatshop worker; this is the independent uneasiness needed for the double relation. The idea of that uneasiness is associated with the greedy, insensitive character of the sweatshop owner by the relation of cause and effect, one of the relations of ideas. The observer's sympathetic feeling of uneasiness resembles the feeling of moral disapproval in being unpleasant; that provides the relation of impressions. These two relations facilitate the conversion of the first feeling into the second. Somewhere in this process (perhaps after she has noticed the connection to the sweatshop owner) the observer imagines herself to occupy the common point of view and her sympathy is thereby adjusted.

Thus the parallels between the moral sentiments and the indirect passions are very striking. As a result, the indirect passions provide a framework for Hume's genetic account of moral approval and disapproval. We have seen how the four principal indirect passions are ways of valuing and disvaluing persons, ways separable from the valuer's expectation of pleasure or pain for herself and so distinct from wanting. This permits a departure from what would otherwise be a rather Hobbesian, mechanistic hedonism about the emotions in Hume. He explains quite unedifying evaluations (such as our admiration for the rich and handsome and contempt for the poor and ugly) in the same way he accounts for more inspiring evaluations such as our admiration of great geniuses: in quasi-Newtonian terms, identifying these passions' efficient causes and showing how they arise in regular patterns from the associations of ideas and impressions, without appeal to any independent standard of human goodness or evil, without any appeal to the purpose of these emotions or their inherent suitability to the proper sorts of objects (McIntyre 2006: 210) – and yet without assimilating them to desires. Once he has done that, he can then ease into explaining, with different details, the efficient causes of the moral sentiments, which are another way of valuing, one similar in all these respects to the valuing that constitutes love and hatred, pride and humility.

One may doubt that the parallel between the main indirect passions and the moral sentiment is as close as I propose, because the main indirect passions all take the person as their intentional object, while the moral sentiments do not always do so, but more frequently and characteristically focus on particular traits (a point raised in a slightly different context by Baier 1991: 134, 308, n. 10, and Ainslie 2000: 475–6). On Hume's view it is normal and appropriate to assess some people as of mixed character, approving some of their traits and disapproving others, and he does this himself in many places. Thus I might approve someone's honesty but disapprove his cowardice, for example; and doing this I need not approve or disapprove him as a whole.

There is probably some difference here, but in fact the objects of those passions are more alike than they seem so far. In approving a single trait I do not think of how I can profit from it, and my attention is not (or certainly need not be) on my own pleasure or pain. So even a moral sentiment that takes a single trait as its object is not desire-like. It is not like the student's appreciation of her professor's leniency. But furthermore, there is a way in which all moral judgments of virtues and vices take the whole person as their object, in that they direct our attention to the person – even judgments about individual traits. In making a moral assessment of a trait, I judge what *kind* of person someone is. The assessment need not be of his entire character, but it is nonetheless always an assessment of him. If I judge a public official to be corrupt, I evaluate *him*. Although this need not be an assessment of him as a bad man over all, it is a judgment of what he is: he is dishonest. If I also judge him to be courageous and kind (and someone might have all three traits, on Hume's view), there too I evaluate him. That is the kind of man he is: dishonest, but brave and kind. This is very like the way the main indirect passions direct our attention to the person, thought of as having a particular trait or possession. I love my friend insofar as he is witty, and I am proud of myself as an elegant dresser. (For a related point see Korsgaard 1999.)

Coda: classifying the moral sentiments

There is a recent debate about where the moral sentiments fit in Hume's taxonomy of the passions. Are they direct passions, indirect passions, or neither? Without stopping to examine the arguments for the existing interpretations, we can briefly see what our argument shows about that issue. We can conclude (in opposition to Kemp Smith 1941/1964: 166–8, and Hearn 1973) that the moral sentiments are not direct passions, for they have the very features that make Hume's four principal indirect passions indirect. Árdal argues that the moral sentiments are specialized forms of pride, humility, love, and hatred, in particular versions of those that are of a generally calm character and are elicited by the contemplation (from the common point of view) of qualities of mind (1977; 1966/1989); and many have agreed (including Penelhum 1993 and Korsgaard 1999). This view does not follow from what we have said here, although it is compatible with it. All that follows is that the moral sentiments are indirect, and not only could there be other indirect passions besides those four with which they might be identified, but there could be indirect secondary impressions not even classified as passions. While some passages strongly support Árdal's view, many passages and other considerations tell heavily against it.[18]

I do not see any way to settle conclusively from the text the precise classification of the moral sentiments (though I do not argue for this textual indeterminacy here). What we can conclude, though, is that the moral sentiments are indirect secondary impressions. As evaluative feelings that can take persons as their intentional objects, and as emotions that "take us out of ourselves" and direct us away from the pursuit and avoidance of our own pleasure and pain, they closely resemble the indirect passions and differ importantly from the direct ones. And in explaining the production and features of the principal indirect passions, Hume shows that one kind of valuing can be explained empirically and naturalistically without too much distortion and without assimilating it to wanting, which leads the way to his similar explanation of moral valuing. It is not just moral emotions but also many other feelings that are not species of desire or aversion, so the moral sentiments are not *sui generis*. Thus there

179

is no whiff of *deus ex machina* about their production; they are one sort of sentiment among many that have this feature. On Hume's view our moral judgments are based on feelings that are not like desires, but there is nothing Platonic or supernatural about that.

See also 10 "Hume on the Direct Passions and Motivation"; 12 "Hume on Moral Rationalism, Sentimentalism, and Sympathy"; 13 "Sympathy and Hume's Spectator-centered Theory of Virtue"

Acknowledgment

I am grateful to Charlotte Brown, Donald Ainslie, and David Owen for indispensable comments on earlier drafts of this paper, and to Bradley Armour-Garb and Corliss Gayda Swain for very helpful discussions.

Notes

1   Hume's predecessors have varied aims in analyzing the passions: dualists such as Descartes seek to explain mind–body interaction, materialists such as Hobbes seek a mechanistic account both of experienced feelings and of deliberation and action, and philosophers of different persuasions pursue other goals such as founding their ethical theories or recommending a strategy to attain human happiness. Their lists of basic and derivative passions differ as well. See for example Fieser (1992), Schmitter (2006) for overviews.

2   Hobbes and Spinoza also eschew final causes in explaining the passions, but we cannot assume that they and Hume all do so for the same reasons.

3   Hobbes, for example, begins his discussion of the passions in *Human Nature* with what Hume would call pride and humility. But they are just items in a list that includes indignation, emulation, revengefulness, hope, lust, and love – which for Hume would cross categorial lines.

4   Two examples: his use of his position on the influencing motives of the will in Book 2 to argue in Book 3 that morals are not derived from reason, and (less often noticed) his analysis of the natural virtues of greatness and goodness as forms of the passions of pride and love.

5   Hume says both that love and hatred are always directed to persons (T 2.2.1.2–3) and that animals feel them toward other animals (T 2.2.12.3–4). So either he thinks animals are persons or he is inconsistent on this point.

6   Of course original impressions also bear resemblance relations to one another: (an impression of) a red fire truck resembles (an impression of) a red apple. But Hume does not claim that as a result of this resemblance, when we see a red fire truck we then immediately *see* – have an impression of – a red apple. This kind of association, where an *impression* is called into being by its related impression, occurs only among the secondary impressions. The main sort of resemblance that has this effect is resemblance in hedonic tone, but in T 2.2.9 and DP, p. 160, Hume also talks about passions calling forth other passions because of a resemblance in their direction.

7   These qualifications are needed because otherwise the account is vulnerable to many objections. Just one example: if a complete stranger who (I know) resembles me in being fair-skinned and unathletic writes a novel I have greatly enjoyed reading, on the initial account I would (in virtue of that resemblance) feel pride as a result of her accomplishment, which

180

is absurd. Her accomplishment is sufficiently related to me to produce joy (in the reading of the book), but since it is far more closely related to her than to me, and its connection with me (unlike that with her) is of short duration, it is not sufficiently associated with myself to produce pride, but rather is likely to produce a form of love for her.

8   I do not assume that for Hume, in order for passions to have intentional objects they must themselves contain within them representations of the things toward which they are directed. That hypothesis is in tension with other things he says, including T 2.1.2.4, in which he treats the passion's object (the idea of the self in this case) as something distinct from the passion and caused by it, not a part of it. Some present-day philosophers think directedness toward the self is a necessary, not a contingent, feature of pride. Were Hume to take this on board (as he might), it would not require him to suppose that pride is a compound impression or composite of impressions and ideas; instead, having a certain cause or effect might be necessary if a passion is to be identified as pride. On this see Davidson (1975) and Radcliffe (2006). Baier (1991: ch. 7) seems implicitly committed to the internal-representation view, and Weller (2002) argues for it. For arguments for a non-representational view of the passions on which passions nonetheless have intentional objects (understood causally), see Árdal (1966/1989), Cohon (1994), and Radcliffe (2007). Nothing in this chapter turns on which interpretation one adopts, but I write as if the causal account of intentionality rather than the internal-representation account is correct. Readers who disagree should be able to reword certain phrases to suit their interpretation without altering my argument. Baier (1991: 163–4) and Penelhum (1993: 128) think Hume (unwisely) denies at T 2.3.3.5 that passions have any intentional objects at all; I do not think he does.

9   Some argue that on Hume's view the passions of pride, humility, love, and hatred do not merely call up an already existing idea of the self or another person but actually create or form a part of a new idea of the self or the other (Rorty 1990; McIntyre 1990; Ainslie 2000). I take no position on this interpretive issue here; either stance is compatible with my point that the indirect passions involve a shift in attention or focus.

10 Sometimes Hume seems to write as though the object of pride is simply *the self*. This does not ring true; pride is pride in something and so directs attention not only to the self but also to that of which one is proud. But at other times he writes as if the object of pride is the self characterized or qualified in a certain way, for example the self-as-snappy-dresser, which is more plausible.

11 Hume seems to use "esteem" and "contempt" as synonyms for "love" and "hatred" throughout T 2.2.1 and a bit later calls them species of love and hatred (T 2.2.5.1), though later still he analyzes "contempt" as a mixture of hatred and pride, and treats "esteem" as a synonym for "respect," which he analyzes as a mixture of love and humility (T 2.2.10). In Book 3 Hume sometimes seems to use "esteem" as a name for the moral sentiment, approbation (e.g. at T 3.1.2.2).

12 It is an entirely different question whether love of other people is properly analyzed as a feeling at all, rather than some other state of a person among whose features is a disposition to have characteristic feelings. I do not address this important issue here, since Hume, rightly or wrongly, clearly thinks the love in which he is interested is a feeling with a pleasant hedonic tone. (The same issue may be raised about pride.)

13 He also invokes pity and malice, which mimic benevolence and anger closely but without the tie to love and hatred; however, pity and malice are explained by means of sympathy and comparison, and while Hume's position on this is not entirely clear, there are strong hints that as motives they function in an egoistic, hedonistic fashion. E.g., "malice is the unprovok'd desire of producing evil to another, in order to reap a pleasure from the comparison" (T. 2.2.8.12).

14   There is a place where Hume seems to waver about whether benevolence and anger are truly "unaccountable" and "produce good and evil, and proceed not from them, like the other affections" (T 2.3.9.8). He says that "benevolence is an original pleasure arising from the pleasure of the person belov'd, and a pain proceeding from his pain: From which correspondence of impressions there arises a subsequent desire of his pleasure, and aversion to his pain" (T 2.2.9.15). This looks like a use of sympathy and desire to provide a causal explanation of benevolence. However, he does not come out and say (as he does about malice) that in benevolence our "subsequent desire of his pleasure" is or comes from a desire to get more sympathetic pleasure *for ourselves*.

15   He may, of course, be quite wrong about what desires are; Lewis and the others would not agree.

16   By "casual" Hume means, I think, *accidental*. See *The Oxford English Dictionary*, "casual," 1a. This meaning remains today in very few contexts; one of them is "casualty insurance."

17   If he takes the moral sentiments to be species of the four main indirect passions (as claimed by Árdal 1966/1989, 1977, and some other interpreters), then he has no need to explain that they are generated in this way, as he has already done it. But in case the moral sentiments are not species of the four main indirect passions, we should consider whether they could be generated by the double relation.

18   The strongest support for Árdal's view comes in T. 3.3.1.3, 3.3.1.4, and 3.3.5.1, all quoted by him (1966/1989: ch. 6). However, some crucial passages (T 2.1.7.5, 3.1.2.4, and DP, p. 139) are incompatible with that view because they indicate that the four main indirect passions typically accompany the moral sentiments but are distinct from and caused by them (Ainslie 1999: 474–5). Indeed, in the right context the moral sentiments provide the independent pleasure or pain that is needed to generate pride, humility, love, or hatred. Another problem with that view is that Hume never calls the moral sentiments "passions," and (as Loeb argues, 1977) the division of the subject he makes at 2.1.1.3 strongly suggests that the distinction between direct and indirect passions is not exhaustive of the secondary impressions and that the moral sentiments belong outside it entirely. Thus perhaps the moral sentiments are not passions at all and not explained in Book 2 or the *Dissertation*. But this interpretation also faces contrary textual evidence: apparently Hume does not adhere to the plan to limit Book 2 and the *Dissertation* to passions properly so-called, i.e. the violent affections (T 2.3.3.8–10; T 2.3.4.1), and so perhaps the division into direct and indirect is exhaustive after all and would need to include the moral sentiments. Furthermore, if the moral sentiment is not a passion (because, according to this interpretation, only violent affections are passions), it is difficult (even more difficult than it otherwise would be) to explain how "morals" influence the *passions*, as Hume famously says they do (T 3.1.1). Charlotte Brown (1994: 33, n. 7), suggests that the issue cannot be resolved on textual grounds alone.

References

Ainslie, Donald C. (1999). "Scepticism about Persons in Book II of Hume's *Treatise*," *Journal of the History of Philosophy*, 37, pp. 469–92.

Árdal, Páll S. (1977). "Another Look at Hume's Account of Moral Evaluation," *Journal of the History of Philosophy*, 15, pp. 405–21.

—— (1966/1989). *Passion and Value in Hume's "Treatise,"* 2nd edn., revd. (Edinburgh: Edinburgh University Press).

Baier, Annette (1991). *A Progress of Sentiments: Reflections on Hume's "Treatise"* (Cambridge, MA: Harvard University Press).

Bricke, John (1996). *Mind and Morality: An Examination of Hume's Moral Psychology* (Oxford: Clarendon Press).

Brown, Charlotte (1994). "From Spectator to Agent: Hume's Theory of Obligation," *Hume Studies*, 22, pp. 19–35.

Clarke, Samuel (1705). *A Discourse concerning the unchangeable obligations of natural religion, and the truth and certainty of the Christian revelation* (The Boyle Lectures), excerpted in D. D. Raphael (ed.), *British Moralists 1650–1800*, vol. 1 (Indianapolis: Hackett Publishing Co., 1991).

Cohon, Rachel (1994). "On an Unorthodox Account of Hume's Moral Psychology," *Hume Studies*, 20, pp. 179–94.

Crane, Tim (1998). "Intentionality," in E. Craig (ed.), *Routledge Encyclopedia of Philosophy* (London: Routledge), retrieved June 20, 2007, from http://www.rep.routledge.com/article/V019SECT2.

Davidson, Donald (1976). "Hume's Cognitive Theory of Pride," *Journal of Philosophy*, 73, pp. 744–56.

Fieser, James (1992). "Hume's Classification of the Passions and Its Precursors," *Hume Studies*, 18(1), pp. 1–17.

Frankfurt, Harry G. (1971). "Freedom of the Will and the Concept of a Person," *Journal of Philosophy*, 68, pp. 5–20.

Hearn, Thomas K., Jr. (1973). "Árdal on the Moral Sentiments in Hume's *Treatise*," *Philosophy*, 48, pp. 288–92.

Hobbes, Thomas (1650). *Human Nature*, excerpted in D. D. Raphael (ed.), *British Moralists 1650–1800*, vol. 1 (Indianapolis: Hackett Publishing Co., 1991).

—— (1651). *Leviathan*, ed. Richard Tuck (Cambridge: Cambridge University Press, 1996, rpt. 1999).

Hume, David (1757). *Dissertation on the Passions*, in *Four Dissertations and Essays on Suicide and the Immortality of the Soul* (South Bend, IN: St. Augustine's Press, 1992, 1995). (Citations are indicated in the text in parentheses by DP followed by a facsimile page number.)

—— (1741–77). *Essays Moral, Political and Literary*, ed. Eugene F. Miller (Indianapolis, IN: Liberty Fund, 1987). (Citations appear as "*Essays*" followed by a page number.)

Hutcheson, Francis (1725). *An Enquiry concerning the original of our ideas of virtue or moral good* (rpt. from 4th edn., 1738), in R. S. Downie (ed.), *Philosophical Writings*, Everyman Library (London: Orion Publishing Group; Rutland, VT: Charles E. Tuttle Co., Inc., 1994).

Kemp Smith, Norman (1941). *The Philosophy of David Hume* (London: Macmillan & Co., rpt. 1964).

Korsgaard, Christine M. (1999). "The General Point of View: Love and Moral Approval in Hume's Ethics," *Hume Studies*, 25 (April/Nov.), pp. 3–41.

Lewis, David (1989). "Dispositional Theories of Value," *Aristotelian Society Supplement*, 63, pp. 113–37.

Loeb, Louis E. (1977). "Hume's Moral Sentiments and the Structure of the *Treatise*," *Journal of the History of Philosophy*, 15, pp. 395–403.

Lovelace, Richard (1649). *Lucasta: On Going to Wars* (Scholar Press, Facs edn., 1972).

McIntyre, Jane L. (1990). "Character: A Humean account," *History of Philosophy Quarterly*, 7, pp. 193–206.

—— (2006). "Hume's 'New and Extraordinary' Account of the Passions," in Saul Traiger (ed.), *The Blackwell Guide to Hume's "Treatise"* (Malden, MA: Blackwell), pp. 199–215.

Penelhum, Terence (1993). "Hume's Moral Psychology," in David Fate Norton (ed.), *The Cambridge Companion to Hume* (Cambridge: Cambridge University Press), pp. 117–47.

Radcliffe, Elizabeth S. (2006). "Moral Internalism and Moral Cognitivism in Hume's Metaethics," *Synthese*, 152, pp. 353–70.

—— (2007). "Representation and Motivation: Hume and His Predecessors," presented at New Philosophical Perspectives on Hume Conference, University of San Francisco, San Francisco, CA.

Rorty, Amelie O. (1990). "Pride Produces the Idea of the Self: Hume on Moral Agency," *Australasian Journal of Philosophy*, 68, pp. 255–69.

Schmitter, Amy (2006). "17th and 18th Century Theories of Emotions," in Edward N. Zalta (ed.), *Stanford Encyclopedia of Philosophy* (summer 2006 edn.), http://plato.stanford.edu/archives/sum2006/entries/emotions-17th18th/.

Spinoza, Baruch (1677). "Ethics," in *Ethics, Treatise on the Emendation of the Intellect, and Selected Letters* (Indianapolis: Hackett, 1992).

Weller, Cass (2002). "The Myth of Original Existence," *Hume Studies*, 28, pp. 195–230.

Yeats, William Butler (1930). "For Anne Gregory," in Oscar Williams (ed.), *The Mentor Book of Major British Poets* (New York: New American Library, 1963).

Further Reading

Alanen, Lilli (2006). "The Powers and Mechanisms of the Passions," in Saul Traiger (ed.), *The Blackwell Guide to Hume's "Treatise"* (Malden, MA: Blackwell), pp. 179–98.

Baier, Annette C. (1978). "Hume's Analysis of Pride," *Journal of Philosophy*, 75, pp. 27–40.

Brown, Charlotte (1988). "Is Hume an Internalist?" *Journal of the History of Philosophy*, 26, pp. 69–87.

Capaldi, Nicholas (1989). *Hume's Place in Moral Philosophy* (New York: Peter Lang).

Descartes, René (1649). *The Passions of the Soul*, trans. Robert Stoothoff, in *The Philosophical Writings of Descartes*, vol. 1, trans. J. Cottingham, R. Stoothoff, and D. Murdoch (New York: Cambridge University Press, 1985).

Gardiner, P. L. (1963). "Hume's Theory of the Passions," in D. F. Pears (ed.), *David Hume: A Symposium* (London: Macmillan), pp. 31–42.

Inoue, Haruko (2003). "The Origin of the Indirect Passions in the *Treatise*: An Analogy between Books 1 and 2," *Hume Studies*, 29 (Nov.), pp. 205–21.

Lecaldano, Eugenio (2002). "The Passions, Character, and the Self in Hume," *Hume Studies*, 28, pp. 175–93.

McIntyre, Jane L. (1989). "Personal Identity and the Passions," *Journal of the History of Philosophy*, 27, pp. 545–57.

—— (2000). "Hume's Passions: Direct and Indirect," *Hume Studies*, 26, pp. 77–86.

Purviance, Susan M. (1997). "The Moral Self and the Indirect Passions," *Hume Studies*, 23, pp. 195–212.

Radcliffe, Elizabeth S. (2004). "Love and Benevolence in Hutcheson's and Hume's Theories of the Passions," *British Journal for the History of Philosophy*, 12, pp. 631–53.

10

Hume on the Direct Passions and Motivation

TITO MAGRI

Hume proposes a powerful and, on the face of it, remarkably simple view of motivation. Its principal goal, and the respect under which it most differs from other theories, is to advance an understanding of motivation in *non-cognitive* terms. As I suggest at the start, motivation consists in mental states, the direct passions (centrally, desire and aversion), that have no representational character and do not, in general, aim to agreement with matters of fact. The motivational import of direct passions derives from their being feelings, or experiential qualities, with causal connections to action. The crucial role, in the explanation of motivational states (as I point out below), is played by the (quite complex) relationship between impressions of pleasure and desires. A major problem Hume and his interpreters have to face is whether, and how, this conception of motivation can still warrant the common sense view of conduct and of agency that Hume himself seems to share. Hume is prepared to acknowledge (as I discuss later) that we will and intend to act; that some beliefs are motivating; that agents have some control on their conduct; that they can grasp, compare, and choose real, intrinsic values; and that there is something like rationality in action. But he is also keenly aware that these facts seem to be inconsistent with the principles about motivation he accepts as true. I think that Hume eventually manages to attenuate the appearance of inconsistency. But, in order to do this, he has to revise and weaken his original commitments to motivational non-cognitivism and hedonism. I suggest below that the core of a revised Humean theory of motivation consists in the idea of natural dispositions to desire, that this theory includes an account of the (ostensible) practical import of reason, and that Hume is even prepared to call in question the identification of motivation with a certain kind of passions. But it is fair to say that he did not fully explore the potentialities of his alternative view of motivation.

Direct Passions

"By direct passions I understand such as arise immediately from good or evil, from pain or pleasure. By indirect such as proceed from the same principles, but by the conjunction of other qualities" (T 2.1.1.4). According to the most prominent line of thought in the *Treatise*, thus, mental states like desire, aversion, grief, joy, hope, fear, despair, and security, are distinguished from other kinds of passions by their being caused "most naturally, and with the least preparation" by the impressions of pleasure and pain (T 2.3.9.2). The direct passions motivate in that they cause agents to act. To understand Hume's theory of motivation, therefore, we must begin by specifying the nature of direct passions as mental causes.

Direct passions as mental states

As mental episodes, passions are secondary impressions, or impressions of reflection, as distinct from original impressions, or impressions of sensation. Impressions of reflection "proceed from some of these original ones, either immediately or by interpositions of its idea" (T 2.1.1.1). The relevant original impressions that are the common root of all sorts of passions, either direct or indirect, are pleasure and pain (T 2.3.9.1). It is fair to assume that in the case of direct passions, the interposition of ideas will be minimal, in contrast to the complex structure of an indirect passion like pride. The direct passions seem to consist just in the return "upon the soul" of the pleasant or unpleasant sensations, in the mind paying protracted attention to them, so that it can respond with the new impressions of desire and aversion (T 1.1.2.1).

As perceptions belonging to the category of impressions, direct passions have two principal features. They occur in the mind as episodes of *feeling*, rather than of thought. And they occur with a certain *causal character* that Hume loosely characterizes in terms of firmness and solidity, force and influence, intensity and weight (T App. 3). (The two features are connected, since the feeling of an impression has influence on cognition and action.) The nature of this causal character is different for the different sorts of impressions. Impressions of sensation impose certain objects on the mind and make it conceive them as real. Indirect passions influence the mind from the inside, as sentiments felt in response to objects under certain descriptions. Direct passions (and they only) have motivational force. They only can impart to the mind a first impulse to internal or external action. This unique causal character might be connected to a further, distinctive mental feature of direct passions. Direct passions neither present objects in experience (like impressions of sensation) nor represent objects (like ideas). As reflective impressions, they are related to objects that impress us as pleasant or painful. They can also be influenced by the representation of what actions are possible for us. But, in themselves, they are only primitive, blank impulses to pursue or avoid such objects, that is, "propense or averse motions of the mind" (T 3.3.1.2). The suggested connection might be that, as mental states that are utterly without representational content, direct passions have only a *dynamic* causal character. In this regard, direct passions are different from the indirect ones. These latter are, in part, individuated by their objects falling under certain descriptions. That is, they are partly individuated by properties and relations of objects, which also makes a difference to their representational quality. For instance, the object of pride is necessarily the self, and this is certainly a representational feature. Pride requires that certain relations, like ownership, hold between the self and certain objects, and this is, again, something that comes to be represented in or about them. Direct passions, by contrast with indirect ones, lack any such cognitive architecture, they follow on the experience of pleasure and pain as such.

186

The thesis of non-cognitivism can be sharpened. Hume is explicit that direct passions are utterly *non-representational*, have neither reference nor truth-value. "Our passions, volitions, and actions" are not susceptible of "truth or falsehood," that is, of "agreement or disagreement either to the *real* relations of ideas, or to *real* existence and matter of fact." They are "original facts and realities, compleat in themselves, and implying no reference to other passions, volitions, and action" (T 3.1.1.9). A direct passion does not contain "any representative quality, which renders it a copy of any other existence or modification." In general, they have "no more a reference to any other object, than when I am thirsty, or sick, or more than five foot high" (T 2.3.3.5). Lack of reference and truth-value, strictly, differentiates direct passions only from ideas (which are representational). But a closely related point can be made in relation to impressions of sensation. Such impressions are, as mental episodes, "original facts and realities" that do not represent anything. But unlike direct passions, they are not blank and empty, but rather count as contents and have structure, possibly even of a judgment-like sort. Impressions of sensation figure into relations of representation, although as contents that are represented, and not as what represents a content.

Direct passions, while non-representational, might however still be, in a broader sense, *cognitive*. A model for this possibility is given by Hume's theory of belief. Belief, as an attitude, is not representational (not consisting in an impression of sensation nor in an idea) but does modify our overall view of the world. The analogy between the attitude of belief and the attitude of desire, however, fails in a way that is crucial for deciding cognitive import. In his agonizing revision of the theory of belief, in the Appendix to the *Treatise*, Hume points out that beliefs, as "conceptions," are similar (in terms of firmness and solidity, force and influence on the mind) to impressions "which are immediately present to us." He must have in mind impressions of sensation, because he then considers, as an alternative, the possibility that "belief, besides the simple conception, consists in some impression or feeling, distinguishable from the conception." On this alternative understanding, the impression of belief "does not modify the conception, and render it more present and intense: It is only annex'd to it, after the same manner that *will* and *desire* are annex'd to particular conceptions of good and pleasure." But Hume *rejects* this view of belief. On Hume's considered view, believed ideas "take faster hold of my mind," are "different to feeling." But "there is no distinct or separate impression attending them." Belief is an "operation" that is "performed by the thought or imagination alone"; it involves "no act of the mind, distinct from the peculiarity of conception" (T App. 3–4).

The attitude of belief, therefore, does not count as representational, since it does not determine reference or truth-conditions (this is exclusively the role of impressions and ideas of sensation). But it can be regarded as broadly cognitive. Firstly, being only a "peculiarity of conception," it does not add to or subtract from representational content. To have a belief is to conceive of ideas in a way that preserves, and responds to, what they refer to and their truth-conditions. Such a mode of conception can well be considered as cognitive, since it ultimately aims at agreement with matters of fact. Of course, there is more to belief than having a representation. But, secondly, the "operation" of belief on ideas (like the "operation" of sense impressions) consists in making us take, or feel, represented contents as present, or real. This sort of feeling certainly affects our cognitive purchase on the world, our view of reality.

187

The attitude of desire, by contrast, does not consist in a peculiarity of the conception of representational content. Rather, it is annexed to impressions or ideas as a separate act of the mind. Therefore, the resulting state (composed of attitude and content) does not respond to reference and truth, nor does it aim at agreement with facts. Furthermore, desire is only annexed to good or pleasant objects, and, while having, as an attitude, robust experiential qualities, and a strong influence, is similar neither in feeling, nor in causal character, with impressions of sensation. Desire does not make us take (as belief does) objects as real, but *moves* us toward them. It does not relate (as belief does) to properties represented in objects, but to the pleasure objects cause us to feel. On both accounts, desire is different from belief, in the way a non-cognitive attitude can be different from a cognitive one. Therefore, direct passions are not only non-representational, but also non-cognitive. Radical non-cognitivism is the fundamental thesis about motivation that Hume advances in the *Treatise*.

The will

Given this non-cognitive approach to motivation, and the prominence of feeling and causal powers, the notion of the will may appear out of place. Hume is of a divided mind whether to count volition, or the will, as one of the direct passions (compare the list of the direct passions at T 2.1.1.4 with that at T 2.3.9.2). His considered view seems to be that the will is the most "remarkable" among the "immediate effects of pain and pleasure," and that, while, "properly speaking," it is not "comprehended among the passions" (we will see presently in what sense), an explanation of them requires the "full understanding of its nature and properties" (T 2.3.1.2). He finds it natural to employ phrases like "the will and passions" (T 2.3.7.8), "the impressions of volition and desire," or "desire and volition" (T 2.3.9.4). And to define the will as a motivational mental episode:

> By the *will*, I mean nothing but *the internal impression we feel and are conscious of, when we knowingly give rise to any new motion of our body, or new perception of our mind.* (T 2.3.1.2)

The will has a distinctive experiential quality and causal powers. The causal role of the will is prominent in Hume's discussion of liberty and necessity. By clarifying it, we can also understand why Hume hesitates to classify the will as a direct passion. The will has, as its object, the choice and the performance of actions. Actions are particulars: "Each action is a particular event" which "must proceed from particular principles, and from our immediate situation within ourselves, and with respect to the rest of universe" (T 3.2.6.9). The will is, thus, radically different from the understanding, which has, "as its proper province," "the world of ideas," while the will "always places us in that of reality" (T 2.3.3.2). But in this respect, the will is also different from the generality of direct passions. "DESIRE arises from good consider'd simply, and AVERSION is deriv'd from evil. The WILL exerts itself, when either the good or the absence of the evil may be attain'd by any action of the mind and body" (T 2.3.9.7). We can have desire or aversion for objects or states of affairs considered in general, independently of what is in our power to do. But we can will only when we take ourselves to be in a position to act. In effect, only our actions are the objects and the possible effects of our will. Conversely, if actions are to be explained as effects, this can only be done by means of a causal antecedent like the will, determining the mind to pass from desire for good, or aversion to evil, to give rise to particular events, here and now ("the will has an influence only on present actions," T 3.2.3.3). Therefore, the will is nothing else but direct passion being exerted in action. In this way, it is not different from any particular kind or episode of direct passion, and thus, properly, not a passion at all. The will is, rather, a role that any direct passion can perform, and the distinctive experience of this role being performed.

Hume discusses the nature of the experience of willing only indirectly, in connection with the "*false sensation or experience*" we have of liberty of indifference. The source of this false experience is the difference between the observer's and the agent's standpoint. When we observe someone else's actions, we usually feel a determination to infer their actions from certain motives, and we seldom feel any "looseness or indifference" in this regard. This is, by contrast, what we feel "in performing the actions themselves." From our agential standpoint, "we feel that our actions are subject to our will on most occasions, and imagine we feel that the will itself is subject to nothing." This is because, if challenged, "we feel that it moves easily every way, and produces an image of itself even on that side, on which it did not settle" (T 2.3.2.2). Hume, of course, rejects this as a proof of liberty of indifference: also in these cases, he contends, the will is determined by some desire. However, what he says implies that, in willing, we have a distinctive experience, one that conveys a feeling of *control* on our conduct. Even more importantly, this experience essentially involves an *image* of a certain action that we could decide to do and as what we would do (if we decided to act). But it should be noticed that, by introducing such a feeling of control, and assigning such a role to the image of action, Hume seems committed to ascribing a minimal form of *content* to the will – as it also follows from his holding it to be the impression of our *knowingly* giving rise to inner or outer actions. Hume is also aware that the will is the source of intentions to act, that "actions themselves are artificial, and are perform'd with a certain design and intention" (T 3.1.2.10). This, again, seems to require that will has content, that it is essentially directed to objects. These views seem clearly to be part of a sound understanding of action and agency. But they also seem clearly to be in contrast with other things Hume says about direct passions. Ascribing content to direct passions, the will included, seems unwarranted, if they can be reduced to causal relations among purely qualitative, blank, original, and reflective impressions, only inexplicably and accidentally attending certain objects. Furthermore, if direct passions are the immediate effects of episodes of pleasure or pain, there seems to be no way an agent can intend to act and have control of actions.

Hume seems to push his non-cognitivism about direct passions and motivation to the extreme of denying their being essentially directed to objects. But at the same time he seems to accept a conception of the will that implies that direct passions have content and that agents have (on this ground) a certain control on their intentions and on their actions. To see whether these apparently contrasting positions (as well as others we will consider below) can be made consistent, we have to look more closely at Hume's view of the springs of action, and, particularly, at the relationship between pleasure and desire.

Pleasure and Desire

The fulcrum of motivational non-cognitivism in the *Treatise* is the immediate depend-ence of desire and aversion on pleasure and pain. This is a strongly hedonistic thesis about motivation, although not one of *psychological*, or *logical*, hedonism. Hume does not say that we are, or could be, only motivated to *achieve* pleasure, but that it is pleasure that *causes* us to pursue whatever object we pursue.

The motivational role of belief

This brand of non-cognitivism, however, is ultimately unstable, since (as we have begun to see) it does not match with facts about motivation that Hume himself accepts. Hume recognizes that direct passions can spring not only from *impressions of*, but also from *beliefs about*, pleasure, or pain. Pleasure and pain may appear "in impression to the actual feeling and experience, or only in idea" and have, according to which is the case, an "influence" "upon our actions" that is "far from being equal": "Impressions always actuate the soul, and that in the highest degree; but 'tis not every idea which has the same effect." This arrangement has clear advantages:

> Did impressions alone influence the will, we shou'd every moment of our lives be subject to the greatest calamities; because, tho' we foresaw their approach, we shou'd not be provided by nature with any principle of action, which might impel us to avoid them. (T 1.3.10.2)

If, on the other hand, every idea influenced our actions, given the "unsteadiness and activity of thought," and the images of goods and evils that are always wandering in the mind, our mind would be "mov'd by every idle conception." Nature, thus, has "chosen a medium":

> The ideas of those objects, which we believe either are or will be existent, produce in a lesser degree the same effect with those impressions, which are immediately present to the sense and perception. (T 1.3.10.3)

In particular, "by making an idea approach an impression in force and vivacity," belief bestows on it "a like influence on the passions." In this way, "our reasonings from causation are able to operate on the will and passions" (T 1.3.10.2).

Hume here is making a sound descriptive and functional point. A motivational role of belief is required if intention is to be detached from occurrent feelings, and if design and minimally efficient conduct (as manifested in everyday behavior and in the experience of willing) are to be possible. But, the similarity of belief and impression notwithstanding, this does not seem to be consistent with the view of motivation that is prominent in the *Treatise*. According to this view, motivation consists in pre-sent, felt pleasure (pain) causing present, felt desire (aversion). (Ideas of pleasure and pain, as we have just seen, do not have by themselves the causal power to motivate.) On this ground, for beliefs concerning goods or evils, that is, objects productive of pleasure and pain, to motivate, would be for such beliefs to *take the place* of occurrent impressions, or feelings, of pleasure and pain. It seems that this might happen either by such beliefs (partly) *consisting of* pleasant or painful impressions or by their *reliably causing* such impressions. I will consider the two points in turn.

Given Hume's conception of belief as an impression enlivening an idea, the first alternative might seem promising. However, it can be quickly dismissed. To believe is to have an idea present to the mind as if it were an impression. But this only means that belief is a specific way of conceiving objects, that is, as present. If a feeling is involved in the enlivening of an idea, it is (as we have seen) not as an independent mental occurrence, but only as a mode of conception, a sense of reality. It follows that to have a belief concerning a pleasant or painful object is to conceive it as present or impending. It might also be that it is to conceive as present or impending an experience of pleasure or pain. But this is not the same as to feel pleasure or pain. This would be a distinct mental episode, and not the mode of conception proper of belief. No feelings with the quality of pleasure or pain need to be included in the belief that pleasant or painful objects or experiences are present. (It should be kept present that Hume firmly distinguishes between believing something and perceiving it.) Thus, beliefs do not consist in the occurrent impressions of pleasure or pain that are required for the causation of direct passions.

It remains that such impressions could be reliably caused by beliefs concerning pleasure or pain. But this might not be a position Hume could really have taken. The relevant belief might be the belief that a certain object is pleasant, that is, the conception as real (present or impending) of an object that has been experienced as pleasant. It is not immediately clear how such a conception might cause an impression of pleasure: perhaps, there is pleasure in anticipating pleasure. Be this as it may, it would not serve Hume's aims, since it would run afoul of his commitment to non-cognitivism. The impressions of pleasure or pain would be caused by objects *represented* as pleasant and painful. Motivating states would thereby be ultimately caused by cognitive states, by the representational content of certain sorts of beliefs. In order to remain faithful to non-cognitivism, we should therefore understand the causation of desire by belief in a way that does not involve any representational content (i.e., that a certain object is pleasant). This might be the case if desire were caused by an occurrent episode of pleasure, that, in turn, is caused by the occurrence of a belief, but not by the content of that belief being that a certain object is good, or pleasant. This might perhaps be a consistent position for Hume to take. But the motivational role of belief would in this way be minimal and, in effect, quite mysterious. What would cause us to be motivated would be episodes of pleasure or pain. Belief could cause them, but not as a function of how its objects are represented. Rather, the original impressions of pleasure, or pain, would be perfectly unaccountable from the standpoint of the content of the relevant belief. (As original impressions, in general, are.) That is, belief would not cause pleasure for, and desire of, a certain object, qua the belief that that object is pleasant, or good. Rather, any belief that would in some way cause pleasure would motivate us by that pleasure causing desire. But Hume had explicitly ascribed motivational import to beliefs *about* goods and evils, pleasant and painful objects. And only if beliefs with this sort of content can motivate, can willing, intending, and controlling our conduct seem to be a possibility. We can conclude that, on Hume's account of direct passions, as we have so far reconstructed it, the motivational import of belief and the possibility of practical control remain unaccounted for.

Natural desires

In the *Treatise*, however, we can find hints of a different conception of the relation between pleasure and desire. Direct passions may arise not only from impressions of pleasure and pain, but also "from a natural impulse or instinct, which is perfectly unaccountable." Passions of this kind (like the "desire of punishment to our enemies, and of happiness to our friends; hunger, lust, and few other bodily appetites") "produce good and evil, and proceed not from them, like the other affections" (T 2.3.9.8). Hume also says of certain calm passions or desires that they are "instincts originally implanted in our natures, such as benevolence and resentment, the love of life, and kindness to children" (T 2.3.3.8).

Direct passions of this sort consist in the mind's responding with pursuit, or avoidance, to certain kinds of objects (that is, to their impressions or ideas), because of the mind's instinctual, original dispositions. We can identify these original dispositions with dispositional desires or aversions for certain kinds of objects (food, drink, mates, and so on). Direct passions are caused, as episodes of desire or aversion, by objects appropriate for the different motivational dispositions being present to, or represented by, the mind. The causal connection between desire and pleasure is still important for motivation. But now the connection is that pleasure can be an *effect* of desiring. Pleasure is not the *first* link in a causal chain leading, through direct passions and volition, to action. It is the *final* link in a causal chain leading from the original disposition of the mind to pursue or avoid certain objects, through impressions or ideas of those objects, to episodes of desire, aversion, and volition, and to action, whose success is accompanied by pleasure. Therefore, what ultimately drives individuals to actions is not *hedonic*, but *conative* states (dispositional and episodic).

On this view, direct passions relate to objects differently from what we have seen before. Their nature as dispositions includes a propense or averse response to certain kinds of objects. As mental episodes, therefore, direct passions are caused, and in part individuated, by the fact that objects are present to the mind, or represented by it, under a certain description. By contrast, on the view that we have just considered, there is no particular kind of object that is assigned to desire or aversion by our pleasant or unpleasant impressions. Episodes of desire are not caused by their objects being of certain kinds, but just by the taking place of a pleasant feeling. This is a remarkable difference. But the view we are now considering does not amount to a complete rejection of motivational non-cognitivism. Desire is not a mode of conception for which a representational grounding is essential and does not aim to agreement with facts. It is still a propense (and potentially pleasure-generating) motion of the mind. But this is a form of non-cognitivism less extreme than the one we considered before, one that has no tendency to call in question the content of desire. This seems sufficient to make place for a more adequate conception of the motivational role of beliefs. The problems for such a conception were set by the failure of beliefs about pleasant objects to constitute or to generate the impressions of pleasure required, in turn, for the causation of desire. On the present view, no such impression must precede motivation. Desire is simply the response of the mind to objects of certain kinds, on the ground of original, object-relative, dispositions. But, then, believing objects of the appropriate kinds to be present can well actuate such dispositions and cause desire. The content of belief has an intrinsic relation to desire, and its motivational role seems robust enough to make possible willing, intending, and controlling action.

Motivation in the second Enquiry

The importance and scope of the desire-based view of motivation might be questioned, since, in the *Treatise*, Hume proposes it alongside the pleasure-based one, without any comment. But the desire-based view is the central one in the later *Enquiry concerning the Principles of Morals*. Any detailed discussion of the differences between these texts would be here out of place. But a new orientation about motivation finds full expression in Appendix 2 (*Of Self-Love*) to the second *Enquiry*. Here the priority of desire over pleasure constitutes the "hypothesis," concerning what we are motivated to do, which has "really more *simplicity* in it" and is "more conformable to the analogy of nature." Certain "bodily wants or appetites" (like hunger and thirst) necessarily precede "all sensual enjoyment," so as to "carry us directly to seek the possession of the object" . . . "from the gratification of these primary appetites arises a pleasure, which may become the object of another species of desire or inclination, that is secondary and interested" (EPM App. 2.12). Thus, there are direct passions that arise from pleasant feelings. But such pleasures can only be caused by the satisfaction of primary, independent, desires, and these desires, and not any pleasant feeling, are ultimately explanatory of motivation. This view is then extended to "mental" passions:

> In the same manner, there are mental passions, by which we are impelled immediately to seek particular objects, such as fame, or power, or vengeance, without any regard to interest; and when these objects are attained, a pleasing enjoyment ensues, as the consequences of our indulged affections. (EPM App. 2.12)

The general point is that, unless we have, "by the internal frame and constitution of the mind" an "original propensity" to objects like fame, praise, power, vengeance, we cannot "reap any pleasure" from attaining them, nor be motivated by the thought of that pleasure, of our happiness, and thus by interest or self-love. Object-related conative dispositions and episodes are the central phenomenon, while feelings of pleasure are only intermediately explanatory:

> In all these cases, there is a passion, which points immediately to the object, and constitutes it our good or happiness; as there are other secondary passions, which afterwards arise, and pursue it as a part of our happiness, when once it is constituted such by our original affections. (EPM App. 2.12)

The view of motivation is still non-cognitive: desire is an "active feeling or sentiment," not a "speculative affirmation." But (as I have already suggested) it is less radically non-cognitive, since relation to objects under a certain description (one that finds response in the natural constitution of the mind) is essential to motivating states. The objects we are naturally disposed to desire are good, or part of our happiness. Therefore, to believe that such an object is present is (non-problematically) motivating, for it is an object we are disposed to desire. There seem to be no restrictions about possible natural objects of desire – if vengeance is intrinsically desired, why not benevolence or friendship? – so that the desire-based view seems to express Hume's considered, general view of motivation. (Notice also that it is proposed in opposition to another completely general view, motivation based on self-love.)

Reason and Passion

The motivational role of belief has thus been shown to be consistent with Hume's considered view of the direct passions. But this, while necessary, is still not sufficient to account for all the ostensible normative features of will and action that Hume recognizes.

Strength of mind and intrinsic value

It is important to distinguish two ways in which beliefs concerning objects of natural desire (or goods) could be motivating. We could be motivated by the belief that we would have certain desires in response to the objects in question. This is a cognitive account of motivation, which does not require that we now have a desire for the object believed. By representing their future desires for certain objects, agents gain control on their present desires, and on volition and action. However, this is *not* how Hume thinks beliefs can motivate. Motivation requires *present desire*. Beliefs do not motivate us because we take as true that we will have certain desires, but by causing us (on the ground of a natural disposition) to have *now* a desire for a distant good. This is a (moderately) non-cognitive account. But if this is the motivating power of belief, we have not yet fully explained how agents can have control on their conduct. Hume recognizes that agents sometimes display the virtue of "strength of mind," the capacity for acting in view of the "greatest possible good," and of counteracting other motivations "in prosecution of their interests and designs"(T 2.3.3.10; EPM 4.1; EPM 6.15). This is, of course, a motivational capacity that is ultimately rooted in motivating beliefs. But the fact that desires can be caused by belief does not cancel the fact that the agent is in the hold of his *present desires* and of their *relative weight*. Strength of mind, intending and controlling conduct, involve the capacity of agents to *distance* themselves from the complex of their present desires. But by introducing motivating beliefs about goods we have merely *added* to that complex.

Hume, furthermore, not only recognizes, but endorses, the distinction between real and apparent goodness. He complains that we "judge of objects more from comparison than from their real and intrinsic merit" and that "we are apt to overlook even what is essentially good in them" (T 2.1.6.4). There is an important contrast to draw between comparative and real value: "So little are men govern'd by reason in their sentiments and opinions, that they always judge more of objects by comparison than from their intrinsic worth and value" (T 2.2.8.2). Correspondingly, it is a task for any agent to examine the principles that influence his judgment and to settle the "just value of every thing." But judgments of goodness or value have motivational import. Therefore, correcting them can contribute to the "easy production of the passions" and "guide us, by means of general establish'd maxims, in the proportions we ought to observe in preferring one object to another" (T 2.1.6.9). However, the possibility of this kind of correction implies that our judgments and our preferences can fall out of alignment, so that the former can be brought to bear, with some interesting normative import, on the latter. But it is not clear how this can be possible, in view of Hume's (even moderate) non-cognitivism. Judgments of value are beliefs concerning what objects are good and how good they are. But (given non-cognitivism) goodness and degrees of goodness are determined by the same dispositions to desire that underlie episodes of desiring and preferences. Therefore, judgment and preference reflect and obey the very same principles and there is no reason why they should diverge in a normatively significant way. In effect, there just seems to be no fact of the matter as to whether what we prefer and value is really, or only apparently, preferable and valuable. Hume's overall position seems thus to involve a paradoxical contrast between his (even considered) non-cognitive view of motivation and of motivating belief, on the one hand, and the strength of mind and the grasp of real value that he recommends to agents, on the other.

The rejection of practical reason

This paradoxical contrast is emphasized by Hume, who rejects any role of reason in action, and does so on non-cognitivist grounds. Hume denies that reason, as a representational faculty, has the causal power to control desire and the will. He also denies that desire and the will can have any normative property that corresponds to what truth is for reason.

> Nothing is more usual in philosophy, and even in common life, than to talk of the combat of passion and reason, to give the preference to reason, and assert that men are only so far virtuous as they conform to its dictates. (T 2.3.3.1)

This widespread view is Hume's target, in his discussion of the influencing motives of the will. The astounding conclusion he wants to draw is that "Reason is, and ought only to be the slave of the passions, and can never pretend to any other office than to serve and obey them" (T 2.3.3.4). Hume's argument for this conclusion is that reason cannot conflict with motivating passions, and thus cannot influence or correct them, either. The first lemma, in turn, is supported by consideration of the representational nature of reasoning and the non-cognitive one of direct passions. Hume examines, in turn, demonstrative and probable reasoning. He takes as obvious that demonstrative reasoning is never the cause of any action, because of its abstract and a priori character (T 2.3.3.2). A practical role could thus only be ascribed to probable or causal reasoning. Beliefs concerning the properties of objects, or how to attain our ends, can clearly influence desiring and willing. However, "'tis evident in this case, that the impulse arises not from reason, but is only directed by it. 'Tis from the prospect of pain or pleasure that the aversion or propensity arises toward any object." This influence on volition and action springs ultimately from non-cognitive sources. Causal reasoning has no independent power on conduct. "But if reason has no original influence, 'tis impossible it can withstand any principle, which has such an efficacy, or even keep the mind in suspense a moment" (T 2.3.3.3).

Reason not only lacks any independent causal influence on conduct. It is also without *any normative relevance*. A direct passion has no "representative quality," no cognitive content.

> 'Tis impossible, therefore, that this passion can be oppos'd by, or be contradictory to truth or reason; since this contradiction consists in the disagreement of ideas, consider'd as copies, with those objects, which they represent. (T 2.3.3.5)

Therefore, motivating states cannot be rational or irrational, and there is no such thing as practical reason. Beliefs often accompany passions, and can be true or false, reasonable or unreasonable. Passions can be founded on a mistaken belief concerning the existence of an object. We can also be mistaken in our beliefs concerning the means for a designed end. In all these cases, affections can be called unreasonable. But this normative assessment does not extend beyond these cases, and, what is more important, is properly addressed not to the passions, but only to the accompanying belief. Desires and intentions, in themselves, are unaccountable to reason. It is not contrary to reason that I prefer "the destruction of the whole world to the scratching of my finger"; or that I choose "my total ruin, to prevent the least uneasiness of an *Indian* or person wholly unknown to me"; or even that I prefer "my own acknowledg'd lesser good to my greater" (T 2.3.3.6). Hume is not shy of acknowledging the paradoxical implications of his non-cognitivism.

Calm passions and distant goods

This is an extremely strong conclusion. But it is one that follows from Hume's non-cognitivism, unless some alternative explanation is given for strength of mind, the possibility of real value, and the (ostensible) conflict of reason and passion. In this last connection, Hume remarks that "the principle, which opposes our passion, cannot be the same with reason, and is only call'd so in an improper sense" (T 2.3.3.4). Thus, if not reason, some other principle does indeed oppose (and influence) our passions, as reason (deceivingly) seems to do. To dissolve the paradoxical consequences of non-cognitivism, Hume's theory should include a consistent and plausible account of this principle.

Hume's position, in the *Treatise*, can be reconstructed (if somewhat speculatively) from two sets of texts, one dealing with the causal, and the other with the normative, aspects of the principle that should substitute for practical reason. The first step consists in replacing reason with *calm passions*. The misconception of a practical reason is rooted in phenomenological error. Reason exerts itself without producing any sensible emotion, pleasure or uneasiness. "Hence it proceeds, that every action of the mind, which operates with the same calmness and tranquillity, is confounded with reason." But it is certain that there are "certain calm desires and tendencies, which, tho' they be real passions, produce little emotion in the mind, and are more known by their effects than by the immediate feeling or sensation." These calm passions are "very readily taken for the determinations of reason, and are suppos'd to proceed from the same faculty, with that, which judges of truth and falshood" (T 2.3.3.8). This mistake is connected with that of not distinguishing "betwixt a calm and a weak passion; betwixt a violent and a strong one" (T 2.3.4.1). Phenomenology is doubly deceitful, since it makes us mistake a non-cognitive faculty for a representational one, on the one hand, and fail to grasp the motivational force of calm direct passions, on the other.

Calm and violent direct passions have the same general nature and general objects: pursuit of the good and avoidance of evil (both in proportion to their greatness). But they are systematically differentiated, and set in opposition, by differences in their causal antecedents. I cannot enter into a detailed examination of the causal factors that differentiate passions into calm and violent. Some of these factors involve imaginative and affective mental processes, like when a particular emotion is associated with the direct passion of desire and gives new force and violence to it. Custom and repetition allow to survey objects with greater tranquility and augment our inclination toward them (T 2.3.5.2–5). Acquaintance and other relations that enliven imagination may influence also our passions (T 2.3.6.1–2). But the causal principle that has the greatest influence on the calmness or violence of the direct passions has to do with the "situation of the object." More in particular, "the same good, when near, will cause a violent passion, which, when remote, produces only a calm one" (T 2.3.4.1). Closeness or remoteness, contiguity or distance in space and time, are the circumstances of objects that most contribute to determining whether the desires and the aversions that arise in response to them are calm or violent (as Hume explains at length, T 2.3.7). These differences in their causal antecedents are reflected in differences in the causal powers of calm and violent passions, which result in their being able to influence conduct in conflicting ways "according to the *general* character or *present* disposition of the person" (T 2.3.4.10). The potential, standing motivational opposition between calm and violent passions is Hume's substitute for what is misleadingly (but understandably) considered as the combat of reason and passion:

> What we commonly understand by *passion* is a violent and sensible emotion of mind, when any good or evil is presented . . . By *reason* we mean affections of the very same kind with the former; but such as operate more calmly, and cause no disorder in the temper. (T 2.3.8.13)

But nothing so far has been said to make intelligible the ostensible difference in authority between reason and passion, nor that between real and apparent value. This introduces us to the second step, one of the most original developments of Hume's theory of motivation. Calm and violent passions are differentiated by Hume not only in causal, but also in normative terms. Calm passion responds to and motivates to action on the ground of "the view of the greatest possible good." It is thus for the sake of their "interests and designs" that it makes men "counter-act a violent passion" (which only expresses their "present uneasiness"). This is a difference in value, and not just in relative strength, among desires. "Strength of mind," which as the disposition to act prevalently on calm passions is the same as practical control, is recommended by Hume as a "virtue" (T 2.3.3.10). But what is the warrant for this normative qualification of calm passion? Hume's answer is that the circumstances of objects that cause direct passions to be *calm* are the *same* that cause them to respond to *real value*, so as to induce a grasp of, and a preference for, the *greatest good*. On the desire-based view of motivation (which Hume in this context is tacitly assuming), the real value of objects is a function of the kind of object and of whether the object is appropriately related to the natural, original dispositions to pursuit or avoidance. If a direct passion is such that it is *only* (or at least *principally*) determined by the kind of object it takes, and by the relation of it to the original dispositions of the mind, then (and only then) we can say that it responds, and is proportioned, to real value and to its degree (the same holds of the preferences and judgments springing from that passion). Now, the features that cause a passion to be calm also cause it to be determined only (or principally) by its type of object and its relation to our original dispositions to desire. Direct passions are principally caused to be calm by the *distance in time and space* of their objects. But distance in space and time ensures that direct passions respond only to the *general and stable features* that, relatively to the original dispositions of the mind, make objects desirable and valuable (T 3.2.7.2). Calm passions having distant objects are only minimally distorted by the accidental features of their situation and of our attitudes. This makes sense of real value, and provides a standard for judgment and control of action. Calmness of direct passions, grasp of and preference for the greatest good, and practical control or strength of mind, are thus neatly tied together. (The possibility of motivating beliefs forms the relevant background.) What we call practical reason is nothing but the result of systematic and (broadly speaking) causal differences and interrelations among (dispositional and occurrent) direct passions.

From passion to taste

The theory of calm passions does much to attenuate the paradoxical consequences of the rejection of practical reason. Pro tanto, therefore, Hume might claim to have vindicated, within the scope of a revised, moderate non-cognitivism, the widespread normative views concerning action he seems to accept. But something may still be missing. Any principle that should substitute for reason should make sense of our capacity for orderly, principled reasoning activity. In Hume's philosophy, this is clearly the case with demonstrative reasoning and also (although in a more complex and controversial way) with probable or causal reasoning. Also in the practical case we seem to have to do (at least in many cases) with the activity of a subject that judges and compares goods and evils, and draws conclusions from such judgments and comparisons. But this kind of activity does not fit easily with Hume's alternative conception of practical reason. Direct passions may be attuned to the general properties of objects and to the ways they are related to our natural dispositions. This is, however, a far cry from establishing an agential standpoint, and a proper activity of judgment and reasoning.

It is possible that Hume had some awareness of this situation, since, shortly after the *Treatise* (in the essay *The Sceptic* 1742; then, much more fully, in the second *Enquiry* 1751; and in the essay *Of the Standard of Taste* 1757) he introduced the notion of *taste*, as the third kind of operation of the mind (besides reason and passion) that is involved in evaluation and motivation. A full discussion of Hume's doctrine of taste is here out of question. But the important point seems to be that, while reason is still denied any motivational import, taste becomes the spring of all the impressions that are involved in motivation:

> Reason, being cool and disengaged, is no motive to action, and directs only the impulse received from appetite or inclination, by showing us the means of attaining happiness or avoiding misery: Taste, as it gives pleasure or pain, and thereby constitutes happiness or misery, becomes a motive to action, and is the first spring or impulse to desire and volition. (EPM App. 1.21)

As the ultimate source of motivation, taste replaces both the original impressions of pleasure and pain and the direct passions that spring from the constitution of the mind.

Taste is a much more complex mental operation than anything that we have so far considered in connection with direct passions. Hume recognizes that "there is something approaching to principles in mental taste" (*Essays*: 163). Later, he even calls in question the view that "all sentiment," since it has "reference to nothing beyond itself," is "right" and "always real" (*Essays*: 230). A "standard of taste," rather, seems to be possible, so that the difference "between judgment and sentiment" is not as wide as it is said to be (*Essays*: 229). This standard consists of rules that are not fixed *a priori*, but have their foundation in experience, and on the observation of the common sentiments of human nature. More in particular, they express information concerning "particular forms or qualities" that, from the "original structure of the internal fabric," tend to please or to displease (*Essays*: 233). The causal facts underlying the general and regular features of evaluation and motivation are the same as before. But, now, these facts are explicitly regarded as the ground for *normative principles* of feeling and sentiment that we ought to follow in judging and (it may be surmised) in preferring. Most importantly, taste is an *active, judgmental* faculty of evaluation and motivation that could make intelligible the capacities ostensibly manifested in practical reasoning. Hume also describes it in explicitly *projective* terms, as having "a productive faculty, and gilding or staining all natural objects with the colours, borrowed from internal sentiment, raises, in a manner, a new creation" (EPM App. 1.21). This makes for an analogy between the operation of taste and certain content-shaping operations of the imagination (those involved in forming the idea of necessary connexion, for instance). In this way, it might be suggested that taste could be constitutive of content, a circumstance that, together with the abandonment (in favor of taste) of the identification of motivation with passion, would radically reshape Hume's theory of motivation. It is regrettable that, in Hume's texts, we only find few hints of these possibilities.

See also 9 "Hume's Indirect Passions"; 11 "Hume on Liberty and Necessity"; 12 "Hume on Moral Rationalism, Sentimentalism, and Sympathy"; 13 "Sympathy and Hume's Spectator-centered Theory of Virtue"; 15 "Hume on Beauty and Virtue"; 26 "The Humean Theory of Motivation and Its Critics"

References

Hume, David (1741–77). *Essays, Moral, Political and Literary*, ed. Miller, Eugene F. (Indianapolis, IN: Liberty Fund, 1987). (Cited in the text as *Essays*.)

Further Reading

Árdal, Páll (1989). *Passion and Value in Hume's "Treatise"* (Edinburgh: Edinburgh University Press).
Baier, Annette C. (1991). *A Progress of Sentiments: Reflections on Hume's "Treatise"* (Cambridge, MA: Harvard University Press). (Especially chs. 6, "Persons and the Wheel of their Passions," and 7, "The Direction of Our Conduct.")

Bricke, John (1996). *Mind and Morality: An Examination of Hume's Moral Psychology* (Oxford: Clarendon Press).

Brown, Charlotte (1988). "Is Hume an Internalist?" *Journal of the History of Philosophy*, 26, pp. 69–82.

Cohon, Rachel (1997). "Is Hume a Noncognitivist in the Motivation Argument?" *Philosophical Studies*, 85, pp. 251–66.

Darwall, Stephen (1995). *The British Moralists and the Internal "Ought": 1640–1740* (Cambridge: Cambridge University Press). (Especially ch. 10, "Hume: Norms and the Obligation to be Just.")

Fieser, James (1992). "Hume's Classification of the Passions and Its Precursors," *Hume Studies*, 18, pp. 1–17.

Hampton, Jean (1995). "Does Hume Have an Instrumental Conception of Practical Reason?" *Hume Studies*, 21, pp. 57–74.

Korsgaard, Christine (1986). "Skepticism about Practical Reason," *Journal of Philosophy*, 83, pp. 5–25.

Kydd, Rachel (1946). *Reason and Conduct in Hume's "Treatise"* (London: Oxford University Press).

Lecaldano, Eugenio (2002). "The Passions, Character, and the Self in Hume," *Hume Studies*, 28, pp. 175–93.

Lloyd Thomas, D. A. (1990). "Hume and Intrinsic Value," *Philosophy*, 65, pp. 419–37.

Mackie, J. L. (1980). *Hume's Moral Theory* (London: Routledge and Kegan Paul). (Especially chs. 3, "Hume's Psychology of Action," and 4, "Morality Not Based on Reason.")

Magri, Tito (1996). "Natural Obligation and Normative Motivation in Hume's *Treatise*," *Hume Studies*, 22, pp. 231–54.

McIntyre, Jane (2000). "Hume's Passions: Direct and Indirect," *Hume Studies*, 26, pp. 77–86.

Millgram, Elijah (1995). "Was Hume a Humean?" *Hume Studies*, 21, pp. 75–93.

—— (1997). "Hume on Practical Reasoning," *Iyyun: The Jerusalem Philosophical Quarterly*, 46, pp. 235–65.

Norton, David (1982). *David Hume: Common-sense Moralist, Sceptical Metaphysician* (Princeton, NJ: Princeton University Press). (Especially ch. 3, "Hume's Common-sense Moral Theory.")

Penelhum, Terence (1975). *Hume* (London: Macmillan). (Especially chs. 5, "The Passions," and 6, "The Will.")

—— (1993). "Hume's Moral Psychology," in David F. Norton (ed.), *The Cambridge Companion to Hume* (Cambridge: Cambridge University Press), pp. 117–47.

Radcliffe, Elizabeth S. (1994). "Hume on Motivating Sentiments, the General Point of View, and the Inculcation of Morality," *Hume Studies*, 20, pp. 37–58.

—— (1999). "Hume on the Generation of Motives: Why Beliefs Alone Never Motivate," *Hume Studies*, 25, pp. 101–22.

Robertson, John (1989–90). "Hume on Practical Reason," *Proceedings of the Aristotelian Society*, 90, pp. 267–82.

Russell, Paul (1995). *Freedom and Moral Sentiment: Hume's Way of Naturalizing Responsibility* (New York: Oxford University Press).

Smith, Michael (1987). "The Humean Theory of Motivation," *Mind*, 96, pp. 36–61.

Stalley, R. F. (1986). "The Will in Hume's *Treatise*," *Journal of the History of Philosophy*, 24, pp. 41–53.

Sturgeon, Nicholas (2001). "Moral Skepticism and Moral Naturalism in Hume's *Treatise*," *Hume Studies*, 27, pp. 3–84.

—— (forthcoming). "Hume on Reason and Passion," in Donald Ainslie (ed.), *Critical Essays on Hume's "Treatise"* (Cambridge: Cambridge University Press).

11

Hume on Liberty and Necessity

JOHN BRICKE

Hume's is one of the classical attempts to display the compatibility of moral responsibility, and so freedom, with a thoroughly naturalistic account of human beings as a
part of nature and so as wholly subject to causal law. He, along with Hobbes and Locke,
and with a host of modern writers, has, in the words of one of the moderns, "done what
can be done, or ought ever to have been needed, to remove the confusions that can
make determinism seem to frustrate freedom" (Davidson 2001b: 63).

Hume offers two extended treatments of liberty and necessity, of freedom and determinism. The first, in his *Treatise of Human Nature*, appears towards the end of his lengthy,
proto-scientific discussion of human conative and affective life, a discussion that is preceded by (amongst many other things) his revolutionary account of causation and that
is followed by his thoroughly naturalistic account of morality. The second treatment
appears nearly a decade later in his *Enquiry concerning Human Understanding*, and
follows immediately upon his recasting of his account of causality: complementary
accounts of the passions and of morality are reserved for other works. The two treatments differ in interesting ways from one another but their contents are – arguably
are – very much the same.

Hume's discussion of the matters in question, expressed with extraordinary economy,
is also extraordinarily complex. To make things manageable we may distinguish,
much more sharply than Hume does, his discussions of necessity, of liberty, and of agency
and responsibility.

Necessity

Hume believes that the concept of causation incorporates the notion of causal necessitation. He denies that such necessitation is either a perceptible feature of causal
transactions or a matter of an intelligible, as it were logical, tie: it's not something one
recognizes, whether by the senses or by reason, to hold between a cause and its effect.
One's conception of causal necessitation is a product, rather, of two linked things,
"constant *union* and the *inference* of the mind" (T 2.3.1.4).

Interpreting the requirement of constant union we may say that an event of type *A*
is cause of an event of type *B* if and only if events of type *A* are regularly followed by

events of type B. Viewed in terms of an inference of the mind, an event of type A is cause of an event of type B if and only if an impression of an event of the first type would determine someone, suitably conditioned, to form an expectation of an event of the second type. The element of necessitation in the concept of causation derives from the ineluctability with which, having been conditioned by exposure to repeated pairs of events of two types, one following the other, one expects an event of the later type given one's awareness of an event of the first type. In effect, causes are sufficient conditions for their effects; and awareness of a cause is sufficient, given appropriate conditioning, for forming an expectation of its effect.

There is some suggestion that Hume takes causes to be necessary as well as sufficient conditions for their effects. Presumably he would then invoke its temporal priority in order to capture the notion of a cause's producing, and thus necessitating, its effect. In what follows we may restrict attention to causes as sufficient conditions.

For Hume, constant conjunctions find expression in causal laws of greater or lesser generality. He represents the task of the scientist as that of progressing from lower-level laws to a unifying set of more general ones. Importantly, he distinguishes what we may call strict laws from probabilistic ones (in the course of distinguishing "proofs" from "probabilities" in both the *Treatise* and the first *Enquiry*): strict laws express uniform correlations, probabilistic laws express less-than-uniform correlations, between events (or sets of events) of two types. It appears to be another part of the task of the scientist to proceed from probabilistic laws to strict ones. Explanation of an event is a matter of deriving it from antecedent conditions with which it is lawfully correlated; explanation of a regularity is a matter of deriving it from a more general one. Some, but not all, laws find mathematical expression: Hume writes of "mixed mathematics." Whether mathematically expressible or not, however, a causal law expresses a "matter of fact," not a "relation of ideas" (in the language of the first *Enquiry*), and so is a synthetic and a posteriori claim, not one that is necessarily true.

Hume maintains a principle of causal determinism: every event has another event (or set of events) as its cause; the occurrence of any event is governed by (strict) causal law. (This is not to say the envisaged laws are currently available.) Of course, the principle of causal determinism, not expressing a relation of ideas, is not a necessary truth. Given a standard reading of Hume's inductive scepticism it is also not a claim supportable by reasoning. Nor is it one to which everyone, peasant as well as philosopher, in fact subscribes. It is, however, a principle to which Hume found natural scientists of his period committed so far as the physical world, at least, was concerned. And it seems, at least, that he offers a naturalistic explanation for their doing so, one deriving from repeated experience of discovering the cause of the *non*-obtaining, on a given occasion, of an expected regularity. They are thus led to "form a maxim, that the connexion betwixt all causes and effects is equally necessary, and that its seeming uncertainty in some instances proceeds from the secret operation of contrary causes" (T 1.3.12.5). Penelhum (2000) argues that, whatever his intentions, Hume here offers an explanation not of belief in the universality of causality but only of commitment to a weaker principle of predictability, the principle that, given the same cause, one gets the same effect.)

What, more specifically, do the natural scientists, and Hume with them, believe?

> [T]hat the operations of external bodies are necessary [= necessitated], and that in the communication of their motion, in their attraction, and mutual cohesion, there are not the least traces of indifference or liberty. Every object is determin'd by an absolute fate to a certain degree and direction of its motion, and can no more depart from that precise line, in which it moves, than it can convert itself into an angel, or spirit, or any superior substance. (T 2.3.1.3)

Given the laws, and the state of the (relevant region of the) physical universe at a given time, its subsequent state is determined.

Hume offers the collision of billiard balls in illustration. He alludes to other illustrations to be found in botany, chemistry, biology, and meteorology. And he contends that the situation is essentially the same when one turns from the "actions of matter" to "actions of the mind." Of course he is committed to the project of a "science of man," and so to the discovery of laws governing mental operations generally, and mental and bodily actions in particular. His associationist laws governing ideas (in Book 1 of the *Treatise*) and the indirect passions (in Book 2) are offered as contributions to that project. So, too, are the accounts of moral sentiments, of the origin and exercise of virtues and vices, and of the origin of complex social and political practices and arrangements, in Book 3. In the sections of both *Treatise* and first *Enquiry* explicitly devoted to the question of liberty and necessity, however, he focuses particularly on the causation of "volitions," or of "actions of the will." In drawing attention to regularities in human behavior, he in effect intimates candidate laws governing the occurrence of volitions, or more broadly of voluntary actions. In thus displaying parallels between the explanatory and evidentiary situations of the physical sciences and the (nascent) behavioral ones he calls into question the commonly made assumption of indeterminism – of the absence of necessity – in the case of human action. In doing that, he advances "the doctrine of necessity" (T 2.3.2.3) – a specification of the principle of causal determinism – for "actions of the mind."

In the case of "motives, volitions and action," Hume argues, just as in the central physical case of "figure and motion" (T 2.3.1.17), one discovers the union and inference that constitute causal necessitation. *Union* appears across the different periods of human history, as well as across differing social and political settings:

> It is universally acknowledged that there is a great uniformity among the actions of men, in all nations and ages, and that human nature remains still the same, in its principles and operations. The same motives always produce the same actions: The same events follow from the same causes.

The "chief use" of history is:

> to discover the constant and universal principles of human nature, by showing men in all varieties of circumstances and situations, and furnishing us with materials, from which we may form our observations, and become acquainted with the regular springs of human action and behaviour. (EHU 8.7)

A similar concern for constant and universal principles informs the human sciences of politics, morals, and criticism. Regularity-based *inference* with respect to human motives, volitions, and actions appears both in speculation and in practice, both in the human sciences and in common, daily activity. Many actions – most obviously and complicatedly those involving the cooperation of others – involve reference to the actions of others; and in the conclusions, including the expectations, thus drawn agents "take their measures from past experience, in the same manner as in their reasonings concerning external objects" (EHU 8.17). On a rough par, then, so far as union and inference go, both psychological and physical considerations can mesh smoothly in our causal investigations: "*natural* and *moral* evidence," Hume writes, "cement together, and form only one chain of argument betwixt them" (T 2.3.1.17).

To be sure, the behavioral regularities Hume remarks are no more than approximations to constant conjunctions: the intimated laws governing human action are probabilistic at best, not strict. But so, too, are many of the regularities and laws governing events in the physical world. In *their* case the absence of genuinely constant conjunctions comports easily with a commitment to causal determinism: the natural scientist, prompted by past experience, need only, and will, invoke "springs and principles, which are hid" (T 1.3.12.5), as yet unidentified factors assumed to play a role in the causation of events of the kinds in question. For Hume, there is every reason for a like response to the less than strictly regular regularities in the case of human behavior.

When making his case for union and regularity in the case of human actions Hume invokes a variety of psychological and (perhaps) other factors: "circumstances," "situation," "temper," "inclination," "character," "view," "disposition." As we shall see, the concept of character plays a critical role in his account of causality, agency, and responsibility. At this point, however, we must attend to the central trio of "motives, volitions and actions."

Both in the *Treatise* and in the first *Enquiry* Hume focuses on *motives* as the causes of volitions, and so of actions. It is only subsequent to the discussion of liberty and necessity in the *Treatise*, however, that he characterizes them as passions, and in particular as desires. Claiming to have "prov'd, that all actions of the will have particular causes" he poses the question "what these causes are" (T 2.3.3.8). He proceeds, in *Treatise* 2.3.3 ("Of the influencing motives of the will") to develop a conativist theory of reasons for action, one that assigns a distinctive and ineliminable role to an agent's desires. He does so while attempting to subvert various cognitivist theories that, emphasizing an agent's beliefs, would reject, restrict, or in some way dilute the causal role of desire in motivated action.

According to Hume, "[h]uman nature . . . is compos'd of two principal parts, which are requisite in all its actions, the affections [= desires] and understanding" (T 3.2.2.14). He displays the differing ways in which the two parts are requisite in an illustration in the second *Enquiry* of the causal role of a reason for action. For Hume, a reason for action is a complex psychological state incorporating both a desire and a belief. Each constituent has a distinctive contribution to make. Having a desire, an agent is in a goal-setting or practical state: in having a desire he has a "*designed end or purpose*" (T 2.3.3.2), is not "indifferent" to some or other actual or possible aspect of his situation, has a "propensity" towards or an "aversion" against some or other ways of behaving (T 2.3.3.3). In having a belief the agent is in a purportedly informational state: he represents, or purports to represent, the way things are. The belief and desire that jointly constitute a reason for action must, of course, be suitably related: the belief must present information pertinent to securing the goal set by desire. Specifically, the belief must represent the bearing of possible actions, or of the action to be explained, on the securing of what the agent desires. In Hume's example, the agent desires to keep his health and believes that exercising will contribute to his doing so; he has, then, a reason for exercising. (He may, of course, have countervailing reasons for not doing so as well.) If the reason thus constituted by his desire and belief causes the agent to exercise it is the reason from which he acts and may be invoked to explain his doing so. The desire constitutes, we may say, the motivational element in the reason for action – in short, the motive.

Hume typically renders desires as phenomenologically distinctive items in consciousness, passions or so-called impressions of reflection that provide the sort of impetus to action indicated above. At times, and more plausibly, he represents them as enduring states of agents, perhaps as dispositions to have impressions of the kind just described.

According to Hume's determinism – specifically, his "doctrine of necessity" – in every instance there are causally sufficient conditions, amongst the antecedents of an agent's having a given reason for action, for the agent's having that reason for action. Similarly, there are sufficient conditions for the agent's having the desires that are ingredient in such reasons for action. There are, that is to say, causally sufficient conditions for the agent's having whatever motives for action that agent has.

On Hume's rendering, motives give rise to actions, whether mental or bodily, by giving rise to acts of will or volitions. "[B]y the *will*," he writes, "I mean nothing but *the internal impression we feel and are conscious of, when we knowingly give rise to any new motion of our body, or new perception of our mind*" (T 2.3.1.2). (It would be well to substitute "volition" for "will" here: it is volitions, or willings, or acts of will that, on Hume's view, constitute the "internal impressions" here described.) Wittgenstein (1958: I, 621) famously posed the question "What is left over if I subtract the fact that my arm goes up from the fact that I raise my arm?" In answer, Hume would invoke an arm-raising volition. On his telling, volitions have a quite different functional location in the mind's economy than motives, or than desires, do. In the standard case, volitions occur in the light of, and so subsequent to, reasons for action. A volition's occurrence constitutes, one might say, an agent's decision to act in a certain way, the choice of a particular action. Having reason to raise his arm, an agent forms a volition to do so and (standardly) does so. Wanting to rehearse a mathematical proof in his head, the agent forms a volition to rehearse the proof, and so (standardly) rehearses it. The volition causes the rehearsing of the proof, the rising of the arm.

Suppose an agent to raise his arm. Within the framework of Hume's determinism, the reason from which the agent acts is causally sufficient (in the circumstances) for the volition the agent forms. There are causally sufficient conditions for the agent's having that reason and for the reason's having the efficacy it then has. The volition is (in the circumstances) causally sufficient for the rehearsing of the proof, the rising of the arm. And, in principle at any rate, all this is governed by some strict law (or laws).

Serious questions can be raised about every element in Hume's articulation of "the doctrine of necessity," and about the argumentation he provides in its support. Does the development of the natural sciences in fact support the assumption of causal determinism? Must probabilistic laws give way, in principle, to strict ones? (Think of quantum indeterminacies in quantum physics.) Is there any reason to think that psychological or psychophysical regularities, assuming there to be such, might or must give way to strict laws? If strict laws governing human behavior are indeed possible, is it also possible that they be laws employing specifically mental or psychological concepts? (Think of the argument in Davidson (2001a) for the anomalism of the mental.) How, in any case, is one to think of the intersection of physical and psychological considerations – an intersection Hume largely neglects while setting out his case of "the doctrine of necessity?" What, in particular, of the threat of overdetermination when one attempts to envisage that intersection in the explanation, via laws, of psychological events? And, in any event, are explanations of actions that cite an agent's reasons for doing them – even granting them to be causal explanations – explanations that work by registering regularities? (Think of Hume's example of exercising for the sake of one's health.)

Having entered this list of familiar caveats, let us turn from Hume's "doctrine of necessity" to the question of liberty.

Liberty

It is tempting to think that if (1) an agent is to be responsible for some intentional action he has done, then (2) he must have been free in doing what he did, and so (3) it must be true that he could have done otherwise. It can be further tempting to think that an agent could have done other than he did only if (4) the motive from which he acted was not, in the circumstances in which he acted, causally sufficient for his acting in that way. Proponents of what Hume terms "the doctrine of liberty" or "the liberty of *indifference*" (T 2.3.2.1) – we may call them Libertarians – subscribe to the intimated contra-causal account of free-will or liberty, and of the link between motivation and action, that (4) represents. As proponents of "the scholastic doctrine of *free-will*," they hold that "motives deprive us not of free-will, nor take away our power of performing or forbearing any action" (T 2.1.10.5). And, taking human agents to be responsible for at least some of the actions they perform, they hold that, in some instances at least, the things agents do are not causally necessitated (in the circumstances) by the motives from which, as we might say, they act.

Hume takes his argument for "the doctrine of necessity" to subvert the Libertarian's central contra-causal claim about motivation and action. But in addition he considers, and counters, a number of Libertarian arguments in support of that claim. Three such arguments may be noted at this point. (The first two occur at T 2.3.2.)

While it is true that in acting we are "influenc'd by particular views and motives," the first argument goes, we normally have no sense of being subject to "force, and violence, and constraint" when so acting. This argument rests, however, on a confusion of the Libertarian's claimed "liberty of *indifference*," or "a negation of necessity and causes," with something quite different, a "liberty of *spontaneity*," a genuine sort of liberty that is indeed "oppos'd to violence."

According to the second argument, we have direct experience of indeterminacy when, as agents, we are moved to act, and we can display that indeterminacy by acting, at a later time, in a way other than that in which we earlier chose to act. In reply Hume insists that the alleged experience is merely a seeming one, a matter of nothing more than being able to imagine ourselves acting in a way other than that in which we in fact act. And that we later act in that other way (perhaps, Hume slyly suggests, with a view to showing that we could have acted that way earlier) goes no way towards showing that we could, indeed, have acted that way earlier.

Don't we, when acting, fail to feel that objective necessary connection that we discover in the physical world? And doesn't that fact reveal the absence of causation in the link between motivation and action? In the first *Enquiry* (EHU 8.21) Hume contends that this third Libertarian argument both misrepresents physical causation (a matter merely of constant conjunction and consequent inference, as he had earlier argued) and makes an obviously illicit inference from the absence of a putative (but unintelligible) objective necessity in the case of human action.

Running the argument represented by (1)–(4), above, the Libertarian claims that unless we have liberty of indifference we cannot be responsible for what we do. Were the doctrine of necessity true we could not do other than we do and so could neither be, nor coherently be held to be, responsible for our actions. Before considering Hume's response to this fourth, and central, Libertarian argument, let us look to his constructive views on liberty.

"[T]he doctrine of liberty" – the Libertarian's doctrine – is, Hume claims, "absurd . . . in one sense, and unintelligible in any other" (T 2.3.2.1). It is absurd, in his view, if taken as a denial, for the case of human action, of the union and inference constitutive of causation. It is unintelligible if taken to rest on the unintelligible assumption of objective necessitation. But there is, he holds, an intelligible conception of liberty, and one that, compatibly with causal determinism, marks a significant contrast amongst the things that human agents do. Indeed, he may hold that there are two such conceptions, or even three.

There is, Hume claims in the *Treatise* (T 2.3.2.1), such a thing as "liberty of *spontaneity*." An agent possesses such liberty provided that, or insofar as, he is not, in acting as he does, subject to "violence" (or, as the context suggests, "force, and violence, and constraint"). This is, Hume says, "the most common sense of the word ['liberty']"; and "'tis only that species of liberty, which it concerns us to preserve." That is all that, in the *Treatise*, he says of it.

In the first *Enquiry*, having rejected the Libertarian's "doctrine of liberty," he writes: "By *liberty*, then, we can only mean *a power of acting or not acting, according to the determinations of the will*; that is, if we choose to remain at rest, we may; if we choose to move, we also may." This "hypothetical [which is not to say bogus or unintelligible] liberty is universally" – and, it seems, correctly – "allowed to belong to every one, who is not a prisoner and in chains" (EHU 8.23). Over the next few pages it is apparently taken to be "opposed . . . to constraint" and to "external violence," and to be compromised by "ignorance and impotence." Hume doesn't give this species of liberty a name in the first *Enquiry*. Not to beg one of the interpretative questions, let us call it "liberty of implementability."

It's a matter of the implementability of an agent's volitions: it has to do not with the causation of the agent's volitions (all of which are, for Hume, effects of his just-prior motives) but with the efficacy of volitions in effecting what the agent wills to do. It's a matter, that is to say, of a power, not to choose what one will do, but to do what one chooses to do. It's not a power to choose whether or not one will raise one's arm but a power to raise one's arm *if* one chooses to do so or to keep it at one's side *if* one chooses to do that instead. It is a "hypothetical" liberty in that its possession by an agent involves the appropriate hypothetical (or conditional) proposition being true of that agent. Clearly the liberty of implementability is compatible with Hume's determinism.

Surprisingly, however, it is not wholly clear just what Hume takes it to involve. On what is surely the standard reading, an agent is free to move if and only if the following is true of him: if he chooses to move he does and if he chooses not to move he does not move. Freedom, that is, is a matter of the implementability of (as we may say) relevant alternatives. On an austere reading, however, the agent is free to move if and only if the following is true of him: if he chooses to move he does. On the austere reading what would happen if he were to choose not to move is, so far as his being free to move is concerned, neither here nor there. Freedom, read austerely, is simply a matter of the implementability of what one chooses to do.

In his *Essay concerning Human Understanding* Locke writes: "Liberty . . . consists in a Power to do, or not to do; to do, or forbear doing as we *will*" (Locke 1690: 270). Marking a distinction between mental and bodily actions, he also writes: "so far as a Man has a power to think, or not to think; to move, or not to move, according to the preference or direction of his own mind, so far is a Man *Free*" (Locke 1690: 237). So far, so Humean, and so, it seems, inexplicit. But Locke is in fact explicit in rejecting the austere view sketched above: "Where-ever any performance or forbearance are not equally in a Man's power; where-ever doing or not doing, will not equally follow upon the preference of his mind directing it, there he is not *Free*, though perhaps the Action may be voluntary" (Locke 1690: 237). Against this Lockean background – and in the absence of any Humean signals to the contrary – it is reasonable to read Hume's doctrine in the standard, non-austere, way: liberty of implementability is the implementability of relevant alternatives.

For some modern proponents of the doctrine, liberty of implementability provides a way to capture, compatibly with determinism, the notion of an agent's being able to do otherwise. Though unable to have *chosen* otherwise than he did, it is said, an agent may have been able to *do* something other than he did. In conditions causally sufficient for his choice, he chose to raise his arm, and he did it; but that's compatible with his having succeeded in keeping it at his side *had* he chosen to do that instead. The link between (2) and (3), above, is thus preserved. Ayer (1954) develops just such a compatibilist rendering of the specific claim that an agent could have done otherwise. (See Chisholm 2003 for a Libertarian critique.) There is, however, no evidence that Hume himself seeks some compatibilist way to support the notion that an agent could have done otherwise, no evidence that he wants to secure a link between (2) and (3), so no reason to think he wishes to deploy the liberty of implementability in the way Ayer does. On the face of it, he has no hesitation in saying, of the things we have done, that "'twas utterly impossible for us to have acted otherwise" (T 2.3.2.1). Apparently he will say of the causation of a volition what, as a determinist, he says of the causation of an event in the physical world: "no other effect, in such particular circumstances, could possibly have resulted from it" (EHU 8.4). It seems not to follow for Hume that if an agent acted freely he could have done otherwise. That said, it can seem puzzling that Hume assigns to liberty of implementability the significance that he clearly does.

It is additionally puzzling given that there is compelling reason to prefer its austere variant as an analysis of freedom of action. On the face of it, it is not a condition on one's being free to raise one's arm that one would refrain from doing so were one to choose to refrain. If it is true that one would raise one's arm if one were to choose to do so (and would do so because one chose to do so) then, no matter what would happen if one chose to refrain, one is free to raise one's arm.

It may be objected that if one cannot refrain then there must be conditions sufficient for one's raising one's arm quite apart from one's choosing to so do. But, the objection continues, if one will raise one's arm willy-nilly (whether one chooses to raise one's arm or chooses to refrain) one's raising one's arm cannot be in one's own hands (as it were), and so cannot be something with respect to the doing of which one is free. Though it is tempting, however, this objection is confused. Even in cases of overdetermination, *something* – the crucial thing – is in the agent's hands, viz. acting *intentionally* (as Davidson 2001b argues).

This brings us back to the austere version of liberty of implementability: an agent is free to move if and only if it is true of him that if he chooses to move he moves (with the caveat, of course, that his choice is the cause of the movement). And one can combine with this austere analysis of *freedom to act* an equally austere analysis of a *free action*. An action is a free action *if* – as well as only if – it is a voluntary action, an action deriving from the agent's volition. An agent can't have voluntarily moved his arm if he was not, at the time he moved it, free to do so.

It remains a puzzle why liberty of implementability (understood non-austerely) is significant for Hume. Let us sink this puzzling question (as Hume might say) in another one, a vexing interpretative question concerning the relationship between liberty of spontaneity, as represented in the *Treatise*, and (what we have called) the liberty of implementability to be found in the first *Enquiry*. Stroud (1977), Bricke (1996), and others appear to view them as identical; according to Garrett (1997) they "correspond"; Botterill (2002) argues them to be quite distinct, while contending that liberty of implementability (he calls it "liberty$_2$"), not liberty of spontaneity, lies at the heart of Hume's enterprise.

They have similar functional roles, of course: each comes on the stage as an alternative to the rejected liberty of indifference. On the other hand, when looked at in isolation from that context, neither looks very much like the other. What scant textual evidence there is points equivocally in several directions. In passages cited earlier liberty of spontaneity is opposed to "force, and violence, and constraint"; but liberty of implementability also appears to be "opposed . . . to constraint" and to "external violence." On the other hand, the thought that liberty of implementability is compromised by "ignorance and impotence" finds no echo in Hume's brief remarks about liberty of spontaneity. Then, too, liberty of implementability is "universally allowed to everyone who is not a prisoner and in chains." Are we to assume that everyone not in prison and in chains is free from force, violence, and constraint? That liberty of spontaneity is the only species of liberty "which it concerns us to preserve" can seem to suggest both that there are several species of liberty (and so perhaps to leave room for liberty of implementability as one of the others) and that it has a significance for us that liberty of implementability lacks. But Hume takes liberty of implementability to be "absolutely essential" (EHU 8.26) to morality and, though Hume doesn't say this himself, we are surely concerned to have options – ranges of options – available as we act, and that's a matter of implementability.

On the textual evidence the interpretative issue is, it seems, undecidable. Perhaps, however, we can shed *some* light on the matter if we consider what Hume has to say of exculpation. To do that we must turn to the question of agency and responsibility.

Agency and Responsibility

A fourth Libertarian argument against Hume's doctrine of necessity, mentioned but deferred earlier, turns on that doctrine's purported "dangerous consequences to ... morality" (T 2.3.2.3), consequences avoided by the Libertarian position itself. While making clear that the alleged danger lies in the undermining of notions of moral responsibility, Hume omits explicit statement of the Libertarian's argument. Presumably, however, the claim is that, absent the liberty of indifference, we cannot be responsible for what we do. And why is that? The Libertarian's contention is that were the doctrine of necessity true we could not do otherwise than we do, and so would not be free in our actions, and so could neither be, nor coherently be held to be, responsible for what we do. The objection amounts to an inference incorporating our earlier propositions (1) through (4).

Omitting explicit statement of the Libertarian's fourth objection, Hume also offers little by way of characterization of the Libertarian's conception of human agency. On the negative side, Hume's Libertarian denies that (in some cases, at least) there are causally sufficient conditions for an agent's motives and that (in some cases, at least) an agent's motives are causally sufficient for his volitions, and so (other conditions assumed) for his actions. We may take it, on the positive side, that Libertarian agents act voluntarily or intentionally, and that they do so for reasons. They form volitions, that is to say, and they do so in light of some consideration or other, or from some motive or other. The motives from which they act are not, however, ones they have by causal necessity. And – the key point – they are not (even given other circumstances that obtain) causally sufficient for the volitions the agent forms. Such volitions are, in a word, undetermined. In just such circumstances, then, we may say that, while acting in a certain way, the agent could have chosen not to act in that way – could, for some other reason, have chosen not to do so. Much of this minimal picture finds expression as what Hume terms "the scholastic doctrine of *free-will*": "motives deprive us not of free-will, nor take away our power of performing or forbearing any action" (T 2.1.10.5). For the Libertarian, it is only on such a rendering of agency that agents can be responsible for what they do.

This minimal Libertarian picture can be complicated in two, among many other, ways. In the first, the Libertarian introduces the possibility of free choices being the source of thenceforward dominating motives, the actions resulting from such motives being derivatively, as one might say, free actions, and so actions for which the agent is responsible (as in Kane 2002). In the second, the Libertarian construes agents, not just events or states, as causes. In free action it is the agent, not some state of, or some event in, the agent, that is the cause of the agent's volition when the agent acts in light of, but not as causally determined by, some reason for action or another. Hume's contemporary Thomas Reid (1788) forwards such a view of free agency, as does Roderick Chisholm (2003), among other moderns.

Hume's bold response to the Libertarian's fourth objection has (though these are nearly inextricably linked together in the texts) two parts. He argues, first, that the Libertarian view is *incompatible* with an agent's responsibility for his actions. He argues, secondly, that the doctrine of necessity is not only *compatible* with, but in fact *required for*, responsibility. (In the *Treatise* (T 2.3.2.3) it is "not only innocent, but advantageous to . . . morality"; in the first *Enquiry* (EHU 8.26) it is both "consistent with morality" and "absolutely essential to its support.")

The Libertarian account is incompatible with responsibility, Hume claims, because it severs the tie – the "relation to the person or connexion with him" – that responsibility requires between an agent and his actions. What, precisely, is the character of that tie? Hume has no non-question-begging way to represent the tie directly, but offers, in effect, a series of criteria for its presence. The tie is one that is absent in "casual and accidental" actions, which is to say unintentional ones, while clearly present in actions that are "design'd and premeditated." It turns on an agent's being "a person or creature endow'd with thought and consciousness," and in particular being capable of "thought and deliberation." It underpins the thought that, in acting as he did, an agent acted from a certain motive. It supports such thoughts as that the horrendousness of an agent's intentional action reveals the horrendousness of the agent himself, and, more generally, the thought that his actions reveal the sort of person an agent is. Were the Libertarian doctrine true, Hume contends, none of these tie-displaying thoughts would have standing. The reason, at bottom, is that as uncaused, and so chance, events, the Libertarian's putative free actions have no explanatory origin in their purported agents. How, as later writers have put the question, can an agent be responsible for something that happens by chance? (For the remarks quoted above see a crucial paragraph at T 2.3.2.6, and a closely matched paragraph at EHU 8.29.)

The Libertarian has, it must be said, ways to reply. His free agents freely choose to act for this reason or for that. Such free actions can be the source of longstanding motivational structures, the foundation of traits of character. Arguably, the inference from "uncaused" to "chance" is too quick, as is that from "uncaused by some state of, or event in, the agent" to "uncaused" (for agents, it may be said, can be causes). Replying in turn, Hume can query the Libertarian's "for" in the phrase "choose to act *for* this reason or that." He can press the merits of his own analysis of causal relations, taking states or events as their terms. He has, famously, an argument that agents are not intelligibly viewed as distinct from, but rather are constituted by, their states and events (their "perceptions"). And he can display the merits of his own constructive account of human agency, including its capacity for illuminating the tie between agent and action that responsibility requires.

Humean agents are not distinct from their perceptions but they are not merely, though the word is Hume's, "bundles" of perceptions. They are, as Pitson (2002) has suggested, embodied systems of perceptions, the perceptions of the several kinds being identifiable by their functional locations in a mind's economy, and being elements in complex and enduring structures. Amongst those structures are motivational ones, structures that undergo changes through the history of the agent, but that are robust and relatively enduring – in Hume's words "durable and constant" – nonetheless. Such motivational structures constitute the agent's being the sort of person the agent is; they constitute, we may say, aspects of his character. They, or their elements, are causally implicated in the agent's voluntary actions. It is as thus structured that an agent is the source of his actions, and thus responsible for his actions. It is largely as thus structured that a human agent is an object of emotional responses, more generally of evaluation, by others – and by himself. The emotional responses in question are, in Hume's taxonomy, the indirect passions of love and benevolence, hatred and anger, when directed towards others, pride and humility (or shame), when directed towards one's self. Attention to the workings of such responses reveals clearly, Hume suggests, the complex causal underpinnings of agency and responsibility.

A confusion must be avoided here. Though actions must, in Hume's view, "proceed . . . from some *cause* in the character and disposition of the person" who did them if that person is to be responsible (EHU 8.29), and though the requisite motivational structures must be "durable and constant," it does not follow that an agent is not responsible for something done that was (as we might say) out of character. After all, his acting or not from a given motive (and so the frequency of his acting from that motive) depends not only on his having that motive but on his beliefs, his other motives, his circumstances, and other factors as well. Even uncharacteristic actions, then, will reveal something of the sort of person the agent is, thus will serve as the basis for affective responses, and judgments of responsibility, of which he is the object. (Contrast Foot 1978.)

Hume supplements his rendering of responsible agency, and its emphasis on "durable and enduring" qualities, with a too-brisk look at circumstances that can affect the blameworthiness of agents for actions (at T 2.3.2.7 and at EHU 8.30). If unsatisfactory in many ways, and in particular in their explanatory emphasis on the momentary or intermittent character of the exculpating factors they identify, these brief remarks are nonetheless illuminating.

"Men are not blam'd for such evil actions as they perform ignorantly and casually, whatever may be their consequences." Why? "[T]he causes of these actions are only momentary, and terminate in them alone." The principal claim is an exaggeration, surely; and the proffered explanation in terms of the momentariness of the causes of such actions is unpersuasive. But it is what an agent does intentionally, and not just unwittingly or by accident, that bears centrally on evaluative and affective responses to that person. And the enduring motivational structures that lie behind particular actions, being general in character, do not – or not necessarily – "terminate alone" in the particular action performed on a particular occasion.

212

"Men are less blam'd for such evil actions, as they perform hastily and unpremeditately, than for such as proceed from thought and deliberation." A "hasty temper," Hume writes in explanation, even if "a constant cause in the mind, operates only by intervals and infects not the whole character." Correcting for the too-narrow way in which haste and absence of forethought are taken to bear on responsibility, there is something to the thought that actions proceeding "from thought and deliberation" are centrally revelatory of the sort of person the agent is: when actions are in question, one might say, it's his motives that make the man.

"[R]epentance wipes off every crime, if attended with evident reformation of life and manners." In explanation, Hume writes: "actions render a person criminal, merely as they are proofs of criminal passions or principles in the mind; and when by any alteration of these principles they cease to be just proofs, they likewise cease to be criminal." Correcting for exaggeration, we may say both that individuals may change their enduring motivational structures, and that – a narrow point – certain evaluative responses to agents presuppose the continuance, in the agent, of the motivational structures that prompted the agent's earlier actions. One can't think him, now, an objectionable cheat if he has in fact changed his stripes.

Hume takes these facts about exculpation to support his determinist insistence on the centrality of "durable and enduring" qualities in human agency. As such, they are urged in support of his striking claim that the doctrine of necessity is not only compatible with but in fact "absolutely essential to" morality. Presumably it is the presence of these strategic concerns that explains his otherwise surprising neglect of other exculpatory considerations, in particular ones intimated in his constructive characterizations of liberty, whether of spontaneity or of implementability.

His doctrine of necessity, Hume claims, is "absolutely essential to" morality. So too, he says, is the liberty of implementability. (The liberty in question, he writes in the first *Enquiry*, is that "as above explained.") It's not at all clear what Hume's argument for *this* contention is. A possible line would run: liberty of indifference being rejected, but the capacity to do otherwise being a condition on responsibility, one requires liberty of implementability because it (it alone?), while compatible with determinism, can meet that condition. As we have seen, however, Hume appears to reject the ability to do otherwise as a condition on responsibility.

Hume writes that no human actions where liberty of implementability is absent can be "objects either of approbation or dislike." To be "objects of our moral sentiment" they must be "indications of our internal character, passions, and affections" (EHU 8.31). Thus far, this is just a restatement of an aspect of his determinist theory of human agency. What he adds, however, is that actions fail to be such indications if they are "derived altogether from external violence" (EHU 8.31). In language that seems to associate implementability with spontaneity, he returns to the issue of exculpation. Let us, if independently and briefly, follow him in this.

Non-implementability seems to mark a class of exculpatory conditions including not only, to use Hume's terms, "impotence and ignorance" but also "force, and violence, and constraint." An agent may be physically unable to implement his volition (as in the example of impotence both Locke and Hume use, the suddenly paralyzed agent unable to implement his volition to move his arm). Non-culpably, let us assume, an agent may not know how to implement his intention. The use, by another, of force or violence or constraint can also prevent implementation of an agent's volitions: the agent may be forced off course, or held back. Assuming the non-occurrence of the intended action to be objectionable or undesirable, the would-be agent is not to blame: the action's non-occurrence had no origin in his motivational structure, as witness his assumed volition.

In the cases just considered, austere implementability is in question. Arguably, absence of its non-austere cousin, implementability of relevant alternatives, is not in fact a condition on blameworthiness. An agent acted in an objectionable way. On the face of it, the action was his: it originated in his motivational structure, and in the volition he formed. That he would not have been able to implement a decision not to perform that action, had he made that decision, appears not to be exculpatory.

Force and violence, at least, can be exculpatory in ways having nothing to do with implementability. That the threat of either was present serves, in easily imagined circumstances, to diminish or eliminate blameworthiness, even for actions arising from the agent's own volitions. Able to implement either of the relevant alternatives, the agent chooses one of them: he forms a volition and acts. He does what would, in other circumstances, be objectionable. Yet he is not to blame. A gun held to his head, the bank-teller can implement the volition to hand over the money, as also the volition not to do so: he can do whichever of the two actions he chooses to do as Stroud (1977) has pointed out. But the threat of violence is present, and his decision will be taken in light of that. The threat introduces not non-implementability but, as we might say, an intrusive motivational factor of an unwelcome sort. The teller is not to blame for handing over the money; indeed, it would have been foolish of him not to do so.

Should one say the teller's action is not wholly his own? Is this, perhaps, suggested as one reflects on Hume's efforts to articulate his constructive determinist account of human agency and action? Do considerations of mental and emotional maturity bear on blameworthiness? For Hume, those viewed as responsible are capable of "thought and deliberation" and, as he elsewhere remarks, young children have no capacity not only for philosophical reasoning but also for "prudent and well-concerted action" (T 2.3.1.7). Do issues of cognitive or affective impairment have a role to play? If for his own reasons, Hume might wish to endorse what is "commonly allow'd," namely, that "mad-men have no liberty" (T 2.3.1.13), and so no responsibility.

When considering the bearing of his doctrine of necessity on theological matters, Hume raises the question whether a divine creator and sustainer of the universe, were there such, would be responsible for the evil actions men do. It is unclear what his own answer is. He takes it the envisaged situation would not render putative human actions non-actions. On the assumption that the actions are indeed evil, however, he seems (EHU 8.32) to vacillate between two very different claims: that God as well as man would be responsible (evil human actions "involve our Creator in the same guilt" as ourselves); and that God alone would be responsible ("the Deity, not man, is accountable for them"). In posing the theological question he at least broaches an important mundane one, that of the bearing of psychological ascendancy and manipulation on agency, responsibility, and exculpation.

To think these unelaborated thoughts and queries to be credibly Hume's is to see him as having conceived the range of exculpatory conditions to encompass not only the original trio of accident, haste, and repentance, and implementability (of the austere sort) as well, but also a set of conditions, not sharply specified, that turn on intuitive notions of what is wholly or fully the agent's own. It is to see a bit more clearly just what he takes human agency to be. It is – perhaps stretching the point – to enrich the content of Hume's own term "spontaneity." It is in any case to find intimations in Hume of what Watson (2003: 4) has called, when characterizing contemporary developments in compatibilist theories of free will, "the refined analysis."

Hume is a naturalist about the mind. He purports to offer naturalistic characterizations and explanations of, among other things, the affective life of human beings, and in particular the so-called indirect passions. Russell (1995) has urged the importance of seeing Hume's treatment of exculpation in just that light. Hume's concern, seen this way, is to identify the many sorts of considerations about agents and their circumstances that, as a matter of fact, do affect, in exculpatory ways, our affective responses to one another. Provided one does not reduce thoughts of responsibility to the affective states consequent upon them, Russell's interpretative recommendation is surely one to follow.

See also 5 "Hume on the Relation of Cause and Effect"; 10 "Hume on the Direct Passions and Motivation"

References

Ayer, A. J. (1954). *Philosophical Essays* (New York: St. Martin's Press).

Botterill, George (2002). "Hume on Liberty and Necessity," in Peter Millican (ed.), *Reading Hume on Human Understanding* (Oxford: Clarendon Press), pp. 277–300.

Bricke, John (1996). *Mind and Morality: An Examination of Hume's Moral Psychology* (Oxford: Clarendon Press).

Chisholm, Roderick (2003). "Human Freedom and the Self," in Gary Watson (ed.), *Free Will* (Oxford: Oxford University Press), pp. 26–37.

Davidson, Donald (2001a). "Mental Events," in Donald Davidson, *Essays on Actions and Events* (Oxford: Clarendon Press), pp. 207–25.

—— (2001b). "Freedom to Act," in Donald Davidson, *Essays on Actions and Events* (Oxford: Clarendon Press), pp. 63–81.

Foot, Philippa (1978). *Virtues and Vices* (Oxford: Basil Blackwell).

Garrett, Don (1997). *Cognition and Commitment in Hume's Philosophy* (New York: Oxford University Press).

Kane, Robert (2002). "Free Will: Ancient Dispute, New Themes," in Joel Feinberg and Russ Shafer-Landau (eds), *Reason and Responsibility: Readings in Some Basic Problems of Philosophy* (Belmont, CA: Wadsworth), pp. 499–512.

Locke, John (1690). *An Essay concerning Human Understanding*, ed. P. H. Nidditch (Oxford: Clarendon Press, 1975).

Penelhum, Terence (2000). *Themes in Hume: The Self, the Will, Religion* (Oxford: Clarendon Press).

Pitson, A. E. (2002). *Hume's Philosophy of the Self* (London: Routledge).

Reid, Thomas (1788). *Essays on the Active Powers of the Human Mind*, ed. B. A. Broady (Cambridge, MA: MIT Press, 1969).

Russell, Paul (1995). *Freedom and Moral Sentiment: Hume's Way of Naturalizing Responsibility* (New York: Oxford University Press).

215

Stroud, Barry (1977). *Hume* (London: Routledge and Kegan Paul).

Watson, Gary (ed.) (2003). *Free Will* (Oxford: Oxford University Press).

Wittgenstein, Ludwig (1958). *Philosophical Investigations*, trans. G. E. M. Anscombe (Oxford: Basil Blackwell).

Further Reading

Árdal, Páll (1966). *Passion and Value in Hume's "Treatise"* (Edinburgh: Edinburgh University Press).

Bayles, M. (1976). "Hume on Blame and Excuse," *Hume Studies*, 2, pp. 17–35.

Bricke, John (1988). "Hume, Freedom to Act, and Personal Evaluation," *History of Philosophy Quarterly*, 5, pp. 141–56.

Dennett, Daniel (1984). *Elbow Room: The Varieties of Free Will Worth Wanting* (Cambridge, MA: MIT Press).

Flew, Antony (1961). *Hume's Philosophy of Belief: A Study of His First Inquiry* (London: Routledge and Kegan Paul).

Helm, P. (1967). "Hume on Exculpation," *Philosophy*, 42, pp. 265–71.

Honderich, T. (1993). *How Free Are You? The Determinism Problem* (Oxford: Oxford University Press).

Honderich, T. (ed.) (1973). *Essays on Freedom of Action* (London: Routledge and Kegan Paul).

Kane, Robert (1998). *The Significance of Free Will* (Oxford: Oxford University Press).

Kemp Smith, Norman (1941). *The Philosophy of David Hume* (London: Macmillan).

Penelhum, Terence (1975). *Hume* (London: Macmillan).

Part III

Morality and Beauty

12

Hume on Moral Rationalism, Sentimentalism, and Sympathy

CHARLOTTE R. BROWN

Introduction

The eighteenth-century sentimentalists based morality in our affections and sentiments. There are two ways they do this. First, what has moral value are certain first-order sentiments, passions, and affections, which motivate us to act, and actions expressive of these sentiments. Second, what makes them valuable are our reflective, second-order sentiments, sentiments we have about our sentiments or those of others. We feel approval or disapproval towards ourselves or others for having and acting on certain first-order sentiments and affections. David Hume traced our reflective second-order sentiments to sympathy, which makes his theory the most powerful version of sentimentalism ever produced. I will explain why his account of morality is powerful, but first I briefly describe the approach he takes in his moral theory.

Hume steps into an ongoing philosophical debate about the foundation of morality that Thomas Hobbes (1588–1679) initiated. Hobbes, as his contemporaries read him, believed we are naturally self-interested, power-hungry creatures. Without some sort of society our lives would be "nasty, brutish, and short." We thus agree to hand over our power to a sovereign, who not only makes the laws that are necessary for us to live together, but who also has the power to make us comply with them. Acting morally is a matter of complying with the laws the sovereign establishes, but the basis of morality is our self-interested desire to preserve ourselves.

Two kinds of moral theory developed in reaction to Hobbes – rationalism and sentimentalism. Both objected to Hobbes's theory, but on different grounds. By the time Hume wrote the *Treatise of Human Nature*, however, almost everyone agreed that Hobbes's theory had been refuted. With Hobbes's theory no longer on the table, there were only two possibilities for Hume to consider – rationalism or sentimentalism. If one falls, the other stands. Thus, he thinks he must show that moral rationalism fails before he can present his sentimentalist account of morality. His arguments against moral rationalism are found in the *Treatise* 3.1.1, 3.2.1, and in *An Enquiry concerning the Principles of Morals*, Appendix I. He presents his version of sentimentalism in Book 3 of the *Treatise*, the *Enquiry*, and in various essays. The *Treatise* account is the most interesting, innovative, and thorough statement of his theory.

In the first section, I provide the philosophical background necessary for understanding both Hume's arguments against moral rationalism and his version of sentimentalism. In the next section, I examine Hume's arguments against the rationalists, and in the following section, I turn to his account of morality, especially his idea that morality springs from sympathy.

Philosophical Background

Hume's rationalist opponents

Hume has two rationalists in mind – Samuel Clarke (1675–1729) and William Wollaston (1660–1724). His primary target is Samuel Clarke, who defends rationalism in the second volume of *A Discourse concerning the Unchangeable Obligations of Natural Religion* (1706). Clarke appeals to reason to explain almost every facet of morality. Moral rules are rules of reason, so acting morally and acting rationally are the same. We perceive moral rules by means of reason alone. The rational awareness that an action is right has the power to obligate us and to motivate us.

Clarke claims that there are certain eternal and necessary relations in which God, human beings and other entities stand. It follows from these relations that certain actions are fit or unfit to be done. He believes that each kind of thing has a nature or essence, knowable by reason. The different natures of things determine the different relations in which things stand to one another. They, in turn, make certain actions fit or unfit. These relations are eternal and necessary, and impart a kind of immutability and necessity to actions. Most of Clarke's examples bring in the idea of comparative fitness: one kind of action is more fit than another in certain circumstances. Because God is infinitely superior to us, it is more fitting that we should worship and obey him than dishonor him. Because He is the supreme ruler, dispensing rewards and punishment, it is more fitting that He should make innocent people happy than miserable.

Clarke frequently compares moral truths to mathematical truths, claiming they are self-evident, certain, and knowable in the same way that fundamental mathematical axioms are. Consider the axiom that the whole is greater than the part. As long as you know what the terms in it mean, you know that it is true and certain. You don't need to make any observations or conduct any research; reason alone enables you to know it. Clarke believes that the fitness and unfitness of actions are self-evident and certain in the same way. Like John Locke (1632–1704), he thinks that if we begin with these self-evident truths, we may demonstratively prove certain moral rules, although neither produced such a demonstration.

Clarke objected to Hobbes's idea that the good person needs to be prodded by sanctions to do what is right. Genuinely virtuous action is rational action, and we do not need sanctions to do what we have a reason to do. We may be motivated simply by the rational intuition that an action is fitting or obligatory, that is, by the motive of duty, the motive from which the morally good person acts.

At one point Clarke says that evildoers, by opposing the nature and relations of things, "endeavor to make things be what they are not, and cannot be," which he thought is as absurd as trying to change a mathematical truth (Clarke 1706: 201). William Wollaston, the second rationalist Hume opposes, constructs his entire moral theory around this idea. But, unlike Clarke, for whom the basic moral notions are fitness and unfitness, Wollaston argues that moral goodness and evil may be reduced to truth and falsehood. His only work, *The Religion of Nature delineated* (1724), was extremely popular during his lifetime, but, as we will see, he later became the butt of jokes.

Wollaston argues that we are able to say things not only with words, but also with actions. Defining true propositions as those that express things as they are, he maintains that actions may express, declare, or assert propositions, by which he means something more than that we understand gestures such as laughing or weeping. To use his example, if one group of soldiers fires on another, the first group's actions declare that the second are their enemy. If they aren't, their declaration is false. Since we can understand actions, they – like sentences – have meaning, and whatever has a meaning is capable of truth and falsity. Immoral actions deny things to be what they are, and thus express false propositions. If I break a promise, I falsely declare I never made one. If I am ungrateful, I falsely assert that I never received favors from you. To treat things as being what they are not is, for Wollaston, as irrational and absurd as denying that $2 + 2 = 4$.

The sentimentalists' reading of the rationalists

Francis Hutcheson (1649–1746), Hume's sentimentalist predecessor, opposes moral rationalism in his book, *Illustrations upon the Moral Sense* (1728). He was a brilliant arguer and Hume freely employs many of his objections to rationalism. Hutcheson claims that God gave us, in addition to the other senses, a special moral sense that disposes us to feel approval or disapproval when we contemplate people's character traits. He argues that the only character trait the moral sense approves of is benevolence. Temperance, courage, prudence, and justice are virtuous only when motivated by benevolence. He distinguishes universal benevolence, which aims at the happiness of all human beings, from particular forms of benevolence, such as patriotism, parental love, and pity. The former is the morally best motive.

Hume follows Hutcheson in translating moral rationalism into a sentimentalist framework. One surprising advantage the sentimentalists had over the moral rationalists is that they had a more fully developed view of reason and they reinterpret rationalism in terms of it. They characterize reason in two ways.

The first is that reason compares ideas to find relations among them. Reasoning is "nothing but a *comparison*, and a discovery of those relations . . . which two or more objects bear to each other" (T 1.3.2.2). Hume calls these relations, the philosophical relations. Later on in the *Treatise*, he divides them into two types – relations of ideas and matters of fact. The four relations of ideas are resemblance, degrees of quality, contrariety, and proportion in quantity. We may find the first three relations simply by inspecting and comparing the ideas themselves. By inspecting my idea of an orange and my idea of a lemon, I find that oranges are sweeter than lemons. To ascertain proportion in quantity, however, we must engage in a more extensive reasoning process – we must produce a demonstration. Hume clearly has Clarke in mind and probably Locke as well.

Matters of fact include identity, contiguity, and causality. To determine whether any of these relations hold, we must consult experience rather than examining our ideas. We discover the first two relations by direct perception. Causal reasoning is the only way to judge matters of fact we don't directly perceive; it involves a more complicated process of reasoning. While Hume doesn't have any particular rationalist in mind who belongs in this group, its inclusion makes his survey exhaustive.

The second way Hume characterizes reason is that it consists in the discovery of truth or falsehood. Hume has Wollaston in mind here, since he tries to reduce moral goodness and evil to truth and falsehood. Like Hutcheson, Hume isn't sure how to interpret Wollaston's criterion of immoral actions, so he looks at a number of possible interpretations, and argues that none of them make sense.

There is another important way in which Hume follows Hutcheson in translating moral rationalism into a sentimentalist framework. Roughly speaking, we may distinguish two different aspects of a moral theory – a spectator component and an agent component. The spectator component is primarily concerned with answering questions that arise when we assess people: when is it appropriate to hold people responsible and to praise or blame them for what they have done? The agent component is primarily concerned with answering questions that arise when we deliberate: what should or ought I to do? Every complete moral theory must include a discussion of both components, although philosophers tend to privilege either the spectator or the agent component.

Hume like Hutcheson takes the basic moral concepts to be spectator concepts – praise and blame, approval and disapproval – rather than the concepts agents use in deciding what to do – right and wrong, fit and unfit. Both build their moral theories around the idea of an admiring and disapproving spectator. Both also think that what we approve and disapprove of in the first instance are people's character traits and the motives that typically spring from those traits. As such they offer a theory about what character traits are morally good and bad – a theory of virtue and vice. Actions, as they see them, are merely external signs of inner character traits and motives. Actions are appropriate objects of praise and blame, but only when they express people's character traits and motives.

Clarke and Wollaston, by contrast, privilege the agent component. According to them, the basic moral concepts are those we use in deciding what we should do – right or wrong, fit or unfit. Moreover, they think these concepts apply in the first instance to actions rather than to character traits. Hume, however, interprets the rationalists as privileging the spectator concepts, as he does. He characterizes the rationalists not only as offering a theory of approval and disapproval, but also as thinking that they primarily apply to character traits and motives. On his reading of the rationalists, they are concerned, as he is, to distinguish virtuous character traits from vicious traits. Keeping this in mind will help in understanding Hume's arguments against moral rationalism and his sentimentalist account of morality.

The moral project

Rationalists and sentimentalists agree that we possess moral concepts and that they have practical and psychological effects on us. We may be motivated to perform an action by the thought that it is our duty and feel ashamed when we fail. Moreover, during this period there is general agreement about the content of morality. Both rationalists and sentimentalists assume that we know more or less what is good or bad, virtuous or vicious. They also agree that the basic moral ideas are simple and can't be defined in terms of their component parts. Although they can't be defined this way, Hume thinks we may explain how we come to have moral concepts and their effects on us.

Along with his empiricist predecessors, Hume took the philosophical project to be investigating the origin of our ideas, passions, and sentiments. In his "Introduction" to the *Treatise*, Hume says that like Locke, Hutcheson, and others, he wants to apply Newton's experimental method to the study of the human mind. He thinks that the proper way to understand an idea's content is to explain its origin. To do that, we need to find the "simplest and fewest" causes of our ideas and to base our explanations solely on experience. Hume's project in *Treatise* 1 is to find the most fundamental laws that explain the operations of the mind in acquiring such ideas as causality and identity. In *Treatise* 2, his aim is to discover the most basic laws that explain passions such as love and hatred, pride and humility, as well as various desires and aversions.

Hume's moral project is of a piece with his overall project. In the first *Enquiry*, he aligns himself with those "abstruse" philosophers who "regard human nature as a subject of speculation; and with a narrow scrutiny examine it, in order to find those principles, which . . . make us approve or blame any particular object, action, or behaviour" (EHU 1.2). He contrasts this with "easy" philosophy, which aims to make us morally good. Hume's task, as he sees it, is to explain the origin of our moral concepts, discovering the laws that explain the causes of our approving virtue, and therefore providing an account of what we mean by "virtue." He isn't directly interested in making his readers morally better.

Our moral approval and disapproval of character traits and the actions that express them, like any other human activity, are to be explained in wholly naturalistic terms. There are two senses in which Hume's moral theory is naturalistic. One concerns his Newtonian ambition of explaining moral sentiments and concepts in a way that is consistent with the scientific picture of the world. The other is that he rejects attempts to ground morality in religion. There is no need to appeal to anything outside of human nature to explain morality. Not only do appeals to God and particular religious doctrines offend against naturalism, but also religion is damaging and dangerous to human beings. We would be happier and morally better without it.

The foundational issue

The foundational issue between rationalists and sentimentalists concerns the source of our moral concepts. Do our basic moral ideas spring from reason alone or from sentiment? Hume frames the debate about the origin of moral concepts in terms of his own theory of the mind. He reminds us that all the contents of the mind are perceptions. On this view, to engage in any type of mental activity – seeing, judging, thinking, or loving – is to have some perception before the mind. Similarly, "to approve of one character, to condemn another, are only so many different perceptions" (T 3.1.1.2). Hume divides perceptions into two types – ideas and impressions – a distinction that is supposed to capture the difference between our experience of thinking of something and our experience of feeling something. Impressions are more forceful and vivacious perceptions than ideas.

The foundational issue is to determine what kind of perceptions approval and disapproval are and then to explain how we come to have these perceptions. The debate between rationalism and sentimentalism about the origin of moral concepts reduces to the question of

> Whether 'tis by means of our ideas or impressions we distinguish betwixt vice and virtue, and pronounce an action blameable or praise-worthy? (T 3.1.1.3)

If the judgment that a person's action is virtuous were simply a matter of comparing and relating ideas, we would be able to arrive at moral ideas by means of reason alone.

Hume offers four arguments to show that reason alone isn't the source of moral ideas. In a fifth argument, Hume challenges the rationalist account of the motive of duty. The arguments are:

1   the argument from motivation (T 3.1.1.4–7);
2   the arguments from truth and falsehood (T 3.1.1.9–16);
3   the argument that reason discovers relations of ideas or matters of fact (T 3.1.1. 18–26);
4   the "is–ought" argument (T 3.1.1.27);
5   the argument concerning the motive of duty (T 3.2.1.2–8).

Several of these arguments are complex, consisting in a number of sub-arguments, but I won't necessarily examine each one.

Before turning to Hume's arguments against moral rationalism, it is important to remember that there are different types of moral rationalism and that his arguments are directed to only one version – dogmatic rationalism. Clarke best exemplifies this view. According to him, the nature and relations of things are part of the framework of the universe. While we know them by means of reason alone, they exist prior to and independently of reason. Today, Clarke would be labeled a realist. Dogmatic rationalism should be distinguished from the sort of rationalism Immanuel Kant went on to develop. On Kant's view, the principles of reason aren't part of the fabric of the universe, but are principles that our minds generate, which we then apply to the world around us and to ourselves.

Arguments against Moral Rationalism

The argument from motivation

Hume's first argument, one he thinks decisive, is the argument from motivation. It is directed primarily against Clarke and has only two premises. The first is that moral ideas have pervasive practical and psychological effects on us, something both experience and philosophy confirms. Experience shows that we are often motivated to perform an action because we think it is obligatory or to refrain from performing it because we think it is unjust. We try to cultivate the virtues in ourselves and are proud when we succeed and ashamed when we fail. If morality did not have these effects on our passions and actions, moral rules and precepts would be pointless, as would our efforts to be virtuous. Philosophy, Hume notes, is commonly divided into two kinds, speculative and practical, and philosophers classify morality as practical because they agree that moral ideas have these practical effects. As Hume puts the first premise, "morals excite passions, and produce or prevent actions" (T 3.1.1.6).

The second premise is that by itself reason is incapable of bringing about any of these effects. It isn't able to excite passions or move us to act or to refrain from acting. Hume's support for this premise appears in *Treatise* 2.3.3, in the section entitled "Of the influencing motives of the will." Hume challenges the widely held view that we ought to govern our actions by reason rather than passion, arguing that "reason alone can never be a motive to any action of the will" and "can never oppose passion in the direction of the will" (T 2.3.3.1).

Hume argues by a process of elimination. Taking it as settled that reason consists in finding relations of ideas or establishing matters of fact, he considers mathematical reasoning from the first group and causal reasoning from the second. He asks us to look at instances of action where these two types of reasoning have a bearing on action. When we do, we will see that reason alone could not have moved us.

No one thinks that mathematical judgments by themselves are capable of motivating us. While we calculate how much money we are owed and how much we owe to stay out of debt, mathematical reasoning is always used in connection with achieving some pre-existing purpose, so it is always used in conjunction with causal reasoning. When causal reasoning figures in the production of action, it always presupposes some pre-existing desire or want. According to Hume, reasoning is a process that moves you from one idea to another idea. If reasoning is to have practical force, one of the ideas must be tied to a desire or affection. Noticing the causal connection between exercise and losing weight will not move you to exercise, unless you want to lose weight. Reason can't give rise to a passion or motive by itself.

Hume now shows that reason alone can't oppose a passion in the direction of the will. To oppose a passion, reason must be able to give rise to a motive by itself, since a motive can only be opposed by another motive, but as he has just shown, reason can't give rise to a motive.

The argument from motivation, then, is that if moral concepts are capable of exciting passions and producing or preventing actions, but reason alone is incapable of doing these things, then moral concepts can't spring from reason alone. If they did, they wouldn't have the practical and psychological effects everyone agrees they have.

In the last several decades, there has been considerable debate about how to interpret and evaluate this argument. Both premises are controversial. The second premise concerns the source of motivation: Is it some sentiment or desire or is it possible for us to be moved by reason alone? Questions have been raised about what sorts of "reason" or "reasoning" Hume is talking about and whether his arguments establish that reason by itself is motivationally inert. The first premise concerns how best to explain the practical and psychological effects of moral concepts. There are two general ways to explain them and accordingly two ways of reading this premise (Brown 1989: 71–8).

One is to claim that the rational intuition that an action is right can move us, but only when it is tied to some pre-existing desire. Philosophers who accept this view claim that everyone possesses a "moral" desire – a desire to do what is right or to do their duty – as part of their psychological makeup. The intuition that a certain course of action is obligatory becomes practical by triggering the pre-existing desire to do our duty. However, on this reading, the argument is invalid. Suppose the source of all motivation is a desire or sentiment. Then it no longer follows that reason alone is incapable of perceiving moral ideas. Reason may give rise to awareness of our duty, which in turn triggers a desire to do our duty, thereby providing a motive for acting as morality directs.

If we interpret the first premise as saying that moral concepts, when grasped, are inherently motivating or intrinsically action guiding, the argument is valid. On this reading, the awareness that an action is right or obligatory by itself provides an agent with a motive to perform it, though not necessarily with one sufficient to outweigh others that might also be present. If an agent perceives that an action is right, she necessarily has some motive to do it. If she doesn't have a motive, she hasn't perceived what her duty is. The conclusion now follows that reason doesn't give rise to moral ideas because reason alone can't motivate, whereas moral concepts do.

Another issue is whether Hume himself is committed to the idea that moral perceptions are inherently motivating, or if only the rationalist is. If we accept the former reading, this suggests that Clarke's and Hume's understanding of the idea must be different. Hume takes the idea that moral concepts must motivate to mean that we first need to look at the sorts of things that are capable of motivating us in order to discover what gives rise to moral concepts. Since Hume thinks that a desire or sentiment must be present if we are to be moved to act, moral concepts must be located in them. For Clarke, the implication of the claim that moral concepts are inherently motivating goes the other way. Since moral considerations by themselves are capable of moving us and we are rational creatures, once reason shows us what is morally required, we have a motive for doing it. Rational creatures respond to reason. If this reading is accepted, Hume must show that the moral sentiments are inherently motivating (Radcliffe 1996). However, if we accept the reading in which only the rationalist is committed to the idea that moral ideas are motivating, no such burden falls on Hume (Baier 1991: 184).

The argument from truth and falsehood

Hume's second argument, which relies on the characterization of reason as concerned to discover truth and falsehood, is directed primarily against Wollaston. Since he isn't sure how to interpret Wollaston's moral theory, he canvasses a number of possibilities, arguing that they don't make sense. These interpretations are based on Hume's understanding of reason's role in the production of action.

Hume first looks at the possibility that morally good actions are those that conform to truth and are reasonable, while morally bad actions are contrary to truth and are unreasonable. He rejects this because, strictly speaking, passions and actions can't be true or false, reasonable or unreasonable. Hume supports this claim by extending an argument he gave in "Of the influencing motives of the will." Reason may judge ideas to be unreasonable because they have representational content and thus may be contradictory to truth or reason. The contradiction "consists in the disagreement of ideas, consider'd as copies, with those objects, which they represent" (T 2.3.3.5). Passions and actions, however, are "original facts and realities, compleat in themselves, and implying no reference to other passions, volitions, and actions" (T 3.1.1.9). Lacking representational content, they can't be true or false, reasonable or unreasonable. Since we judge actions to be good or bad, but actions cannot be reasonable or unreasonable, their goodness and badness cannot be a matter of their being reasonable or unreasonable.

Although actions can't be reasonable or unreasonable, Hume thinks there are several ways in which, figuratively speaking, they may be. One, where Hume explicitly mentions Wollaston, is that actions may give rise to false judgments in others. On this reading, the criterion of immoral actions is the intention to cause false beliefs in others. Wollaston, however, claimed that immoral actions express falsehoods, not cause them. But Hume's parody of his view allows him some fun, as his example makes clear. Someone walks by an open window and sees Hume cavorting with his neighbor's wife and is thereby caused to falsely believe that she is his wife. He responds that the wrongdoing in this example is unintentional, since the adulterer's intention is to satisfy his lust, not to cause false beliefs in others. Furthermore, if he had taken the precaution of shutting the window, his actions would not have been immoral, since they would not have caused false beliefs in others.

Another criticism is directed against Wollaston's actual view that wrong actions express falsehoods. His criterion is circular. It is wrong for me to take off with your property because I falsely declare it to be mine, not yours. But if we ask why this is what my action means, the answer is that the fact that it is yours *means* that I should not steal it. The truth that is supposedly denied by a wrong action already has moral content.

Reason discovers relations of ideas or matters of fact

Hume's third group of arguments relies on the characterization of reason as comparing ideas to find relations among them. If we were able to determine what is virtuous or vicious by means of reason alone, the basis of moral distinctions must lie either in one of the relations of ideas or in some matter of fact. His real opponents are those who hold that moral relations consist in some relation of ideas. Philosophers such as Clarke and Locke, he remarks, have "industriously propagated" the idea that morality is as susceptible of demonstration as is mathematics.

In his *Enquiry* account, Hume reverses the way in which he proceeds in the *Treatise*, first looking at the suggestion that the virtuousness or viciousness of an action consists in some matter of fact and then turning to the idea that it lies in or is based upon some relation of ideas. This way of proceeding is better, since it sets up the rationalist view that morality lies in some relation of ideas.

Hume's argument in the *Treatise* is this:

> Take any action allow'd to be vicious: Wilful murder, for instance. Examine it in all lights, and see if you can find that matter of fact, or real existence, which you call *vice*. In which-ever way you take it, you will find only certain passions, motives, volitions, and thoughts. There is no other matter of fact in the case. (T 3.1.1.26)

227

Hume puts his point more clearly in the *Enquiry*. Here the crime is ingratitude. He points out that it is isn't bad in every situation. It is bad only when directed toward someone who has already shown you goodwill or has helped you. The badness of ingratitude, therefore, cannot lie in any particular fact surrounding the case. If it doesn't lie in any particular fact, maybe it lies in some relation among the facts. So Hume considers that view.

Hume argues that if you think that the virtuousness or viciousness of an action lies in one of the four relations of ideas, "you run into absurdities," since these relations hold not only among human beings, but also among inanimate objects and non-human animals. Spruce trees and pine trees resemble each other; oranges are sweeter than lemons; an elephant weighs more than a mouse. If these relations hold for these sorts of things, it should be appropriate to praise and blame them.

In his *Enquiry* discussion, Hume focuses on the relation of contrariety, a relation that has at least some initial plausibility. Consider again ingratitude. Suppose I respond to your kindness with indifference or, even worse, by treating you badly. The relation of contrariety holds between your conduct and mine, which might tempt us into thinking that the viciousness of ingratitude lies in that relation. However, it is equally contrary, if I respond to your meanness with indifference, or, even better, by helping you. In the first example, my conduct is blamable; in the second example, it is laudable. The relation of contrariety can't distinguish morally good actions from bad actions.

No rationalist, however, ever claimed that the virtuousness and viciousness of actions lies in one of Hume's four relations of ideas. Nevertheless, rationalists such as Clarke think we arrive at moral ideas by means of reason alone. Hume realizes that he arrived at his list of the four relations of ideas empirically, she imagines that the rationalist will respond that his list is incomplete. He may have overlooked a relation – specifically, the "ought" relation.

Hume offers a reductio of the idea that virtue and vice consists in some relation discoverable by reason alone. He considers parricide and incest, which are among the most horrible crimes we are capable of committing. His strategy is to show that any relation the rationalist might propose to account for these crimes will also be found among trees and animals. Everyone agrees that while we may act immorally, trees and animals can't. If the same relations are found in human beings and for trees and animals, the viciousness of these crimes cannot lie in any relation of idea.

Hume's first example concerns an oak tree. When a sapling grows big enough to overtop and destroy its parent, no one thinks it has acted badly. The "parent" tree is the cause of the "child" tree and the "child" tree is the cause of the destruction of the "parent" tree. Exactly the same relations are found in cases of human parricide. Since the same relations are found in both cases, but we agree that only human beings can act immorally, the moral viciousness of parricide cannot lie in any relation.

Hume makes the same argument about animals. Everyone agrees that when non-human animal siblings have sexual relations, it isn't morally bad, but all the same relations are found in incest among humans. Hume anticipates that the rationalists will reply that incest in animals is innocent "because they have not reason sufficient to discover its turpitude" whereas a human, "being endow'd with that faculty, which *ought* to restrain him to do his duty, the same action instantly becomes criminal to him" (T 3.1.1.25). But this is circular. For:

before reason can perceive this turpitude, the turpitude must exist; and consequently is independent of the decisions of our reason, and is their object more properly than their effect. (T 3.1.1.25)

Hume clearly has Clarke's dogmatic rationalism in mind. On his view, the relations upon which moral fitness and unfitness are based exist prior to and independently of our rational perception of them. If they didn't, there would be nothing for reason to perceive.

One implication of this view is that the question whether someone knows what he is doing is immoral is independent of the question whether what he is doing is immoral. Animals, as the rationalist acknowledges, can't perceive their moral duties, given their limited rational capacities. But, argues Hume:

> Their want of a sufficient degree of reason may hinder them from perceiving the duties and obligations of morality, but can never hinder these duties from existing; since they must antecedently exist, in order to their being perceiv'd. (T 3.1.1.25)

Thus rationalists are in the unfortunate position of having to say that when animal siblings have sex they act badly, but don't know it.

The "is–ought" argument

The final argument that Hume offers in *Treatise* 3.1.1 is the "Is–Ought" argument. He remarks that most moral theorists begin by establishing that God exists or make some observation about human beings – that we are naturally sociable or that society is necessary if we are to preserve ourselves. But after a while, instead of finding propositions with an "*is* and *is not*," he encounters propositions with an "*ought, or an ought not*," which he finds troubling

> For as this *ought*, or *ought not*, expresses some new relation . . . 'tis necessary that it shou'd be observ'd and explain'd; and at the same time that a reason shou'd be given, for what seems altogether inconceivable, how this new relation can be a deduction from others, which are entirely different from it. (T 3.1.1.27)

Hume is assuming that the "ought" relation can't be basic in the sense that it doesn't need to be explained in terms of some other relation. Thomas Reid (1710–96), one of Hume's rationalist successors, complained that Hume's criticism is unfair, since even Hume must think that some relations are basic in this sense. For example, the relation of resemblance is basic for Hume. He doesn't try to explain it in terms of other relations and there is no other relation available that could explain it. The rationalist may be thinking that the "ought" relation is basic in the same way.

Twentieth-century philosophers thought the "is–ought" argument was pivotal. Many believed it supported the dictum that no "ought" can be legitimately derived from an "is," which in turn supported a non-cognitivist position in ethics. Non-cognitivism is the view that ethical judgments cannot be true or false, since they do not describe facts. While many maintained that this argument commits Hume to a non-cognitivist view of moral judgments, others point to passages that they think show that Hume was a cognitivist (Stroud 1977: 185, 186; Cohon 1997). Still others remind us that Hume was concerned with the question of the origin of our moral concepts, not with the analysis of moral language.

The motive of duty argument

One of Hume's strongest arguments against moral rationalism occurs in *Treatise* 3.2.1, the opening section on the artificial virtues, and is aimed at Clarke's view that the morally good person acts from the motive of duty. Hume counters that doing your duty because you see it is your duty can't be the *first* or *original* motive for dutiful actions. As with many of his other arguments, he tends to couch his objection in terms of virtuous actions and their motives.

Hume claims that virtuous actions by themselves aren't meritorious. They have merit only as "signs or indications" and thus "derive their merit only from virtuous motives" (T 3.2.1.4). We would be reasoning in a circle if we held that virtuous actions were motivated by a regard for their virtuousness:

> Before we can have such a regard, the action must be really virtuous; and this virtue must be deriv'd from some virtuous motive: And consequently the virtuous motive must be different from the regard to the virtue of the action. A virtuous motive is requisite to render an action virtuous. An action must be virtuous, before we can have a regard to its virtue. Some virtuous motive, therefore, must be antecedent to that regard. (T 3.2.1.4)

If virtuous actions are those performed from virtuous motives, no action can be virtuous unless there is at least initially a motive for doing it other than the desire to do it because it is virtuous. Before you can perform a virtuous action from the desire to do what is virtuous, the action must already be virtuous. What makes an action virtuous is the virtuousness of the motive, so the motive must be something other than the desire to do the virtuous thing.

Hume's point is that you cannot perform virtuous actions for the sake of their virtuousness until you know what actions are virtuous, and the desire to do virtuous actions won't tell you what actions are virtuous. To use Hume's examples, we blame a father for neglecting his children because it shows a lack of parental affection, a duty incumbent on every parent. If parental affection were not a duty, caring for your children would not be a duty. If Hume's argument is successful, the rationalist view that the motive of duty is primary is incoherent. Kant, however, took great pains to respond to this argument in section 1 of the *Groundwork*.

There is considerable debate today about what type of motive is morally best. Is the good person motivated by the sense of duty or by such natural and spontaneous motives as benevolence? Hume tried to give the rationalist view that we do the virtuous thing because it is virtuous a limited place within the sentimentalist framework. With respect to the natural virtues, he holds that the morally best person acts from spontaneous and natural motives such as benevolence, parental affection, and so on. With respect to the artificial virtues of justice, fidelity in promises, and obedience to government, however, the normally operative and morally best motive is the sense of duty and not, as Hutcheson claimed, benevolence. The just person does what is just because she perceives it to be just.

The Moral Sentiments and Sympathy

The positive phase

Hume takes the defeat of rationalism to be the triumph of sentimentalism. He concludes that "morality . . . is more properly felt than judg'd of" (T 3.1.2.1). The moral sentiments are feelings of admiration or contempt, praise or blame that arise when we survey a person's character. Most of the time he refers to them as feelings of approval and disapproval.

In several key passages, Hume describes the moral sentiments as calm forms of love and hatred. Approval and disapproval, he says, are "nothing but a fainter and more imperceptible love or hatred" (T 3.3.5.1). When we evaluate our own character traits, pride and humility replace love and hatred. As calm species of love and hatred, they are distinguished from the more personal love and hatred we have for family members, friends, and other associates. Our personal loves and hatreds are violent, variable, and often biased.

There is some debate about how to interpret the passages in which Hume links the moral sentiments with love and hatred. He explicitly says that the moral sentiments are calm rather than violent and that approval is a pleasant feeling, while disapproval is a painful feeling. The debate concerns whether approval is a unique pleasure that causes love or whether approval is to be identified as a species of love – a calm sort of love (Árdal 1989: 111–15; Korsgaard 1999: 9–12) Since there are passages that lend support to both views, the issue can't be resolved on textual grounds alone. Ultimately, we need to ask which view makes better sense of Hume's moral theory as a whole. I read Hume as thinking that the moral sentiments are calm forms of love and hatred.

Hume asks two questions about the moral sentiments. First, what kind of sentiments are they? Second, how do we explain how we come to have them? The answer to the first question, he says, is obvious. Approval is a pleasant or agreeable feeling and disapproval is a painful or disagreeable feeling. Hume appeals to experience for support. A noble and generous action strikes us as pleasant and beautiful; cruelty and treachery are painful and repulsive to us. He adds that:

> No enjoyment equals the satisfaction we receive from the company of those we love and esteem; as the greatest of all punishments is to be oblig'd to pass our lives with those we hate or contemn. (T 3.1.2.2)

Hume's point isn't merely that we like being around people we love and dislike being around those we hate. He is saying that morality is primarily about what is lovable or hateful in the characters of those with whom we interact.

Hume concludes that "to have a sense of virtue, is nothing but to *feel* a satisfaction of a particular kind from the contemplation of a character. The very *feeling* constitutes

231

our praise and admiration" (T 3.1.2.3). We don't approve of an action because it is virtuous; an action is virtuous only because we approve of it.

Hume turns next to the question about the causes of the moral sentiments, and he criticizes Hutcheson for failing to explain the moral sense – how we come to feel approval and disapproval. He also says that he will show that there are many other virtues besides benevolence. If there are many different virtues, Hutcheson must think that there is some "instinct" disposing us to approve of each one. This goes against scientific economy. Instead, we should look for a few general principles to explain why we approve of the different sorts of virtues and disapprove of the different sorts of vices.

Hume takes up that task in *Treatise* 3.3.1. His project is to "discover the true origin of morals, and of that love or hatred, which arises from moral qualities" (T 3.3.1.6). He reminds us that our moral love and hatred are primarily directed to people's character traits and that actions are virtuous or vicious only if they proceed from some durable character trait of the person. He then introduces the most distinctive feature of his version of sentimentalism – the idea that the moral sentiments spring from sympathy.

The sympathy mechanism

Hume treats sympathy as an important mechanism of the mind and explains how it works in *Treatise* 2.1.11. Sympathy is our capacity to receive the passions, sentiments, and even beliefs of others. It is not itself a passion, so it should not be confused with such feelings as compassion, pity, or empathy. It also shouldn't be confused with a love of humankind – Hutcheson's universal benevolence – since Hume denies that we have such a feeling. Rather, it is a mechanism by means of which the feelings of others are imparted to us. Sympathy explains how we literally enter into the feelings of others, feeling what they are feeling. If you walk into a room where everyone is cheerful, you will tend to feel cheerful. If your friend is sad, you will tend to feel sad. Sympathy is a deep principle of human nature and even animal nature. It explains a wide range of phenomena: our interest in history and current affairs, our ability to enjoy literature, movies, novels, and, more generally, our sociability. It is central to Hume's account of the passions, the sense of beauty, and morality.

Hume explains how sympathy works in terms of the more fundamental principles of the mind, the associative principles – resemblance, contiguity in time or place, and causation. He believes there is a pattern or regularity in the way the mind works. Certain ideas tend to go together; certain passions tend to go together. The principles of association explain how one idea naturally introduces another idea and how one passion naturally introduces another passion. Contiguity in time, for example, explains why there is a tendency for the mind to move from thoughts about Vietnam to thoughts about miniskirts. The principle of resemblance explains why grief is often followed by disappointment and anger. Hume describes the associative principles as "gentle forces." There is only a tendency for certain ideas as well as certain passions to follow one another, not a necessary or inevitable connection. Moreover, he thinks of association, whether of ideas or passions, as immediate and unreflective. It is something that happens to us, not something we deliberately do.

Sympathy involves a four-step process. First, you arrive at the idea of what another person is feeling. Reflection on your own past experience tells you what feelings are regularly associated with what bodily expressions, actions, or verbal behaviors. When you see similar expressions and behaviors in others, you infer that they are caused by similar passions. Second, you are aware that the other person resembles you. Hume thinks that every human being resembles every other human being to some extent. We tend to experience the same sorts of passions in similar situations and we express them in similar ways. But we also resemble some people more than others. You resemble individuals who are your own age and sex, from your own country, and in the same profession more than individuals who differ from you in these ways. Third, Hume claims that you always have available to you a forceful, lively and vivacious impression of yourself. Fourth, he appeals to two points he established in Book 1. The principles of association not only relate two perceptions, they also transmit force and vivacity from one perception to the other. Since the difference between an idea and an impression is a matter of force and vivacity, the difference between experiencing a passion and having an idea of that passion is that the former is more forceful and vivacious than the latter.

Sympathy explains how you move from merely having an idea of what someone is feeling to your actually feeling what the other person is feeling. You arrive at an idea of what another person is feeling and, at the same time, you are related to that person by some sort of resemblance. Your lively and vivacious idea of yourself transmits its force and vivacity to your idea of the other person's feeling by means of the associative principle of resemblance. In this way, your idea of the other person's passion becomes forceful, lively, and vivacious. If an idea of a passion is lively and forceful enough, it becomes the very passion itself.

Hume's explanation of sympathy implies that our natural and spontaneous sympathetic reactions are variable and biased. We sympathize more easily with people who speak our language, share our culture, and are the same age or gender as us. Because the associative principles transmit force and vivacity from one perception to another, the more we resemble someone, the more liveliness and vivacity gets transmitted from my impression of myself to my idea of the other person's passion. The more vivacious and lively my idea of a passion, the more I feel what the other person is feeling.

Hume thinks the other two associative relations also influence our capacity to react sympathetically to others. We sympathize more strongly and easily with those to whom we are related by causation and who are spatially or temporally contiguous to us – friends, family, neighbors, and fellow citizens. If I am related to someone in all three ways, I will be able to conceive of that person's passion "in the strongest and most lively manner." Although sympathy enables us to enter into the feelings of anyone – we resemble everyone to some extent – our capacity to react sympathetically to others varies with the variations in the associative relations. For shorthand, call the natural and spontaneous operation of sympathy, "unregulated" sympathy.

Sympathy, like the associative principles that explain it, operates in us as a "gentle force." It isn't a mechanism that we may turn on or off at will. Instead, it is something that happens to us, immediately and unreflectively. If you are watching a scary movie, you can't help but feel afraid. If you happen to live with people who are

233

always criticizing you, you can't help but inherit their disapproval, which, in turn, makes you miserable and unhappy. Although we can't directly control whether and with whom we sympathize, we may modify the effects of sympathy in various ways. For example, Hume suggests that we move away from critical parents or friends, since distance weakens their feelings of disapproval.

One final point about sympathy is that by itself it doesn't motivate action. Although it isn't by itself a motive, it may enter into the explanation of why someone performs certain actions. For example, Hume explains why we feel pity when we see or read about the distressing experiences of others by appealing to the sympathy mechanism. While sympathy explains how we come to feel their pain, it doesn't explain how we are going to react to those painful feelings. Our inherited pain may move us to help them, but it may also motivate us to walk away or to take an aspirin.

The general point of view and the regulation of sympathy

Hume develops his theory of moral evaluation in 3.3.1 of the *Treatise* in response to two objections to his idea that the moral sentiments spring from sympathy. The first begins with the acknowledgment that the loves and hatreds resulting from unregulated sympathy are variable and biased. This poses a problem for Hume because he thinks we tend to morally love and hate the same sorts of character traits in people. It doesn't matter whether we are causally related to the person, contiguous to her, or resemble her in special ways. If someone in Scotland has the same "good" character trait as someone in China, the trait is equally loved and esteemed. Moral love can't be based on sympathy, because our moral approvals don't vary, but the loves and hatreds that result from the natural and spontaneous workings of sympathy do vary.

The second objection is that "virtue in rags" is still esteemed. Sympathy works by looking at the actual effects of a person's character traits. But sometimes misfortune or lack of opportunity prevents someone from exercising a good character trait, and as a consequence, it doesn't bring about the beneficial results it normally would. However, even when the beneficial results aren't realized, we still esteem the person for her virtuous character trait. As Hume puts it, "virtue in rags is still virtue; and the love, which it procures, attends a man into a dungeon or desart, where the virtue can no longer be exerted in action, and is lost to all the world" (T 3.3.1.19).

Hume responds that moral love and hatred arises from sympathy, but only when it is regulated by "some steady and general points of view." There are two regulative features of the general point of view. The first is that we survey a person's character from the perspective of that person's narrow circle – the people with whom she regularly interacts. Typically these will include the person herself and her usual associates: her family, friends, neighbors, co-workers, and so on. We sympathize with the people who make up a person's narrow circle, and we judge character traits to be virtuous or vicious in terms of whether they are good or bad for those in her narrow circle.

The second feature is that we regulate sympathy further by relying on general rules that specify the usual effects and tendencies of character traits, rather than the actual effects of a person's character traits. For example, if some misfortune prevents a person from exercising her kindly impulses, we judge her kindness to be morally good because in normal circumstances it is beneficial to others.

Although Hume explicitly introduces only two regulative components of the general point of view, others may be derived from them. For example, the actual composition of a person's narrow circle will vary from person to person and for an individual over her lifetime. Moreover, in most cases we know nothing or very little about the actual composition of a person's narrow circle. Since we are able to morally love and hate people who are unfamiliar to us – people who live in remote countries or are from distant ages – this suggests that we do not survey a person through the eyes of her actual narrow circle, but rather through the eyes of what would be a person's normal or usual narrow circle.

Hume maintains that sympathy, when regulated by the general point of view, causes us to admire four kinds of character traits – those that are useful or immediately agreeable to the possessor or useful or agreeable to others. As an empirical hypothesis, he thinks it must be confirmed by experience, a task he takes up in his discussion of the individual virtues.

The general point of view is, for Hume, the moral perspective. Its regulative features define a perspective we can share with everyone, from which we may survey a person's character traits. When we occupy the general point of view, we sympathize with the person herself and her narrow circle, and come to love the person for those traits that normally are useful and pleasant for everyone in her narrow circle. The moral evaluations that result when we take up the general point of view differ in important ways from the judgments that arise from two other perspectives – the perspective of self-interest and the perspective of unregulated sympathy.

From the point of view of self-interest, I tend to love anyone who serves my interests and benefits me, and hate anyone who opposes my interests and harms me. From a self-interested point of view, I will dislike my rival's industriousness because it counteracts my own interests. But by viewing my rival through the eyes of her narrow circle and by sympathizing with the effects her character trait would typically have on them, I will be constrained to see her industriousness as worthy of love. In the same way, what we love and hate from the perspective of unregulated sympathy may be opposed to our moral loves and hates. From the perspective of unregulated sympathy, if someone is causally related to me, contiguous to me, or resembles me, I will esteem her good qualities – her loyalty – more strongly than someone who isn't associated with me in these ways. For example, I will love my friend more than the ancient Roman, Marcus Brutus, even though Brutus's loyalty is greater and more impressive. But by sympathizing with Brutus's narrow circle and by relying on general rules that specify the usual tendencies of character traits, I will be constrained to admire his loyalty.

One advantage of Hume's account of the moral point of view is that he provides a wholly naturalistic account of moral judgment. He begins with our more personal, variable, and violent loves and hatreds – feelings that aren't themselves moral – and he then describes the process whereby we transform them into moral loves and hates. The effect of taking up the general point of view and regulating our sympathetic responses is to make these violent, variable, and irregular loves and hatreds more calm, stable, and regular.

Another advantage of Hume's account of the general point of view and, in particular, the regulation of sympathy is that it brings a kind of impartiality and objectivity to our moral judgments. The regulation of sympathy ensures that we put to one side considerations of self-interest as well as considerations derived from the special ways we may be related to others, effectively excluding bias and partiality from the moral point of view. In judging others we discount not only the fact that they may be our rivals, but also that they resemble us in special ways or are related to us by contiguity or causality. In this sense, the judgments that result when we take up the general point of view are impartial.

The regulation of sympathy allows Hume to explain why there tends to be agreement in moral judgments. Although approval and disapproval are feelings, they are distinct from our mere likes or dislikes and from our more personal and violent loves and hatreds. Approval and disapproval are calm forms of love and hatred that arise when we survey people from the same perspective – through the eyes of the person's normal narrow circle, taking into account the usual or regular tendencies of people's character traits. In this sense, the judgments that result from the general point of view are objective.

Hume's conception of the general point of view enables him to generate an ideal of character, a picture of our moral selves that goes beyond what is given in experience (Brown 1994). The ideal element is brought in with the regulation of our sympathetic loves and hates. In the case of unregulated sympathy, we love or hate someone if their character traits are actually beneficial or harmful for their narrow circle. If someone is unable to exercise one of his character traits because of some misfortune, there will be nothing with which to sympathize, so we won't love them. But regulated sympathy may operate quite independently of the actual world. In the case of regulated sympathy, we respond sympathetically to the usual tendencies of a person's character for her normal narrow circle. In fact, we may be sympathizing with the non-existent pleasures of non-existent people.

According to Hume, the ultimate test of "merit and virtue" is this:

> if there be no relation in life, in which I cou'd not wish to stand to a particular person, his character must so far be allow'd to be perfect. If he be as little wanting to himself as to others, his character is entirely perfect. (T 3.3.3.9)

We arrive at the ideal of character by surveying a person's character from various perspectives – that of friend, fellow-worker, neighbor, and fellow-citizen. The ideal of character that results is a picture of ourselves as essentially social beings. The effect of the regulating features is to idealize this picture. We imagine a person in all possible roles and relationships, and by relying on general rules we know what character traits usually have good effects. The ideal of character is a kind of artificial construct: an ideal of someone who is beneficial in all possible roles and relationships.

While it is true that moral character is an ideal construct, the ideal is not very exacting. This is especially true with respect to the natural virtues. On Hume's account of the natural virtues, the ideal does not demand that human nature be radically altered or reformed, or that our relationships must be impartial. Our sympathetic reactions are guided by what is normal and usual in human nature. Thus, it is normal and usual for us to love our children better than our nephews, nephews better than cousins, and cousins better than strangers, where everything else is equal. Moreover, with respect to the natural virtues, Hume thinks that the best person acts from natural and spontaneous affections rather than from the motive of duty. From the perspective of the general point of view, human nature is lovable as it is.

The idealizing character shows up more in the artificial virtues. The duties that arise from the artificial virtues – respecting property rights, fidelity in promises, and obedience to government – are not owed to people because of any special relationship we might have with them, but simply because they are fellow-citizens. With respect to the artificial virtues, Hume holds that the usual and morally praiseworthy motive is the sense of duty.

Hume's theory also has the resources to explain why we try to live up to the moral ideal. Sympathy ensures that we will inherit other people's moral judgments about us, which, in turn, pressures us to see ourselves as others see us. If we fall short of the moral ideal by having a trait that is harmful or disagreeable to others, but not to ourselves, sympathy will get us to disapprove of it. Sympathy may go so far as to make us disapprove of our own vices, even when they are beneficial to us.

> And this sympathy we sometimes carry so far, as even to be displeas'd with a quality commodious to us, merely because it displeases others, and renders us disagreeable in their eyes. (T 3.3.1.26)

The capacity to survey ourselves as others do may be developed to the point where we come to see ourselves not just as we actually appear to others, but as we *would* appear to them. According to Hume, we may respond sympathetically to what we anticipate someone else would feel, if they were aware that an event or action was occurring or was about to occur. The internalization of the moral judgments of others may thus have the effect that even the *idea* that others would disapprove of us may make us hateful in our own eyes. In this way, we come to see ourselves through the eyes of someone who fully regulates her sympathy – from the general point of view.

The result is that we will be lovable in our own eyes only if we are or would be morally lovable in the eyes of others. Being morally loveable in our own eyes is an important ingredient of happiness since it gives us peace of mind. Both our sense of ourselves as a lovable person and our happiness are dependent upon living up to the ideal of character. When a person is aware that he falls short of the character ideal, he

> may hate himself upon that account and may perform the action without the motive, from a certain sense of duty, in order to acquire by practice, that virtuous principle. (T 3.2.1.8)

The motive of duty arises when our self-conception clashes with the ideal of character. We hate ourselves for failing to live up to the character ideal and this makes us unhappy. We may thus be motivated to cultivate the virtues. In this way, we move from being a spectator who surveys his own character to being an agent who is motivated to live up to the moral ideal.

237

There are several other advantages Hume's account of morality has over his rationalist opponents and his sentimentalist predecessors. Clarke and Hutcheson failed to explain why we are able to perceive people's characters and their actions in moral terms. Clarke simply asserts that reason perceives the relations of fitness and unfitness, while Hutcheson asserts that we possess a unique moral sense. By tracing the moral sentiments to sympathy, Hume is able to produce an explanation of how we come to have the moral sentiments, one that explains many other aspects of our lives, such as our social tendencies. More importantly, he explains sympathy in terms of the even more fundamental associative principles of resemblance, contiguity, and causality. Our capacity to see the world in moral terms, on Hume's view, is not an arbitrary or merely contingent feature of our lives, but is something that is deeply rooted in us. If we lacked the capacity to respond sympathetically to others, along with these other associative tendencies, we would be unimaginatively different than we are.

In the concluding section of the *Treatise*, Hume describes one other advantage his account of morality has over Clarke's and Hutcheson's. He remarks that "all lovers of virtue" must be pleased to see the distinction between virtue and vice traced to such a noble source as sympathy. He thinks "it requires but very little knowledge of human affairs to perceive, that a sense of morals is a principle inherent in the soul," which has powerful effects on us (T 3.3.6.3). He continues by saying that:

> This sense must certainly acquire new force, when reflecting on itself, it approves of those principles, from which it is deriv'd, and finds nothing but what is great and good in its rise and origin. Those who resolve the sense of morals into original instincts of the human mind, may defend the cause of virtue with sufficient authority [*Hutcheson*]; but want the advantage, which those possess who account for that sense by an extensive sympathy with mankind [*Hume*]. According to the latter system, not only virtue must be approv'd of, but also the sense of virtue: And not only that sense, but also the principles from whence it is deriv'd. So that nothing is presented on any side, but what is laudable and good. (T 3.3.6.3)

When the moral sense reflects on itself, it approves both its source and its workings. When we reflect on the origins of the moral sentiments and come to understand their basis in sympathy, we have no reason to want to reject our nature as moral creatures. We come to accept the moral sentiments along with the deep and fundamental principles of human nature in which it is rooted. Hume's account of morality is reflectively stable (Rawls 2000: 99–100; Baier 1991: 277–88; Korsgaard 1996: 51–66).

See also 9 "Hume's Indirect Passions"; 28 "Hume's Metaethics: Is Hume a Moral Noncognitivist?"

References

Árdal, Páll (1989). *Passion and Value in Hume's "Treatise"* (Edinburgh: Edinburgh University Press).

Baier, Annette C. (1991). *A Progress of Sentiments: Reflections on Hume's "Treatise"* (Cambridge, MA: Harvard University Press).

Brown, Charlotte (1988). "Is Hume an Internalist?" *Journal of the History of Philosophy*, 26, pp. 69–82.

—— (1994). "From Spectator to Agent: Hume's Theory of Obligation," *Hume Studies*, 20, pp. 19–35.

Clarke, Samuel (1706). *A Discourse concerning the Unchangeable Obligations of Natural Religion*, in D. D. Raphael (ed.) (1991), *British Moralists: 1650–1800*, 2 vols. (Indianapolis, IN: Hackett, 1991).

Cohon, Rachel (1997). "Is Hume a Noncognitivist in the Motivation Argument?" *Philosophical Studies*, 85, pp. 251–66.

Hobbes, Thomas (1641). *Leviathan*, ed. Edwin Curley (Indianapolis, IN: Hackett, 1994).

Hutcheson, Francis (1728). *An Essay on the Nature and Conduct of the Passions and Affections, with Illustrations upon the Moral Sense*, ed. Aaron Garrett (Indianapolis, IN: Liberty Fund, 2002).

—— (1725). *An Inquiry into Our Ideas of Beauty and Virtue in Two Treatises*, ed. Wolfgang Leidhold (Indianapolis, IN: Liberty Fund, 2004).

Kant, Immanuel (1785). *Groundwork of the Metaphysics of Morals*, ed. Mary Gregor (Cambridge: Cambridge University Press, 1997).

Korsgaard, Christine (1999). "The General Point of View: Love and Moral Approval in Hume's Ethics," *Hume Studies*, 25, pp. 3–41.

—— (1996). *The Sources of Normativity*, ed. Onora O'Neill (Cambridge: Cambridge University Press).

Locke, John (1690). *Essay concerning Human Understanding*, ed. Peter H. Nidditch (Oxford: Clarendon Press, 1975).

Radcliffe, Elizabeth (1996). "How Does the Humean Sense of Duty Motivate?" *Journal of the History of Philosophy*, 34, pp. 383–407.

Rawls, John (2000). *Lectures on the History of Philosophy*, ed. Barbara Herman (Cambridge, MA: Harvard University Press).

Reid, Thomas (1788). *Essays on the Active Powers of Man*, in D. D. Raphael (ed.), *British Moralists: 1650–1800*, 2 vols. (Indianapolis, IN: Hackett, 1991).

Stroud, Barry (1977). *Hume* (London: Routledge and Kegan Paul).

Wollaston, William (1724). *The Religion of Nature Delineated* (London: S. Palmer; repr. New York: Garland Publishing, 1978).

Further Reading

Darwall, Stephen (1995). *The British Moralists and the Internal "Ought": 1640–1740* (Cambridge: Cambridge University Press).

Mackie, J. L. (1980). *Hume's Moral Theory* (London: Routledge and Kegan Paul).

Penelhum, Terence (1975). *Hume* (London: Macmillan).

Schneewind, J. B. (1998). *The Invention of Autonomy* (Cambridge: Cambridge University Press).

Snare, Francis (1975). "The Argument from Motivation," *Mind*, 84, pp. 1–9.

—— (1991). *Morals, Motivation, and Convention: Hume's Influential Doctrines* (Cambridge: Cambridge University Press).

Stroud, Barry (1993). " 'Gilding or Staining' the World with 'Sentiments' and 'Phantasms'," *Hume Studies*, 19, pp. 253–72.

13

Sympathy and Hume's Spectator-centered Theory of Virtue

KATE ABRAMSON

In the following sense, Hume's moral theory is unquestionably spectator-centered: Humean moral approval and disapproval arises – in the first instance – from the standpoint of a judicious spectator contemplating the praiseworthiness of traits and motives, rather than that of an agent contemplating what to do. Whether this alone constitutes grounds for objection is one issue. It is a separate issue whether, as some scholars have claimed, this feature of Hume's account of moral evaluation also entails (or is entailed by) other purportedly spectatorial features of his ethical theory, ranging from his views about moral motivation and ethical normativity, to character, responsibility, and personal identity. And whether Hume's views on these latter topics are objectionable as well is yet a further question.

Additionally complicating discussion of any of these questions is Hume's claim that the standpoint of Humean moral evaluation is sympathetic, a claim that appears to be at odds with the thought that Humean moral evaluation is spectatorial. We tend to assume that "sympathizing" with someone involves adopting *that person's* perspective, and thus cannot be spectatorial. But, as Stephen Darwall points out, this is not Hume's primary conception of sympathy (2002: ch. 3; 1999: 143–4; 1998). According to Hume, sympathy typically works like this: I see in another's "countenance or actions" the usual indications of some passion, and infer that she feels that passion. Sympathy then "enlivens" my idea of her passion, thereby allowing me to feel, in some measure, what she feels (T 2.1.11.3). There appears to be no point in this process at which I adopt another person's *perspective*, and hence no point at which sympathy will force the judicious Humean spectator out of her spectatorial standpoint.

All this makes it difficult to so much as survey the territory marked out by references to "sympathy and Hume's spectator-centered theory of virtue." Here I address three of the most significant objections to the spectator-centered aspects of Humean moral evaluation. First among these is the complaint that the spectatorial character of Humean moral sentiments makes them ill-suited to play a role characteristic of moral sentiments as such, i.e. sentiments through which we hold one another accountable (Darwall 1999: 163–4). A second charge is that Humean sentiments of moral disapproval are paradigmatically exclusionary in their practical import, a disturbing feature that comes hand-in-hand, it is thought, with their spectatorial character (Baier 1994: 281; Darwall 1999: 163). A third complaint makes the more general claim that the standard of virtue embedded in Hume's spectatorial account of moral evaluation is in fact no standard at all: not only the "monkish virtues," so famously condemned by Hume, but nearly any trait, ought to qualify as a virtue for Hume (Hursthouse 1999: 71).

It should be noted that these are not the objections that lie behind most contemporary objections to "Hume's spectator-centered ethics." Such complaints usually target Hume's views about moral motivation – the charge being that Hume is committed to the wildly implausible view that an agent's moral commitments play no essential role in motivating her virtuous conduct (Abramson 2002; and Abramson forthcoming).

Yet the objections examined in what follows pose the most serious of threats to Hume's moral theory. Were any of them well founded, it would, to borrow Hursthouse's words, spell "disaster" for Hume (1999: 71). A moral theory that cannot provide a plausible account of our moral sentiments as responsibility-conferring is a theory that cannot account for one of the most distinctive aspects of our ethical practices as such. A theory that sees moral disapproval as characteristically exclusionary is a theory that commits us – as Baier notes – to the ridiculous proposition that we all ought to be running around shunning one another for each other's vices (1994: 282). And a "theory of virtue" on which nearly all traits qualify as virtues cannot qualify as a theory of virtue in the first place.

Fortunately, Hume can be acquitted of all these charges. What will emerge in the process is a significantly new understanding of Hume's conception of moral evaluation.

Humean Moral Sentiments as Responsibility Conferring

On the supposition that Humean moral sentiments not only arise from the standpoint of "an observer, rather than a participant in ethical life," but are themselves felt from such a spectatorial standpoint, Stephen Darwall complains that for Hume,

> morality has nothing essentially to do with judgments we render from *within* the moral life as agents and patients interacting with each other. It is not concerned, in any fundamental way, with reciprocity between equals or with any mutual accountability that expresses equal respect. It is akin, rather, to aesthetics, and moral value is like a kind of beauty, as Hume explicitly says. (1999: 141)

The first of Darwall's claims follows straightforwardly from the thought that Humean moral sentiments are felt from an observer's standpoint, and the analogy to aesthetic judgments is indeed Hume's own. But the notion that for these reasons, Humean morality is not fundamentally concerned with "mutual accountability" is initially puzzling. Why should the premise that Humean sentiments of moral approval and disapproval are spectatorial be thought to entail *this* conclusion?

Answers Darwall:

> We don't deserve praise, our own or others', of course, unless our motives and character are proper. But we are not accountable before others for general impropriety. Imprudently wasting my fortune may rightly make me subject to disesteem, but not to any emotion, like resentment or anger, that makes a claim on how I should act.

241

Here again we see a fundamental difference between Smith's form of sentimentalism and Hume's. For Hume, all negative ethical judgment expresses a kind of disengaged, aesthetic reaction ("disdain," as Annette Baier terms it), an attitude or sentiment whose natural expression is some form of disengagement or distancing – revulsion, turning away from, looking down on, and so on. As Smith understands them, however, judgments of justice express reactions that demand a distinctive form of engagement, namely, a mutually respectful accountability that recognizes the dignity of the other to be treated as an equal. (1999: 163)

In outline, Darwall's argument seems to be as follows: (1) Humean moral sentiments arise from the standpoint of an observer; (2) Humean moral sentiments must then themselves be felt from a spectatorial standpoint; (3) because it is spectatorial, Humean moral disapproval is "naturally" expressed in "some form of disengagement" – as opposed to being a "reaction that demands . . . mutually respectful accountability"; (4) moral attitudes are characteristically responsibility-conferring, and in at least some cases, this comes in the form of a demand for accountability; (5) thus, Hume cannot offer an adequate account of our moral attitudes.

There is much that's compelling about this argument. It's certainly true, for instance, that our moral attitudes are responsibility-conferring, whereas not all evaluative sentiments are. To see another as beautiful, for instance, I needn't view her as responsible for that on account of which I find her beautiful. And Darwall is surely right to see it as characteristic of moral sentiments that they are responsibility-conferring. To say, "I morally disapprove, but I don't think she's responsible for it" either involves a deep misunderstanding of moral disapproval or is merely a confused way of excusing (or forgiving) her.

Having granted these modest claims, we who wish to dispute Darwall's anti-Humean conclusion are left only with the following options. We might contend that spectatorial sentiments can be responsibility-conferring, or at least responsibility-conferring in morally significant ways that do not involve holding another *accountable* in the Kantian sense. Alternatively, we might argue that Humean moral sentiments are not spectatorial. Or, third, we might dispute Darwall's contention that spectatorial sentiments, as such, are "naturally expressed" in "disengagement" rather than "demands for accountability" – either by arguing that spectatorial sentiments needn't be expressed in disengagement, or by arguing that disengagement can be a way of holding someone accountable.

Here I want to pursue what many will undoubtedly think the least promising of these avenues. I will contend that Humean moral sentiments are not paradigmatically spectatorial. There are two apparently daunting obstacles in the way of this thought. First, there is an etiological consideration. The standpoint from which Humean moral assessments arise in the first instance is that of a judicious spectator. It seems *prima facie* implausible to suppose that a spectatorial standpoint could give rise to sentiments that are felt from something other than a spectator's standpoint. Second, on Hume's own description, at least some sentiments to which the Humean moral point of view gives rise – love, hatred, pride, and humility – do indeed seem to be felt from a spectator's standpoint. Add to this the common scholarly presumption that all Humean moral sentiments can be reduced without loss to a form of Humean love, hatred, pride, or humility, and the conclusion that Humean moral sentiments are felt from the standpoint of a spectator seems unavoidable.

Let's begin with the standard view about the role of love, hatred, pride, and humility in Humean moral evaluation.

Consider this key passage from T 3.3.1.31:

> As to the good or ill desert of virtue or vice, 'tis an evident consequence of the sentiments of pleasure or uneasiness. These sentiments produce love or hatred; and love or hatred, by the original constitution of human passion, is attended with benevolence or anger; that is, with a desire of making happy the person we love, and miserable the person we hate. We have treated of this more fully on another occasion.

The "sentiments of pleasure and uneasiness" first mentioned in this passage are those that take traits as their objects – e.g. moral approval of liberality. The consequent love or hate is directed towards a person who has that trait – e.g. esteem for Sally's liberality. Finally, in the punch line of the passage, Hume reminds readers of the connections between love and benevolence, and between hatred and anger. Why does he do so?

One answer is that benevolence and anger, unlike hatred and love, are motivating, and so prompt conduct (partly) constitutive of Humean morality's sanctions and rewards. In other words, one might think that Hume's concern here is with ethical sanctions and rewards which are expressed in the appraiser's conduct towards others (Brown 1988: 86 n.). But this reading strains the text. For one, the issue just described is tangential to Hume's main concern in the *Treatise* section in which the passage appears, namely, the nature of Humean moral assessment. The proposed interpretation reads the section's last paragraph as an abrupt digression concerning how we treat those whom we praise or blame, a topic just as abruptly dropped in the next *Treatise* section. And to see Hume as here concerned with ethical sanctions and rewards is an awkward interpretation of his claim to be interested in "the good or ill *desert* of virtue or vice."

A more natural interpretation of this passage is that Hume is concerned with the responsibility-conferring dimensions of ethical assessment. Not only is this a straightforward reading of Hume's use of the term "desert" at T 3.3.1.31, but it also fits nicely with the fact that Hume's general topic in 3.3.1 is moral assessment. But if that's right, then Hume's invocation of benevolence and anger in the punch line of the passage suggests something interesting, namely, that there is a special form of approval and disapproval that the virtuous and vicious deserve, one which confers responsibility upon them and which is constituted by moralized benevolence and anger.

Anger is both felt from a participant's standpoint, and a sentiment that responds to another as an accountable equal (Darwall 1999: 163). So too, albeit surprisingly, is moralized Humean benevolence. For Hume, benevolence is any "desire of making happy the person we love." But the specific form of this desire to which another's virtuous conduct gives rise is *gratitude* (e.g.: T 2.2.3.3–4, T 3.2.5.8; EPM 5.17). And gratitude *is* felt from the standpoint of a participant in ethical life (see Darwall 1999; Strawson 1982).

Although Hume does not say so at T 3.3.1.31, anger and gratitude are not the only sentiments to which love and hatred give rise. They are merely the most usual attendants of moralized love and hatred (T 2.2.6.5). Moralized Humean hatred can also be attended with contempt, disdain, indignation, resentment, shame, and reproach (e.g.: EHU 5.8; EPM 1.10, 5.1, 9.5, App. 4.1–2, App. 4.9; T 2.2.14; HENG vol.1, ch. 5, p. 332; vol.4, ch. 39, pp. 79–80).

Resentment, reproach, and indignation are also all participant sentiments, by Darwall's own lights. This leaves us only with contempt, disdain, and shame, three concomitants of Humean love and hatred commonly taken to be spectatorial sentiments. Yet even if we grant that they are such, it's worth noting that Adam Smith – whose account of moral assessment is anything but spectatorial – also includes contempt, disdain, and shame on his list of specifically moral attitudes (Smith 1982: e.g. 44, 62, 84, 85, 115). At the very least, then, we have no reason to suppose that the fact that Hume includes these sentiments on his list of moral attitudes is a result of his spectatorial account of moral evaluation.

The interpretation I am pressing, in short, is this. T 3.3.1.31 tells us that adoption of the Humean moral point of view gives rise to approval or disapproval of character traits, and then to a form of love or hatred for the agent with those traits. But T 3.3.1.31 also speaks of a third set of sentiments to which the Humean moral point of view gives rise. My thesis is that Hume thinks only the sentiments in this third category are responsibility-conferring, and for that reason qualify in the full-fledged sense as *moral* sentiments. This is why Hume goes out of his way to refer to this third category of sentiments in the punch line of his brief discussion of the "good or ill desert of virtue and vice" – the final sentence of the *Treatise* section on moral evaluation. The vast majority of the sentiments in this third category are participant sentiments, rather than sentiments felt from a spectator's standpoint. So, if I'm right that Hume regards only the sentiments in this third category as responsibility-conferring, and hence as full-fledged moral sentiments, then Darwall's objection dissolves.

One might object that if Hume had intended T 3.3.1.31 to carry this much weight, we ought to have expected him to at least mention self-directed forms of praise and blame (like guilt). Yet insofar as such self-directed sentiments have clear other-directed counterparts (e.g., guilt to anger), there's little reason for Hume to have made separate mention of the former at T 3.3.1.31. Furthermore, there's good reason for Hume to have avoided entering into this territory. Hume holds that the psychological connections between self-directed reactive attitudes like guilt and humility/pride are more complicated than those which link anger to hatred, or gratitude to love. To discuss the precise nature of these complicated connections would have required a long digression into the philosophical psychology of Book 2. Better to close T 3.3.1.31, by simply remarking, as Hume does, "We have treated of this more fully on another occasion."

What are we to then say about the standard interpretation which not only holds that a subspecies of the indirect passions qualifies as Humean moral sentiments, but that all Humean moral sentiments are reducible to a form of love, hatred, pride, or humility? If we grant that moral attitudes as such are responsibility-conferring, and stipulate that the spectatorial character of these four Humean attitudes precludes their being responsibility-conferring, then the most we might say is that so-called "moralized" Humean love, hatred, pride, and humility are *proto*-moral sentiments – sentiments that do not have the full, responsibility-conferring normative force of properly moral attitudes like resentment or gratitude.

Yet, contrary to the standard interpretation, Hume himself in fact never claims otherwise. There are, to begin with, straightforward reasons for Hume to repeatedly highlight the link between vice/virtue and love, hatred, pride, and humility, reasons which pose no difficulties for the proposed interpretation. For instance, while Hume holds that resentment, anger, contempt, guilt, resentment, and gratitude may all arise independently of one of the indirect passions, he also holds that these sentiments usually arise by being prompted by one of the moralized indirect passions (e.g., T 2.2.6.3–6). In this *causal* sense, love, hatred, pride, and humility have priority in Hume's account of moral assessment over anger, gratitude, reproach, resentment, and so on. But this is entirely compatible with the thought that these four indirect passions do not and cannot themselves qualify as full-fledged moral sentiments.

In all of Hume's works, I can locate only a single passage that appears to be in tension with the proposed understanding of the role of love, hatred, pride, and humility in Humean moral assessment:

> It has been observ'd, in treating of the passions, that pride and humility, love and hatred, are excited by any advantages or disadvantages of the *mind, body* or *fortune*; and that these advantages or disadvantages have that effect, by producing a separate impression of pain or pleasure. The pain or pleasure, which arises from the general survey or view of any action or quality of *mind*, constitutes its vice or virtue, and gives rise to our approbation or blame, which is nothing but a fainter and more imperceptible love or hatred. (T 3.3.5.1)

The final sentence in this passage not only seems to qualify love and hatred as forms of genuine moral approval and disapproval, but to also identify Humean moral approval and disapproval as a particular subspecies of these passions.

In fact, however, Hume does not say that the love and hatred at issue in the final sentence are sentiments of *moral* approval and disapproval. He does say that the pain or pleasure arising from the "general survey of any action or quality of mind" constitutes its "vice or virtue," and in that sense, the sentence as a whole is focused specifically on moral (as opposed to aesthetic) qualities. But the sentiments that constitute a quality's viciousness or virtuousness are not sentiments of love and hatred; the former, Hume tells us, "give rise" to the latter. And Hume does not refer to the latter as specifically *moral* sentiments.

Moreover, in the sentence that immediately follows the passage just quoted above, Hume writes:

> We have assign'd four different sources of this pain and pleasure; and in order to justify more fully that hypothesis, it may here be proper to observe, that the advantages or disadvantages of the body and of fortune, produce a pain or pleasure from the very same principles.

Hume's goal in T 3.3.5, in other words, is to argue that just as vice and virtue give rise to pride, humility, love, and hatred on account of their usefulness/disutility or agreeableness/disagreeableness to ourselves or others, so the advantages and disadvantages of body and fortune give rise to pride, humility, love, and hatred on account of "the very same principles." In this light, what is important about the love to which virtue gives rise is, as Hume says, that such love is a kind of "approval" of the virtuous person, just as the "esteem" to which a person's wealth gives rise constitutes a kind of "approval" of that person (T 3.3.5.5). Whether the former sort of "approval" is properly *moral* approval in the full-fledged sense, and in what ways moral approval differs from other sorts of approval or esteem, are separate questions not at issue in this section. Hume himself gestures to this fact in the penultimate sentence of T 3.3.5:

> a convenient house, and a virtuous character, cause not the same feeling of approbation; even tho' the source of our approbation be the same, and flow from sympathy and an idea of their utility. (T 3.3.5.6)

The apparently intractable sentence at T 3.3.5.1 is hence compatible with the interpretation for which I've been arguing. Hume does not there say that the species of love and hatred which play a role in Humean moral assessment are themselves properly *moral* sentiments, nor does the claim for which he is arguing in this *Treatise* section rely on the thought that they are properly *moral* sentiments.

Most of the other passages in which Hume links virtue and vice to the indirect passions of Book 2 claim only that virtue and vice do produce love and hatred (T 2.1.11.1, 2.2.1.4–7, 2.2.2.9–14, 2.2.7.5, 3.1.2.2–5, 3.3.1.19–25, 3.3.3.10, 3.3.4.8–10; EPM 1.6, n.25). A few passages assert that virtue and vice can be safely treated as the power of a mental quality to produce love, hatred, pride, or humility (e.g., T 3.3.1.3–5). And twice Hume tells us that the heart does not regulate "all its love or hatred, by the universal, abstract differences of vice and virtue" (EPM 5.27; T 3.3.3.2). All of these claims are compatible with the proposed interpretation. Even if, for instance, we identify vice and virtue as the power of producing love or hatred, we may regard this love and hatred as the necessary concomitant of, and antecedent to, those sentiments which fully qualify as *moral* sentiments.

We are left only with the etiological objection. But to suppose that because Humean moral sentiments arise, in the first instance, from a judicious spectator's standpoint, they must themselves be felt from a spectator's standpoint is to seriously oversimplify the etiology of Humean moral sentiments. The initial spectatorial standpoint of Humean moral evaluation gives rise only to approval or disapproval of traits. On Hume's account, a separate associative mechanism (or imaginative exercise) takes us from approval of a trait to love or hatred (pride or humility) for someone who has that trait, and yet a further imaginative exercise moves us to feel gratitude, anger, resentment, etc. One might argue that these latter associative mechanisms cannot be made sense of in the absence of implausible details of the philosophical psychology of Book 2, or constitute mere hand-waving on Hume's part. But the fact remains that these additional aspects of the etiology of specifically moral Humean anger, gratitude, reproach, and so on, effectively open up the space Hume needs to hold that such sentiments may be felt from the standpoint of a participant in ethical life. The shift from spectatorial to participant standpoint in Humean moral evaluation may be located in the associative mechanisms that follow the generation of love, hatred, pride, or humility. If it is, there is nothing incoherent about Hume's presuming that some sentiments which originate partly in a spectatorial standpoint are themselves participant sentiments.

246

Exclusion and Humean Moral Disapproval

Whereas Darwall presumes that Humean moral disapproval is characteristically expressed in disengagement as part of an argument directed toward the responsibility-conferring aspects (or lack thereof) of Humean moral sentiments, Annette Baier takes aim directly at the purportedly exclusionary character of Humean moral disapproval. Her central worry is that this feature of moral disapproval will spoil Hume's otherwise "gentle" morality (1994). Baier suggests that the only solution for the good Humean is to refrain as much as possible from actually expressing our disapproval to those of whom we disapprove (1994: 286–7).

Just why Baier supposes the spectatorial standpoint of Humean moral evaluation must give rise to forms of moral disapproval that are exclusionary is not obvious. Perhaps, with Darwall, she supposes that all sentiments originating in a spectator's standpoint must themselves be felt from a spectator's standpoint, and that disapproval felt from a spectator's standpoint is characteristically exclusionary. Or perhaps the thought is that any form of disapproval which originates in a spectator's standpoint must be exclusionary for that reason alone. In either case, one may wonder why one should suppose there to be such a connection.

Baier claims that the evidence for the exclusionary character of Humean moral sentiments lies in the terms of disapproval Hume uses when discussing vices and vicious persons. She writes, "the range of reactive terms [Hume] uses definitely falls more into what Gibbard calls the disdain and shame family" (sentiments Baier treats as characterized primarily by their exclusionary import) "than the anger and guilt family" (sentiments that are not exclusionary) (1994: 282).

Baier might mean that most of the forms of disapproval Hume employs are exclusionary, or alternatively, that Hume employs exclusionary forms of disapproval more often. Either way, the text doesn't give Baier what she needs. Relatively few of the forms of disapproval Hume invokes when discussing vice are exclusionary. He speaks of vice as properly occasioning not only the exclusionary sentiments of contempt, disdain, and shame, but also as properly occasioning anger, guilt, resentment, indignation, antipathy, and reproach. Nor does Hume invoke exclusionary sentiments with substantially greater frequency. "Contempt" and its cognates appear often in Hume's works. But most of these are either references to contempt for something other than a person (e.g. contempt for "riches"), or to a sentiment felt *by* vicious persons. In the *Treatise* and EPM, there are only thirteen passages that invoke contempt as a morally appropriate response to vice (T 2.2.1.4, 2.2.1.7, 2.2.2.27, 2.2.10.8; EPM 1.10, 2.3, 6.13, 7.10n, App. 1.11, App. 4.3, App. 4.5, App. 4.8–9, App. 4.20). Five passages invoke "shame" or one of its cognates as an appropriate response to vice, and at most one passage can plausibly be read as using "disdain" in this way (T 1.4.7.6, 3.2.12.4, 3.3.1.11; EPM 5.13, 6.1, 7.4). By comparison, Hume writes of vice as warranting the judgment that one is guilty five times, resentment five, indignation six, anger twice, guilt four, and reproach five times (T 1.3.13.13, 2.2.3.7, 2.2.8.11, 3.1.1.12, 3.1.1.15n, 3.1.1.25, 3.2.2.8, 3.2.2.24, 3.2.8.7, 3.3.1.31, 3.3.3.9; EPM 2.13, 3.18, 3.38n, 5.16, 5.21, 5.27, 5.34, 5.39, 7.4, 8.10, App. 1.3, App. 1.16, App. 4.1, App. 4.19, Dialogue. 2, Dialogue. 48n).

247

All told, then, there are nineteen passages in the *Treatise* and EPM that mention an exclusionary sentiment as a morally appropriate response to vice, and twenty-seven that invoke an attitude that is not exclusionary. Even if we set aside all of Hume's references to "reproach" (on the grounds that his use of that term is arguably ambiguous), and all of his references to the *judgment* that one is guilty (on the grounds that this is not strictly speaking a reference to the sentiment of guilt), we are still left with seventeen instances in which Hume invokes a sentiment that is not exclusionary as a morally appropriate response to vice. The difference between this reckoning and the nineteen times Hume makes similar use of an exclusionary sentiment is far too slim a reed on which to hang the claim that "the range of reactive terms [Hume] uses definitely falls more into" the family of exclusionary sentiments.

One might try to get mileage out of the fact that Hume invokes "contempt" as a response to vice more often than any other *single* sentiment of disapproval I have thus far mentioned. But this fact – taken on its own – is misleading for a variety of reasons, not least because I have yet to discuss the two sentiments of disapproval that Hume mentions most frequently in connection to vice: hatred and humility.

I've already argued that the forms of hatred and humility to which adoption of the Humean moral point of view gives rise are not, strictly speaking, specifically *moral* sentiments. But let's set that aside for the moment. Whatever our conclusions on that score, neither Humean hatred nor Humean humility is properly thought exclusionary.

Considered in and of itself, moralized human hatred has *no* characteristic expression, for on Hume's account, hatred is not intrinsically motivating (T 2.2.7.3–5). Nor does moralized Humean hatred typically *give rise to* exclusionary sentiments. To the contrary, "by the original constitution of the human mind" moralized Humean hatred characteristically gives rise to anger (T 3.3.1.31), a sentiment whose expression, in turn, is a form of engagement with the agent even according to Kantians (see, e.g., Darwall 1999).

In the same vein, Humean humility is hardly identical with the exclusionary sentiment of shame; it is rather a brand of "modesty" or "self-diffidence," of feeling oneself undeserving of praise and deserving of condemnation, based an accurate perception of one's own vice(s) (EPM 8.8–9). And it would be false to the experience of due moral modesty – as well as Hume's analysis of it – to claim that due moral modesty is characteristically expressed like shame in a desire to hide from view. For his part, Hume seems to think that the characteristic expression of due modesty is a desire to reform one's own character. In one of the most famous examples in the *Treatise*, for instance, he speaks of a person who upon having a due sense of his own vice "hate[s] himself upon that account," and tries "to acquire, by practice, that virtuous principle" he lacks (T 3.2.1.8).

Of course, Hume does include exclusionary sentiments in his catalogue of attitudes that can be appropriate responses to vice, and in that respect alone, he differs from Kant. But we have no reason to trace this difference between Hume and Kant to the spectatorial aspects of Hume's account of moral evaluation. Adam Smith, for instance, like Kant offers a participant-centered account of moral evaluation (Darwall 1999). And Smith, as we've seen, thinks that exclusionary sentiments such as contempt and shame can be morally appropriate responses to vice.

Thus, even if Hume is misguided in conceiving of exclusionary sentiments as morally appropriate responses to vice, we have no reason to see this view as the inevitable outgrowth of his spectator-centered account of moral evaluation. At most, we Humeans may need to prune a few small branches from our theory of moral assessment. We have as yet no reason to dig up the whole "spectator-centered" tree, roots and all.

A Spectator's Standard of Virtue

A third complaint targets the Humean standard of virtue itself. For Aristotle, virtuous conduct is whatever the perfectly virtuous agent would see as such. For Smith, the standard of virtue is constituted by a combination of agent and patient perspectives (Darwall 1999). But the Humean standard of virtue is constituted by a judicious spectator's conclusions about the typical effects of traits. More specifically, on the traditional interpretation, traits qualify as Humean virtues if they satisfy a disjunctive criterion of being useful or agreeable to their possessor or others.

While Hume argues that many traits fail to satisfy his criterion of virtue, his most infamous such claim is that the "monkish virtues" of "celibacy, fasting, penance, mortification, self-denial, humility, silence, [and] solitude" are in fact vices (EPM 9.3). Following earlier critics, Rosalind Hursthouse contends that the "monkish virtues" do satisfy Hume's criterion. Moreover, says Hursthouse, self-indulgence, self-abnegation, licentiousness, and injustice are all also agreeable or useful to the agent or others in some respect, and hence ought also to qualify as Humean virtues.

One might alternatively propose that Hume ought to regard all these traits as virtuous in some respects (insofar as they are useful or agreeable to the agent or others), and vicious in other respects (insofar as the opposite is true). But Hursthouse anticipates this line of defense, pointing out that if celibacy and licentiousness warrant mixed verdicts for this reason, so should other traits that Hume regards as virtues, such as justice and courage (1999: 71–2, 76). After all, courageous and just acts often have disutility for the agent, no matter what their other salutary effects. Furthermore (though Hursthouse does not herself say this), if every trait that is useful or agreeable in some respect, and disagreeable or has disutility in other respects, warrants a mixed verdict, all traits would seem to warrant such mixed verdicts. And were this the case, we would lose our concept of a virtue – of an *excellency of character* – altogether.

So, the "mixed verdict" defense will get us nowhere. The result, Hursthouse concludes, is "disastrously obvious": "just about any vice" ought to qualify as a Humean virtue (1999: 71).

Much of Hursthouse's brief argument for these bold claims is easily refuted. Contrary to Hursthouse (1999: 71–2), Hume does give courage a mixed verdict. Courage is clearly virtuous (and agreeable to its possessor), Hume argues, *only* insofar as it is an aspect of her greatness of mind – a virtue whose content Hume draws from Cicero's *magnitudo animi*, and the agreeable Aristotelian *megalopsychia* (Abramson 2002). Nor does Hume argue, as Hursthouse claims (1999: 71–2), that justice is *only* useful to others but neither agreeable to others, nor useful nor agreeable to the agent. Rather, the implicit contrast in Hume's 3.1.1 that "public utility is the *sole* origin of justice" is to those who claim that reflections on the benefits of the institutions of justice could never have given rise to those institutions.

Other aspects of Hursthouse's argument are problematic for reasons that go beyond the exegetical. For instance, she imagines a celibate defending himself thus:

> I am serving a very useful role in society by exemplifying the idea that sexual gratification is something that human beings can willingly and happily put to one side in pursuit of finer ends . . .
>
> my celibacy in no way hinders my capacity to be entertaining company. . . But what I actually think is more important, is that I expect reasonable women to find it agreeable to be occasionally in the company of a man whom they know is not trying to get into their knickers, nor responding to them in accordance with how sexually attractive they are. (1999: 76)

Sexual desire would have to be an all-consuming business indeed for its mere presence to prohibit pursuit of "the finer things in life." And while I'm uncertain whether to take Hursthouse's second remark as indicative of her views about men or else women, in either case I find it remarkable. Does Hursthouse imagine (heterosexual) men *so* ruled by sexual desire that its mere presence – and/or the absence of a vow not to act on it – inevitably leads them to respond to every woman "in accordance with how sexually attractive they are"? Is the idea that in the absence of vows of celibacy *women* will assume that this is how all men regard them?

Still, there's something to Hursthouse's critique. Consider the final defense she imagines the celibate offering: "I assure you that my renouncing of the pleasures of the flesh has brought me a serenity and joy that was entirely lacking in my life" (1999: 76). If we grant the celibate her claims to serenity, we appear committed to regarding celibacy as a Humean virtue on account of its agreeableness to the agent. But licentiousness, self-indulgence and injustice may also be agreeable to the agent in some respect or another, and self-abnegation is useful in some respects to others (Hursthouse 1999: 71–2).

All of these traits seem therefore to qualify as Humean virtues, for on the four-fold disjunctive of "useful to others, or useful to ourselves, or agreeable to others, or agreeable to ourselves," once we have discovered that a trait is in one respect or another agreeable or useful to someone or another, there is *nothing more to debate*. It is, for that reason, virtuous. This may not be enough to qualify *all* traits as virtues, but it would certainly qualify far too many.

The real question is whether scholars have rightly interpreted Hume's standard of virtue. The pleasure and pain "on which moral distinctions depend," Hume writes,

> may arise from four different sources. For we reap a pleasure from the view of a character, which is naturally fitted to be useful to others, or to the person himself, or which is agreeable to others, or to the person himself. (T 3.3.1.30)

This certainly *looks* like a set of criteria for virtue and vice, i.e. virtues are those traits that are [1a] useful or agreeable to others, or [1b] useful or agreeable to ourselves.

Only a few pages later, however, Hume writes:

[2a] 'tis a most certain rule, that if there be no relation of life, in which I cou'd not wish to stand to a particular person, his character must so far be allow'd perfect. [2b] If he be as little wanting to himself as to others, his character is entirely perfect. (T 3.3.3.9)

Hume describes the criteria in this passage I've labeled as [2a] and [2b] as together constituting "the ultimate test of merit and virtue." But [2a] is an explicitly interpersonal criterion: the issue is whether or not others are left "wanting" in some "*relation of life*" with the agent. For this reason, [2a] seems more restrictive than [1a]: i.e. a trait might pass the test of [1a], and yet fail to qualify as a virtue on the criterion specified in [2a]. In many ways, for example, it would be useful to my students for me to be the sort who is weak-willed in the face of pleas for higher grades and less work, though were I of such character, they would surely be "left wanting" in their student–teacher relationship with me. In contrast, [2b] appears just as permissive as is [1b]. Accordingly, scholars consistently claim that [2b] and [1b] both qualify as virtuous any trait that is useful or agreeable to the agent (e.g. Baier 1991: 212; Brown 1994; Martin 1992). But how can we reconcile [2a] and [1a]? And why, with respect to [2a] and [2b], does Hume seem to be more liberal in qualifying traits as virtuous on account of their service to the agent, than on account of their benefits to others?

Suppose we approach these questions by examining Hume's analysis of the traits that he claims to be virtuous on account of their service to the agent, i.e. those which fit under the rubric of [1b] and [2b]. In so doing, we ought to ask: on the basis of *which* benefits to the agent – of what *sort* of advantages – does Hume claim that these traits are virtues?

"Industriousness," for instance, might be thought laudable because it allows one to avoid the anxiety that the indolent face on having failed to carry out their designs. Yet the reason Hume regards industriousness as virtuous is "its advantages, in the acquisition of power and riches, or in raising what we call a fortune in the world . . . The tortoise, according to the fable, by his perseverance gained the race of the hare" (EPM 6.10). What makes industriousness a Humean virtue is a specific subset of its advantages to the agent, namely, its advantages to the agent *in her relations with others*.

In the same vein, Hume remarks that discretion is laudable because it allows one to "carry on a safe intercourse with others" (EPM 6.8), while "meanness" is vicious because it leads one to "submit to the basest slavery in order to gain his ends, fawn upon those who abuse him, and degrade himself by intimacies and familiarities with undeserving familiars" (EPM 7.10). The reason the merit of honesty, fidelity, and truth consists partly in their service to the agent, Hume says, is that once established as virtuous on other grounds, they serve the agent in her relations with others by being "the source of that trust and confidence, which alone can give a man any consideration in life" (EPM 6.13). Still other traits Hume classifies as "useful or agreeable to ourselves" can *only* be thought of service to the agent *in her relations with others*: consider, for instance, "secrecy," "insinuation," "considerateness," and "facility of expression" (EPM 6.10).

Similarly, Hume claims that the reason cheerfulness qualifies as a trait "immediately agreeable to ourselves" is that it "readily communicates itself to all . . . the most sullen and morose are often caught by it." Why does this show the agreeableness of cheerfulness to the *agent*? Because it is pleasant for me to be a person who is pleasant to be around (EPM 7.1; T 2.2.5.21). The sense in which cheerfulness is "*immediately*" agreeable

251

is that its *being* agreeable does not require any "reflexions on the tendencies of actions" (T 3.3.1.27). Cheerfulness, in other words, is agreeable irrespective of whether we reflect upon its tendency to be agreeable, though reflections on its tendency to be agreeable are requisite for finding it virtuous.

Even "greatness of mind" – Hume's primary example of a trait "immediately agreeable to ourselves" – fits this pattern. The pleasure of Humean greatness is the pleasure of a fully virtuous person's "invaluable enjoyment of a character with [himself]" (EPM 9.25; Abramson 2002). If the value of other Humean virtues is based on their role in interpersonal interactions, this must also be derivatively true of Humean greatness. That is, what the truly great-minded man enjoys is that he is fully virtuous, and by hypothesis, what makes him fully virtuous is that none of his traits leaves either himself or others "wanting" in their relations with one another.

In short, traits tending to the advantage of the agent are Humean *virtues* just insofar as they do not leave the agent "wanting" *in her relations* with others. This fits with Hume's [2a] claim that traits are virtuous if they do not leave others "wanting" in some "relation of life" with the agent. On both criteria, the value of traits is derivative of their role in the agent's interactions with others. And [2b] is then no more permissive than [2a]. Finally, [2a] and [2b] together qualify as virtuous any trait that makes an agent "fitted," in one of these two ways, for some "relation of life."

It's tempting to read "relation of life" as here meaning "relationship" or "role." But this would suggest, misleadingly, that Hume thinks of all virtues as role-specific (cf. e.g.: T.3.3.3.3). We come closer to Hume's meaning if we say that T 3.3.3.9 qualifies as virtuous any trait that makes one well suited for participation in some sphere of interpersonal interactions. The sphere of interpersonal interactions for which a particular trait makes one well suited then may or may not be coextensive with those involved in a particular relationship or role.

The reason there is no tension between the proposed reading of Hume's standard of virtue and the famous "useful or agreeable" passage of T 3.3.1.30 is that it is a mistake to read the latter as an answer to the question of what makes a trait a virtue or a vice. T 3.3.1.30 is addressed to a substantially more narrow question. This passage appears nearly at the end of a section devoted to an account of precisely what is involved *in* adopting the Humean moral point of view. T 3.3.1.30 offers a summary of the conclusions reached in this section. The first conclusion summarized – that which is at issue in the infamous "useful or agreeable" passage – is that there are four features of traits we see as *salient* when we adopt the "common point of view" from which moral assessments arise: their fitness to be useful to ourselves, or others, or agreeable to ourselves, or others. In Hume's terms, this passage answers the question, "what features of traits give rise to pleasure or pain when we consider traits from a 'common point of view'?"

In contrast, at T 3.3.3.9, Hume is concerned not with enumerating particular aspects of the general point of view, but with providing an overview of the Humean conception of virtue. *This* passage concludes two sections of the *Treatise* in which Hume's goal has been to "illustrate [his] general system of morals" (T 3.3.2.1). What has been illustrated, Hume writes, is that when we judge of a person's virtue, "we consider him with all his relations in society; and love or hate him, according as he affects those, who have any immediate intercourse with him" (T 3.3.3.9). Virtues, accordingly, are those traits that make a person well-suited for participation in some sphere of interpersonal interactions – i.e., they are traits which either do not leave an agent "wanting" in her interpersonal interactions, or which do not leave others "wanting" in their interactions with the agent. This, Hume writes, is the "*ultimate*" test of virtue.

Read this way, T 3.3.3.9 also provides Hume's first-level response to the long-debated question, "why do we adopt the general point of view?," i.e., a moral purview in which we treat as salient only the agent and those with whom the agent has "commerce" (T 3.3.1.18). What we are trying to determine is whether a trait makes one well suited for some sphere of interpersonal interactions. In that light, the only relevant persons *are* those who interact with – who have "commerce" with – the agent.

We have our answer to Hursthouse's objection. The problem with Hume's standard of virtue, recall, is that it seems to qualify far too many traits as virtuous. If, for instance, celibacy gives the agent an agreeable "serenity," we seem committed to thinking it virtuous. There is, at that point, *nothing more to debate*, for even if celibacy also has innumerable deleterious effects, the mere fact that it is – in one way – agreeable ought to be sufficient to qualify it as virtuous. That, says Hursthouse, is the force of Hume's four-fold disjunction.

The Humean standard of virtue isn't in fact susceptible to this objection, for the disjunction implicit in Hume's standard is two-fold, not four-fold. A trait is a Humean virtue if it does not leave the agent wanting in her interactions with others, or if it does not leave others wanting in their interactions with the agent. The fact that a trait is in some way agreeable or useful, to the agent or others, may be relevant to whether it is a virtue, but it is not determinative thereof.

Suppose, for instance, that you convince me that celibacy gives one "serenity." This will be relevant to the status of celibacy as a virtue only if you can also show me that the celibate's serenity is agreeable to her *in her interactions with others*. Let's say you do so. That still does not answer the question of whether the celibate is "left wanting" in her relations with others. Here, celibacy's other typical effects are relevant. I might, for instance, point out the obvious sense in which a celibate is "left wanting" in her relations with others. Or I might argue that the celibate is left wanting in the sense of being excluded (to some extent) from the whole sphere of interpersonal interactions which in our own social milieu we call "romantic" interactions. Or I might contend that to the extent the celibate succeeds in actually extirpating her sexual desires, she suffers to some degree by limiting the extent to which she can sympathize with, and so commiserate with or share in the joys of others still moved by sexual desire. To point to any typically deleterious effects that celibacy has for the agent in her interpersonal interactions is to *directly dispute* the claim that celibacy is virtuous, for any such deleterious effect constitutes a respect in which the agent is "left wanting" in her relations with others.

We might similarly concede to Hursthouse that self-indulgence, licentiousness, and injustice are also all agreeable to the agent without conceding that they satisfy the Humean standard of virtue. The self-indulgent are left wanting that intimacy which is only possible when we trust that another will sometimes sacrifice her interests for our own. Licentiousness robs the agent of the benefits of a trust that would otherwise be reposed in her (EPM 6.14), while the unjust are left wanting a "satisfactory review of [their] own conduct" (EPM 9.23). And even if Hursthouse is right to suppose that self-abnegation is useful to others, it still leaves others wanting in that no true intimacy is possible with the servile. None of these traits qualifies as a Humean virtue.

Looking Forward

I'd like to close with a few speculative remarks about just a few of the many issues raised by our new anatomy of Humean moral evaluation. First, one of the most intriguing features of the answers to each of the three objections addressed here is that not a single one relies on the role of sympathy in Humean moral evaluation. Perhaps, then, sympathy's role in Humean moral evaluation is just what Hume claims it to be, namely, the imaginative means through which the objects of our moral evaluations become objects of our concern (T 3.3.1.25).

Consider also the role of the indirect passions in Humean moral evaluation. If, as I've argued, the forms of love, hatred pride, and humility implicated in Humean moral evaluation are not themselves responsibility-conferring, then why does Hume repeatedly insist that these are the typical causal antecedents of responsibility-conferring, full-fledged moral sentiments? Here is one explanation. On my account, Hume treats as full-fledged moral sentiments not only sentiments in which the notion of responsibility at play is that of accountability (e.g., anger, guilt), but also sentiments that involve a different form or mode of moral responsibility, namely, that of responsibility for achieving or failing to achieve an excellency of character (e.g., shame, contempt). Perhaps Hume thought he needed to provide an account of moral evaluation which could explain how appraisers are generally able to identify all these various sentiments *as* ethical. To do so, he needs to offer an account that does not require that in order to see for herself which of her various attitudes qualify as ethical, the average appraiser must engage in such "fine reflections" about virtue as we philosophers engage in when considering the responsibility-conferring force of moral sentiments and the various modes and forms of responsibility intrinsic to ethical attitudes as such (EPM 1.10). The close causal association of all the differing responsibility-conferring attitudes with a particular species of love, hatred, pride, and humility might just do the trick. But then, and for just that reason, it would be important that the causal antecedents of the responsibility-conferring sentiments have a contingent relationship to any particular mode or form of moral responsibility, as do Hume's indirect passions.

Finally, what should we say about Hume's standard of virtue itself? For Hume, asking whether a trait is virtuous is asking, "what difference would this trait make to people involved in interpersonal interactions with someone who has that trait?" This strikes me as precisely the right question in several respects. To the extent that this is the basis of our judgments of virtue, our judgments reflect a consideration of individuals *as* the kind of individuals who can be subject to moral assessment. After all, only persons are subject to moral assessment, and only persons can engage in inter*personal* interactions. Hume's question also speaks directly to what matters to us as persons who interact with one another, namely, how those interpersonal interactions actually go for the parties concerned. If we lose sight of this, we risk constructing moral theories about the ethical life of a creature unrecognizable as one of *us*. "Be a philosopher; but, amidst all your philosophy, be still a man" (EHU 1.6).

See also 9 "Hume's Indirect Passions"; 10 "Hume on the Direct Passions and Motivation"; 12 "Hume on Moral Rationalism, Sentimentalism, and Sympathy"; 15 "Hume on Beauty and Virtue"; 16 *Enquiry concerning the Principles of Morals*: Incomparably the Best?"

Acknowledgments

My gratitude to all those who provided commentary on earlier versions of this piece, including Daniel Garber, Don Garrett, Florence Hsia, Agnieszka Jaworska, Rachana Kamtekar, participants in the 2003–4 Rockefeller Center for Human Values workshop, the symposium audience of the 2003 International Hume Society Conference, and the participants in the 2005 Mid-Atlantic Early Modern Seminar. A special note of thanks to Elizabeth Radcliffe for the invitation to contribute to this collection, and for all of the work she put into seeing the collection through to publication.

References

Abramson, Kate (2002). "Two Portraits of the Humean Moral Agent," *Pacific Philosophical Quarterly*, 83, pp. 301–34.

—— (forthcoming). "What's So 'Natural' about the Natural Virtues?" in Donald Ainslie (ed.), *Critical Essays on Hume's "Treatise"* (Cambridge: Cambridge University Press).

Baier, Annette C. (1991). *A Progress of Sentiments: Reflections on Hume's "Treatise"* (Cambridge, MA: Harvard University Press).

—— (1994). *Moral Prejudices, Essays on Ethics* (Cambridge, MA: Harvard University Press).

Brown, Charlotte (1994). "From Spectator to Agent," *Hume Studies*, 20, pp. 19–35.

Darwall, Stephen (1998). "Empathy, Sympathy, Care," *Philosophical Studies*, 89, pp. 261–82.

—— (1999). "Sympathetic Liberalism," *Philosophy and Public Affairs*, 28, pp. 139–64.

—— (2002). *Welfare and Rational Care* (Princeton, NJ: Princeton University Press).

Hume, David (1754–78). *The History of England* (Indianapolis, IN: Liberty Fund, 1983). (Cited in text as HENG.)

—— (1741–77). *Essays Moral, Political and Literary*, ed. Eugene F. Miller (Indianapolis, IN: Liberty Fund, 1987).

Hursthouse, Rosalind (1999). "Virtue Ethics and Human Nature," *Hume Studies*, 25, pp. 67–82.

Martin, Marie (1992). "Hume on Human Excellence," *Hume Studies*, 18, pp. 383–400.

Smith, Adam (1792). *The Theory of Moral Sentiments*, eds. D. D. Raphael, D. D. and A. L. Macfie (Indianapolis, IN: Liberty Press, 1976).

Strawson, P. F. (1982). "Freedom and Resentment," in Gary Watson (ed.), *Free Will* (Oxford: Oxford University Press).

Further Reading

Hume's "spectator-centered" account of moral evaluation and critiques thereof

Abramson, Kate (1999). "Correcting *Our* Sentiments about Hume's Moral Point of View," *Southern Journal of Philosophy*, 37, pp. 333–61.

Cohon, Rachel (1997). "The Common Point of View in Hume's Ethics," *Philosophy and Phenomenological Research*, 57, pp. 827–50.

Garrett, Don (1997). *Cognition and Commitment in Hume's Philosophy* (New York: Oxford University Press).

Gordon, Robert M. (1996). "Sympathy, Simulation, and the Impartial Spectator," in May, Freidman and Clark (eds.), *Mind and Morals* (Cambridge, MA: MIT Press).

Hampton, Jean (1997). "The Hobbesian Side of Hume," in Herman, Korsgaard, and Reath (eds.), *Reclaiming the History of Ethics* (Cambridge: Cambridge University Press).

Harman, Gilbert (1986). *Moral Agent and Impartial Spectator*, The Lindley Lecture (Lawrence, KS: University of Kansas).

Korsgaard, Christine (1999). "The General Point of View: Love and Moral Approval in Hume's Ethics," *Hume Studies*, 25, pp. 3–42.

Loeb, Louis E. (1977). "Hume's Moral Sentiments and the Structure of the *Treatise*," *Journal of the History of Philosophy*, 4, pp. 395–403.

Sayre-McCord, Geoffrey (1994). "Why Hume's General Point of View Isn't Ideal – and Shouldn't Be," *Social Philosophy and Policy*, 11, pp. 202–28.

Wiggins, David (1997). "A Sensible Subjectivism," repr. in Darwall, Gibbard, and Railton (eds.), *Moral Discourse and Practice* (Oxford: Oxford University Press).

The relationship between Hume's account of moral evaluation and his account of moral motivation

Baron, Marcia (1988). "Morality as a Back-up System: Hume's View?" *Hume Studies*, 14, pp. 25–53.

Bricke, John (1996). *Mind and Morality* (Oxford: Oxford University Press).

Brown, Charlotte (1988). "Is Hume an Internalist?" *Journal of the History of Philosophy*, 26, pp. 69–82.

Radcliffe, Elizabeth (1996). "How Does the Humean Sense of Duty Motivate?" *Journal of the History of Philosophy*, 34, pp. 383–407.

Moral sentiments and moral responsibility

Frankfurt, Harry G. (2004). *The Reasons of Love* (Princeton, NJ: Princeton University).

Russell, Paul (1995). *Freedom and Moral Sentiment: Hume's Way of Naturalizing Responsibility* (New York: Oxford University Press).

Taylor, Gabriele (1985). *Pride, Shame and Guilt* (Oxford: Clarendon Press).

Wallace, R. J. (1996). *Responsibility and the Moral Sentiments* (Cambridge, MA: Harvard University Press).

Contain critiques of "Humean" theories of virtue

Darwall, Stephen (1995). *The British Moralists and the Internal "Ought"* (Cambridge: Cambridge University Press).

Herman, Barbara (1993). *The Practice of Moral Judgment* (Cambridge, MA: Harvard University Press).

Hursthouse, Rosalind (1999). *On Virtue Ethics* (Oxford: Oxford University Press).

Schneewind, Jerome (2003). "The Misfortunes of Virtue," *Ethics*, 101, pp. 42–63.

Watson, Gary (1990). "On the Primacy of Character," in Flanagan and Rorty (eds.), *Identity, Character, and Morality: Essays in Moral Psychology* (Cambridge, MA: MIT Press).

14

Hume's Theory of Justice, or Artificial Virtue

EUGENIO LECALDANO

When Hume sought the chair in ethics and pneumatic philosophy at the University of Edinburgh in 1744, his adversaries – a group which probably included Hutcheson but which chose as its representative the *principal* of the University William Wishart – published a pamphlet which brought together a series of attacks on the theses sustained in Hume's *Treatise on Human Nature*. One of the principal accusations in this pamphlet was that Hume had undermined the foundations of morality by denying the natural and essential difference between good and evil, justice and injustice, and recognizing among them only an artificial distinction, born of the conventions and agreements of men. In so doing, Hume had gone beyond even Thomas Hobbes, in that Hobbes, even though he eliminated and abolished all other natural obligations, had found it necessary to allow the obligation inhering in promises and pacts to subsist. Hume they claimed, had instead insisted on his thesis of artificiality, even with regard to obligations of this kind.

Hume made an effort in *A Letter from a Gentleman to his Friend in Edinburgh* (Hume 1745) to minimize this result of his theory, arguing that in his *Treatise* he had limited himself to a critique of the thesis of an eternal difference between the just and the unjust along the path already taken by the ancient moralists and by Hutcheson. The accusation that Hume had furthered the skeptical negation of moral distinctions through his conceptions of justice as an artificial virtue achieved in the short term the result of sinking Hume's candidacy at the University of Edinburgh, and would be repeated often in the following decades. Hume's decision, in his *Enquiry concerning the Principles of Morals*, to put aside the distinction between artificial and natural, labeling as "merely verbal" all the disputes raised by the use of this distinction, did not help to render his theory of justice more acceptable (EPM, App. 3.9, footnote). Hume's critics certainly were not right at the normative level in accusing him of moral skepticism. They did however have the merit of grasping that Hume's theory of justice presented an entirely innovative theory that could be reconciled neither with traditional conceptions of natural rights, nor with the attempt made a century before by Hobbes to drive the validity of just laws from a contract or a pact. They understood that Hume's theory, more generally, brought into crisis the thesis of a close connection between justice and human rationality. Hume's conception was novel for the way it offered an account of the origin of justice, for the way it reconstructed the motivations that make the rules of justice obligatory, and finally, for the way it explained the content of these rules. Now we may see with greater clarity that Hume's theory of justice not only seemed scandalous and unacceptable to the majority of the philosophers of his time. It also delineated an entirely unique and particular conception that, over the course of the centuries, would come more and more clearly to be considered the source of a quite specific philosophical paradigm (Baier 1991; Russell 1995; Snare 1991).

In this chapter I will illustrate Hume's peculiar concept of justice, which, in analogy with the arguments of many of his readers today, I will characterize as a form of sentimental conventionalism. At the same time, I will also indicate those elements because of which his theory cannot be reduced to the other principal means – natural law, contractualism, and utilitarianism – with which philosophical reflection has sought to explain the nature and scope of justice.

The Origin of Justice

According to Hume, the rules of justice were invented by human beings in the course of their natural history and thus cannot be considered original, or as innate principles made known to men by nature's Author. More specifically, to deny that the laws of justice were original for human beings meant for Hume that these were not directly rooted in what could be considered the constitutive passions of human nature. Accounting for the origins of justice was, then, the same thing as to explain how the conditions had come about in which the rules that characterize justice had become able to motivate and guide the conduct of human beings. To think that human beings had come to accept the obligatory force of the rules of justice through reasoning would have been equivalent to going against that which Mackie (Mackie 1980: 44–50) has correctly presented as the central thesis of Hume's psychology of action: that is, that human conduct is guided principally by passions and sentiments rather than by reason. This thesis is broadly illustrated in Book 2 of the *Treatise*, dedicated to the passions, and in particular in the pages in which Hume addresses the question of which motives influence the will (T 2.3.3).

According to Hume there is no reasoning able to establish that a certain order is just for eternity and at the same time to give it compelling, obligating force for human beings. The medieval and modern theorists of natural law committed serious errors, according to Hume, on precisely this point. Already in the period in which he studied at the University of Edinburgh, Hume's reading of texts by Heinnecius had brought him closer to Grotius and Pufendorf. But Hume's reflection on Justice cannot be seen, as suggested first by Forbes (Forbes 1975) and more recently by Haakonssen (Haakonssen 1993), as "an exclusively secular because exclusively empirical . . . version of the fundamental principles of natural law, an attempt to lay the foundation of a science of morality and law in a science of man which had no need of the religious hypothesis, or for that matter of the atheistic hypothesis of Hobbes, which had thrown off 'all prejudices', and was 'consistent', as Grotius and Pufendorf were not" (Forbes: 68).

In reality, it was precisely the use of the experimental method in the study of human nature that brought Hume, at the same time that he of course proposed a secular concept which put religious hypotheses aside, to push himself still further, and to abandon completely the project of limiting himself to presenting "a modern theory of natural law." This is because the manner in which he was able empirically to explain the genesis of the rules of justice was entirely irreconcilable with the path followed by theorists of natural law who appealed to human rationality in their arguments.

Through his experimental study of human nature Hume also took his distance from the attempt to base the rules of justice directly upon the natural passions of the human being. From this point of view, Hume agreed with Hobbes's critique of Aristotle's ethics that assumed the problem of explaining the genesis of juridical and political institutions was already resolved from the beginning, through Aristotle's character-ization of the human being as a "political animal." But for Hume this meant also to distance himself from the manner in which Hutcheson explained justice as a natural virtue that represented an aid to that universal benevolence with which the author of nature has provided man, while in addition giving them the unique capacity of moral sense to perceive and approve it. In reality, Hume's experimental enquiry into human nature shows that human beings possess at the most a limited benevolence.

Indeed it was precisely Hume's effort to present an empirical hypothesis on the gen-esis of justice that indicated that no rule of the kind would ever have come into being if human beings had indeed had the capacity for some kind of universal love or a natural and spontaneous interest in the common good. According to Hume, if human beings possessed a passion of that kind they would have no need for the rules of justice precisely because they would be naturally driven to complete certain actions and avoid others, such that neither the rules of justice nor the sanctions of law would be necessary. Hobbes was thus in part correct to demonstrate the artificial origin of justice. But then not even Hobbes's picture could be accepted. Indeed, Hume distanced himself decisively both from the manner in which Hobbes reconstructed the con-stitutive passions of human beings, as well as from the paths along which Hobbes had proceeded in order to explain the genesis of justice. On one hand, Hobbes erred in considering human beings as completely devoid of even a limited form of benevolence. On the other, Hobbes was wrong to present society and justice as the product of a pact or a promise that human beings exchanged as the rational result of a process of contract formation.

Hume again explicitly explains the manner in which justice is formed as a correc-tion of human beings' natural affections, which are characterized by partiality. In presenting justice as an artificial product of evolution of human nature, Hume, in order to avoid confusion, immediately adds, "the remedy . . . is not deriv'd from nature, but from *artifice*, or more properly speaking, nature provides a remedy in the judge-ment and understanding, for what is irregular and incommodious in the affections" (T. 3.2.2.9). He further clarifies:

> To avoid giving offence, I must here observe, that when I deny justice to be a natural virtue, I make use of the word, *natural*, only as oppos'd to *artificial*. In another sense of the word; as no principle of the human mind is more natural than a sense of virtue; so no virtue is more natural than justice. Mankind is an inventive species; and where an invention is obvious and absolutely necessary, it may as properly be said to be natural as any thing that proceeds immediately from original principles, without the intervention of thought or reflection. Tho' the rules of justice be *artificial*, they are not *arbitrary*. Nor is the expression improper to call them *laws of nature*; if by *natural* we understand what

259

is common to any species, or even if we confine it to mean is inseparable from the species. (T 3.2.1.19)

The steps, therefore, through which the process of creation of the notions of justice is realized are to be considered in a certain sense necessary and inevitable. Indeed, even if justice is an artificial result of the development of the original conditions of the life of human beings, the points of departure, the context in which the process of the creation of justice is realized, and finally, the results achieved are so obvious and inevitable that the institution of justice and several of its fundamental laws can be found in all human societies. They may, in this sense, be characterized as natural and universal laws. With regard to the context from which human beings move to create their ideas of justice, Hume seeks to determine this both from the point of view of subjectivity as well as from that of objective or, as it were, environmental conditions. He writes,

> Thus, the rules of equity or justice depend entirely on the particular state and condition, in which men are placed, and owe their origin and existence to that UTILITY, which results to the public from their strict and regular observance. Reverse, in any considerable circumstance, the condition of men: produce extreme abundance or extreme necessity: implant in the human breast perfect moderation and humanity, or perfect rapaciousness and malice: by rendering justice totally *useless*, you thereby totally destroy its essence, and suspend its obligation upon mankind.
>
> The common situation of society is a medium amidst all these extremes. We are natur- ally partial to ourselves, and to our friends; but are capable of learning the advantage resulting from a more equitable conduct. Few enjoyments are given from the open and liberal hand of nature; but by art, labour, and industry, we can extract them in great abundance. Hence the ideas of property become necessary in all civil society: hence justice derives its usefulness to the public: and hence alone arises its merit and moral obligation. (EPM 3.12–13)

Viewing the matter from the point of view of human passions, justice may, therefore, be generated precisely insofar as human beings are a mixture of egoistic self-interest and limited benevolence. In reality, human beings begin to appreciate the advantages of cooperative relations through personal relations within the family, which, accord- ing to Hume, are natural to the human species from its origins, rooted in strong instincts like those that drive humans toward sexual activity and procreation. With the broad- ening of personal relations beyond restricted familial or clan groups, human beings, already aware of the benefits to be derived from cooperative relations, arrive at an under- standing of the need for a more stable equilibrium. They recognize, that is, the need for implicit or explicit rules of conduct, that place them in the condition of being able to coexist peacefully with other families and clans, thus forming real societies.

Examining the issue from an objective point of view, it should be emphasized that the realization of this shared equilibrium is necessary in that sphere of human activ- ity that deals with a particular class of goods. Hume explains this as follows:

> There are three different species of goods, which we are possess'd of; the internal satisfaction of our mind, the external advantages of our body, and the enjoyment of such possessions we have acquir'd by our industry and good fortune. We are perfectly secure in

the enjoyment of the first. The second may be ravish'd from us, but can be of no advantage to him who deprives us of them. The last only are both expos'd to the violence of others, and may be transferr'd without suffering any loss or alteration; while at the same time, there is not a sufficient quantity of them to supply every one's desires and necessities. As the improvement, therefore, of these goods is the chief advantage of society, so the *instability* of their possession along with their *scarcity*, is the chief impediment. (T 3.2.2.7)

The rules of justice, therefore, were invented in order to make it possible for human beings peacefully to enjoy those external goods that they can exchange and which, furthermore, exist in nature in a reduced quantity with relation to the amount thereof that humans might aspire to possess. The explanation Hume offers of the genesis of justice is not only generically evolutionary, but also, in a stricter sense, historical. The rules of justice are not only a casual and contingent product of the real human condition, marked by its passions and set in a context of material scarcity, but rather are by their nature changeable. We can imagine, for example, a change in the situation whereby an external good that had been removed from the sphere of justice because of its overabundance (say, water or air) ends up entering within the sphere of application of rules once it has become scarce.

But to understand fully Hume's theory of justice we must bring into sharper focus the creative process through which are generated what can now unequivocally be called "the three fundamental laws of nature, *that of the stability of possession, of its transference by consent*, and *of the performance of promises*" (T 3.2.6.1). Indeed, the scientist of human nature observes,

> 'Tis on the strict observance of these three laws, that the peace and security of human society entirely depend; nor is there any possibility of establishing a good correspondence among men, where these are neglected. Society is absolutely necessary for the well-being of men; and these are as necessary to the support of society. Whatever restraint they may impose on the passions of men, they are the real offspring of those passions, and are only a more artful and more refin'd way of satisfying them. Nothing is more vigilant and inventive than our passions; and nothing is more obvious, than the conventions for the observance of these rules. Nature has, therefore, trusted this affair entirely to the conduct of men, and has not plac'd in the mind any peculiar original principles, to determine us to a set of actions, into which the other principles of our frame and constitution were sufficient to lead us. (T 3.2.6.1)

As we see, Hume insists on reconstructing the genesis of justice in such a way as to explain that the principal rules that characterize justice were discovered by human beings in an entirely casual manner. These rules were consolidated over the course of a process that was not governed in any way by a sort of intentional end, or by an explicit effort to imagine the results to be reached. Humans came only slowly to realize that their civil relations could proceed in a more stable, secure, and ordered manner if in their reciprocal relations they let themselves be guided by a few fundamental rules of justice. These aspects of the casual, non-intentional, and gradual nature of the process through which justice developed have been emphasized by many of Hume's readers, especially in the second half of the twentieth century. For example, Friedrich August von Hayek opposed conventionalism to the rationalist constructivism of Hobbes

(Hayek 1963). This interpretation is undoubtedly illuminating if it is not pushed so far as to make the process through which Hume claims the rules of justice are generated appear identical with the procedure of an economic market that casually creates the growth of wealth. For where the market is dominated by the mechanism of competition, the rules of justice on the other hand are created only when human beings are inspired in their conduct by a principle of cooperation.

That which makes Hume's reconstruction of the origin of justice an explanation that cannot be reduced to the others is, however, another particular component of the evolutionary context in which Hume places his reconstruction. This evolution does not in any way call upon reason, but involves the passions, human sentiments, and those same notions that have to do with justice – notions which present themselves more as a function of the sentimental nature of human beings than as the result of some kind of intellectual awareness (Snare 1991). Not only is justice not the fruit of reasoning, it is rather the casual result reached through trial and error. Justice is structured as the outcome of those same passions, their correction, and their projection. Precisely on this point Hume is particularly attentive in his language to highlight the difference between his explanation and that offered by those who, like Hobbes, see justice as born of an explicit accord of a rational nature, that is, the contract. To mark this difference Hume introduces the specific concept of convention:

> It has been asserted by some, that justice arises from HUMAN CONVENTIONS, and proceeds from the voluntary choice, consent, or combination of mankind. If by convention be here meant a *promise* (which is the most usual sense of the word) nothing can be more absurd than this position. The observance of promises is itself one of the most considerable parts of justice; and we are not surely bound to keep our word, because we have given our word to keep it. But if by convention be meant *a sense of common interest*; which sense each man feels in his own breast, which he remarks in his fellows, and which carries him, in concurrence with others, into a general plan or system of actions, which tends to public utility; it must be owned, that, in this sense, justice arises from human conventions . . .
>
> Thus two men pull the oars of a boat by common convention, for common interest, without any promise or contract: Thus gold and silver are made measures of exchange; thus speech and words and language are fixed by human convention and agreement. Whatever is advantageous to two or more persons, if all perform their part; but what loses all advantage, if only one perform, can arise from no other principle. There would otherwise be no motive for any one of them to enter into that scheme of conduct. (EPM, App. 3.7–8; see also T 3.2.2.10)

Hume derives his reconstruction of the origin of justice as a convention, as a casual product of an evolutionary process – as the only identifiable result on the basis of the experience of the natural history of the human species – from his more general reconstruction of human nature. In fact, his conclusion, that human conduct cannot be influenced by reasoning, leads him to locate the origin of justice not in an explicit, rational formation of a contract, but on the basis of a sense of the common utility of a certain practice, and this feeling emerges as an achievement of the passionate and emotive development of human beings.

Furthermore, it is precisely Hume's experimental reconstruction of human passions that allows him to put aside earlier efforts to reconstruct the origins of justice through myths, like those of the state of nature or of the golden age. Hume attributes these myths to philosophers and poets respectively, both characterized by a projection at the symbolic level of an unrealistic image of human nature. In the first case it is an image of human nature as a condition presented by Hobbes as a war of all against all among rapacious and vain human beings. In the other case it is a state characterized by the great abundance of all goods and by the universal benevolence among all human beings. But as Hume explains:

> This *state of nature*, therefore, is to be regarded as a mere fiction, not unlike that of *golden age*, which poets have invented; only with this difference, that the former is describ'd full of war, violence and injustice; whereas the latter is painted out to us, as the most charming and most peaceable condition, that can possibly be imagin'd. (T 3.2.2.15)

There are, finally, two distinct clauses of application of the rules of justice explicitly enunciated in EPM that help us understand the process through which these rules come into effect, find an application, or are suspended. On one hand, in order to clarify the historic nature of the rules of justice and their dependence, once created, on the perception of their utility, Hume offers the following example:

> Suppose . . . that it should be a virtuous man's fate to fall into the society of ruffians, remote from the protection of laws and government; what conduct must he embrace in that melancholy situation? He sees such a desperate rapaciousness prevail; such a disregard to equity; such contempt of order, such stupid blindness to future consequences, as must immediately have the most tragical conclusion, and must terminate in the destruction to the greater number, and in a total dissolution of society to the rest. He, meanwhile, can have no other expedient than to arm himself, to whomever the sword he seizes, or the buckler, may belong: to make provision of all means of defence and security: and his particular regard to justice being no longer of USE to his own safety or that of others, he must consult the dictates of self-preservation alone, without concern for those who no longer merit his care and attention. (EPM 3.9)

But on the other hand the process of creation of the rules of justice can be better understood when, according to Hume, one does not lose sight of the fact that these rules are in a certain sense exclusively a human matter:

> Were there a species of creatures, intermingled with men, which though rational, were possessed of such inferior strength, both of body and mind, that they were incapable of all resistance, and could never, upon the highest provocation, make us feel the effects of their resentment; the necessary consequence, I think, is, that we should be bound, by the laws of humanity, to give gentle usage to these creatures, but should not, properly speaking, lie under any restraint of justice with regard to them, nor could they possess any right or property exclusive of such arbitrary lords. Our intercourse with them could not be called society, which supposes a degree of equality; but absolute command on the one side, and servile obedience on the other. Whatever we covet, they must instantly resign: our permission is the only tenure, by which they hold their possessions: our compassion and kindness the only check, by which they curb our lawless will: and as no inconvenience ever results from the exercise of a power, so firmly established in nature, the restraints of justice and property, being totally *useless*, would never have place in so unequal a confederacy.

> This is plainly the situation of men with regard to animals; and how far these may be said to possess reason, I leave it to others to determine. (EPM 3.18–19)

Hume explicitly refuses the thesis that an exclusion of this kind from social relations and from the application of the rules of justice may apply also to those populations held by Europeans to be barbarian or to the female sex.

The Particular Motivation for the Obligatory Nature of Justice

Hume's explanation is not however complete after having offered a reconstruction of the evolutionary genesis of a convention shared by human beings to abstain from taking others' goods. Indeed, given the way Hume explains in general the capacity of moral distinctions to influence human conduct, he must identify, for the idea of justice as well, a root in the passionate structure of human nature that is able to render these ideas operative at the level of motivation. As I said above, it is precisely Hume's experimental research into human nature that led him to establish as a secure fact that the human being is motivated in his conduct not by reason but rather by the passions. Only the sentiments and the passions can motivate human beings to take one position rather than another. Thus natural motivations like self-interest and limited benevolence could explain all those situations in which humans undertook actions that could be seen as fitting in the list of what Hume, in the last part of the book of the *Treatise* dedicated to morals, called the natural virtues. But these natural motivations cannot be considered the source that drives people to just actions. Hume faces the problem of finding a suitable motivation for the rules of justice principally in the *Treatise*, leaving the matter in the background in the EPM.

In the *Treatise*, therefore, we find a series of detailed arguments aimed at demonstrating clearly that the ideas of justice cannot be moved directly by natural motives like private benevolence, concern for our personal interest or reputation, solicitude for the public interest, or love of humanity. For each of these motivations, Hume cleverly demonstrates that each of these will eventually suggest actions that are contrary to the rules of justice. For example, it is obvious that if human beings were to let themselves be guided by their personal interest alone, they would end up taking actions that suit themselves and thus actions that are entirely unjust. Similarly, one who is guided by limited benevolence will not approve actions that are just in general, but rather those actions that privilege the interests of those to whom he or she is connected, and that are, therefore, entirely unjust. Hume discards furthermore the argument that there might, at the root of just actions, be a motivation directed at achieving the public interest that is itself stimulated by ideas of justice. In reality this public interest presents itself as an object of motivation only *after* our notions of justice have been constituted. In natural terms, there cannot be any sort of direct motivation with regard to a common or general good, just as, according to Hume, there can be no such thing as a love for humanity.

The solution to the question of what it is that makes the rules of justice obligatory at the level of motivation must be sought in a basis of sentiment that cannot be identified with any natural passion.

From all this it follows, that we have naturally no real or universal motive for observing the laws of equity, but the very equity and merit of that observance; as no action can be equitable or meritorious, where it cannot arise from some separate motive; there is here an evident sophistry and reasoning in a circle. Unless therefore, we will allow, that nature has establish'd a sophistry, and render'd it necessary and unavoidable, we must allow that the sense of justice and injustice is not derive'd from nature, but arises artificially, tho' necessarily from education and human conventions. (T 3.2.1.17)

But the fact that Hume is constrained to conclude that justice does not have a motivation among the natural sentiments does not for that reason lead him, as some have suggested (Harrison 1981) entirely to exclude the possibility that justice may be a virtue of the human character. In reality we are able, as Tito Magri has suggested (Magri forthcoming), to retrace in Hume's writings a presentation of a passionate motivation for justice that is entirely unique. Indeed Hume explains how, for this artificial virtue, there can be found a passionate motivation that is a mixture of a sense of obligation toward it and a natural approbation of its moral value. The decisive elements of this explanation are, on one hand, the mechanism of sympathy already illustrated in detail in the second book of Hume's *Treatise* and, on the other, by the explanation offered at the beginning of the second part of Book 3, but then taken up again also in the third part of Book 3, of the sense of obligation, or duty.

To begin with the sense of duty, Hume explains clearly how this is generated:

In short, it may be establish'd as an undoubted maxim, *that no action can be virtuous, unless there be in human nature some motive to produce it, distinct from the sense of morality.*

But may not the sense of morality or duty produce an action, without any other motive? I answer, it may: but this is no objection to the present doctrine. When any virtuous motive or principle is common in human nature, a person who feels his heart devoid of that principle, may hate himself upon that account, and may perform the action without the motive, from a certain sense of duty, in order to acquire by practice, that virtuous principle, or at least, to disguise to himself, as much as possible, his want of it. A man that really feels no gratitude in his temper, is still pleas'd to perform grateful actions, and thinks he has, by that means, fulfill'd his duty . . .

Now to apply all this to the present case; I suppose a person to have lent me a sum of money, on condition that it be restor'd in a few days, and also suppose, that after the expiration of the term agreed on, he demands the sum: I ask, *What reason or motive have I to restore the money?* (T.3.2.1.7–9)

In this case, as in the case of an action done out of gratitude without really feeling the sentiment of gratitude, the act of keeping the promise and repaying the loan is done out of a sense of duty, and is not driven by any natural sentiment. But here the explanation is more complex than in the case of gratitude, because the sense of duty that accompanies the rules of justice is not the surrogate of an affection present only in human nature, but, rather, the projection at the level of motivation of an absence of natural affections. The element of artificiality in justice is linked therefore with a motivation that only civilized human beings have acquired through education and human conventions. But the sense of duty could not guide our action if we were not aware of the moral value of the passionate motivation in which we are lacking. In this sense, according to Hume, the sense of obligation that leads us to respect the rules of justice depends on our sympathy with the sentiment of moral approbation that accompanies the conduct of those who let themselves be guided by the rules of justice.

According to Hume's explanation, sympathy as a natural process is always contextualized and thus aimed toward the good of this or that particular person. The constitution of justice and of the rules that belong to it broadens however the range of interests that can be observed with the aid of the imagination. This is because, in effect, the rules of justice seem aimed at preserving or defending not so much a particular good as a public good in which our private good is also included (even if there are cases in which the public good is realized to the detriment of our own more particular interest). Thus it is with the help of imagination that we learn to sympathize with the public good that is safeguarded by the rules of justice. Hume explains, too, that the common citizen does not sympathize directly with the public good. Rather, in our imaginations we evaluate two different forms of conduct, the first aimed at fulfilling a personal interest, and the second, more impartial one, aimed at following the rules of justice. Our moral sense will approve of the more impartial and equitable conduct. It is here that the natural component of sentimental approbation for this type of conduct as opposed to another is inserted into the sense of duty that moves us to be just.

After societies have evolved to the point of forming governments, the rules of justice may find additional support from a more direct and concrete sympathy with those who are invested with the public role of preserving the rules of justice. This is the process, delineated with precision by K. Haakonssen (1993: 197–9), that Hume reconstructs by explaining how our sympathy is transmitted to those governing leaders who suitably distribute the rules of justice (Hume, "Of the Original Contract" in *Essays*). These governors, for their part, will feel a direct motivation in favor of the rules of justice on the basis of their personal interest in continuing to apply them by governing.

There is another way in which the rules of justice find motivation support in Hume's theory, and that is through establishing a habit of following these rules more and more as their general utility comes to be confirmed. Notions of justice seem useful both to the single individual and to the human species in general. But surely this cannot be an entirely sure and sufficient motivation, as there is no shortage of cases in which personal interest and utility could best be served by going against the rules of justice. Here the motivational drive, as said above, must come from moral sentiment, which cannot but lead us to prefer impartial conduct to egotistical and interested behavior.

The Whole of Artificial Virtues: Property, Promises, Government, and Chastity

Hume's explanation of the genesis of those ideas of justice and of motivation that enable people to recognize their obligatory nature provide the basis on which we may understand the choices Hume makes with regard to justice and the principal artificial virtues. When, as we have said, Hume presents as "fundamental laws of nature" the principal articulations of justice, or indeed the recognition of the "stability of possession, its transfer through consent, and the maintenance of promises" (T 3.2.6), he does not do this by converting to the philosophy of natural law. He does this instead by presenting the values that constitute the field of justice in an evolutionary system both of priority in time as well as ethical relevance. The area of the artificial notions of justice opens up in Hume's reconstruction with the recognition of property, or rather, with the consolidation of a tendency to abstain from the goods of others. The privileging, for the constitution of civil life, of this negative virtue of abstaining from taking others' goods from them, seems to occupy the same space in Hume's theory that negative duties and rights, as opposed to positive ones, do in theories of natural law. In so doing, Hume opens the path for the more explicit argumentation of Adam Smith, who in his *Theory of Moral Sentiments* would go on to locate the cement of society precisely in justice, understood as a negative virtue (Smith 1759: 100–7).

As I have noted above, for Hume property concerns only external goods, and specifically those external goods that are scarce relative to the needs and desires of humans. Again, this characterization of the extension of application of property bases its validity in history, given that in different periods there may be conditions that will render scarce certain goods that were not scarce before, and that will thus bring these goods under the power of reciprocal recognition of others' possession of them. It is precisely a constitutive trait of external goods – the fact of their being able to change hands and thus to be exchanged and transferred to others – that creates, in Hume's explanation, the conditions for the genesis of that later convention that constitutes the area of justice: the invention of the formula of the promise and of the rules linked to keeping promises. Since it is too complex to exchange goods only through barter, and thus with the good to be exchanged always physically present, human beings come to invent a linguistic formula – the promise – that allows them to undertake the exchange even without all the goods involved for the parties directly present. The original promise is the one that guarantees that the good to be exchanged can be given or received at another time. After this restricted use, the range of application of the practice of promising broadens progressively. Hume puts his general theory of the nature and necessity of the artificial virtues to the test, explaining why promises are kept (T 3.2.5). Even in the case of the promise, one can imagine that the genesis of the verbal formula could have been entirely casual and unintentional, and that this practice was consolidated slowly, as humans came to discover its utility. As in the case of the rules of reciprocal respect of possessions, so with regard to the making and keeping of promises it is only *a posteriori* that human beings recognize that they have invented a practice that works. Naturally, according to Hume, the motivation to recognize the obligatory nature of promises cannot be considered original. It is, rather, in social life that human beings learn to give significance and the power of obligation to the formulas with which they promise.

Certainly, the capacity of the formula of the promise to obligate those who use it, if not seen in this context of growing civil relations, seems quite mysterious. In this regard, Hume offers an analogy between the mysteriousness of the promise and that of "transubstantiation, or holy orders, where a certain form of words, along with a certain intention, changes entirely the nature of an external object, and even of a human creature." But beyond this apparent similarity, transubstantiation and promise differ broadly, as their origins are completely different.

> As the obligation of promises is an invention for the interest of society, 'tis warp'd into as many different forms as that interest requires, and even runs into direct contradictions,

rather than lose sight of its object. But as those other monstrous doctrines are merely priestly inventions, and have no public interest in view, they are less disturb'd in their progress by new obstacles; and it must be own'd, that after the first absurdity, they follow more directly the current of reason and good sense. (T 3.2.5.14)

Even that area of the ideas of justice that has to do with the transfer of the property of goods through consent is introduced as a means of perfecting the fundamental need to make possible the exchange of goods in a broader way on the basis of reciprocal trust. In effect it is precisely after the invention of the promise that this practice is perfected and can be developed in a systematic manner.

Just how far Hume's analysis is from that of the theorists of natural law is documented furthermore by Hume's ample treatment of the various rules according to which one can attribute ownership to one person instead of another. In Hume's discussion of these rules we do not find only, as Stephen Buckle has suggested, a program "to complete" the natural law (Buckle 1991: 298), but rather "to replace" it with a completely different approach. The rules that determine property recognized by humans have shared the essential prerequisite of being able to guarantee, through the stability of possessions, peace and social stability. These rules, according to Hume, are fundamentally four: "occupation, prescription, accession, and succession" (T 3.2.3.5), with occupation understood as the first possession. Hume's analysis seems to put aside the normative exigencies of the theorists of natural law, from Grotius, to Pufendorf, to Locke, who sought the most valid among diverse possible criteria, and seems instead to privilege the need to explain how this process works. On one hand, Hume seeks to explain that the rules for determining ownership share a common origin in the sense that all can be seen as an exemplification of the rules through which the imagination associates the perceptions in the human mind, and applying them to the determination of the ownership of a certain good. The principles that human beings follow in deciding questions of property and external goods are nothing other than the application of the rules of association that are most natural and habitual for them.

A good portion of his analysis is then devoted to making the criteria for the functioning of different rules for determining ownership square with the principles Hume fixed with regard to the way in which the imagination associates the contents of the mind in part one of Book 1 of the *Treatise* on understanding. Thus Hume is concerned to explain how, in spite of the fact that he "already observ'd, that the imagination passes with greater facility from little to great, than from great to little," in the rules with which human beings determine property there are cases in which, instead, "a small object naturally follows a greater one as its accession." Hume points out that this does not represent an objection to his system but only a further element of observation that makes us aware of the "agility and unsteadiness of the imagination, with the different views, in which it is continually placing its objects" (T 3.2.3 fn. 75, 4–5).

When therefore Hume's discussion of the criteria that determine ownership seems to go beyond mere description and to take a normative turn, we can see that this is possible because the explanatory picture drawn on the basis of Hume's observation of human behavior leads him not only to exclude certain criteria as impractical, but to indicate the pragmatic advantages of a certain way of proceeding. The advantages of the guarantee include not only the stability of individual possession, but more generally the stability and continuity of the social order and thus of the conditions for peaceful coexistence. In this context, Hume holds that the view of those who want to make the attribution of ownership depend upon the evaluation of the merit of the persons involved is unacceptable, because "were mankind to execute such a law; so great is the uncertainty of merit, both from its natural obscurity, and from the self-conceit of each individual, that no determinate rule of conduct would ever result from it; and the total dissolution of society must be the immediate consequence" (EPM 3.23).

In the same way, Hume also refuses any rule that makes ownership depend upon some criterion of perfect equality and communion of goods. Indeed, he writes,

> historians, and even common sense, may inform us, that however specious these ideas of *perfect* equality may seem, they are really, at bottom, *impracticable*; and were they not so, would be extremely pernicious to human society. Render possessions ever so equal, men's different degrees of art, care, and industry will immediately break that equality. Or if you check these virtues, you reduce society to the most extreme indigence; and instead of preventing want and beggary in a few, render it unavoidable to the whole community. The most rigorous inquisition too is requisite to watch every inequality on its first appearance; and the most severe jurisdiction, to punish and redress it. But besides, that so much authority must soon degenerate into tyranny, and be exerted with great partialities; who can possibly be possessed of it, in such a situation as is here supposed? Perfect equality of possessions, destroying all subordination, weakens extremely the authority of magistracy, and must reduce all power nearly to a level, as well as property. (EPM 3.26)

The path that seems, finally, most acceptable to Hume for assigning ownership is the recognition of present possession. Acknowledging the possession that is already effectively present can be a first step toward the construction of peaceful civil relations. One must not, however, incorrectly interpret Hume's predilection for rules that turn out to be useful as a form of normative utilitarianism and thus an acceptance of utility as the decisive ethical criterion. As we know, Hume repeatedly explains how practices created in an entirely casual manner reveal themselves to be useful only after they have been consolidated. Certainly, then, in his theory this choice cannot be made to derive from an explicit pursuit of maximum utility. As far as the overall validity of the rules of justice is concerned, Hume again calls upon an idea of utility, but this is a utility that can be discovered only after such rules have been consolidated and reinforced by the presence of governments. Indeed, according to Hume, for a full recognition of their validity, ideas and notions of justice demand that persons be able to appreciate the utility not only of single rules and actions, but indeed of the possession of a comprehensive system of justice that impartially limits and restrains behaviors that are guided exclusively by personal interest.

The concept of justice Hume presents turns out, we can see, to be only marginally concerned with satisfying distributive criteria for a readjustment of the possession of goods. This concept seems engaged, rather, in an effort to demonstrate that there exist minimal notions of justice that have been consolidated in all human societies because they are necessary conditions for stability and security. It is as if Hume chose not to address further questions about equity and redistribution because these seem secondary, insofar as they arise only after notions of justice in Hume's minimum sense have been stabilized. Thus one sees that Hume's theory of justice seems not to take upon itself a whole series of questions related to the rights of the person. Indeed, among the natural laws or in the various tasks of the government that Hume identifies, we do not find discussion of murder, or other safeguards of personal liberty or integrity. We must not however lose sight of the fact that in Hume's moral theory such rights and demands relative to the preservation of persons from suffering, from pain, or from the absence of consideration are addressed with reference to the natural virtues. These situations are addressed by an extension, demanded by the general point of view, of the outcomes that are arrived at by a sympathy that is restricted to those who are similar and near to us.

Practically it is enough to keep in mind the way that Hume reconstructs situations of sympathy with persons who have been subjected to cruelty from others – for example those who suffered the cruelties of Nero – in order to recognize that precisely the natural motivations of human beings, such as for example their limited benevolence, represent for him a sufficient guarantee against this type of action. The sphere of natural virtues and that of more direct personal relations already include the elements for the protection of life and personal liberty. If we examine the distinction between the sphere of moral sentiments assigned by Hume to the natural virtues and that sphere created by the artificial virtues we can identify in Hume's philosophy a treatment that anticipates (as revealed by Whelan 1985: 356–63) some of the formulations of philosophical liberalism. In particular Hume anticipated the separation between the sphere of morality and that of law established for example by Jeremy Bentham and John Stuart Mill. Hume's evolutionary and conventionalist argument leads him for example to consider the constitution of a specific political obligation, after the conventions of property and promising have become established, as the step that follows the development of the artificial virtues. The natural basis of this plan of artificiality lies, according to Hume, in the difficulty that human beings have in taking care of their more long-term interests, and in their tendency to prefer more immediate satisfactions, even when this is not reasonable. Rulers can intervene to correct this tendency. They may do this where a situation becomes institutionalized which allows for the creation of rulers as a class that has a personal interest in the success of the long-term public interest.

Hume also locates questions of international law in an evolutionary and historical frame. Hume understands international law as a perfection of the process of civilization, in which ethical relations come progressively to determine relations among states. Hume does not embrace, therefore, the realist thesis that argues that relations among states constitute a sort of no man's land for moral evaluation. While Hume admits that moral bonds are less stringent in the case of the actions of princes, in particular in the relations among nations, he recognizes however that these bonds continue to have a residual force when those general needs are satisfied through which the whole system of artificial virtues is constituted. The general constitutive needs are to have a set of "human conventions" useful for "the preservation of peace and order" (T.3.2.11.5). While the prince is on some occasions justified by the demands of these objectives in not respecting moral rules, on other occasions he is not so justified. In this sense the history of international relations itself indicates the presence of an ongoing process of civilization, in the course of which a plan is consolidated that is, in one way or another, valid for those needs of humanity that are connected with the natural virtues. It is enough indeed that we not lose sight of the stabilization of the "laws of nations" such as "the sacredness of the person of ambassador, the declaration of war, the abstaining from poison'd arms, with other duties of that kind, which are evidently calculated for the commerce, that is peculiar to different societies" (T 3.2.11.1).

In order to demarcate more clearly the area of civil relations entrusted to the artificial virtues, Hume concludes his presentation by occupying himself with the demands made by chastity and modesty, almost exclusively for the female sex. The fact that Hume considers these virtues as artificial virtues, and thus historical and conventional and not natural; that he denounces certain points of incoherence at the level of the natural sentiments of impartiality; that he applies this exclusively to women; and that Hume connects the genesis of these moral laws to the need of fathers to be assured of the biological derivation of the offspring in their care (T 3.2.12) – all of these facts clearly demonstrate the ironic nature of this discussion.

In the end, chastity and modesty in no way go together with the natural tendencies of human beings. Thus a sexual morality that revolves around these concepts is entirely historical, as Hume explains in EPM: "The long and helpless infancy of man requires the combination of parents for the subsistence of their young; and that combination requires the virtue of CHASTITY or fidelity to the marriage bed. Without such a *utility*, it will readily be owned, that such a virtue would never have been thought of" (EPM 4.5). Thus, as in *A Dialogue* (EPM, A Dialogue), Hume explicitly suggests that this is only a norm connected to the customs of historical societies. This, too, is another step toward the naturalization and secularization of traditional religious moralities.

See also 10 "Hume on the Direct Passions and Motivation"; 21 " 'One of the Finest and Most Subtle Inventions': Hume on Government"

References

Baier, Annette C. (1991). *A Progress of Sentiments: Reflections on Hume's "Treatise"* (Cambridge, MA: Harvard University Press).

Buckle, Stephen (1991). *Natural Law and the Theory of Property* (Oxford: Clarendon Press).

Forbes, Duncan (1975). *Hume's Philosophical Politics* (Cambridge: Cambridge University Press).

Haakonssen, Knud (1981). *The Science of a Legislator: The Natural Jurisprudence of David Hume and Adam Smith* (Cambridge: Cambridge University Press).

—— (1993). "The Structure of Hume's Political Theory," in David Fate Norton (ed.), *The Cambridge Companion to Hume* (Cambridge: Cambridge University Press), pp. 182–221.

Harrison, Jonathan (1981). *Hume's Theory of Justice* (Oxford: Clarendon Press).

Hayek, Friedrich August von (1963). *The Legal and Political Philosophy of David Hume. Il Politico*, XXVIII, from V. C. Chappell (ed.), *Hume: A Collection of Critical Essays* (Garden City, NY: Anchor Books, 1966), pp. 335–60.

Hume, David (1741–77). *Essays Moral, Political and Literary*, ed. Eugene F. Miller (Indianapolis, IN: Liberty Fund, 1987). (Cited in the text as *Essays.*)

—— (1745). *A Letter from a Gentleman to His Friend in Edinburgh containing Some Observations on a Specimen of the Principles concerning Religion and Morality, said to be Maintain'd in a Book Lately Publish' d Intituled "A Treatise of Human Nature,"* ed. Ernest Campbell Mossner and J. V. Price (Edinburgh: Edinburgh University Press, 1967).

Mackie, J. L. (1980). *Hume's Moral Theory* (London: Routledge and Kegan Paul).

Magri, Tito (forthcoming). "Hume's Justice," in Donald Ainslie (ed.), *Critical Essays on Hume's "Treatise"* (Cambridge: Cambridge University Press).

Norton, David Fate (1982). *David Hume: Common-sense Moralist, Sceptical Metaphysician* (Princeton, NJ: Princeton University Press).

Rawls, John (2000). *Lectures on the History of Moral Philosophy*, ed. Barbara Herman (Cambridge, MA: Harvard University Press).

Smith, Adam (1759). *The Theory of Moral Sentiments*, ed. Knud Haakonssen (Cambridge: Cambridge University Press, 2002).

Snare, Francis (1991). *Morals, Motivation and Convention: Hume's Influential Doctrines* (Cambridge: Cambridge University Press).

Whelan, Frederick G. (1985). *Order and Artifice in Hume's Political Philosophy* (Princeton, NJ: Princeton University Press).

Further Reading

Allan, James (1998). *A Sceptical Theory of Morality and Law* (New York: Peter Lang).

Árdal, Páll S. (1966). *Passion and Value in Hume's "Treatise"* (Edinburgh: Edinburgh University Press).

Baillie, James (2000). *Hume on Morality* (London: Routledge).

Bricke, John (1996). *Mind and Morality: An Examination of Hume's Moral Psychology* (Oxford: Clarendon Press).

Lecaldano, Eugenio (1991). *Hume e la nascita dell'etica contemporanea* (*Hume and the Birth of Contemporary Ethics*) (Roma-Bari: Laterza).

Magri, Tito (1994). *Contratto e convenzione: razionalità, obbligo e imparzialità in Hobbes e Hume* (*Contract and Convention: Rationality, Obligation and Impartiality in Hobbes and Hume*) (Milan: Feltrinelli).

Miller, David (1981). *Philosophy and Ideology in Hume's Political Thought* (Oxford: Clarendon Press).

Russell, Paul (1995). *Freedom and Moral Sentiment: Hume's Way of Naturalizing Responsibility* (New York: Oxford University Press).

Stewart, John Benjamin (1963). *The Moral and Political Philosophy of David Hume* (New York: Columbia University Press).

Stroud, Barry (1977). *Hume* (London: Routledge and Kegan Paul).

15

Hume on Beauty and Virtue

JACQUELINE TAYLOR

In this essay, I examine Hume's views on beauty and our aesthetic taste alongside his views on virtue and our moral taste. In each of the major works on moral and aesthetic theory, Hume deliberately presses a comparison between our perception of beauty and that of virtue. The examination of Hume's comparisons of beauty and virtue helps us to track and make sense of his evolving methodological concerns. In the *Treatise*, Hume first compares beauty and virtue in order to highlight the success of the theory of association in explaining how certain passions originate. He also uses the comparison in both the *Treatise* and the *Enquiry concerning the Principles of Morals* to show that both our moral sentiments and our sentiments concerning beauty have their source in sympathy. In his 1757 essay, "Of the Standard of Taste," Hume uses the comparison for a different purpose, and he presents a sophisticated case for how we might reconcile both moral and artistic pluralism with a standard that allows us to withhold endorsement of some evaluative outlooks.

Background for Hume's Views

Hume is part of the sentimentalist tradition in both morals and aesthetics. I will give a brief overview of this tradition so that we may better appreciate Hume's distinctive contribution to it.[1] Anthony Ashley Cooper, the Third Earl of Shaftesbury (1671–1713), is often regarded as the philosopher who initiated modern sentimentalism. Shaftesbury developed his account of internal senses in response to the Hobbesian doctrines that good or evil is relative to individual desire or aversion, and that morality is grounded in self-interest. Hobbes famously pronounced in chapter 6 of the first part of *Leviathan*, "These words of good, evil, contemptible, are ever used with relation to the person that useth them: there being nothing simply and absolutely so; nor any common rule of good and evil, to be taken from the nature of the objects themselves." Hobbes argued that man is a material system, perpetually moving and changing, so that "it is impossible that all the same things should always cause in him the same appetites, and aversions" (*Leviathan* 1.6.6–7). The good differs not only among men, but also for the same man given his fluctuating desires. Hobbes traces a chief source of social instability to these changeable judgments regarding what is good. The only way to have fixed notions of moral good and evil is by means of a political convention establishing a sovereign with absolute power, and whose rule determines what is morally good or bad. Each person enters into the social compact and keeps his covenants because it is in his interest to do so. Moral obligation is thus founded on artifice, and moral motivation grounded in self-interest.

Shaftesbury responds critically to Hobbes, arguing that a completely self-interested creature would have to be a self-contained system. Human beings, in their anatomy, physical needs, and psychology, clearly have a relation to one another, showing that they are part of a social system. Each part must cooperate to support the whole. While we each have a private good and concern for ourselves, this need not be inconsistent with the public good. Indeed, virtue and an appropriate self-interest can be in agreement. Not only are social affections natural to us, but "the charm of kind affection is superior to all other pleasures," so much so that it regulates our other passions and "remains as the master-pleasure and conqueror of the rest" (*Inquiry* 2.21). But virtue lies not merely in the strength of social affection. Rather, we are able to form "general notions" of our various affections and of the public good, and "by means of this reflected sense, there arises another kind of affection towards those very affections themselves, which have been already felt and have now become the subject of a new liking or dislike" (*Inquiry* 1.2.3). Shaftesbury's positive theory extends Lockean ideas of reflection to include the perceptions of internal senses. According to Locke, ideas of reflection are the ideas arising from our observations of the mind's workings; these so are the ideas we have of mental operations such as thinking, imagining, or doubting. Shaftesbury argues that the mind not only conceives of its own operations, but also has an internal sense that responds to the beauty and deformity of its affections. He speaks figuratively of the mind having "its eye and ear so as to discern proportion, distinguish sound and scan each sentiment or thought which comes before it." When this inner "reflex sense" presents the various affections that are the "springs of action," the mind cannot "withhold its admiration and ecstasy, its aversion and scorn." Only a creature who possesses social affections, on which he can reflect, taking notice of what is worthy, and then make that "conception of worth and honesty to be an object of his affection," can cultivate virtue and have a sense of morality (*Inquiry* 1.2.3).

In his dialogue, *The Moralists*, Shaftesbury argues that both beauty and virtue are real qualities, perceived by the mind's internal sense. Beauty and goodness are the same, and although men may argue about what is good, the "standard, rule and measure" of goodness is "ever presupposed." Virtue is the highest of three orders of beauty. The first order is comprised of those "dead forms" created by man or nature, but without their own forming power, while the second is the "double beauty" of mind, which is a form whose activity is to form the works of art. But the "supreme and sovereign beauty," the highest order and "what may be more truly termed our issue," are our sentiments, resolutions, and actions, "whatsoever is handsome and noble in the kind." Reflecting his tutelage under Locke, Shaftesbury does not argue for innate ideas, but instead asserts that we instinctively recognize the beauty of virtue, "exclusive of art, culture or discipline." Instinct provides us with certain "pre-conceptions" or "pre-sensations" of beauty, which belong only to a mind that can reflect on its own sentiments, and consciously advance in its own beauty (*Moralists* 3.2).

Francis Hutcheson (1694–1746), whose early work on beauty and virtue defends and extends Shaftesbury's views, develops a more complex view of internal senses and a more systematic analogy between them and the physical senses. Hutcheson posits several distinct internal and instinctive senses, including a public sense and a sense of honor in addition to a sense of beauty and a moral sense. In his *Inquiry into the Original of Our Ideas of Beauty and Virtue*, he proceeds systematically, examining first the sense of beauty and then the moral sense, and also comparing these two senses with physical sense and with each other. According to Hutcheson, beauty, whether natural or artistic, or the beauty of mathematical theorems, arises from our perception of "uniformity amidst variety," where that ratio is a real (theoretically measurable) quality in the object (*Inquiry into Beauty* 2.3). Like sensible perception, beauty is mind-dependent; as Hutcheson puts it, "beauty is taken for the idea rais'd in us," that is, the perception of some mind (*Inquiry into Beauty* 1.9). More precisely, beauty depends on our having a sense of beauty, which Hutcheson defines as a power to receive the idea of beauty. Someone without a sense of beauty may perceive the uniformity–variety ratio, but will fail to find anything beautiful. Yet the uniformity–variety ratio is what makes the object beautiful to someone with a sense of beauty. Our response to beauty is an immediate and necessary perception of pleasure. Moreover, it is distinct from and antecedent to any consideration of the object's utility, which arises from the prospect of interest or advantage (although these latter may "super-add a distinct rational pleasure"). Without a sense of beauty, Hutcheson argues, self-interest will lead us to find objects convenient or advantageous, but not beautiful (*Inquiry into Beauty* 1.16). We perceive beauty, and likewise virtue, independently of custom or education; indeed, these latter can lead us to form "wild associations" that corrupt our senses of beauty and virtue.

Just as the sense of beauty responds with admiration or scorn to a uniformity–variety ratio that gives objects their beauty or deformity, the moral sense approves of benevolence and disapproves of unkind affections. The kind or unkind affections of agents elicit from our moral sense a pleasure or pain in precisely the same way that the uniformity–variety ratio elicits pleasure or pain from the sense of beauty. And just as "beauty" denotes the perception of a mind, "moral goodness . . . denotes our idea of some quality (i.e., kind affection) apprehended in actions, which procures approbation" (*Inquiry into Virtue*, Intro.). Our sense of morality, like that of beauty, operates immediately, without reflection, and without any consideration of advantage.

While Hume's moral theory is clearly indebted to his moral sense predecessors, his approach differs from theirs in several key ways. Rather than positing internal senses, Hume locates sympathy, a principle that allows us to communicate emotions and beliefs, as a common source of our sentiments of beauty and of virtue. As we shall see, this allows him to emphasize the social character of both kinds of sentiment. While we naturally find things valuable or disagreeable, our sentiments are shaped in a social context where we receive a particular education, internalize customary beliefs and values, and learn how to reflect on the useful or harmful tendencies of the qualities to which we ascribe value or disvalue. In contrast to the teleological explanations that Shaftesbury and Hutcheson offer to explain how we achieve the right balance of our different affections, Hume uses sympathy and the principles of association to account for the *efficient* causes of our sentiments. That is, he explains how some of our perceptions of pain or pleasure along with our ideas about value produce the complex sentiments that express approval or blame. This approach enables him to include a wide variety of features among those that we find morally valuable or harmful. So for example Hume includes among the virtues some not obviously moral qualities such as wit or cleanliness, or self-regarding qualities such as industriousness, and his broader catalogues of virtue and vice stand in marked contrast to the views of Shaftesbury and Hutcheson, in which only the social affections, especially benevolence, count as virtues.

Beauty, Virtue, and the Double Association

In the *Treatise*, his earliest work, Hume seems to be recasting the notion of reflection when he introduces impressions of reflection, a category that includes all our passions and desires as well as the sentiments of beauty and virtue. He argues that our perceptions of beauty and deformity are calm impressions of reflection, or sentiments. Impressions of reflection are so called because they derive from some antecedent sensation or idea of pleasure or pain, yet they are nevertheless "original existences," and not themselves copies of prior perceptions as are ideas. Sentiments of beauty are in part naturally calm, frequently causing less agitation or disturbance than other emotions such as fear, joy, pity, or love. But some of our sentiments of beauty, particularly those directed towards beautiful or deformed characters or towards works of art, arise from a process that corrects an initial biased response. This process of correction yields calmer sentiments, and Hume likens them to judgments of reason. The *Treatise* is the work in which Hume takes most pains to show the distinctiveness of his own theory of value and our sentiments of beauty and virtue. We will thus look in some detail at the comparisons he draws between beauty and morality in this work.

Hume identifies several different kinds of beauty, including the physical beauty of persons, the beauties of nature, beautiful artworks and other manmade objects, and the beauty of human character (i.e., virtuous character). The main focus, especially in Book 3 of the *Treatise*, is on our moral sentiments, the objects of which are virtuous or vicious characters. Hume compares our perception of natural or artistic beauty with moral perception to show that all our sentiments of taste, while directed towards different objects, arise from the same principles and have similar effects. For example, both beauty and virtue produce the passions of pride and love, while deformity and vice produce humility and hatred. Hume uses the cases of virtue and beauty as support for his causal explanation of how certain passions and sentiments originate in the mind, and in particular to showcase how the theory of association, first set out in Book 1, plays a role in generating pride and love. In turn, the indirect passions of pride, humility, love, and hatred, along with the principle of sympathy, are crucial to our sense of identity with regards to the passions, and play a central role in producing the moral sentiments.

The comparisons between beauty and virtue provide confirming evidence in favor of Hume's explanatory hypothesis regarding the origin of the indirect passions and moral sentiments. The first comparison, between virtuous character and the beauty of persons, arises in the context of a discussion of the causes of pride. Pride is an indirect passion, that is, a passion that does not arise directly in response to good and evil, but instead requires "the conjunction of other qualities" (T 2.1.1.4). These other qualities are comprised of what Hume refers to as "a double association of ideas and impressions." In brief, pride is a passion directed towards the self in virtue of something about oneself that produces pleasure; it thus contrasts with a passion such as joy, which is a direct response of pleasure to something good. Pride requires a relation of two ideas that both refer to the self: the idea of something good related to oneself, and the idea of oneself as the object of pride. Pride also requires two related impressions, which are two resembling forms of pleasure: the pleasure of pride itself and a separate pleasure in response to the good feature related to oneself. After giving a detailed discussion of the double association, and introducing some limitations governing the appropriate experience of pride, Hume examines various natural causes of pride in order to show that they support this explanation in terms of double association.[2] Virtuous character and the physical beauty of persons are introduced first, as "the natural and more immediate causes" of pride since they are "the qualities of our mind and body, that is self." These qualities contrast with other things such as wealth, which are "foreign and extrinsic" to the self, but may nevertheless acquire a "particular relation to ourselves" and thus become a cause of pride (T 2.1.9.1).

Hume argues that the essence of both virtue and beauty is pleasure, and this pleasure is the "real" cause of pride. Whatever the quality, the pleasure it arouses in us in turn produces pride "by a transition along related ideas," that is, the two ideas of self. If the beautiful quality has no connection to me, it may still please me, but will not produce pride (T 2.1.8.7). With respect to virtue, Hume considers two allegedly competing theories, the so-called "selfish" theory (advocated, for example, by Bernard de Mandeville) that morality is founded on self-interest and education, and the sentimentalist view (for example, of Shaftesbury or Hutcheson) that holds we naturally have a moral sense by means of which we perceive virtue and vice. He argues that in either case, the essence of virtue is pleasure, while that of vice is uneasiness. Either virtue redounds to our advantage, which we find pleasant, or we naturally approve of virtue and that approbation is pleasant. So virtue is something that produces pleasure independently of pride, and when related to oneself will also produce the passion of pride. Similarly, beauty "gives us a peculiar delight and satisfaction," and when "plac'd upon our own bodies," this pleasure is converted into pride (T 2.1.8.1). This natural tendency to produce pleasure "is the distinguishing characteristic of beauty, and forms all the difference betwixt it and deformity, whose natural tendency is to produce uneasiness" (T 2.1.8.2). So pleasure and pain constitute the "very essence" of beauty and deformity, and of virtue and vice (T 2.1.8.2). Indeed, "there is nothing common to natural and moral beauty, (both of which are the causes of pride) but this power of producing pleasure; and as a common effect supposes always a common cause, 'tis plain the pleasure must in both cases be *the real and influencing cause* of the passion" (T 2.1.8.3, my emphasis). The examination of beauty and virtue gives "proof" that the hypothesis concerning the double association of ideas and impressions does explain the origin of the indirect passions. Notice that this explanation deploys the theory of association to explain the origin of the indirect passions in terms of their efficient causes, comprised of the double association of ideas and impressions (as Hume notes explicitly in "Dissertation of the Passions"). The theory of association, along with sympathy, likewise explains the origin of our sentiments of beauty and morality. Hume thus dispenses with the teleological explanations, favored by predecessors such as Shaftesbury and Hutcheson, of both the natural balance of our passions and the internal senses of morality and beauty.

Beauty and Virtue as Powers of Producing Pleasure

Let us examine more closely the claim that beauty and virtue are powers of producing pleasure. Some commentators have argued that in the *Treatise*, as well as in his essay "The Sceptic," Hume intends the claim about the power of virtue or beauty to produce pleasure to evoke something akin to Locke's notion of a secondary quality. According to Locke, the content of a sensible perception (e.g., a sound) does not literally resemble the object perceived. That content depends both on our having the senses we do and on the microphysical (or for Locke, "corpuscular") structure of the object. It is the encounter between the object and our sense organ that produces the non-resembling sensible perception; hence we say that the object has a power to produce that perception. In his initial discussion of virtue and vice in Book 3, Hume explicitly draws an analogy between moral qualities and sensible qualities. When we consider, for example, a crime of murder, we cannot perceive vice as a quality independently of the internal sentiment that responds to the malicious killing of another. The dead body, the motive of malice, and the deliberate stabbing are all identifiable matters of fact. But:

> the vice entirely escapes you, as long as you consider the object. You never can find it, till you turn your reflection into your own breast, and find a sentiment of disapprobation, which arises in you, towards this action . . . So that when you pronounce any action or character to be vicious, you mean nothing, but that from the constitution of your nature you have a feeling or sentiment of blame from the contemplation of it. Vice and virtue, therefore, may be compar'd to sounds, colours, heat and cold, which according to modern philosophy, are not qualities in objects, but perceptions in the mind. (T 3.1.1.26)

Virtue and vice are "perceptions in the mind" insofar as the perceptions are not resemblances of any fact in the situation, just as our sensible perceptions do not resemble any actual quality of the object.

But Hume does not always use "power" in a way that could be considered analogous to Locke's use of the term when theorizing about secondary qualities. In the section on beauty in Book 2, Hume explicitly distances himself from the secondary quality analogy. He asks "whether beauty be not something real, and different from the power of producing pleasure" (T 2.1.8.6). Rather than answering this question directly, he introduces the notion of surprise, asserting that something that is surprising and connected to us is yet another cause of pride, since "surprise is nothing but a pleasure arising from novelty" (T 2.1.8.6).[3] Setting aside the fact that what we find surprising about one another can also be distinctly *un*pleasant, the main point Hume wants to make here is that the pleasure of something surprising that is also connected to us makes it apt to produce pride. We may, for example, be proud of our surprising bodily accomplishments, or of the surprising adventures or dangers we have met with and can boast about to others. When we find something surprising it is not because of any conformity between our capacity for surprise and the physical qualities of the object. Surprise is not like the perception of a secondary quality, since the latter depends on

278

the object having the physical qualities that comprise the object's power to produce in us a sensible perception. Attributing to the object a power of producing in us a sensible perception usually entails everyone with nondefective senses will or should have the same perception, and that our having the senses we do necessitates our perceiving things in terms of their sensible qualities; there are facts of the matter about the objects of our sense perception. In contrast, surprise is a subjective response on our part, not to anything about the object as such, but to what is *to us* novel, unusual, or exciting in our encounter with it. We may feel surprise in response to someone because, for example, we did not expect him to have a certain talent, or have not previously encountered it, or because he displays it in unexpected circumstances. Not everyone need find the same things surprising, and what once surprised us may no longer do so. But if enough people love or admire someone for something surprising that he himself finds pleasant, that is sufficient for his feeling pride.

Nevertheless, the discussion of surprise does not answer the question about beauty. Novelty notoriously wears off, and what was once surprising becomes familiar. Yet we often continue to find an object beautiful no matter how familiar it becomes to us. Some cases of beauty and virtue, at least, garner an enduring and widespread admiration. Are beauty and virtue more like secondary qualities or like something surprising? Hume's answer, I think, is neither, and a more complex story must be told to explain our perception of morality and beauty. Let us first consider whether there is something about beautiful objects or virtuous characters that specifically comprises a power to produce pleasure. We can then turn to Hume's discussion of the particular kind of feelings that the pleasures of beauty and virtue consist in.

Hume's claim that the power of producing pleasure is the essence of beauty is a general conclusion he arrives at after comparing the difference between beauty and deformity according to "philosophy or common reason" (T 2.1.8.2). The differences "resolve into this, that beauty is such an order and construction of parts, as either by the *primary constitution* of our nature, by *custom*, or by *caprice*, is fitted to give a pleasure and satisfaction to the soul" (T 2.1.8.2). Perhaps superficially, this description suggests that beauty produces pleasure analogously to the way in which the secondary qualities of objects produce in us sensible perceptions. Given our natural capacity to experience pleasure, something about the construction of the parts of the beautiful object will evoke pleasure in us when we contemplate it. But Hume's elaboration of his view stands distinctly at odds with that of Francis Hutcheson, who did attempt to show that the internal senses worked analogously to our physical senses (see esp. *Inquiry concerning Beauty* 1.7).

Beauty, Utility, and Sympathy

While Hume acknowledges that a beautiful appearance can consist in regular features, or a uniformity that we find pleasing, he argues that the "more considerable part" of beauty is owing to the *utility* of objects (T 3.3.5.3–4). We admire the order and construction of parts that renders an object useful or convenient. For example, we admire certain animals because their bodies equip them to be particularly strong, agile, or swift.[4] Powerful shoulders or hindquarters give an animal the advantage of greater strength, and make it appear beautiful to us. The beauty of persons often consists of features advantageous to both the possessor and others, a claim Hume illustrates through his description of the well-built "good women's man" whose body promises "extraordinary vigor" (T 3.3.5.2). Similarly, the beauty we admire in an architectural masterpiece may derive as much from the convenience for the inhabitants – sweeping views, easy to heat or cool down, high-quality building materials – as from the ornamental design. Even with works of art, their beauty is proportional "to their fitness for the use of man, and even many of the productions of nature derive their beauty from that source" (T 3.3.1.8; see also 3.3.5.2–3). Beauty and utility are not distinct, and Hume cites Quintilian who wrote that "true beauty and usefulness always go hand in hand" (T 3.3.1.8, n. 83). He makes a similar case for virtue, beginning with the virtues of justice which we approve for their utility. In general, the traits of character that we find most valuable are those we admire because they are useful either for their possessor or for others.

Yet Hume is mindful of Hutcheson's concern about utility being relative to individual interest. According to Hume, utility *is* for someone's advantage, but not necessarily the advantage of the individual approving of the useful object or character. He appeals to sympathy, the principle of imagination by means of which we communicate our passions and sentiments to one another, and asserts that our sense of beauty, and similarly our sense of virtue, "depends on sympathy" (T 3.3.1.8). Regarding beauty Hume writes, "Wherever an object has a tendency to produce pleasure in the possessor, or in other words, is the proper *cause* of pleasure, it is sure to please the spectator, by a delicate sympathy with the possessor" (T 3.3.1.8). This same principle of sympathy produces our sentiments of morals as well as those of beauty. Recall from the discussion of beauty that Hume has emphasized *whatever* is connected to oneself and produces pleasure will in turn produce pride. So any mental quality that produces pleasure, either because it is useful or agreeable, is a source of pride for the possessor and a source of love for those on whom the agent's character has beneficial effects. The observer who sympathizes with that pride or love will in turn approve of the agent's virtuous character. Hume now extends his claim from Book 2 that beauty and virtue are powers of producing pleasure, and writes: "These two particulars are to be consider'd as equivalent, with regard to our mental qualities, *virtue* and the power of producing love or pride, *vice* and the power of producing humility or hatred. In every case, therefore, we must judge of the one by the other; and may pronounce any *quality* of the mind virtuous, which causes love or pride; and any one vicious, which causes hatred or humility" (T 3.3.1.3).

Virtues are powers of producing love or pride, and our sympathy with those latter passions will produce in us a moral approbation that we direct towards the agent's character.

Hume views our moral life as more varied than does Hutcheson. The qualities we consider virtues are not limited to social affections. An instinctive sense cannot accommodate all the variety. According to Hume, we do direct our moral approval towards kind affections – compassion, friendship, generosity, gratitude – and so on. But there are other "mental qualities" of which we approve that are quite distinct from benevolence, including such traits as patience, fortitude, industriousness, loyalty, discretion, good sense, and frugality. As a source of value, utility unifies a broad range of traits. The category of "useful" traits can be further divided between those that are useful to society and those useful to their possessor. The merit of justice, for example, is explained by its public utility and our sympathy with the public good. Indeed, "we carry our approbation of" the virtues of justice "into the most distant countries and ages, and much beyond our own interest" (T 3.3.1.9). It is "only by sympathy" that we approve of the merit of justice wherever we find it, even when our own interest is not concerned: "It follows, that sympathy is the source of the esteem which we pay to all the artificial virtues" (T 3.3.1.9). Sympathy with others' pleasures also explains our approval of natural social virtues, friendship and gratitude for example. Sympathy with the pleasure others get from self-regarding qualities, such as industriousness or frugality, as well as from other mental qualities, such as wit, that are not so much useful as they are immediately agreeable, explains our approval of these qualities as virtues. Hume even blunts the distinction between the physical beauty of persons and virtue when he observes that "besides all those qualities which render a person lovely or valuable, there is also a certain je-ne-scai-quoi of agreeable and handsome" that is immediately pleasing, and which we thus denominate virtuous (T 3.3.4.11).

Sympathy and the Standard of Virtue

Our perception and admiration of qualities as virtuous or beautiful reflects our sympathy with the pleasure of those who benefit from them. Without sympathy we frequently would not recognize beauty or virtue, and would not appropriately admire or approve of them. Sympathy thus has an epistemological function: it moves us beyond self-interest and corrects the distorting effects of distance so that we gain a clearer view of what characters are like. And although sympathy's natural partiality and limited scope can make us prone to erroneous evaluations, Hume invokes the notion of a standard of virtue or merit to show that we can easily correct these errors, at least in a way that is adequate for our moral purposes. Rather than relying on our own "peculiar" perspective, we need to find a common point of view with others if we want to "converse together on any reasonable terms" (T 3.3.1.15).

> Every person's pleasure and interest being different, 'tis impossible men cou'd ever agree in their sentiments and judgments unless they chose some common point of view, from which they might survey their object, and which might cause it to appear the same to all of them. Now in judging of characters, the only interest or pleasure, which appears the same to every spectator, is that of the person himself, whose character is examin'd; or that of persons, who have a connexion with him. And tho' such interests and pleasures touch us more faintly than our own, yet being more constant and universal, they counter-ballance the latter even in practice, and are alone admitted in speculation as the standard of virtue and morality. They alone produce that particular feeling or sentiment, on which moral distinctions depend. (T 3.3.1.30)

The common point of view helps us to move beyond our present and particular situation, and so to disregard the variations in sympathy and sentiment due to interest, vivacity or distance. Through sympathy, we extend our concern to the perspective of those most familiar with the character. Their responses are "more constant and universal," so that they "counter-balance" our own interests "even in practice." Taking up this shared perspective has a steadying or stabilizing effect on our judgment. The responses of the agent and her acquaintances "are alone admitted in speculation as the standard of virtue or morality," since they fix our view of what the agent's character is really like and thus help us to calibrate our sense of someone's praiseworthiness or blame-worthiness. By following this method of evaluation, we gradually form a "general un-alterable standard" to which our moral sentiments should conform, so that our moral evaluations become correspondingly "constant and establish'd" (T 3.3.3.2).

The requirement to adopt a common point of view and sympathetically engage with the responses of others in order to praise or blame appropriately is further evidence that Hume does not view beauty or virtue as like secondary qualities. One might think that just as Hutcheson views benevolent affections as the real qualities that elicit our approval, Hume too appeals to the real psychological traits of persons as the equival-ent of powers that will cause us to feel approval or blame. Annette Baier points out that Humean characters are comprised of real psychological traits, the "durable mental qualities" that are exhibited in someone's habits of feeling, attitude, and con-duct. Baier also notes that Hume's talk of character is often of the character "given one," since he took the mental qualities, themselves unseen, to be inferred by those attending to the person's conduct. The character that is the object of moral sentiment is, according to Baier, "a cultural artifact and a somewhat abstract thing, abstracted out of the array of persons and personalities that we encounter" (Baier 1991: 190). In a similar vein, Simon Blackburn suggests that in modern terms we might say that character "is a theoretical entity, or possibly a logical construction." A character is "a construct from occasions of acting, [and] thoughts about likely motivation," and has to be judged "in light of a historical record" (Blackburn 1993). Blackburn explicitly offers this description to highlight the disanalogy between sensible perceptions and moral perception. We can extend the disanalogy by noting that when Hume refers to the actions and attitudes of persons as signs of character, he sometimes means that they are signs that are in need of decoding and interpretation, skills we acquire by way of sympathy. Hume makes this point in the first *Enquiry*, writing: "we mount up to the knowledge of men's inclinations and motives, from their actions, expressions, and even gestures; and again, descend to the interpretation of their actions from our knowledge of their motives and inclinations" (EHU 8.9). Moreover, as Hume makes clear in the second *Enquiry*, the common point of view is best regarded as an arena in which we must dis-cuss, debate and negotiate our understandings of persons' characters.

Beauty and Virtue in Hume's Later Philosophy

Hume's *Treatise* project is ambitious. On the one hand, he wants to explain the causal origin of the indirect passions and sentiments of beauty and virtue in terms of the prin-ciples of association and sympathy. Yet he also wants to show that moral evaluation is a reflective social process yielding a shared fund of moral knowledge, grounded in our common sentiments, upon which we draw to shape policy, provide moral instruc-tion and illustration. It is important to consider that Hume does not successfully meet the aims of his dual agenda. The emphasis on the causal origin of the moral sentiments suggests that moral evaluation, while perhaps impartial insofar as we overlook our own interests and take up the perspective of the agent and her associates, is something of an unreflective process. The impartiality of moral evaluators is guaranteed by their taking up the common point of view, yet Hume gives no indication of how the evaluators might assess the appropriateness of what he refers to as the "constant and universal" responses of the agent's associates. If there is disagreement among them, or if their responses are informed by such factors as envy, dependency, enmity, or bias, then we should not take such responses to attest adequately to the agent's character. In EPM and "Of the Standard of Taste," Hume seems aware of this difficulty. He no longer relies on an associationist account of sentiment, and offers different criteria that evaluators must meet if their sentiments are to set or conform to the standards of virtue or taste.

There are several significant differences between the *Treatise* and the later works. New weight is given to the role of reasoning and reflection in our appreciation of beauty and virtue. Moral and aesthetic evaluation continue to be characterized as social processes, where people reflect on their experience and education, but Hume also attends to the importance of discussion and debate, of reasoning well and the role of good sense in forming good judgments about character and art. A noteworthy development concerns the delicacy of feeling or taste, which Hume connects both with moral or artistic discernment and the cultivation of internal attitudes, including tranquility and a sense of humanity. Finally, he shows an appreciation, not evident in the *Treatise*, for the historical and cultural variability of both moral and artistic values.

The *Enquiry concerning the Principles of Morals*

As I noted in the introduction, Hume carries the comparisons between beauty and virtue into his later works, notably the *Enquiry concerning the Principles of Morals* (EPM) and the essay, "Of the Standard of Taste." But there are significant differences between these works and the *Treatise*. First, Hume sets aside the first task of the *Treatise*, noted above, namely, to show how the theory of association explains the origin of our passions and sentiments.[5] Hume clearly intended the theory of association to have substantial explanatory power with regard to our mental life, including the formation of belief, and as we have seen, the origin of the indirect passions, the sentiments of beauty and the moral sentiments. At the same time, the theory of association requires Hume to set limits on what counts as legitimate philosophical inquiry. As he noted, the effects of association "are everywhere conspicuous; but as to its causes, they are mostly unknown, and must be resolved into original *qualities* of human nature, which I pretend not to explain." To attempt such explanation would lead "into obscure and uncertain speculations" (T 1.1.4.6). At other points in the *Treatise*, including the discussions of our sentiments, Hume points to the limits of our philosophizing. For example, although our capacity for sympathy makes possible "the flexibility of our sentiments," including both the diversity of sentiments we feel and the variety of their objects, Hume notes that "'tis what we have experience of with regard to all our passions and sentiments," yet "there is something very inexplicable in" this diversity, for which he again pretends not to give a philosophical account (T 3.3.5.6).

But these limits are more tightly drawn in EPM, where explanation is based on observable attitudes and conduct rather than on a theory of the principles of association. Hume again points to the limits of philosophizing about some virtues and kinds of beauty. A quality, such as manners and grace, which seems to combine both virtue and beauty, and "catches our affection" so powerfully, still has "something mysterious and inexplicable" about it. In contrast to the obviously useful virtues, "this class of accomplishments . . . must be trusted entirely to the blind, but sure testimony of taste and sentiment; and must be considered as a part of ethics, left by nature to baffle all the pride of philosophy, and make her sensible of her narrow boundaries and slender acquisitions" (EPM 8.13). Without the associationist explanation, it is "sufficient" that sympathy "is experienced as a principle in human nature. We must stop somewhere in our examination of causes; and there are, in every science, some general principles, beyond which we cannot hope to find any principle more general" (EPM 5.17, n. 19). In the *Treatise*, detailed explanations of the connections between the indirect passions, sympathy, and the moral sentiments were important for explaining how the common point of view works, as well as how a person's character affected her sense of pride or humility. In contrast, in EPM, the indirect passions and their various mixtures such as envy, respect, and contempt, are merely noted as "a subject of speculation to such as are curious with regard to moral enquiries" (EPM 6.33, n. 34). Instead, Hume's task is to explain the relevant common features of the group of traits we in fact admire, and which contribute to "personal merit," rather than explaining the origin of our perceptions of moral pleasure, hence the indirect passions are of less importance. Moreover, Hume characterizes rather differently the role of sympathy and the common point of view in establishing a standard of virtue, as we shall see below.

The emphasis in EPM instead falls more squarely on utility and agreeableness as the sources of value, and Hume provides more precise arguments to show that our praise for utility need not refer to our own individual interest. While philosophers might think only moral skeptics appeal to utility, "in common life . . . utility is always appealed to" in considerations of what merits praise, while the person "whose habits and conduct are hurtful to society . . . [is] an object of disapprobation" (EPM 5.1). "A more public affection" than self-interest explains our approval of benevolence, justice, and other virtues useful for society or the individual (EPM 5.17). This more public affection is sympathy, or a "general benevolence" that we experience at least as much as we do self-interest. Sympathy interests us in the lives of others even when "we have no friendship or connexion or esteem for the person" (EPM App. 2, n. 60), and it may arouse no more on our part than "a cool preference of what is useful and serviceable to mankind, above what is pernicious and dangerous" (EPM 9.4). While we have more intimate affections towards those for whom we care, sympathy, in making us sensitive to the happiness or misery of others generally, and taking us beyond our more partial concerns, is the source of our attention to moral distinctions and of our moral sentiments (EPM 5.39). Sympathy always has "*some* authority" over our moral sentiments, and without it we would be indifferent to virtue and vice (EPM 5.39).

In EPM, Hume stresses the positive contribution of both reason and sentiment or taste, and he suggests that the person in whom the two faculties are working together properly will possess the virtues of good evaluation. The final evaluation of characters and actions as praiseworthy or blameworthy, "which stamps on them the mark of honour or infamy . . . and . . . which renders morality an active principle, and constitutes virtue our happiness, and vice our misery," depends on sentiment. But a moral sentiment that properly discerns its object requires the concurrence of reason, so that "in order to pave the way for such a sentiment, and give a proper discernment of its object, it is often necessary, we find, that much reasoning should precede, that nice distinctions be made, just conclusions drawn, distant comparisons formed, complicated relations examined, and general facts fixed and ascertained." We thus need to develop skills of good reasoning, learning to identify relevant facts and relations, which distinctions to make, how to form relevant comparisons and draw a just conclusion. Some of "the natural kinds" of beauty charm us immediately and, indeed, often cannot be changed by reflection or reasoning. But with the beauties of morality and the finer arts, we cannot "feel the proper sentiment" without "the assistance of our intellectual faculties" and "a false relish may frequently be corrected by argument and reflection" (EPM 1.9). Hume repeats the point in the first Appendix, insisting that an "accurate reason and judgment" must inform our moral sentiments (EPM App. 1.2).

Hume continues to argue that utility is a considerable source of our approbation of both beauty and virtue. But in EPM, he appeals to the expert as someone whose specialized training (breadth of knowledge, appropriate comparative experience, etc.) leads her to find beautiful what is useful, convenient, or well-made (EPM 5.1). The appeal to the expert is an important addition, since it helps to make the point that the utility with which we are concerned is not what, perhaps short-sightedly, serves narrow self-interest, but that which any well-informed person with the relevant experience might reasonably prefer. In addition to her training and experience, the expert or the connoisseur also has an appreciation for that which is done well or finely crafted. Hume notes that the more experience a person gains of moral matters, and the warmer her concern for humankind, the more likely she will acquire a "delicate feeling of the most minute distinctions" (EPM 5.5).

There is a difference between moral reasoning and the craft-knowledge or expertise of the connoisseur of the arts, however. Hume acknowledges that in some moral matters we may at times need the help of experts, for example some matters of justice and social policy are particularly difficult to resolve without the contributions of precedence, and of "civilians" and other experts (EPM App. 1.2). But the cultivation of moral taste, and moral evaluation as a social practice where we expect the concurrence of others, typically requires active debate and discussion about everyday moral matters rather than a specialized training. In EPM, Hume reconceives the standard of virtue, arguing that it is grounded in our moral conversations and debates about the general preferences of society insofar as these are informed by reflection on past experience to establish which stable traits of character tend over time to promote or detract from the happiness of the agent or others (EPM 5.42, n. 25).

The Standard of Taste

In his essay, "Of the Standard of Taste," Hume separates (although not as clearly as one would like) the issue of what makes a work of art beautiful from that of what makes someone qualified to judge the work's beauty. As we saw above, in the case of morality, when we are considering what makes someone virtuous, we examine the character traits, such as loyalty, industriousness, or wit, that render her useful or agreeable to herself or others. A proper judgment of character will take account of what Blackburn referred to as the person's historical record, that is, her decisions, attitudes and actions as these are displayed over time and in the various circumstances she encounters. Of course, as Hume makes clear in EPM, it is only because our capacity for sympathy interests us in the happiness and misery of others that we recognize moral distinctions and feel an approval for virtue and abhorrence for vice.

Hume suggests something analogous in the case of our consideration of works of beauty. There are first of all the qualities that we use in describing beautiful art. Hume mentions eloquence or "spirit of writing" as qualities that contribute to the beauty of the well-written essay. There are also the rules of art or composition, general rules that we derive from experience of what has pleased universally. An artist conforms, either by "genius or observation," to the rules of art that give the work its eloquence, spirit, and other qualities comprising its beauty (*Essays*: 231). The artist's talent or genius is an important element in assessing the work (and the talented artist may produce beautiful work despite transgressing some of the rules of art). The good poet, for example, has a talent for moving "the pathetic and sublime of sentiment" and pleases us even when describing tragic events (EPM 7.27). In the essay "Of Tragedy," Hume observes that fine drama speaks to the artist's skill in depicting human passion, as well as his eloquence and deft deployment of devices that heighten or soften the emotional responses of the audience. Notice that beautiful art pleases by arousing passions and enlivening the imagination; Hume makes no reference to utility in these essays. The artist must also succeed in achieving her ends with respect to the audience and as appropriate to discipline or genre; for example, the successful history instructs, while the eloquent oration persuades and fine poetry pleases (*Essays*: 240). Finally, good art survives over time, eliciting a "durable admiration" that transcends the envy or jealousy that may have characterized the artist's "narrow circle," or the flattery accorded to what is merely fashionable (*Essays*: 233).

The works of art that have stood the test of time serve as "established models" to which we can turn in learning how to discern beauty or to try to correct some defect of taste (*Essays*: 235). Even if most people may admire the enduring and beautiful works of art to which they are exposed, we should not expect "that in every individual the pleasure will be equally felt," or that their admiration goes beyond the whole rather than an appreciation for the particular qualities that make the work beautiful (*Essays*: 234). There are various obstacles that hinder the proper appreciation of works of art. We may consider it in the wrong setting, for example, viewing a picture in the wrong light, or hearing part of a poem out of context. In addition to eliminating external hindrances, we must also be in the right frame of mind, and need "a perfect serenity of mind, a recollection of thought, a due attention to the object," or we risk obscuring the relation between the form or qualities of the work and our sentiment (*Essays*: 232).

In addition, there are the "general principles of approbation or blame," on which the sentiments of beauty and deformity depend. While these principles of taste are "universal," few people have cultivated their taste in such a way that they can "establish their own sentiment as the standard of beauty" (*Essays*: 233–4, 241). In "Standard of Taste," Hume's systematic presentation of the virtues that comprise good taste makes clearer the relation between reasoning well and feeling appropriately. He begins with delicacy. Someone with delicacy of taste is able to discern in the work of art its particular qualities, in their several degrees and mixtures, perceiving "every ingredient" in the work (*Essays*: 235). The person without a delicate taste has confused sentiments, the result of being unable to "perceive the several excellencies of the performance; much less distinguish the particular character of each excellency, and ascertain its quality and degree" (*Essays*: 237). While everyone pretends to this form of delicacy, it is something that must be cultivated (*Essays*: 234). Here is where the established models of beautiful art can help us cultivate good taste, as we study them and learn to discern what makes them beautiful. Repeated experience of considering the works "in different lights" or situations will gradually improve the judgment, allowing the feeling to become "more exact and nice" (*Essays*: 237). To master any order of beauty, the critic must be able "to form comparisons between the several species and degrees of excellence" (*Essays*: 238). She must have exposure to the different genres of each form of art (e.g., the genres of literature, music, or painting), and acquire an ability to "weigh the several performances, admired in different ages and nations" (*Essays*: 238).

The proper comparison of artworks from different times and cultures requires that the critic "preserve his mind free from all prejudice." In the case of a work that lies at either a temporal or cultural distance, the critic must "place himself in the same situation as the audience" for whom the work was intended. If he does not, but instead "obstinately maintains his natural position," and makes no allowance for the views and prejudices of the original audience, then he is apt to condemn "rashly . . . what seemed admirable" to that audience. The critic who considers the work of a friend or enemy must, in contrast, "depart from this situation," and forget his particular connection to the artist. If he fails here, then he "never sufficiently enlarges his comprehension." In either case, the prejudiced person has "perverted" sentiments, which fail to register the proper influence of the beauty under consideration. His taste thus "departs from the true standard; and of consequence loses all credit and authority" (*Essays*: 239–40). Prejudice can undermine sound judgment on factual or theoretical matters as well as corrupt our sentiment of beauty. Hume argues that "it belongs to *good sense* to check its influence in both cases" (*Essays*: 240). In an early essay, "Of the Delicacy of Taste and Passion," published for the first time in 1741, shortly after Book 3 of the *Treatise*, Hume argues that a "fine taste" regarding the sciences and liberal arts "is, in some measure, the same with strong sense, or at least depends so much on it that they are inseparable" (*Essays*: 6). Similarly, in "Standard of Taste," he observes that "reason, if not an essential part of taste, is at least requisite to the operations of this latter faculty" (*Essays*: 240). Moreover, the improvement of reason and true taste both require "the same clearness of conception, the same exactness of distinction, the same vivacity of apprehension," and it would be "rare to meet with a man who has a just taste without a sound understanding" (*Essays*: 240–1).

If these general principles of taste – delicacy, practice, comparison, freedom from prejudice, and good sense – fail to have "their full play" because the person labors under one or more defects of taste, we may pronounce his judgments "erroneous." In fact, Hume thinks the character of the "true judge" is rare. It is the "joint verdict" of these true judges that establishes a standard of taste: "strong sense, united to delicate sentiment, improved by practice, perfected by comparison, and cleared of all prejudice, can alone entitle critics to this valuable character; and the joint verdict of such, wherever they are to be found, is the true standard of taste and beauty" (*Essays*: 241). As with the standard of virtue, the standard of taste serves to guide the sentiments of others. Whether someone possesses the virtues of good taste is a factual matter, Hume claims, although the character of the aesthete, like any other character, must be interpreted in light of her historical record of judging, and a final determination may depend on the best arguments about who is best qualified to judge. Hume adds that the modern critic must also cultivate a sense of humanity which will not permit her to endorse wholeheartedly works in which the worst vices are approvingly depicted by the artist.

More on Delicacy and the Pleasures of Beauty

Hume identifies a delicate taste as a virtue. He writes that it "must always be a desirable quality; because it is the source of all the finest and most innocent enjoyments of which human nature is susceptible," and "is sure to meet with approbation" (*Essays*: 236–7). In EPM, delicacy of taste is counted among the virtues immediately agreeable to oneself, and "is itself a beauty in any character, as conveying the purest, most durable, and most innocent of all enjoyments" (EPM 7.28). In the essay, "Of the Delicacy of Taste and Passion," Hume argues that cultivating a more delicate taste is also useful to the possessor because it helps to extinguish those delicate passions that make us overly sensitive to (especially our own) happiness and misery. A delicate taste is thus a means to internal tranquility. By studying the liberal arts, such as literature and history, which are critical to cultivating good taste, a person can "form juster notions of life." Hume also cites Ovid, who wrote that studying the liberal arts "humanizes the character and permits it not to be cruel" (*Essays*: 6, n. 4).

In the essay, "The Sceptic," Hume again emphasizes that inner tranquility and a sense of humanity can result from study of the liberal arts. It is important to note that a key theme of this essay concerns the limited and yet real way in which philosophical reflection can make a difference to how we live. The skeptic asserts several times in this essay that beauty and deformity are not qualities of objects but belong entirely to the mind that praises or blames (*Essays*: 162–6). The skeptic also points to the authority nature has over the mind's affections, changing the objects we desire or renounce. Custom, education, prejudice, or caprice can change our preferences without any change in the objects themselves. Some scholars think that the skeptic's seemingly subjectivist position with regard to value represents Hume's own views. But the point of the discussion is to show that even if beauty is nothing, it does not follow that we should just choose our ends "at adventures." Rather, in keeping with the common sense view of "Standard," the skeptic argues that there are better and worse ways of selecting and pursuing our ends (*Essays*: 160–1). However much our desires or sentiments may vary, the cultivation of the internal, more contemplative sentiments, rather than acquisitive desires or immoderate passions, tends to protect us against unhappiness. Recall that we have seen that Hume's own position is subtler than the subjectivist one. The useful objects we find beautiful also have describable qualities that we take to contribute to the beauty. Likewise, in the characters we praise as virtuous or blame as vicious we can identify and describe particular traits, the value or harm of which we can discuss intelligently with one another. Even the skeptic subscribes to a relational view of value, not a purely subjectivist one. It is because our mind has a "particular fabric or structure," such that we are sensitive to beauty and deformity, virtue and vice, that we respond as we do to the qualities of objects and characters; we perceive beauty and virtue because of the relation, or "conformity," between those qualities and our sentiments. When we contemplate a beautiful object or virtuous character we do not merely survey it and content ourselves with ascertaining the facts and relations, but instead feel "a sentiment of delight or uneasiness, approbation or blame, *consequent to that survey*" (*Essays*: 164; emphasis added). As we saw earlier, the more complex forms of beauty, such as those of morality or art, can have a suitable influence on the mind only when they has been assisted by reason, reflection, experience, and argument.

Beauty and Morality in "Of the Standard of Taste"

We will conclude with an examination of Hume's comparison between morality and beauty in "Standard of Taste." He appeals to a comparison between artistic beauty and morality in order, first, to make a point about the cultural and historical variability of taste, and then to argue that a certain kind of moral standard must inform our taste with respect to beauty. He begins by noting that when it comes to art, most of us notice a diversity of taste even in the narrow circle of our acquaintances and despite the fact that we have had a similar education and "imbibed the same biases" (this point about diversity in the narrow circle is relevant to the point I made above about the inadequacy of Hume's *Treatise* characterization of the common point of view and the standard of virtue). As we saw above, such diversity is frequently due to some defect of taste, either because we have not fully developed skills of reasoning well, have not had enough practice, cannot develop a sensibility to beauty, or have failed to overcome the biases that prevent us from appreciating what is done well but is foreign to us. And of course some diversity is "blameless," as when people prefer one form (literature vs. painting) or genre (tragedy vs. comedy) of art to another. Here, however, there is still, among those of good taste, agreement about what count as the good models among the different genres or forms (*Essays*: 244).

But there is another kind of diversity, familiar to those who have taken a broader survey of human nature, namely, the historical or cultural variability with respect to what is regarded as beautiful. Hume points out that we find a similar diversity with respect to morality and the depiction of virtue and vice. This diversity is frequently masked because everyone uses the same type of general evaluative discourse. Across cultures and epochs, people have used a similar vocabulary to identify and evaluate the works regarded as beautiful or deformed, or the characters that are virtuous or vicious. There are general terms such as "beautiful" or "virtuous" that imply praise, and their opposites, "deformity" or "vicious" that imply blame. We also have more specific terms that purport to identify the features that make a work beautiful, such as "eloquence," or that make a person virtuous, such as "courageous" or "just." Some of these terms, those naming virtues, for example, imply praise, as others imply blame. There is agreement on how to apply the terms, and unless someone is purposefully using the terms in a nonstandard way, for example, ironically or to dispute a standard meaning, then we think that the misapplication of the term betrays ignorance about how we use the language.

Despite this "seeming harmony due to the nature of language," when we examine what different peoples actually mean by the particular terms we find that there can be considerable difference in the descriptive content of the terms, and hence in the application of them. For example, everyone applauds courage, but what courage meant in Homer's time is different from the eighteenth-century characterization of it by Fénelon in his retelling of the Homeric epic. The heroism of Achilles as depicted by Homer includes more ferocity than an eighteenth-century depiction finds appropriate. While we should in general put aside our own prejudices when we evaluate the works of past eras or other cultures, our moral prejudices are harder to overcome. We cannot enter into an artist's or author's sentiments if we find them blamable. Nor, indeed, should we: "where a man is confident of the rectitude of that moral standard, by which he judges, he is justly jealous of it, and will not pervert the sentiments of his heart for a moment" simply in deference to the artist (*Essays*: 247). As Michelle Mason notes, Hume's discussion sets out a "taxonomy" of prejudices (Mason 2001). Some prejudices are blameless, such as preferring music to literature, or film noir to screwball comedy. In overlooking one's moral prejudices, on the other hand, one risks betraying one's commitment to standards of decency and humanity. Nevertheless, we might ask whether Hume has created puzzles for himself here. Is it not true that any culture, in judging another whose values differ from its own, is likely to jealously preserve its own moral standard, and so "call barbarous whatever departs widely from" it (*Essays*: 227)? And while everyone may agree that the person with good taste is a valuable character, Hume seems now to have introduced the possibility that the meaning of delicacy or good sense, those virtues of the good judge, which were supposed to be identifiable as matters of fact not of sentiment, may also be historically and culturally variable.

Notice that Hume does not think the same kind of problem arises for us with regard to scientific facts and theories. We are open to revising our scientific knowledge in the light of new evidence, and embracing new theories when they offer greater explanatory or predictive power. Our commitment to discovering the truth about the way the universe works makes us ready to revise our opinions because we want them to be tracking the truth. When it comes to art, it is thus easy to forgive representations of old-fashioned theories that we no longer take seriously. We can still find beautiful a seventeenth-century painting of the alchemist at work since the fact that alchemy is not now regarded as a legitimate scientific endeavor does not detract from the beauty of the work. While moral values may vary historically or culturally they are not in such flux, or not in flux in the same way, as scientific facts and theories. "A very violent effort is requisite to change our judgment of manners, and excite sentiments of approbation or blame, love or hatred, different from those to which the mind has long been familiarized," so that "where a man is confident of the rectitude of that moral standard, by which he judges, he is justly jealous of it, and will pervert the sentiments of his heart for a moment" (*Essays*: 247).

Hume suggests we might find a solution to setting a standard with regard to culturally and historically distinctive uses of moral terms by "examining the celebrated controversy concerning ancient and modern learning" (*Essays*: 245). This debate, which took place in both France and England during the seventeenth century, was over which age showed the greater knowledge and wisdom. Hume clearly admires the ancients; he regularly draws on them as sources of wisdom and for their illustrations of moral character. He also endorses their characterization of personal merit, and the diverse qualities we may possess that help us to live well; and he clearly disapproves of the modern theological views that take a narrow view of which qualities we can admit as virtues. But he also thinks that citizens of the modern age can learn from the mistakes, ignorance, and more limited views of their forebears. The ancient heroic societies had to put courage and other martial virtues above the "softer," more social ones, given the difficult circumstances under which they lived where they lacked "full experience of the advantages attending beneficence, justice, and the social virtues." At the extreme, the celebration of courage extinguishes humanity (EPM 7.14–15). Uncultivated societies also tended to take a narrower view of what makes a quality useful: praise and blame tended to be regulated "by the ideas of private utility and injury," in the absence of the "more enlarged reflections" of modern society (EPM 9.8, n. 57). That narrower evaluative outlook and lack of experience would similarly constrain the principles of taste. Hume's modern person of taste has both a cultivated sense of morality and the delicacy of taste required to assess works of art. She allows for pluralism in both schemes of moral value and the standards for assessing works of art. Yet her sense of humanity informs her sense of taste so that she cannot endorse ethical outlooks that promote inhumanity or traits of that kind to the detriment of a sense of humanity. For this judge, consideration of the artists of such societies who approvingly depict inhumanity in their work leads her to lower her estimate of both the works and the artists' merit.

It may seem odd that Hume's person of good taste with regard to art also has a cultivated sense of humanity, while the person with a cultivated sense of morality may lack good taste and yet still be a good judge of moral character. But we should keep in mind that Hume thinks that among our important purposes in making accurate evaluations of ideal, good, and bad characters is the moral illustration provided by "the theatre" and other forms of art. The exemplars of virtue portrayed in the arts are important sources of moral education. The person of good taste thus shares with others of good moral sense in the task of molding virtuous characters.

See also 13 "Sympathy and Hume's Spectator-centered Theory of Virtue"; 16 "*Enquiry concerning the Principles of Morals*: Incomparably the Best?"

Acknowledgments

I presented versions of this essay at the Royal Flemish Academy in Brussels in November 2005, at the AAP meetings at the University of Otago in New Zealand in December 2005, and at the Pacific Division meetings of the APA in Portland, Oregon, in March 2006. I'm grateful to audiences on those occasions, and to Elizabeth Radcliffe, for helpful comments.

Notes

1 Although there are other important influences on Hume's thought besides the moral sense theorists. Of particular importance to his views on beauty was the Abbé J. B. Dubos. (See Jones 1982.)
2 The causes are natural, he notes, in the sense that the same kind of things (mental and bodily qualities, wealth and advantages, and others' opinions of us) produce pride or humility across cultures and throughout history.
3 Hutcheson also defines surprise as a pleasure arising from novelty and says he is following Addison's usage in his 1711 *Spectator* article on "Pleasures of the Imagination."

4   Hume is a bit inconsistent, and sometimes refers to features such as strength as something that we admire in addition to beauty; see, e.g., T 2.1.8.4.
5   Hume sets the theory of association aside without abandoning it altogether. There are two fairly important references to the customary association of ideas in EPM. And Hume retains the associative explanation of the origin of the indirect passions in his "Dissertation of the Passions."

References

Baier, Annette C. (1991). *A Progress of Sentiments: Reflections on Hume's "Treatise"* (Cambridge, MA: Harvard University Press).

Blackburn, Simon (1993). "Hume on the Mezzanine Level," *Hume Studies*, 19, pp. 273–88.

Hobbes, Thomas (1668). *Leviathan*, ed. Edwin Curley (Indianapolis, IN: Hackett Publishing Co., 1994). (Cited in the text by part, chapter, and paragraph.)

Hume, David (1741–77). *Essays, Moral, Political and Literary*, ed. Eugene F. Miller (Indianapolis, IN: Liberty Fund, 1987). (Cited in the text as *Essays*.)

Hutcheson, Francis (1724). *An Inquiry into the Original of Our Ideas of Beauty and Virtue*, ed. Wolfgang Leidhold (Indianapolis: IN: Liberty Fund, Inc., 2006). (Cited in the text as *Inquiry concerning Beauty* and *Inquiry concerning Virtue* by part and section.)

Jones, Peter (1982). *Hume's Sentiments: Their Ciceronian and French Context* (Edinburgh: University of Edinburgh Press).

Mason, Michelle (2001). "Moral Prejudice and Aesthetic Deformity: Rereading Hume's 'Of the Standard of Taste'," *Journal of Aesthetics and Art Criticism*, 59, pp. 59–71.

Shaftesbury (Anthony Ashley Cooper) (1699). *An Inquiry concerning Virtue or Merit*, in *Characteristics of Men, Manners, Opinions, Times*, Shaftesbury (1711), ed. Lawrence Klein (Cambridge: Cambridge University Press, 1999). (Cited in the text as *Inquiry*, by book, part, and section.)

—— (1709). *The Moralists: A Philosophical Rhapsody*, in *Characteristics of Men, Manners, Opinions, Times*, Shaftesbury (1711), ed. Lawrence Klein (Cambridge: Cambridge University Press, 1999). (Cited in the text as *Moralists* by part and section.)

Further Reading

Árdal, Páll (1966). *Passion and Value in Hume's "Treatise"* (Edinburgh: Edinburgh University Press).

Costelloe, Timothy M. (2004). "Hume's Aesthetics: The Literature and Directions for Research," *Hume Studies*, 30, pp. 87–126.

Dees, Richard H. (1997). "Hume on the Characters of Virtue," *Journal of the History of Philosophy*, 35, pp. 45–64.

Korsmeyer, Carolyn W. (1976). "Hume and the Foundations of Taste," *Journal of Aesthetics and Art Criticism*, 35, pp. 201–15.

McIntyre, Jane L. (1990). "Character: A Humean Account," *History of Philosophy Quarterly*, 7, pp. 193–206.

Mothersill, Mary (1984). *Beauty Restored* (Oxford: Oxford University Press).

Norton, David Fate (1982). *David Hume: Common-sense Moralist, Sceptical Metaphysician* (Princeton, NJ: Princeton University Press).

Sayre-McCord, Geoffrey (1995). "Hume and the Bauhaus Theory of Ethics," *Midwest Studies in Philosophy*, 20, pp. 280–98.

Taylor, Jacqueline (2002). "Hume on the Standard of Virtue," *Journal of Ethics*, 6, pp. 43–62.

Townsend, Dabney (2001). *Hume's Aesthetic Theory: Taste and Sentiment* (New York: Routledge).

16

Enquiry concerning the Principles of Morals: Incomparably the Best?

ANNETTE C. BAIER

Hume, in his brief and somewhat disingenuous autobiography, found *An Enquiry concerning the Principles of Morals* (EPM) to be, "of all my writings, historical, philosophical or literary, incomparably the best." (He presumably meant the best of those published in his lifetime – no comparison or, strictly speaking, impossibility of comparison, with his *Dialogues on Natural Religion* is implied.) Nor can this be dismissed as a bit of farewell irony, to be put with his claim later in "My Own Life" that he had been untouched by the baleful tooth of calumny. Twenty years earlier he had told a correspondent, Le Blanc, that EPM was his "favorite Performance" (Hume's Letters, Greig 1969: i., 227.). So his preference for this work seems to have been considered and stable. It challenges us to try to understand what it was about it that so particularly pleased its author. He wrote, in that same remarkable little memoir, that it was more the manner than the matter of "the unfortunate *Treatise*" that he believed to have led to its initial lack of success. He had therefore decided to "cast anew" the matter of its three books in his two *Enquiries*, and the "Dissertation of the Passions." EPM is definitely a "performance," and has fairly obvious literary as well as philosophical pretensions (not to mention a fairly stiff dose of history) in its examples. It is the mark of a fine literary performance to suit the manner to the matter. I think Hume set himself, in EPM, to do just that. In what follows, I shall largely be concerned with its ostensible "matter," but matter and manner cannot be kept entirely separate. I begin with some remarks about EPM's structure, and I will end with some questions about the relation of that to the work's matter and its chosen manner.

EPM's nine main sections are followed by a series of appendices, in the first edition two (the first and what became the third), four by the 1777 edition. In the first edition, and in all later ones until Selby-Bigge's in 1894, a final dialogue, which had been written separately, and may have been inspired by Montesquieu's *Persian Letters*, was included, as a final touch. Possibly it is an afterthought, but the appendices to EPM, unlike the appendix to the *Treatise*, are not second thoughts. If EPM is seen as a grand villa, then they are its workrooms, its kitchen, scullery, laundry, and cellars, lying behind, or under, the nine grandly furnished reception rooms with their many portraits, while off to one side is a more frivolous independent little building, a summerhouse or gazebo. Some of the materials for the main building, especially for its workrooms, are taken from one of the three wings of an earlier, condemned building, and the summerhouse may be partially modeled on a French one, but the main effect is of a fresh start, not an adaptation.

In *Treatise* 3, Hume had invoked facts about our moral capacity in support of a general and abstruse thesis about the limits of "reason," the derivative status of all "ideas," their association, and their subordinate role in motivation. It, after all, was the third book in a *Treatise of Human Nature*. The concern of EPM is to understand morality in its own right, and it is not so much moral motivation, as human recognition of human merit, that is now under scrutiny. Its avowed aim is to reveal "the true origin of morals"; its method, "to analyze that complication of mental qualities, which form what, in common life, we call Personal Merit" (EPM 1.10). Shaftesbury had undertaken a project of this sort, half a century earlier, in his *Inquiry into Virtue or Merit* (first published in 1699), and not just Hume's preference for the term "merit," but many other choices of words (dresses for morality, the interested obligation to virtue, a character with oneself and others, what it is to wear a human heart, etc.), echo Shaftesbury. He is the first philosopher to be named in EPM, on its second page, and it is not only his predecessor's possible confusion over the roles of reason and sentiment (mentioned there), nor his interest in the relation of religion to morality (clearly shared by Hume), nor his thesis about reflex affections (which seemed so important in the *Treatise*), that are now on Hume's mind. It is also Shaftesbury's concern about how reflections on manners of life are best presented to a general, well-educated readership. EPM is no more a compendium for students than is Shaftesbury's *Characteristics of Men, Manners, Opinions, Times*, in which, in 1711, a revised version of his *Inquiry* was imbedded. Both Shaftesbury's and Hume's mature writings about morality are more like Theophrastus' amusing portrayal of unwelcome "characters," than like Aristotle's (or for that matter Hutcheson's) lecture notes. EPM is a book for well-read adults with a sense of humor, not a solemn moral manual for the young. It is definitely no *Whole Duty of Man, Laid down in a Plain and Familiar Way . . . Necessary for all Families, with Private Devotions for several Occasions* (Anon. 1684: title page); indeed it continues the case against religion that Hume had begun in EHU, sections 10 and 11 (see Gaskin 2002).

Despite its impressive display of learning ("so much ingenious knowledge so genteelly delivered"), EPM is a genuine enquiry. It has a "conclusion," but that is by no means its last word. This enquiry, unlike EHU, is left fairly open-ended and inconclusive. A firm finding is reached about the "true origin" of morals, but the morals with this human origin are not so firmly set in stone. EPM is in its main sections an empirical investigation into what human judges have recognized as human merit, in a variety of conditions of life, and, as such, it must be left unfinished, just as a history of Britain has to be left off, "to be continued." As long as conditions of human life continue to change, the perceived value of some particular mental traits can be expected also to change. Hume gives the example of good memory as one that, in eighteenth-century Europe, had lost the special value it once had, and he mentions some fearsome skills that had been understandably prized in "barbaric" conditions of life. He makes it quite clear which traits he himself esteems, but he is also engaged in a sort of moral anthropology, which includes some comparative anthropology. His own selective index to EPM includes entries on the Athenian, the French, and the Irish conceptions of merit, and the Spanish conception of politeness. Facts about what has been praised in human persons are assembled, and the terms in which the praising has been done are examined. (See Taylor 2002; Price 1991: 82; King 1976: 343–61.) EPM's wealth of examples, mostly historical, contrasts strikingly with *Treatise* 3. There we were offered only Marcus Brutus, Alexander, Caesar, and Cato. Now they are joined by a host of others, and in almost every case, Hume quotes someone else's assessment of their character, before endorsing or disagreeing with that judgment. He is not just giving exemplars of the virtues; he is giving empirical evidence about what traits have in fact been praised and condemned, and by whom. So we have Diodorus Siculus on Epaminondas, Plutarch on Phocian, Demosthenes on Philip of Macedon, Livy on Hannibal, Sallust on Pompey, Tacitus on Vitellius, St. Evremont on Turenne, and so on, down to Hume's own assessment of the fictional Cleanthes, the perfect son-in-law. All these panegyrics and censures show as much about the one praising or censuring as about the character of the one assessed, but this is precisely what Hume's bootstraps method involves. Just as Samuel Johnson compiled his *Dictionary* by citing evidence from "the best writers," so Hume cites the best historians, orators, and satirists to show what has been praised and criticized in human persons. (Must we agree on who the good historians, orators, and satirists are, before we can agree on what makes a good person? And to what critics shall we turn, for assessing historians, orators, and satirists?)

In *Treatise* 1 and 2 Hume had attempted to analyze persons, their motivation, and the mechanics of their mutual sympathy, before giving, in *Treatise* 3, any analysis of how they correct the bias of natural sympathy in order to assess each other's merit. In EPM we have to do without any such "metaphysics" or mechanics of morals. Sympathy still plays a major role, and there is some moral epistemology, mostly in the first appendix, where Hume gives a very judicious settlement to "a controversy started of late," the one that had been at the forefront of his attention in *Treatise* 3.1.1. Neither this debate, about the roles of reason and sentiment in discerning virtues, nor any other abstruse topic, is the main business of the nine sections. Their task is to analyze personal merit, and so to compile a richly illustrated "catalogue of laudable qualities" (EPM 6.21), in every case suggesting the reasons why that particular trait in a person is welcomed, and identifying the principles or sources from which that welcome springs. All more intricate matters are discussed in the appendices, the workrooms, and Hume a month before his death was still busy revising his decisions about what should be transferred to them. Because they link EPM most closely with the most famous theses of *Treatise* 3, and because I do not see what Hume put in them to have been "relegated to a subordinate place" (Raphael 2001: 91), I shall look first at them. But we should note that one change Hume made from the *Treatise* was to let any conclusions he drew about how we recognize virtues, and what this shows about our nature, wait until after considerable virtue-recognition has been conducted.

The Appendices

It is in the first Appendix that we find Hume's reconsideration of the famous *Treatise* claim about the "impotence" of "reason alone" to motivate us, or serve as a basis for morals. He repeats that it is the "sentiments and affections of mankind, without any dependence on the intellectual faculties," that determine "the ultimate ends of human actions" (EPM App. 1.5), but it is no longer as certain as it seemed in *Treatise* 3.1.1 that moral considerations do provide an independent source of motivation, for most of us, most of the time. And for discerning which natural motives and mental abilities should count as virtues, he finds that our intellectual faculties have a very important role to play. In place of the master-slave pair, lively passion and inert reason, we now have the cooperating partners, warm sentiment and cool reason. The "distinct boundaries" of reason and taste are still firmly drawn, and we get the famous metaphor of the "gilding and staining" by sentiment of "objects, as they really stand in nature" (EPM App. 1.21). Morality may well be "a new creation," the creation of human sentiment, but before we, the creators, can select which natural mental traits to "gild," making them into virtues, many facts must be assembled, and many utilities weighed.

> One principal foundation of moral praise being supposed to lie in the usefulness of any quality or action; it is evident, that *reason* must enter for a considerable share in all decisions of this kind; since nothing but that faculty can instruct us in the tendency of qualities and actions, and point out their beneficial consequences to society and to their possessor. (EPM App. 1.2)

Reason in the form of tracing consequences and weighing utilities seems, in EPM, to have acquired considerable potency. The contrast between lively "impressions," without representational content, and "inert" ideas, with such content, which was essential to the *Treatise* argument for reason's limited moral role, in EPM is not even drawn. Reason is still "cool and disengaged," but taste and sentiment must secure its "concurrence" before there can be any moral outcome. Hume has not really altered the substance of his position, which all along was that both reason and sentiment are vital to discernment of moral merit, but there is, in Selby-Bigge's words, "a very remarkable change of tone or temper" (Selby-Bigge 189: xxiii; but see also Laird 1932: 236ff.). Gone are the provocative anti-rationalist pronouncements, and master-slave reversals. Logicians will search in vain here for any re-issuing of "Hume's Law," supposedly forbidding inferences from "is" premises to "ought" conclusions; the most they will find is the distinction between mistake of fact and mistake of right.

The fourth appendix, with its dismissal of the importance of the distinction between what is and what is not voluntary, its rejection of a punitive or pre-punitive role for disapprobation, and its consequent disdain for the question of whether the vicious person could have helped having the vices he has, is the one which, along with the third (which elaborated on the already controversial theses of section 3), gave most offense to Hume's contemporaries, and still upsets some readers (Penelhum 2000: 173ff.). The theses are familiar from the *Treatise* section "Of natural abilities," but now Hume compounds the offense by associating the sharp distinction between virtues and abilities, which he is rejecting, with religious doctrines of divine retribution for vice. The offended eighteenth-century "philosophers, or rather divines under that disguise," included not only James Balfour, Thomas Reid, and James Beattie, but also Adam Smith, a believer in natural and divine justice and in moral responsibility in a stronger sense than Hume can accommodate. Smith complains that, by his refusal to restrict moral assessment to those traits showing proper "self command," and by his emphasis on utility, Hume makes moral beauty of character not essentially different from the beauty of a chest of drawers (Smith 1759: 188). Hume, in a footnote which was apparently added in reply to his upright friend, significantly does not say that the reason why we respond to beautiful human characters differently from the way we respond to beautiful furniture is that the former, through their self-command, are responsible for their own moral beauty. What he says is that we have a special interest in "rational thinking" beings like ourselves, the objects of our love and hate, while we cannot be in love with a chest of drawers (EPM 5.1, n. 17). The fourth appendix was originally part of section 6, where some other factors influencing whom we fall in love with are discussed, to Balfour's at least pretended embarrassment (Balfour 1989: 118). Beattie too speaks bitterly of those, like Hume, whose corrupted morals "seduce others to vice and perdition" (Beattie 1810: 204).

Hume put his restatement of his views, not only on providence, but on "liberty and necessity," into EHU, not EPM. The morals of the latter are, however, definitely designed for determinists. (For lapsed Calvinists? Within two years of its publication, a move was afoot in Edinburgh to have Hume charged by the General Assembly of the Church of Scotland with infidelity and immorality.) Like Spinoza, Hume contents himself with listing and commenting on the character traits we have reason to welcome, and pointing out the consequences, such as loss of trust, that usually follow if the worst vices are displayed. There is occasional talk of what we "ought" to do, and there is talk of "blame," especially when the rules of "justice" have been broken, but the language of morals that Hume invokes in EPM's conclusion is not a deontology. It is a descriptive-cum-evaluative language ascribing the character traits that make a person "amiable or odious" to other human beings. As for moral responsibility, the only overt ascription of that in EPM is to "the Supreme Will," which, in a mischievous aside at the end of the first Appendix, which echoes the line of thought expressed in the last paragraphs of EHU 8, is credited with control over all human sentiments and reactions, presumably including human choices. Hume, while casting off most of his paternal Calvinist heritage, retains the belief that our given natures, together with the culture and institutions into which we are born, "predestine" our adult characters. (See Emerson 1990: 34, and Russell 1995: ch. 9.)

Morals without any mention of a moral law, or much concern with moral responsibility, are not morals as most of Hume's British contemporaries knew them. By 1753 Balfour was publishing his alternative "delineation" of morality and its divinely sanctioned obligations, cold-shouldering Hume's invitation to a civilized discussion of their differences, and trying, in his later lectures, to protect his Edinburgh students from Hume's dangerous influence (Sher 1990: 110–12; Hume's Letters, Greig 1969: i., 172). Balfour's version of our obligations is certainly more suitable "for families" than is Hume's, but prudery is not all that is at issue. More fundamental differences are at stake – the relation of religion to morality, and the freewill question. Since Hume's time, morality without God has become fairly standard, but a determinist version of morals is still controversial (see Haji 2003). Hume does of course include intentional action in the scope of moral assessment, and he does talk of "duty," of "a rule of right," and of the "obligations" not to steal, break promises, or disobey magistrates. But moral assessment goes beyond and behind the will. Even the virtue of self-command is, he notes, not within our will's command (EPM App. 4, 2). The normative-sounding idioms Hume sometimes uses are easily translated into factual claims about community expectations, and about what will be found "odious," "contemptible," or punishable by magistrates. Hume "defines virtue to be *whatever mental action or quality gives to a spectator the pleasing sentiment of approbation;* and vice the contrary. We then proceed to examine a plain matter of fact, to wit, what actions have this influence" (EPM App. 1.10). If it is a fact that we cannot but be displeased by extreme stupidity, as well as by malice, since both can do great harm, then both go into the demerit column, in Hume's moral ledger.

Hume's least controversial appendix, and the last that he gave that status, is the second, on self-love, originally the first part of the section on benevolence. It is probably its abstruseness, its indulgence of a speculative curiosity about human nature, rather than anything very controversial in the position taken, that led Hume to move it to an appendix. If it "may be esteemed, perhaps, a superfluous task to prove, that the benevolent or softer affections are ESTIMABLE," it will seem even more superfluous to prove that there are any such affections. But since writers of the stature of Epicurus, Horace, Hobbes, and Locke, who were no strangers to these affections, had taken them all to be (possibly unconscious) modifications of self-love, a philosopher engaged in "the speculative science of human nature" will want to examine "the selfish system." Hume says that the question is not very material to "morality and practice," since "I esteem the man whose self-love, by whatever means, is so directed to give him a concern for others, and render him serviceable to society" (EPM App. 2.4). As a speculative scientist of human nature, he suggests that it has been an exaggerated love of simplicity that has led thinkers to try to reduce the apparently disinterested affections to self-love, and that, where human passions are concerned, the obvious cause is probably the true one. In the end, he thinks, there is "really more simplicity" in the hypothesis that allows disinterested benevolence to exist than in the selfish hypothesis.

Like Butler before him, and Balfour after him, Hume distinguishes self-interest or "cool self-love" from particular propensities or passions, such as the desire for power, for fame, or for vengeance, and finds in human nature plenty evidence of disinterested, sometimes even self-sacrificial, benevolence. Butler, however, might not have appreciated one of Hume's arguments for its existence – that "the rules of analogy" require us, if we allow that "inferior species" of animal exhibit some benevolence, to grant that it is also to be found in "superior species" of animal, namely us human animals (EPM App. 2.8). This was not quite "the analogy of nature" Butler wanted us to draw (even though, in his *Analogy of Religion,* he was open-minded about the prospects of "the brutes" for possible progress and immortality). Maybe the second appendix is not so inoffensive.

One way to read all four appendices is as saying "If you thought I have, in the nine main sections, taken back the substance of what offended the reviewers and readers of *Treatise* 3, think again." There are some concessions to rationalists, and some bad arguments against them are gone, but readers like Balfour were not misled about the main message, nor about the challenge it presented to a religious and puritan culture.

The Analysis of Personal Merit

Postponing comment on the third Appendix, which differs only in degree of detail from section 3, I turn now to the nine sections. Their main task is to compile the catalogue of virtues, with illustrations and annotations. The list itself does not differ from what could be compiled from *Treatise* 3, and there are the same significant absentees, namely piety, humility, self-denial, and obedience, but we are now offered a more extensive gallery of dubious characters. To the *Treatise's* province-devastating military heroes, insipid conversationalists, and debauched bachelors shocked at any lewdness in a woman, are added effeminate men and rough mannered women, pompous declaimers, sloth-encouraging alms-givers, pernicious inquisitors, splenetic misanthropes, griping misers, indiscreet gossips, drinking companions with too good a memory, serious melancholics, egregious blockheads, harmless liars, ferociously coiffed Swabians, scalp-collecting Scythians, hair-brained enthusiasts, sour-tempered monks, and sensible knaves. This gallery is instructive as well as entertaining – the Swabians, for example, who dress their hair more to make themselves hateful to enemies than attractive to friends, are for this very reason deemed laudable by as esteemed a historian as Tacitus (EPM 7.13). To martially minded historians, the odious as well as the amiable can be found laudable. (Does this mean that their esteem should be discounted?)

The first section begins by raising the question of the roles of reason and sentiment in morals, and, while postponing the final decision on that until the catalogue has been compiled, correctly predicts what it likely will be. Hume then raises the question of how a cataloguer of virtues is to proceed. He says that, to frame the catalogue, all that we need do is ask ourselves which traits we would be pleased to have ascribed to us. He optimistically thinks we cannot be mistaken in this, and that language will guide us, since "every tongue possesses one set of words that are taken in a good sense, and another in the opposite." It is interesting that the acid test is not "would I want to have this trait?" (nor even "would I want my child, or my son-in law, to have it?") but rather "would I want to be taken to have it?" In the fourth Appendix, Hume draws a distinction between what he most wants for himself (to have a friendly humane heart), and how he wants the world to see him ("one endowed with extensive genius and intrepid courage"). "Character," for Hume, is close to reputation and name; it is a person's mental characteristics as shown to others. So to frame the catalogue of meritorious character traits one asks how one would like others to see one. This means that the knave, although proud of his successful secret knavery, can put honesty on his version of the catalogue, and a person who would feel damned with faint praise if described as "very good-natured" should have doubts about its presence on Hume's list. It may not be as easy as Hume here makes out to compile this catalogue, and in section 2 he allows that reflection and "sounder reasoning" often leads us "to retract our first sentiment, and adjust anew the boundaries of moral good and evil" (EPM 2.17).

In the second section Hume begins his disentangling of the different strands that, in his judgment, make up personal merit. (There are 67 named ones, by my count, although only a select 17 get onto Hume's own brief index. That short list is: benevolence,

299

chastity, cheerfulness, cleanliness, courage, decency, delicacy of taste, discretion, frugality, honesty, justice, memory, modesty, politeness, tranquility of mind, wisdom, wit.) First to be examined are the two main "social virtues," or rather groups of virtues, benevolence (which includes "beneficence and humanity, friendship and gratitude, natural affection and public spirit") and the conformity to various conventions that comprises Hume's "justice." He predicts that explicating these will "probably give us an opening by which the others may be accounted for." He reverses the *Treatise* order, by dealing first with benevolence, which Hutcheson had made practically the whole of virtue. Justice had been the first virtue to be examined in *Treatise* 3, giving the title of the lengthy part 2, which detailed a series of "artifices or contrivances," those presupposed by the approbation we give to respect for property, promises, magistrates, marriage vows, and treaties. Some commentators (see especially Taylor 1998) have found that early placing of a discussion of social artifice, and the coordination of attitudes it requires, important for Hume's later specification of the shared point of view from which any virtue, including benevolence, is discerned, but Hume now seems to see no need for such a tactic. He is first assembling all the traits admired by reflective people, before making any generalization about why they are all admired, or drawing any conclusion about the point of view needed for their recognition. And he looks first, and more carefully than in the *Treatise*, at forms of benevolence that deserve admiration. Whereas for the other virtues that Hume lists on his index, we get entries of the form, "Chastity, its merit, whence," for benevolence the entry has to be much more complicated, and to include, "its kinds."

His finding is that benevolence has many kinds, not all of them admirable. The virtue he endorses, whose merit comes both from its immediate agreeableness and from its social usefulness, is humane, thoughtful beneficence, not mere good will, nor impulsive charity. "Giving alms to common beggars is naturally praised because it seems to carry relief to the distressed and indigent: but when we observe the encouragement thence arising to idleness and debauchery, we regard that species of charity rather as a weakness than a virtue" (EPM 2.18). This observation about giving to beggars is the first intimation that the Christian virtues, not only Knox's stern ones but also Hutcheson's gentler ones, are in for a hard time, on Hume's analysis. From the "humane beneficent man" the hungry will indeed receive food, and the naked clothing. But not necessarily from handouts, since the humane beneficent man will also give "the ignorant and slothful skill and industry" (EPM 2.6). Utility, and utility of the sort Hume was attending to in his essays on economics, is a constraint on the merit of benevolent intentions. It is merchants and manufacturers, the makers of machines, the planters of trees and the cultivators of fields, not the members of charitable religious orders, who show the meritorious thoughtful benevolence that Hume wants us to appreciate. Any "heedless praises" we might be tempted to give to the ostentatious liberality of princes are to be retracted. (Replaced by praises of Caxton, Arkwright, and some of Hume's own relatives who were improving farming practices in the Scottish Lowlands?) Hume's pretense that all he is doing is recording agreed approbations, rather than educating and "adjusting" them, is fairly hollow, right from the start. His treatment of benevolence is as distinctly revisionary as his later treatment of the "monkish virtues." Hutcheson is not mentioned, but his shade is surely a background presence, subjected to polite correction. Cicero is quoted twice, and it is his views, not those of Christian writers, that Hume is largely following. Even when he disagrees, as he does on tyrannicide, it is Cicero's questions that are being addressed (see Moore 2002). For Hume, a well-disposed will is not the only thing we should want in each other; indeed benevolence without wisdom can do more harm than good. In a human community we also need wisdom and knowledge, enterprise and industry. Some people, indeed, Hume says at a later point, may be "too good." But to say that of someone is to praise as well as to criticize. He concludes this second section:

> Upon the whole, then, it seems undeniable, *that* nothing can bestow more merit on any human creature than the sentiment of benevolence in an eminent degree; and *that* a *part*, at least, of its merit arises from its tendency to promote the interests of our species, and bestow happiness on human society. (EPM 2.22)

(This sentence incorporates the last small correction Hume sent to his publisher, two weeks before his death, namely the deletion of the clause, "that there is such a sentiment in human nature as benevolence," which came after "undeniable." I presume Hume deleted the clause since the defense of the claim it makes had been transferred to Appendix 2.)

Having established the importance of "public utility" in the valuing of benevolence, and in the selection of which forms of benevolence are really to be welcomed, Hume moves on, in the third section, to explicate an equally essential virtue, this time one whose "*sole* origin" is public utility. This is the complex virtue Hume calls "justice," the virtue of respect for recognized rights and entitlements. This is a "curiously narrow" sense to give the word (Raphael 2001: 87ff.), omitting the traditional elements of concern for equality and for desert. (Is this just a "verbal dispute?") Hume reiterates the *Treatise* thesis that it is scarcity, and the need for cooperative schemes to prevent a disorderly scramble for the scarce goods, that make room for what he arguably misnames "justice." He characterizes it as the "cautious, jealous virtue." Frugality too is a virtue that depends on scarcity, but not on social measures to distribute the scarce goods peaceably, and it is these distributive schemes that give Hume's justice its special features. Justice has been famously declared, by John Rawls, to be the first virtue of social institutions. Hume takes the virtue he calls "justice" to be closely linked with, indeed inseparable from, social institutions, but what he means by it is not the fairness that institutions can have, or lack. (Like Aristotle, he lists equity as a separate virtue, one he never calls "artificial.") Hume's "justice" is not any sort of virtue of institutions, but is rather an individual person's acceptance of the need for them, and willingness to conform to their rules as long as others are doing the same. (A sort of unfairness or inequity would be involved in exempting oneself, while counting on others' conformity, and Hume does speak of justice as requiring "equitable conduct.") Justice, or what might better be called "conformity to cooperative schemes," is cautious, compared with generosity and benevolence. In our "necessitous condition," it restrains immediate self-interest, and we accept that restraint cautiously, only on the understanding that others are doing the same. And justice is "jealous," because its rules determine what each can count as exclusively "mine," what is each person's "due" or "*ius.*"

The point of inventing property and other rights depends on general scarcity. "Why call this object *mine*, when upon the seizing of it by another, I need but stretch out my hand to possess myself of what is equally valuable?" (EPM 3.3). What had not been said in the *Treatise*, and is now said, to Balfour's and Broad's outrage, is that just as "profuse abundance" would make justice pointless, so extreme scarcity, say in a shipwreck or a famine, would suspend its rules (Balfour 1753; 1989: 80–1; Broad 1944: 98). Whatever might lead Broad to share the last biscuit with his starving wrecked shipmates, and so starve "decently, and in order," it would not be a sense of Humean justice. Balfour cites Cicero and Lactantius against Hume on the "injustice" of seizing a plank to which another survivor had been clinging, in order to save one's own life. Hume could easily allow that humanity or equity, or even Broad's "decency," might stop one from being so ruthless in extreme conditions, but for him justice will have nothing (except possibly rowing in stroke) to contribute to lifeboat ethics. By balancing the psychological condition, moderate selfishness, with the external circumstance, moderate scarcity, Hume completes his account of "the circumstances of justice" (an account admired by Rawls 1971: 127–8; 1999: 110). He goes on to face and answer a very important question left unasked in the *Treatise*, that of who exactly are parties to these cooperative schemes, the ones who get to have rights. The answer is "all those who can make resentment felt," and Hume makes it clear that this excludes other animals, but includes all human beings. It definitely includes women, on whom men depend, not merely for charming company, but for "the propagation of his kind," and, most importantly, the knowledge that he has done so. (Hobbes, who said that it was our mutual vulnerability that makes acceptance of moral rules rational for us, and who took women to be strong enough, in the "state of nature," to rear their children without help from the children's fathers, would certainly have approved.) These are important clarifications of the *Treatise* account of justice. Despite the brevity of the section, compared with *Treatise* 3.2, it is more theoretically complete.

Another clarification, given in the second part of the section, concerns inequality of material possessions. Just as Hume's version of the virtue of benevolence/beneficence is a proto-capitalist version, so too is his version of what sort of inequality of wealth has to be tolerated. Although the cooperative schemes in which we are required to do our part were supposed to be adopted because they were "infinitely advantageous to the whole, and to every part" (T 3.2.2.22), and although they presuppose "some measure of equality" in all human persons, some end up doing a lot better than others from the adoption of property rights and from particular ways of transferring them. Hume expresses some sympathy with the "Levellers," but believes that egalitarian measures, such as redistributive taxation, would be too socially costly. If there were insufficient incentive to enterprise and hard work, we would soon have general indigence. And "rigorous inspection" by official re-distributors of property would be offensive, even bringing the risk of "tyranny." Inequality of material possessions has to be accepted, as the price of liberty. Should the wealthy have the virtues of generosity and public beneficence, this inequality may be slightly mitigated, but only slightly. And after all, the poor, to make up for having to go without "the feverish empty amusements of luxury and expence" (EPM 9.25), may have the consolation of "the unbought satisfaction of conversation, society, study, even health and the common beauties of nature" (EPM 9.25). (Their conversation, however, may have to be with the equally poor, since their "dirty furniture, coarse and ragged cloaths, nauseous meat and distasteful liquor" will, Hume believes, be off-putting to the more fortunate [EPM 6.33].)

Are there corrections, as well as clarifications, in the revised version of Humean justice that we find in section 3, supplemented by Appendix 3? (The "further considerations" advanced in the latter are said to give "a more particular explication of the origin and nature of justice, and . . . mark some differences between it and the other virtues" [EPM App. 3.1].) We still get the *Treatise* contrast between a virtue like beneficence, which does good act by act, and does some good even if it is rarely shown, and justice, where the benefit "arises from the whole scheme or system concurred in by the whole, or the greater part of the society" (EPM App. 3.3). We are now offered the simile of the "wall" of benevolence, built stone by useful stone, versus the more contrived "vault" of justice, where "each individual stone would, of itself, fall to the ground" unless it had the support of the others. Since these schemes and systems are of collective human making, are still given an account of a *human* "origin of justice," but, and not merely because of the compression of the account, we are no longer given the *Treatise's* sequential story. In that story, property rights were first fixed, and then various ways of exchanging and transferring property and services were invented, before magistrates were given authority to give the "*execution* and *decision* of justice" (T 3.2.7.8). By the time Hume completed his *History*, he had come to acknowledge, in that work's first appendix, that rights to command might, as in the Germanic tribes, precede property rights in land. Here, in EPM, we find him noting that rights of inheritance can be recognized in a pre-agricultural society, and that rights to water are mentioned in the biblical book of Genesis before rights to land (EPM 3.6). (It was a nice touch on Hume's part to invoke the Bible to show the human origin and culturally varying content of justice, as, in App. 4, he quotes the 49th psalm on the praiseworthiness of doing well to oneself. He was clearly pleased with himself about this, since both passages are included in his own selective index, under the entry for "Scriptures, holy, quoted" [EPM 2.91].) Different sorts of scarcity in different places will determine the sequence in which different sorts of property right come to be recognized, and there is no particular reason why promissory rights, and rights to inherit from relatives, should not be established in a pre-agricultural society. Promissory rights, however, will become of central importance in a commercial society, with various forms of "paper money" used in exchanges.

Hume speaks throughout of justice and fidelity (to promises) as if they arise together, and at times brings in, not only equity, which he takes to be "natural virtue" (T 3.3.1.11), but also veracity and integrity (EPM 3.48), whose status as natural or artificial is less clear. (The offense-giving adjective, "artificial," kept out of section 3, is allowed back in, in a footnote to Appendix 3.) He has not given up what may be his most original thesis in ethics, the thesis that promises have to be humanly invented before they can be used to bind. (Hobbes, whose "artificial man," Leviathan, lurks in the background to Hume's discussion, had said that neither property rights nor rights to allegiance existed in a "state of nature," but he seemed to take the force of "covenant" to be natural and unproblematic.) Hume makes it clear, in Appendix 3, that the sort of "agreement" that sets up these convention-dependent rights and obligations is an informal one, arising out of a sense of common interest, like that of rowers who coordinate their strokes. It cannot itself be a contract or promise. "The observance of promises is itself one of the principal parts of justice, and we are not surely bound to keep our word because we have given our word to keep it" (EPM App. 3.7). But nothing in the account now given rules out the possibility that the invention of some sort of promise, say between co-parents, might precede the invention of property rights. Hume had all along supposed property conventions to be adopted by people who already know the benefits of cooperation in the natural family, and now he is less dogmatic about what the first, most urgent convention will be. In some conditions, the first convention will create rights to command, in some rights to wells, in others rights to land, in others rights to navigation on rivers and seas. In almost all conditions there will very soon be rights arising from some sort of binding agreement between individuals, be it a form of marriage, of employment, or of tutelage and apprenticeship.

Existent customs and institutions can of course be subject to criticism, and Hume occasionally talks of what laws and customs ought to allow, as well as what they do. He was already writing his political and economic essays at this time, and he has firm views about such matters. "Who sees not . . . that whatever is produced or improved by a man's art or industry ought, for ever, to be secured to him, in order to give encouragement to such *useful* habits and accomplishments?" (EPM 3.28). However, most of the "oughts" in Hume's version of morals arise within existent artifices of "justice," that is, they are "deduced" from the fact of a particular social institution, along with a general sense of its public utility, and the consequent moral approbation of conformity to its rules.

> By the laws of society, this horse, this coat is mine, and *ought* to remain perpetually in my possession: I reckon on the secure enjoyment of it: By depriving me of it, you disappoint my expectations, and doubly displease me, and offend every bystander. (EPM App. 3.11)

Without customary rules, "the distinction between *mine* and *thine* would be unknown in society" (EPM App. 3.11), but once it is known then, if anyone takes Hume's splendid coat, he will be doubly displeased: displeased to lose what he reckoned on securely enjoying, and displeased, as any honest bystander would be, on the public's behalf, that its laws are being flouted. Hume in this passage calls these rules "the rules of equity," since equity demands that we not excuse ourselves from rules we want others to keep. If we do, we must expect "universal blame," and, if found out, loss of trust. Hume takes equity and impartiality very seriously, and the one unequivocally endorsed "ought" in EPM outside the scope of "justice" occurs when Hume agrees with Polybius that a historian ought to list the strengths as well as the weaknesses of those whose deeds he relates (EPM App. 4.9). Hume himself certainly showed this basic virtue when he turned historian, and it brought him the attention of Hyppolite de Saujon, who in her first letter to him praised his account of the Stuarts for its "divine impartiality."

The short fourth section, "Of Political Society," looks only in a cursory fashion at government, to which so much of *Treatise* 3.2 was devoted, and which provides the topic for many of the essays that Hume was writing at this time. Section 4 quickly moves on from the state to the great variety of other convention-governed circles we move in, from marriages, friendships, and leagues to loose communities of road-users, drinking clubs, and boxing fraternities. Some interesting virtues are recognized, such as selective and considerate forgetting, and some unwelcome characters are sketched – the gossip, the person who opens and reads others' mail, the nosey person who "plays the spy" upon his neighbor's "words and looks and actions," the person who presumes upon casual acquaintance. The background presence of Theophrastus and la Bruyère, in Hume's library, can now be felt, lightening the Ciceronian *gravitas* of sections 2 and 3, and their influence will continue, when Hume gets to the "agreeable" virtues.

In the central fifth section, Hume pauses and reflects on where his analysis of the virtues is taking him. So far it has led him to an emphasis on utility. But since a virtue, by Hume's definition, is a quality we are pleased to find in others, and pleased to have found in ourselves, utility must please, to have any moral importance. The last virtues Hume will go on to survey, in sections 7 and 8, are those that are directly pleasing, rather than pleasing for their utility. The question now arises of what the relation is, for Hume, between what pleases and what has utility, between Theophrastus' properly salted soup, and the Ciceronian prudence and enterprise of those who make salt available.

For Bentham, utility is simply stock of pleasure, although he has nice and possibly Hume-derived distinctions between what has hedonic "fertility" and what yields pleasure more directly. For him, the question of why utility pleases could not arise. As Sidgwick noted (1902: 209, n. 2), Hume does not use "utility" in this "utilitarian" way, but restricts it to "what advances some *ulterior* good." For Hume, utility is what advances someone's interest (EPM 5.15), and one's "interest" is not the same as one's pleasure. It is a fact that most of us are concerned for our futures, and so pleased when our interests are advanced. Utility usually pleases, but voluptuaries who live for the day may not care much about their interests, nor always welcome what advances them. It is also a fact, important for the refutation of "the selfish hypothesis," that most of us care about others' interests, as well as our own, so are pleased about public benefits, even when we personally will not profit from them. There may be occasional people with "affected spleens" who welcome public catastrophe, just as there are a few misers who get no pleasure except from what advances their own pecuniary interests, but most of us get pleasure from many sources, including what advances our own and other people's interests. What is in our interest matters, on Hume's version of morals, but so do "play, frolic and gaiety."

Hume's look at the role of utility in explaining what we value in the social virtues has, as he had predicted, given him an opening for accounting for other virtues. These include those, such as enterprise, economy, perseverance, and common sense, that are discussed in the sixth section as "useful to ourselves" (as well as being, very often, useful to others), and also the directly "agreeable" virtues, those discussed in sections 7 and 8. These three sections, like the fourth, contain some provocative inclusions in Hume's catalogue of endorsed virtues, and he deliberately rubs in the fact that many of them, such as quickness of conception and facility of expression, are no less "involuntary" than are the breadth of shoulders, taper legs, and sexual potency, that are listed as "bodily endowments" in 6.2. His ostensible reason for discussing these last, non-moral, endowments, is to confirm the link between beauty and utility, but he surely knows

305

he is asking for trouble when he reduces moral merit to a "beauty" of character that is as much a gift of fortune as is physical beauty, or sexual attractiveness. Moral charm and moral potency were new and offensive notions to many of his contemporary readers, and many, including several professors of moral philosophy in eighteenth century Scotland, and some in other universities since, duly took offense. However mischievous, this second part of section 6 does mediate nicely between the mainly "useful" virtues, discussed from sections 2–6, and the mainly agreeable ones, discussed in sections 7 and 8.

The directly agreeable traits are important since "something must be desirable on its own account, and because of its immediate accord or agreement with human sentiment and affection" (EPM App. 1.19). Health, wealth, and our other important interests, point us to the "ultimate ends" of pleasure and absence of pain. Once something, such as money, has been shown to be an instrument of pleasure, "it is an absurdity" to keep asking for a reason why it should be wanted. Hume is unabashedly Epicurean on this point. Some virtues please because of their means-value, or utility; others, such as wit and delicacy of taste, please directly, before the special pleasure of approbation gets added on. And since all of them must give this special pleasure, to be accounted virtues, then "virtue is an ultimate end, and is desirable on its own account, without fee or reward, merely for the immediate satisfaction it conveys" (EPM App. 1.20). A useful virtue, such as justice or frugality, may have its costs, but no contrived "fee," and the benefits and satisfaction that virtues bring their possessors are not "rewards," in the sense of contrived recompense. Like Shaftesbury, Hume believes that belief in specially arranged rewards for virtue and punishment for vice, including divine arrangements, tend to corrupt virtue. "The steady attention to so important an interest as eternal salvation is apt to extinguish the benevolent affections, and beget a narrow, contracted selfishness" (*Dialogues* [1947; Kemp Smith]: 222). The only dependable human response to perceived virtue is the harmless uncorrupting one of approbation, and that is a natural and inevitable reaction, not a contrived "reward."

Hume says that a virtue, such as benevolence, can be valued mainly for the utility of its results, yet also be "sweet, smooth, tender and agreeable" to its possessor, and agreeably contagious. This immediate agreeableness will presumably be independent of the extra pleasure the virtue brings by occasioning "the pleasing sentiment of approbation." Virtues can be both useful and immediately agreeable, and "qualities often derive their merit from complicated sources." A virtue, such as "fidelity to promises," may be first valued for its usefulness to society, making transactions secure, and trust in future delivery of goods and services a possibility, but it soon, by a "progress of sentiments," also becomes something a person wants for himself, if he is not to be "contemptible, no less than odious" (EPM 6.13). Is this not only because we need a reputation for honesty, but also because we like being approved of? Certainly such a shift in valuation is assisted by our supposed need to share our self-evaluations, and have them confirmed by others. What begins by being valued for its utility can become valued for the approbation it occasions, and can end by being taken to be intrinsically valuable. (Bernard Williams has recently given a Hume-inspired account of a similar "progress of sentiments" with respect to the virtue of truthfulness [Williams 2002: chs. 2 and 3].)

The True Origin of Morals

Hume does not claim to have completed his catalogue of virtues; it is left open-ended. (In the sixth section, after listing 24 qualities "useful to ourselves," he waves his hand toward "a thousand more of the same kind.") But everything he has surveyed that is "admitted to the honourable denomination of virtue or merit" (EPM 9.1) has been found to be "useful or agreeable to the person himself or to others" (where these "or"s are definitely not exclusive). He is now in a position, in the "Conclusion," to turn (or rather, to return, since the fifth section prepared the ground for the ninth), to the question of "the true origin" of the morals he has outlined, and to specify the point of view from which recognition of moral merit is made. For theological moralists, God's will is the "true origin" of morals. For Hume, its origin is entirely human. Despite slight differences in terminology, *EPM*'s finding is pretty much the same as that of the *Treatise*, that virtues are discerned from a general human point of view, requiring extensive but regulated sympathy in those who manage to take it up. It cannot be the viewpoint of self-love, which, however strong, has not "a proper direction for that purpose."

> The notion of morals implies some sentiment common to all mankind, which recommends the same object to general approbation, and makes every man, or most men, agree in the same opinion or decision concerning it. It also implies some sentiment, so universal and comprehensive as to extend to all mankind, and render the actions and conduct, even of the persons the most remote, an object of applause or censure, according as they agree or disagree with that rule of right which is established. These two requisite circumstances belong alone to the sentiment of humanity here insisted upon. (EPM 9.5)

The "sentiment of humanity," as a name for the virtue-recognizing moral sentiment, is new, and underlines what Hume had written in a famous letter to Hutcheson in 1740, that morality "regards only human nature and human life" (Hume's Letters, Greig, ed., 1969: i, 40).

The double requirement, that the moral sentiment be shared by almost all human beings, and that all be subject to its findings, is similar to the requirement that Hume's later friend/enemy, Rousseau, made for his authoritative "general will," which governs all and only those who go to comprise it. It is just as stringent, and just as unlikely to be met with in the real world, where moral judges do not always agree, and are not always judged by the same standards that they impose on others. It makes "the rule of right" (not to be confused with the culturally varying rules of "justice") cosmopolitan, rather than local, and makes it democratically arrived at. Taken seriously, it means that the most we usually do when we judge actions and character is aspire to the point of view from which truly moral judgements would be made, make judgements that we hope but cannot be sure have the requisite commonality and universality. James Beattie found Hume's ethics elitist, a concession to the tastes and views of the fashionable French circles that Hume went on to move in, and this is ironical, if the official theory is radically democratic. Hume, in an intemperate moment, called Beattie "that bigotted silly Fellow" (Hume's Letters 1969: ii, 301), but his theory seems to require him to get Beattie's and Balfour's agreement, as much as that of Shaftesbury, Cicero, or the judicious Polybius.

Or can Hume properly dismiss the disagreement of those he has reason to think bigots or silly fellows? His theory does require that moral judges rid themselves of "the deceptive glosses of superstition and false religion," and does allow that reason needs to be "fully assisted and improved" if it is to "instruct us in the pernicious or useful tendency of qualities and actions" (EPM App. 1.2), so that we can, where necessary, "adjust anew the boundaries of moral good and evil." Ignorant or silly persons, who do not discern these tendencies, or splenetic misanthropes who do not care about them, or hidebound traditionalists who are unwilling to do any adjusting, are, on Hume's theory, disqualified as moral judges. Beattie is, I think, right to judge that Hume's morals are elitist, but the elitism is more intellectual than social, more a matter of having the right education and cast of mind than of wearing the right waistcoat. Hume's list of virtues is likely to prove acceptable only to peaceable, sociable, intelligent, reflective, not-zealously religious persons (and it will help if they like reading history).

Hume of course speaks of "false religion" as the enemy of his humane and human version of morals, not of religion as such, and always disclaimed being an atheist. It is pretty clear that neither Pascal's nor Knox's religion is his "true" acceptable one. It was the grandfather of "the elegant Lord Shaftesbury" who set the fashion for avoiding being Bacon's double fool (*Dialogues* [Kemp Smith 1947]: 139) by claiming to be an adherent of the religion of all sensible men, and then, when asked what that religion was, responding: "Sensible men never say." Hume, in EPM, as elsewhere, preserves a truly Shaftesburian reticence on the true religion. In this, as in so much else, he is also following the prudent Cicero. Certainly the Christian virtues, not just "celibacy, fasting, penance, mortification, self-denial, humility, silence, solitude" (EPM 9.3), but also charity in the form of handouts to beggars, are judged to be "rejected by men of sense." Hume, as most of his contemporaries realized, as Leslie Stephen (Stephen 1902: vol. 1, ch. 6) saw very clearly, and as J. B. Schneewind, Isabel Rivers, and G. C. A. Gaskin have more recently emphasized (Schneewind 1983: 1–9; Rivers 1991: ii, ch. 4; Gaskin 2002: 369), is fairly openly defying the officially Christian culture in which he was writing. Gerhard Streminger even finds EPM to be blasphemous, for its implicit denial of original sin, and dismissal of the possibility of an afterlife where punishments and rewards await us (Streminger 1994: 357). On his deathbed Hume joked with Adam Smith about wanting to delay his death till he had completed the revisions he was making to his works, including EPM, works intended to "open the eyes of the public." He wished, he said, that he could live long enough to see if they would hasten the downfall of "superstition," but knew that that would not happen for "these many hundred years." Hume's case against religion is not only its superstition, but its socially divisive force and incitement to violence, when its devotees and enthusiasts go to war for their faith. It is not just that the "monkish" virtues/vices sour the lives of the monks, it is that they "harden the heart" and lead to persecution and religious wars. Even when the heart of the religious believer is not hardened, it may be corrupted by the prospect of divinely ordained reward for virtue, or deranged by fear of punishment for vice.

Despite our disagreements about religion, and our varying cultures, we are supposed to be able to come to agreement on what mental traits we should welcome in each other, at least once our reason has been assisted by reading enough history. The point of view from which we are to discern true moral merit is one that looks beyond self-interest, but not beyond the good of humankind. Hume's moral judge does not, like Shaftesbury's admirer of moral beauty, look beyond human communities to the wider "systems" in which they are included, eventually to the whole cosmos, but limits herself to the good of the human species. (She will, however, look with a cold eye on those who do not "give gentle usage" to other sentient beings, without rights though they may be.) It is therefore appropriate that Hume renames the attitude that is needed for discerning virtues "the sentiment of humanity." Its viewpoint is no God's eye view, no "view from nowhere," but an earthly perspective, that of a representative of "the party of humankind." Hume's version of morals is unashamedly humanist, and those who want a more "ecological" and less "speciesist" version would do well to turn to Shaftesbury, rather than Hume, for inspiration.

What is the relation of Hume's "sentiment of humanity" to two of the main virtues it discerns, the virtues of impartiality and benevolence? Do we have to possess the main Humean virtues in order to recognize them as such? Hume's terminology is a bit sloppy, and has changed. In *Treatise* 3, "humanity" was the name of a particular virtue, associated with the attempt to relieve human misery, so was close to compassion and pity. It was not the same as sympathy, which can be felt for any passion, not just for suffering. Like benevolence, of which it was one form, it was more a motive than a sentiment. In EPM, "humanity" has become a sympathy-based sentiment, "fellow feeling," and, in its extensive form, generates the point of view from which moral merit is discerned. (See Abramson 2001, for a discussion of the relation of sympathy to the sentiment of humanity.) Benevolence the virtue is a tendency to have "good" *intentions*, to try to *do good* to others, and to relieve their suffering. It may have quite a limited object, say one person whose welfare can be improved by the benevolent person's action. Indeed Hume says that it is best if the focus of our affections and well-meaning actions be limited, otherwise they might "be dissipated and lost for want of a proper limited object (EPM 5.42, n.). The sentiment of humanity is sympathetic concern for all human persons, and need not lead to any intentions or action, except the expression of its findings. To reach them, it has to "correct" the "inequalities" of natural sympathy and natural benevolence by "reflection" (EPM 5.42 n.), and it is impartiality that does the correction. Still, some benevolence, in addition to impartiality and extensive sympathy, seems a prerequisite. "A creature absolutely malicious and spiteful," just as much as a hopelessly partial person, or one without any fellow feeling, will be constitutionally unfitted to take up this moral point of view, so there may be what we could call a virtuous circle in recognition of the components of true merit.

Hume's moral point of view, despite the formal similarities noted above to Rousseau's law-generating general will, is not that of a would-be world legislator, pretending to issue binding and enforced laws, nor even that of a person forming a policy for her own life, but rather that of a reflective surveyor of human character who, through the breadth of her sympathies, her humanity (Adam Smith says humanity is a woman's sentiment; Smith 1759: 190), and her impartiality, admires beneficent human traits, and dislikes those whose "tendency is pernicious to society." The mood of its expressed findings is optative, not imperative, and they will be only indirectly action-guiding. Hume cites, but does not commit himself to, the view of some "modern enquirers," perhaps including himself in *Treatise* 3.1.1, that "the end of all moral speculations" is to "engage us" to embrace virtue and avoid vice (EPM 1.7). His "speculative" enquiry (EPM 2.5) does not find that our possession of the sentiment of humanity need make very much difference to the way we actually behave. Sometimes strong private passions may "yield the dominion of our breasts to those social and public principles" which, although "somewhat small and delicate," are "cherished by society and conversation" (EPM 9.9); at other times the moral sentiments are lulled into lethargy. But even if our "generous sentiments" be "ever so weak . . . insufficient to move a hand or finger of our body, they must still direct the determinations of our mind, and where everything else is equal, produce a cool preference of what is useful and serviceable to mankind, above what is pernicious and dangerous" (EPM 9.4). The sentiment of humanity reliably enables us to "discern" virtues, to have a cool and expressed preference for them, perhaps to love those who possess them, but not to come to acquire those we lack. It may give us some sort of "rule of right," but the only pressure it can exert to get conformity to this rule is through its own expressed find-ings, in "conversation, in the pulpit, on the theatre, in the schools." Should a person not care about being judged a bigot, a fool, a tyrant, a hypocrite, a busybody, or a knave, then Hume's version of morality is powerless, unless magistrates, or the tyrant's vic-tims, take action to limit the harm done by persons with the undesirable character traits. Hume's answer to the "sensible knave," to which I now turn, makes it very clear how little coercive force he takes his gentle non-vengeful morality to have.

In the second part of the "Conclusion," after his account of the viewpoint from which virtues are discerned, Hume takes up the question that Shaftesbury had turned to in the second book of his *Inquiry*, that of the interested obligation to virtue. This is a rather pressing question for moralists who disdain appeal to divine sanctions to underwrite moral obligations. Is there enough incentive for a Humean to show virtue, given the likelihood, recognized by Shaftesbury in his *Sensus Communis*, "that knaves are advanced above us, and the vilest of men preferred before the honestest?" (Cooper 1999: vol. 1, 60–4). Shaftesbury discusses the bid for happiness of the "accomplished knave," his willingness to sacrifice "a character with himself and others" for the sake of tempting "plums," and Hume takes up this discussion in the second part of his "Conclusion." For him, as for Shaftesbury, to establish the presence of an "obligation" is to establish that the obligated person risks some cost if the obligation is not met. Obligations had barely figured in EPM, except where justice was concerned. There were "obligations" not to cheat and steal, nor to break promises, since we withdraw trust from those known to be offenders, and magistrates may punish some of them. So it is appropriate that it is obligations to this sort of convention-governed conduct that Hume's knave is seen to be neglecting. But such obligations will not restrict a clever knave, who is confident he can get away with his knavery. Hume allows that judicious dishonesty may serve a "sensible knave" better than honesty. As Shaftesbury says, hon-esty is a "sober mistress," despised by those who are intent at all costs on worldly suc-cess. If one has the knave's preference for "toys and gewgaws" over "consciousness of integrity," then one's interest may indeed lie in taking advantage of the loopholes in the law and the gullibility of one's fellows, and so making additions to one's fortune without "causing any considerable breach in the social union and confederacy." Hume's unanswerable knave is "sensible," and so sensitive to his own dependence on the social union, and he may have some virtues along with his profitable vice of dishonesty. (Hume, as his summaries of monarchs' characters in his *History* make clear, is no believer in the unity of the virtues.) The knave sacrifices "invaluable enjoyment of a character, with himself at least" to his ill-gotten luxury. But if luxury matters more to him than such supposedly higher pleasure, then there is no "satisfactory and convincing answer" that can be given him. Everything depends on his preferences and his tastes in pleasures. Just as there is no arguing with Diogenes, who opts for his "beastly" offensive pleasures, nor with Pascal, who prefers his spiritual satisfactions to ordinary innocent ones, so there is no arguing with the knave who forgoes "enjoyment of a character" for the sake of monetary gain. Hume dutifully says the knave is "the greater dupe," but allows that he cannot convince the knave of that. It is a standoff. Hume hopes that few are tough enough, or clever enough, to live as successful and happy knaves, but he does not pretend that his version of ethics offers a way to turn knaves honest. (Nor does it promise compensation in kind to the knaves' victims. So does the interested obligation to honesty exist only for those of us who are not cut out to be accomplished knaves? Hume leaves this question as unanswered as the knave's challenge.)

Why did the knave's challenge not arise in the *Treatise*? The sensible knaves, along with the conspiracy-breaking women, and the self-denying Christians attended by theologians disguised as philosophers, were significant absentees from *Treatise* 3, however close the women got to getting a hearing in the section on chastity and modesty, and however sly the satire of inefficacious hellfire moralists in the Book 1 section with the disarming title "Of the effects of other relations, and other habits." We were warned, in *Treatise* 3.2.2, that in developed societies the interested obligation to justice can become "remote," and not so readily perceived. Some extra artifices of politicians and educators may be needed to "inculcate the principles of probity," and get each person to "fix an inviolable law to himself, never, by any temptation, to violate those principles, which are essential to a man of probity and honour" (T 3.2.2.27). Hume's knave has slipped through these educational and political safeguards, as some inevitably do. He cares little for probity, although he likely does care more about honor and reputation. Hume, in the *Treatise*, left it to educators and politicians to show warmth in the cause of virtue, while he concentrated on doing the "anatomy" of our moral sense, but, in the very last paragraph, he did a little "painting" of the happy man of virtue, who will not sacrifice "peace and inward satisfaction" for any "advantage of fortune." This was an advance notice of his reply to the knave in EPM. Despite his earlier claim that his enquiry into merit is speculative, rather than practical, he seems, in its conclusion, to be making an effort to "represent virtue in all her genuine and engaging charms" (EPM 9.15). The analysis of panegyrics of virtuous people slips into a panegyric of virtue. The answer to the knave begins in candid calculation of interest, but ends in rather unconvincing edifying rhetoric. Hume performs better as skeptic than as painter, preacher, or rhapsodist, and it is not clear that it will be with his help that "truths, which are pernicious to society, if any such there be, will yield to errors that are salutary and advantageous." He is more open in EPM than in the *Treatise* about the godlessness of his moral philosophy, and about its generally Epicurean character, and his concessions to the knave should be seen in this light. He has no hellfire to threaten the knave with, nor even a rigorously inquisitorial human police, only the possibility of self-disgust, and the need for secrecy and psychic isolation. Shaftesbury wrote that his only reply to the man who asks why he should not be "nasty" (dirty) when alone and in the dark is, "because you have a nose" (Cooper 1999: 58). Should the man claim to have no sense of smell, then the conversation has to cease, and the company of that man be avoided, just as one would try to keep clear of the man whose only reason for being honest is fear of the gibbet, or of hellfire.

It is only with respect to "the interested obligation" to justice, not with respect to virtue in general, that Hume allows that virtue may prove costly to the virtuous, especially if they become prey to accomplished knaves. The other Humean virtues, as David Gauthier puts it, "do not curb self-interest but rather instruct it in the means necessary to the greatest happiness of sociable and sympathetic creatures" (Gauthier 1990: 41). Hume says that the morality he has endorsed

> talks not of useless austerities and rigours, suffering and self-denial. She declares that her sole purpose is to make her votaries and all mankind, during every instant of their existence, if possible cheerful and happy; nor does she ever willingly part with any pleasure but in hopes of ample compensation in some other period of their lives. The sole trouble which she demands is that of just calculation, and a steady preference for the greater happiness. (EPM 9.15)

(It was *Treatise* 3, not EPM, that Bentham said made the scales fall from his eyes, but this passage seems a clearer anticipation of his hedonic calculus than anything in the *Treatise*.) Hume's version of morality is neither austere nor rigorous, and has no inquisitorial function. "Who would live amidst perpetual . . . scolding, and mutual reproaches?" Dugald Stewart, in a book intended for students at Edinburgh University in the decades after Hume's death, criticized Shaftesbury for neglecting "conscience" and its authority (Stewart 1818: 151). In Hume's ethics too, as Balfour, Kant, and even T. H. Huxley complained, its stern and scolding voice is replaced by an agreeable "dance measure" (Huxley 1894: 239). Hume takes up Shaftesbury's question of the appropriate dress for "the moral dame" to wear. Penitential robes, and even sober gowns, are discarded in favor of more attractive dress.

Part of Hume's case for saying that virtue should bring happiness, without any divine intervention, is that we can cultivate a taste for the pleasures of surveying our own "inward beauty and moral grace" (EPM 9.10). Should we fail to do this, fail to have a "continual and earnest pursuit of a character, a name, a reputation in the world," a "constant habit of surveying ourselves as it were, in reflection" (EPM 9.10), perhaps because we have retired from society into "solitary and uncultivated nature," where Hume thinks we risk falling into moral "lethargy," then his case for virtue may fail. Some may find the prospect of this constant moral self-inspection distasteful, and prefer "the common beauties of nature," even enjoyed in anti-social solitude, to the narcissistic delights of "peaceful reflection on one's own conduct." It is therefore appropriate that Hume puts some emphasis on the need for moral education, and encouragement of this cultivation of character. The moral sentiments are to be given expression in schools, as well as in literature, from the pulpit and on the stage. (And he himself supported the production of the controversial play, *Douglas*, a moral tale about a woman's virtuous suicide, and may even have acted in it, so he did his public bit for the version of morality he endorsed. A wit, John Maclaurin, later Lord Dreghorn, summed up Hume's ethics thus: "that suicide is a duty we owe ourselves; adultery a duty we owe to our neighbour; that the tragedy of *Douglas* is the best play ever was written" (Mossner 1980: 367).

Is there a social need to monitor the incidence, not merely of knaves, fools, dismal delirious monks, and hare-brained enthusiasts, but also of those with a distaste for the self-inspection that Hume seems to be counting on to make us care about our own merit? The only pressure to conform to Humean morality comes from pride in good character, from concern lest we appear "odious" in the eyes of others, and in our own eyes. Where the Christian has to please an all-seeing God, Hume's moral person has to please fellow-persons, and bear her own survey. But the threat of inability to bear one's own survey will not work if one can manage to avoid self-survey. Others' less avoidable reactions seem essential, if Hume's version of morality is to work.

Hume says his version of morality displays "the force of many sympathies" (EPM 9.11). Sympathy was first brought in, in the *Treatise*, to account for "the love of fame," and was found to be particularly influential, indeed a necessary prompt, "when we judge of our own worth and character." "The minds of men are mirrors to one another," and the magic of Hume's morality is all done with these mirrors. Should we lack "a care for preserving a character with ourselves," or should we not "find it necessary to prop our tottering judgement on the correspondent approbation of mankind," then even the gentle force of the Humean sympathy-dependent morality, which the likes of Balfour and Kames found much too gentle, may be lost. Hume made lack of self-sufficiency a condition for the perceived need for cooperation on which one important virtue, justice, rests, but it is more than lack of self-sufficiency, it is positive sociability, a concern to be acceptable to others, and to have them prompt and confirm our self-assessments, that are needed if his version of morality itself is to be of more than speculative interest to us. In EPM, Hume is not, as he was in the *Treatise*, putting forward a theory of human nature, the mechanics of sympathy, and the sources of human motivation, and then confirming that theory by looking at how our moral natures work. He is, however, sticking with his earlier conclusions about human nature, about the average person's sociability, capacity for sympathy, consequent tendency to self-survey, and need for confirmation of the self-assessments that are made. Morality is not, on his view, an "artifice of politicians," as it was for Mandeville, and certainly is not sired by flattery, but it is "begot upon pride," and it needs both midwifery and nurturing from others' candid appraisals of our merit.

The reliance on a form of pride, pride in one's "inward beauty and moral grace," as moral incentive, can be taken as another slap by Hume at the moral psychology of the Christians, for whom humility, not pride, is the mainspring of righteousness. Just as Hume relied on self-interest to curb itself, for justice to be a possibility for us, so he relies on a new direction to self-conceit, and the desire to be admired, for morality as a whole to be a possibility for us. Although the "selfish hypothesis" is rejected, and fellow feeling emphasized, "partiality in our own favour" is accepted as innate. But it is the original of virtue, not of sin. Just as "there is no passion . . . capable of controlling the interested affection but the very affection itself, by an alteration of its direction" (T 3.2.2.13), so the thing to be done with self-conceit is not just veil it decently, but direct it on "character." Hume had spoken enigmatically, in the *Treatise*, of vanity as "a social passion and a bond of union among men" (T 3.2.2.12). Now we see just how it can be that, since it is vanity's redirection that enables us to care enough about our own characters.

In EPM's "conclusion," Hume speaks the same Newtonian language as in the *Treatise's* "Of the origin of justice and property," both of the "force" and of the "direction" of passions on which morality might be thought based. Self-interest had the needed force, and once regulated, the right direction, to control the love of personal gain, and motivate initial conformity to cooperative schemes. But it does not have the right direction to explain the whole of morality, neither to explain all that we praise in others, nor to explain why we are pleased ourselves to be possessors of the recognized virtues. "Would you have your character coveted, admired, followed; rather than hated, despised, avoided? Can anyone seriously deliberate in the case?" (EPM 9.18). The sympathy-based "sentiment of humanity" has the right direction to explain all the mental qualities that we praise, however weak its intrinsic force as a motivator. Fortunately it has a stronger ally: "Another spring of our constitution, that brings a great addition of force to moral sentiment, is the love of fame; which rules, with such uncontrolled authority, in all generous minds" (EPM 9.10). Moral self-conceit, and concern for "character with others," explains why we want to measure up to shared moral standards.

What Pleased the Author

Hume has, in EPM, completed his account of how vanity can become a bond of social union, can replace fear of divine anger as the engine that drives human morality. Mandeville had spoken of "millions endeavoring to supply each other's lust and vanity." Hume shows us how two not very attractive passions, lust for gain and self-conceit, can replace dehumanizing fear of hell as moral incentive. With the appropriate redirection, and a little guidance from the "sentiment of humanity," they can become the guardians of a functioning morality, indeed of "the most perfect morality with which we are acquainted" (EPM 9.11). The Christian vices of greed and pride have, in Hume's hands, become the driving forces of a perfect, and almost perfectly non-punitive, morality. The inversion of Christian morality is complete.

It is a measure of how well Hume's campaign for a secular and humane morality succeeded that many of the readers of EPM now find it uncontroversial, even "bland" (Box 1990: 225). But to most of his contemporaries, to Balfour, to Beattie, to Reid, it was, both in its secular and Epicurean matter and in its playful manner, a dangerous threat, and one they felt obliged to try to counter. It takes some historical imagination to see what in EPM offended, and what Hume was so pleased with. Leslie Stephen judged the latter to be the demonstration that the good was the useful, and definitely not because of divine rewards and punishment (Stephen 1902: vol. 2, 92). This utilitarian inversion would be offensive to the religious, and surely at least part of what pleased Hume was precisely what offended, namely EPM's challenge to his own religious and puritan culture. A restrictive culture often produces its own subversives. Hume, descendant of Covenanters, devoted son of a pious mother, friend till the end of moderate clergymen in Edinburgh, teases his Christian contemporaries in this work, and invites them to let their "natural sentiments" prevail over their "delirious and dismal" religious proclivities. These humane sentiments, he says, "form, in a manner, the *party* of humankind against vice and disorder." It has to be seen still as a "party," opposed by other parties, in particular by the grimmer sentiments played on by the hellfire moralists.

Still, it was not just as anti-Christian manifesto that Hume had reason to be pleased with this book. His "Natural history of religion" easily outdoes it on that score. EPM makes several substantive adjustments to *Treatise* 3's version of moral good and evil, while keeping unchanged the essentials of the account of the point of view from which they are discerned. "The circumstances of justice" are revised, and attention is belatedly given to the question of who it is that justice protects. Some concessions are made to rationalists, and some hasty arguments against them are removed, preparing the way for Hume's final judgment, in the first Appendix of his *History of England*, that virtue is "nothing but a more enlarged and more cultivated reason." In EPM, the main opponent is identified as the theological moralist, whether rationalist or not, who treats "all morals as on a like footing with civil laws, guarded by the sanctions of reward and punishment." The emphasis on "mankind" as the only judge of human morality is louder and clearer, and the authoritative moral sentiment is appropriately renamed "the sentiment of humanity." These are important adjustments. And of course EPM has literary as well as philosophical finesse. It suits its manner to its matter by displaying some of the virtues it recognizes – wit, wisdom, politeness, decency. It avoids "pompous declamations," but its polite contributions to reflections on morality are scarcely "insipid."

When EPM appeared in 1751, James Wodrow, moderate Presbyterian son of the Calvinist preacher, Robert Wodrow, read it eagerly to see what the "great infidel" had produced this time, then reported with some disappointment that it contained nothing new, but was about "Hutcheson's disinterested scheme." It was, however, "mighty fine polished, beautiful & entertaining, & which is odd, nothing at all Sceptical." (My information about this unpublished letter from December 1751, in Dr. William's Library, London, comes from M. A. Stewart.) Wodrow cannot have been a very perceptive, nor even a very careful reader. Entertaining and mighty fine polished EPM certainly is, and plenty others have found it Hutchesonian. But nothing new? And without a trace of scepticism? The "civil" Balfour, and even the "silly" Beattie, saw and complained of the new anti-religious emphasis, and the skepticism.

For EPM's ambitious structure, Hume may be indebted, not so much to the benign but humorless Hutcheson, as to the eloquent and humor-loving Shaftesbury. He imbedded his "Inquiry into Virtue or Merit" in a longer, more methodologically exploratory and skeptical work, his three-volume *Characteristics of Men, Manners, Opinions, Times*. In the first volume we find, in *Sensus Communis*, a discussion of various types of knave and their not-altogether-to-be-dismissed chances of happiness, and then, following the somewhat didactic *Inquiry* in the second volume, Shaftesbury placed a dialogue, *The Moralists*, which, like Hume's "whimsical" one, has a skeptic as one participant, curbing the main (theist) speaker's rhapsodies in praise of virtue. Then, in the third volume, in the *Miscellanies*, Shaftesbury continues to comment on and to some extent distance himself from the "positive" and "dogmatic" claims of his own *Inquiry*. Hume too has much more to say after the official conclusion of his inquiry into merit. His dialogue queries whether we in fact find that agreement on which morality is supposed to be based (see Mazza 2005). Palamedes points out that we do not all agree

315

on the rule of right for regulating sexual relations, or for regulating the killing of human beings. Nor, as the "I" of "A Dialogue" acknowledges, does Pascal agree that friendship, wit, and eloquence are always valued, even by those disagreeing on tyrannicide, homosexuality, infanticide, and abortion. The metaphor of differing customs flowing, like the Rhine and the Rhone, in differing directions from the same mountain, does little to alter the fact of moral disagreements, and disagreements about which of them are more important. Hume's whimsy, in the dialogue, is as teasing as his pretense, in the work it follows, that his catalogue of virtues will be acceptable to all his readers. (He does not expect Scythian scalp-collectors nor Topinamboue cannibals to be reading him, but he does expect some communicant Christians.)

Both Shaftesbury's and Hume's skeptical wrappings for their more positive inquiries into morals leave the reader in healthy doubt as to just what is going on, and in both cases, this is surely intentional. Hume had at one point conceded the "uncertainty" and "natural obscurity" of merit (EPM 3.23) and had referred along the way to some very ugly human traits that have been admired, even by respected historians. In his official "Conclusion," after his relative warmth in the cause of his version of virtue, he drops a hint. Were he right about what we admire in each other, and why, he muses, then there would not be the disputes there undoubtedly are about morals. His conclusions would, "long ere now, have been received by the unanimous suffrage and consent of mankind" (EPM 9.13). In EPM, Hume gives us the case for a shared sentiment of humanity that can give us an agreed list of virtues. In various dropped hints and in "A Dialogue," he balances that with the contrary case. His enquiry is left open and inconclusive. As "a true sceptic," and one who is reputed to have taken skepticism to be a "sturdy virtue," (even if it did not get named in EPM's catalogue), he has reason to be proud of his performance in this teasing work. Could he even be one of those disingenuous moralists, apparently censured in EPM's first sentence, who have "a desire of showing wit and ingenuity, superior to the rest of mankind"?

The next pronouncements Hume went on to make about morals, after EPM (if we leave aside the considerable moral content of his history of the Stuarts) were in his *Four Dissertations*, six years later. His "Natural history of religion" continues and intensifies his attacks on Christianity, adding ridicule to his calmer diagnosis of the doctrines of popular religion as "sick men's dreams." Intolerant mutually warring monotheists, those who imitate their vengeful god, and those who "make and then eat their god," are added to the rogues' gallery begun in EPM. If EPM shows "extensive genius," it is the "Natural History" that shows more "intrepid courage." In the accompanying dissertation, "Of the Standard of Taste," Hume, more explicitly than in EPM, keeps his near promise at the end of EHU to make the fixing of a standard of beauty the object of his reasoning and enquiry. And he begins by warning us that such agreement about moral beauty as we may think we find is more verbal than substantive. Even when we appear to agree on a list of virtues, we may not mean quite the same by, say, "courage," or "prudence" (*Essays*: 228). He also says there that, although in judging works of literature we should make allowance for the author's culture and religion, we are, rightly, always jealous of our own moral standards (247). And whose taste in morals is an expert taste? Hume instances Bunyan as an inferior author, compared with Addison (231), despite the great popularity of *Pilgrim's Progress* in his own culture, so the tastes of the people are not counting for much. The secular, humane, enlightened and peace-loving morality that Hume had delineated in EPM, and was so jealous of, is, as he well knew, not to everyone's taste, not even to every historian's taste.

Final Note

Should we confirm Hume's own assessment of his "performance" in EPM? As he allowed, he was not the best person to judge it. But to what judges, then, should we turn? To his contemporary readers in Britain, who, more than most of us today, were in a position to have some preference between Suetonius and Tacitus, or know what Fabius and Scipio achieved by their differing military styles? They however were more likely than most of us are to be prejudiced by some "false religion." To his enlightened French admirers and translators? To any cultural heirs of the elegant Shaftesbury? Hume hoped that his works would be judged by "posterity." But a suitably educated and in other ways well-qualified readership may not yet be available to confirm, or disconfirm, his verdict on EPM. Few of his commentators have followed his request to let it, not the *Treatise*, be taken to give his "sentiments and principles" in ethics. (As far as I am aware, only Henry Sidgwick, C. D. Broad, and more recently Frederick Rosen, have complied.) Of those who have looked at both, most twentieth-century commentators (such as Laird, Greig, Noxon, and Mackie) prefer the less diplomatic and less polished *Treatise*.

This Hume reader, who appreciates the intricacies and boldness of the *Treatise*, nevertheless admires EPM's intellectual acuteness, especially on "justice," welcomes its clear-eyed working out of the implications of determinism, its "humane and beneficent" version of a gentle morality, and its refusal to look for any secular substitutes for hellfire as moral inducement. (The contrast with Adam Smith here is great. Even when Smith, in later editions of his *Theory of Moral Sentiments*, plays down the terrifying prospect of the "Great Judge," he still waxes edifyingly eloquent about the horrors of remorse.) Also admirable are EPM's literary craft, its demonstration of some of the virtues it discusses, its Shaftesburian and Theophrastan resonances, its lightness of touch, playful wit and teasing doubleness of message. But are these what its author hoped we would admire? Who is to know? "I fall back into diffidence and scepticism."

See also 11 "Hume on Liberty and Necessity"; 12 "Hume on Moral Rationalism, Sentimentalism, and Sympathy"; 13 "Sympathy and Hume's Spectator-centered Theory of Virtue"; 14 "Hume's Theory of Justice, or Artificial Virtue"; 15 "Hume on Beauty and Virtue"; 17 "Hume's Views on Religion: Intellectual and Cultural Influences"; 22 " 'The Most Illustrious Philosopher and Historian of the Age': Hume's *History of England*"; 26 "The Humean Theory of Motivation and Its Critics"; 27 "The Sources of Normativity in Hume's Moral Theory"; 28 "Hume's Metaethics: Is Hume a Moral Noncognitivist?"

Note

The study of Hume is gradually converting me to his sort of skepticism, and the history of this essay about him has given me plenty of cause for diffidence. Generous critics have alerted me to some places needing adjustment, as well as making helpful suggestions at the start of the project. For both sorts of aid I am greatly indebted to James Moore and M. A. Stewart. For adjustments along the way I also thank Donald Ainslie, Tom Beauchamp, Stephen Buckle, Stephen Darwall, David Gauthier, Maurice Goldsmith, James Harris, James King, Elizabeth Radcliffe, and Robert Shaver.

References

Abramson, Kate (2001). "Sympathy and the Project of Hume's Second *Enquiry,*" *Archiv für Geschichte der Philosophie,* 83, pp. 45–78.

Anon. (1684). *The Whole Duty of Man* (London: R. Norton for Robert Pawley, at the Sign of the Bible in Chancery Lane, near Fleetstreet).

Balfour, James (1753). *A Delineation of the Nature and Obligation of Morality* (Edinburgh: Hamilton, Balfour and Neill; repr. Bristol: Thoemmes Antiquarian Books Ltd., 1989).

Beattie, James (1770). *An Essay on the Nature and Immutablity of Truth, in Opposition to Sophistry and Scepticism,* 10th edn. (London: Lackington, Allen and Co., 1810).

Box, M. A. (1990). *The Suasive Art of David Hume* (Princeton, NJ: Princeton University Press).

Broad, C. D. (1944). *Five Types of Ethical Theory* (London: Kegan Paul, Trench, Trubner and Co.)

Cooper, Anthony Ashley, Third Earl of Shaftesbury (1711). *Characteristics of Men, Manners, Opinions, Times,* 3 vols., ed. Lawrence E. Klein (Cambridge: Cambridge University Press, 1999).

Emerson, Roger L. (1990). "Science and Moral Philosophy in the Scottish Enlightenment," in M. A. Stewart (ed.), *Studies in the Philosophy of the Scottish Enlightenment* (Oxford: Clarendon Press).

Gaskin, J. C. A. (2002). "Religion: The Useless Hypothesis," in Peter Millican (ed.), *Reading Hume on Human Understanding* (Oxford: Oxford University Press).

Gauthier, David (1990). *Moral Dealing: Contract, Ethics, and Reason* (Ithaca, NY: Cornell University Press).

Greig, J. Y. T. (1931). *David Hume* (Oxford: Oxford University Press).

Haji, Ishtiyaque (2002). *Deontic Morality and Control* (Cambridge: Cambridge University Press).

Hobbes, Thomas (1641). *Leviathan,* ed. Edwin Curley (Indianapolis, IN: Hackett, 1994).

Hume, David (1741–77). *Essays Moral, Political and Literary,* ed. Eugene F. Miller (Indianapolis, IN: Liberty Fund, 1987). (Cited in the text as *Essays.*)

—— (1754–78). *The History of England* (Indianapolis, IN: Liberty Fund, 1983).

—— (1777). "My Own Life," in J. Y. T. Greig (ed.). *The Letters of David Hume,* 2 vols. (Oxford: Clarendon Press, 1932), vol. 1, pp. 1–7.

—— (1779). *Dialogues concerning Natural Religion,* ed. Norman Kemp Smith (Indianapolis, IN: Bobbs-Merrill, 1947).

—— (1969). *The Letters of David Hume,* 2 vols., ed. J. Y. T. Greig (Oxford: Clarendon Press).

Hutcheson, Francis (1725). *An Inquiry into Our Ideas of Beauty and Virtue in Two Treatises,* ed. Wolfgang Leidhold (Indianapolis, IN: Liberty Fund, 2004).

Huxley, T. H. (1894). *Hume: With Helps to the Study of Berkeley, Essays* (New York: D. Appleton and Company).

King, James T. (1976). "The Place of the Language of Morals in Hume's Second *Enquiry,*" in Donald W. Livingston and James T. King (eds.), *Hume: A Re-evaluation* (New York: Fordham University Press).

Laird, John (1932). *Hume's Philosophy of Human Nature* (London: Methuen).

Mackie, J. L. (1980). *Hume's Moral Theory* (London: Routledge and Kegan Paul).

Mazza, E. (2005). "Cannibals in 'A Dialogue' (in Search of a Standard of Morals)," in E. Mazza and E. Ronchetti (eds.), *"Instruction and Amusement": Le ragioni dell'illuminismo britannico* (Padua: Il Polygrato).

Montesquieu, Baron de (Charles-Louis de Secondat) (1721). *Persian Letters*, ed. George R. Healy (Indianapolis, IN: Bobbs-Merrill, 1964).

Moore, James (2002). "Utility and Humanity: The Quest for the *honestum* in Cicero, Hutcheson, and Hume," *Utilitas*, 14, pp. 356–86.

Mossner, Ernest Campbell (1980). *The Life of David Hume*, 2nd edn. (Oxford: Clarendon Press).

Noxon, James (1973). *Hume's Philosophical Development: A Study of His Methods* (Oxford: Clarendon Press).

Penelhum, Terence (2000). *Themes in Hume: The Self, the Will, Religion* (Oxford: Clarendon Press).

Price, John Valdimir (1969/1990). *David Hume* (Boston: Twayne Publishers).

Raphael, David Daiches (2001). *Concepts of Justice* (Oxford: Clarendon Press).

Rawls, John (1971/1999). *A Theory of Justice* (Cambridge, MA: Harvard University Press).

Rivers, Isabel (2000). *Reason, Grace and Sentiment: A Study of the Language of Religion and Ethics in England, 1660–1780*, 2 vols. (Cambridge: Cambridge University Press).

Rosen, Frederick (2003). *Classical Utilitarianism from Hume to Mill* (London: Routledge).

Russell, Paul (1995). *Freedom and Moral Sentiment: Hume's Way of Naturalizing Responsibility* (New York: Oxford University Press).

Schneewind, J. B. (1983). "Introduction," in David Hume, *Enquiry concerning the Principles of Morals*, ed. J. B. Schneewind (Indianapolis, IN: Hackett Publishing).

Selby-Bigge, L. A. (1894). "Editor's Introduction," in David Hume, *Enquiries concerning Human Understanding and concerning the Principles of Morals*, 3rd edn., ed. P. H. Nidditch (Oxford: Oxford University Press, 1975).

Sher, Richard B. (1990). "Professors of Virtue: The Social History of the Edinburgh Moral Philosophy Chair in the Eighteenth Century," in M. A. Stewart (ed.), *Studies in the Philosophy of the Scottish Enlightenment* (Oxford: Clarendon Press).

Sidgwick, Henry (1902). *Outline of the History of Ethics, for English Readers* (London: Macmillan and Co.)

Smith, Adam (1759). *The Theory of Moral Sentiments*, ed. D. D. Raphael and A. L. Macfie (Oxford: Clarendon Press, 1976).

Stephen, Sir Leslie (1902). *History of English Thought in the Eighteenth Century*, 2 vols. (London: Smith Elder & Co.)

Stewart, Dugald (1818). *Outlines of Moral Philosophy, for the Use of Students at Edinburgh University* (Edinburgh: Archibald Constable and Co., Fairbairn and Anderson, successors to Mr. Creech).

Streminger, Gerhard (1994). *David Hume: Sein Leben und sein Werk* (*David Hume: His Life and Work*) (Paderborn, Munich, Vienna, Zurich: Ferdinand Schoeningh).

Taylor, Jacqueline (1998). "Justice and the Foundations of Social Morality," *Hume Studies*, 24, pp. 5–30.

—— (2002). "Hume on the Standard of Virtue," *Journal of Ethics*, 6, pp. 43–62.

Williams, Bernard (2002). *Truth and Truthfulness: An Essay on Genealogy* (Princeton, NJ: Princeton University Press).

Further Reading

Baier, Annette C. (1991). *A Progress of Sentiments: Reflections on Hume's Treatise* (Cambridge, MA: Harvard University Press) (esp. ch. 10, "A Catalogue of Virtues").

—— (1998). Hume, David (1711–76), in Edward Craig (ed.), *Routledge Encyclopedia of Philosophy*, vol. 4 (London: Routledge), pp. 543–62.

—— (2001). Hume, David (1711–1776), in Lawrence C. Becker and Charlotte B. Becker (eds.), *Encyclopedia of Ethics*, vol. 2 (New York: Routledge), pp. 803–15.

Darwall, Stephen (1995). *The British Moralists and the Internal "Ought," 1640–1740* (New York: Cambridge University Press).

Haakonssen, Knud (1981). *The Science of a Legislator: The Natural Jurisprudence of David Hume and Adam Smith* (Cambridge: Cambridge University Press).

Taylor, Jacqueline (forthcoming). "Hume's Later Moral Philosophy," in David Fate Norton and Jacqueline Taylor (eds), *The Cambridge Companion to Hume* (Cambridge: Cambridge University Press).

Part IV

Religion

17

Hume's Views on Religion: Intellectual and Cultural Influences

TERENCE PENELHUM

All major philosophers transcend the influences that help to form their views. But a knowledge of those influences will often assist us in understanding what those views were. This is especially true when we consider Hume's philosophy of religion. He often expresses his opinions on religion in guarded and indirect ways, and he chose not to publish his most important work on this subject during his lifetime. These facts alone suggest that a knowledge of the context of his thinking is an important aid in the determination of his opinions.

For all their clarity of presentation, Hume's writings on religion present some puzzles. There can be no doubt that Hume is for the most part hostile to religion in general and to the Christian religion in particular. He uses his superlative critical skills to emphasize what he sees as the intellectual baselessness of faith. He also offers an account of the nature of morality that leaves no role for the belief in Providence or for the promise of divine rewards and punishments. But he also seems from time to time to express concurrence with some of the teachings that his arguments undermine. More importantly, his system has, as one of its core epistemological results, the claim that our basic secular common sense beliefs (in real objects, causal regularity, and self-identity) are not due to rational argument, and cannot be successfully defended by such argument against skeptical doubts; they are due to fortunate instincts that supply us with doxastic commitments that fit us for the needs of common life. Yet Hume does not seem to accord the same status to religious beliefs, even though common life seems full of them, and his occasional protestations of religious conformity seem insincere. The crowning example of his apparent ambivalence on the subject is to be found in the concluding part of the *Dialogues concerning Natural Religion*, where Philo, the character whom most consider to represent Hume himself, seems to concede the theism to which he has been raising objections throughout the work, while suggesting that the right preparation for this form of religion is philosophical skepticism!

In these circumstances it is not surprising that there is disagreement on what Hume's ultimate judgments on religion are. A look at his relation to the society in which he lived and worked, and at the controversies about religion to which he responded, may help to make the nature of these judgments clear. So, at least, I shall suggest.

Hume in Scotland

In the quadrangle of New College, on the Mound in Edinburgh, there is a statue of John Knox, the famous Reformer. It has been there since 1895. Knox's effect on Scots life has been very great, and he was arguably the most important personal influence in the forging of the modern Scottish identity. A few hundred yards away, at the top of the Royal Mile, there is a statue of David Hume. It has been there only since 1997. The sculptor has carved him in classical attire, as if to emphasize the distance that has always separated him from the mainstream of the culture of which he is arguably the most famous figure. While Edinburgh's current pride in him is quite real, it is quite recent, and in his own day his opinions put him at odds with the prevailing culture in a way that did him significant damage, and could well have done him more.

Hume might write disparagingly of Knox in the *Natural History* as a "rustic apostle," but there can be no doubt of Knox's success in establishing the dominance of the Calvinist Reformation in Scotland, a success that survived the attempts of the Stuart monarchs to force the Scots into Episcopal conformity. After the accession of William III to the British throne in 1688, the supremacy of the Presbyterian kirk in Scotland was complete, and Hume was born into a world where its teachings and practices were all around him. It taught a dour and largely unlettered form of Calvinism, complete with the doctrines of predestination, election, and the total depravity of fallen human nature, doctrines which of course entail the salvific uselessness of unaided moral effort. Hume appears to have reasoned himself out of these religious teachings during adolescence, and never to have felt anything but hostility towards them afterwards. They caused him to hold a view of popular religion as bigoted, life-denying, and inimical to the social needs of human nature. They were replaced for him, at the moral level, by a desire to return to the classical virtues, which he extols to the detriment of the "monkish virtues" of humility and self-denial. In the second and third books of the *Treatise of Human Nature*, he gives an account of the nature and basis of morality that allows no place for divine commands or for doctrines of ultimate rewards and punishments.

Even though the *Treatise* contains no sections devoted explicitly to religion, Hume's anti-religiousness was widely realized, and led to two important episodes. The first and better-known is his failure to gain appointment to the chair of Ethics and Pneumatical Philosophy at Edinburgh University in 1745 (Mossner 1970). In the anonymous *Letter from a Gentleman to His Friend in Edinburgh* (which, though published without his permission, was clearly written by him) he argues, disingenuously, that the *Treatise* was not religiously objectionable, but his arguments did not move the electors from their determination not to let him teach the young of their city. It must always be remembered that the *Enquiry concerning Human Understanding*, which appeared in 1748, was written in the aftermath of this affair, in which he clearly felt himself to have been the victim of bigotry and superstition. The second episode was an attempt to censure and excommunicate him at the General Assembly of the Church of Scotland in 1755 and 1756. By this date, however, another party in the church was able to exert influence: the group known as the Moderates (Sher 1985).

The Moderates were the inevitable contrast to the popular church party that had dominated the kirk for so long. They were learned, urbane, and anxious to free the church from narrowness and bigotry. They were also skilled in the art of debate and manipulation, and it was these skills that enabled them to save Hume from the attacks that the popular party (or "High Flyers") mounted on him at the General Assembly. The Moderates included such personages as Hugh Blair, William Robertson, and Alexander Carlyle, whom Hume numbered among his friends. It was the prominence of these men, as much as that of Hume himself and even of Adam Smith, that sustained the period of cultural development commonly referred to now as the Scottish Enlightenment. Hume's friendship with them must be taken into account in the understanding of his attitudes toward religion, especially his concept of what he calls "true religion." The preaching of the Moderates inculcated a form of Christian Stoicism that could not have contrasted more with the fervor of their theological opponents, whose "enthusiasm" they deplored.

It is worthwhile here to take a brief look at one of the sermons of their most famous preacher, Hugh Blair (Blair 1825). In his sermon "On Devotion" he explores the proper Christian religious attitude. He defines devotion as "the lively exercise of those affections which we owe to the Supreme Being," these affections being veneration of God, gratitude to him, desire for his favor, and resignation to his will. These he recommends as rational attitudes, which are to be carefully distinguished from superstitious attachment to ritual, and enthusiastic obsession with "internal emotions." He is at pains to emphasize that proper devotion requires neither retreat from the world and contempt for its concerns, nor perpetual rapture or spiritual joy. Blair's emphasis throughout is on a moderate and restrained attachment to the religious life. Theological underpinnings are hard to find, in spite of the fact that scriptural quotations abound. Religion in such a form was wholly compatible with toleration and freedom of opinion, and was clearly something with which Hume's skeptical temper and dislike of acrimonious public controversy could easily coexist.

The Enlightenment is commonly thought of as anti-religious; but this cannot be said without heavy qualification of the *Scottish* Enlightenment. It was not even anticlerical, since so many of its prominent figures were clerics. The Moderates were rather men who attempted to integrate religious life and secular society. They did not find Hume's views on religion to their liking, but were even more repelled by the stance of those who strove to condemn him. He in his turn allowed them to persuade him to leave the *Dialogues concerning Natural Religion* unpublished during his lifetime, and it is at least in part a result of their influence that his negative views on religion were usually expressed in a way that Norman Kemp Smith describes as following a policy of "stating his skeptical positions with the least possible emphasis compatible with definiteness" (DNR 73).

I also think that his recognition of the value of the Moderates' influence must be taken into account when we decide how to read the puzzling twelfth part of the *Dialogues*. In this part Cleanthes and Philo argue about the nature and limits of "true religion." Cleanthes, whose natural theology has been the subject of the previous eleven parts, gives this rather startling account of it:

> The proper office of religion is to regulate the heart of men, humanize their conduct, infuse the spirit of temperance, order, and obedience; and as its operation is silent, and only enforces the motives of morality and justice, it is in danger of being overlooked, and

325

confounded with these other motives. When it distinguishes itself, and acts as a separate principle over men, it has departed from its proper sphere, and has become only a cover to faction and ambition. (DNR 220)

This is a fair enough description of the religion of the Moderates; but for all its doctrinal emptiness, it is clear that Cleanthes does not see it as equivalent to no religion at all, and sets great store by the retention of those institutions that embody it. Philo voices obviously Humean sentiments about the evils of "false" (that is, really religious) religion, but Cleanthes rebukes him, and tells him not to be so concerned about the dangers of false religion that he jettisons "the true." Hume uses Cleanthes at this point as representative of his Moderate friends, and the deference Philo accords him indicates that Hume conceded that the unbridled questioning of religious credentials in which Philo indulges needed to be kept in check in the face of the ever-present risk of a High-Flying backlash.

This does not mean, however, that Hume thinks, any more than Philo does, that "true religion" is *true*. But having done all he can in the *Dialogues* to drain it of doctrinal content, he settles for having Pamphilus, the supposed narrator, award the official victory to Cleanthes.

Hume, Cicero, and the Skeptical Tradition

The device of having Pamphilus declare Cleanthes "nearer to the truth" than his friends is one that Hume, for his own purposes, copies from Cicero, who has the same thing happen at the close of his dialogue *On the Nature of the Gods* (Cicero 1972). Cicero, who, unlike Hume, reports the conversation in his own person, says that in his view Balbus, the Stoic who propounds the natural theology at issue in the work, rather than Cotta, the Academic skeptic, has the best of the argument. However we are to judge Cicero's sympathies, we can see that Hume, by copying this formal conclusion, is able to soften the impact of Philo's skeptical arguments, which most readers agree represent his own opinions.

The importance of Cicero to Hume is very great (Jones 1982). The wider question of the nature and extent of Hume's skepticism cannot be fully explored here, but is important for deciding how his philosophy of religion is to be interpreted.

Hume himself states in section 12 of the first *Enquiry* that he adopts what he calls "mitigated" skepticism, and he identifies it with "academical" skepticism – the form of skeptic thought which was represented in the Academy in Athens in Cicero's day, and on which he reported in *On the Nature of the Gods* and the *Academics*. The skeptic tradition of antiquity had a lengthy and complex history, beginning with Pyrrho in the fourth century BC and lasting seven hundred years (Burnyeat 1983). What Cicero reports to us is one of its phases. Many of its representatives are only known to us by report. Aside from the work of Cicero, the most important embodiment of the Skeptic tradition is to be found in the writings of Sextus Empiricus which date from the third century AD, especially his *Outlines of Pyrrhonism* (Sextus Empiricus 1967). The writings of Sextus were rediscovered in the sixteenth century, and became an important intellectual influence, which Descartes tried to defeat. It is not clear how far

Hume made any detailed study of Sextus, as distinct from Cicero, although he was certainly well acquainted with the work of Pierre Bayle, whose writings are full of Pyrrhonian influences. It is important to distinguish between Hume's views about skepticism regarding secular beliefs, and his views about skepticism and religion.

The skeptic tradition of Hellenistic times competed for the allegiance of the intelligentsia with Epicureanism and Stoicism, and like them had a critically important moral dimension. All three Hellenistic traditions sought to provide an antidote to the anxieties consequent upon the demise of the city-state tradition in which the good of the individual and that of the state could be integrated or even identified. Each sought to offer its adherents inner calm in the face of an impersonal world. The Epicureans claimed to provide this by recommending a life devoted to simple pleasures and the avoidance of unattainable objectives. The Stoics argued that it could be found in the practice of virtuous identification with the dictates of cosmic reason and the suppression of desire. The Skeptics saw the source of anxiety as commitment, in particular commitment to dogmas, or theoretical claims about reality that are believed to ground the pursuit of objectives that people judge to be good. They therefore used philosophical reasoning to undermine attempts (especially Stoic attempts) to use the philosophical intellect to prove the existence of a cosmic backing for human opinions. As their techniques are described by Sextus, the Skeptic would examine the philosophical arguments for and against dogmatic opinions, and becoming sated with such arguments, reach a stage of suspended judgment (*epoché*), which would in turn lead to an unperturbed state of mind, called *ataraxia*.

The natural response to this philosophical stance is to say, as opponents of Skepticism have indeed regularly said, that suspense of judgment can only lead to practical paralysis, and that one cannot doubt everything in the way this method seems to suggest one can. As Sextus reports it, the Skeptics had a well-thought-out response to this: that one lives according to appearances (*phainomena*). One reverts to the opinions and ways of life that one has always been inclined to accept, but one now follows them undogmatically – that is, in a way that is freed from the attempt to ground them in some supposed knowledge of ultimate reality. The message here is conservative and relativistic, and implies that the right use of philosophical reasoning is to induce an abandonment of attempts to arrive at final truth. Such a stance is not (or not self-evidently) unlivable, though many would find it morally enervating. It entails a life of external conformity to the beliefs of one's community, without inner commitment to them, and without expectation that philosophy can justify them. The particular modification of this stance that is associated with the Academic version of Skepticism reported by Cicero is the suggestion that among the appearances we encounter some which, though still lacking ultimate justification, can nevertheless be classed as probable, and therefore deserving of something resembling assent.

Hume's attitude to the Skeptic tradition is roughly as follows. He agrees that philosophical reasoning is unable to provide justification for our primary beliefs, but he goes further in one critical respect by denying that the negative arguments of the Skeptic can dislodge them. They can at most weaken them for short periods in the study. Human beings are by nature believing beings, and are therefore incapable of the belieflessness the Pyrrhonian tradition claimed to be a feature of the Skeptic life. Our instinct to believe is human nature's answer to the skeptic, though it is not a philosophical refutation of his arguments. It is an instinct which saves us from paralysis and anxiety, which would be the actual result of suspense of judgment if it were possible for us. Hume thus rejects what he sees (correctly or not) as the Pyrrhonian form of skepticism, and in his detailed exploration of the concept of probability he embraces and develops what he calls mitigated, or Academic, skepticism. He expounds this most fully in section 12 of the first *Enquiry*, and incorporates into it the crypto-positivist recommendation that the philosopher is best advised not to stray beyond the methodizing and correcting of the beliefs of "common life," and to eschew attempts to ground them in reason or add to them in metaphysical speculation.

What, however, about religious beliefs? These, after all, seem to be, or to have been, a substantial element in common life. The Skeptics of antiquity were fully conscious of this, and although in our own day the term "skeptic" tends to connote a rejection of religious beliefs, the skeptics of antiquity did not respond to them in this way. For them the wise man would conform to the religious traditions and practices of his own community, but would do this undogmatically: that is, without supposing that they have cosmic backing and without attempting to support them by reason. Cotta, in Cicero's dialogue, speaks as a practitioner, indeed a functionary, of the state religion. What he rejects is not the religion but the attempt to use philosophy to establish its teachings. Hume is fully cognizant of this strand in the Skeptic tradition, and of the fact that it implied an acceptance of religion as a form of social cement, while keeping one's inner distance from the doctrines to which one outwardly and verbally conforms. But this raises a difficult question: if the secular beliefs of common life (in the regularity of nature, the existence of physical objects, and the identity of the self) are not beliefs we can detach ourselves from, might not the same be true of religious beliefs? Hume's response here is a twofold one. He enters into a substantial examination of the origin and place of religious belief in human nature, in *The Natural History of Religion*. He is at pains to separate this enquiry from the philosophical examination of natural theology in the *Dialogues*, where he scrutinizes the attempt to ground religious beliefs in philosophical argument. The upshot of this twofold procedure is a famous statement at the end of part 12 of the *Dialogues*: "To be a philosophical skeptic is, in a man of letters, the first and most essential step towards being a sound, believing Christian."

The implications of this statement of Philo are complex ones. In the first instance, the sound, believing Christian to whom Philo refers will be the secularized believer whose doctrinal commitments have been reduced to those minimal tenets that Philo has allowed Cleanthes to stay with by the end of part 12 – tenets which Philo summarizes in the notorious statement that "the cause or causes of order in the universe probably bear some remote analogy to human intelligence." Secondly, the skepticism he refers to will be the Humean mitigated skepticism that Philo explicitly espouses in the first part of the *Dialogues*. It is part of that sort of skepticism to maintain that the philosopher should not investigate vast questions such as the origin of the world because they are beyond the reach of our faculties to determine. The arguments Hume puts into the mouth of Philo do not presuppose the correctness of this view, but are designed to demonstrate its truth. Cleanthes offers, in his version of the Argument from Design, an attempt to establish the reality of God on the basis of observation and experience, and what Philo seeks to show is that it is a bad argument that at best yields a far less nourishing result.

Hume is thus far at one with the classical Skeptics in rejecting the philosophical attempt to ground religious doctrines in argument. The sentence in which Philo speaks of the value of skepticism for the Christian, however, seems to suggest something more: that the Skeptics were right to think of religion as being properly based solely upon tradition, to which the skeptic could undogmatically conform. Is this also Hume's opinion? Or is this sentence of Philo's a merely verbal form of deference to the religion Philo has left over for his friend?

I do not think a full answer to this is possible until we have looked at some of the French influences on Hume's thought. But it is closely allied to another issue we can answer. If skeptical arguments cannot hinder us from believing those things without which we cannot live this life, why suppose they can hinder us from believing those things that we are told we need to believe in order to prosper in the next? Perhaps religious beliefs are as inescapable as the secular natural beliefs. Hume is deeply aware that his system has to confront this issue, and he gives us his answers to it in *The Natural History of Religion.*

The first answer is that although religious beliefs are very widespread among human beings, they are not universal. The second is that religious beliefs vary so much from society to society that they have to be due to "secondary" causes, that is, to environmental or historical factors rather than to basic instincts in our natures. The implication is that it is possible for those who are suitably fortunate to escape them, so that our reasoning powers do not have to be subordinated to religious beliefs in the way that mitigated skepticism tells us they have to be subordinated to our secular natural beliefs. The actual causes of religion, Hume says, are the anxieties that humans suffer in the face of calamitous events, which they ascribe to invisible personal powers that they hope to propitiate. This theory of the origin of religious beliefs locates it in special events whose causes are not understood – the exact opposite of the law-abiding natural uniformity which is the basis of the Argument from Design. An additional implication of this fact is that those who are aware of the orderliness of the natural world will not be plagued by the anxieties that generate religious hypotheses in the first place.

So Hume feels he can deflect the suggestion that since our natures determine our commitment to the secular natural beliefs whose status is the core concern of his epistemology, they must also determine us to hold some form of religious belief. But this could still leave him open to the view of the classical Skeptic that we would be wise to conform to its institutions and practices in a suitably detached fashion. Indeed, Philo's concluding comment on skepticism seems to embody this very suggestion. Is this Hume's own opinion?

Hume and the French

Hume went to France in 1734 and stayed there until 1737, and most of the *Treatise* was composed during these three years. Readers who have viewed him primarily as an empiricist successor of Locke and Berkeley have inevitably overlooked the immense importance of French influences on his thinking. This is especially odd when one considers that the skeptical strand in Hume, which the "Locke–Berkeley–Hume" tradition tends to emphasize, has largely French sources.

One of the many debts philosophical scholars owe to Richard Popkin is his exploration of the influence of the Catholic Pyrrhonists of the sixteenth and seventeenth centuries (Popkin 1979; Penelhum 1983). The recovery of the writings of Sextus led some to think that they could draw upon his batteries of arguments against the power of human reason and use them in the service of a particular form of Fideism – the view that faith should avoid all attempts to recommend itself by appeals to reason. This form of apologetic was used in the debates between Catholics and Protestants to reinforce the Catholic claim that a traditional authority was necessary to interpret scripture, and was used more generally to reinforce the claims of faith against reason, whose alleged impotence was said to leave a gap that only faith could fill. Forms of this position are to be found in such otherwise opposed thinkers as Montaigne and Pascal, to mention only the most famous and influential figures. Hume will have been familiar with this apologetic tradition, in spite of being unsympathetic to it. He makes use of its language for his own purposes, as when he says at the end of his discussion of miracles that "I am the better pleased with the method of reasoning here delivered, as I think it may serve to confound those dangerous friends or disguised enemies to the CHRISTIAN religion, who have undertaken to defend it by the principles of human reason. Our most holy religion is founded on *Faith*, not on reason, and it is a sure method of exposing it to put it to such a trial as it is, by no means, fitted to endure" (EHU 10.40). He appropriates it further when he makes Philo say that philosophical skepticism is the first step towards sound Christianity.

In this appropriation he is following in the footsteps of a thinker whose influence he acknowledges, namely Pierre Bayle. Bayle's importance as a source of understanding of the Enlightenment is very great. A French Protestant who had briefly converted to Catholicism and then relapsed, he lived as a refugee from French persecution in Rotterdam. His immense erudition and prolific journalistic and literary writings were a bottomless storehouse of skeptical comment and argument throughout the eighteenth century. He gained notoriety through his *Various Thoughts on the Occasion of a Comet*, which first appeared in 1682 (Bayle 1682). In it he decisively undermined a common assumption of ethical and religious writers of his time, that atheism entailed moral depravity, arguing on the contrary that a society of righteous atheists was indeed a possibility, especially in view of the lack of righteousness in many Christian societies. We can see Hume as the first major moral philosopher to attempt to demonstrate the truth of Bayle's contention by producing in Book 3 of the *Treatise* an ethic in which religion has no place as a source of moral judgment or moral motivation, and by arguing in section 11 of the first *Enquiry* that the only sort of knowledge of God that natural religion could provide is irrelevant to our moral decisions. Bayle is best known for his *Historical and Critical Dictionary* of 1697, an immense work that is nominally a series of biographies of greater and lesser historical figures, but in which phenomenal learning, skeptical argument, and cynical cunning combine to produce what was regarded by the major figures of the Enlightenment, including Hume, as a mine of anti-religious ammunition. The intellectually exciting material for which the work is known had to be mined from the footnotes, and the footnotes to the footnotes, to the frequently rather bland articles – a device to deflect orthodox authorities from the work's frequently explosive contents. Bayle's intentions are in fact a matter of controversy. His stance throughout is that the limitations of reason are such that faith must sustain itself without philosophical support, since the key teachings of Christianity are not merely beyond, but are frequently contrary to, reason. This apparently extreme form of fideism may in fact have been Bayle's real opinion, and his major motive in scholarship may merely have been that of defusing the religious controversies from which he and his family had suffered by suggesting the faithful had best be content with the sort of conformist religiosity into which the classical Pyrrhonists had retreated. But his obvious relish for exposing the intellectual difficulties in orthodox doctrine, and his aggressively naturalistic readings of classical and biblical history and mythology, were commonly read throughout the succeeding century as anti-religious in their purpose. As far as Hume is concerned, Bayle's influence is to be seen in at least four aspects of his writing on religion: first, as a major conduit of the Skeptic tradition on a multitude of subjects; second, as a source of the naturalistic interpretation of religion that Hume develops in *The Natural History of Religion*; third, as an obvious inspiration for Hume's occasional resort to indirection and nominal reportage in his presentation of some of his key arguments (as in the *Dialogues* and section 11 of the *Enquiry*), and the adoption of a light and bantering manner while dealing with themes on which he felt very strongly; and fourth, as a model for the presentation of unorthodox views in a form that retains at least a verbal conformity with current religious conventions.

One more of the many French influences on Hume's writing must be mentioned here. David Wootton has shown that the form and the content of the famous section "Of Miracles" was determined in large part by the fact that Hume appears to have composed its key argument during his stay at La Flèche, and that its primary target was not (or not initially) any English writers on miracles, but Antoine Arnauld, who had argued in *La logique, ou l'art de penser*, known in English as *The Art of Thinking*, that testimony of high quality could override the intrinsic unlikelihood of miraculous events, and thus justify us in accepting that miracles have occurred. Hume's main argument against miracles is that when the testimony is to an event that is genuinely miraculous, and not merely extraordinary, the reverse is true. The fact that Hume's target was originally Arnauld explains the fact that his essay confines itself to the evaluation of miracle testimony (Wootton 1990; Arnauld 1662; Hunter 1996). It also explains the fact that Hume goes out of his way in a footnote to ridicule a particular miracle story associated with the monastery of Port-Royal, where Arnauld's sister Angélique was abbess, namely the miracle of the Holy Thorn. Marguérite Perrier, the niece of Pascal, was a young pupil at a school attached to Port-Royal, and was afflicted with a tumor in the corner of her left eye, which had grown worse over the years, and on which the doctors were planning to perform a dangerous cauterization. In 1656 Port-Royal received the loan of a holy relic, said to be a thorn from the crown of Christ. Marguerite was told to touch the thorn to her eye, and when she did so, the discharge ceased and the tumor dried up. It would seem that this event was in Arnauld's mind in *The Art of Thinking*, although it is not mentioned explicitly. Hume uses it as an example, which his English Protestant readers would interpret as he did, of a person of the highest intellectual attainments (Pascal) being taken in by collective hysteria (EHU 10.27n25). It is noteworthy also that the other examples of erroneous beliefs in miracles that Hume draws upon from his own time are French.

331

The Deists and Butler

However much Hume's mind was influenced by French thinkers, he wrote for an English readership. The second part of the Miracles section contains arguments that will have been familiar in type to all those who had followed what R. M. Burns has called the Great Debate on Miracles (Burns 1981). This debate had raged for years among the British intelligentsia, and Hume joined it quite late. It had been dominated by two groups, whom Burns accurately names the orthodox and the deists.

The orthodox took the traditional apologetic position, deriving from Aquinas, in which proofs of the existence of God are followed by secondary arguments designed to show that the God whose being had been demonstrated in the proofs has revealed additional truths about himself in the history of Israel, the events of the New Testament, and the miracles alleged to have attended the history (especially the early history) of the Christian church. In *The Evidences of Christianity*, Paley later complained that Hume had attacked miracles in a manner that ignored the fact that their defenders presupposed the existence of a God who might well reveal himself to us in history (Paley 1794). Hume had in fact carefully confined himself to the claim that testimony can never be enough to establish a miracle so as to make it a "foundation for a system of religion." There is room for debate on how far this fact vitiates Paley's argument, but it is striking that Paley says nothing about Hume's independent attacks on the sort of proof of God that Paley himself uses, but proceeds as though the *Dialogues*, and section 11 of the *Enquiry*, which immediately follows the argument on miracles, had never been written.

It is important, however, to bear in mind that the orthodox use of miracle evidence and testimony did indeed follow on from a supposed demonstration of God's existence and his providence. The deists' role in the miracles controversy was that of separating these two parts of the traditional apologetic, by arguing that the proof of God did not make miracles more likely, but less. Deists believed that God's being had indeed been shown by the Design argument. That argument sought to establish the existence of a Designer of the world, whose modus operandi had been shown to us by the labors of Newton. The deists maintained that a being of such intelligence would have no need to intervene in his creation subsequently; and just as his cosmic design was open to the understanding of all, so his moral and spiritual requirements must be open to all and not be known only to those who happen to have lived in or near ancient Palestine.

So they rejected special revelation, believing only in whatever divine message was contained in the order of nature and in the deliverances of the individual conscience. All additional claims to revealed authority were dismissed as mystery-mongering, due to "priestcraft." Many deists claimed to be Christians, and saw their mission as the demonstration that Christianity was, in the words of the title of John Toland's book, not mysterious, and consisted of the sort of natural religion that was, in the words of the title of Matthew Tindal's work, as old as creation (Toland 1696; Tindal 1730). Hume's attack on miracles put him, as far as this ongoing English debate was concerned, on the side of the deists. But only, of course, as far as *this* debate was concerned.

The deists met their intellectual match in Joseph Butler, for whom Hume expressed admiration, and whose support he tried to solicit before the *Treatise* was published.

(He even excised material on miracles from it in order to make it less unpalatable to him.) In *The Analogy of Religion* of 1736, Butler argues with his opponents where they are. He assumes what they assume, namely that there is a God who has created an orderly world and placed us in it. His main argument against them is that they infer too much from this about our ability to decide what God's purposes are, or what they cannot be. His most important apologetic work outside the *Analogy* is his fifteenth sermon, "Upon the Ignorance of Man." The message, both there and in the larger work, is that we should be properly aware of our epistemological limitations. His position, however, owes nothing to skepticism. We know that we live under a providential order, governed by God, but this does not mean that God intends us to understand all the principles of this order, only that we can learn enough to enable us to practice that mode of life to which he calls us. (God may, in fact, conceal from us some features of his plans that we are capable of understanding, but which he thinks it best we should not know.) Butler then proceeds, in the *Analogy*, to argue that there is a probable case for natural religion, and no sound case against revealed religion. On the first, when we reflect that the natural order is the work of God, and that in it we are able to learn from our experience early in life how best to conduct ourselves in later years, so, by analogy we can infer that this life is a training ground, or sphere of "probation," in which we can equip ourselves for whatever God has in store for us in a future life. On the second, he argues that since God may have intentions for us that we do not understand fully, he may "attest" those intentions by prophecies and miracles that authenticate scriptural pronouncements. Even though these phenomena may be exceptions to the natural laws we learn from science, they may well be in accordance with "general laws of wisdom" that will make fuller sense to us in time (Butler 1736).

Butler's arguments have serious force against the deists, and succeed in undermining their confidence that God would not place us in a world that had mysteries in it. But his arguments have their power largely because they assume the common conviction that the being of God has been proved. If one holds this, it follows that apparent evils in the world, or puzzling facts such as the special status Christianity ascribes to a chosen people, must have a reason even though we do not presently see what it is. It is not accidental that Butler, who is praised by Hume at the outset of the *Treatise* for his empirical methods, and certainly seeks to use such methods in the *Analogy*, presupposes that God's being is not only rendered certain by the argument from Design, but accepts the cogency of Samuel Clarke's *a priori* demonstration of it (see *Analogy* 2.6). In section 11 of the *Enquiry*, and later in the *Dialogues*, Hume insists, on the assumption that no matter of fact can be proved *a priori*, that phenomena that may perhaps be reconciled with divine perfection if that is assumed beforehand, have to be weighed in the evidential balance when the nature, and even the being, of God is considered solely in the light of the sort of cosmos we can see ourselves to inhabit. Such a cosmos does not of itself suggest that our life we live here is the prelude to another, or that the deity, if such there be, who governs it, has the power or inclination to produce a world better than we find here and now.

But Hume does not only have negative things to say at the level of philosophical theology. He also pioneers the study of comparative religion, and argues that the deists and (by implication) Butler run afoul of the evidence at that level also. In the

Natural History he distinguishes at the outset between religion's "foundation in reason" and its "origin in human nature." He pays lip-service to the former, which is not to be his topic in this work; he then makes it clear at once that an investigation into the latter shows that it had nothing to do with the contemplation of natural order which is the basis of the Design argument:

> It appears to me, that, if we consider the improvement of human society, from rude begin-nings to a state of greater perfection, polytheism or idolatry was, and necessarily must have been, the first and most ancient religion of mankind. (NHR Intro.)

He then ascribes the origin of religious belief to human fears arising from special events and calamities such as monstrous births. Such events are ascribed to "invisible, intelligent" powers which resemble the personal forces with which primitive humans are already familiar. Early humans did not have the leisure to contemplate nature as a whole; they merely reacted to aberrant and unpleasant forces in it. Monotheism is a much later development that comes, in Hume's story, from competition between competing groups of devotees.

So idolatry precedes, and does not follow upon, monotheism, which Hume ironically says could never be dislodged once the mind was convinced of its cogency. In this Hume opposes the orthodox view, found famously in the beginning of Calvin's *Institutes*, that humanity began with a clear awareness of the one true God, an awareness that was defaced and corrupted because of the Fall, and was manifested in sinful form in all later history, in which the human soul became a "factory of idols" (Calvin 1536). But Hume also undermines the deists' view that idolatry requires a special explanation in view of the obviousness of God's unity and rationality – a special explanation that often ascribed it to the wiles of priests. Butler, in defending revelation against the deists, also supposes that it took an initially monotheistic form at the time of creation. Hume sweeps all these views aside by an appeal to evidence.

Conclusion

I will take, in order, sections 10 and 11 of the first *Enquiry*, *The Natural History of Religion*, and the *Dialogues concerning Natural Religion*, and indicate how each embodies Hume's responses to the influences described in the preceding sections.

Section 10 of the *Enquiry*, "Of Miracles," opens with a general argument that tries to establish that if we confine ourselves to the evidence, even impeccable testimony to a miracle must contend with the fact that if the event reported is genuinely miraculous in character, all the evidence that established the natural law of which it would be a violation has to be weighed in the balance against the reports of it; so that even the best reports of witnesses can do no more than produce a stalemate in which one "proof" balances an opposite one. It seems that Hume originally developed this argument to respond to the claims for miracle testimony found in Arnauld, though it clearly has wider application. The second part of the section is designed to join the prior English debate on miracles by giving a series of reasons why we should never accept the miracle testimony we actually have, since it has never been impeccable and has never, therefore, amounted to a "proof" in Hume's sense. In section 11, "Of a Particular Providence and of a Future State," one of Hume's most elegant and carefully-constructed essays, he argues that the Design argument can at most show the reality of a God great enough to produce the world we have. Such a conclusion is irrelevant to our practical decisions. The essay also undermines Butler's apologetic by showing that the evidence on which the Design argument rests cannot lend support to any theory that draws analogies between this life and another.

The Natural History of Religion is noteworthy for three things. First, by arguing that the forces that lead to religious belief are "secondary" in our natures, so that religion is not universal, Hume seeks to evade the criticism that in tracing our common sense commitments to non-rational instincts in our nature, he has opened the way to a philosophical legitimation of religion. Second, by insisting that religion is initially polytheistic, or idolatrous, Hume undermines both the orthodox and the deistic views of the nature of humans' initial awareness of the divine. Third, by trying to show how monotheism evolves from primitive polytheism, Hume paves the way for many of the later arguments in the *Dialogues* which make it clear that the evidence on which the Design argument relies is not evidence that naturally suggests its conclusion. The story told in the *Natural History* explains why it is that the monotheism whose origin is described there is ready to hand in our minds as a supposed conclusion from that evidence.

The *Dialogues* is too complex a work for any summary of the influences upon it to be comprehensive. I will try, however, to draw together some of the themes that have arisen earlier.

In part 1, Philo is made to propound the mitigated skepticism of section 12 of the *Enquiry*, and to hold, in opposition to Cleanthes, that our reason, which should be confined to matters of experience and common life, should avoid theological argument. While Cleanthes also thinks that reason should argue from experience, he thinks such reasoning can indeed lead us to knowledge of the being and nature of God. The next ten parts put this matter between them to the test; and Philo's dialectical victories throughout justify his concluding statement that being a philosophical skeptic is the first step towards "sound" Christian belief. The whole argument, therefore, puts Hume on the side of the Christian Pyrrhonists in maintaining that reason cannot justify religion or provide intellectual foundations for it. It also provides his refutation of Butler's defense of orthodoxy by showing, against both Butler and his deistic opponents, that if one really does confine one's reasoning to the analogies and probabilities to which Butler said he was restricting himself, the result, at the very best, is a pared-down recognition that the cause or causes of the world's order may resemble human intelligence: a conclusion that is less than Butler's starting-point, and which Philo merely presents as a position that "some people maintain." Any more doctrinal content in religion must come, as Philo says, from revelation, if any should turn out to be available. It is hard for a reader of the *Natural History* to think that Philo speaks for Hume, or even for himself, in expressing a longing for it.

The Pyrrhonists, and the early modern fideists who followed them and whose language Hume uses, saw revealed and institutionalized religion as a matter of tradition and convention, like Cicero's Cotta and the fictional Epicurus of section 11 of the *Enquiry*. It is not totally clear that Hume has no sympathy for this view of religion, at least if the institutions that embody it are in suitably urbane hands, such as those of his Moderate friends. This must be at least part of the reason behind his making Philo, in part 12, talk as though he has been at one with Cleanthes all along in recognizing the divine source of the world's order, and as sharing in spiritual objectives that they can agree upon now that Demea, who represents orthodoxy, has left the scene. He can even live with Cleanthes' continuing and obtuse belief that the theism he represents has rational foundations, since he has long since shown that the price of maintaining this claim is the abandonment of all doctrinal content. At this stage I suggest Philo is no longer Hume, any more than Cleanthes is any longer Butler (if he ever was). Philo is rather the skeptic who concedes as much as Hume's epistemological principles can permit anyone to concede in theology, and in so doing adopts the wording of the secularized religious functionaries of Hume's day as a concession to the value of a tolerant religious establishment. What of Hume himself? He chooses in the *Dialogues* not to speak in his own person; but we can recall that in section 11 of the *Enquiry* the argument that he presents as his own, rather than through his fictional friend or that friend's fictional Epicurus, is the argument that causal reasoning cannot be extended beyond the realm of experience. In the *Dialogues* this appears as one of Philo's earliest objections to Cleanthes, which suggests that Philo speaks for Hume in those negative early arguments, and may well not do so at the close, when he seems to embrace "true religion." If this inference is a sound one, then Hume himself probably does not concede even the little that Philo agrees to. He keeps his atheism in the closet, a closet to which even Philo does not have the key.

See also 18 "Hume on the Nature and Existence of God"; 19 "Hume on Miracles and Immortality"

References

Arnauld, Antoine and Nicole, Pierre (1662). *The Art of Thinking*, ed. James Dickoff and Patricia James (Indianapolis, IN: Bobbs-Merrill, 1964).

Bayle, Pierre (1682). *Various Thoughts on the Occasion of a Comet*, trans. Robert C. Bartlett (Albany, NY: State University of New York Press, 2000).

—— (1697). *Historical and Critical Dictionary*, trans. Richard H. Popkin (Indianapolis, IN: Bobbs-Merrill, 1965).

Blair, Hugh (1825). *Sermons*, 2 vols. (Edinburgh: T. and W. Nelson).

Burns, R. M. (1981). *The Great Debate on Miracles: From Joseph Glanvill to David Hume* (Lewisburg, PA: Bucknell University Press).

Burnyeat, Myles (ed.) (1983). *The Skeptical Tradition* (Berkeley: University of California Press).

Butler, Joseph (1736). *The Works of Bishop Butler*, 2 vols., ed. J. H. Bernard (London: Macmillan, 1900).

Calvin, John (1536). *Institutes of the Christian Religion*, ed. John T. McNeill, trans. Ford Lewis Battles (Philadelphia: Westminster Press, 1960).

Cicero (1972). *The Nature of the Gods*, trans. Horace C. P. McGregor (Harmondsworth: Penguin).

Clarke, Samuel (1738). *Works*, vol. 2: *A Demonstration of the Being and Attributes of God* (New York: Garland Publishing Inc., 1978).

Hume, David (1745). *A Letter from a Gentleman to His Friend in Edinburgh*, ed. Ernest C. Mossner and John V. Price (Edinburgh: Edinburgh University Press, 1967).

—— (1779). *Dialogues concerning Natural Religion*, ed. Norman Kemp Smith (Indianapolis, IN: Bobbs-Merrill, 1980). (Cited in the text as DNR.)

—— (1757). *The Natural History of Religion*, ed. H. E. Root (Stanford: Stanford University Press, 1957). (Cited in the text as *Natural History*.)

Hunter, Graeme (1996). "Arnauld's Defence of Miracles and Its Context," in Elmar J. Kremer (ed.), *Interpreting Arnauld* (Toronto: University of Toronto Press).

Jones, Peter (1982). *Hume's Sentiments: Their Ciceronian and French Context* (Edinburgh: Edinburgh University Press).

Mossner, Ernest C. (1970). *The Life of David Hume* (Oxford: Clarendon Press).

Paley, William (1794). *The Works of William Paley*, vol. 2: *The Evidences of Christianity* (London: Longmans, 1838), 4 vols.

Penelhum, Terence (1983). *God and Skepticism* (Dordrecht: Reidel).

Popkin, Richard (1979). *The History of Skepticism from Erasmus to Spinoza* (Berkeley: University of California Press).

Sextus Empiricus. *Sextus Empiricus*, trans. Robert Gregg Bury (Loeb Classical Library. Cambridge, MA: Harvard University Press, 1976), 4 vols.

Sher, Richard B. (1985). *Church and University in the Scottish Enlightenment* (Edinburgh: Edinburgh University Press).

Tindal, Matthew (1730). *Christianity as Old as the Creation* (New York: Garland Publishers, 1978).

Toland, John (1696). *Christianity Not Mysterious*, ed. Gunther Gawlick (Stutttgart-Bad Cannstatt: Friedrich Frommann, 1964).

Wootton, David (1990). "Hume's 'Of Miracles': Probability and Irreligion," in M. A. Stewart (ed.), *Studies in the Philosophy of the Scottish Enlightenment* (Oxford: Clarendon Press).

Further Reading

Fogelin, Robert J. (2003). *A Defense of Hume on Miracles* (Princeton, NJ: Princeton University Press).

Gaskin, John (1988). *Hume's Philosophy of Religion*, 2nd edn. (London: Macmillan).

Manuel, Frank E. (1959). *The Eighteenth Century Confronts the Gods* (Cambridge, MA: Harvard University Press).

Penelhum, Terence (1985). *Butler* (London: Routledge).

—— (2000). *Themes in Hume: The Self, the Will, Religion* (Oxford: Clarendon Press).

Sessions, William Lad (2002). *Reading Hume's Dialogues: A Veneration for True Religion* (Bloomington, IN: Indiana University Press).

Stewart, M. A. and Wright, John P. (eds.) (1994). *Hume and Hume's Connexions* (Edinburgh: Edinburgh University Press).

Yandell, Keith E. (1990). *Hume's "Inexplicable Mystery": His Views on Religion* (Philadelphia: Temple University Press).

18

Hume on the Nature and Existence of God

MARTIN BELL

This chapter is restricted to Hume's account of what philosophical reasons can be given for beliefs about the existence and nature of God, and so is restricted to the subject that in Hume's time was called "natural religion." Natural religion consists in religious beliefs that can be given a foundation in reason, and natural theology is the enterprise of formulating reasons in support of these beliefs. I shall say a little about section 11 of *An Enquiry concerning Human Understanding* (1748) and concentrate on *Dialogues concerning Natural Religion* (posthumously published 1779). Hume's philosophical examination of religious beliefs and practices is much wider than this. The chapters in this volume by Michael Levine and Terence Penelhum discuss some of these wider aspects.

The term "natural religion" contrasts with "revealed religion," which means beliefs derived from supposed divine revelations, made by God to people such as Abraham, Moses, Jesus, and Mohammed, preserved in holy books, and transmitted through the institutions of the religions they founded. The distinction has a long history. The medieval theologian, Thomas Aquinas, for example, says that natural theology can establish that there exists just one God who created the world and guides it providentially, but human reason alone cannot establish all the doctrines that a Christian should believe, such as the doctrine of the Trinity. Revealed truths can neither be understood nor made credible by human reason alone.

The position of Aquinas on the distinction between natural and revealed religion became dominant in the Catholic tradition of Christianity. Some later Protestant theologians, such as Luther and Calvin, were more skeptical about the possibilities of natural theology. For them, human reason, like all other parts of human nature, is so weakened and blinded through the Fall, the wilful turning away from God that Adam and Eve made in Eden, that it cannot arrive at a knowledge of the being and nature of the one true God without the aid of his grace of which faith is the gift. Some theologians went even further, arguing that religious beliefs can be paradoxical and so incredible when judged simply from the point of view of reason. For example Pierre Bayle (1647–1706), a French Calvinist philosopher and theologian, some of whose writings were read by Hume, argued that from the point of view of human reason the belief that God is both omnipotent and wholly good is incompatible with the existence of evil in the world. Nevertheless, the Christian must, contrary to reason, have faith in God's goodness and omnipotence, and so should distrust the powers of reason. The combination of the views that reason is unable to arrive at truth (skepticism) and that religious truth can be grasped only by faith (fideism) is called "skeptical fideism." As will be come apparent, skeptical fideism has an important role in Hume's exploration of natural religion (although Hume certainly was not a skeptical fideist).

At the opposite end of the spectrum of theologies from fideism was deism. This was not a term that had a precise meaning, but roughly it means the view that natural theology alone is a sufficient basis for religion. It is essential to revealed religion to believe that God communicates with human beings and responds to their hopes and fears expressed through prayer and worship. The deist conception of God was of the great architect who made the universe and established its unalterable laws but does not act to reveal himself at particular times and places. As a result "deism" is often used for belief in a God who does not intervene in his creation and "theism" is often used for belief in a God who does so intervene and is concerned with the everyday lives of human beings. Penelhum (this volume, ch. 17) contains a discussion of the importance of skeptical fideism and deism for Hume's thought.

Differing positions about the importance of revelation as against reason in theology were found in the Christian church in Scotland in Hume's time. "Orthodox" clergy in the tradition of Calvin and Knox emphasized faith as a God-given gift that opened the heart and the mind to revealed truths and biblical teachings, and they were skeptical about philosophical reasoning in religion. "Moderate" clergy, like those in the "Latitudinarian" movement in the Church of England, aimed at a synthesis of natural religion, revealed religion, and ethical teaching. Philosophers and theologians of this movement hoped to give systematic theories that would show how the truths of revealed religion gained support from natural religion (Rivers 2000; Moore 2000; Ross 2000). Natural theology should be able to give good reasons for the belief that the world is not only made by a wise, good and powerful God, but is providentially ordered and guided for the good of human beings. This God of natural theology is consonant with the God revealed in Christianity, a God who desires the salvation and happiness of human beings, and provides them with a moral law, a conscience, or a moral sense by which they can live in obedience to God's will, be happy in this life, and through the salvation of Christ be united with God in heaven. Ethics therefore rests on religion, and religion can be shown to be reasonable.

Hume's writings disrupt this program, breaking the assumed connections between its components. In his moral philosophy he argues that the foundation of morality lies in human nature not in divine nature, and that it is a matter of human sentiments, their communication through sympathy, and their regulation by institutions that are human inventions justified by their utility. Here he breaks the connection between ethics and revealed religion. In his examination of natural religion he breaks the connection on the other side, arguing that philosophy gives no reason to believe in the existence of the providential God of Christianity.

In a time when the conviction that morality and the welfare of society depends on religious beliefs was so dominant, Hume had to exercise prudence in his discussions of religion. He used a number of stylistic and rhetorical devices for this purpose. One device was provided by the fact, noted earlier, that theologians such as Calvin, and the orthodox clergy of Hume's time, were themselves skeptical about appealing to philosophical reasoning to support religious teachings. This enabled Hume often to represent his skepticism about the prospects for natural religion as consistent with orthodox religious faith. Another device was to write in the form of a dialogue, or to put some of his criticisms into the mouth of a fictional character. These literary devices are used in both EHU 11 and DNR, and as a consequence any reader who is not already familiar with these texts, and who comes to this chapter in the reasonable expectation of a clear account both of Hume's conclusions about the existence and nature of God and of his reasons for such conclusions, is warned that rather more of it than might have been expected is concerned with questions of interpretation.

The structure of the rest of this chapter is as follows. The first section concerns section 11 of EHU where, in a fictional conversation between a narrator and a friend, Hume gives an argument to show that natural religion has no practical implications for how humans should live. The next section summarizes the first eight parts of DNR, in which the three main characters in the *Dialogues* are introduced and state their initial positions about the scope of natural religion, and debate the strengths and weaknesses of the design argument. (DNR part 9 is a brief examination of another classic argument in natural religion, the cosmological or "first cause" argument, which is presented as an *a priori* argument in contrast to the *a posteriori* design argument. I shall not examine this part of DNR, because to do so requires reference to details of Hume's accounts of the nature of ideas, of meaning, of logic, and of reasoning, which there is not space adequately to do.) I then review the discussion of the problem of evil in parts 10 and 11 of DNR. The discussion here assumes that *a priori* proofs of the infinite power and benevolence of God are unsuccessful, which is why Hume discusses the cosmological argument in part 9 first. I then go on to examine some of the interpretative problems posed by DNR, and especially the puzzling concluding part 12. In conclusion, I briefly make a further proposal about reading Hume on natural religion.

Natural Religion in EHU

The design argument was the argument most favored in the natural theology of Hume's time. It is an *a posteriori* argument based on features of the universe both those that are open to unaided observation and those that are revealed by science. Its dependence on scientific discoveries was what made it especially favored in Hume's time. For its proponents, Newton's laws of motion and his discoveries in the science of optics showed that the universe is anything but chaotic. It is very highly ordered and regular, and governed by a small set of laws expressible in precise, mathematical terms. In many parts, the universe is also purposive. Living things have bodies that are structured and organized in order to enable them to live and flourish within their environments. Some of the purposes of nature are easily observed. But science, by the use of microscopes, reveals the vast extent of purposiveness in the minute structures of plants and animals. It was generally held that all this evidence pointed to just one conclusion. Not only is there a God who created the universe, but this God must be very powerful and also very wise and intelligent. The universe is made by a divine designer; it is the product of a divine mind.

In the traditions of revealed religion such as Christianity, God is not only the designer and maker of the world but is also concerned with the happiness and salvation of human beings. There is not only God's "general providence," his intelligence and design displayed in the laws of nature, but also his "particular providence," his concern with justice and benevolence according to which those who live by God's moral commands will be rewarded with eternal bliss and those who do not will be punished with eternal damnation. It was because of the belief in the particular providence of God and in a "future state," a life after death, that belief in God was seen as essential to the foundations of morality and the well-being of society.

Section 11 of EHU, "Of a Particular Providence and of a Future State," is written as a conversation between a narrator, "I," and a friend who is described as someone "who loves skeptical paradoxes" and who "advanced many principles of which I can by no means approve" but which "seem to be curious, and to bear some relation to the chain of reasoning carried on throughout this enquiry" (EHU 11.1). Here Hume indicates that the antireligious arguments of the friend are consequences of his own epistemological and metaphysical theories developed earlier in EHU.

Speaking through the friend Hume says that the design argument is "the chief or sole argument for a divine existence . . . derived from the order of nature." He says that he will not challenge this inference but he argues that it yields only a strictly limited conclusion. All that can be inferred from the order of nature is that its cause, God, has such attributes as power, intelligence, and design only to the extent needed to explain the effects from which the cause is inferred: "when we infer any particular cause from an effect, we must proportion the one to the other, and can never be allowed to ascribe to the cause any qualities, but what are exactly sufficient to produce the effect" (EHU 11.12). Consequently, the belief that God will eventually in the afterlife reward the virtuous with bliss and punish the vicious with torment gets no support from the design argument, for those divine intentions go beyond the evidence in nature to which the argument appeals. As a result, accepting the design argument gives no reason or motive to pursue virtue and avoid vice, beyond those that experience of life already gives, while rejecting it takes nothing away from those motives and reasons. In this argument, Hume breaks a link between natural and revealed religion.

The narrator challenges the Humean principle invoked by the friend. Suppose there is just one human footprint in the sand. Is it not legitimate to infer, first, that it was caused by a human being and, second, that it is probable there was a footprint of the other foot which has been obliterated? The reply to this is that the second inference depends on knowledge of the anatomy of human beings that was obtained by experience other than just the observation of the one print. But in the case of the inference from nature to a divine designer, there is no other relevant experience to draw on. "The Deity is known to us only by his productions, and is a single being in the universe, not comprehended under any species or genus, from whose experienced attributes or qualities, we can, by analogy, infer any attribute or quality in him" (EHU 11.26).

The section therefore not only limits what can be inferred about the nature of God by the design argument, but also raises the question of whether it has any force at all. This is the main topic of *Dialogues concerning Natural Religion*.

341

The Critique of the Design Argument in DNR

Dialogues concerning Natural Religion is a dialogue between three characters, Cleanthes, Demea, and Philo, whose conversation is reported by a young man, Pamphilus, to a friend, Hermippus. Pamphilus makes a few comments on the debate as it goes along, and writes an introductory letter and supplies a closing comment neither of which represents Hume's own opinions. Despite the use of classical Greek names for the characters, the context is set by early-eighteenth-century debates on the possibility of natural religion.

In part 1 Demea expresses the orthodox view that true religious convictions rest on faith in the traditions of revealed religion, which should be taught to children. Philosophical arguments about the nature of God should be treated with caution because human reason is a weak instrument. Philo gives a brief outline of Hume's mitigated skepticism. In "common life" experience, custom and habit lead us to form beliefs and act upon them even though reason alone cannot answer skeptical doubts about the rational bases of these beliefs. But, he says, the arguments of natural theologians about the nature of God, the origin of the world, and the afterlife are purely speculative and are beyond the scope of the custom, habit, and experience which form and maintain our everyday beliefs. They are therefore always open to skeptical challenges. Cleanthes, in contrast, is optimistic about the possibility of establishing conclusions about the nature of God on the basis of evidence drawn from our experience of the world and our scientific understanding of it. He rejects both Demea's orthodoxy and Philo's skepticism.

The arguments of Philo in DNR are based mainly on Hume's empiricist theory of human thought and reason which limits both to what experience provides. Thought cannot go beyond ideas derived from impressions and reason cannot go beyond the data provided by observation and experiment. Nearly all commentators on DNR agree that Philo's arguments are derived from Hume's philosophy. Gaskin (1988) contains a discussion of the evidence for taking Philo to be Hume's main spokesman. But although this seems to me quite correct, I also think that in interpreting DNR we need to recognize that Hume constructs the drama in such a way that neither Demea nor Cleanthes understands Hume's philosophy, and as a result, neither understands Philo to be a spokesman for Hume's mitigated skepticism. At a number of places Hume has Philo fit in with Demea's and Cleanthes's interpretation of him, and this affects our reading of DNR, especially the rather puzzling last part, as I shall suggest below.

At the start of part 2 Demea uses biblical language to express the orthodox Christian position that God is not *a* being, an entity of a kind, species, or genus, but is infinitely perfect Being, beyond human comprehension. For him, the nature of God is expressed only in the language of faith and revelation, but he does not doubt that there *is* something this language expresses. His doubts about the capacity of human reason to produce a substantive natural theology come from his orthodox religious conception of God as so unlike human minds that reason cannot comprehend him. Philo, in contrast, hints at the view that this language is meaningless because there are no ideas expressed by the terms used for the traditional attributes of God, such as omniscience, omnipotence, and eternity: "Our ideas reach no farther than our experience:

We have no experience of divine attributes and operations: I need not conclude my syllogism" (DNR 142). As he says, "just reasoning" (his own) and "sound piety" (Demea's) "concur in the same conclusion"; but the conclusion is obtained by different means. Demea does not understand Philo, but sees the apparent agreement as indicating that Philo's skepticism is combined with a fideism that accepts traditional religious doctrine.

For Cleanthes, too, Philo is a skeptical fideist, one who combines acceptance of the traditional theism of revealed religion with pyrrhonian skepticism about the capacity of human reason to arrive at truth and reality. Such excessive skepticism, he argues, is inconsistent with accepting, as he knows Philo does, the discoveries in natural philosophy made by Copernicus, Galileo, and Newton. If a skeptic accepts the arguments of natural philosophy, then the skeptic should also accept the design argument because it is an argument of the same form and is, indeed, stronger because simpler and more immediately persuasive than arguments in natural philosophy.

The argument for this, which he gives in part 2, is that science shows that the world is a great machine, composed of parts that are themselves machines, all obeying the same natural laws that constitute the order of nature. Furthermore, many of these parts of nature are "adjusted to each other" in such a way as to achieve the purposes of these machines. The whole world (or universe – Hume often uses these terms interchangeably) displays both order and purposiveness wherever we look. There is therefore a resemblance between the world and its parts, and machines and their parts made by human beings. In the latter cases, order and purposiveness is the effect of the design, thought, wisdom, and intelligence of human beings. The conclusion Cleanthes draws is that, by analogy, "the author of nature is somewhat similar to the mind of man" (DNR 143).

From part 2 to part 8 Philo makes a series of criticisms of this argument, based on Hume's philosophy. At the core of these criticisms is the point already suggested in EHU 11. If we consider the universe as a whole and ask what is the nature of any cause it may have, as something prior to and outside the universe as a whole, then we have no experience on which we can base any conclusion. This universe is the only universe of which we have experience. But all inferences from an effect to a cause depend on previous experience of the causes of similar effects. The features of the universe to which Cleanthes draws attention, order and regularity, and the adaptation of structures to functions ("the adjustment of final causes") are not in themselves "proof of design; but only so far as [they have] been experienced to proceed from that principle" (DNR 146). Consequently, Cleanthes's argument is based on no more than an analogy between the universe and one small part of it, machines made by human beings. The conclusion is therefore no more than a guess or conjecture, not a proof.

The cases of order and purposiveness whose external cause we do know, machines made by the exercise of human intelligence and design, are only a small fraction of those parts of the universe that exhibit order and purposiveness, such as plants and animals. Plants and animals derive these features from their parents through reproduction, where the parents already possess these features. The analogy of the universe with a plant or animal is just as plausible as the analogy Cleanthes makes (DNR, part 7). But if we make the analogy with plants or animals, the argument would suggest

343

that this universe is just one offspring of another that is already ordered and purposive, so the explanation of these features lies in a previous state of affairs that already possesses them. Such an argument does not lead to a God.

Cleanthes seems to be assuming that to infer a cause that is a mind with intelligence and intentions is more explanatory than to infer a previous material universe already ordered and structured. But that tacitly assumes that the order and structure of ideas is inherent to a mind, and so does not need further explanation, whereas the order and structure of any wholly material thing is not inherent to it. But "to say that all this order in animals and vegetables proceeds ultimately from design is begging the question; nor can that great point be ascertained otherwise than by proving *a priori*, both that order is, from its nature, inseparably attached to thought, and that it can never, of itself, or from unknown original principles, belong to matter" (DNR 179).

In part 8 Philo suggests that a wholly material universe might come to be ordered and structured by chance. Suppose that the universe is infinite in time but that there is only a finite stock of elementary particles constantly in motion. In infinite time, we may suppose, all possible configurations of particles are formed and perish many times. Among these configurations, a configuration in which there is order, regularity, and purposiveness might be simply one of the possibilities which, in infinite time, is going to appear. A universe like this one is, therefore, only one possible universe. If the order, regularity, and purposiveness found in it were to be lost, the particles of matter would then become reconfigured in some other perhaps more chaotic state. In such a universe in which order and purposiveness arise from "unguided matter" (DNR 184) it will be pointless to insist on the order and purposiveness found in it as evidence of design, for its parts would not exist in the first place unless they were ordered and purposive.

These criticisms are all based on Hume's theory of causal reasoning. Cleanthes does not accept this theory, rejecting it as excessively skeptical. In part 3 he complains that Philo's objections amount to no more than "perverse, obstinate metaphysics" (DNR 154). He gives two thought experiments that are supposed to show imagined instances where the inference from certain phenomena to an intelligent designing cause would be immediate and compelling, even though Philo's kinds of objections to the design argument could still be made. In fact he thinks that there clearly are such cases in reality. Consider, he says, the anatomy and physiology of an organ like the human eye "and tell me, from your own feeling, if the idea of a contriver does not immediately flow in upon you with a force like that of sensation." His position is that the persuasiveness of the design argument is a matter of "common sense and the plain instincts of nature" (DNR 154). He says that Philo may fault this on the basis of his (Hume's) logic of causal reasoning but insists that such "irregular" arguments will persuade anyone who is not a determined skeptic (DNR 155).

One of the thought experiments Cleanthes uses is the idea of a world in which books are works of nature rather than of human production, things which reproduce themselves like animals and vegetables. They still, however, contain meaningful content in a universal language that everyone can read. No one, he says, would doubt that these natural books are produced by the action of a vast intelligence. Demea objects to the analogy between God and human authors. Human thinking is "fluctuating, uncertain, fleeting, successive, and compounded" (DNR 156), and these features, while essential to what we mean by "mind" and "thought" in the case of human beings, cannot be applied to God, who is traditionally said to be simple and unchanging. In part 4 Cleanthes responds to Demea's "mysticism" by insisting that the only content that can be given to talk of the divine nature is through analogy with the human mind, because a mind "that is wholly simple, and totally immutable . . . in a word, is no mind at all" (DNR 159).

Philo has a further set of criticisms, now based on taking seriously Cleanthes's insistence that the design argument postulates a God whose mind is like a human mind. If God's thought is like human thought, a complex order of different ideas that change over time, then it seems as necessary to ask what causes this thought as it seems necessary to ask what causes the complex and changing order of the material world. Further, if the divine mind is like human minds, there is no ground for ascribing to God infinite or perfect attributes. Yet to postulate a finite God is to invite even further problems. In the human world, large and complex structures are often the product of a number of people working together; often a machine exists and operates long after the original designer is dead; often the best way to make a structure is discovered by trial and error; often a number of different models and prototypes are made before the final version is achieved; and so on. In parts 4 and 5 Philo argues that by insisting on the similarity between human and divine minds Cleanthes becomes unable to rule out that something similar could be true of the creation of the universe.

Cleanthes dismisses all this as "rambling" objections, again showing that he takes Philo to be arguing like a pyrrhonian, simply opposing any argument with a contrary argument. He draws comfort from what he sees as Philo's concession – "a man, who follows your hypothesis, is able, perhaps, to assert or conjecture, that the universe, some time, arose from some thing like design" – and says, "to this concession I adhere steadily; and this I regard as a sufficient foundation for religion" (DNR 169). Thus Cleanthes shows that he misunderstands the nature of Philo's criticisms, and rashly takes Philo's minimal concession of "some thing like design" to be "a sufficient foundation for religion."

The Problem of Evil

Parts 10 and 11 of DNR are concerned with the problem that the existence of natural and moral evil poses for belief in a God who is both almighty and morally perfect. At the start of part 10 Demea and Philo combine to describe the kinds and extent of pains and suffering, that is, natural evils, that afflict both human and other sentient beings, and the kinds of crimes and cruelties, that is, moral evils, that people inflict on each other. Demea does this because for him suffering is not a challenge to the truth of his belief in an omnipotent and benevolent deity; rather that belief offers hope and consolation and the more people are aware of suffering and evil the more they will turn to it. Philo does this because for someone like Cleanthes who claims to rest religious beliefs on evidence drawn from the nature of the world, evil and suffering are a major obstacle, as he intends to make clear.

345

Cleanthes recognizes the challenge: "If you can make out the present point, and prove mankind to be unhappy or corrupted, there is an end at once to all religion" (DNR 199). He at first proposes merely to deny that the evidence is as bad as it looks; in general "health is more common than sickness: pleasure than pain: happiness than misery" (DNR 200). Philo replies that the question of the overall balance between goods and evils is highly uncertain; but the problem for Cleanthes is that if the arguments of natural theology are supposed to prove that the divine attributes are as traditionally stated – "infinite power, infinite wisdom, and infinite goodness" – then the question is not whether good predominates over evil, but "why is there any misery at all in the world?" If God intends there to be suffering and misery, he is not perfectly benevolent. If suffering and misery is contrary to God's intention, he is not infinitely powerful. "Nothing can shake the solidity of this reasoning . . . except we assert, that these subjects exceed all human capacity" (DNR 201). Even if one concedes the inference from the nature of the world to divine power and intelligence, says Philo, and concedes to the natural theologian these "natural attributes," even so "there is no view of human life or of the condition of mankind, from which, without the greatest violence, we can infer the moral attributes, or learn that infinite benevolence, conjoined with infinite power and infinite wisdom, which we must discover by the eyes of faith alone" (DNR 202).

At the start of part 11 Cleanthes makes a concession in his turn. If goodness and justice are to be ascribed to God in anything like the sense they have when ascribed to human beings "we must for ever find it impossible to reconcile any mixture of evil in the universe with infinite attributes; much less can we ever prove the latter from the former" (DNR 203). So, he suggests, the natural theologian would do better by assuming that God's goodness, power, and wisdom are very great but finite. There are limits to what God can do; he may be "limited by necessity" and unable to make a world without natural and moral evil.

Philo shows that this move does not help the natural theologian as much as Cleanthes hopes it does. If necessity of one form or another limits what God can do, then the existence of evil may indeed be consistent with the existence of a good, wise, powerful, but limited God. But this is only speculation, an imagined solution to the problem. The question that a natural theologian must address who argues as Cleanthes does is: what evidence is there that evil is unavoidable? Philo enumerates four circumstances that, he suggests, produce most of the pain and suffering of sentient beings, and argues that none of them appears unavoidable from the point of view of human reason. If, arguing from experience rather than from speculative hypotheses, we have no reason to think that suffering is inevitable, then we have no reason to infer that God is just and good, but limited.

Philo suggests (DNR 212) four hypotheses about the moral attributes of God. (In fact he switches at this point to talking in the plural of "the first causes of the universe" because he wants to give as one of these hypotheses the Manichean theory that the universe is a scene of struggle between a good and an evil deity.) The gods may be perfectly good; or perfectly malicious; or some are good and some malicious; or the gods are indifferent to the happiness or misery of sentient beings. The mixture of good and evil in nature cannot be evidence for either of the first two of these. The third, Manichean, hypothesis is, he says, improbable. His reason for this is "the uniformity and steadiness of [the] general laws" of nature, implying, presumably, that if there is more than one deity, they work together in harmony. This leaves the fourth hypothesis, that God is indifferent to the happiness and misery of his creatures. Finally, Philo applies his argument to virtue and vice, as well as to happiness and misery. Here, too, the conclusion that he thinks a natural theologian like Cleanthes ought to reach is that God is indifferent to vice and virtue. Furthermore, on this argument, God is the ultimate cause of both, a conclusion that is unacceptable to Cleanthes, and horrifies Demea, who leaves the discussion at this point.

Part 12 and the Interpretation of DNR

What were Hume's conclusions about the nature and existence of God? Arriving at an answer is difficult because the main sources we have been examining, section 11 of EHU and DNR, are written in the forms of conversation and dialogue in which the arguments and objections are put into the mouths of fictional characters. Hume, the author, does not speak directly in his own voice. All the same, it is not difficult to identify in both EHU 11 and DNR a number of criticisms of the design argument which are very forceful, summarized above, and of which Hume is the author. Although Hume drew on a number of sources for these arguments, there is no doubt that these powerful criticisms are essentially his creation. In DNR they are mainly voiced by Philo, and so when we consider what were Hume's final conclusions about natural religion it is natural to look to the concluding part of DNR and to what Philo says there. But what we find is initially rather puzzling.

Demea has left, and the final dialogue is between Cleanthes and Philo only. Philo speaks of his intimate friendship with Cleanthes, implying that the conversation is to be carried on in a new register of candor and directness. Immediately, he declares that Cleanthes must know from their close acquaintance that

> no one has a deeper sense of religion impressed on his mind, or pays more profound adoration to the divine being, as he discovers himself to reason, in the inexplicable contrivance and artifice of nature. A purpose, an intention, a design strikes everywhere the most careless, the most stupid thinker. (DNR 214)

This declaration certainly comes as a surprise to the reader, given all that Philo has previously argued, and the shock is intensified in the next paragraph where Philo speaks of the pleasure he takes in a passage from Galen (a Greek authority on medicine writing in the second century AD) in which Galen gives a detailed description of parts of human anatomy and concludes from the complexity of the ways in which structure is adapted to function that the best explanation is that human anatomy is the product of intelligent design. So Philo endorses an argument that is a classic instance of the kind of design argument against which he has put so many objections. Cleanthes is pleased at last to have Philo agree with him that "the comparison of the universe to a machine of human contrivance is so obvious and natural, and is justified by so many instances of order and design in nature, that it must immediately strike all unprejudiced apprehensions, and procure universal approbation" (DNR 216).

The language Cleanthes uses here reminds us of the passages in part 3 where Cleanthes asks Philo to consider the structure and function of the eye and "tell me, from your own feeling, if the idea of a contriver does not immediately flow in upon you with a force like that of a sensation," and suggests that even if this is not a strong argument when judged by logical criteria and is in that sense "irregular," nevertheless its "irresistible influence" makes all objections to it appear simply "cavils." We should also remember that Philo gave no answer to this, and that in part 10 he stated that "in many views of the universe, and of its parts, particularly the latter, the beauty and fitness of final causes strike us with such irresistible force that all objections appear (what I believe they really are) mere cavils and sophisms." There seems to be agreement between the two characters that the design argument's power comes from a "force" that "strikes" the mind with an "irresistible" immediacy like a sensation or feeling. When the mind is so struck, the kinds of objections made by Philo appear merely cavils and sophisms.

What are we to make of this? It was mentioned earlier that Hume intended to disrupt the program of showing that natural religion, revealed religion and ethics cohere together and are supported by philosophical arguments. It seems clear that the arguments of EHU 11 and DNR parts 10 and 11 do show that belief in the providential and morally good Christian God gets no support from philosophy, and there is no reason to think that Hume did not conclude this much. Nor does Philo say anything in DNR part 12 against this conclusion. So much is agreed by many commentators, for example Gaskin (1988), Millican (2002), Penelhum (2000). However, Philo seems in part 12 to accept a belief in a divine intelligence despite all his earlier arguments. Could this also be Hume's conclusion? Is what Philo says at the start of part 12 consistent with Hume's philosophy?

In EHU sections 4 and 5 Hume argues that all reasonings from past experience to predict future events depend on a principle of the uniformity of nature that cannot be established by either *a priori* or *a posteriori* reasoning, but which cannot be abandoned. In THN 4.2 he says something similar about the belief in the distinct and continued existence of the objects of our senses. Beliefs of this kind have come to be referred to by Kemp Smith's phrase "natural beliefs" (Kemp Smith 1941). Hume's mitigated skepticism is partly a matter of showing that not all the beliefs we accept as reasonable can actually be based on reasons, a position that he makes more intelligible by his theory that belief is in the end a certain kind of naturally occurring sentiment or feeling arising in certain circumstances.

In broad terms, this element of Hume's mitigated skepticism raises the question whether, for him, some religious beliefs might fall in the category of natural beliefs. Could it be that, by the agreement he stages between Philo and Cleanthes in part 12, Hume is indicating that the objections to the design argument he gives to Philo are ones that reason cannot answer, but that, as with the natural beliefs in the principle of causal inferences and in the distinct and continued existence of the objects of the senses, the belief in a divine power and intelligence is irresistible and unaffected by arguments that then appear merely skeptical? Butler (1960), Penelhum (1979), and Tweyman (1991) all give substantial and illuminating readings to try to show that this is indeed Hume's view.

However Gaskin (1974, 1978, 1988) shows that there are at least two strong reasons why the belief in an intelligent designer on which Cleanthes and Philo appear to agree would not have been classed by Hume as a natural belief. Gaskin says that the belief in a divine designer that Philo eventually accepts is one that is so heavily qualified and limited that it amounts to no more than what he calls "minimal deism," but it is a belief based on analogical reasoning of the kind Cleanthes gives and in that way is a rational not a natural belief. Penelhum (1983) accepts Gaskin's arguments against taking the belief to be a Humean natural belief, as against his view in Penelhum (1979), but still finds a puzzle. If Philo's acceptance of minimal deism is based on analogical reasoning, this is reasoning that he has already shown to be seriously flawed. In Penelhum's words, "In the case of divine intelligence, the theist has merely to refer us once again to the intricacies of nature, and it is as though we had never heard how inadequate a reason they give us to infer it." A belief that is a conclusion from reasoning that the believer simultaneously judges to be too weak to support the conclusion is, Penelhum suggests, "an anomaly in Hume's system" and to call it "rational" as Gaskin does is questionable.

Gaskin's response to Penelhum is to separate the design *argument* from what he calls a *feeling for design*, which is a feeling of wonder and admiration at the intricacies of nature that finds expression in the idea of an intelligent designer. This feeling, he insists, is not a natural belief, and is not universal. It is what moves Philo at the start of part 12 to endorse Galen's praise of the divine designer. But later in part 12 Philo gives his considered judgment of what the design *argument* shows, and here he does accept that on balance divine design is more probable than not. In reply to Penelhum, therefore, Gaskin claims that Philo does *not* think that his earlier criticisms have shown that the design argument is totally flawed, so his belief is rational, and is not an anomaly in Hume's system (Gaskin 1988).

Conclusion

Although Philo is evidently Hume's hero, and in that sense speaks for Hume, I do not think that in reading DNR we are required to make everything Philo says cohere with Hume's philosophy. We can also consider Philo as he is understood within the drama of the *Dialogues*, that is, how he is understood and his arguments interpreted by the others and by Pamphilus, the person who, within the work, is its author and makes occasional authorial comments. Pamphilus is Cleanthes's pupil, who accepts his views as more authoritative than those of the others. Pamphilus's opening letter to Hermippus asserts that Philo is a "careless skeptic," meaning, I suggest, a pyrrhonian skeptic, able and willing to argue both pro and con, careless of which side he argues precisely because he aims to produce a total suspension of judgment. Presumably Pamphilus here repeats what Cleanthes, his teacher, has told him. In part 1 Cleanthes claims that Philo proposes "to erect religious faith on philosophical skepticism" and he follows this with criticisms of the "ridiculous . . . principles of the ancient Pyrrhonians" (DNR 132–3), which are close to Hume's own criticisms of pyrrhonism in EHU section 12. Philo replies with a brief explanation of Hume's mitigated skepticism, but this seems to be too subtle for Cleanthes. His speech to Demea shows him lumping together academic and pyrrhonian skepticism, and complaining of the use made of ancient skepticism by fideists such as Bayle. He cannot see any significant difference between pyrrhonian skepticism and the Humean mitigated skepticism that Philo actually expresses, and he takes Philo to be a skeptical fideist somewhat in the style of Bayle.

Nothing Philo says ever changes Cleanthes' opinion that Philo is just a careless skeptic whose objections are, however unanswerable, in reality no more than "whimsies" that "may puzzle, but never can convince us" (DNR 181). It is, I suggest, part of Hume's strategy to maintain this space between the mainly Humean position that Philo's speeches for the most part express and the skeptical fideism that Cleanthes, with Pamphilus dutifully echoing him, ascribes to Philo and in terms of which he understands him. This sets the scene for the conversation in part 12, which opens with Philo referring to how intimately he and Cleanthes know each other, and how there is no real danger that his intentions in arguing as he has done will be misunderstood. He implies not only that he is now to deliver his true opinions but that his close friend Cleanthes has been right all along in his view of him.

He therefore plays the part of the pyrrhonian, suddenly arguing as strongly for a divine designer as he has previously argued against. Hume lets us know that Philo is playing a role here by his choice of the passage about Galen and human anatomy. As Rivers (1993) has shown, Hume has taken this instance of the design argument from a book by John Wilkins, *Of the Principles and Duties of Natural Religion*, published in 1675 and reissued nine times up to 1734. Hume gives to Philo a classic and widely admired statement of the design argument in a form that was then taken to be extremely persuasive. A Humean mitigated skeptic could not employ such an argument, but a skeptical fideist such as Bayle could. As Labrousse (1983) says, Bayle

> continues to use the time-honoured a posteriori argument which proves God's existence from the order and beauty of the Creation. The Heavens proclaim the glory of God, and the universal clock attests the existence of the Clockmaker. Bayle is aware that this is not a rigorous logical proof, but he sees it as a persuasive one. Above all it has the advantage in his eyes of refuting the kind of materialist argument which ascribes the order of the cosmos to pure chance. In other words, it is not so much a positive proof as one that negates a particular form of atheism. This, however, is characteristic of philosophical proofs. Since God is the object of faith, only a revelation can positively assure us of his existence.

The paragraph that follows the passage from Wilkins about Galen is further evidence that Philo is playing the part of a skeptical fideist, regarding the design argument as rhetorically persuasive rather than logically rigorous, and using it against dogmatic atheists. Every instance of apparent design in nature counts as "an argument" and there are therefore innumerably many such arguments: "no human imagination can compute their number, and no understanding estimate their cogency" (DNR 216). This is an unusual sense of "argument" but it fits, I think, the pyrrhonian idea of reasoning as persuasive rather than leading to truth. I am proposing, then, that in part 12 Hume has Philo play along with Cleanthes's assumption that he is a skeptical fideist, leading up to his closing remark, made for the benefit of Pamphilus, that "to be a philosophical skeptic is, in a man of letters, the first and most essential step towards being a sound, believing Christian" (DNR 228).

I say that Philo only plays along with the role that is assigned to him internally within the *Dialogues* because he does not, in fact, suggest that the outcome of the debate is a pyrrhonian suspense of judgment leaving room for true faith that comes from God's grace, although he pretends to have concluded this. Instead he concludes that the debate between theist and atheist is "merely verbal, or, perhaps, if possible, still more incurably ambiguous" (DNR 218). At the end of part 12 Philo reduces "the whole of natural theology" to the proposition "that the cause or causes of order in the universe probably bear some remote analogy to human intelligence" (DNR 227). So I agree with Blackburn (1999) that when Philo says that the dispute is merely verbal, he means that whether or not this proposition is said to express theism, deism, atheism, or agnosticism is itself purely verbal, and that it is therefore a proposition which no skeptic (whether pyrrhonian or mitigated) will think worth contesting.

My reading of part 12 claims that Hume has Philo play along with a role assigned to him internally within the work. But I have not speculated about why Hume should have done this. It seems to me possible that the way in which Philo is never fully understood by the others may itself enact something of Hume's own experience in the difficulties he encountered in getting his philosophy properly understood by his contemporaries. Here I think the interesting discussion of these questions in Penelhum (2000) and in his chapter in this volume gets us a long way. Perhaps Hume's own views cannot be fully ascertained from his writings. However, it is with Hume's writings rather than with his personal biography that philosophers must be concerned. As with all great philosophical writings, they do not constrain us to a single interpretation.

See also 17 "Hume's Views on Religion: Intellectual and Cultural Influences"; 19 "Hume on Miracles and Immortality"

Acknowledgment

I am grateful to the Arts and Humanities Research Council for a research leave award during which this chapter was written.

References

Blackburn, Simon (1999). "Playing Hume's Hand," in D. Z. Phillips and Timothy Tessin (eds.), *Religion and Hume's Legacy* (Basingstoke and New York: Macmillan and St. Martin's Press).

Butler, R. J. (1960). "Natural Belief and the Enigma of Hume," *Archiv für Geschichte der Philosophie*, 42, pp. 73–100.

Gaskin, John (1974). "God, Hume and Natural Belief," *Philosophy*, 49, pp. 281–94.

—— (1978). *Hume's Philosophy of Religion*, 1st edn. (Basingstoke: Macmillan).

—— (1988). *Hume's Philosophy of Religion*, 2nd edn. (Basingstoke: Macmillan).

Hume, David (1779). *Dialogues concerning Natural Religion*, ed. Norman Kemp Smith (Indianapolis, IN: Bobbs-Merrill, 1963). (Cited as DNR.)

Kemp Smith, Norman (1941). *The Philosophy of David Hume* (London and New York: Macmillan and St. Martin's Press).

Labrousse, Elisabeth (1983). *Bayle* (Oxford and New York: Oxford University Press).

Millican, Peter (2002). "The Context, Aims and Structure of Hume's First *Enquiry*," in Peter Millican (ed.), *Reading Hume on Human Understanding* (Oxford: Clarendon Press).

Moore, James (2000). "Hutcheson's Theodicy: The Argument and the Contexts of *A System of Moral Philosophy*," in Paul Wood (ed.), *The Scottish Enlightenment: Essays in Reinterpretation* (Rochester, NY: University of Rochester Press), pp. 239–66.

Penelhum, Terence (1979). "Hume's Scepticism and the *Dialogues*," in David Fate Norton, Wade Robison, and Nicholas Capaldi (eds.), *McGill Hume Studies* (San Diego: Austin Hill Press).

—— (1983). "Natural Belief and Religious Belief in Hume's Philosophy," *Philosophical Quarterly*, 33, pp. 266–82.

—— (2000). *Themes in Hume* (Oxford: Clarendon Press).

Rivers, Isabel (1993). " 'Galen's Muscles': Wilkins, Hume, and the Educational Use of the Argument from Design," *Historical Journal*, 36, pp. 577–98.

—— (2000). *Reason, Grace, and Sentiment: A Study of the Language of Religion and Ethics in England 1660–1780*, vol. 2 (Cambridge: Cambridge University Press).

Ross, Ian (2000). "The Natural Theology of Lord Kames," in Paul Wood (ed.), *The Scottish Enlightenment: Essays in Reinterpretation* (Rochester, NY: University of Rochester Press).

Tweyman, Stanley (1991). "Introduction," in Stanley Tweyman (ed.), *David Hume: Dialogues concerning Natural Religion in Focus* (London and New York: Routledge).

Further Reading

Gaskin, John (1993). "Hume on Religion," in David Fate Norton (ed.), *The Cambridge Companion to Hume* (Cambridge: Cambridge University Press).

Noxon, James (1976). "Hume's Concern with Religion," in K. R. Merrill and R. S. Shahan (eds.), *David Hume: Many-sided Genius* (Norman, OK: University of Oklahoma Press).

O'Connor, David (2001). *Hume on Religion* (London: Routledge).

Oppy, Graham (1996). "Hume and the Argument for Biological Design," *Biology and Philosophy*, 11, pp. 519–34.

Swinburne, Richard (1991). *The Existence of God*, revised edn. (Oxford: Clarendon Press).

19

Hume on Miracles and Immortality

MICHAEL P. LEVINE

Context: Irrelevant and Relevant

A great deal of scholarship has gone in to situating Hume's writings on religion in various contexts – historical, cultural, religious, and personal. As interesting as this may be, none of it is necessary for understanding Hume's argument in part 1 "Of Miracles" against justified belief in miracles. The substance of Hume's argument is independent of contexts that many have claimed essential to its understanding. Nevertheless, one cannot read Hume's essay like you are reading the morning paper and hope to understand it. The context essential to its interpretation is Hume's own metaphysics – his account of *a posteriori* reasoning, which ultimately rests on his empiricism. The following explanation of Hume's argument supports these views.

Instead of reiterating historicist scholarship, I begin by locating Hume's writings on religion in what is in my view the context of *most* contemporary western analytic philosophy of religion. This will not help in interpreting Hume's argument, but it does heighten the contrast between Hume's achievements and contemporary ones, as well as between Hume's understanding of natural as opposed to revealed theology, and contemporary views where the two are purposefully, sometimes artfully, jumbled for religious, even evangelical, purposes. It is worth noting that contemporary Christian analytic philosophers of religion not only believe that we can justifiably believe in miracles – so do I, *in principle* – but they also believe miracles have occurred.

Philosophy of religion is now dominated by Christian fundamentalists (or close to it) like Alvin Plantinga, Richard Swinburne, R. M. Adams, William Alston, Nicholas Wolterstorff, John Haldane, and Peter van Inwagen. Such philosophy of religion rejects views central to contemporary biblical hermeneutics and religious studies. They are mostly at odds with non-fundamentalist theologians. Haldane and Van Inwagen are *creationists*, though neither explicitly acknowledges this. Wolterstorff defends the acceptability of the belief that God literally speaks though scripture. Van Inwagen (1995: 100, n. 4, 106; Levine 2000) believes in our descent from Adam and Eve. And Haldane has a view of how scripture came to be in its current form that was repudiated by biblical scholars in the nineteenth century, and is utterly at odds with contemporary biblical scholarship – a fact he does not acknowledge. He thinks the New Testament was written shortly after the time of Jesus by those who received the stories from eyewitnesses who relayed them (more or less) truthfully and accurately for no other purpose then to tell it like it was. Incidentally, comparative philosophy of religion is no antidote to such philosophy of religion since it too is engaged in apologetics.

While Hume's *Dialogues concerning Natural Religion* is often regarded as the single greatest work in natural theology, the distinction between natural theology or religion (enquiry into religion based on reason apart from revelation) and revealed religion (enquiry into religion based in part on revelation), is a distinction that contemporary philosophers of religion seek to undermine on philosophical grounds. However, the most general way in which they undermine it is to hold firm – *no matter what* – to "revealed truths," and then construct intricate, sometimes fanciful, and at times intriguing arguments that could *possibly* be true given their inviolable premises. Thus, Van Inwagen will allow no evil, no matter what kind or how much of it, to count in any way whatsoever in any degree against the claim that God exists, or if he exists, is omniscient, omnipotent, and perfectly good. For Van Inwagen, Plantinga, Swinburne, etc., there really is no problem of evil, whether logical, empirical, or existential – just a bit of a puzzle.

Anthony Flew (1955) was on to something when he noticed the tendency on the part of some believers not to allow anything to count against certain assertions about God, and therefore claimed that their assertions about God "died the death of a thousand qualifications." In arguing their case with regards to the problem of evil the new fundamentalists seem unaware that their position is in contrast to classical religious (Christian, Jewish, Islam, Hindu) positions on the matter – that the existence of evil is a *mystery* given the nature of God. It is incomprehensible, at least in this world, why God allows the kinds and amounts of evil undeniably present in the world. *Job*, and also Dostoyevski, in *The Brothers Karamazov*, and Hume, all see evil as a problem *for the believer as a believer*. It is not something solvable by asserting the omniscience of God or value of human freedom. It is in the context of contemporary philosophy of religion that Hume's *Dialogues concerning Natural Religion*, "Of Miracles," and "Of the Immortality of the Soul" should be read. The juxtaposition is stark. Whereas contemporary philosophy of religion, as described above, relies on revelation, Hume was a natural theologian through and through.

Hume's Argument against Justified Belief in Miracles Explained

The *locus classicus* for modern and contemporary philosophical discussion of miracles is chapter 10 ("Of Miracles") of David Hume's *Enquiry concerning Human Understanding* (1748). He says "A miracle may accurately be defined, *a transgression of a law of nature by a particular volition of the Deity, or by the interposition of some invisible agent*" (EHU 10.12n23). His slightly different definition of a miracle as "a violation of the laws of nature" is central to his argument against justified belief in miracles. "A miracle is a violation of the laws of nature; and as a firm and unalterable experience has established these laws, the proof against a miracle, from the very nature of the fact, is as entire as any argument from experience can possibly be imagined" (EHU 10.12).

"Of Miracles" is probably the most widely discussed essay ever in philosophy of religion, and the vast majority of that discussion is critical. Many commentators claim that the essay is ambiguous at key points. Thus, the most straightforward question as to whether or not Hume concludes that one could ever be justified in believing in a miracle on the basis of testimony is subject to dispute. I find Hume's essay neither ambiguous nor successful. In part 1 of the essay he is indeed arguing, *a priori*, that one can never be so justified. Hume's position on miracles cannot be understood apart from his account of causation, *a posteriori* reasoning, and the most fundamental elements of his empiricism – his analysis of "impressions" and "ideas" (T 1.1.1). Hume's essay has been contextualized in various ways, but never in the most important way – in the context of the *Treatise* – apart from which it is virtually unintelligible. (I draw on my previous interpretations of Hume [Levine 2002; 1996; 1989; 1988a; 1988b; 1984].)

Gaskin (1993: 317) says that Hume "excised . . . some version of 'Of Miracles' . . . and possibly some version of 'Of the Immortality of the Soul'" from the *Treatise* (1739–40) before publication. See Wootton (1990: 199). R. M. Burns (1981: 133) cites a passage from a letter of Hume's to George Campbell (1762) whose *Dissertation on Miracles* was a reply to Hume. It shows that Hume took his argument against miracles to be integrally connected with the *Treatise*. Hume writes:

> It may perhaps amuse you to learn the first hint, which suggested to me that argument which you have so strenuously attacked. I was walking in the cloisters of the Jesuits College at La Fleche . . . engaged in conversation with a Jesuit . . . who was relating to me, and urging some nonsensical miracle performed in their convent, when I was tempted to dispute against him; and as my head was full of the topics of my *Treatise of Human Nature*, which I was at that time composing, this argument immediately occurred to me.

Burns (1981: 140–1) sees Hume's argument as not especially original – the same argument occurring in earlier writers Hume may have read. If the thesis that Hume's essay *must* be interpreted in the context of his theory of *a posteriori* reasoning is correct, then his argument in part 1 is highly – *completely* – original.

Burns argues that some allegedly problematic passages in Hume's essay, should be interpreted as ironic or sarcastic (chs. 6–7); most notably where Hume (EHU 10.13) says "If the falsehood of his testimony would be more miraculous than the event which he relates; then, and not till then, can he pretend to command my belief or opinion." He also argues (ch. 7), contrary to Flew (1967), that Hume's argument in part 1 is *a priori*; and contrary to Gaskin (1978), that Hume intended his argument to apply to cases of seeing a miracle as well as to belief based on testimony (295, n.120). On all of these points I agree. Burns is the only author I know of who also contends that Hume's argument against miracles is, in a sense, superfluous given his view that divine activity is impossible to know. However, he does not see how this view, aside from logically pre-empting Hume's *a priori* argument, also plays a crucial role in it. If, contrary to Hume's empiricism, it were possible to know divine activity as such, then it would be possible to justifiably believe a miracle.

Miracles and laws of nature

Hume's argument against miracles, as well as much subsequent discussion, depends heavily on the premise that "a miracle is a violation of the laws of nature." However, the role such a premise plays in Hume's argument, and whether he meant to define a miracle as a violation of a law of nature, or merely to characterize it, in some epistemologically relevant sense, as "contrary" to the ordinary course of nature, is controversial. It is clear, however, that on most commonsense *or* "scientific" accounts of what a law of nature is, miracles are not violations of laws but are instead positive instances of them. This is because laws of nature do not, and are not meant to, account for or describe events with supernatural causes – but only those with natural causes. If an event is assumed to have a supernatural cause, it is, by that very fact, outside the scope of laws of nature and so cannot violate them. Only if one disregards the possibility of supernatural causes can exceptions to laws be regarded as violations of laws (Levine 1989: ch. 6; 1996). However, in such a case, and this is relevant to Hume's argument in part 1, there might be better reason to suppose that the exception shows that what was taken to be a law is not really a law, rather than that the exception is a violation of a genuine law of nature. A miracle should not be understood as a violation of the laws of nature in a technical sense. But this does not undermine the possibility of a miracle, since the crucial element in the notion of a miracle of "a supernatural interference with the natural order" is not ruled out in showing that a miracle cannot, strictly speaking, be a violation of a law of nature.

If "violation" is not being used in a technical sense, then a miracle can still be described as a violation of a law of nature – where "violation" would mean "contrary to what could have happened had nature been the only force operative." An event may be contrary to a law of nature without invalidating it if it is caused by non-natural forces, or in epistemic terms, if its occurrence can only be correctly explained in terms of non-natural forces. Even if the laws of nature were logically necessary, there could be events contrary to those laws once it is assumed that the scope of those laws is limited.

A violation of a law of nature by *natural* means is what should be taken, normatively, as a contradiction in terms – assuming insistence on generality (i.e., non-local empirical terms) in the statement of the law. One does not want to hold the occurrence of an event contrary to a law of nature due to non-natural means as a contradiction – at least not on the basis of an analysis of laws of nature. To hold this position, an analysis of laws would have to be combined with an argument against the possibility of non-naturally caused events. (This is more or less what occurs in Hume's argument in part 1. His empiricism and theory of meaning are the basis of his implicit rejection of the possibility of an event being supernaturally caused.) To say that miracles are imposs-ible *because* violations of laws of nature are impossible is to improperly assume either: (1) that a miracle must involve a violation of a law; or (2) that nothing contrary to a law of nature can occur because laws of nature circumscribe what is possible. But apart from distinct arguments to the contrary – for example, an argument against the pos-sibility of non-natural interference – neither assumption is *prima facie* warranted.

Belief in a miracle assumes that God caused an event that is not the sort of occur-rence that can be satisfactorily explained in terms of laws of nature. I am here suppos-ing supernatural explanation to be a viable alternative, and one that might plausibly be chosen in a case like the Red Sea parting as depicted in the movie *The Ten Commandments* (i.e., not simply a low tide). If causal statements did require refer-ence to laws of nature, then this would appear to rule out the possibility of miracles, since a miracle refers to a type of causal statement whose nature rules out reference to laws of nature taken as generalized cases of which they are instances. (John Locke [1706] denies that miracles are not instances of laws. They are not, however, instances of laws of nature according to Locke. He thinks that to say they are not instances of any laws whatsoever [e.g., not even of supernatural laws] is to say that they are random occurrences, and he thinks that this is absurd.) Miracles are contrary to laws of nature, *not* "violations" of them and *not* instances of them. Actually, miracles are *vacuous* instances of true laws of nature (Levine 1989: 72–5). Note that it is not simply a miracle's *uniqueness* that rules out reference to laws, since even repeatable miracles, such as raising one from the dead, cannot in principle refer to laws of nature for a complete explanation. They must also refer to divine intervention. Flew (1967: 349) may be right in his claim that "it be neither arbitrary nor irrational to insist on a definition of a law of nature such that the idea of a miracle as an exception to a law of nature is ruled out as self-contradictory." But this has nothing – nothing at all – to do with Hume's argument. A miracle is not self-contradictory according to Hume, nor should it be understood technically as a violation of a law.

If the explanation (below) of Hume's argument against belief in miracles is correct, then the premise that "a miracle is a violation of a law of nature" plays no significant role in his argument. The premise is a gloss for the underlying supposition that one cannot have an "impression" of a supernatural event. Because no such impression can be had, any allegedly miraculous event, simply because it is allegedly miraculous, cannot *ex hypothesi* be judged relevantly similar to any other event in experience. And *any* event that cannot be judged relevantly similar to others in our collective experience cannot *justifiably* be believed to have occurred in accordance with Hume's principles of *a posteriori* reasoning. Nor can one justifiably believe, with any degree of probability whatsoever, that such an event will occur.

Hume's argument against justified belief in miracles

Remarkably, the philosophical discussion of Hume on miracles has not been principally concerned with whether Hume was correct. It has focused instead on exegetical issues. There is, for example, no generally accepted view on whether his argument (in part 1) against justified belief in miracles is (1) an *a priori* or *a posteriori* argument; or (2) if that argument can be, or is meant to be, generalized to include first-hand experience of an alleged miracle. (For a defense of the view that Hume's argument in part 1 is meant to be *a priori* see Levine [1989: 13–14]. If the argument in part 1 is meant to be *a priori*, then part 2 of the essay appears to be superfluous. But the reasons against belief in miracles Hume gives in part 2 can be seen as additional arguments – though they also support some of his reasoning in part 1.) Hume does not appear to claim that miracles are impossible. In fact he explicitly denies this. However, some interpreters have sought to show that miracles are impossible according to Hume, given what he says in his essay in relation to his wider empiricist views. These conundrums must be dealt with in the context of an explanation of his argument in part 1.

Hume's position on miracles cannot be properly understood apart from his analysis of causation, *a posteriori* reasoning, and the most fundamental element of his empiricism – his analysis of "impressions" and "ideas" (T 1.1.1). The argument hinges on making these connections explicit, and to understand it the following question must be answered. Why did Hume think that under certain circumstances one could justifiably believe that an extraordinary event had occurred, but that under identical circumstances one could never justifiably believe a miracle had occurred? The proposed interpretation of Hume's argument in relation to his account of causation and empiricism yields the only plausible answer. It also shows why it makes no substantial difference whether we interpret Hume's argument in part 1, against justified belief in the miraculous based on testimony, as an *a priori* or *a posteriori* argument since the arguments essentially coalesce.

Hume (EHU 10.36) gives the following example of an extraordinary event he thinks could be rendered credible on the basis of testimony.

> suppose, all authors, in all languages, agree, that from the first day of JANUARY 1600, there was a total darkness over the whole earth for eight days: Suppose that the tradition of this extraordinary event is still strong and lively among the people: That all travellers, who return from foreign countries, bring us accounts of the same tradition, without the least variation or contradiction: It is evident, that our present philosophers, instead of doubting the fact, ought to receive it as certain, and ought to search for the causes whence it might be derived. The decay, corruption, and dissolution of nature, is an event rendered probable by so many analogies, that any phaenomenon, which seems to have a tendency towards that catastrophe, comes within the reach of human testimony, if that testimony be very extensive and uniform.

Not only is testimony to the alleged event "very extensive and uniform," but also to justifiably believe it Hume thinks it necessary that our past experience must not render the event completely improbable. Assuming it is testified to extensively and uniformly, he claims the eight-day darkness can be "rendered probable by so many analogies." In such a case Hume assumes that the event is natural and that "we ought to search for the causes." Hume immediately compares this with another imaginary case (EHU 10.37).

> suppose, that all historians who treat of ENGLAND, should agree, that, on the first of JANUARY 1600, QUEEN ELIZABETH died . . . and that, after being interred a month, she again appeared, resumed the throne, and governed ENGLAND for three years: I must confess that I should be surprized at the concurrence of so many odd circumstances, but should not have the least inclination to believe so miraculous an event.

Since both events are assumed to be more or less equally well testified to, the reason Hume thinks the former can be judged credible, *but not the latter*, is that the former "event is rendered probable by so many analogies." (Some claim that Hume does not see this later event is not as equally well testified to. If that were the case, Hume would have said so in no uncertain terms. But the supposition that they are equally well testified to is also supported by my interpretation of Hume's argument.) Perhaps this appears to be little more than a subjective judgment by Hume. His experience suggests analogies for the former type of event but not the latter. The eight-day darkness "sufficiently resembles" events Hume has experienced, or believes in on the basis of experience, to warrant belief in it given that the event is particularly well attested to. In the latter case (Elizabeth), Hume can find no analogies to draw upon from experience. Given the similarity in relevant respects of most people's experience, Hume thinks that if people base their judgments on their experience (in accordance with his principles of *a posteriori* reasoning [Levine 1989: 5–12] extrapolated from his analysis of causation), they will agree that the former *extraordinary* alleged event can be judged credible, but not what would be the *miraculous* latter event. Hume would agree that if an individual's experience were very different from his own in relevant respects, then that individual could justifiably believe things that he himself could not.

So Hume claims that evidence may justify belief in the occurrence of an extraordinary event as long as we have experienced events analogous in type. However, an extraordinary event is not necessarily a miraculous one. In the case of extraordinary events that are well attested to and for which we have suitable experiential analogies, Hume thinks that the most we are justified in believing is that the event did occur – but *not* that the event is a miracle. We are to "search for the [natural] causes whence it might be derived." Such cases may require us to reassess our estimation of what nature is capable of. Sometimes laws of nature must be reassessed and altered in light of new experience. Also, we must be careful not to extend our judgments as to what to believe or expect of nature to situations where the relevant circumstances are not the same. This requires explanation.

Hume relates the case of the Indian who refused to believe that water turned to ice. According to Hume, the Indian "reasoned justly" on the basis of his past experience. He refused, at first, to believe that water turned to ice, despite the fact that it was well attested to, because the event had the Indian's "constant and uniform experience to count against it, and it also "bore so little analogy to that experience (EHU 10.10). The Indian "reasoned justly" but he extended his judgments about water to cases where all the circumstances were not the same, the relevant circumstance here being temperature. In certain situations in which we hear testimony to extraordinary events we may be in situations similar to that of the Indian. Indeed, according to Hume, if we justifiably believe that an extraordinary event did occur, then we *should* assume that we are in a situation like that of the Indian. We should assume this because, as I shall show, there are compelling reasons why the consistent Humean, in accordance with his principles of *a posteriori* reasoning, his analysis of causation, and his empiricism, can do nothing else. The extraordinary event should be judged "[not] contrary to uniform experience of the course of nature in cases where all the circumstances are the same" (EHU 10.10n22).

Why should we judge our situation to be like that of the Indian's? Hume does not explicitly say, but it must be because our experience has shown us that situations like the Indian's arise. On the basis of *experience*, when we are justified in believing in the occurrence of an extraordinary event, we should liken ourselves to the Indian. That is why, in a case like the eight days of darkness, "we ought to search for the [*natural*] causes whence it might be derived." Experience demands it. According to Hume, when an extraordinary event is extraordinarily well attested to we have two options. One is to accept the testimony and look for the event's natural causes. The other is to reject the testimony on the grounds that the event testified to bears no *significant* analogy to events experienced.

If we reason in accordance with the principles of *a posteriori* reasoning – a type of causal reasoning, according to Hume, he thinks that testimony, no matter how reliable, *can never* warrant belief in a miracle. He says (EHU 10.5), "It being a general maxim, that no objects have any discoverable connexion together, and that all the inferences, which we can draw from one to another, are founded merely on our experience of their constant and regular conjunction; it is evident, that we ought not to make an exception to this maxim in favour of human testimony." Thus, Hume thinks that if we justifiably accept testimony to an extraordinary event, then on the basis of past experience, we must liken ourselves to the Indian and search for its natural causes. This would be for us the equivalent of the Indian moving north to "Muscovy during the winter" (EHU 10.10n22). Underlying Hume's argument is his insistence that his principles of reasoning about empirical matters, and his philosophical empiricism – based in turn on his theory of "impressions" and "ideas" – show that supernatural explanation cannot be justified experientially.

We need to ask: What is it about experience, in the sense of expectations about future events, or judgments about past ones, that could justify the positing of a supernatural cause? Positing such a cause is necessary if one is to justifiably believe an event to be a miracle. For Hume, positing such a cause is speculative and can have no basis in experience. Even if some event really were a miracle, whether a resurrection, or "the raising of a feather, when the wind wants ever so little of a force requisite for that purpose" (EHU 10.12n23), we would not be justified in believing that it was anything more than an extraordinary event. Extraordinary events are at the limits of our experience, the supernatural beyond it. Hume (EHU 10.38) says:

> Though the Being, to whom the miracle is ascribed, be . . . Almighty, it [the miracle] does not, upon that account, become a whit more probable, since it is impossible for us to know the attributes or actions of such a Being, otherwise than from the experience of his productions, in the usual course of nature. This still reduces us to repeat observations, and obliges us to compare the instances of the violation of truth in the testimony of men with those of the violations of the laws of nature by miracles, in order to judge which of them is most likely and probable.

For Hume, a "cause," insofar as it can be used as an item in reasoning from experience, can only be something that we can have an "impression" of. The cause of a miracle would have to be identified as something we could perceive, even if we were to attribute it speculatively (nonempirically) to God. The "cause" of Lazarus's coming forth from the grave would have to be identified with Christ's beckoning – either his voice or some physical gesture – both of which we have "impressions" of and both of which are events "in the usual course of nature."

If a resurrection were well enough attested to warrant belief, then that event could still only be assigned status as an extraordinary event with a natural explanation. Hume is thus constrained by his empiricism. He is constrained in such a way that had he been at the shore of the Red Sea with Moses when they were being chased (as in the C. B. De Mille movie version); and had Moses raised his staff and the Red Sea split up the middle (no low tide but raging waters on both sides); and had the Red Sea crashed to a close the moment the last Israelite was safe – killing those in pursuit – and had Hume lacked grounds for assuming he was hallucinating or perceiving events in any way other than as they were actually happening, Hume would still be constrained by his principles to deny that what he was witnessing was a miracle. This example suffices to show the unacceptability of Hume's argument. Indeed, assuming Hume would have agreed that had he been there with Moses, and had events transpired in a manner suitably similar to the way they are depicted in the film, then he would have (readily) agreed that he was justified in believing a miracle occurred; then his argument against justified belief in miracles can be used as a *reductio ad absurdum*.

A resurrection could only be well enough attested to be justifiably believed if it could be judged somehow analogous with something in past experience. If it is, then it must be considered a natural event because, for Hume, anything analogous to our experience is at least analogous in the sense of suggesting that it too has a natural cause. We experience only what occurs in nature and judgments based on that experience cannot warrant positing causes outside of that experience. Suppose some event actually was supernaturally caused. (Let us suppose Hume recognizes this as a logical possibility in his essay, though I do not think it is given his analysis of causation and his empiricism.) Hume would say that we could not, on the basis of experience, attribute a supernatural cause to the event because we experience only natural causes (i.e., events occurring in the usual course of nature). If an event were supernaturally caused we could legitimately say that we "experienced" some supernatural event, but the sense of experience used here would be an equivocation on Hume's usage. This "cause," being transcendent, and not discernible by means of "sense impressions," "internal impressions," or "impressions of reflexion" could not be an item of experience at all as Hume sees it. Thus, because Hume thinks that every cause must be regarded as natural, he is committed to the view that one *could* justifiably believe that an extraordinary event had occurred, but *never* a miracle.

Hume's *a priori* argument against justified belief in miracles actually coalesces with his *a posteriori* argument. On *a posteriori* grounds we could never justifiably believe testimony to the miraculous because we could never judge the occurrence of such an event to be similar, in relevant respects, to anything we have experienced. However, that a miraculous occurrence could never be judged relevantly similar to anything in experience (i.e., that there must be "a firm and unalterable experience" counting against belief in it) is something we can know *a priori*, since *a priori* we know that we cannot have an "impression" of a supernatural cause. It follows from this that, for Hume, we can also rule out the possibility of justified belief in the miraculous, either from testimony or from first hand experience, on *a priori* grounds.

It follows from what has been said that unless one accepts Hume's analysis of *a posteriori* reasoning as a type of causal reasoning, and also accepts his analysis of causation that ultimately rests on his theory of impressions and ideas – a theory that even staunch empiricists should reject as simplistic – there is no reason to accept *his* argument against the possibility of justified belief in miracles.

Of course, nothing in this critique of Hume's argument should be taken to suggest that miracles have ever occurred, or that we are justified in believing that any have occurred. Some of Hume's arguments in part 2 of his essay are problematic, but the reasons he gives for rejecting reports of miracles are more or less sound and more or less common sense. The arguments he gives here are the kinds of reasons, based on experience, why people do reject reports of miracles. But it would be surprising if some people at some time and in certain circumstances have not been, and will not again be, justified in believing in the occurrence of a miracle. However, nothing I have said suggests that the evidence available for the occurrence of any alleged miracle warrants justified belief in miracles for most people – including those who believe in them.

Bayesian analyses of Hume's argument concerning miracles

Bayesian analyses are prominent among recent and allegedly novel interpretations of Hume's argument. Bayes's theorem is a formula that allows us to calculate a conditional probability – that is, in its basic form, it allows us to calculate the probability of one event given another if we know the probability of the second given the first and the probabilities of each event alone. There are various versions of Bayes's theorem. Earman (2000: 27) employs the following:

$$Pr(H/E\&K) = \frac{Pr(H/K) \times Pr(E/H\&K)}{Pr(E/K)}$$

He says (2000: 27; cf. Earman 1993):

> It is helpful to think of *H* as a hypothesis at issue, *K* as the background knowledge, and *E* as the new evidence. *Pr(H/K&E)* and *Pr(H/K)* are called, respectively, the *posterior* and *prior probability* of H. *Pr(E/K&H)* is called the *likelihood* of H; it is a measure of how well *H* explains E. Pr(E/K) is variously called the *prior likelihood or* the *expectancy* of E; it is a measure of how surprising the new evidence E is.

However, since there is no consensus on what Hume's argument is, or exactly what he is trying to establish, it is impossible that any Bayesian analysis, or recasting of the argument in terms of Bayes's theorem, will not beg crucial issues of interpretation. In so doing, such analyses will also beg epistemological issues concerning, for example, evidence. Furthermore, it is difficult to see how recasting Hume's argument in a Bayesian form can clarify the structure or substance of the argument, as Earman claims, without presupposing what the argument is. There may be many useful applications of Bayesian analyses of probability, but they are not useful to figuring out what is going on in Hume's essay.

The balancing of probabilities is useless until it is decided what goes into the balance; that is, what constitutes the evidence that is to be subject to the balancing of probabilities. Hume's argument is all about what constitutes the evidence – what we can and cannot legitimately count as evidence, and how to figure out the probability of what is testified to *given* his theory of *a posteriori* reasoning. Bayesian analyses beg the question by *ignoring* Hume's account of *a posteriori* reasoning in favor of accounts of their own. The Humean will not agree with the Bayesian as to what $Pr(H/K\&E)$ and $Pr(H/K)$, or $Pr(E/K)$ is. So casting the argument in Bayesian terms only obfuscates it. Bayesian analyses are of no use in disputing Hume on miracles because they ignore Hume's entire argument in part 1. Apart from independent philosophical arguments – arguments that would in effect undermine the relevance of a Bayesian analysis to the question of the credibility of reports of the miraculous – no such analysis can, in principle, prove that testimony can (or cannot) establish the credibility of a miracle.

Immortality

Hume's essay, "Of the Immortality of the Soul" contains none of the interpretive problems that "Of Miracles" does, nor is it intrinsically linked to his more basic metaphysical positions to the extent that "Of Miracles" is. ("Of the Immortality of the Soul" and "Of Suicide" were not published, though they were printed, in Hume's lifetime. He decided not to publish them out of "abundant prudence" [*Letters*, II, 253].) To be sure, Hume still employs his empiricism and principles of *a posteriori* reasoning at various points in the essay, and near the end of it he cites an argument similar to the one he used against justified belief in miracles. He says ("Of the Immortality of the Soul," 1783, in Paul Edwards, ed., 1997: 140): "By what arguments or analogies can we prove any state of existence, which no one ever saw, and which no way resembles any that ever was seen? Who will repose such trust in any pretended philosophy, as to admit upon its testimony the reality of so marvelous a scene?" However, neither his empiricism nor his principles of *a posteriori* reasoning are used to construct any *a priori* argument against belief in immortality. His *a posteriori* reasoning is employed in the service of his analogies.

There is another important difference between miracles and immortality that Hume either overlooked or simply did not mention. One might believe in a miracle on the basis of testimony (even though its source is in scripture and so based on revelation), or first hand experience. But belief in immortality is more closely linked to the acceptance of a revelatory promise rather than to testimony (even though accepting revelation is itself accepting testimony), first hand experience or reliance on analogical reasoning, as with belief based on the argument from design. Some might believe in immortality on account of testimony or alleged encounters with ghosts and spirits, but that is rare. So in a sense, part of Hume's essay misses its mark by missing its audience. It seems to regard grounds for belief in immortality as experiential or analogical when, as Hume acknowledges later in the essay, they are not.

Nevertheless, in the essay Hume does what he does best. He argues more or less successfully as a natural theologian and largely from analogy and on moral grounds, against justified belief in immortality. Even though the essay on immortality is straightforward and unencumbered, it is perhaps more philosophically interesting than "Of Miracles." Whereas Hume's argument in part 1 "Of Miracles" fails but is of considerable interest, "Of the Immortality of the Soul" largely succeeds. It is a mistake to regard Hume's essay on immortality as simply drawing analogies that are open to the charge of being weak. Like Russell, Sartre, Camus, and others who followed, Hume recognized that one's views about immortality could be crucial to the way in which one lives; not in the sense that denying immortality gives one license to act immorally, but that how one lives is informed by such a denial (Levine 1988c; 1987). One's pursuit of goals, relationships, and the manner in which one lives may be affected by assuming annihilation. Hume thought that *whether or not* one believes in immortality is not without its ramifications in life.

Hume's first argument against immortality suggests that processes like consciousness and thought which are often taken to be properties of the immaterial soul might, for all we know, actually be material properties. He says (Hume in Edwards, ed.: 135): "Matter . . . and spirit, are at bottom equally unknown; we cannot determine what qualities inhere in the one or the other . . . nothing can be decided a priori concerning any cause or effect; and the experience, being the only source of our judgments of this nature, we cannot know from any other principle, whether matter, by its structure or arrangement, may not be the cause of thought." The suggestion seems to be that since the only thinking things we experience are linked to material bodies, we should conclude that whatever the nature of the mental may be, we have no reason to suppose, experientially, that they can exist apart from material substance or embodiment. He makes this explicit later in the essay. He says (138–9):

> Where any two objects are so closely connected, that all alterations which we have ever seen in the one, are attended with proportionable alterations in the other: we ought to conclude, by all rules of analogy, that, when there are still greater alterations produced in the former, and it is totally dissolved, there follows a total dissolution of the latter . . . Judging by the usual analogy of nature, no form can continue when transferred to a condition of life very differ from the original one in which it was placed. Trees perish in the water; fishes in the air; animals in the earth. Even so small a difference as that of climate is often fatal. What reason then to imagine, that an immense alteration, such is made on the soul by the dissolution of its body, and all organs of thought and sensation, can be effected without dissolution of the whole? . . . Our insensibility, before the composition of the body, seems to natural reason a proof of a like state after dissolution.

Given the close relation between soul (or consciousness) and body, Hume (139) thinks that on experiential grounds, a stronger case can be made for metempsychosis – the passing of the soul at death into another body either human or animal – than for the immortality of a bodiless soul.

Furthermore, suppose we grant (1) there is an immaterial substance in which the mental inheres and (2) the immortality of such a substance if it exists. If we reason in accordance with experience we still cannot justifiably believe in personal immortality – where the notion of personal immortality is connected to memory. Hume says (135):

Abstract reasonings cannot decide any question fact or existence. But admitting a spiritual substance to dispersed throughout the universe . . . and to be the only inherent subject of thought, we have reason to conclude from *analogy*, that nature uses it after the manner she does the other substance, *matter* . . . As the same material substance may successively compose the bodies all animals, the same spiritual substance may compose their minds: their consciousness . . . may be continually dissolved by death, and nothing interests them in the new modification. The most positive assertors of the mortality of the soul never denied the immortality of its substance; and that an immaterial substance, as well as a material, may lose its memory or consciousness, appears in part from experience, if the soul be immaterial.

Thus, even allowing for the existence of an immaterial and immortal substance in which the mental inheres, if we reason in accordance with experience we cannot justifiably believe in personal immortality.

Hume is most forceful in his attack on the moral arguments for immortality – "those derived from the justice of God, which is supposed to be further interested in the further punishment of the vicious and the reward of the virtuous" (136). These same or similar arguments are also moral arguments for the existence of God and are directly concerned with the problem of evil. In fact, Hume is less concerned about the immortality issue than about evil, and his real concern (like Dostoevsky in *The Brothers Karamazov*) is to reject the facile notion that after death God is somehow going to make everything all right in terms of the evil we have endured. Heaven and hell will take care of it even if we do not quite know how – a view prominent, if not prevalent, among Christian analytic philosophers. Like Russell after him, Hume is concerned to show that such views are not so much or merely conceptually flawed as they are morally flawed. Hume regarded these arguments as easy targets. Despite the principal focus of contemporary analytic philosophy on the problem of evil, not only has there has been no serious conceptual advance in analytic philosophy of religion on the problem of evil since Hume, but in my view, most efforts in theodicy (for example, Van Inwagen, Swinburne, etc.) are regressive. The interesting philosophical work, conceptually and morally, on the problem of evil has been in literature and continental philosophy.

He attacks the notion of heaven and hell as places where one gets one's just deserts conceptually and morally. In doing so, Hume is again fundamentally at odds with contemporary Christian philosophers like Swinburne. (See Levine 1993; Swinburne 1995.) Consider, for example, the question of who gets to go to heaven and hell. Hume (137) says "Heaven and hell suppose two distinct species of men, the good and the bad. But the greatest part of mankind float betwixt vice and virtue. Were one to go round the world with an intention of giving a good supper to the righteous and a sound drubbing to the wicked, he would frequently be embarrassed in his choice, and would find, that the merits and demerits of most men and women scarcely amount to the value of either." This is, in many ways, a profound attack on the alleged criteria as traditionally understood for separating good people from bad, and also on the cogency of the idea of a heaven and hell. What sense can be made of heaven as a place where the good go, and hell as a place for the bad if most people are good and bad? Arguing on moral grounds alone against the notion of both eternal and retributive punishment Hume says (137) "Punishment, without any proper end or purpose, is inconsistent with *our* ideas of goodness and justice; and no end can be served by it after the whole scene is closed. Punishment, according to *our* conception, should bear some proportion to the offence. Why then eternal punishment for the temporary offences of so frail a creature as man?"

Preceding these remarks on the injustice of eternal punishment Hume (137) says, "By what rule are punishment and rewards distributed? What is the Divine standard of merit and demerit? Shall we suppose that human sentiments have place in the Deity? How bold that hypothesis! We have no conception of any other sentiments. . . . To suppose measures of approbation and blame, different from the human, confounds every thing. Whence do we learn, that there is such a thing as moral distinctions, but from our own sentiments." Hume is making essentially the same point made later by J. S. Mill (1865; 1874). If we are to attribute moral predicates of God, then we must suppose that such predicates mean much the same as when applied to people. "Good" as applied to God must mean more or less what it means as applied to anyone else. Otherwise the term "good" would be completely equivocated upon. We might as well invent another term entirely.

In addition, Hume (137) rejects the "one size fits all" conception of reward and punishment. "According to human sentiments, sense, courage, good manners, industry, prudence, genius, etc., are essential parts of personal merits. Shall we therefore erect an elysium for poets and heroes like that of ancient mythology? Why confine all rewards to one species of virtue?" It is worth comparing this view with Swinburne's, who regards it as virtually self-evident that certain pleasures are higher and better than others no matter who you are – that, for example, it is fundamentally – even *morally* – better to drink with company then to drink alone (Levine 1993).

Hume also raises what is perhaps the most pointed of all questions in regard to evil. He says, "As every effect implies a cause, and another, till we reach the first cause of all, which is the *Deity*; every thing that happens is ordained by him, nothing can be the object of his punishment or vengeance." In other words, since God is ultimately responsible for this world, he is also ultimately responsible for the evil in it and his punishing others for what he is responsible for makes no sense. God's responsibility mitigates our own moral responsibility – even for acting immorally. It renders the notions of just punishment and vengeance problematic on the part of a deity responsible for how we are constituted. If God created things as they are, then it is God who is fundamentally responsible – free will (though Hume does not say so) notwithstanding. See, Mackie (1982), Plantinga (1967), and the literature on whether God could have created us so as to always freely choose the good.

Many problems related to immortality and evil that Hume briefly addresses in his essay, he does not go on at length about any of them, have generated a contemporary literature of their own. One such problem, taken without acknowledgment from Lucretius's *De Rerum Natura*, has to do with our asymmetrical attitude toward pre-natal and post-mortem non-existence. The latter but not the former is a cause of concern. But if the former is of no concern, why is the latter? Hume says (135–6)

> Reasoning from the common course of nature and without supposing any new inter-
> position of the Supreme Cause, which ought always to be excluded from philosophy;
> what is incorruptible must also be ingenerable. The soul, therefore, if immortal, existed

before our birth; and if the former existence noways concerned us, neither will the latter. Animals undoubtedly feel, think, love, hate, will, and even reason, though in a more imperfect manner than men: are their souls also immaterial and immortal?

Hume, of course, is not suggesting that a lack of concern with pre-natal non-existence is mistaken or that the asymmetry in our attitudes in any way supports the view that there is no immortality of the soul. He is claiming what some recent philosophers have taken issue with, namely that the asymmetry in attitudes is unwarranted (Fischer 1993). He thinks that if we are unconcerned with our non-existence before we were born, then we should be unconcerned with our non-existence after we are dead. This view is at least problematic, and it is uncharacteristic of Hume not to see it as such and pursue the difficulties.

The capacities that people share with animals may be sufficient reason for supposing that animals ought to be treated differently than they are treated. But not many who believe in human immortality are inclined to believe in the immortality of animal souls on the basis of shared capacities. Hume denies that the capacity to feel or reason is sufficient grounds for believing the soul to be immortal since if it was, then at least some animals too would have immortal souls.

Even when Hume is most polemical, there is truth in what he says. "There arise indeed in some minds some unaccountable terrors with regard to futurity; but these would quickly vanish were they not artificially fostered by precept and education. And those who foster them, what is their motive? Only to gain a livelihood, and to acquire power and riches in this world. Their very zeal and industry, therefore, are an argument against them." This is not *always* true. Hume did not say it was. But the gross criminal activity and corruption endemic in the Catholic Church (and others) would come as no surprise to Hume. (See the footnote on the hypocrisy of the clergy in Hume's essay "Of National Characters" [1748].) It didn't come as a surprise to many.

The strangest of Hume's arguments for mortality of the soul is the one from the inferiority of women. He says (137) "On the theory of the soul's mortality, the inferiority of women's capacity is easily accounted for. Their domestic life requires no higher faculties either of mind or body. This circumstance vanishes and becomes absolutely insignificant on the religious theory: the one sex has an equal task to perform as the other: their powers of reason and resolution ought to have been equal, and both of them infinitely greater than at present." The argument is archaic. As with Hume's (or Kant's, or Aristotle's) sexist and racist remarks elsewhere, one is left wondering why he (or Kant, or Aristotle), of all people, could not see through the prejudices of his age, or how difficult it might be to see through the prejudices, no matter how stupid, of any age – of our own age. Religious fundamentalism – Christian, Islamic, Jewish, or Hindu – is by far the most dangerous prejudice of our age. To interpret this as anti-religious is indicative of the orectic (desiderative or wishful), Manichaean way fundamentalists think.

Hume thinks that when all is said and done, the reasons people believe in immortality has nothing to with rational argument or experience. It has to do with wish fulfilment – with wanting and needing to believe. He says (140) "All doctrines are to be suspected which are favored by our passions. And the hopes and fears which gave rise to this doctrine [immortality] are very obvious." (See Hume's essay, "Of

Superstition and Enthusiasm" [1741].) It should not have to be pointed out that Hume is being sarcastic and protecting himself when he closes his essay with this: "Nothing could set in a fuller light the infinite obligations which mankind have to Divine revelation, since we find that no other medium could ascertain this great and import truth."

See also 5 "Hume on the Relation of Cause and Effect"; 17 "Hume's Views on Religion: Intellectual and Cultural Influences"; 18 "Hume on the Nature and Existence of God"

Acknowledgments

My thanks to Sam Gross for the wonderful cartoon; James Fieser for his comments and sharing his work on early responses to Hume's essay with me; and to Elizabeth S. Radcliffe for comments and a mountain of editing.

References

Adams, R. M. (1992). "Miracles, Laws of Nature and Causation – II," *The Aristotelian Society*, supplementary vol. 60, pp. 207–24.

Alston, William P. (1991). *Perceiving God: The Epistemology of Religious Experience* (Ithaca, NY: Cornell University Press).

Burns, R. M. (1981). *The Great Debate on Miracles: From Joseph Glanvill to David Hume* (Lewisburg, PA: Bucknell University Press).

Campbell, George (1762). *A Dissertation on Miracles* (New York: Garland Publishing, 1983).

Dostoevsky, Fyodor (1964). "Rebellion" (from *The Brothers Karamazov*), in Nelson Pike (ed.), *God and Evil: Readings on the Theological Problem of Evil* (Englewood Cliffs, NJ: Prentice-Hall), pp. 6–16.

Earman, John (2000). *Hume's Abject Failure: The Argument against Miracles* (New York: Oxford University Press).

—— (1993). "Bayes, Hume, and Miracles," *Faith and Philosophy*, 10, pp. 293–310.

Fischer, John Martin (ed.) (1993). *The Metaphysics of Death* (Stanford: Stanford University Press).

Flew, Antony (1967). "Miracles," *Encyclopedia of Philosophy*, vol. 5 (New York: Macmillan and Free Press), pp. 346–53.

Flew, Antony, Hare, R. M., and Mitchell, Basil (1955). "Theology and Falsification," in Antony Flew and Alasdair MacIntyre (eds.), *New Essays in Philosophical Theology* (London: SCM Press), pp. 66–105.

Gaskin, J. C. A. (1978). *Hume's Philosophy of Religion* (London: Macmillan).

—— (1993). "Hume on Religion," in David Fate Norton (ed.), *The Cambridge Companion to Hume* (Cambridge: Cambridge University Press), pp. 331–44.

Greig, J. Y. T. (ed.) (1932). *The Letters of David Hume*, 2 vols. (Oxford: Clarendon Press). (Cited as Letters.)

Haldane, John J. and Smart, Jack J. C. (1996). *Atheism and Theism* (Oxford: Blackwell).

Hume, David (1779). *Dialogues concerning Natural Religion*, ed. Norman Kemp Smith (Indianapolis, IN: Bobbs-Merrill, 1947).

—— (1783). *Essays on Suicide and the Immortality of the Soul* (Bristol: Thoemmes Press, 1992).

—— (1783). "Of the Immortality of the Soul," in Paul Edwards (ed.), *Immortality* (Amherst, NY: Prometheus Books), pp. 134–40.

—— (1741–77). *Essays Moral, Political and Literary*, ed. Eugene F. Miller (Indianapolis, IN: Liberty Fund, 1987).

Levine, Michael P. (1984). "Hume's Analysis of Causation in Relation to His Analysis of Miracles," *History of Philosophy Quarterly*, 1, pp. 195–202.

—— (1987). "What Does Death Have to Do with the Meaning of Life?" *Religious Studies*, 23, pp. 457–65.

—— (1988a). "Belief in Miracles: Tillotson's Argument against Transubstantiation as a Model for Hume," *International Journal for Philosophy of Religion*, 23, pp. 125–60.

—— (1988b). "Hume on Miracles: The Coalescence of the a priori with the a posteriori Arguments against Justified Belief," in Venant Cauchy (ed.), *Philosophy and Culture*, vol. 3 (Montreal: Ed-Montmorency), pp. 340–4.

—— (1988c). "Camus, Hare, and the Meaning of Life," *Sophia*, 27, pp. 13–30.

—— (1989). *Hume and the Problem of Miracles: A Solution* (Dordrecht: Kluwer Publishers).

—— (1993). "Swinburne's Heaven: One Hell of a Place," *Religious Studies*, 29, pp. 519–31.

—— (1996). "Miracles," in E. Zalta (ed.), *Stanford Encyclopedia of Philosophy* (http://plato.stanford.edu/).

—— (2000). "Contemporary Christian Analytic Philosophy of Religion: Biblical Fundamentalism, Terrible Solutions to a Horrible Problem, and Hearing God," *International Journal for Philosophy of Religion*, 48, pp. 89–119.

—— (2002). "Review of John Earman, *Hume's Abject Failure: The Argument against Miracles*," *Hume Studies*, 28, pp. 161–7.

Locke, John (1706). *A Discourse on Miracles*, ed. I. T. Ramsey (London: A. and C. Black, 1958).

Mackie, J. L. (1982). *The Miracle of Theism: Arguments for and against the Existence of God* (Oxford: Oxford University Press).

Mill, John Stuart (1865). "Mr Mansel on the Limits of Religious Thought," in Nelson Pike (ed.), *God and Evil: Readings on the Theological Problem of Evil* (Englewood Cliffs, NJ: Prentice-Hall, 1964), pp. 37–45.

—— (1874). *Three Essays on Religion* (London: Longman).

Plantinga, Alvin (1967). *God and Other Minds* (Ithaca, NY: Cornell University Press).

—— (1983). "Reason and Belief in God," in Alvin Plantinga and Nicholas Wolterstorff (eds.), *Faith and Rationality* (Notre Dame: University of Notre Dame Press).

Swinburne, Richard (1970). *The Concept of Miracle* (London: Macmillan).

—— (1995). "Theodicy, Our Well-being, and God's Rights," *International Journal for the Philosophy of Religion*, 38, pp. 75–91.

Van Inwagen, Peter (1995). *God, Knowledge and Mystery: Essays in Philosophical Theology* (Ithaca, NY: Cornell University Press).

Wolterstorff, Nicholas (1995). *Divine Discourse* (Cambridge: Cambridge University Press).

Wootton, David (1990). "Hume's 'Of Miracles'," in M. A. Stewart (ed.), *Studies in the Philosophy of the Scottish Enlightenment* (Oxford: Oxford University Press).

Further Reading

Ahern, Dennis (1975). "Hume on the Evidential Impossibility of Miracles," in Nicholas Rescher (ed.), *Studies in Epistemology* (Oxford: Blackwell), pp. 1–32.

Armstrong, Benjamin F. (1995). "Hume's Actual Argument against Belief in Miracles," *History of Philosophy Quarterly*, 12, pp. 65–76.

Bagger, Matthew C. (1997). "Hume and Miracles," *Journal of the History of Philosophy*, 35, pp. 237–51.

Basinger, David (1986). *Philosophy and Miracle: The Contemporary Debate* (New York: Mellen Press).

Beckwith, Francis J. (1989). *David Hume's Argument against Miracles: A Critical Analysis* (Lanham, MD: University Press of America).

Buckle, Stephen (2001). "Marvels, Miracles, and Mundane Order: Hume's Critique of Religion in *An Enquiry concerning Human Understanding*," *Australasian Journal of Philosophy*, 79, pp. 1–31.

Clarke, Steve (1999). "Hume's Definition of Miracles Revised," *American Philosophical Quarterly*, 36, pp. 49–57.

David, Philip and Gillies, Donald (1989). "A Bayesian Analysis of Hume's Argument concerning Miracles," *Philosophical Quarterly*, 39, pp. 57–65.

Ellin, Joseph S. (1993). "Again: Hume on Miracles," *Hume Studies*, 19, pp. 203–12.

Flew, Antony (1961). *Hume's Philosophy of Belief* (London: Routledge and Kegan Paul).

Gower, Barry (1990). "David Hume and the Probability of Miracles," *Hume Studies*, 16, pp. 17–31.

Houston, J. (1994). *Reported Miracles: A Critique of Hume* (New York: Cambridge University Press).

Langtry, Bruce (1990). "Hume, Probability, Lotteries and Miracles," *Hume Studies*, 16, pp. 67–74.

Levine, Michael (1998). "Bayesian Analyses of Hume's Argument concerning Miracles," *Philosophy and Theology*, 10, pp. 101–6.

Millican, Peter (1993). "Hume's Theorem concerning Miracles," *Philosophical Quarterly*, 43, pp. 489–95.

Penelhum, Terence (1971). *Religion and Rationality* (New York: Harper and Row).

Schoen, Edward L. (1991). "David Hume and the Mysterious Shroud of Turin," *Religious Studies*, 27, pp. 209–22.

Slupik, Chris (1995). "A New Interpretation of Hume's 'Of Miracles'," *Religious Studies* 31, pp. 517–36.

Smart, Ninian (1964). *Philosophers and Religious Truth* (London: SCM Press).

Stewart, M. A. (1995). "Hume's Historical View of Miracles," in M. A. Stewart (ed.), *Hume and Hume's Connexions* (University Park, PA: Pennsylvania State University Press), pp. 171–200.

Tweyman, Stanley (ed.) (1996). *Hume on Miracles* (Bristol: Thoemmes Press).

Wilson, Fred (1989). "The Logic of Probabilities in Hume's Argument against Miracles," *Hume Studies*, 15, pp. 255–75.

Part V

Economics, Politics, and History

20

Hume's Economic Theory

TATSUYA SAKAMOTO

Hume as Economist

Hume's place in the history of economics is considerable. Adam Smith, Hume's closest compatriot and friend, and the illustrious economists after Smith – Karl Marx, John M. Keynes, F. A. Hayek – regarded Hume as a pioneer and original thinker in economics. It will always remain true that Hume's greatest contribution to the history of modern science was that he woke Kant up from his slumber of philosophical dogmatism. But we always ought to remember that Hume's social-scientific works, ranging over economics, politics, and history, were intended as essential parts of his philosophical project of the "Science of Man." While great Enlightenment thinkers in the eighteenth century, Smith, Montesquieu, Rousseau, and Kant, more or less attempted to achieve a philosophical synthesis of their social science in similar fashion, it was in Hume's project that the attempted synthesis succeeded to such a remarkable degree. The basic principles of Hume's economics developed in the *Political Discourses* (1752) directly or indirectly derived from his fundamental theories of knowledge, passions, and morality as presented early on in *A Treatise of Human Nature* (1739–40).

The theoretical significance of Hume as economist has been examined in mainly three areas. The first is the theory of economic development. Hume has been recognized as the most important predecessor of Adam Smith's economic liberalism as well as the most effective critic of the so-called "mercantilist" economic doctrines that had been prevalent for over a century until Hume's time in Britain and Europe. In this area, Hume's chief contribution was his clear vision of the autonomous course of economic development as propelled by the "arts" and "industry" of the people. His theoretical formulation was so impressive that it has been believed to have effectively undermined the prevalent mercantilist notion that the economic growth of a nation should start from a constant inflow of trade surplus as a result of systematic regulation of international trade by the government. He attempted to demonstrate that the stable economic growth of a nation should originally arise from people's growing demand for a higher standard of living and the subsequent growth of agricultural, industrial, and commercial sectors of a national economy. This attempt played a pivotal role in Hume's account of why and how any substantial economic growth could occur in one nation's history and not in another's.

The second area is Hume's theory of money. This part of Hume's economics has arguably exerted the most visible influence upon the succeeding generations of economists to this day, especially in its application to the theory of international trade (to be discussed shortly). Although his view of money as the medium of exchange and evaluation was largely preceded by a number of writers since the late seventeenth century including John Locke, it nevertheless provided the later economists with the most sophisticated formulation of the quantity theory of money. The theory argues for the neutrality of money and suggests that any change in the quantity of circulating money has no substantial effect upon producers and consumers besides causing a merely proportional change in the nominal price level of goods and services. This led to a further discovery of the misguided nature of the prevalent doctrine of "benign infla-tion" as a result of the favorable balance of trade. It was particularly important for Hume to use his view of money as having only a secondary importance to explain several historical facts. Mercantilist writers took those facts to show the "benign" effects of the inflow of money and considered those facts illustrated historically by the constant economic growth in European countries in varying degrees ever since the discovery of the West Indies.

Third, Hume's version of quantity theory developed its theoretical application in the theory of free trade. Since mercantile regulations of international trade were founded upon the idea that the national wealth principally accumulated through trade surplus over time, Hume's attack upon this idea with his quantity theory provided the rising free-trade ideology of the time with a reliable scientific foundation. Hume's account of the irrelevance of traditional attempts to maintain trade surplus by protectionist policies was so brilliant that by the early nineteenth century, even after the publica-tion of Smith's masterpiece, Hume was regarded by the leading economists of the time as the founding father of the new ideology of free-trade. This is so, even though a number of similar arguments had been made by his predecessors. The theory of free-trade was to dominate the public mind of Britain for more than a century.

Hume's Philosophical Economics

Hume's economics was presented primarily in the *Political Discourses* published in Edinburgh in 1752. Eight chapters out of the whole twelve are devoted to specifically economic subjects. Notwithstanding its apparent want of systematic character, it con-tains almost every important subject of political economy, with an extensive coverage of commerce, luxury, population, money, the balance of trade, interest, and public debt. Of this work, Hume was later to recall in *My Own Life*, written in 1776, that it was "the only work of mine that was successful on the first publication. It was well received abroad and at home" (Hume 1776: xxxvii). The high reputation of this par-ticular work attained for Hume British and European status as one of the truly great thinkers after Montesquieu. Although a clear contrast with the anonymous and the "dead-born" *Treatise* is noticeable here, there is ample reason to believe that the later work's principles had its philosophical origins in the *Treatise*.

In the formal and systematic sense, Hume's economic theory in the later work was designed to be a specific realization of what he called in the Introduction to the *Treatise*

"Politics," one of the four departments of the Science of Man. In contrast with the other departments – Logic, Morals, and Criticism, which deal with the internal activities of reasoning, the passion, and sentiments – Politics "consider men as united in society, and dependent on each other" (T Intro. 5). This obviously suggests that politics inquires into the external facts and phenomena that arise in history and society. Laws of proper causal reasoning as described in Book 1 of the *Treatise* find the ideal arena of their full exercise here in the world of social phenomena. "Politics" in Hume's sense of the term is virtually the same as "social science" today.

It is easy to identify at least three substantial connections between the two works. First, the theory of knowledge and empirical reasoning developed in Book 1 of the *Treatise* provided a methodological groundwork for whatever causal political and economic analysis Hume was to make in the *Political Discourses*, illustrated by his essays on money and the balance of trade. Second, the theory of the passions and sympathy formulated in Book 2 of the *Treatise* formed the psychological framework within which Hume went on to discuss in the later work the way in which the passions and interests generate men's economic behavior. Third, the theory of justice, property, and government in Book 3 of the *Treatise* continued to provide Hume's economic discourse with the legal and institutional structure in which men's economic behavior in market relations is supposed to operate.

Thus, unlike his contemporary economic writers, who were mostly merchants, journalists, or politicians by profession, Hume's economics was deliberately designed by the author himself as a strictly philosophical and scientific treatise. Hume believed that the science of "politics," as an empirical science, ought to follow the same rules of investigation as the other empirical sciences, such as physics and astronomy. At the same time, social science must deal with some practical disadvantages not found in the natural sciences. The foremost difficulty is the impracticability of artificially planned experiments. Since the world of political and economic behaviors of men is the total sum of an infinite number of individually motivated actions, the social scientist is not able in principle to create an ideal condition for observation or to remove all the factors that would obstruct the projected outcomes of planned experiment or observation. What Hume proposes for coping with this "peculiar disadvantage" is to "glean up our experiments in this science from a cautious observation of human life and take them as they appear in the common course of the world" (T Intro. 10). This means that a moral philosopher must attempt to reach the more common and repetitious phenomena and their underlying causes by using many other less common and exceptional phenomena, and do so by means of a massive collection and careful comparison of empirical facts and data.

This methodological principle is more elaborately repeated in the opening part of "Of Commerce," the first essay in the *Political Discourses*. Hume distinguishes between the vulgar and "shallow" thinkers and the philosophical and "abstruse" thinkers and characterizes the former as those who "cannot enlarge their view to those universal propositions, which comprehend under them an infinite number of individuals, and include a whole science in a single theorem." These universal propositions certainly seem too intricate and refined to the eyes of the vulgar in many cases, but the philosopher must stand these accusations because the philosopher is convinced that "however intricate they may seem, it is certain, that general principles, if just and sound, must always prevail in the general course of things" and "it is the chief business of philosophers to regard the general course of things" (Hume 1752: 253). Hume's social scientist is required to execute two opposite scientific activities at the same time. One is an extensive empirical observation of "the general course of things," and the other is a highly abstract theorizing of those facts. This explains why Hume's works in economics, politics, and history are so distinctive among the contemporary works: they offer the highest syntheses of empirical and historical research with theoretical and abstract speculation.

Hume was aware that this feature of his social science was particularly evident in the case of his economics. He warns his enlightened readers that "there will occur some principles which are uncommon, and which may seem too refined and subtle for such vulgar subjects." He also seeks their understanding of the unusual novelty and originality of his economic arguments. "No one ought to entertain a prejudice against them, merely because they are out of the common road" (Hume 1752: 255). This strongly suggests that his theoretical position was designed to be highly critical of common views on a number of important subjects. At least three subject areas in his economics could be characterized as "out of the common road." First is Hume's comparative view of the ancient and the modern European societies. Second is his famous theory of money and trade. Third is his outright economic liberalism. As is clear by now, his three contributions to the history of economic thought outlined at the outset largely overlap with these problem-areas. Undoubtedly this did not happen purely by chance. On the contrary it clearly demonstrates that Hume's economic discourses were designed to be strictly philosophical as an indispensable part of his Science of Man.

Luxury, Knowledge, and Economic Development

In Hume's time, the view that the ancient Greek and Roman societies were significantly more populous than the modern European societies was prevalent and influential. The root cause of this demographic difference was usually traced to the want of luxury in the former and its extreme growth in the latter. There were three moral and political justifications for the common negative view of luxury. First was the Christian moral condemnation of luxury. Both traditional Catholic and Protestant views regarded the gratification of the senses as nothing but a moral corruption. No less fierce was the Classical Republican argument against luxury on the ground that it constituted the fundamental cause for the decline of Roman liberty and for its disintegration into Imperial rule. This traditional criticism was reinforced by the Country Party view that British liberty as realized by the Glorious Revolution of 1688 was being ruined by the "corrupt" politicians whose avarice was fueled by the pursuit of luxury. Moreover, the critics believed that luxury turned the concern of the common people from public affairs and caused the love of liberty and public spirit to deteriorate. Last, but far from least, those writers who emphasized the special importance of low-wages economy offered the mercantilist argument against luxury. They had long argued that the general increase of wages as a result of prevailing luxury would always result in the increase of the cost of production and then in the decrease of competitiveness in international markets.

In opposition to all these accusations against modern luxury and claims of its root cause in modern commercial or market society, Hume attempts to present a full consistent vindication of luxury by a radical reformulation of it as "the refinement in the arts." In the modern age "where luxury nourishes commerce and industry," the industrial class such as "the peasants" become "rich and independent" while the commercial classes such as the tradesmen and merchants "acquire a share of the property, and draw authority and consideration to that middling rank of men, who are the best and firmest basis of public liberty" (Hume 1752: 277–8). By claiming that modern luxury is essentially one with the industrious manners of the people, Hume effectively replaced the negative sounding term "luxury" with the more positive sounding "refinements in the arts" and discovered in it the driving force of the industrious and commercial people. Since these people historically constituted "the best and firmest basis of public liberty," he could simultaneously refute both the traditional Christian and the Classical Republican accusations that luxury was morally and politically corrupting. Hume presents by these arguments three counter-theses against the traditional cases. First, luxury as newly defined as refinement in the arts is not vicious in itself. Second, in the modern market society, as opposed to the non-market and slavery-based ancient agrarian community, luxury as the chief driving force of the middle and lower classes forms the social foundation for moral and political liberty and equality. Third (as I will discuss in more detail later), increase in a luxurious way of life would necessarily improve the nation's trade competitiveness and create the economic conditions for international free trade among civilized nations, contrary to the belief of mercantilist writers.

Thus, Hume's counter-theses against the three traditional criticisms of luxury inevitably led to the formulation of his theory of economic development. It presents a moral, political, and even philosophical demonstration of the long-term viability of modern commercial civilization. The theory was a practical outcome of Hume's methodological strategy that he would not shy away from doubting even the most widely accepted view of the subject. The common belief that the ancient and agrarian society was more populous and happy than modern society partly derived from the contemporary observation that the medieval agrarian community and its succeeding stage of free and independent farmers were violently transformed into a full fledged system of capitalist agriculture in mid-eighteenth-century Britain. Since this historical process was carried out forcibly by parliamentary measures of "enclosure," dissolving independent farmers either into new farming capitalists or agricultural and industrial workers, many contemporary writers condemned the policy. These writers, among them Robert Wallace, Hume's Scottish friend and the pioneer in the theory of population, lamented the miserable condition into which so many peasants were thrown. Hume's methodological skepticism helped counter-balance this sentimental criticism of the time and made it possible to present a long-term theoretical vindication of modern society at the dawn of the Industrial Revolution. This was practically what he intended to do in his economics as a result of his belief that "the general principles, if just and sound, must always prevail in the general course of things."

As to the general course of things in the theory of economic development, Hume says,

> Every thing in the world is purchased by labour; and our passions are the only causes of labour. When a nation abounds in manufactures and mechanic arts, the proprietors of land, as well as the farmers, study agriculture as a science, and redouble their industry and attention. The superfluity, which arises from their labour, is not lost; but is exchanged with manufactures for those commodities, which men's luxury now makes them covet. By this means, land furnishes a great deal more of the necessaries of life, than what suffices for those who cultivate it. (Hume 1752: 261)

At one decisive point, Hume's argument opposed not only his colleague writers' scientific beliefs but also the more common belief widely shared among the general public. His contemporaries had the serious fear that the growth of industry might undermine the basis of agriculture and eventually result in the decline of the nation's population and then in the decline of national wealth and power. As a matter of course, Hume did not neglect the fundamental importance of agriculture as the material basis of human life. On the contrary, he firmly believed that in modern commercial civilization where ancient slavery is long abolished and an individual's desire and passion for better living becomes the only driving force of the economy, the growth of mechanical arts and industry as the engine of market economy is the key element of the growth of agriculture itself. Without a steady growth of arts and industry, agriculture itself would not be able to grow without limit. That agriculture became the peculiar modern type of commercial agriculture and one component of the system of division of labor that naturally grows and expands among agricultural, industrial and commercial sectors.

In the above allusion to "agriculture as a science," Hume's view was distinctive: it contained knowledge as an essential force for economic development. Hume identifies at least three social functions of knowledge in the framework of the theory of civilization. First is knowledge as the source of technological and industrial progress. In Hume's view, industry promotes knowledge, and knowledge promotes industry. But here the relationship between the two is neither simply mutual nor reciprocal. Hume places an unequivocal emphasis on the fact that industry originally produces knowledge and not vice versa. Hume is not a simple Baconian or an Enlightenment philosopher who believes in knowledge as the sole original spring of every human progress without a due regard to its historical and social conditions. At the same time Hume believes that once the knowledge-producing pattern of industrial growth is set in motion, the knowledge-produced pattern of economic growth necessarily begins with an almost equal force. This is further confirmed by a well-known remark that "We cannot reasonably expect, that a piece of woollen cloth will be wrought to perfection in a nation, which is ignorant of astronomy, or where ethics are neglected" (Hume 1752: 271).

The second role Hume assigns to knowledge in the theory of economic development is knowledge as the source of the principle of the rule of law in modern market society. Hume says that "Laws, order, police, discipline; these can never be carried to any degree of perfection, before human reason has refined itself by exercise" and further clarifies his point by adding "by an application to the more vulgar arts, at least, of commerce and manufacture" (Hume 1752: 272–3). As indicated before, Book 3 of the *Treatise* had provided the theoretical account of how the social

378

institution of justice, private property, and promise would arise through mutual and spontaneous convention among individuals. The present account supplements the theory with the social and historical foundation of "commerce and manufacture" upon which the regular system of modern European government and law could establish itself.

Third, knowledge in modern society becomes the source of the moral as well as the intellectual improvement of the people. Intellectual enhancement of a society naturally inclines people to get together to show each other the fruits of their learning, and this exchange of knowledge disseminates it throughout the society. This stimulates scientific inquiry and learning and further widens people's communication and strengthens their sociability. The following vivid passage by Hume describing the process of socialization by means of exchange of knowledge in modern society is convincing enough to demonstrate modern commercial civilization as the historical arena for the full realization of the principles of human nature and, for that matter, the full vindication of the moral worth of modern civilized society.

> The more these refined arts advance, the more sociable men become: nor is it possible, that, when enriched with science, and possessed of a fund of conversation, they should be contented to remain in solitude, or live with their fellow-citizens in that distant manner, which is peculiar to ignorant and barbarous nations . . . Particular clubs and societies are every where formed: Both sexes meet in an easy and sociable manner; and the tempers of men, as well as their behaviour, refine apace . . . Thus *industry, knowledge*, and *humanity*, are linked together by an indissoluble chain, and are found, from experience as well as reason, to be peculiar to the more polished, and, what are commonly denominated, the more luxurious ages. (Hume 1752: 271)

Money and International Trade

The second subject on which Hume's ideas were "out of the common road" was the theory of money and its application to the theory of international trade. As outlined at the outset, Hume is now widely known as the prominent founder of the quantity theory of money. Results of the theory seem quite opposite to the economic common sense of ordinary people and even of traditional politicians and vulgar authors.

The theory's argumentative structure consists of three parts. First, Hume famously declares that "Money is not, properly speaking, one of the subjects of commerce; but only the instrument which men have agreed upon to facilitate the exchange of one commodity for another." The same thing is said in a rhetorical manner. "It is none of the wheels of trade: It is the oil which renders the motion of the wheels more smooth and easy" (Hume 1752: 281). Should it be the case that money is no more than the means of exchange, it follows that money is not wealth or riches by itself. Riches are necessities and conveniences of life to be gained with money and *not* vice versa. People want as much money as possible not because they want money itself but because they want those goods and services that they can purchase with money. No matter how convincing this reasoning is, this is opposite of economic common sense because people take it for granted that a man is rich because he or she owns much money.

379

Second, given this maxim that money is not wealth by itself for individuals, it should also be true that money as such is not wealth or riches for a state or nation. Hume simply says that "If we consider any one kingdom by itself, it is evident, that the greater or less plenty of money is of no consequence" (Hume 1752: 281). Again in opposition to the common and vulgar belief that a country is rich because its government or people have a lot of money, Hume claims that no matter how much money any country possesses, it never means that the country is rich and wealthy because the plentitude immediately means that the general price level is proportionately higher than when it possesses a smaller amount of money. In exactly the same way as individuals' purchasing power is proportionately reduced by the larger amount of money that they have, the purchasing power of a nation is simply reduced and counterbalanced by a larger amount of money that circulates in the market in proportion to the increase of money that flows into it by a trade surplus.

Third, should these two sets of reasoning be sound and correct, they obviously undermine the theoretical foundation of the mercantilist and protectionist trade policy that had consistently and systematically been pursued by merchants and politicians since the late seventeenth century. According to Hume's critical reasoning, the theoretical ground of this trade policy, the theory of the balance of trade, proves to be wrong and misguided both logically and empirically. Any increase or decrease of the circulating money in a nation would merely bring about the proportionate increase or decrease of the general price level and this in turn means the corresponding decrease or increase of purchasing power. Any change of the amount of circulating money would not change a national wealth in the true sense of the term. Hume poses a hypothetical question in order to trace what would logically happen following a sudden decrease of the amount of money in a country.

> suppose four-fifths of all the money in GREAT BRITAIN to be annihilated in one night, and the nation reduced to the same condition, with regard to specie, as in the reigns of the HARRYS and EDWARDS, what would be the consequence? Must not the price of all labour and commodities sink in proportion, and every thing be sold as cheap as they were in those ages? (Hume 1752: 311)

The immediate result would be a proportionate decline of the general prices in the country and this should further cause a sudden rise of the nation's competitiveness in the foreign market. "What nation could then dispute with us in any foreign market, or pretend to navigate or to sell manufactures at the same price, which to us would afford sufficient profit?" Then Hume traces the final result up to the point of the return of the once drained money. "In how little time, therefore, must this bring back the money which we had lost, and raise us to the level of all the neighbouring nations" (Hume 1752: 311)? All in all, the three component parts of Hume's logical reconstruction of the empirical process (so-called "specie-flow mechanism") that would start from a sudden and externally caused change of the quantity of money in the market obviously intends to demolish the narrow-minded and highly nationalistic idea and theory of protectionism.

Hume's formulation and rhetoric was so brilliant that it easily overshadowed several important predecessors who proffered the same theory, such as John Locke and

Jacob Vanderlint, and has long been understood as the single most important pre-cursor of the modern quantity theory of money presented by Irving Fisher. However, if one traces the deep original intention of Hume's argument, the above classic state-ment may be reinterpreted, rather than taken at its face-value. His formulation of the quantity theory was certainly brilliant, but this was because of the model's rhetorical purpose and its highly abstract and mechanistic nature. Viewed from this perspective, Hume's rhetorical expressions always involve an element of ambiguity. The first remark that money is not a wheel but "the oil which renders the motion of the wheels more smooth and easy" can be interpreted as indicating the indispensable role of money for a stable working of market economy in addition to the secondary and subservient role of money. The second claim that money is not wealth in itself for a state or nation includes a careful reservation: "It is only the public which draws any advantage from the greater plenty of money; and that only in its wars and negotia-tions with foreign states" (Hume 1752: 281). This clearly suggests Hume's belief in the importance of a bounty of money for any government in particular circumstances of war and diplomatic negotiations. Hume indeed develops this line of argument con-sistently throughout his economic writings.

Quantity Theory Reconsidered

The most striking instance where Hume substantially limits the theoretical validity of his own theory is a key passage added to his famous case that begins with 'suppose four-fifths of all the money in GREAT BRITAIN to be annihilated in one night . . ."

> Now, it is evident, that the same causes, which would correct these exorbitant inequal-ities, were they to happen miraculously, must prevent their happening in the common course of nature, and must for ever, in all neighbouring nations, preserve money nearly proportionable to the art and industry of each nation. All water, wherever it com-municates, remains always at a level. Ask naturalists the reason; they tell you, that, were it to be raised in any one place, the superior gravity of that part not being balanced, must depress it, till it meet a counterpoise; and that the same cause, which redresses the inequality when it happens, must for ever prevent it, without some violent external operation. (Hume 1752: 312)

This clearly shows that the rhetorical model was no more than a thought experiment over what would happen in unrealistic circumstances. The proviso that "were they to happen miraculously" shows that Hume regards the sudden and drastic flowing-out of money as a pure hypothesis. Hume believes that it would never happen in "the com-mon course of nature." Therefore, these rhetorical models do not intend to provide the true ground upon which he develops a fundamental criticism of the balance of trade theory and its practical outcome of a protectionist trade policy. Why does Hume use such unrealistic rhetoric and models? It is simply because he wishes to demonstrate the existence of the universal law of international trade that governs the balance of trade and distributes the proper quantity of money among nations and across national borders. The fundamental law is the law of the distribution of money that "preserve[s] money nearly proportionable to the art and industry of each nation."

381

The mechanistic model of the specie-flow mechanism was certainly effective and "out of the common road" enough to refute the widely prevalent theory of the balance of trade. Now that the model proves to be a mere rhetorical device to convince the readers of the principle of free trade, what becomes of Hume's original concept of money as strictly neutral to the workings of the market, as suggested at the outset? This question can be answered only by a proper definition of the quantity of money in a national market "nearly proportionable to the art and industry of each nation." Here we turn to the third question concerning how Hume landed "out of the common road" in his economics. This is exactly where he presents a systematic vision of the international division of labor and free trade. The theoretical core is an extended argument of the first part of his economic theory. It is the theory that economic development is the foundation for refuting the common belief about the ancient Greek and Roman societies as more populous and happy than the modern European societies. Hume says,

> Nature, by giving a diversity of geniuses, climates, and soils, to different nations, has secured their mutual intercourse and commerce, as long as they all remain industrious and civilized. Nay, the more the arts encrease in any state, the more will be its demands from its industrious neighbours . . . The industry of the nations, from whom they import, receives encouragement: Their own is also encreased, by the sale of the commodities which they give in exchange. The encrease of domestic industry lays the foundation of foreign commerce. Where a great number of commodities are raised and perfected for the home-market, there will always be found some which can be exported with advantage. But if our neighbours have no art or cultivation, they cannot take them; because they will have nothing to give in exchange. (Hume 1752: 329)

This passage suggests that while it is true that the law of international division of labor and trade tends to operate universally across borders, the extent, speed, and quality of economic activities and economic development in general would depend heavily upon the specific historical and social circumstances of a nation. This ambiguous relationship in Hume's account between the neutrality of money, which is prominently argued for in his quantity theory, and the non-neutrality of money, which Hume confirms in various contexts of his economic theory, has been the focus of debate to this day, not only in Hume studies but also in the studies on the quantity theory of money. As a Nobel Prize winner claimed, "This tension between two incompatible ideas . . . has been at the center of monetary theory at least since Hume wrote" (Lucas, Jr. 1996: 664).

To examine this question in a proper manner, it is useful to remember that the larger part of Hume's essay, "Of Money," is devoted to an analysis of money that is broadly favorable to the non-neutrality view. After giving a brief account of the essence of quantity theory as if it were a commonly held opinion, along with a critique of paper-credit and bank notes, Hume begins an extended argument for the apparent non-neutrality of money. He says, "I shall finish this essay on money, by proposing and explaining two observations, which may, perhaps, serve to employ the thoughts of our speculative politicians" (Hume 1752: 285). One of the two observations discusses the unquestionable rise of commercial activities in Europe as a consequence of the steady inflow of money since the discovery of the West Indies. The other concerns the poverty of some European countries, which seems to have equally derived from monetary causes and from the scarcity of money. However, the way in which Hume relates the cause to the consequence in each case is quite different. In the former case, Hume endorses the common view by saying "this may justly be ascribed, amongst other reasons, to the encrease of gold and silver" (Hume 1752: 286). In the latter, he emphasizes "the fallacy of the remark, often to be met with in historians, and even in common conversation, that any particular state is weak, though fertile, populous, and well cultivated, merely because it wants money" (Hume 1752: 293). Nonetheless, Hume regards the two cases as having essentially the same theoretical significance because they equally seem to contradict his own belief in the neutrality of money with respect to the wealth and political strength of a nation. Thus Hume had an obvious reason to say, "The contradiction is only apparent; but it requires some thought and reflection to discover the principles, by which we can reconcile reason to experience" (Hume 1752: 290).

Manners and Diversity of Economic Development

I argue that Hume achieves this theoretical reconciliation by the concept of manners. Regarding the first example, he carefully excludes Spain and Portugal from those countries where monetary causes actually worked by saying "industry has encreased in all the nations of Europe, except in the possessors of those mines" (Hume 1752: 292). This suggests his belief that the increase of money from America resulted in a positive increase of industry only in the countries where industrious manners had already been in existence independently of or prior to that increase. About England Hume says in "Of Interest" that, "if the industry of England had risen as much from other causes, (and that rise might easily have happened, though the stock of money had remained the same) must not all the same consequences have followed, which we observe at present" (Hume 1752: 306)? Hume believes that only on this condition could an additional increase of money supply provide an incentive or encouragement to industrious activities in those countries. By contrast, Hume explains in "Of the Balance of Trade" why Spain and Portugal have had difficulty in maintaining the abundance of money that they got from their colonies: namely, the total want of industrious manners in those countries. Hume asks, "Can one imagine, that it had ever been possible, by any laws, or even by any art or industry, to have kept all the money in Spain, which the galleons have brought from the Indies?" He answers, "What other reason, indeed, is there, why all nations, at present, gain in their trade with Spain and Portugal; but because it is impossible to heap up money, more than any fluid, beyond its proper level" (Hume 1752: 312)?

Concerning the second case, Hume draws readers' attention to "a greater disproportion between the force of Germany, at present, and what it was three centuries ago, than there is in its industry, people, and manufactures." On the other hand, Hume allows that "The Austrian dominions in the empire are in general well peopled and well cultivated, and are of great extent; but have not a proportionable weight in the balance of Europe; proceeding, as is commonly supposed, from the scarcity of money" (Hume 1752: 289). This seems to contradict "that principle of reason, that the quantity of gold and silver is in itself altogether indifferent." He attempts to solve "these difficulties" by asserting that "the effect, here supposed to flow from scarcity of money, really arises from the manners and customs of the people; and that we mistake, as is too usual, a collateral effect for a cause" (Hume 1752: 290). Hume undoubtedly regards "the manners and customs of the people" as the chief cause of the political power of a nation, and the plenty or scarcity of money should be taken as merely "a collateral effect" of the same cause. In other words, Austria is weaker than it could have been not because it wants money but because the country is not industrious enough to make the fullest use of whatever quantity of money happens to exist in the country. Hume here implicitly introduces the idea of the velocity of money and incorporates it into his precise formulation of quantity theory by saying "It is the proportion between the circulating money, and the commodities in the market, which determines the prices" (Hume 1752: 291). Germany has achieved its present national power by circulating the quantity of money available with utmost velocity, and this was possible only on the condition that the country had independently nurtured industrious manners and customs of the people.

Hume further generalizes this analysis into a theoretical account of the reason why the general price level of European countries has "only risen three, or at most four times since the discovery of the West Indies" while the total quantity of money in Europe must have increased during the same period infinitely more by any calculation. Hume solves this problem by clearly distinguishing the increase of money from the West Indies from the more endogenous industrious manners of European peoples after they "depart from their ancient simplicity of manners" (Hume 1752: 292). This distinction explains the basis on which Hume wrote the following answer to the historical question.

As Hume understands it, this change of manners was initiated by city merchants' importing foreign luxurious products for satisfying the vanity of country nobility and gentry. This practice generated a new way of life and manners among these wealthy classes, but the manners immediately spread and developed by imitation and sympathy into new ways of living and spending among the common people. This account might appear to contradict Hume's claim that industrious manners must have been developed prior to the inflow of money in order to cause an accelerated economic development. However, this doubt is resolved when we recall that Hume made a consistent and clear distinction between the increase of money on the one hand, and that of luxurious products and consumption on the other. The latter, and not the former, was the very thing that Hume believed to have caused the most fundamental transformation of European society and to have generated a new motivation for economic activities in the name of "manners." Thus, Hume made the neutrality of money theoretically compatible with those empirical observations that make us believe in the non-neutrality of money. The two contrasting views of money are unified at a deeper level by the concept of manners. Indeed, "The absolute quantity of the precious metals is a matter of great indifference," as Hume says. But the relative quantity of money as a necessary manifestation of a people's industrious manners is certainly significant and has actually caused momentous historical consequences by shaping modern civilized society in Europe. We now easily understand the profound sense in which Hume is happy to remark, "There are only two circumstances of any importance, namely, their gradual encrease, and their thorough concoction and circulation through the state" (Hume 1752: 294).

For Hume, this "concoction and circulation" ought not to be done by politicians and magistrates on the basis of protectionist policies and the narrow spirit of nationalism. Rather, it should be skilfully managed by a new type of politician and leader in the spirit of enlightened cosmopolitanism. Leaders should care first and foremost about the level of arts and industry in their nation based on open free trade rather than about the quantity of money by itself. In so doing, they could possibly envision open and free international trade across borders. Hume concludes this message by an impressive and bold rhetoric at the time when a major war with France could be breaking out at any moment.

> I shall therefore venture to acknowledge, that, not only as a man, but as a British subject, I pray for the flourishing commerce of GERMANY, SPAIN, ITALY, and even FRANCE itself. I am at least certain, that GREAT BRITAIN, and all those nations, would flourish more, did their sovereigns and ministers adopt such enlarged and benevolent sentiments towards each other. (Hume 1752: 331)

Conclusion: Economics and Civilization

The hallmark of Hume's economic writings is their consistent philosophical character combined with the methodology of social science. Careful and extensive observation of the "common course of the world" is neither an acceptance of the commonly held view of the world nor a mere generalized description of the facts and phenomena of the world. On the contrary, by being identified clearly as one of the central subjects comprising the Science of Man, his economic arguments were presented as a grand synthesis of extensive and detailed historical research and scientific analysis and model-building. Hume characterizes his way of doing this synthesis as an act of getting off the "common road," and this methodological feature gives to an apparently fragmentary collection of eight essays in *Political Discourses* the character of a systematic treatise on economics.

However, no matter how novel and provocative his arguments were, Hume's economics never departed from what was regarded by many as sound and commonsensical judgment. Hume's theories of luxury, money, and international trade all represent this dual character. Indeed the simple truism that luxury is vicious or that money is wealth was flatly rejected and refuted by Hume. But he was quick to substitute another set of more profound commonsense truths: that the enjoyment of an improved standard of living is good by nature and that money is merely a representation of goods and services, which compose the true substance of riches and wealth. Even the traditionally held view of inflationism – that a steady inflow and the consequent rise in the quantity of circulating money, was economically beneficial – was only conditionally allowed to survive under Hume's scrutiny, with his strict analysis of what historical and social conditions were required to make it generally true. Hume's answer was that only in the country or region where industrious manners are widely established and deeply rooted among people could monetary inflow from outside further encourage the already growing economic activities. The "common" view of money as a useful boost to economy was effectively replaced by a profound understanding of the "common course of the world," an understanding which, reconstructed at a deeper level, created a historical consciousness of a new emerging civilization.

As historians of economics have almost unanimously agreed in the literature, economic theories propounded by Hume had a number of significant predecessors. Nonetheless the place that has been accorded to Hume by the same scholars is significantly greater than those predecessors. Why is it? As illustrated by the case of quantity theory, Hume's outstanding ability to synthesize and formulate his views in an impressive rhetoric was certainly one reason. But something more than that must have worked to record his name as possibly the greatest author before Adam Smith. Not only did he synthesize the existing body of economic knowledge and theories in an admirable fashion, but also he completely reformulated and reconstructed them in an original way. In particular, the philosophical and methodological groundwork of economics was strengthened incomparably by contemporary standards, and Hume's message was an enlightened vision of free trade among civilized nations.

Certainly, Hume's economic analysis was still far from satisfactory even by the standard of the pre-Smithian stage of economics. Nevertheless, the two Scottish economists after Hume, his close friends, James Steuart and Smith, could never have created their great systems of political economy as they did without the rich and profound groundwork prepared by Hume. What they learned from Hume was not just the theories of economic development, money, and international trade. The greatest legacy of Hume left to those who came after him was the forceful vindication of the philosophical, moral, and political viability of modern civilized society. Hume's triad of "industry, knowledge and humanity" was exactly what lay at the heart of this intellectual legacy.

See also 21 " 'One of the Finest and Most Subtile Inventions': Hume on Government"; 22 " 'The Most Illustrious Philosopher and Historian of the Age': Hume's *History of England* "

References

Hume, David (1752). "Political Discourses," in Eugene F. Miller (ed.), *Essays, Moral, Political and Literary* (Indianapolis, IN: Liberty Fund, 1987).

—— (1776). "My Own Life," in Eugene F. Miller (ed.), *Essays, Moral, Political and Literary* (Indianapolis: Liberty Fund, 1987).

Lucas, Jr., R. E. (1996). "Nobel Lecture: Monetary Neutrality," *Journal of Political Economy*, 104, pp. 661–82.

Further Reading

Blaug, M. (ed.) (1995). *The Quantity Theory of Money: From Locke to Keynes and Friedman* (Aldershot: Elgar).

Caffentzis, C. G. (2001). "Hume, Money, and Civilization; Or, Why Was Hume a Metalist?" *Hume Studies*, 27, pp. 301–35.

Hont, I. and Ignatieff, M. (eds.) (1983). *Wealth and Virtue: The Shaping of Political Economy in the Scottish Enlightenment* (Cambridge: Cambridge University Press).

Norton, David Fate and Taylor, Jacqueline (eds) (forthcoming 2008). *Cambridge Companion to Hume*, 2nd edn. (New York: Cambridge University Press).

Pocock, J. G. A. (1985). *Virtue, Commerce and History* (Cambridge: Cambridge University Press).

Redman, D. A. (1997). *The Rise of Political Economy as a Science* (Cambridge, MA: MIT Press).

Rostow, W. W. (1990). *Theorists of Economic Growth from David Hume to the Present* (New York: Oxford University Press).

Rotwein, E. (1970). "Introduction," in E. Rotwein (ed.), *David Hume: Writings on Economics* (Madison: University of Wisconsin Press).

Sakamoto, T. (2003). "Hume's Political Economy as a System of Manners," in T. Sakamoto and H. Tanaka (eds.), *The Rise of Political Economy in the Scottish Enlightenment* (London: Routledge), pp. 86–102.

Schabas, Margaret (2001). "David Hume on Experimental Natural Philosophy, Money and Fluids," *History of Political Economy*, 33, pp. 411–35.

Teichgraeber, III, R. F. (1986). *"Free Trade" and Moral Philosophy: Rethinking the Sources of Adam Smith's "Wealth of Nations"* (Durham: Duke University Press).

Wennerlind, C. (2005). "David Hume's Monetary Theory Revisited: Was He Really a Quantity Theorist and an Inflationist?" *Journal of Political Economy*, 113, pp. 223–37.

21

"One of the Finest and Most Subtile Inventions": Hume on Government

RICHARD H. DEES

Hume's theory of government has been appropriated by nearly every part of the political spectrum, from conservatives (Livingston 1999: chs. 8–10) to liberals (Stewart 1992: chs. 5–6). Such labels, of course, belong to a world that did not exist until after Hume died, but the fact that the many sides to contemporary debates can find comfort in Hume demonstrates both the enormous appeal of Hume's sensible pronouncements on politics and the complexity and subtlety of his account. To understand fully Hume's theory of government, however, requires an interpretation that goes beyond the pronouncements Hume makes in the *Treatise* (or in the *Second Enquiry* [EPM 4.1–4], which is so sparse that it adds nothing); it must delve deeply into the *Essays* and even more deeply into the *History of England*. For Hume includes in his account of government not only the broad observations that apply to all human institutions that touch on how large groups of people can live together, but he also offers broad thoughts on the political institutions of his age and a subtle historical perspective on the origins of the institutions and values of modern governments, particularly those of Great Britain in the eighteenth century.

The Origins of Government

Of the actual origins of government, Hume is distinctly uninterested. In the *History*, he skips any account of or speculation about the origins of government in Britain, dismissing them as unsuited for civilized interest:

> [T]he sudden, violent, and unprepared revolutions, incident to Barbarians, are so much guided by caprice, and terminate so often in cruelty that they disgust us by the uniformity of their appearance; and it is rather fortunate for letters that they are buried in silence and oblivion. (H 1; I 3–4)

The annals of the distant pasts when governments came into being can only disgust us now, and more importantly, they teach us no lessons that will be useful to us. Nevertheless, Hume is interested in the conceptual issues that arise at the origins of government, if only to explain what our relationship to government is. Indeed, Hume

388

presents *three* different accounts of the origins for government: (1) a natural history of government, in which he explains how government develops as a natural response to the problems that can not be addressed within the institutions of justice and promise-keeping; (2) a speculative history of the circumstances under which governments are likely in fact to develop; and (3) a natural history of the moral obligation of government, in which he explains how we come to have duties towards government. All three are interrelated, and Hume himself treats them together (T 3.2.7–8), but it will be useful to treat them separately.

The natural history of government is a story based on the traits of human nature that would naturally lead people to adopt government. Justice and promise-keeping arise as stable conventions that people construct to secure their property and to facilitate their relationships with others. Government arises because, although adhering to these conventions is in everyone's interest in the long run, we are sometimes impressed by a short-term gain of breaking our promises or of seizing someone else's property (T 3.2.7.2–3). Sometimes, we find the objectively greater long-term good overwhelmed by the prospect of short-term benefit:

> Tho' we may be fully convinc'd, that the latter object excels the former, we are not able to regulate our actions by this judgment; but yield to the sollicitations of our passions, which always plead in favour of whatever is near and contiguous. (T 3.2.7.2)

Of course, each of us separately has a similar temptation, and if I think that others will act on these impulses, then I have a further incentive to commit injustices, lest I become "the cully of my integrity" (T 3.2.7.3). Seen from enough distance, we understand that our own interests are not served by these lapses, so we will endeavor to set up institutions that will enable us to resist the temptations when they come (T 3.2.7.4–5). Thus, we empower some people to enforce the rules of justice and contracts. In doing so, we insure that everyone knows that both their short-term and their long-term interests are served in following the demands of justice (see Whelan 1985: 268–73).

On this view, governments come into existence to solve two logical-psychological problems. First, we have an internal problem between our long-term self-interest and our short-term self-interest. The situation is a one-person variant of a Prisoners' Dilemma (Parfit 1984: 92–3). At each moment in time, I am tempted to violate justice, but it will be worse for me over time if I do so. Structurally, this situation looks like this (Mackie 1980: 106–7):

		Me-later	
		Follow	Defect
	Follow	2, 1	4, 4
Me-now			
	Defect	1, 3	3, 2

Numbers are ordinal rankings of options, Me-now first, followed by Me-later. Of course, both parties in the matrix do not really have a choice. What my future self wants me to do now is irrelevant to what I want to do now, and – as Parfit (1984:

ch. 6) argues – creating an argument that shows why I am irrational to prefer my present aims to my interests considered over the course of my life is surprisingly difficult. Since the problem is fundamental, we can solve it not by changing human nature, but only by changing human circumstance:

> 'Tis evident such a remedy can never be effectual without correcting this propensity; and as 'tis impossible to change or correct any thing material in our nature, the utmost we can do is to change our circumstances and situation, and render the observance of the laws of justice our nearest interest, and their violation our most remote. (T 3.2.7.6)

The only way to get out of problems like Prisoners' Dilemma is to change the incentive structures. Setting up an institution that will more reliably punish me if I stray tilts the balance in favor of following the rules in the short-run. We can rationally do so because we can look at the above conflict from afar, as one between Me-later and Me-still-later, and since the objective good lies with the Me-still-later, we can set up a mechanism by which Me-later will be induced to follow justice too. For that very purpose, we establish a civil magistrate, who, with the threat of punishment, can give all the Me-nows incentive to do what is the interest of Me-in-the-long-run.

The second problem government is meant to solve is a similar interpersonal Prisoners' Dilemma. Even if I personally can resist the temptation to injustice without government, I might not be confident that you can do so, and if I think you will violate the rules of justice, I will think that society will fall apart no matter what I do. Then it would be in my interest to violate justice before you can take advantage of me. In this case, we are in a more traditional Prisoners' Dilemma, in which we will both do something that is worse for us because we can not trust the other to take the option that would be better, but only if we both take it:

		You	
		Follow	Defect
	Follow	2, 2	4, 1
Me			
	Defect	1, 4	3, 3

Once again, government provides the incentive structure that solves the problem: once I know that you are likely to be punished if you defect, then I know that you are unlikely to defect, and so – even setting aside the risk that I will be punished if I defect – I no longer have any reason to defect (see Charron 1980).

Although government is one means by which we can solve these two Prisoners' Dilemmas, it is not the only means. Indeed, in a society that is small enough, I can expect that people will find out if I break my promises or if I steal. When a society is small, there is no place to hide, and a person's reputation can quite literally be his livelihood. An outside force is not needed to enforce the rules, because the society itself will be able to do so. The temptation to stray is removed, because there is little hope that I can gain from any transgressions. Such societies, then, have little need for any formal governmental structures. So only when the society is large enough that the agreement to follow justice does not enforce itself do we need government. But when we do have reason to set up government, we have self-interested reasons both to set it up and to obey it. Such self-interested reasons to obey government are what Hume deems our "natural obligation" to it (see T 3.2.2.23).

Of course, Hume rightly notes, governments do not form simply because they may prove useful, so he offers an account of the circumstances under which governments are likely to form. Societies in the past have been small, and, as we have seen, such societies do not need governments. Large societies, on the other hand, are extremely difficult, if not impossible, to sustain without government. So, we seem caught in a Catch-22: societies can not grow large without government, but governments are not needed unless the society is already large, so there seems to be no reason that governments would ever be formed. The flaw in this reasoning is that it assumes that small societies never need structures that resemble government just because they do not always require them. But a little reflection will show why that premise is false. Even small societies need a centralized form of authority to wage war. As Hume puts the point: "Camps are the true mothers of cities" (T 3.2.8.2). Wars require a central command to direct the action, so only then does some one person come to have authority over the others. Usually, of course, once the threat is over, the need for such authority disappears, and the war leader returns to his position in society. Of course, he may not: he may simply take the opportunity to set himself up permanently. But even in the cases that are benign, the example of a central power, Hume thinks, will present itself in the future as a means to solve other kinds of problems as they arise. Such an example also explains why governments tend to be monarchical. In any case, as a society gradually becomes larger and wealthier, the need for a more permanent and more formal mechanism to enforce justice will become evident. Thus, only "an encrease of riches and possessions" (T 3.2.8.2) makes government necessary. When it is established, then, it will be because people see the need for it and put it into effect. In that sense – but only in that sense – people consent to government (T 3.2.8.3). Indeed, the first governments may even be established explicitly by consent. They are designed to enforce the laws of nature – justice and promise-keeping – so using a promise to secure the agreement would seem natural (T 3.2.8.3).

Once government is in place, it stays in place because it enforces the laws of nature, and so no further consent is needed:

> tho' the duty of allegiance be at first grafted on the obligation of promises, and be for some time supported by that obligation, yet so soon as the advantages of government are fully known and acknowledg'd, it immediately takes root of itself, and has an original obligation and authority, independent of all contracts. (T 3.2.8.3)

Because it serves a separate function from the institution of promise-keeping, however, we do not need to suppose, as Locke does, that consent is essential to government (T 3.2.8.4–6; see Locke 1689: sections 95–9). Only philosophers, committed to a theory in which promise-keeping is seen as outside human conventions when governments are so clearly human inventions, need to maintain that the latter is based on the former (T 3.2.8.4; see Miller 1981: ch. 4). But our own experience, Hume says, shows that such an account must be mistaken. Most people do not think they are obligated by anything they have said or done, but by their mere presence in a country, and

Hume claims, "the opinion of men, in this case, carry with them a peculiar authority" (T 3.2.8.8; see E 2.12.7; M 470). Promises require a conscious intent, but because people do not generally think they have made such a promise, their obligation to obey government is not based on it. Consent theory thus gets the basic facts about our obligations completely wrong. For that reason, Hume rejects the traditional Whig theory of government of his day in favor of a more skeptical "scientific Whiggism" (Forbes 1975: ch. 5).

However, Hume's account of the origins of government has two significant problems. First, wars need not be fought with a single leader, and before government institutionalizes hierarchies, no plans can be formed without the cooperation of a number of different groups, even within a relatively small society. So while Hume's argument may show why some form of democracy is not the first government, the first structures need not be monarchical. Second, and much more importantly, the relationship Hume posits between government and riches seems backwards. Without a government to enforce justice, no one can muster the economic forces to accumulate any real wealth. Once there is significant wealth, government is essential, but the government must come into existence *before* anyone could even try to possess very much. So effective government makes economic progress possible, not vice versa. So we need to posit a different reason for why governments would form in the first place. But we need not exercise ourselves too much over this question since a number of scenarios are plausible: sometimes, wars last a long time, so a leader becomes entrenched in power; sometimes, respected members of a community are looked upon to decide disputes and more formal mechanisms evolve; or perhaps, they develop for other reasons. In the end, the explanation of how exactly governments form is less important than the explanation of why they remain in place once they are formed. Hume's important point here, then, is that because government clearly serve a useful function in enforcing justice among larger groups, it will tend to stay in place because everyone sees it in their interests to support it, however it came into being.

The Moral Obligation to Government

The third history that is relevant is how the *moral* obligation to obey government arises. While a natural obligation is based on self-interest, a moral obligation is the "sentiment of right and wrong" (T 3.2.2.23) which we attach to traits of character. In general, Hume argues that we call character trait a virtue if we feel pleasure contemplating it from a general point of view. Any trait that is either useful or agreeable to oneself or to others may qualify (T 3.3.1). Traits like justice and allegiance to government are virtues because they are useful to the public at large: "a *sympathy* with *public* interest is the source of the *moral* approbation, which attends that virtue" (T 3.2.2.24). Unlike natural virtues like benevolence which are always either useful or agreeable, these virtues are artificial because they depend on conventions and human institutions for their existence, and their usefulness may not be found in every observance of the virtue. In the case of justice, we may be required to restore the money of a dissolute profligate from the poor man who stole it to provide bread for his family. In the case of allegiance, we are required to obey government even if in a particular case, we can benefit from not doing so. Indeed, we are even required to obey in most cases, even if the public interest would be better served by disobedience. Governments will not be stable if people are constantly claiming that our interests are better served by disobedience. Too often, those judgments are simply mistaken. But even when they are not, the stability of government itself has benefits that go beyond any particular case. So, even though the moral obligation rests on the natural one, obedience to government is one of those general rules which "extend beyond the principles, on which they are founded" (T 3.2.9.3).

For that reason, when we ask to whom we owe our allegiance, our primary guide about what we should do rests on what is established:

> In the particular exertions of power, the question ought never to be forgotten, *What is best?* But in the general distribution of power among the several members of a constitution, there can seldom be admitted any other question, than *What is established?* (H App. 3; IV 354)

Working within a framework of a particular government, we can ask what the best course of action is, but in the broader questions of what form of government we should endorse, we must simply accept what has already been established. Given the benefits of government, we must settle the government on someone, and the most obvious candidate is the person, group, or set of institutions that is already in place. Indeed, very strong reasons are needed to overturn that judgment. "Long possession" is then the first principle that determines to whom we owe our allegiance (T 3.2.10.4–5). This principle has the paradoxical result that

> a king, who during his life-time might justly be deem'd a usurper, will be regarded by posterity as a lawful prince, because he has had the good fortune to settle his family on the throne, and entirely change the antient form of government. (T 3.2.10.19)

If the family of a usurper survives on the throne, then we come to regard that family as a salient solution to the problem of who should govern, and it thereby gains legitimacy after the fact, when the initial usurpation only caused instability. If no such long-standing government exists, then we should defer to "present possession," for much the same reason: as long as the goals of government are met, then whoever currently hold the reins of power should be allowed to do so (T 3.2.10.6–7). If no government qualifies as the present possessor, we should accept the conqueror (T 3.2.10.8), and failing that, we should look to the right of succession (T 3.2.10.9– 13). Only then should we look to the laws passed by a legislature to settle these questions (T 3.2.10.14).

All of these rules really amount to ways of finding a salient solution to the problem of empowerment. We need someone to rule, and it is more important that we get someone – virtually anyone – than that we fight over whom it should be. So we should alight on some rule and then stick to it (see Hampton 1986: 173–86). For that reason, Hume argues, we simply should not take questions about who should rule too seriously:

> Whoever considers the history of the several nations of the world; their revolutions, conquests, encrease, and diminution; the manner in which their particular governments

are establish'd, and the successive right transmitted from one person to another, will soon learn to treat very lightly all disputes concerning the rights of princes, and will be convinc'd, that a strict adherence to any general rules, and the rigid loyalty to particular persons and families, on which some people set so high a value, are virtues that hold less of reason, than of bigotry and superstition. (T 3.2.10.15)

Some of the questions about the title to rule simply do not have any rational answer, and since the purpose of government is to provide peace and stability, we should focus more on ensuring that we achieve peace than on the particular rights of one person or another to wield this power or that.

The Right to Revolution

Although Hume thinks we should follow the general rule that we should obey the established government, he does recognize some exceptions to that rule – as long as the exceptions themselves "have the qualities of a general rule, and be founded on very numerous and common instances" (T 3.2.9.3). We can, then, refuse to obey when the exercise of power begins to undermine the security which we hoped to gain from government:

'Tis certain, therefore, that in all our notions of morals we never entertain such an absurdity as that of passive obedience, but make allowances for resistance in the more flagrant instances of tyranny and oppression. (T 3.2.9.4; see E 2.1.3; M 488–92)

In extreme circumstances, then, the people are morally permitted to rebel. Government is formed because it benefits people on the whole, and when it ceases to benefit them, they need not cling to it. Indeed, if the right to revolution did not exist, we could expect only tyranny:

For as no rights can subsist without some remedy, still less rights exposed to so much invasion from tyranny, or even from ambition; if subjects must never resist, it follows, that every prince, without any effort, policy or violence, is at once rendered absolute and uncontroulable. (H 63; VI 174)

So we have a moral obligation to obey government, and we should err on the side of obedience; otherwise, governments will cease to be effective. However, we are not bound to it to suffer great harms to the public interest by obedience.

So far, Hume's conclusion seems properly balanced; it is a politics, as Duncan Forbes remarks, for "moderate men" (Forbes 1975: ch. 3). We have a moral obligation to obey government because doing so is greatly to our benefit, but it will not be to our benefit if the government can abuse its power indiscriminately. By this route, as Hume himself recognizes (T 3.2.9.1), we come to roughly the same conclusions about our obligation to government as the consent theorists who base the right to rebel on the government's breach of its contract with the people. For Hume, then, consent theory gets the right answer, but since its premises are factually inaccurate, its normative case is undermined. Nevertheless, we cannot simply think of Hume as the person who put what is right about consent theory on its proper footing, for two reasons. First, Hume misses an essential element in the argument of consent theorists. The important point in Locke's theory is not that governments did in fact arise by consent or that they are maintained by tacit consent, but that the only *legitimate* governments are the result of consent. So consent theory is not based on the claim that people *do* consent to government, but that they are obligated to obey only if they do so. It is thus an entirely normative theory, not a normative theory based on falsities. The modern conviction that only democratic forms of government are legitimate is an expression of the ideal that consent *should* play a crucial role in the everyday operations of government, down to who should serve as the county dogcatcher. Moreover, because we have accepted something like consent theory, it is now false to say that if consent theorists "look abroad into the world, they would meet with nothing that, in the least, corresponds to their ideas" (E 2.12.7; M 469–70). Because we have come to regard consent theory as *morally* true, it has become *factually* true. The consequences of the modern view is, of course, a conclusion that Hume would have found absurd: no government that existed during his lifetime was legitimate. Locke himself, of course, tried to argue that the British government, if none other, had acquired the active consent of the people in the Glorious Revolution of 1688 and that it maintained that consent by the freedom people had within that government. But a Lockean could simply accept the contention that no eighteenth-century government was truly legitimate – though even then, she could still think that some governments were better than others because they better respected the basic rights of people to "the mutual *Preservation* of their Lives, Liberties and Estates" (Locke 1689: §123). But Locke would not regard the result that no government counted as legitimate as an absurd outcome; it may simply be the logical result of his inquiry. The difference between Hume's view and Locke's is then fundamental: for Hume, as long as government serves the basic functions of providing for peace and stability, then it is legitimate in the sense that we owe it our allegiance. Locke sets a higher standard for what counts as a legitimate government, and if the result is that few governments existing qualified, then so be it. For just that reason, Hume's arguments against consent theory are not decisive.

Second, Hume does not simply give us a new face for consent theorists' enthusiasm for governmental changes, because Hume fundamentally distrusts revolutions. Locke sees them as sometimes necessary and, when necessary, heroic. Hume, on the other hand, disdains them.

> Some innovations must necessarily have place in every human institution . . . but violent innovations no individual is entitled to make: they are even dangerous to be attempted by the legislature: more ill than good is ever to be expected from them. (E 2.12.27; M 477)

New governments, Hume complains, "must commonly be supported with more expence and severity than the old" (H 59; V 520). Revolutionaries, as such, are always in the wrong, and even in those cases in which the representatives of the people support change, they are still unlikely to benefit most people. For that reason, Hume thinks, "it is dangerous to weaken, by these speculations, the reverence, which the multitude owe to authority" (H 59; V 544). Teaching consent theory is a mistake, since revolutions are hard to stop once they start. Instead,

> the doctrine of obedience ought alone to be *inculcated*, and that the exceptions, which are rare, ought seldom or never to be mentioned in popular reasonings and discourses. (H 59; V 544)

So passive obedience, though false, should be taught to the people so that they are not tempted by revolutions. When a real exception comes, he says,

> it must, from its very nature, be so obvious and undisputed, so as to remove all doubt, and overpower the restraint, however great, imposed by teaching the general doctrine of obedience. (H 59; V 544)

Consent doctrine, even if it were true, would be too dangerous to teach, and its conclusions, while just, are just as bad. So, while Locke thinks a check on the rulers is their knowledge that the people know they can rebel if the rulers take too much power, Hume thinks that giving the people such knowledge is playing with fire. Thus, Locke fundamentally trusts the will of the people; Hume does not.

On whether Hume's distrust of the people is justified, history gives a mixed record. Hume is thinking of English Civil Wars, of the Wars of Religion in France, and of other incidents in English history, like the revolts of Simon Montfort (H 12; II 46–61) and Henry Bolingbroke (H 17; II 315–22). We could add, just for starters, the French Revolution, the Russian Revolution, Rwanda, and Bosnia-Herzegovina. From that perspective, the relative peace and ease of the Glorious Revolution is the exception. Since Hume's time, however, we also have several other instances of relatively peaceful transformations, like those in Eastern Europe in 1989 and of orderly violent revolutions, like the American. Nevertheless, Hume's caution is still clearly applicable. Locke, focusing on just the Glorious Revolution, probably has a more distorted view. On the other hand, democratic government itself demonstrates that Hume's pessimism is, in the end, unwarranted.

The Further Uses of Government

Once government is in place as a tool for enforcing the rules of justice, we find that we naturally turn to it to solve other tasks, in what Annette Baier (1991: ch. 11) notes is a "progress of sentiments." First, to fulfill its basic function of enforcing justice, government will also have to decide when a rule has been broken. As any prosecuting attorney will attest, deciding what crime, if any, has been committed is the most important task that the judicial system performs. So the task of deciding issues of justice is intimately connected with the execution of justice. For just that reason, government will be in a position to arbitrate conflicting property claims and contract disputes. It serves, then, not just as the executor of the laws, but also as the judge of those laws and, more generally, as a judge of any disputes that might arise.

To these tasks, not even the most ardent libertarian would object. However, Hume's argument goes beyond what a minimalist about government would endorse. Hume realizes that once we have a government, we might come to see it as a useful means to solve other problems, even if it is not designed explicitly for those purposes:

> Two neighbours may agree to drain a meadow, which they possess in common; because 'tis easy for them to know each other's mind . . . But 'tis very difficult, and indeed imposs-ible, that a thousand persons shou'd agree in any such action; it being difficult for them to concert so complicated a design, and still more difficult for them to execute it; while each seeks a pretext to free himself of the trouble and expence, and wou'd lay the whole burden on others. Political society easily remedies both these inconveniences . . . Thus bridges are built; harbours open'd; ramparts rais'd; canals form'd; fleets equip'd; and armies dis-ciplin'd every where, by the care of government. (T 3.2.7.8)

We often have projects that are mutually beneficial, so government can enforce an agree-ment between us. But with government, we can also create projects on a much larger scale, with an even greater benefit, projects that would be impossible to coordinate, much less pay for, without a centralized authority to enforce the complex contract that such projects require. But Hume goes even further in this passage: some goods would benefit society as a whole, and they would be cheaper and more beneficial if everyone had access to them. But for that very reason, each individual person can want others to pay for those projects, as long as she can then use them. But of course, if everyone thinks this way, no such projects will ever be realized. Governments, through taxation, thus solve a multi-player Prisoners' Dilemma by forcing everyone to contribute to projects for the common good. Governments thus solve the "public good problem," and in doing so, they create a new environment in which society can evolve and prosper. After all, public roads, for example, are not merely good for people visiting their relatives; they also make possible an economy based on trade. Indeed, one of the crucial public goods for which government is essential is the creation of the marketplace itself. Assuring every-one that contracts will honored and that every trader will be treated fairly creates the environment in which an economy can grow and in which capitalism can work its magic. For this reason, Hume thinks government is "one of the finest and most subtile inventions imaginable" (T 3.2.7.8).

In addition, government is essential for a very different kind of public good: liberty. For most of his account of government in the *Treatise*, Hume writes about the role of government in preserving justice and the role of justice in keeping the peace. Peace and stability, then, seem to be the only goals. But when he discusses who should govern, Hume concludes that there are no philosophically exact rules:

> the study of history confirms the reasonings of true philosophy; which . . . teaches us to regard the controversies in politics of incapable of any decision in most cases, and as entirely subordinate to the interest of peace *and liberty*. (T 3.2.10.15; emphasis added)

Suddenly, peace and security are not the only issue. Government should provide for *liberty* as well. Indeed, he proclaims, "nothing is more essential to public interest, than the preservation of public liberty" (T 3.2.10.16).

Liberty is what was distinctive about the British government in the eighteenth century, the product of its free press, its religious toleration, and its proto-democratic institutions. All of these elements either came into existence or were greatly streng-thened by the Glorious Revolution of 1688, which deposed the Catholic proponent of absolute monarchy, James II, in favor of his Protestant and more liberal son-in-law, William III. Since that time, Hume declares,

we, in this island, have ever since enjoyed, if not the best system of government, at
least the most entire system of liberty, that ever was known amongst mankind. (H 71;
VI 531)

Liberty made the Glorious Revolution worthwhile. Even though Hume says that
James's actions were "pernicious and tyrannical" (T 3.2.10.16), he does not mean
that they threatened peace and stability. Indeed, Hume admits that the similar actions
of another monarch in another era would have been "beneficial to the public" (T
3.2.10.16). The problem with James was not that he failed to enforce the laws
or that he endangered the peace; the problem was that he violated the understanding of his subjects about the limits of his power. In 1688 – though not in 1588 –
liberty was an essential part of the British constitution, and for that reason, Hume endorses
the Revolution Settlement that ousted James. The context makes all the difference.
Because Hume regards liberty as an important goal for government, his position on
revolution once again edges closer to Locke's. When the people have an established
role in government, they have the right to protect that role from the intrusion of
the magistrate.

However, unlike Locke, Hume does not think liberty is the most important goal of
government. "Liberty," he argues, "is the perfection of civil society; but still authority
must be acknowledged essential to its very existence" (E 1.5.7; M 41). Liberty is nice,
but it can not exist without authority: "a regard to liberty, though a laudable passion,
ought commonly to be subordinate to a reverence for established government"
(H 71; VI 533). Because authority is always more important than liberty, Hume, unlike
Locke, does not think absolute monarchy, in which liberty does not exist, is an inherently illegitimate form of government. Before the modern age, monarchs could change
laws on a whim, and so no long-term stability was really possible. But modern monarchies, like that embodied by the government of Louis XV, are not so capricious; the
king operates through laws and through a regular process so that people feel secure
in their persons and their property:

> Property is there secure; industry encouraged; the arts flourish and the prince lives secure
> among his subjects, like a father among his children. (E 1.12.12; M 94)

Security is the key to good government for Hume. Thus, order, the chief virtue of
government is well-served in such a government (see Whelan 1985: 348–63):

> It may now be affirmed of civilized monarchies, what was formerly said in praise of
> republics alone, *that they are a government of Laws, not of Men*. They are found susceptible
> of order, method, and constancy, to a surprizing degree. (E 1.12.12; M 94)

Any government that provides security and stability fulfills its most important duty and
should therefore be considered legitimate, and modern absolute governments can do
so (Miller 1981: ch. 7).

Because they were always less arbitrary, free governments of the past fulfilled the
basic functions of government well, and they had certain other advantages. They gave
rise not only to liberty, but also to knowledge and to the arts:

> Though a republic should be barbarous, it necessarily, by an infallible operation, gives rise to LAW . . . From law arises security: From security curiosity: And from curiosity knowledge. (E 1.14.14; M 118)

A regular system of law is needed to foster creativity, both scientific and literary, and such a system of law is a necessary part of free governments (Whelan 1985: 351). Absolute monarchies in the past, on the other hand, were "somewhat oppressive and debasing" (E 1.14.11; M 116). But because they are no longer arbitrary, modern monarchies like that in France can support the arts and many fields of knowledge. If they do not offer liberty, they do offer quite a spectacle of the arts and of refinement. Because advancement comes from social superiors, monarchies best promote a "refined taste." A person gets ahead by becoming "*agreeable, by his wit, complaisance, or civility*" (E 1.14.28; M 126). Moreover, "they have, in great measure, perfected that art, the most useful and agreeable of any, *l'Art de Vivre, the art of society and conversation*" (E 1.12.6; M 91; see Livingston 1999: 263–4).

Yet even if a modern absolute monarchy would be preferable to many kinds of republics, Hume does not, as Nicholas Phillipson (1989: 59–60, 113) contends, actually prefer it. Against a refined taste, republics produce "strong genius," and because office comes from elections, "it is necessary for a man to make himself *useful*, by his industry, capacity, or knowledge" (E 1.14.28; M 126). In addition, philosophy is likely to be promoted better in a republic because monarchies depend on "a superstitious reverence to priests and princes" and so they have "abridged the liberty of reasoning, with regard to religion, and politics, and consequently metaphysics and morals" (E 1.14.29; M 126; see Forbes 1975: ch. 5). Because he values philosophy and science, Hume's judgment falls on the side of a free government, but as David Miller notes, "this preference was expressed in such a cautious way that it could have very little practical impact" (Miller 1981: 159). To modern sensibilities, however, the arguments in favor of free governments seem even stronger, and they show why a republic should be preferred to an absolute monarchy – even if nothing in the nature of the latter warrants a revolution against it simply from its form. Yet Hume reaches a different conclusion: he argues that when the delicate balance of the British constitution fails – as inevitably it must – he would prefer to see it become an absolute monarchy rather than a republic. A republic would rest the entire government in the House of Commons, a situation he thinks would be highly unstable:

> If the house of commons, in such a case, ever dissolve itself, which is not to be expected, we may look for a civil war every election. If it continue itself, we shall suffer all the tyranny of a faction, subdivided into new factions. (E 1.7.7; M 52)

The result in either case is civil war and the establishment of a monarchy, so he would prefer a peaceful "*Euthanasia*" directly to monarchy rather than the violent path through a republic (E 1.7.7; M 53).

Hume's pessimistic assessment of republics is based on his interpretation of the Commonwealth years, in which the House of Commons did rule and refused to dissolve itself until the factions led by Cromwell simply established a new form of monarchy under the title of a "protectorate." Given that history, Hume's conclusions are understandable, but of course, the history of the two hundred years since Hume wrote shows that the old British constitution could die a peaceful death in a parliamentary government as well. None of the evils Hume predicted for such a government have in fact come to pass. So we have even more reason to prefer republican government than Hume did. Because we accept for moral reasons the contract theory Hume rejects and the democracy he finds untenable, republicanism has in fact become our "established practice" of government. For us, then, even Hume would endorse a republic. And so for us, Locke and Hume finally converge.

The History of Liberty

Hume's respect for modern monarchies almost overshadows his fondness for liberty. But even if liberty is not essential for legitimacy, it is a public good that is worth fostering and protecting – with violence in some rare cases. But while Hume constructs a "natural history" of government, there is no similar natural history for liberty. Human needs and powers will give rise to government of some form almost everywhere. The process is not literally inevitable: we can imagine societies that, because they lack sufficient natural resources or because they never come into contact with other humans who would threaten their lifestyle, never develop a form of central authority that we would recognize as a true government. But given a set of circumstances that is common, governments will result. Liberty, on the other hand, is not the product of broad causal forces that make its rise inescapable. It is a monumental historical accident. Indeed, Hume suggests, the chief benefit of the study of history for "a civilized nation, like the English, who have happily established the most perfect and most accurate system of liberty that was ever found compatible with government" is that it teaches them to "cherish their present constitution"

> by instructing them in the great mixture of accident, which commonly concurs with a small ingredient of wisdom and foresight, in erecting the complicated fabric of the most perfect government. (H 23; II 525)

Liberty was not an inevitable product of history. The English, Hume says, were deeply and profoundly lucky.

The most important factors in the rise of liberty in England lie not in human nature, nor do they originate in some ancient constitution. Liberty, first and foremost, requires a steady government. Without it, even the most powerful men have little freedom since they must constantly guard their possessions (H App. 1; I 168–9). On Hume's reckoning, even the Magna Charta was not particularly important: although it gave the people some freedom to enjoy their property, its primary purpose was to enshrine the power of the barons (H 11; I 443–6). The establishment of the House of Commons, while significant, was of limited importance, since its power was obliterated during the reigns of Henry VIII and Elizabeth I. During Henry's rule, "when they [the people] laboured under any grievance, they had not the satisfaction of expecting redress from parliament" which was so servile to the king that the people "had reason to dread each meeting of that assembly, and were then sure of having tyranny converted into law"

(H 32; III 264). And in summing up Elizabeth's reign, he says, "we have seen, that *the most absolute* authority of the sovereign . . . was established on above twenty branches of prerogative . . . every one of them, totally incompatible with the liberty of the subjects" (H App 3; IV 367; see Miller 1981: 169–70). Liberty for the people, then, was completely absent until the seventeenth century. Its roots, then, lie in the relatively recent past. Before then, the constitution of Britain had "been in a state of continual fluctuation" (H App. 3; IV 355; see Miller 1990; Livingston 1999: ch. 8).

The story of liberty is, for Hume, deliciously ironic. The heroes of that story are the Puritans, who were interested not in liberty, but in their own peculiar notion of salvation. In the absolutist age of Elizabeth I,

> the precious spark of liberty had been kindled, and was preserved, by the puritans alone; and it was to this sect, whose principles appear so frivolous and habits so ridiculous, that the English owe the whole freedom of their constitution. (H 40; IV 145–6)

Since the Puritans wanted to resist Elizabeth's religious edicts, they had to maintain that it was proper for them to do so and they appealed to a liberty that only later became established. The Reformation that Henry VIII began in England itself led to the idea that authority could be questioned:

> But in proportion as the practice of submitting religion to private judgment was acceptable to the people, it appeared, in some respects, dangerous to the rights of sovereigns, and seemed to destroy that implicit obedience, on which the authority of the civil magistrate is chiefly found. The very precedent, of shaking so ancient and deep founded an establishment as that of the Romish hierarchy, might, it was apprehended, prepare the way for other innovations. (H 31; III 212)

However, Hume's own account shows that the mere idea of innovation was not enough: the government of England became, if anything, more absolutist in the sixteenth century, rather than less. But the Puritan party, as they became more powerful in the reign of James I, still linked together the ideas of religious and civil liberty:

> The spirit too of enthusiasm; bold, daring, and uncontrouled; strongly disposed their minds to adopt republican tenets; and inclined them to arrogate, in their actions and conduct, the same liberty, which they assumed, in their rapturous flights and ecstasies. (H 48, n. J; V 559)

People who were willing to take religion into their own hands were only too willing to put the more mundane matters of government into those same hands. But the situation, Hume argues, was in fact more complicated, since there were actually three parties who were called Puritans:

> political puritans, who maintained the highest principles of civil liberty; the puritans in discipline, who were averse to the ceremonies and episcopal government of the church; and the doctrinal puritans, who rigidly defended the speculative system of the first reformers. (H 51; V 212)

401

These three groups were mixed together in complicated ways, so the triumph of the Puritans at the end of the Civil War did not create a simple or stable political order, and so their legacy was decidedly mixed.

The pretenses of the Puritans would have had no effect whatsoever, however, if two other factors had not been in their favor. First, a broad trend favored them: the general rise of the middle class created a group whose interests were not sufficiently represented as long as the power of the House of Commons remained weak (H App. 3; IV 384). Many of the middle class were also Puritans, so their interests coincided and indeed were co-mingled. The general prosperity of the kingdom in the first half of the seventeenth century also created a demand for liberties from a middle class that was increasingly wealthy and educated (H 46; V 39–40). But even France had its Puritans – the Huguenots – and a rising middle class, so these factors alone do not account for the rise of liberty. The other important factor is peculiar to England, and without it the more the general factors would have had no effect: the relative poverty of the English crown. Elizabeth had maintained her power and independence by fostering a scrupulous frugality, if not a stinginess. She was thereby able to husband her funds and then supplement them as necessary by selling off many crown lands. By the time the Stuarts came to power, the Crown had little independent revenue and the Stuarts had no option but to appeal to Parliament for funds (H 46; V 38). But the leaders of the Commons had little personal regard for either James I or Charles I, and they saw it as their duty to establish a more firm liberty for the people:

> Animated with a warm regard to liberty, these generous patriots saw with regret an unbounded power exercised by the crown, and were resolved to seize the opportunity, which the king's necessities offered them, of reducing the prerogative within more reasonable compass. (H 50; V 160)

With the power of the purse, the Commons were able to extract concessions from Charles I in the Petition of Right of 1628 which gave the people sufficient liberty and to curb the discretionary power of the monarchy that had, in Hume's view, become too great (H 51; V 196–7).

To make a long story – and for Hume, this story is the main focus of the 1,100 pages of the two Stuart volumes of the *History* – short, the new circumstances in which England found itself in the seventeenth century, combined with the peculiar factors of the politics of the time made a greater liberty for the people both attractive and possible in a way it was not elsewhere in Europe. Of course, the Puritans did not stop at the reasonable liberty they had secured in the Petition of Right, but carried it further until Charles was provoked to act stupidly in suppressing Parliament both in 1629 and later in 1641, actions which eventually forced him to defend his crown in open warfare. In Hume's view, however, the English Civil War was not inevitable. Parliament went too far because it was driven by religious fanaticism: "[H]ad not the wound been poisoned by the infusion of theological hatred," Hume argues, "it must have admitted of an easy remedy" (H 54; V 303). The Puritans were the impetus behind liberty, but their religious zeal led them into the Civil War. They won that war, but the disastrous Commonwealth that followed undermined their cause. The forces of liberty had to struggle during the tumultuous reign of Charles II and the absolutist pretensions of James II, until a stable plan of liberty emerged after the Glorious Revolution of 1688.

For our present purposes, the important point to see is that although Hume thinks that liberty is "so necessary to the perfection of human society" (H 48; V 96), its rise depended on contextual features: the inability of the crown to support itself after Elizabeth, the political deafness of James I, the unwillingness of the people to accept unquestioningly the pronouncement of this "foreign" prince, the obstinacy of Charles I faced with the delicate and precarious position in which he found himself, and the "arbitrary disposition" of James II and the "bigotry of his principles" (H 70; VI 451) were all crucial factors in the emergence of liberty. But, as Hume argues elsewhere:

> What depends upon a few persons is, in a great measure, to be ascribed to chance, or secret and unknown causes: What arises from a great number, may be often accounted for by determinate and known causes. (E 1.14.2; M 112)

So we must ascribe the rise of liberty to chance rather than to cause – or, more accurately, the causes are of a particular rather than of a general nature (Schmidt 2003: 270–2). For that reason, we cannot have a true natural history of liberty, only a political history of it.

Such a history of liberty, however, undercuts another piece of traditional Whig ideology: the myth of the ancient constitution (Forbes 1975: ch. 8). For Hume, the constitution was a constantly shifting affair, and the liberty of the Anglo-Saxons to whom the Whigs pointed was really just "an incapacity of submitting to government" (H 23; II 521). In truth, Hume argues,

> notwithstanding the seeming liberty or rather licentiousness of the Anglo-Saxons, the great body even of the free citizens, in those ages, really enjoyed much less true liberty, than where the execution of the laws is the most severe . . . The reason is derived from the excess itself of that liberty. Men must guard themselves at any price against insults and injuries. (H App. 1; I 168–9)

Nor did any meaningful liberty develop in the years of the Norman kings, much less during the more absolutist period of the Tudors, which many traditional Whigs promoted as a kind of golden age. Yet despite its recent genesis, Hume is no less enthusiastic than the most rabid Whig about the blessings of liberty. Although Hume backs away from his more florid panegyrics for liberty during the Wilkes and Liberty riots of the 1760s (Forbes 1975: 187–92; Miller 1981: 182–4; Livingston 1999: ch. 10), the change is really one of emphasis. Liberty is only valuable, he insists, in a society in which order and authority are firmly in place. The value of liberty itself, however, he never seriously questions.

Conclusion

Hume's theory of government is thus a complicated affair. Government has a basic responsibility to protect people and property, but it also has an important role both

403

in creating the circumstances in which liberty can arise and in promoting liberty itself. As government takes on such responsibilities, its structures become more complex as well. Even modern absolute monarchies are not the simple structures found in early governments. The reasons for the many different interpretations of Hume's political views thus become clear. Like conservatives, Hume values established practices and conventions, but like liberals he cherishes liberty. Elsewhere, of course, he dismisses the traditional liberal ideal of equality (EPM 3.26), and he shows utter contempt for the organized religion that is the bulwark of much conservative thought (DNR 12.11, 16–19, 25; KS 220, 222, 224–5). Hume himself, of course, preaches "moderation" in politics, a quality that "is of advantage to every establishment" (E 2.14.17; M 500). Ultimately, I think, we should see Hume's appeal for moderation and his general political theory as a kind of pragmatism: governments are set up to solve certain problems. As other problems and possibilities arise, governments often prove to be useful tools. But like any tool, they can be used for bad purposes, and so the people have the right to insure that the tool remains only in the hands of those who will use it well. That much, Hume can say in a perfectly general way. But most of the concerns of government concern particular problems in particular places operating under particular practices. To see its purposes there requires local knowledge and the refined sensibilities of that person whom Hume calls an "impartial patriot" (E 2.15.4; M 506). The task of demonstrating how to become such a patriot is, I believe, the implicit work of both Hume's philosophical and his historical writings.

See also 22 " 'The Most Illustrious Philosopher and Historian of the Age': Hume's *History of England*"

References

References to Hume's texts besides the *Treatise* and the *Enquiries* are as follows:

DNR   *Dialogues concerning Natural Religion* (1779). DNR is followed by the part and paragraph number, then by KS followed by the page number in the edition edited by Norman Kemp Smith, Indianapolis: Bobbs-Merill, 1947.

E   *Essays: Moral, Political, and Literary* (1752). E is followed by the part, essay, and paragraph number, then an M followed by page number in the edition edited by Eugene Miller, Indianapolis: Liberty Classics, 1985.

H   *The History of England, from the Invasion of Julius Caesar to The Revolution in 1688* (1762). H is followed by chapter number, then by volume and page of the edition edited by William Todd, Indianapolis: Liberty Classics, 1983.

Baier, Annette C. (1991). *A Progress of Sentiments: Reflections on Hume's "Treatise"* (Cambridge, MA: Harvard University Press).

Charron, William C. (1980). "Conventions, Games of Strategy, and Hume's Philosophy of Law and Government," *American Philosophical Quarterly*, 17, pp. 327–34.

Forbes, Duncan (1975). *Hume's Philosophical Politics* (Cambridge: Cambridge University Press).

Hampton, Jean (1986). *Hobbes and the Social Contract Tradition* (Cambridge: Cambridge University Press).

Livingston, Donald (1999). *Philosophical Melancholy and Delirium: Hume's Pathology of Philosophy* (Chicago: University of Chicago Press).

Locke, John (1689). *Two Treatises of Government*, ed. Peter Laslett (Cambridge: Cambridge University Press, 1960).

Mackie, John (1980). *Hume's Moral Theory* (London: Routledge and Kegan Paul).

Miller, David (1981). *Philosophy and Ideology in Hume's Political Thought* (Oxford: Clarendon Press).

Miller, Eugene (1990). "Hume on Liberty in Successive English Constitutions," in N. Capaldi and D. Livingston (eds.), *Liberty in Hume's History of England* (Dordrecht: Kluwer Academic Publishing), pp. 53–103.

Parfit, Derek (1984). *Reasons and Persons* (Oxford: Clarendon Press).

Phillipson, Nicholas (1989). *Hume* (London: Weidenfeld and Nicolson).

Schmidt, Claudia (2003). *David Hume: Reason in History* (University Park, PA: Pennsylvania State University Press).

Stewart, John B. (1992). *Opinion and Reform in Hume's Political Philosophy* (Princeton, NJ: Princeton University Press).

Whelan, Frederick (1985). *Order and Artifice in Hume's Political Philosophy* (Princeton, NJ: Princeton University Press).

22

"The Most Illustrious Philosopher and Historian of the Age": Hume's *History of England*

MARK SALBER PHILLIPS

"I believe that this is the historical Age, and this the historical Nation" (Hume's Letters in Greig 1932: v. 2, 230). Hume's often quoted words speak to eighteenth-century Scotland's confidence in its historical achievements, as well as to Hume's pride in his own contribution to his country's unexpected glory in this branch of literature. Though his historical interests began well before, Hume devoted a decade at the prime of his life to the composition of the *History*, and he continued to revise the text, both for style and for content, as long as he lived. By the time he composed his autobiographical farewell, "My Own Life," he could look back with some complacency on the work's apparently inauspicious beginnings. The attacks, he recalled with satisfaction, came from every possible quarter:

> English, Scotch, and Irish, Whig and Tory, churchman and sectary, freethinker and religionist, patriot and courtier, united in their rage against the man, who had presumed to shed a generous tear for the fate of Charles I. and the Earl of Strafford. (Hume 1777: xxxvii)

In truth, the *History* was never without its political and religious critics, but it is also evident that ideological controversy did not stand in the way of literary fame. Hume's deft blend of national narrative, philosophical history, and literary pathos soon established the *History* as the outstanding example of the new historical style, and such was its success, that by the time he died in 1776, Hume was better known to British readers as a historian than as a philosopher. For two more generations, though critics increasingly found fault with his methods as well as his religious and political views, the *History* held on to its place as the preeminent narrative of the British past – a record of longevity difficult to match even amongst the greatest works of history (Phillips and Smith 2005). Inevitably, however, advancing scholarship and new approaches to historical writing brought the eclipse of the work – the publication of Macaulay's *History* at the mid-century provides a convenient terminus – and in time Hume's historical reputation came to be completely overshadowed by his philosophical one. Only relatively recently, in fact, has it become possible again to think seriously about Hume's historical work except as a minor adjunct to his philosophical writings, and even now there remains a natural tendency to fashion the historian in the image of the philosopher. It may be that we will never succeed in recovering the evenhanded admiration of Adam

Smith, for whom his friend was simply "the most illustrious philosopher and historian of the age" (Smith 1776: vol. 2, 790). Thanks, however, to a growing understanding of the historiographical challenges of the eighteenth century, it now seems possible to address Hume's great narrative in a manner that is more closely attuned to Hume's own ambitions and achievements as a writer of history.

Frameworks of Interpretation

Despite the recent revival of interest in Hume's historical work, the body of scholarly commentary remains relatively small, and much of it has focused selectively on either ideological, conceptual, or formal issues, depending upon the disciplinary framework of the commentator. Historians, in particular, following in the wake of Duncan Forbes's pioneering study of Hume's "philosophical politics," have tended to approach the work primarily as a vehicle of ideological critique. On this view, the book seems to be shaped by Hume's skepticism towards prevailing historical myths, especially the dominant Whig dogma that England had enjoyed a unique and more or less continuous tradition of political liberty rooted in the "ancient constitution." In the fundamentals of his idea of historical development, it is argued, Hume remained a Whig, but a Whig of a "scientific" rather than political stripe (Forbes 1975; Stewart 1992; Miller 1981). Other commentators, however, have discovered in the *History* a skepticism of a more philosophical character, and have pictured Hume as closely attuned to Enlightenment discussions of probability and evidence (Norton 1965; Popkin 1976; Wooton 1993). This approach has the virtue of aligning aspects of the *History* with some famous arguments in the *Treatise*, thus drawing Hume's preoccupations as a historian closer to his philosophy. Another strand of philosophical commentary has engaged with the question of Hume's relationship to problems of historical understanding as defined by the historicist tradition of Dilthey and Croce. Some of those who have explored this avenue have found Hume essentially ahistorical in his outlook (Collingwood 1993; Pompa 1990) but others, especially more recently, have mounted a strong defense (Livingston 1984; Blackburn 2005). Hume was also a "philosophical" historian in the rather different and looser eighteenth-century meaning of that word. In this light, the *History* has been described as belonging to a group of histories and historical essays that trace the rise of modern Europe back to its roots in the fall of Rome and on through successive stages of feudal and commercial society (Pocock 1999). Scholars concerned with this "Enlightened narrative" have focused their interest on the grand arc of Hume's macronarrative, but they have tended to ignore the textures or conventions of the narrative as such. As a result, we learn a good deal about the *History* as a structure of ideas, but comparatively little about some formal features of the narrative which Hume and his contemporary readers valued very highly. Other critics, however, especially those coming from literary disciplines, have been attracted to the *History* precisely by the stylistic and narrative gifts for which Hume was so famous in his day. For some of the scholars who have pursued these dimensions of Hume's work, the *History* is not only a philosophical history, to be compared with the work of Montesquieu, Millar, or Gibbon, but a sentimental one, allied in its sensibilities to the novels and poetry of the period (Hilson 1978; O'Brien 1997; Phillips 2000).

Each of these approaches sheds light Hume's grand and multifaceted narrative, but like any great work, the *History of England* eludes our attempts to anatomize. It is not easy, in truth, to hold steadily in view the full range of what Hume achieved as a writer of history. To broaden our appreciation of his standing as a historian, however, it will be useful to begin by situating the *History of England* in its largest historiographical context.

The Moment of Hume's *History*

Much of what any author accomplishes lies in the moment of the work. By this I mean not only the public setting that is shared by everyone living in a particular community at a particular time, but also the pre-existing challenges and resources that shape the possibilities that confront someone bidding for a place of distinction in the chosen field. In the case of the *History*, a great deal of the fame Hume achieved, as well as the controversy he stirred up, begins from two elementary facts: namely, that in relation to the events of British history, he must be seen as a post-revolutionary observer, while in relation to some key aspects of European historiographical tradition, he wrote from an essentially post-classical vantage. The first is largely a matter of ideological engagements, the second of both aesthetic forms and explanatory structures.

Hume began his work a scant half-decade from "the forty-five," the second and final uprising of the Scottish clans in favor of the exiled house of Stuart. The brutal military suppression that followed the defeat of the Highlanders at Culloden ended forever the hope of reversing the effects of the revolutions of the previous century. Henceforth, Jacobitism would survive primarily as a politics of nostalgia and a literature of romance – most famously in Walter Scott's recreation of these events in the first of his novels, *Waverley, or 'Tis Sixty Years Since.*

Sixty years was also the interval that separated the time of Hume's writing from the great event that, as the terminus of his *History*, measured the distance between the living present and its written past. The Revolution of 1688, as Hume wrote at the end of volume 6, formed "a new epoch in the constitution" and put its "nature . . . beyond all controversy" (H 6: 531). Like *Waverley*, then, Hume's narrative took the form of a look back on a world that was both recent enough to retain its hold on living memory and distinct enough to be past all reclaiming. The difference lay in the fact that while Scott's decision to write a Scottish fiction allowed him to indulge the romance of the vanquished, Hume interpreted the challenge of becoming the historian of Britain as requiring him to strip bare the myths of the victors. "The Whig party," he wrote in a passage that serves as a summary of his historiographical mission,

> for a course of nearly seventy years, has, almost without interruption, enjoyed the whole authority of government: and no honours or offices could be obtained but by their countenance and protection. But this event (i.e. the Whig ascendency), which in some particulars, has been advantageous to the state, has proved destructive to the truth of history, and has established many gross falsehoods, which it is unaccountable how any civilized nation could have embraced.

The result, Hume added, naming the best known works of Whig historiography, has been that the most despicable histories, "both for style and matter, have been extolled, and propagated, and read; as if they had equaled the most celebrated remains of antiquity" (H 6: 533).

Hume's antagonism to Whig historiographical tradition has often been elided with a hostility to the Whig cause itself – a much more disputable point. In fact, Hume liked to picture himself as an even-handed observer capable of displaying both analytic detachment and comprehensive sympathies: the man who had shed "a generous tear" for Charles and Strafford, but also "the only historian that had at once neglected present power, interest, and authority, and the cry of popular prejudice" (Hume 1777: xxxvii). This defense was undoubtedly sincere, but there is a degree of disingenuousness in the accompanying expressions of surprise and hurt. In important ways, the deepest provocation Hume offered his critics lay in assuming precisely that posture which for him was the principal source of pride, namely the presumption that he could write with philosophic detachment about events and ideas still so vital to national memory. Hume, in short, assumed a decidedly *post*-Revolutionary vantage and prided himself in the expanded understanding that this distancing made possible. For his opponents on the other hand, the seventeenth-century remaking of the British state was not yet so much a thing of the past as to permit old instincts to be suspended. Thus the same vantage that nourished Hume's sense of opportunity to win fame in his new field of literary endeavor also ensured a lasting and bitter response from his critics.

If Hume's historiographical politics were post-revolutionary, in important ways his sense of historical form and historical explanation were distinctly post-classical. In this camp, however, the deficiencies of British historiography were widely acknowledged, and the same factors that made Hume hopeful of fame disposed his countrymen to pay proper tribute to his accomplishments.

Eighteenth-century historiography's relation to its classical tradition was far from simple, especially when we take into account its conceptual as well as its formal inheritance. Some useful guidance, however, can be taken from the way in which contemporary British commentators celebrated two distinct, but overlapping achievements in historical writing. First, Britons were conscious of lacking a historical literature worthy of their standing in the world (Hicks 1996), and they welcomed Hume – along with Robertson and (eventually) Gibbon – for his outstanding literary achievement. At last, it was felt, Britain had produced a historian whose polish and dignity placed him on a level to bear comparison with the best writers of continental Europe or even the greatest historians of antiquity. Second, contemporaries celebrated the fact that historical writing had expanded its scope considerably beyond the military and political events that preoccupied historians in the classical tradition. The boast of the times, in a word, was not simply to have made history *polite* but also *philosophical*. History written in the new manner would not, of course, neglect the traditional business of the historian, but it would give older questions new depth and meaning by encompassing questions of manners, commerce, and the history of the arts.

The problem of fashioning a polite historical style existed in anticipation – an artifact of Britain's long tutelage to Italy and France in so many branches of letters. The challenge of rendering history "philosophical," on the other hand, only came into focus retrospectively, as historians began to create narratives or essays of a distinctively modern kind and critics turned back to measure the extent of what had been gained. This sense of accomplishment is nicely summed up in a review in the *Monthly* of Sir John Sinclair's *History of the Public Revenue*:

> History, till of late, was chiefly employed in the recital of warlike transactions . . . The *people* were not known; the circumstances that affected *their* domestic prosperity and happiness were entirely overlooked; and the records of many ages might have been perused without obtaining the least information concerning any fact that led to a knowledge of the internal economy of the state, or the private situation of individuals. (*Monthly Review* 1790: 93–4)

As this reviewer's comments make clear, many eighteenth-century historians regarded themselves as confronting a substantially new challenge. In essence, classical historiography had accepted the boundaries of the *vita activa* as determining both its ethical ideal and its literary form; but if history continued to define itself as a narrative of public actions, the effect would be to continue to exclude a wide range of social groups, institutions, and experiences that eighteenth-century audiences increasingly understood as being essential features of modern life (Phillips 2000). As Robert Henry put it in his widely read *History of Great Britain* (1771–93), "No apology is necessary for introducing the history of Commerce into the history of Britain, which hath derived so many advantages from that source" (Henry 1823: vol. 6, 255).

Hume made similar observations, but he also emphasized how recently Europeans had come to understand the importance of this central institution of modern life. The ancients had completely ignored the question of trade, he pointed out, and even the Italians – Machiavelli, Guicciardini, and their successors – had barely taken it into account, though it was now a preeminent concern of everyone involved in government (*Essays*: 88–9). Commerce, however, did not stand alone as a marker of the distance separating the moderns from their classical and early modern ancestors; it was only the most visible sign of the striking expansion that was in the process of transforming historical studies. The horizon, indeed, was almost without a definable limit. Manners, opinion, arts, industry – all this and more would need to be thought of if (to quote the *Monthly* reviewer again) modern histories were to take it upon themselves to investigate everything that affected the internal economy of the state or "the private situation of individuals."

The "philosophical" approach to history conferred an added measure of moral consequence on an art whose dignity had always been a central part of its definition – a step that added to the confidence with which Enlightenment historians confronted their predecessors: their histories would not just be well written, but history as it had never been written before. It is easy to forget, however, the degree of formal adaptation that would be required to join the new historical approach to older, but still prestigious narrative traditions (Phillips 2000). Classical conventions of historical writing had been devised to narrate the deeds of warriors and statesmen, not alterations in the balance of trade or changes to the texture of manners, and even those who welcomed this expansion of historical understanding could be made uneasy by the sense that history might overload itself with ponderous dissertations. Adam Smith, for example, though soon to become the foremost political economist of the age, began his academic career as a teacher of rhetoric, in which he mounted a very strict defense of history's traditional adherence to narrative form (Phillips 1997; 2005). "Long demonstrations," Smith argued, "as they are no part of the historian's province are seldom made use of by the ancients. The modern authors have often brought them in" (Smith 1762: 101–2). The same objections, he went on to say, apply to reflections and observations that go on for longer than two or three sentences. "The historian who brings in long reflections . . . withdraws us from the most interesting part of the narration; and in such interruptions we always imagine that we lose some part of the transaction" (Smith 1762: 102).

Smith's successor in rhetoric teaching at Edinburgh, Hugh Blair, repeated much the same view, while also applauding just those recent advances that had disturbed the old balances. "But when we demand from the historian profound and instructive views of his subject," Blair wrote, it is not meant that he should be frequently inter-rupting the course of his History, "with his own reflections and speculations." When a historian is "much given to dissertation," Blair wrote, adding a new objection of his own, we grow suspicious that "he will be in hazard of adapting his narrative of facts to favour some system which he has formed to himself" (Blair 1965: 270–1). Despite these warnings, however, Blair ended his chapter on historical writing with yet another summation of the achievements of the age. "I cannot conclude the subject of History," he wrote,

> without taking notice of a very great improvement which has, of late years, begun to be introduced into Historical Composition; I mean a more particular attention than was formerly given to laws, customs, commerce, religion, literature, and every other thing that tends to show the spirit and genius of nations. It is now understood to be the busi-ness of an able Historian to exhibit manners, as well as facts and events.

Assuredly, he continued, "whatever displays the . . . life of mankind, in different periods, and illustrates the progress of the human mind, is more useful and interest-ing than the detail of sieges and battles" (Blair 1965: 288).

Intelligibility and Instruction

Blair's summary of improvements in historical writing takes us back to Hume's pioneering efforts in the new historiographical style and particularly to his famous appendices, which were such influential demonstrations of the new program. These interludes were designed (much as Blair suggested) to set the political narrative into a wider framework of manners, commerce, and the arts. At the same time, the place-ment of the appendices also articulates the history into four broad epochs – roughly Roman and Anglo-Saxon Britain, the Middle Ages, the Tudor monarchy, and the crisis of revolution and civil war that followed on the death of James I. The fourth of these appendices (though the first in order of composition, since Hume began with the seventeenth century and then worked his way backward) clearly states the agenda Hume intended to follow. "It may not be improper at this period, to make a pause:" Hume wrote, "and to take a survey of the state of the kingdom, with regard to government, manners, finances, arms, trade, learning. Where a just notion is not formed of these particulars, history can be little instructive, and often will not be intelligible" (H 5: 124).

Hume's list spells out clearly the topics that would emerge as the essential themes of Enlightenment historiography – government, manners, finances, arms, trade, learning. But there is also a subtler indication of a shift in direction implied in the prominence he assigned to the association between intelligibility and instruction, with its hint that earlier histories, lacking such investigations, would have failed such a test entirely. Coming from one of the pioneers of a new historical school, the claim was necessarily partisan; it is true, however, that humanist historiography, with its Roman rhetorical roots, had focused most of its attention on the *effectiveness* of historical teaching, while Hume's Whig predecessors left no doubt that the lessons of history were straighforwardly political. In neither case was the intelligibility of history brought into question.

What, then, from Hume's standpoint, made history explicable? One important answer can be found in the fourth Appendix itself. It is easy to overlook the fact that this proud assertion of the new historical outlook is structured not only by its roll-call of the topics of philosophical history, but also by its repeated and insistent comparison of past and present. "We may safely pronounce," Hume wrote, taking up the first of his announced themes, "that the English government, at the accession of the Scottish line, was much more arbitrary, than it is at present; the prerogative less limited, the liberties of the subject less accurately defined and secured" (H 5: 124). With respect to religion, similarly, Hume noted that the liberty of conscience "which we so highly and so justly value at present" was utterly suppressed, and he underlines "the (religious) bigotry which prevailed in that age" (H 5: 125–9). Politically, the principles that "prevailed during that age" were entirely favorable to monarchy, but "by the changes which have since been introduced," the liberties of individuals have become more secure, while those of the public have become more uncertain (H 5: 129). Manners, too, were shaped by the prevailing form of monarchy, and they lacked that "strange mixture, which, at present, distinguishes England from all other countries. Such violent extremes were then unknown, of industry and debauchery, frugality and profusion, civility and rusticity, fanaticism and scepticism" (H 5: 132). Amongst the aristocracy, "high pride of family then prevailed" and the nobility distinguished themselves from the common people by their "dignity and stateliness of behaviour." Great commercial wealth was "more rare, and had not, as yet been able to confound all ranks of men, and render money the chief foundation of distinction" (H 5: 132).

Often, of course, the contrast of past and present was implied rather than spelled out, but the hunt for intelligibility through then/now comparison remains a central and consistent impulse. When, for example, Hume noted, "The expenses of the great consisted in pomp and show, and a numerous retinue, rather than in convenience and true pleasure," it is evident that he intended both a temporal and a moral contrast between two stages in the life of the British aristocracy. "Civil honours," he went on to say,

> which now hold the first place, were, at that time, subordinate to the military . . . The fury of duels too prevailed more than at any time before or since. This was the turn, that the romantic chivalry, for which the nation was formerly so renowned, had taken. (H 5: 132–3)

These examples are all drawn from the first two divisions of Hume's "survey" (i.e., government and manners), but the contrastive habit carries through the broad range of observation that makes up the remainder of the Appendix. When Hume speaks about the amount of the king's revenue "as it stood in 1617," for instance, or remarks on the high rate of interest in James's reign, or details the relatively meager "supplies" voted by parliament, or lists the "price of corn during this reign" ("no lower, or rather higher than at present"), or writes of the absence of the "danger and expense of a standing army," or estimates the number of men in England capable of bearing arms according to a review of 1583, not one of these items stands as an autonomous datum. Rather, we have to take every single statistic, observation, or judgment as forming a part of an extended comparison whose whole purpose is to measure the distance between then and now.

Cumulatively these allusions to contemporary conditions not only establish the importance of present-mindedness to Hume's understanding of history, but also the self-consciousness with which he embraces it. For Hume, it is clear, historical thinking implies something more than a knowledge of the four previous epochs of the history of Britain; it also requires a critical thinking-back from a particular present, from which both the historian and his reader take the measure of earlier times. This vantage – post-revolutionary, Hanoverian, Enlightened – stands as an unapologetic reference point in the narrative, where it constitutes the fifth and crucial epoch of the *History of England*.

Decipherment and the History of Opinion

The then/now comparison that is so prominent in the Appendix was not, of course, the only tool Hume had to hand in his search for intelligibility and instruction; two passages in the *Essays* serve as a further guide to problems of social explanation. As Hume wrote in the essay on "The Rise and Progress of the Arts and Sciences," "What depends upon a few persons, is, in a great measure, to be ascribed to chance, or secret and unknown causes: What arises from a great number, may often be accounted for by determinate and known causes" (*Essays*: 112). Going by this "general rule," Hume continued,

> the domestic and gradual revolutions of a state must be a more proper subject of reasoning and observation, than the foreign and the violent, which are commonly produced by single persons, and are more influenced by whim, folly, or caprice, than by general passions and interests.

For this reason, the economic factors leading to the rise of the Commons in England are easier to understand than the personal motives that made for the decline of the Hapsburg dynasty in Spain, just as the rise of commerce is more easily accounted for than the progress of learning – avarice being a more universal passion than curiosity for knowledge (*Essays*: 112–13).

Hume's observation was not meant to interdict investigations that demanded recourse to subtler and less obvious causes; instead, it provided guidance to the success

413

with which broader structures of explanation could be invoked in relation to specific situations, some less, some more susceptible to generalization. The fact is that in practice a great deal of what he wanted to describe lay in territories that by his own "rule" were necessarily more difficult to assess than the rise of commerce. This challenge is particularly evident if we take note of a second maxim, articulated in the essay "Of the First Principles of Government." "Nothing appears more surprizing to those, who consider human affairs with a philosophical eye," he wrote,

> than the easiness with which the many are governed by the few; and the implicit submission, with which men resign their own sentiments and passions to those of their rulers. When we enquire by what means this wonder is effected, we shall find, that, as FORCE is always on the side of the governed, the governors having nothing to support them but opinion. It is therefore, on opinion only that government is founded. (*Essays*: 32)

Elsewhere he put the point still more sweepingly. "[T]hough men be much governed by interest; yet even interest itself, and all human affairs, are entirely governed by *opinion*" (*Essays*: 51).

The historiographical implications of this maxim are as far reaching as the political ones. After all, the initial impulse of Hume's narrative (never abandoned despite the extension of the history to earlier and earlier epochs of English history) was to describe a decisive shift in the terms by which the many would continue to consent to be governed by the few. Considered in this light, even the "gradual and domestic revolutions of the state" – apparently so favorable to general explanation – would ultimately have to be understood in terms of something rather more elusive than the movements of commerce. In fact, though Hume generally endorsed the Harringtonian view that the "rise of the commons" was owing to a change in the balance of wealth, he would never be able to narrow his narrative to economic factors alone. Questions of property and power undoubtedly established the grounds for a great constitutional revolution, but it remained the crucial task of the historian to chronicle what (in a related context) he would call "a sudden and sensible change in the opinions of men" (*Essays*: 51).

In the next century Hume's task would have been an easier one – which is to say that it would have become a different task altogether. Nineteenth-century writers identified the idea of opinion with public debate and the influence of the press – a view captured in the idea of the "fourth estate" (Gunn 1983). Institutionalized in this way, *public* opinion acquired a sense of agency that permitted an easier integration into historical narrative. By contrast, Hume's more generalized understanding may sometimes appear abstract and disembodied, with little of the dramatic interest with which Carlyle or Macaulay could invest their representations of the collective sentiment. Nonetheless, as filled out by complementary terms like manners and "ancient precedent and example" (H 5: 128) (which a later age would call "tradition"), Hume's understanding of opinion represents a crucial recognition that a deeper understanding of historical experience would require a much wider framework than humanism's relatively narrow preoccupation with the *vita activa*. Only when mediated by a new consciousness of the vicissitudes of opinion would the chronicle of events become broadly intelligible.

Hume possessed a variety of resources for writing the history of opinion. Like his nineteenth-century successors, he did not hesitate to generalize about the "spirit of the age" or to identify crucial shifts in national manners, but less direct strategies were also available. One device, both frequent and characteristic, was the oration, a typical feature of ancient historiography, but one that could easily be modified to serve substantially new purposes. We are aware of the shadow of the classical tradition when, for example, Hume pairs opposing parliamentary and royalist arguments in order to draw the lines of the coming conflict (H 5: 93–4). It is soon apparent, however, that Hume's approach to such occasions lacks the formal rhetoricism of his predecessors; in fact, he usually avoids the fiction of representing direct address, offering instead a catalogue of attitudes and ideas that more often resembles a set of notes and headings than a polished oration. The consequence is to shift the oration from being a display of character and an exercise in eloquence towards a more analytic purpose as an index of conflicting views.

When history departs in this way from its classical definition as a narrative of public actions and devotes itself instead to the diagnosis of social change, one of the consequences is to modify the long-standing convention that only weighty matters could be worthy of the dignity of history. In fact, given a desire (as Hume wrote of the age of Elizabeth) "to show the genius of that age, or rather the channels in which power then ran" (H 5: 14), it did not necessarily matter whether an incident resulted in public consequences. It would be enough that the historical object, whatever it might be – an event, an institution, a manner of speaking – was indicative of the mental habits of another time, especially where it revealed a pattern that cut across the grain of present expectations. "It may not be unworthy of remark," he wrote,

> that (Sir Edward) Coke, in the trial of Mrs. Turner, told her, that she was guilty of the seven deadly sins. She was a whore, a bawd, a sorcerer, a witch, a papist, a felon, and a murderer. And what may more surprise us, Bacon, then attorney general took care to observe, that poisoning was a popish trick. Such were the bigoted prejudices which prevailed: Poisoning was not, of itself, sufficiently odious, if it were not represented as a branch of popery. (H 5: 62)

Where religious bigotry was the target, Hume was never shy about adding the twist of irony to the thrust of argument. But while the tone of the closing remarks is unmistakable, the stylized note of hesitation that comes at the opening of the passage might more easily be overlooked. In a text of such elegant smoothness, however, these introductory apologetics – entirely conventional though they may be – are worth noting; they are a muted gesture that signals Hume's consciousness of introducing a novel element into the canons of historical composition, and thus, however modestly phrased, they are intended to reinforce Hume's claim to have moved beyond the now outmoded proprieties of his models.

"My View of Things"

Early in his career as a historian Hume summed up the politics of his *History* in a way that both acknowledges its tensions and hints at their rationalization. "My views of things

415

are more conformable to Whig principles," he wrote to a friend; "my representation of persons to Tory prejudices. Nothing can so much prove that men commonly regard more persons than things, as to find that I am commonly numbered among the Tories" (Hume's Letters in Greig 1932: vol. 1, 237). The formula seems deceptively easy – a simple matter of party allegiances – but it points towards some of the more complex balances that characterize the work, raising questions about explanation and affect, as well as complicating the central ideological issue.

Hume's Whig critics would have scoffed at the notion that his "views of things" were close to those of their own party, but (as has already been said) we should not confuse his condemnation of the partisanship of Whig historiography with a wholesale rejection of fundamental Whig principles. Hume questioned neither the legitimacy nor the desirability of the present constitution; what he did oppose was an entrenched historical doctrine about how the mixed constitutional state had come into being – specifically the creed that the English Revolution represented the culmination of an old and largely continuous history of British freedoms.

Hume's recasting of British history would ultimately reach back to Roman times, but its most dramatic effects related to the two most recent dynasties and especially to the reigns of Elizabeth I and Charles I. For Hume, the revolutionary crisis of the seventeenth century was rooted in broadly based economic and social changes. Exploration and New World commerce had brought increasing commercial wealth, which had "thrown the balance of property into the hands of the commons," and created a situation in which "the dispositions of men became susceptible of a more regular plan of liberty" (H 5: 40). From this broad social observation, a more pointed political argument followed. In the constitutional struggle of the times, Hume argued, the real initiative did not come from the efforts of the Crown, seeking (as the Whigs insisted) to expand its authority at the expense of traditional freedoms. Rather, beginning in the reign of James I, it was an increasingly confident Commons that pressed for political change and overturned the existing balances of the constitution which had leaned so heavily to monarchical power. In fact, if one looked back to the reign of James's predecessor – the much beloved Elizabeth – it was obvious that parliament had been entirely subservient to royal authority and meekly accepted instruction from their extraordinarily imperious monarch. In those days, however, the arrangement of social forces had been very different from the new disposition that began to manifest itself in the following century: commerce, it is true, had already begun to quicken, but at this stage the new wealth served largely to undermine the landed power of the aristocracy without as yet setting the commons on to new paths (H 4: 383–4). As a result, the monarchy found itself in a position of unrivaled power, and it exercised an absolute authority in England very little different from the despotisms that ruled in Turkey or Muscovy.

Thus far an essentially social revolution, but the "domestic and gradual revolutions of the state" become more complex when we have to take into account the circuitous pathways of opinion. Witness the absolutism of the early Stuarts; for many observers the overweening pretensions of Crown seemed the clearest justification for a revolution pursued in defense of traditional British freedoms, but for Hume the meaning was nearly the opposite. Monarchical power had long been close to absolute, but prior to the accession of James I there was very little evidence of any sentiment on the side of the Commons to oppose it. Ironically, the real reasons that royal authority made more strident claims for itself in the seventeenth century were dialectical and essentially defensive. It was only at this time that prerogative found itself opposed by contrary doctrines, "which *began* to be promulgated by the puritannical party" (H 5: 127).

Looking back from the perspective of a later age, Hume repeatedly emphasized the comparative weakness of the state in the seventeenth century, both with respect to arms and to revenues. This was a monarchy whose authority, though very extensive in theory, rested simply "on the opinion of the people," which in turn was shaped by "ancient precedent and example" – which is to say the power of tradition. (No wonder then, as Hume went on to say, James and Charles were "so extremely jealous of their pre-rogative.") But if the extreme claims of royal authority were "more speculative than practical," on the parliamentary side the reverse was true. Supported by the favorable conditions of the time, the Commons succeeded in enlarging their powers, but with-out as yet codifying their new position in "systematical principles and opinions" (H 5: 44). No one, in fact, as yet properly understood the new importance of the Commons, which was one reason that Charles I was so often impolitic in his relations with his parliament: history had not prepared him for the new realities and "nothing less than fatal experience could engage the English princes to pay a due regard to the inclina-tions of that formidable assembly" (H 5: 170).

Charles was hardly alone in suffering from such limitations of vision; of necessity, some degree of historical blindness is the fate of all those who are required to act in the face of new or emergent conditions. For Hume this was a crucial point because it implied an invitation to abandon partisanship and to approach individuals on both sides of the great conflict with a warmer appreciation of the pathos of their situation. The irony of historical judgment, in other words, is that achieving a measure of ideolo-gical detachment can lead to possibilities for closer affective engagement – once again the "generous tear." On another level, however, Hume's sensitivity to the changing basis of opinion made him less interested in individual failures of insight than in the shared ideologies and experiences that conditioned the perspectives of generations. Who in the time of Elizabeth, for example, could have foretold the historical importance of the Puritans to the history of English liberty, though in fact "it was to this sect, whose principles appear so frivolous and habits so ridiculous, that the English owe the whole freedom of their constitution" (H 4: 146). By the same logic, too, Hume recognized that it would be inappropriate to condemn the arbitrary and haughty conduct of Elizabeth; the "maxims of her reign were conformable to the principles of the times," and she continued to be the most popular monarch England ever had. It is only the continued growth of the popular party since her day that has "so changed our ideas in these matters" that her autocratic ways now "appear to us extremely curious, and even at first surprising." Nonetheless, they were so unremarkable at the time that "neither Camden . . . nor any other (contemporary) historian has taken any notice of them" (H 4: 144–5).

Despite the frequency in the *History* of this sort of commentary, Hume has often been derided as a philosopher-historian whose commitment to the uniformities of human nature left no room for a "true" understanding of historical change. Whatever the force of the charge – and it is hard to see how human understanding can operate without a commitment to some universals (Blackburn 2005: 215–18) – by now it should be clear that Hume's supposed "uniformitarianism" offered no barrier to a sharp aware-ness of changes in British manners and institutions. It is evident, too, that Hume did not hold back from drawing the logical conclusions regarding the need for appropri-ate perspective in historical judgment. It "seems unreasonable," he wrote (repeating much the same point on a number of occasions) "to judge of the measures, embraced during one period, by the maxims, which prevail in another" (H 5: 240). Even in the matter of religion, Hume recognized the need to exercise a strenuous effort to comprehend a form of opinion that to him was most recalcitrant to ordinary explanations. This does not mean, of course, that Hume was ever sympathetic to the religious spirit; only that he understood its strength and had some respect for its consequences. Though many of the scruples of the Puritans now seem quite "frivolous," he explained with a characteristic mixture of irony and historical insight, we should not think that these issues only troubled those who were small minded or foolish. "Some men of the greatest parts and most extensive knowledge, that the nation, at this time, produced, could not enjoy any peace of mind; because obliged to hear prayers offered up to the Divinity, by a priest covered with a white linen vestment" (H 5: 159).

In defending Hume against the charge of ahistoricism, however, it is also important to add one caution. Hume's recognition that we need to adjust our judgment to the condition of opinion in another time should not be elided with later historicist doctrines. (For contrary views, see Livingston 1984; Blackburn 2005). Hume was not a proto-Romantic calling for the historian to lose himself in the emotions of the past, nor (like Collingwood) did he envision historical knowledge as a form of reenactment. Rather than imaginative identification with the past, Hume's *History* proceeds upon an operation of continued comparison calculated to produce a heightened awareness of difference. The result is a binocularism that by definition was unavailable to the historical actor, but is the historian's chosen instrument for tracking the complex movements of opinion.

"My Representation of Persons"

Hume, it seems, coupled the assertion that the civil war and its aftermath could at last be regarded as a thing of the ever-receding past with the promise of a warmer sympathy for those who took part in its struggles. The result was a narrative that some readers admired for its pathetic and elegant style, while others criticized it for show-ing a bias to the royalist cause. But though Hume's "representation of persons" was closely tied in this way to his "view of things," his understanding of character has con-sequences well beyond the politics of the *History*. For most of his readers (as Hume had predicted) the portraits were a particularly salient feature of the *History*, providing much of the affective coloration of the narrative and helping to shape its moral psychology.

Hume's predecessors in the humanist tradition regarded history as the pedagogy of public life and, in service to this purpose, they aimed to draw as direct a line as pos-sible from character to action. For his part, Hume was inclined to loosen this link, which had been so crucial to rhetorically conceived ideas of history since ancient Rome. One reason, certainly, was Hume's conviction that individual motive counted little in explanatory terms when weighed against deeper causal patterns. In the context of the *History*, however, this preference for more general forms of explanation was joined to a continued attention to the problem of historical distance – a preoccupation that made him alert to the blindness of historical actors as well as tolerant of their failings (Phillips 2004). If human beings have no option but to operate in a world of changeable circumstances and unforeseen consequences, it is hard to construct historical narrative as the direct consequence of individual will and virtue.

Character, then, had lost much of its traditional authority as a form of explanation or as a focus of emulation, but this did not mean that the subject had exhausted its appeal. Instead, as a historian whose literary sensitivities were shaped by a culture of sensibility, as well as a philosopher much concerned with the operations of sympathy, Hume embraced portraiture for quite different reasons, finding in it an opportunity to display his stylistic gifts and to engage his readers' attention with those elements of historical experience that lay closest to their own humanity (Hilson 1978; Phillips 2003). Fortunately for Hume's literary reputation, if not for his country, British history provided ample opportunities for depicting virtue in distress. "To be oppressed with calamity was at all times sufficient to excite the sympathy of Mr. Hume"; wrote an early nineteenth-century commentator. "To rouse his indignation, it was enough to place before his eyes a scene of cruelty, hypocrisy, or injustice" (Allen 1825: 4). The result is a work whose more somber or skeptical themes find a continued counterpoint in pathetic tableaux designed to serve as a release for sympathetic emotions – notably in such scenes as the many tribulations of Mary Queen of Scots, the execution of Strafford, and (most famously) the final days of Charles I.

"There is no necessity," Hume wrote in the *Enquiry on Morals*, "that a generous action, barely mentioned in an old history or remote gazette . . . should communicate any strong feelings of applause and admiration." Virtue "placed at such a distance" is like a star: visible to the eye of reason, but without power to warm us.

> Bring this virtue nearer, by our acquaintance or connexion with the persons, or even by an eloquent recital of the case; our hearts are immediately caught, our sympathy enlivened, and our cool approbation converted into the warmest sentiments of friendship and regard. (EPM 5.43)

Turning away from the idea that history teaches by depicting exemplary virtue and vice, Hume's "eloquent recital" aimed to place virtue *nearer*, not higher. Immediacy was the key, not ideality, a shift in emphasis that meant that historical writing (like other literatures in this age of sensibility) would be valued as an opportunity to exercise the moral sentiments and that the successful historian, no less than the novelist, might be judged by his capacity for pathos. As the Whig historian James Mackintosh would later put it,

> The effect of the death of Clarissa, or of Mary Stuart on the heart by no means depends on the fact that the one really died, but on the vivacity of the exhibition by the two great pathetic painters, Hume and Richardson. (Mackintosh 1853: vol. 2, 127–35)

Hume's mastery of affective narrative was widely acknowledged in his day, but the time would soon come when such "calm entertainment" no longer seemed sufficient and a more intense engagement with the emotions was demanded. John Stuart Mill, for instance, writing in the full flush of Carlylean enthusiasm, dismissed Hume as an author so imbued with the rationalism of his age and so lacking in genuine insight into human experience that his work could hardly be called a history at all (Mill 1985). Mackintosh's assessment was far more sympathetic and much closer to the sense of Hume's own generation. For him, the *History* was not only Hume's greatest work, but one of the greatest histories ever written. He praised Hume's ease of manner and the unforced air with which he was able to bring in his more abstract reflections; but above all Mackintosh admired Hume's ability to mix pathos and philosophical distance, thereby combining the highest attractions of sensibility and Enlightenment.

> No other narrative seems to unite, in the same degree, the two qualities of being instructing and affecting. No historian approached him in the union of the talent of painting pathetic scenes with that of exhibiting comprehensive views of human affairs. (Mackintosh 1853: vol. 2, 168)

Mackintosh's sketch can hardly be bettered as a synopsis of eighteenth-century historiographical tastes, but even Mackintosh – carried along by rising standards of antiquarian scholarship and especially by a new demand for intense imaginative engagement – had to acknowledge the limitations of this great work. Hume's preference was for reflection over research, he wrote, and it cannot be denied that he "sometimes trusted to his acuteness to supply the place of industry in the investigation of evidence." Still more problematical, however, was the suspicion that at bottom Hume was too abstract in his understanding of history to probe the real depths of earlier times. "He was too habitually a speculator," Mackintosh admitted,

> and too little of an antiquary, to have a great power of throwing back his mind into former ages, and of clothing his persons and events in their moral dress; his personages are too modern and argumentative – if we must not say too rational. (Mackintosh 1853: vol. 2, 169)

As views like these became increasingly representative, the *History of England* – once the focus of fierce political antagonism as well as of cultural pride – inevitably slipped into a new role as a safe literary classic, suitable for the young and the genteel.

See also 21 " 'One of the Finest and Most Subtle Inventions': Hume on Government"

References

Allen, John (1825). "Review of John Lingard's *A History of England*," reprinted in James Fieser (ed.), *Early Responses to Hume's History of England*, 2 vols. (Bristol: Thoemmes, 2002).

Anderson, James (1790). "Review of Sir John Sinclair's *History of the Public Revenue*," *Monthly Review*, 2nd series, 3, pp. 93–4.

Blackburn, Simon (2005). *Truth: A Guide* (Oxford: Oxford University Press).

Blair, Hugh (1965). *Lectures on Rhetoric*, 2 vols., ed. Harold F. Harding (Carbondale, IL: Southern Illinois University Press).

Collingwood, R. G. (1993). *The Idea of History*, ed. J. van der Dussen (Oxford: Clarendon Press).

Forbes, Duncan (1975). *Hume's Philosophical Politics* (Cambridge: Cambridge University Press).

Giarizzo, Giuseppe (1962). *David Hume, politico e storico* (*David Hume, Political Theorist and Historian*) (Turin: Einaudi).

—— (1971). "Ancora su Hume storico," *Rivista storica italiana*, 83, pp. 429–49.

Greig, J. Y. T. (ed.) (1932). *The Letters of David Hume*, 2 vols. (Oxford: Clarendon Press).

Gunn, J. A. W. (1983). *Beyond Liberty and Property* (Kingston: McGill Queens University Press).

Henry, Robert (1823). *The History of Great Britain, from the First Invasion of It by the Romans . . . Written on a New Plan*, 6th edn. (London: T. and J. Allman), 12 vols.

Hicks, Philip (1996). *Neoclassical History and English Culture* (New York: St. Martin's Press).

Hilson, J. C. (1978). "Hume: The Historian as Man of Feeling," in J. C. Hilson, M. M. B. Jones, and J. R. Watson (eds.), *Augustan Worlds: New Essays in Eighteenth-century Literature* (Leicester: Leicester University Press).

Hume, David (1741–77). *Essays, Moral, Political and Literary*, ed. Eugene F. Miller (Indianapolis, IN: Liberty Fund, 1987). (Cited in the text as *Essays*.)

—— (1754–78). *The History of England* (Indianapolis, IN: Liberty Fund, 1983). (Cited in the text as H, followed by volume and page number.)

—— (1777). "My Own Life," in Eugene F. Miller (ed.), *Essays, Moral, Political and Literary* (Indianapolis, IN: Liberty Fund, 1987).

Livingston, Donald (1984). *Hume's Philosophy of Common Life* (Chicago: University of Chicago Press).

Mackintosh, Sir James (1853). *Memoirs of the Life and Writings*, ed. R. Mackintosh (Boston: Little, Brown), 2 vols.

Miller, David (1981). *Philosophy and Ideology in Hume's Political Thought* (Oxford: Oxford University Press).

Norton, David Fate (1965). "History and Philosophy in Hume's Thought," in D. F. Norton and R. Popkin (eds.), *David Hume: Philosophical Historian* (Indianapolis, IN: Bobbs-Merrill).

O'Brien, Karen (1997). *Narratives of Enlightenment: Cosmopolitan History from Voltaire to Gibbon* (Cambridge: Cambridge University Press).

Phillips, Mark Salber (1997). "Adam Smith and the History of Private Life: Social and Sentimental Narratives in Eighteenth-century Historiography," in D. R. Kelley and D. H. Sacks (eds.), *The Historical Imagination in Early Modern Britain* (Cambridge: Cambridge University Press).

—— (2000). *Society and Sentiment: Genres of Historical Thought, 1740–1820* (Princeton, NJ: Princeton University Press).

—— (2003). "Relocating Inwardness: Historical Distance and the Transition from Enlightenment to Romantic Historiography," *Publications of the Modern Languages Association*, 118, pp. 436–49.

—— (2005). "Adam Smith, Belletrist," in K. Haakonssen (ed.), *Cambridge Companion to Adam Smith* (Cambridge: Cambridge University Press).

Phillips, Mark Salber and Smith, Dale R. (2005). "Canonization and Critique: Hume's Reputation as a Historian," in Peter Jones (ed.), *The Reception of Hume in Europe* (London: Continuum).

Phillipson, Nicholas (1989). *Hume* (London: Weidenfeld and Nicolson).

Pocock, John (1999). *Barbarism and Civilization* (Cambridge: Cambridge University Press).

Pompa, Leon (1990). *Human Nature and Historical Knowledge: Hume, Hegel, and Vico* (Cambridge: Cambridge University Press).

Popkin, Richard (1976). "Hume: Philosophical versus Prophetic Historian," in K. Merill and R. W. Shahan (eds.), *David Hume, Many-sided Genius* (Norman, OK: University of Oklahoma Press).

Smith, Adam (1762). *Lectures on Rhetoric and "Belles Lettres,"* ed. J. C. Bryce (Indianapolis, IN: Liberty Fund, 1985).

—— (1776). *An Inquiry into the Nature and Causes of the Wealth of Nations*, ed. R. H. Campbell, A. S. Skinner, and W. B. Todd (Oxford: Clarendon Press, 1976).

Stewart, John (1992). *Opinion and Reform in Hume's Political Philosophy* (Princeton, NJ: Princeton University Press).

Wootton, David (1993). "David Hume, 'the Historian'," in D. F. Norton (ed.), *Cambridge Companion to Hume* (Cambridge: Cambridge University Press), pp. 281–312.

Further Reading

Bongie, Laurence (1965). *David Hume: Prophet of the Counter Revolution* (Oxford: Clarendon Press).

Braudy, Leo (1970). *Narrative Form in History and Fiction: Hume, Fielding, Gibbon* (Princeton, NJ: Princeton University Press).

Capaldi, Nicholas and Livingston, Donald (1990). *Liberty in Hume's History of England* (Dordrecht: Kluwer).

Emerson, Roger E. (1984). "Conjectural History and Scottish Philosophers," in *Historical Papers: Communication Historique*, pp. 63–90.

Fieser, James (2002). *Early Responses to Hume's History of England*, 2 vols. (Bristol: Thoemmes).

Kidd, Colin (1993). *Subverting Scotland's Past* (Cambridge: Cambridge University Press).

Levine, Joseph (1987). *Humanism and History: Origins of Modern Historiography* (Ithaca, NY: Cornell University Press).

Livingston, Donald (1998). *Philosophical Melancholy and Delirium: Hume's Pathology of Philosophy* (Chicago: University of Chicago Press).

Okie, Laird (1991). *Augustan Historical Writing: Histories of England in the Enlightenment* (Lanham, MD: University Press of America).

Smith, R. J. (1987). *The Gothic Bequest: Medieval Institutions in British Thought, 1688–1863* (Cambridge: Cambridge University Press).

Wexler, Victor G. (1979). *David Hume and the History of England* (Philadelphia: American Philosophical Society).

Part VI

Contemporary Themes

23

Hume's Naturalism and His Skepticism

JANET BROUGHTON

Introduction

Hume set out to discover the principles of human nature by observing the ways the mind works. He claimed that by discovering these principles, he would be able to explain important aspects of our ideas and reasonings, our moral and aesthetic judgments, and our political institutions. He predicted that these explanations would in turn lead to many changes and improvements, not just in our understanding of ourselves, but also in our understanding of mathematics, natural philosophy, and natural religion. This is a highly optimistic and constructive outlook; it is at the core of what is often called Hume's "naturalism."

Yet Hume goes on to make claims that seem radically pessimistic and destructive. He denies that philosophers really have the basic tools they thought they had: abstract ideas; their distinction between substance and mode; their concepts of pure space and time and of causal power; their concept of external objects; a direct awareness of the self. He denies that the human mind is capable of rational insight into the natural world: our much-vaunted reason is just the operation in us of habit and feeling. There is no way to rationalize belief in the existence of physical objects; and when we look at ourselves, we find we have no grounds for believing even in our own existence as enduring minds or selves. Hume confesses that

> [t]he *intense* view of these manifold contradictions and imperfections in human reason has so wrought upon me, and heated my brain, that I am ready to reject all belief and reasoning, and can look upon no opinion even as more probable or likely than another. (T 1.4.7.8)

Thus two very different outlooks seem to coexist in Hume's philosophy. Unsurprisingly, some readers of Hume have thought that only one of these outlooks was truly his. During his lifetime, and for more than a century after his death, many readers stressed the skeptical side of Hume's philosophy. Thomas Reid, the leading "common sense" philosopher of the Scottish Enlightenment, interpreted Hume in this way, and his understanding of Hume was highly influential. According to Reid, Hume accepted the common philosophical assumption that

> nothing is perceived but what is in the mind which perceives it: That we do not really perceive things that are external, but only certain images and pictures of them imprinted upon the mind. (Reid 1764: 4)

Reid understood Hume's philosophy as showing that from this assumption followed "a system of scepticism, which leaves no ground to believe any one thing rather than its contrary" (1764: 4), and he treated the seemingly optimistic and constructive side of Hume's outlook as back-sliding: even the arch-skeptic must sometimes slip and yield to "the dominion of Common Sense" (1764: 20).

In the twentieth century, the tide of interpretation turned, starting with the work of Norman Kemp Smith. He argued that Reid's interpretation was wrong: far from being a negative and destructive skeptic, Hume was a positive and constructive naturalist. Hume's aim, Kemp Smith argued, was to show that feeling and imagination play central roles in our lives. His way of showing this was to produce a "science of MAN" (T Introduction 4), a study of the human mind modeled after Newton's study of the physical world. In different ways, most leading commentators in recent decades have agreed with Kemp Smith that we must take Hume's naturalism seriously, and that it is central to his philosophy. But something that was not entirely clear in Kemp Smith's pioneering work is still hotly debated: if we take the naturalism seriously, where, if anywhere, does the seeming skepticism fit in? If Hume is not really a skeptic at all, then what does he mean by saying such things as, "I am ready to reject all belief and reasoning, and can look upon no opinion even as more probably or likely than another"? But if he really is in some way a skeptic, then exactly how can his skepticism co-exist with his naturalism?

In what follows, I will first lay out in more detail some of the claims and arguments that we must examine before we can address these questions. I will focus mainly on Book 1 of the *Treatise of Human Nature*, though at the end of the chapter I will compare the *Treatise* with the *Enquiry concerning the Human Understanding* and the *Dialogues concerning Natural Religion*.

Hume's Naturalism

The Introduction to the *Treatise* is brief and programmatic, but in it Hume tells us several important things about his philosophical project. Its subject matter is us: not us as biological organisms, but us as human minds. Its goal is explanation: it is supposed to explain the nature of our ideas and the principles according to which our minds work. He thinks his results may lead us to make "changes and improvements" (T Introduction 4) in what we say, not just about logic, morals, criticism, and politics, but also about other subjects, including mathematics, natural philosophy, and natural religion. That much does not sound especially original; arguably a philosopher very different from Hume – Descartes, perhaps – could make much the same proposal, with a few adjustments of emphasis. But Hume's distinctive ambitions emerge more clearly when he adds that his basis for his claims about human nature will be "experience and observation" (T Introduction 7) rather than any supposed insight into "the essence of the mind" (T Introduction 8). Although he will try to explain the widest variety of phenomena by establishing principles as simple and general as possible, he promises that he will not "go beyond experience" to form any "hypothesis" about the "ultimate original qualities of human nature" (T Introduction 8). This means that although we may hope to understand human nature better, we cannot hope to explain everything about it. For example, once we have arrived at the most simple and general principles that experience and observation can show us, we must forgo any pretensions to explain why those principles, and not some other principles, are at work in human nature.

In describing his project in these ways, Hume is drawing analogies between the science of man and the kinds of investigations of the natural world undertaken by scientists like Newton. This is one important sense in which his project is a naturalist one, but we should be careful. Hume does not see the science of man as simply one science among many. While its results may lead to changes and improvements in other sciences, Hume never suggests that the results of other sciences may lead to changes or improvements in the science of man.

One of the analogies Hume sees between his project and Newton's is that he aims to identify mental principles that are causal in their general character. Among the causal principles that he appeals to most frequently are principles of the association of ideas in the imagination: he claims that the mind will tend to form an idea of something that resembles the object of the mind's previous state, or is contiguous to that object, or is its cause or effect. He also makes ingenious use of the principle of custom or habit: when the mind has repeatedly experienced things of one sort in conjunction with things of another sort, then when it once again experiences a thing of the one sort, it will tend to form an idea of a thing of the other sort. And he argues that one of the basic principles of the mind's operation involves a tendency to make a distinctive sort of mistake: the mind tends to mistake a given idea or sequence of ideas for some other idea or sequence that closely resembles it. In establishing such principles of the mind as these, Hume offers direct empirical support; indirect support comes from the way these principles help to explain a range of puzzling kinds of mental phenomena.

The Introduction to the *Treatise* suggests two further important points. One is that Hume is adopting the *standards of evidence* that he believes were adopted by such figures as Newton. His principles of human nature will be well supported by observation and experience when they are supported in the same general way that a Newton would support his principles of the natural world. The other point the Introduction suggests is that Hume is at least beginning his investigation by sharing with the rest of us some basic, commonsense assumptions: that there *is* a natural world, that there are human beings, and that we find out about these various sorts of things by observing them. Reid thought that Hume's starting point was the assumption that all a philosopher has available to him for direct study are his own, private mental states. But if Hume is making this assumption, he is certainly not making it explicitly, and indeed he is saying things that at least on the surface seem to be inconsistent with it. For example, he says that we must "glean up our experiments in this science [of man] from a cautious observation of human life, and take them as they appear in the common course of the world" (T Introduction 10). This strongly suggests that we can study people and the world around us, not just our own mental states. Still, Reid might

427

reply that for Hume, we can study the world around us at best *indirectly*, by drawing inferences from our own mental states. I will return to this point later.

A number of the "changes and improvements" that Hume goes on to propose arise from his use of two principles. One is the "copy principle," that all our simple ideas are derived from simple impressions, and Hume offers empirical support for this principle. But he also relies heavily on the principle that different ideas are distinct and therefore separable, and although this principle concerns our perceptions, Hume does not really treat it as a principle whose main support comes from experience. At any rate, with the help of these two principles, Hume launches a number of deflationary criticisms against claims central to the philosophical tradition as he sees it. His treatments of general ideas, of the ideas of substance, space, time, and causal necessity, and of the causal maxim (that every event must have a cause) are all deflationary in character. By this I mean that according to Hume, philosophers – and in some cases, ordinary people too – assume that their concepts can have more content than in fact they have. If Hume is right about this, then what we can think about comes to less than we might suppose. The cumulative effect of these claims is deflationary in an additional sense, because the missing content is, broadly speaking, what we would need in order to have the sort of rational insight into reality that philosophers like Descartes attributed to us.

Hume's discoveries about the human understanding are deflationary in another arena: the nature of our beliefs. He argues that we do not form our beliefs by bestowing and withholding our assent to various propositions in light of the evidence available to us. Rather, our minds operate in such a way that our beliefs are typically automatic. When we have certain sorts of impressions, we are caused to have certain sorts of ideas, and caused to entertain those ideas with a vividness that is constitutive of belief. Belief is our natural reaction to our experiences, in something like the way that fear is our natural reaction to our perils. When we form beliefs about what we haven't experienced on the basis of what we have experienced, the basic way our mind works is simply to form habits of expectation after repeatedly experiencing sequences of kinds of events. In these central cases, belief in us is like the expectant salivation of Pavlov's dogs: "*belief is more properly an act of the sensitive, than of the cogitative part of our natures*" (T 1.4.1.8). More broadly, "reason is nothing but a wonderful and unintelligible instinct in our souls, which carries us along a certain train of ideas, and endows them with particular qualities, according to their particular situations and relations" (T 1.3.16.9), and in this respect we are basically no different from a "dog, that avoids fire and precipices, that shuns strangers, and caresses his master" (T 1.3.16.5).

So far, we have seen some respects in which Hume's philosophy could be described as negative, or perhaps even skeptical: it acknowledges limits to what we can explain or understand about ourselves, it concludes that many of our basic concepts allow us to think about less than we might have supposed, and it endorses a kind of determinism about our beliefs. In all of these ways, it cuts us down to size, or more precisely, cuts down to size our estimation of our intellects. But none of these deflationary conclusions conflicts in any obvious way with Hume's constructive effort to explain the workings of the human mind. The deflation leaves intact the general standards of empirical evidence to which Hume is holding himself, and it seems to leave untouched our general beliefs that there is a natural world, that there are human beings, and that we find out about these various sorts of things by observing them. It was surely not these deflationary results alone that left Hume "ready to reject all belief and reasoning" (T 1.4.7.8). Indeed, in some senses of the term "naturalism," these deflationary results themselves constitute a kind of naturalist outlook: Hume is resolutely treating human beings as basically very smart animals, not as beings that are in some way higher than, or fundamentally different in kind from, animals like dogs.

Hume's Skepticism

There are two places to look for argumentation that is more radically negative in scope and depth. One is in Hume's famous account of causal inference in part 3 of Book 1 the *Treatise*; the other is in the investigations that occupy him in part 4, where he considers the mind's general powers of reflection and its beliefs in both an inner and an outer world.

Hume's analysis of causal inference has seemed to many readers to have the radical skeptical consequence that none of our causal inferences is in any way justified. To justify our causal inferences, Hume appears to say, we must be able to justify the general principle that the patterns of regularity that hold within the scope of our observation also hold uniformly throughout the natural world. But any attempt to justify the general principle appears to be doomed: we cannot claim that we know it to be true a priori, and yet any attempt to justify it by appeal to experience will be fatally circular (T 1.3.6.4–7).

This skeptical reading of Hume's argument is, however, hard to square with the later sections of part 3 in which he unapologetically distinguishes between causal inferences that are justified and those that are not. (See chapter 6.) Indeed, he devotes an entire section toward the end of part 3 to "[r]ules by which to judge of causes and effects," and he assures the reader that by following these rules we will be able to "know" which objects have which effects (T 1.3.15.2). These points suggest to some scholars that in his account of causal inference, Hume's concern is not primarily with justification but rather with explanation. He aims to show what aspect of the mind is responsible for our making causal inferences, and he concludes that the faculty of reason cannot be the responsible faculty. This then prepares the way for his own account, which identifies custom or habit as the aspect of the mind that is at work when we draw causal inferences.

For present-day readers, it may seem odd to think that Hume did not intend his account of causal inference to be skeptical. *We* find it very easy to see a powerful skeptical argument – the "problem of induction" – right beneath the surface of Hume's text, and it is difficult for us to see how Hume could not himself have felt the pull of that reasoning. But it is a line of thought that relies on the assumption that to justify our causal inferences, we must justify the "uniformity principle," and at least in the *Treatise*, Hume appears not to have accepted that assumption. The assumption itself will seem especially plausible if we think that justification requires us to rule out "skeptical counterpossibilities": for example, the possibility that, compatibly with all we have observed, the sun will not rise tomorrow. But there are other ways of thinking about justification. Hume may have thought instead that so long as our causal beliefs are clear and consistent, then they are justified whenever they meet our evidentiary standards: standards like those he himself implicitly adopts in undertaking an empirically based science of man.

But are we right in thinking that our most basic commonsense assumptions are clear, consistent, and in accord with evidentiary standards for belief? Are we justified in thinking that there is a world around us that we find out about through sense experience? Those questions bring me to the second place we might look for radical skeptical conclusions. In part 4 of Book 1 of the *Treatise*, Hume traces out several complex lines of thought that lead him to attribute a fundamentally incoherent set of beliefs to the human mind. He knits these lines of thought together in the final section of part 4, producing the argument that leaves him "ready to reject all belief and reasoning" and unable to look upon any "opinion even as more probable or likely than another" (T 1.4.7.8). Here he is not responding to a problem about skeptical counter-possibilities; he is facing some other sort of quandary.

To see its character, we need to see at least in outline Hume's complex train of thought. He starts by investigating a basic belief that we all have: the belief that the things we touch and see, hear, taste, and smell, are mind-independent, physical objects that continue to exist when we are not perceiving them. He argues that our natural and non-reflective belief about the things we sense is the belief that what we *immediately* perceive continues to exist unperceived. But this vulgar view, he argues, is inconsistent with other, reasonable beliefs that we hold, for example, that pressing the eye does not double the number of chairs in the room (cf. T 1.4.2.44–5). Reflective people, when they recognize this inconsistency, are then naturally driven to embrace the "opinion of the double existence of perceptions and objects" (T 1.4.2.46). Although this belief is consistent with pressing-the-eye beliefs, it fails to meet our standards of reasoning from effects to causes, because we could never have had any experience of the conjunction of the effects (our experiences) with the causes (the external objects) (T 1.4.2.54). So our natural beliefs in physical objects either lead us to embrace inconsistent beliefs or lead us to embrace beliefs that fail to meet our standards for causal reasoning.

Next, Hume argues that if we reflect on some general features of our sense perception, we will find that our standards for good causal reasoning require us to distinguish between primary and secondary qualities (T 1.4.4.3–4). The distinction is one we must make in order to obey one of the rules by which to judge of causes and effects: "the same effect never arises but from the same cause" (T 1.3.15.6). But once we have drawn that distinction, we cannot coherently attribute *any* qualities to bodies: "nothing we can conceive is possest of a real, continu'd, and independent existence; not even motion, extension and solidity" (T 1.4.4.6). If we limit the materials for our conception of body to the primary qualities, we limit our materials to zero: the idea of motion depends on the idea of extension or solidity; the idea of extension depends on the idea of the disposition of colored or solid points; the idea of color is not the idea of a primary quality; and the idea of solidity depends on the idea of body (which depends on the idea of extension, which depends on the idea of colored or solid points, and so on).

There is, then, "a direct and total opposition . . . betwixt those conclusions we form from cause and effect, and those that persuade us of the . . . existence of body" (T 1.4.4.15). In the final section of Book 1, Hume reflects on this "opposition":

[The imagination] makes us reason from causes and effects; and 'tis the same principle, which convinces us of the continu'd existence of external objects, when absent from the senses. But tho' these two operations be equally natural and necessary in the human mind, yet in some circumstances they are directly contrary, nor is it possible for us to reason justly and regularly from causes and effects, and at the same time believe the continu'd existence of matter. How then shall we adjust those principles together? Which of them shall we prefer? Or in case we prefer neither of them, but successively assent to both, as is usual among philosophers, with what confidence can we afterwards usurp that glorious title, when we thus knowingly embrace a manifest contradiction? (T 1.4.7.4)

To avoid "contradiction" we would have to give up drawing causal inferences, or we would have to give up our commonsense belief in the existence of the external world.

Hume suggests that we will find it impossible to answer the question, "Which of them shall we prefer?" though it is not completely clear why. It seems better to keep drawing causal inferences and disown the belief in the existence of the external world, since both the prereflective and the reflective versions of the belief in body have problems of their own. But of course even to make this choice is to opt for a radical skeptical conclusion: it is to concede that we cannot rationalize our beliefs in the external world. The causal beliefs we would hold would have to be beliefs simply about our experiences, rather than beliefs about the world.

In any case, Hume himself presses his negative thoughts even further, asking the question what, in light of these difficulties, we "ought" to do (T 1.4.7.6). Ought we to stop holding some of our most basic beliefs? I think that his response to this question is that it is not possible to give it a reasoned answer. He starts by considering the question whether we ought to give up our beliefs in the external world, but hold on to our causal inferences. To answer this question, he draws upon a complex argument he had given earlier about the diminution of probabilities under reflection (T 1.4.1.5–6). He had argued that by reflecting upon our fallibility in any judgment we make, and then upon our fallibility in that reflective judgment, and so on, we will progressively reduce our confidence that the original judgment is correct. We then can see that continued reflection would, by "all the rules of logic require a continual diminution, and at last a total extinction of belief and evidence" (T 1.4.1.6). So if we want to defend the view that we ought to believe the results of our good causal inferences, we must somehow block the complex argument about the diminution of confidence. But the only way to do that would be to dismiss all complex argumentation, and our reason for doing so would itself be a complex piece of argumentation (the whole line of thought about what we ought to believe). Hume sums up by saying, "We have, therefore, no choice left but betwixt a false reason and none at all" (T 1.4.7.7): either we defend causal inferences by giving a complex argument for dismissing complex arguments, or we acknowledge that all belief is extinguished under reflection. When we ask, then, what we ought to believe in the face of the manifold contradictions in our beliefs, we cannot consistently defend believing in anything. Hume finds that when he thinks about all these considerations and the conclusions to which they lead, he is "ready to reject all belief and reasoning, and can look upon no opinion even as more probable or likely than another" (T 1.4.7.8).

Unlike Hume's earlier deflationary conclusions, these conclusions are broadly and deeply skeptical. His line of thought here is perhaps not as compelling to us as the "problem of induction"; we may especially wonder whether Hume is right to say that good causal reasoning requires us to distinguish between primary and secondary qualities, and that belief diminishes under reflection on our fallibility. We may feel greater sympathy with his criticisms of our belief in the external world: it is indeed difficult to articulate, much less defend, our commonsense belief, and clearly the philosophical doctrine of double existence is indefensible.

What about Reid's diagnosis of the source of Hume's skepticism? Recall that Reid thought Hume's skepticism resulted from his making the assumption that in sense experience we are immediately aware only of the contents of our own minds. I think Hume would regard this as a misdiagnosis. He himself, like the rest of humankind, takes it that in sense experience we are aware of a world of independent, physical objects. While we normally do not ask ourselves whether we are aware of objects immediately or mediately, clearly in everyday life we do not endorse the doctrine of double existence. Hume thus describes the vulgar, or ordinary, view as the view that we are aware of objects immediately, and he appears himself to share this vulgar view whenever he is not reflecting philosophically on his beliefs. When he does reflect, he finds that the vulgar view is defective, and he explains how this reflection gives rise to belief in the philosophical view that Reid rejects. He himself then criticizes this view as defective too.

I think that all of these features of Hume's work certainly show that he thought a great deal about the assumption that Reid attributes to him, and that his reactions to it are far more nuanced than Reid suggests. But it is not easy to evaluate the real strength of Hume's reply: much turns on his characterization of the vulgar view, and he may in the end be guilty of building into it crucial fragments of the philosophical view, especially when he says that if the vulgar do not endorse the doctrine of double existence, then they must believe they perceive objects immediately. Perhaps the question "Mediate or immediate?" is one that already makes an important philosophical assumption. Here lie some important and difficult questions about how to characterize our commonsense beliefs about the world.

The Relation between Hume's Naturalism and His Skepticism

Now let us turn to the general question how Hume's radically negative skeptical conclusions could co-exist with his constructive naturalism. He has argued that we cannot consistently draw good causal inferences and believe in the external world, and he has further argued that we cannot wiggle out of this bind by giving a reason for holding on to some of our beliefs and discarding others. Yet anyone who engages in the constructive project of the science of man is committed to using observations of people and the world we inhabit in order to draw inferences about the workings of the mind. If Hume is committed to doing this, then he must himself hold many of the beliefs that he is condemning as impossible to justify.

When we think about Hume's ambitions and conclusions in this way, I think we must regard his naturalism and his skepticism as incompatible. His naturalism requires him to endorse beliefs that his skeptical conclusions condemn. If our interpretative goal is to show that Hume is first and foremost a constructive naturalist, then we cannot simply add that he also reaches the incompatible skeptical conclusions. We must say more than that.

One broad interpretative strategy we might deploy is to deny that Hume himself actually endorses the skeptical conclusions of the arguments he has presented. Then although the skeptical conclusions of the arguments would be incompatible with Hume's naturalism, we would not have to say that Hume himself was being inconsistent, since he would not himself be committed to the correctness of the skeptical arguments he gives. In the end, I do not think such interpretations are satisfactory, and I will sketch an alternative way to understand Hume. But first I want to explain several ways of developing such a "not-really-skeptical" reading, and to do that, I must begin by describing what Hume himself goes on to do after he arrives at what at least seem to be his skeptical conclusions.

We might expect that what rational people will do when they reach skeptical or negative conclusions about various of their beliefs is simply give the beliefs up. That is certainly what we often do in everyday life. For example, we may start by believing someone who tells us that a particular nation has a stockpile of weapons of mass destruction, and then we may realize that our belief is unsupported by direct evidence and incompatible with other things we know. In light of these skeptical or negative conclusions, we will then stop holding the belief. If Hume were to behave in a similar fashion, then when he reached his sweeping skeptical conclusions, he would stop holding all of his beliefs. This would mean he would stop holding the beliefs that his naturalism requires, and thus he would no longer be able to continue the project with which he began, the project of explaining the workings of the mind through observation and experiment.

But it is one thing to give up a single, specific belief, like the belief about the weapons stockpile, and quite another to give up all causal inference and all belief in an external world. Hume thinks it is not an option for him or for anyone else actually to forgo all these basic beliefs, at least for more than a brief while. This is just not humanly possible: "Nature, by an absolute and uncontroulable necessity has determin'd us to judge as well as to breathe and feel" (T 1.4.1.7).

In the final few pages of Book 1, Hume traces out these workings of nature within his own mind, as it "cures [him] of [his] philosophical melancholy and delirium" (T 1.4.7.9). He is diverted by the company of his friends, and when he looks back at his philosophical thoughts, they leave him unmoved, except for the resolve "never more to renounce the pleasures of life for the sake of reasoning and philosophy" (T 1.4.7.10). This is his mood of "spleen and indolence" (T 1.4.7.11); when we find ourselves in such a mood, we believe "that fire warms, or water refreshes" only because "it costs us too much pains to think otherwise" (T 1.4.7.11). While in the grip of spleen and indolence, Hume holds various unavoidable beliefs, but he is in no mood to be a naturalist philosopher, investigating the broad principles that explain the workings of the human mind.

But for him, at any rate, this mood does not persist. "[C]uriosity and ambition" (T 1.4.7.13) rise up in him again, and once more he finds himself naturally inclined to raise questions about at least some philosophical matters: "the principles of moral good and evil, the nature and foundation of government, and the cause of those several passions and inclinations, which actuate and govern" us (T 1.4.7.12). Some people might want to address such questions through religion, but Hume recommends addressing them through philosophy, because "errors in religion are dangerous; those in philosophy only ridiculous" (T 1.4.7.13). Taking his own advice, Hume finds himself once more pursuing the naturalist project: "'Twill be sufficient for me, if I can bring [science of man] a little more into fashion; and the hope of this serves to compose my temper from that spleen, and invigorate it from that indolence, which sometimes prevail upon me" (T 1.4.7.14).

Hume thus describes his engagement with skepticism as a brief interlude: his return to his naturalist project is rapid and seems definitive; and clearly it is in a naturalist spirit that he goes on, in Books 2 and 3 of the *Treatise*, to investigate further aspects of human nature. These facts have led some readers of Hume to conclude that the skeptical conclusions were not, after all, really his conclusions. For such readers, when we understand Hume properly, we see that his naturalism is not incompatible with any skeptical conclusions that he truly reaches, since in some crucial way he does not truly reach those conclusions after all.

One way to develop such a reading would be to see Hume as successively taking up different perspectives: first naturalist and constructive, then skeptical and destructive, then naturalist and constructive again (see Fogelin 1993). He would not be claiming that one perspective is correct: he would not be identifying one of them as somehow representing his all-things-considered view about the prospects for human knowledge. Although the perspectives would be incompatible in the sense that they could not consistently be occupied simultaneously, the fact that Hume thinks the skeptical perspective is available would not show that he thinks it is correct. And although the same could be said for the naturalist perspective, it is unlike the skeptical perspective in being a perspective that we are naturally suited to occupy. Support for such a reading might come from Hume's remark that it is "proper" for us to "yield to that propensity, which inclines us to be positive and certain in *particular points*, according to the light, in which we survey them in any *particular instant*" (T 1.4.7.15). But this reading faces a serious challenge: it must explain why Hume represents the skeptical standpoint as the one that is the outcome of rationally compelling argumentation. That certainly sounds as though he thinks it is the one that is correct.

We might instead want to say that Hume's skepticism does not prevail over his naturalism because for Hume the skeptical interlude is somehow inauthentic. We might, for example, want to say that Hume sees his skeptical conclusions as depending upon a doctrine or outlook that he himself does not endorse (see Baier 1991). The skeptical argumentation might be rationally compelling, but Hume would be obliged to accept its conclusion only if he also accepted the doctrine or outlook upon which the argument depends. Indeed, we might see his skeptical arguments as a kind of *reductio ad absurdum* of an underlying doctrine or outlook. Suppose, for example, that he thought the skeptical argumentation proceeded only on the underlying assumption that we perceive the objects of our senses indirectly, and perceive directly only the ideas in our own minds. Then Reid's diagnosis and criticism of him would be off by one hundred and eighty degrees. Far from assuming the truth of this doctrine himself and then building a skeptical system upon it, Hume would be rejecting this doctrine on the grounds that if we accepted it, skepticism would follow.

A challenge for this kind of reading would be to show that Hume really did think that his argumentation in part 4 depended on premises that he does not himself accept. At least on the surface, his aims and arguments seem to be smoothly continuous with those in the earlier parts of Book 1. For example, in part 4, he aims to explain the causal origins of our belief in physical objects and in the self, just as earlier he had aimed to explain the causal origins of our beliefs in the possibility of empty space, or the mechanisms that produce our causal inferences. In part 4, he seems to rely upon just the same sorts of explanatory material – the mind's perceptions and the principles of its operations – that he used earlier. And his acute distress at his skeptical conclusions strongly suggests that he thinks his own beliefs are at stake, not those of a philosophical opponent.

On a somewhat different reading of this same general type, we could say that the *reductio* concerns a misguided readiness to subject every belief to rational reflection. Hyper-reflective people end up with skeptical conclusions about all of their beliefs, which just goes to show that there is such a thing as too much reflection (see Loeb 2002). Someone who reads Hume in this way could allow that he thinks strenuous reflection really does lead to skepticism, while saying that for Hume, strenuous reflection is not a good thing. A particular challenge to this reading would be to explain why Hume thinks that strenuous reflection is not a good thing. Of course, it clearly is not good in the sense that it leads to unhappiness, to "melancholy and delirium." But many things that lead to unhappiness are nevertheless things we think we ought to do.

Suppose we decide that Hume was not implicitly offering a *reductio* of some doctrine or outlook that he wanted to repudiate. How then can we understand his resumption of a naturalist program that he himself has undercut with radical skeptical conclusions? It is worth noticing that Hume describes himself as passing through a series of moods: first melancholy, then spleen, and finally a surge of curiosity. He is describing his own successive reactions to his discoveries, giving us a kind of history or chronicle of what goes on in his mind. And his emphasis on mood, feeling, and inclination suggests that a given thought in this succession may arise not because it is the rational consequence of the preceding thoughts, but simply because it is the natural effect of the mind's thoughts and feelings. Perhaps, then, Hume is describing how and why he resumes the naturalist project *even though* it is inconsistent with his own, authentic skeptical conclusions. That is, his skepticism and naturalism might be inconsistent and yet co-exist in the life-history of a philosopher. We could read Hume as genuinely endorsing his skeptical conclusions, while nonetheless finding that he abandons them under pressure from the principles of human nature that operate within him (see Broughton 2004).

This would be to see Hume as taking up a distinctive kind of attitude toward himself. As he chronicles what passes through his mind, he recognizes that he will not, and humanly cannot, maintain the skeptical outlook that he ought, rationally, to maintain. Although he resumes normal belief, and even once more picks up the complex naturalist project with which he began, he resumes his cognitive life with a subtle difference. He is now detached from his own cognitive commitments – his beliefs – in a peculiar way. In effect, as he once more believes this and that, he accompanies his belief with some such general thought as this: "Well, I would, wouldn't I?" On this reading, Hume would be indicating this kind of detached attitude by describing himself as "careless" (meaning "unconcerned") and as "diffident" of both his philosophical doubts and his philosophical convictions (T 1.4.7.14).

Hume would be thinking about his current and future states in a way that we usually adopt when we think about other people, or about our own past states. But perhaps we are sometimes detached from our own current and future mental states in something like Hume's way. Suppose that through intense self-scrutiny you arrive at an unwelcome realization about yourself. You realize, say, that you form critical beliefs about people for reasons you regard as trivial – their clothes, or their taste in home furnishings – and you realize that this attitude has its roots in aspects of your nature over which you have little control. No sooner do you arrive at your self-understanding than you find yourself thinking what a jerk that passerby must be if he wears a shirt like that. But although perhaps you cannot help having the thought, what your insight into yourself may enable you to do is to add, "Well, I would think that, wouldn't I?" You may be in some way detached from your critical belief, even as you have it.

Skepticism and Naturalism after the *Treatise*

It is not easy to describe the sort of post-skeptical return to naturalism that Hume tries to indicate at the end of Book 1 of the *Treatise*, and I suspect that Hume himself was not entirely satisfied with his account of it there. His later accounts of post-skeptical naturalism seem in some ways different from the account he gave in the *Treatise*.

In section 12 of the *Enquiry concerning Human Understanding*, Hume again sketches lines of thought that lead to radical skeptical conclusions; in giving such arguments, he says, the skeptic "shows his force" (EHU 12.22). But he immediately calls such skepticism "excessive" (EHU 12.23), not because he can defend our beliefs against "objections, which may be raised against them" (EHU 12.23), but because "no durable good can ever result from [radical skepticism]; while it remains in its full force and vigour" (EHU 12.23). In part this is because we are humanly able to withhold all assent for only a brief while; but it is also partly because even if we could suspend judgment for days on end, no good would come of it: "[a]ll discourse, all action would immediately cease; and men remain in a total lethargy, till the necessities of nature, unsatisfied, put an end to their miserable existence" (EHU 12.23). Here Hume raises a question he did not explicitly raise in the *Treatise*: what good would come of adhering to the rational dictates of radical skepticism? We might have the satisfaction of conforming our cognition to the irrefutable conclusions to which reflection leads us, but if we stayed in a state of suspended judgment, we would refrain from judging that here is some water, and from judging that if we do not drink, we will die, and so on – until we *did* die.

Here Hume is disagreeing with the view he took the Pyrrhonian skeptics to have held centuries earlier. They too found that reflection drove them to suspense of judgment, but they found this to be a good thing, because, they claimed, it brought them a kind of serenity or tranquility of mind. Of course, they did not sit down and die, nor did they think their suspense of judgment would involve any such radical change in their ordinary way of life. They claimed that they could suspend judgment but still adhere to the "appearances" and "live in accordance with the normal rules of life" (Sextus

Empiricus: 17). Hume is insisting, however, that if a skeptic really did withhold assent from everything, then he could not live a normal life, much less a serene and tranquil one. There is considerable scholarly debate about whether the Pyrrhonian skeptics were really giving up what Hume would call belief; possibly what they meant by adherence to appearances was fairly close to what Hume meant by belief modulated by post-skeptical detachment.

In any case, Hume does think there is some good that can come from going through the skeptical arguments and reaching the skeptical conclusions, so long as we do not linger in a state of suspended judgment. He approvingly describes two kinds of *"mitigated* scepticism" (EHU 12.24) that can result from a brush with radical skepticism. One involves beneficial changes in our intellectual temperaments. Ordinary people would be less dogmatic if they could see "the strange infirmities of human understanding, even in its most perfect state, and when most accurate and cautious in its determinations"; this would make them more like reflective people, most of whom are "diffident" (EHU 12.24). And if some reflective people lack diffidence and have tendencies toward haughtiness and obstinacy,

> a small tincture of PYRRHONISM might abate their pride, by showing them, that the few advantages, which they may have attained over their fellows, are but inconsiderable, if compared with the universal perplexity and confusion, which is inherent in human nature. (EHU 12.24)

Here Hume seems to be describing less the acquisition of a distinctive kind of attitude toward oneself, and more a kind of modification of general temperament. And while he continues to suggest that the modification would arise naturally, he also suggests that it could arise from a line of reflective thought something like this: "If humankind's best cognition is defective, then I cannot justify being dogmatic (or haughty, or obstinate) about *this* cognition." That is, here he seems to suggest that if we reach the skeptical conclusions, then we are rationally required to be less dogmatic, haughty, and obstinate. "In general, there is a degree of doubt, and caution, and modesty, which, in all kinds of scrutiny and decision, ought for ever to accompany a just reasoner" (EHU 12.24).

Hume goes on to describe a second type of beneficial mitigated skepticism that may result from going through the skeptical arguments and seeing their devastating conclusions. We will come to limit our inquiries to *"abstract reasoning concerning quantity or number"* and *"experimental reasoning concerning matter of fact and existence"* (EHU 12.33), and we will forgo inquiries into subjects that we cannot explore simply by using those kinds of reasoning – prime among them, religious subjects. While Hume again suggests that we will naturally rein ourselves in after we have seen the skeptical conclusions, he again seems to add that the skeptical conclusions give us rational grounds to rein ourselves in:

> While we cannot give a satisfactory reason, why we believe, after a thousand experiments, that a stone will fall, or fire burn; can we ever satisfy ourselves concerning any determination, which we may form, with regard to the origin of worlds, and the situation of nature, from, and to eternity? (EHU 12.25).

437

It is difficult to understand the force of Hume's apparent claim that mitigated skepticism is somehow rationally required of people who have understood the arguments for radical skepticism. On the surface, he seems to be saying something analogous to this: "If you cannot lift this weight, you should not try to lift a larger weight." But Hume's unmitigated skeptical conclusion is that we cannot justify any of our beliefs about the world. That suggests that he is saying something more closely analogous to this: "If you cannot lift any weight at all, then you should not try to lift a large weight." But if we cannot lift any weight at all, then surely we should not try to lift even a small weight, either. That is, if the point is that we should refrain from holding beliefs about the origin of worlds because we cannot justify them, then for the same reason we should refrain from holding beliefs about stones and fires too, since we cannot justify our belief that a stone will fall or fire burn.

The question about the relation between radical skepticism and the character of post-skeptical life comes up again in the *Dialogues concerning Natural Religion*. Philo is the character who has reached the radical skeptical conclusions, and his outlook is complex and subtle. In some places he seems to have the diffidence that characterized the post-skeptical outlook in the *Treatise*. In other places he seems to repeat the kinds of claims about mitigated skepticism that Hume made in the *Enquiry*, as when he says,

> When these [skeptical] topics are displayed in their full light . . . who can retain such confidence in this frail faculty of reason as to pay any regard to its determinations in points so sublime, so abstruse, so remote from common life and experience? (Hume 1779: 33)

But Philo also goes on to offer a novel account of how grasping skeptical conclusions leads to a limitation on the scope of human enquiry. Here he does not say that grasping the skeptical conclusions rationally requires us to limit the scope of human enquiry. Rather, he produces an account of the workings of the human mind that would explain why post-skeptical inquirers naturally limit their enquiries. He reminds us that skeptical reasonings are

> not able to counterpoise the more solid and more natural arguments, derived from the senses and experience. But it is evident, whenever our arguments lose this advantage, and run wide of common life, that the most refined scepticism comes to be upon a footing with them, and is able to oppose and counterbalance them. The one has no more weight than the other. The mind must remain in suspense between them. (Hume 1779: 37–8)

Philo is sketching here an empirical claim about how our minds work: when we conduct inquiries into questions that lie beyond the scope of possible experience, the beliefs we form are not vivid enough to pull us away from our radical skeptical conclusions, and those conclusions, even though they exert only a weak hold on us, are nonetheless powerful enough to counterbalance our feeble beliefs about the origins of worlds, the afterlife, and so on.

Cleanthes, one of Philo's interlocutors, challenges this claim by arguing that a belief in God as a designing intelligence is as vivid as any of our beliefs:

438

Consider, anatomize the eye: Survey its structure and contrivance; and tell me, from your own feeling, if the idea of a contriver does not immediately flow in upon you with a force like that of sensation. (Hume 1779: 56)

Philo responds vigorously to this challenge in the last part of the *Dialogues*, offering a concession so highly qualified as to be virtually no concession at all.

Clearly Hume continued to wrestle long after the *Treatise* with the question exactly how radical skeptical conclusions fit into human life, including a life like his own, dedicated to the naturalist study of human nature. In 1776, knowing that he soon would die, Hume wrote a brief autobiography. Toward the end of it, he described his declining health but remarked on his continued good spirits, adding, as if in explanation, "It is difficult to be more detached from life than I am at present" (Hume 1776: 9). I believe Hume thought that skeptical conclusions about human cognition are correct, but that our lives can be better – happier – for knowing this sad truth.

See also: 6 "Inductive Inference in Hume's Philosophy"; 7 "Hume on Belief in the External World"; 18 "Hume on the Nature and Existence of God"; 24 "Is Hume a Realist or an Anti-Realist?"; 25 "Hume's Epistemological Legacy"

References

Baier, Annette (1991). *A Progress of Sentiments: Reflections on Hume's "Treatise"* (Cambridge, MA: Harvard University Press).

Broughton, Janet (2004). "The Inquiry in the *Treatise*," *Philosophical Review*, 113, pp. 537–56.

Fogelin, Robert (1993). "Hume's Scepticism," in David Fate Norton (ed.), *The Cambridge Companion to Hume* (Cambridge: Cambridge University Press), pp. 90–116.

Hume, David (1776). "My Own Life," in David Hume (1779), *Dialogues concerning Natural Religion*, ed. J. C. A. Gaskin (Oxford: Oxford University Press, 1993), pp. 3–10.

—— (1779). *Dialogues concerning Natural Religion*, ed. J. C. A. Gaskin (Oxford: Oxford University Press, 1993).

Kemp Smith, Norman (1941). *The Philosophy of David Hume* (London: Macmillan).

Loeb, Louis (2002). *Stability and Justification in Hume's "Treatise"* (New York: Oxford University Press).

Reid, Thomas (1764). *An Inquiry into the Human Mind on the Principles of Common Sense*, ed. Derek Brookes (Edinburgh: Edinburgh University Press, 1997).

Sextus Empiricus (1933). *Outlines of Pyrrhonism*, trans. R. G. Bury (Cambridge, MA, and London: Harvard University Press).

Further Reading

Bell, Martin and McGinn, Marie (1990). "Naturalism and Scepticism," *Philosophy*, 65, pp. 399–418.

Broughton, Janet (2004). "Hume's Naturalism about Cognitive Norms," *Philosophical Topics*, 31, pp. 1–19.

Buckle, Stephen (2001). *Hume's Enlightenment Tract: The Unity and Purpose of "An Enquiry concerning Human Understanding"* (Oxford: Clarendon Press).

Capaldi, Nicholas (1975). *David Hume: The Newtonian Philosopher* (Boston: Twayne).

Falkenstein, Lorne (1997). "Naturalism, Normativity, and Scepticism in Hume's Account of Belief," *Hume Studies*, 23, pp. 29–72.

Fogelin, Robert (1985). *Hume's Skepticism in the "Treatise of Human Nature"* (London: Routledge and Kegan Paul).

Garrett, Don (1997). *Cognition and Commitment in Hume's Philosophy* (New York: Oxford University Press).

—— (2004). "'A Small Tincture of Pyrrhonism': Skepticism and Naturalism in Hume's Science of Man," in Walter Sinnott-Armstrong (ed.), *Pyrrhonian Skepticism* (Oxford: Oxford University Press), pp. 68–98.

Hatfield, Gary (1995). "Remaking the Science of Mind: Psychology as Natural Science," in Christopher Fox, Roy Porter, and Robert Wokler (eds.), *Inventing Human Science: Eighteenth-century Domains* (Berkeley, Los Angeles, and London: University of California Press).

Livingston, Donald (1984). *Hume's Philosophy of Common Life* (Chicago and London: University of Chicago Press).

Millican, Peter (2002). "Sceptical Doubts concerning Induction," in Peter Millican (ed.), *Reading Hume on Human Understanding* (New York: Oxford University Press).

Mounce, H. O. (1999). *Hume's Naturalism* (London: Routledge and Kegan Paul).

O'Shea, James (1996). "Hume's Reflective Return to the Vulgar," *British Journal for the History of Philosophy*, 4, pp. 285–315.

Passmore, John (1968). *Hume's Intentions* (London: Gerald Duckworth).

Popkin, Richard (1966). "David Hume: His Pyrrhonism and His Critique of Pyrrhonism," in Vere Chappell (ed.), *Hume: A Collection of Critical Essays* (Garden City, NY: Doubleday), pp. 53–98.

Singer, Ira (1995). "Hume's Extreme Skepticism in *Treatise* I IV 7," *Canadian Journal of Philosophy*, 25, pp. 595–622.

Strawson, Peter (1985). *Skepticism and Naturalism: Some Varieties* (New York: Columbia University Press).

Stroud, Barry (1991). "Hume's Scepticism: Natural Instincts and Philosophical Reflection," in Margaret Atherton (ed.), *The Empiricists: Critical Essays on Locke, Berkeley, and Hume* (Lanham, MD: Rowman & Littlefield), pp. 229–52.

Winkler, Kenneth (1999). "Hume's Inductive Skepticism," in Margaret Atherton (ed.), *The Empiricists: Critical Essays on Locke, Berkeley, and Hume* (Lanham, MD: Rowman & Littlefield), pp. 183–212.

24

Is Hume a Realist or an Anti-realist?

P. J. E. KAIL

Introduction

The two broad interpretative stances that concern us are skeptical realism, the so-called "New Hume" and non-skeptical anti-realism, the so-called "Old Hume." At first pass, skeptical realists read Hume as *assuming* a world beyond sensory impressions populated by mind-independent objects in space and time standing in causal relations sustained by unreduced causal powers. Our knowledge of this world is limited by the deep, but contingent, fact that our cognitive transaction with it is mediated by sensory impressions. One of Hume's principal lessons is that our capacity to form a fully perspicuous understanding of this world is thereby limited, a lesson concerning our cognitive powers only.

Skeptical realism is in conscious opposition to anti-realist readings of Hume, which see him as offering a *reduction* or *rejection*, either *semantically* or *ontologically*, of key areas of commitment, namely causal power, external objects, or substantial selves. John Passmore (1952: 151–2), for example, wrote that for Hume "it is not our incapacity which prevents us from discovering ultimate causes, but the fact that there are no causes to discover." Such claims run against Hume's frequent, and apparently sincere, preparedness to make reference to unknowable powers, especially, but not only, in the first *Enquiry*. Similar claims appear in the *Treatise*, and, more ambiguously, in the *Dialogues concerning Natural Religion*, together with related talk of ignorance, the limitations of our faculties, and the deficiencies of our ideas (for a catalogue and commentary see Strawson 1989). Furthermore, much of what Hume says seems to presuppose the existence of "external objects," and some realists argue that his "bundle theory" of self is not a reductive account of what selves *are*, but merely an account of what we can *know* of otherwise unknowable selves.

The work of John Wright (1983), Edward Craig (1987), and Galen Strawson (1989) are points of reference for the realist, but others feature on the map (Ayers 1996; Buckle 2001; Broughton 1987; Costa 1989; Kail 2001 and 2007; Livingston 1984). Univocality lies in rejecting readings like Passmore's but different melodies ring to this common chord. Craig (1987) takes Hume to be agnostic about the existential claims: Hume can allow for *thought* about external objects and causal power, but whether there *are* such things is another matter. Costa (1989) takes causal beliefs to be *unjustified*, and opts for agnosticism, whereas for Wright some justification for the problematic beliefs is forthcoming, but rests "ultimately on a kind of faith" (1983: 27). Strawson, in one passage (1989: 100), makes a claim that Hume takes it that we can *know* that there are external objects and causal powers, but this, Strawson says, is "to put the point more provocatively." Officially, Strawson argues that Hume never bothered to question the existence of objects and power, something quite different from the provocative claim to knowledge.

Given this diversity, it is mistaken to characterize skeptical realists as claiming "that Hume believed we can *know* that causal powers . . . exist in the world" (Richman 2000: 1, my emphasis). What makes realists "realists" is the idea that Hume does not argue for anti-realism, i.e. that *all there is* to causation is regular succession, that *all there is* to selves is bundles of perceptions, that *all there is* to perceptual objects is captured by a species of phenomenalism. Characterizing the "Old Hume" as "a strict epistemic skeptic," opposed to a "New Hume" who takes the relevant beliefs to meet "some minimal epistemic standards for assent" (Richman 2000) fails both to capture the original target and some self-consciously realist positions. Interpreting Hume as *assuming* the existence of external objects and necessity does not imply that he thinks the beliefs "meet some minimal epistemic standards for assent." Whether we are permitted to maintain beliefs in the face of Hume's skepticism is a substantial interpretative question, connected to, but logically independent of, realism. For it may turn out that Hume recommends the retention of belief despite the unavailability of some epistemic justification for it. This may leave us and him in an uncomfortable position (see Craig 2000), but to feel this discomfort a significant New Hume battle must have been won: namely the battle for significance of external object and causal power talk.

This brings us to a key objection against skeptical realism. Calling agnosticism "realism" may seem peculiar, but it makes sense against well-entrenched targets. "Realism," like any term of art, is elusive, and often gets its bite as a contrast term with e.g. reductionism, expressivism, or eliminativism. The line of thought against which realist positions articulate themselves is that Hume gets negative ontological conclusions from the severe restrictions on thought and understanding imposed by his theory of ideas. In order to get to the position to be agnostic, existentially speaking, about unreduced selves, objects, or causal powers, we need to be in a position to form appropriate *thoughts*. But Hume tells us that a term "lacks a meaning" if we lack an idea of its putative object, and, further, ideas get their content by being derived from appropriate impressions. But we have no appropriate impression with respect to selves, causal power, and "external objects," and so no content is available even to *think, wonder, doubt,* or *deny* that there are powers and the like. Even the mildest form of realism is stopped in its semantic tracks. Kenneth Clatterbaugh writes:

> In Hume's own theory of knowledge, when we talk of ultimate principles, etc., we are literally speaking nonsense; we are using words without ideas associated with them . . . To take Hume's talk about secret powers seriously, even to think that such sentences are meaningful, would mean that Hume would have to set aside the entire epistemological framework of his philosophy in the *Treatise* and the *Enquiry*. (1999: 204)

Since skeptical realism readings invite us to reconsider the framework of Hume's philosophy, statements like this simply beg the question. Understanding "the entire framework" of Hume's philosophy requires us to understand the text as a whole, and not impose a particular understanding of one feature of Hume's writings upon the rest. We must reconcile talk of "meaninglessness" on the one hand with Hume's talk of hidden powers, or external objects, ignorance, and the limitations of our faculties, on the other.

Opponents of the "New Hume" offer subtle readings of the realist-sounding passages to show that they need not be taken at face value. Even if they are successful (which I doubt), offering interpretations whereby we *need* not take those passages at face value doesn't amount to an independent case for why we *should*: a silent assumption is that the burden of proof has been on the realist side. *All* readings need to look to their own resources, including the old story which, although well entrenched, doesn't carry with it anything to recommend it as any more (or any less) obvious than the new one, when judged by the textual evidence alone. We need a sustained case for the assumptions on which anti-realist readings rest: not merely their assumption.

A further point: the "New Hume" is not a coinage of the skeptical realists, but currency introduced by Kenneth Winkler in an important article of 1991 (reprinted with a postscript as Winkler 2000). The term has stuck, but it has some misleading implications. Skeptical realists need not make any claim to novelty, and recognizably realist positions pre-date Wright's work. Livingston (1971), all too infrequently cited, is recent enough to seem novel. Constance Maund (1937: 295) wrote of the claim "so hotly disputed that there is no necessary connection between events," that "Hume . . . would wish only to say that we cannot know that there is any necessary connection." William Knight (1886: 156) wrote that Hume tells us "that one thing is the *signum memoriale* of another, that they are associated in experience; but the tie connecting each with each – like the inner substance of them all – is unknown and unknowable." Henry Calderwood, writing in 1898 states that Hume's conclusion is that "knowledge of a cause is unattainable" (p. 58). Such examples could be multiplied (e.g. Kemp Smith 1941; Anderson 1966), but Wright's (2000) "Hume's Causal Realism: Recovering a Traditional Interpretation" is a title which does not mislead.

Realist readings are not offered in isolation from a general consideration of Hume's aims and context. Strawson wants to emphasize Hume's skepticism, Wright the importance of eighteenth-century science, and its relation to Cartesianism, in understanding Hume's naturalism. Craig takes Hume to be offering an attack on the deep assumption that humanity is made in the Image of God (see also Livingston 1984; Buckle 2001, for realism as a natural attendant to Hume's wider concerns). These differences in emphasis lead to differences in interpretation (e.g. agnosticism in Craig, commitment in Wright), so to focus on the realism without the general readings that inform it can lead to a danger of not fully understanding the grounds for the realism. This danger is especially evident in an article of this length. I will nevertheless attempt to give some reasons to think that skeptical realism is a substantial exegetical option. That is not to say that I think realism is unproblematic: the point is rather that it is not *obviously* false, and it offers a useful perspective from which to question the assumptions of other readings, putting key issues into sharp focus.

Meaning and the Copy Principle

Hume's first principle is that "all our simple ideas in their first appearance are deriv'd from simple impressions, which are correspondent to them, and which they exactly represent" (T 1.1.1.7). This Copy Principle (see chapter 2) is accompanied by a claim, scattered in the body of the *Treatise*, and announced more strenuously in the *Abstract* and the first *Enquiry*, that, if no impression can be related to a "pretended idea," the relevant term is "insignificant" (T Abstract 7) or lacks a "meaning" (EHU 2.9). These remarks suggest that he is groping towards some criterion of meaning or significance, the basis of a "theory of meaning," which he will subsequently use polemically, to show that terms like "necessary connection" have no meaning.

Notoriously, Hume's *actual* formulation of the Copy Principle makes it, in Jonathan Bennett's words, "largely irrelevant to the matters which he wants it to illuminate" (Bennett 1971: 230). The Copy Principle is genetic, contingent and *a posteriori*, leaving it vulnerable to counter-examples. One such counter-example, the missing shade of blue, is admitted at the outset. Hume's use of the Copy Principle is peculiar as well: again, as Bennett says, when it comes to particular topics, Hume "often proceeds by detailed, down-to-earth argument rather than by blanket applications of his meaning-empiricism" (p. 233). He also shows a peculiar lack of interest in the resources of his theory; he tends to ignore the possibility that some complex idea may specify the "meaning" of the problematic term.

The inadequacies in the Copy Principle as a criterion of meaning are duly noted and commentators then offer Hume a way of saving his blushes: construe the Copy Principle as an *analytic*, rather than a genetic thesis, and restore the edge to a semantic weapon blunted by its original formulation. Such a move is explicitly revisionary, motivated by a desire to make sense of words like "meaninglessness." But to make such a revision goes against the genetic spirit of Hume's philosophy in general, both inside and outside Book 1 of the *Treatise*, where he is interested in *sources* of commitment. The way to resist the revision is to restore the priority where Hume places it – namely in his geneticism – and attempt to understand terms like "meaninglessness" in that light. More often than not, Hume presupposes some description that purports to pick out the problematic item to an argument to the effect that our idea of that item cannot owe its origin to us having *encountered* or *detected* it, either by the senses or by reason. This is why Hume is uninterested in trying to offer some complex idea to give "the meaning" of the particular term: no description of *what* it is that we cannot detect shows that we are in a position to detect it. Furthermore, since why we can't detect some item will depend on the relevant area in question, Hume, as Bennett says, "often proceeds by detailed, down-to-earth argument."

That we cannot *detect*, e.g. power relates to the status of the associated belief as a "projection." Roughly put, a key sense of the metaphor of projection trades on a contrast with explanations of commitment which make use of sources which are detective of the relevant item (see Kail 2001 and 2007). Hume shows that our belief in necessity cannot be the result of our detecting necessity but it owes its origin to the imagination. So when Hume says the term "necessary connection" loses "its true meaning by being wrong apply'd" (T 1.3.14.14), and in order "perfectly to understand any idea" we trace its origin in the relevant impression (T 1.3.2.4), the suggestion is that we understand this as a claim about the belief's true *origin*, not its *content*. *Mutatis mutandis*, the claim that necessity "is something that exists in the mind": the point is that the belief's aetiology lies in the non-detective features of human psychology, not that "necessity" is identical with that feature.

All this is neutral between a stronger and weaker sense of "meaninglessness." The stronger sense is that, because we cannot detect necessity, no *thought at all* can be formed, and a negative ontological conclusion follows. The weaker sense is simply that we are not in a position to detect that item, but this epistemological conclusion is all that follows. Necessity is such and such, but we cannot be acquainted with necessity, so beyond some quasi-Ramsification, I have no idea – no understanding of – what a description like "the such and such" picks out. Hume's use of words like "meaninglessness" does not by itself decide between these views: all depends on the details of the arguments, not on some prior conviction of what Hume means by "meaningless."

None of this implies that Hume is unprepared to infer ontological conclusions from the emptiness of a word. He certainly does, though this point is independent of any *theory* of in what meaning consists. To see this, and its threat to skeptical realism, compare Richman's characterization of a skeptical realist – a "realist about [an] entity's existence, but agnostic about the nature or character of that thing because it is epistemically inaccessible to us in some non-trivial way" (2000: 1) – with the mystic Demea's view of God:

> The question is not concerning the *being* but the *nature* of God. This, I affirm, from the infirmities of human understanding, to be altogether incomprehensible and unknown to us. The essence of that supreme mind, his attributes . . . these and every particular, which regards so divine a Being, are mysterious to men. (DNR, II, p. 43)

Surely the sentiments of a skeptical realist *à la* Richman: Demea is a realist about God's existence, but agnostic with respect to His nature. The danger is that one becomes *too* agnostic, draining the term "God" of all content, a danger Cleanthes fully exploits, implying that Demea is an atheist "without knowing it" (DNR, IV, p. 61). To give the notion of God some content, we must think in terms of an *intelligent* cause of the universe, and the word "intelligence" had better have some content as well:

> It seems strange to me, said CLEANTHES, that you, DEMEA . . . should still maintain the mysterious, incomprehensible nature of the Deity, and should insist so strenuously, that he has no manner of likeness or resemblance to human creatures . . . if our ideas, so far as they go, be not just and adequate, and correspondent to his real nature, I know not what there is in this subject worth insisting on. Is the name, without any meaning, of such mighty importance? (DNR, IV, p. 60)

If the terms "God," "external object" or "necessity" are to have any significance we need to have some sense or description sufficiently rich to move beyond the bare claim that there is an "unknown something." We need to ensure that what is unknown is, precisely, *God, external objects* or *necessary connection* if we are to secure a realism about *those items* rather than a bare admission of "something" beyond experience.

445

External Objects

This threat is apparent in realist treatments of "external objects." Realists appeal to Hume's talk of a "relative idea," in order to single out an unknown item as an "external object," taking such a notion to be ancestor of a Ramsey sentence (e.g. Strawson 1989: 51). Relative ideas are coupled with a distinction between what we can *suppose* and what we can *conceive*. What we can conceive is determined by what is directly available to us through impressions, whereas what we can suppose is, roughly, some description or "relative idea" rich enough to single out some object which is not so available. Such moves are criticized on various grounds (Winkler 2000; Blackburn 2000; Flage 2000), though realists remain unimpressed. One point of contention is whether what we suppose is rich enough to count as the supposition of, precisely, external objects. A crude Ramsification of "external object" as "the cause of our perceptions" leaves us with too many candidates (e.g. our own minds or God – see T 1.3.5.2), or simply an unknown "something." Indeed, Hume's discussion of the senses in the first *Enquiry*, seems to leave us with "a certain unknown, inexplicable *something*, as the cause of our perceptions; a notion so imperfect, that no skeptic will think it worth while to contend against it" (EHU 12.16; cf. T 1.4.5.15).

This is an unwelcome conclusion for a realist, but it is not obvious that it is Hume's. There are, for the Hume of the first *Enquiry* two "profound" philosophical objections to the senses. The first turns on the rejection of the vulgar conception of perception, a view more fully articulated in the *Treatise*. On this view we are directly acquainted with objects that (1) *continue* to exist when unperceived and (2) whose existence is *distinct* from our experience of them. This false view is replaced by the "doctrine of double existence." Perceptions are directly available to the mind, constituting the medium by which external objects are made *indirectly* available. What singles out those objects as, precisely, external objects, is that objects are supposed to *resemble* perceptions. The profound objection is that we cannot establish that objects do resemble perceptions. "It is a question of fact, whether the perceptions of the sense be produced by external objects, resembling them . . . [but] [t]he supposition of such a connexion is . . . without any foundation in reasoning" (EHU 12.12). The supposition (at this stage) is at most unjustifiable, but it is not meaningless. Nowhere does Hume show any allegiance to Berkeley's likeness principle (that only ideas can resemble ideas). Certainly Hume claims that all philosophers ever do is invent a "new set of perceptions" (T 1.4.2.56), but the point seems to be that objects, if we can conceive them, must, in key respects, be like perceptions, but not *be* perceptions. The difference between a perception and an object consists in objects having "different relations, connexions and durations" (T 1.2.6.9), primarily continuing to exist when not perceived.

We can *suppose* such a resemblance, though the supposition is not the causal product of reason (see T 1.4.2 for Hume's natural history of that belief). Indeed it is a moot point whether he thinks it is epistemically unjustifiable. Certainly he thinks its aetiology is dubious, but its causal providence is a different matter from normative endorsement (see Garrett 1997: 208–20). It is the second "profound objection" that seems to "annihilate" external objects. Modern philosophy distinguishes between primary and secondary qualities, whereby our impressions are "resemblances" of the former but not of the latter. In the *Treatise*, Hume takes an argument from variation to be the "most satisfactory" argument for the distinction, augmented by the principle that like effects have like causes. Given that sensory impressions of e.g. color often "arise from causes, which no ways resemble them" (T 1.4.4.4), the like effects, like causes principle implies that *no* causes of color impressions resemble those impressions. Hume thinks this argument applies to *all* sensible qualities, and so the application of such a principle leaves us without any way of conceiving the "external object": we are left with the "certain unknown, inexplicable *something*." Reason, guided by the maxim of like effects, like causes, leaves us with little in which to believe.

Hume, as we said, does not *endorse* this conclusion. Instead, he presents this argument as a "very decisive" objection to the doctrine of modern philosophy (T 1.4.4.6). Its function is to adduce an opposition between indirect realism and the doctrine of modern philosophy, one way of showing the "whimsical condition" of humanity, and the limits of philosophical reasoning. The consistent application of reasoning leads to unacceptable conclusions, which "admit of no answer but produce no conviction." This argument tells us about the infirmity of our cognitive faculties, and the "signal contradictions" generated by them, raising questions about which conclusions one *ought* to endorse, and how – and to what extent – one should be guided by reason. These are deep and complex issues, which cannot be properly addressed here. Many commentators appeal to Hume's allusion to the permanent, useful, and irresistible principles of the imagination. Outside the study, we feel the pull of the vulgar view, but Hume tells us that this is false. Inside the study, it is unclear whether the doctrine of the philosophers, namely indirect realism, exerts a sufficiently similar pull. Certainly under intense reflection he questions it, but it is a further question whether such *intense* reflection is a normative requirement for Hume.

All this pushes us to questions concerning belief-fixation and not the availability of content for realism, but nevertheless a last point concerning realism and resemblance is worth making. I said that the consistent application of the principle that like effects have like causes, together with a claim about resemblance, evacuates the belief of content. This applies equally in the religious case. To prevent Demea's mystical position from being unknowingly atheistic, we must think in terms of a resemblance between human minds and the mind of God. The bulk of the *Dialogues* turns the argument *a posteriori*, an argument based on the "like effects, like causes" maxim. But, as part XII makes clear, this "rule of good reasoning," or "proportional analogy," renders the dispute between the theist and the atheist merely *verbal*. The conclusion is that "the cause or causes of order in the universe probably bear some remote analogy to human intelligence" (DNR, XII, p. 129), a notion so imperfect that no atheist will think it worth while to contend against. Reasoning, on the like effects, like causes principle, diminishes the resemblance, and hence the belief's content, to vanishing point. The question now for realists is whether the indirect realism is, for Hume, on a par with the belief in God.

Causal Power

When it comes to necessary connection, the anti-realist seems on firmer ground. Here we "talk without a meaning" when we suppose power to exist "in the object," and Hume is prepared to say that "necessity is something that exists in the mind, not in the objects" (T 1.3.14.22). Furthermore, Hume's two "definitions" of cause seem to run against skeptical realism.

These undeniable textual facts are of course matched by Hume's talk of ignorance, of secret and hidden powers, the limitations of knowledge and so forth. The realist argues these avowals indicate the following: Hume countenances the possibility, or, stronger, assumes the existence, of some mind-independent feature which underpins causal regularities, namely power or necessary connection.

Another way of putting the matter is that skeptical realism is a repudiation of the view that Hume *reduces* causation to regular succession. Such a reduction need not be *semantic*, though some have thought it to be. The target is the claim Hume allows nothing to causation, objectively speaking, over and above regular succession. One may be, for example, an expressivist about the distinctly modal aspect of our commitment to cause, without admitting any irreducible class of modal fact which those commitments aspire to represent. The semantic content of "cause" is not thereby reduced or given an error-theoretic interpretation: we can talk the modal talk without walking the metaphysical walk (see Blackburn 2000). Nevertheless, all there is objectively speaking is regular succession, the screen upon which we project habits of modalizing. It is this skeptical realism resists: regular succession is all that is *available* to us, and the powers or forces underlying these regularities are secret or hidden.

Before we come to discuss what might be hidden from us, we need to comment on Hume's notorious "two definitions" of cause. The first roughly defines a cause as an object (token) which stands in a relation of constant conjunction with effect (token) ("D1"). The second definition, again roughly, includes a reference both to constant conjunction and the psychological effect that experience of constant conjunction has on thinkers ("D2"). Emphasis on the word "definition," and concentration on D1, can suggest a semantic reduction of causation to constant conjunction, the classical regularity analysis. But this cannot be Hume's final word on the matter, for a whole number of reasons, two of which are (1) the claim that necessary connection is "essential" to causation (T 1.3.2.9–11) and (2) the sheer presence of D2. Indeed, the presence of D2 casts doubt on the idea that we have *any* form of semantic reduction anyway, since D1 and D2 are neither intensionally nor extensionally equivalent. Unless we can be confident that Hume rejects one in favor of the other, viewing these definitions as semantic reductions looks mistaken. It is possible, as Garrett (1997) ably does, to exploit Humean materials to render the two extensionally equivalent, but the materials required to do so seem too far from Hume's concerns about causation to be fully persuasive.

Some realists think that Hume accepts neither definition. Both, says Hume, are "drawn from circumstances foreign to the cause" (EHU 7.29), and this is taken to mean that the definitions do not comprehend the hidden causal powers. Alternatively, and in line with Hume's geneticism, one can read Hume endorsing both definitions but not as *definitions*, i.e. attempts to give intensional or extensional equivalent explications of "cause" (see Craig 1987: 102ff.; Strawson 2000). Instead, D1 captures the input available to the cognitive machine, D2 its effect upon the mind. Jointly they tell us what is involved in our causal inferences, revealing to us our "idea of causation" from this genetic perspective. Hume tells us that they are "just" and "exact" definitions, and this is compatible with his saying that our ideas of cause are "imperfect" (EHU). They represent the key features operative in casual transactions in minds that are unable to penetrate the real powers of objects.

Realists think such considerations tell against an anti-realist move of Winkler's. Winkler argues that a footnote, added to the 1750 edition of the first *Enquiry*, undercuts the referential force of many "secret power" passages. There, Hume tells us that the term "power . . . is used in a loose and popular sense," pointing us to section 7, where the two definitions occur, for a "more accurate explication" (EHU 4.16n). The suggestion is that Hume's use of "secret powers" is the talk of the vulgar, not the thought of the learned, and the definitions reveal the real meaning of power. In addition to the worry of whether we should think of the definitions as *definitions*, it is unclear that their "accuracy" is intended to undercut the earlier talk of ignorance. Immediately before the introduction of the definitions, Hume announces a discovery is "concerning the weakness and narrow limits of human reason capacity. And what stronger instance can be produced of the surprising ignorance and weakness of the understanding than the present?" (EHU 7.28–9). Even in the thick of the definitions, talk of ignorance continues, and continues after section 7. They are less frequent to be sure, but that is because our ignorance has been established.

But of what are we ignorant? Power, of course, but merely saying that is hardly an advance. To avoid the "unknown somethings" trap, we need something richer, and the obvious place to look is where – and why – Hume denies that we have an impression of genuine necessity. His central point, made repeatedly, is that if we had an impression of the power or force of some particular object we would (1) be able to infer *a priori* its causal upshots and (2) find it impossible to conceive of that cause independently of its effect. Since we cannot make the requisite *a priori* inferences – we have to learn what causes what *a posteriori* – and we can, it seems, conceive any cause independently of its effect, we have no impression, and no idea, of power, "after that manner." We *do* have an idea of power "without which we can never arrive at a distant notion of it, or be able to attribute it either to external or internal objects" (T 1.3.14.20), but its source is an unexpected one. To this we shall return, but notice that it seems we have a way of specifying that of which we are ignorant: power is that feature, acquaintance with which would yield *a priori* knowledge of its effect, and a correlative closure of conception. This particular description is enough to avoid that accusation of "unknown somethings" peddling.

This view of causal power may be unfamiliar, but has a long history. Causes, on this view, are *intelligible*, and our knowledge of them is reflected in conceptual connections. But necessity does not reduce to conceptual necessity: the necessity is *metaphysical* and the corresponding conceptual connections (or "significance" relations – see below) are reflections of that nature and not merely artifacts of description. It is sometimes said that our predecessors "conflate" conceptual necessity with natural necessity, but if they do, it is something done quite self-consciously. The frequent talk of "cause or reason" is no mere slip of the pen.

The debate in which Hume participates is how to place the intelligibility of causes in the world. One view – which Michael Ayers (1996) has dubbed "naturalism" – identifies causal power with the essences of created objects. Some saw causation as the unfolding of created substance directed towards a view of the Best, constrained by will-independent modal fact (i.e. logic) grounded in God's understanding. This Leibnizian view is a form of naturalism since each object has its own essence, though its nature would only be revealed through infinite analysis. Some saw the intelligibility of cause on the model of geometrical essence (Hobbes). Locke, who falls into the naturalist camp, thought that causes were intelligible but not to us: the real essences of objects lie hidden.

Modifying Ayers's formulation of the second option, "voluntarism," we can distinguish between occasionalism and full-blooded voluntarism. In neither case do created objects have causal powers. According to occasionalism, all causal power owes to the metaphysical necessity of the relation between God's will and action, constrained by will-independent and unreduced modal fact (Malebranche and a slightly modified Berkeley, who allows *finite* spirits volitional power). Malebranche's God is constrained by logic, whereas according to full-blooded voluntarism all power resides in God's will, unconstrained by *any* modal facts at all. All (alleged) modal fact (including logic) is simply the result of God's will, morally constrained by his benevolence (Descartes, on some readings). The former view places emphasis on God's understanding and omniscience, the latter his will and omnipotence.

The intelligibility of causation is understood either in terms of unreduced necessary consequence or, for Berkeley and perhaps Bayle, in what we might call the "narrative significance" of humdrum regularity, and our interpretation of it. No finite object has its own causal powers, but instead stands in relation to other objects as sign and signified, semantic components in a language constituting worldly events. For Malebranche, real causation requires the metaphysical impossibility of some cause not being followed by its effect, and the relation between God's will is the only relation which could thereby count as a true cause. A naturalist, like Locke, by contrast, thinks that created objects have powers that have their effects as necessary consequences.

Much of what Hume says puts him in the naturalist tradition, though Malebranche's version of intelligibility (will constrained by logic) is in his sights as well. But it is one thing to work in such a tradition, and another to endorse it. For it is evidently possible that his whole discussion is a *reductio* of that version of intelligibility. No doubt it is: but the *reductio* may force the conclusion that we cannot *know* causes, a deep limitation on our cognitive powers, which is what realists argue. But a cluster of considerations seemingly imply a stronger conclusion, namely that the whole notion is incoherent. The accusation of incoherence gives good ground for the notion being *meaningless* in a stronger sense than mere lack of acquaintance. Acquaintance with necessity, *ex hypothesi*, would render it impossible for us to conceive a cause without its effect. But since we can *always* conceive a cause without its effect, necessity so specified is incoherent.

A more nuanced view of the terrain shows that this attack is not as devastating as it may seem. First, in order to avoid question-begging on Hume's part, we will need to know just why we should believe that we can *always* conceive cause without effect. This invites consideration of what counts as *conceivability* for Hume, and the operative notion here is *separability* in the imagination. Separation in the imagination is a cognitive operation with ideas whose separability is grounded *phenomenologically*. We can conceive A apart from B in virtue of A's phenomenological *distinctness* from B, rendering B *distinguishable* from A and allowing us to *separate* A from B. Separation contrasts with the traditional notion of a "distinction of reason." Take, for example, a particular shape and its colors. The two features of that particular may be *separately attended* to, but not *separated*: one cannot form an idea of that object's color separated from its shape or vice versa. But I may separate two circles standing beside each other in imaginative space. One is phenomenologically salient on the left-hand side, the other on the right, and I can separate the left-hand side from the right by imagining the one without the other. To put the matter another way: they are "distinct existences," in a way in which the color and shape of the phenomenological particulars are not. If these distinct existences were necessarily connected, I could not conceive one apart from another: but I can, so they are not.

Construing "distinct existence" phenomenologically avoids the otherwise nascent circularity in the term. If "distinct existence" simply *means* "independently conceivable," it cannot be exploited to explain conceivability. It also explains Hume's confidence that we can always conceive cause apart from effect. It is plausible to think that all the ideas standing in that relation are phenomenologically distinct, and so we can always separate them in the imagination.

The next question to be asked is this: what has conceivability got to do with metaphysical modalities? Certainly it was the paradigm route to modal knowledge in the early modern period, a fact which demands explanation. Unless one *reduces* modal facts to facts about conceivability, there is a standing question why conceivability should be a guide to modal fact in the first place. I suspect it struck many as plausible when the background assumption was that God made the world in principle intelligible to us, and wouldn't equip us with desire to know and withhold the instruments to satisfy it. Be that as it may, Hume bought the idea that conceivability reveals metaphysical possibility (see e.g. T 1.2.2.8), so it seems we have all the materials in place to mount the *reductio* against necessary connection.

So it seems. We should remember that Hume, like everyone, places restrictions on when conceivability delivers the modal goods. Spinoza, for example, took our conceiving a range of possibilities as reflecting the *inadequacy* of the ideas involved: when our ideas are adequate such possibilities are revealed as illusory. Descartes demands that to make the "real distinction" our ideas of extension and thought must be "clear" and "distinct" (for some sharp criticism of Descartes' modal claims, see Arnauld's objections to the *Meditations*). For Hume the ideas involved must be "clear" or "adequate" representations of objects. But of what "objects" are ideas "clear" or "adequate" representations? The answer is impressions, so the imagination might reveal modal facts about them. But are *impressions* "adequate" or "clear" representations of objects *in re*? Conceived as blank effects, impressions may be "clear perceptions" (i.e. easily discernible), but this does not entail that they are clear *qua representations*. Neither does he claim they are "adequate" in the traditional sense of revealing all the properties of their objects (see e.g. T 1.4.5, and for discussion Kail 2003a). The resemblance view of representation need not entail that every fact about objects is revealed to us. As Hume put it elsewhere:

> any conclusion we form concerning the connexion and repugnance of impressions, will not be known certainly to be applicable to objects . . . As an object is suppos'd to be different from an impression, we cannot be sure, that the circumstance, upon which we found our reasoning, is common to both, supposing we form the reasoning upon the impression. 'Tis still possible, that the object may differ from it in that particular. (T 1.4.5.20)

451

Wright, Ayers, and I see such considerations as Hume's grounds for ignorance of necessary connection. *If* one sees Hume as allowing a natural, but unknowable, world beyond sense impressions, his talk of hidden connections is perfectly compatible with causes as intelligible, but not intelligible *to us*. Given that the materials of the mind – impressions – are loose and separable, we can conceive of anything we dub "cause" and "effect" as separate. But this cognitive operation is powerless to reveal the modal structure of the world.

This view also has an advantage over more deflationary attempts to deal with Hume's talk of hidden power. For Blackburn, talk of causal power for Hume is a non-metaphysically loaded expression of inferential habit, and so talk of necessity in nature is perfectly compatible with a sophisticated non-realism. Winkler sees Hume's rejection of real necessity as compatible with talk of hidden connections, since talk of "hidden connections" can be harmlessly parsed as underlying "micro-regularities." Martin Bell (2000) sees this as a shift away from intelligibility to a Newtonian view. But these strategies fail to relate what it is we are supposed to be ignorant of (namely hidden powers) with the reasons adduced by Hume for that ignorance. These are precisely the same reasons for why we *lack* an idea drawn from the objects, namely that we cannot make the requisite *a priori* inferences and we can conceive the cause independently of its effect. No *further* grounds for ignorance are given, which indicate a *different* sense of "hidden power" amenable to the regularity reading. Whatever makes secret connections secret for us cannot simply be the fact that our microscopes are insufficiently powerful. The "hidden regularities" interpretation of secret connections cannot make sense of why Hume thinks it is a *deep* fact about our cognitive limitations that we cannot perceive causal necessity.

At this point the anti-realist might take a different, but related tack. Power is a feature of an object such that, were we acquainted with it, would yield *a priori* knowledge of its effect and a corresponding closure of conception. If it is granted that conceivability doesn't reveal genuine metaphysical possibility since impressions are not clear or adequate representations of objects, it may seem that the notion of acquaintance is the point of weakness. For the only objects of acquaintance are sensory *impressions* so we can never be acquainted with necessary connection: the "meaninglessness" of necessity is located here. To put the matter differently, we cannot "in principle" be acquainted with necessary connection, and that is why the notion is meaningless in a sense stronger than mere lack of acquaintance.

But Hume does not argue that, in principle, we can only be acquainted with sensory impressions: the Copy Principle is a matter of deep contingency. The alternative non-sensory mode of representation – the intellect of the rationalists – is certainly rejected by Hume, but not as an "in principle" impossibility (see e.g. EHU 2.7).

All these features come together in a passage concerning the "meaninglessness" of a modal relative, necessary existence, from the *Dialogues*:

> [T]his necessity is attempted to be explained by asserting, that, if we knew [God's] whole essence or nature, we should perceive it to be as impossible for him not to exist as for twice two not to be four. But it is evident that this can never happen, *while our faculties remain the same as at present*. (DNR 189 [my emphasis])

We can conceive of the non-existence of any object whilst our faculties remain the same as at present. Furthermore, knowledge of essence would close down our conceptual capacities. As Hume puts it in the *Treatise*, we can "never penetrate into the essence and construction of bodies to perceive the principle on which their mutual influence depends." We are ignorant of essences and so ignorant of power: that is what we cannot detect – be acquainted with – and necessity is in that sense "meaningless."

Given that we have no idea of necessary drawn from acquaintance with genuine power, our belief in power is a projected one. The effect of constant repetition of pairs of objects produces a new impression in the mind, a "new determination." About this, two things should be said. First, Hume thinks the vulgar think that we *perceive* causal power, and it is here the tendency to "spread the mind" on external objects is invoked to account for this phenomenology. But though that might explain *why* it is thought to be perceived, it does not explain *what* is supposed to be perceived: why, that is, the perception or idea is supposed to be *modal* in character. Some think that Hume has nothing interesting to say here (see, e.g. Stroud 1977), but he does better than is commonly supposed. Remember a genuine impression of necessity would allow us to infer *a priori* causal upshots and prevent us from conceiving the cause without its effect (the two would be "inseparable"). The customary transition of the imagination, the internal impression spread onto objects, mimics a genuine impression in this way: repeated experience of connected pairs causes us to think of an effect *immediately* when a cause is perceived, as though we are simply "reading off" the effect from the presence of the cause. This phenomenological feature makes it seem as if we are inferring *a priori* the effect from the cause. The second effect of repeated experience is a psychological inseparability: we cannot think of fire without thinking of warmth. This psychological inseparability is the surrogate for genuine inconceivability. Crude as Hume's psychology may be, some genuine attempt is made to show how a fully fledged modal belief can emerge from non-modal materials.

The Self and Necessary Connection

An anti-realist reading of Hume on the self is that that it is nothing but a bundle of perceptions. One can see this either as a semantic reduction or an error theory. Realists like Craig see no such reduction or error: instead the essence of the mind is unknowable, and bundles of perceptions are all that we can know of the mind (Craig 1987: 111ff.; and, for a slightly different account, Strawson 1989: 128ff.), making Hume's position rather like Malebranche's.

But it may seem inevitable that Hume held an ontological bundle theory. Hume's introspective claim – that he only stumbles upon particular perceptions – is not a forceful argument for the bundle theory. There is however a modal argument in play. Hume asks:

> But farther, what must become of all our particular perceptions upon this hypothesis [of self]? All these are different, and distinguishable, and separable from each other, and may be separately consider'd, and may exist separately; and have no need of any thing to support their existence. (T 1.4.6.3)

We can conceive of perceptions existing separately, and so they *may* exist separately. That they *may* does not entail that they *do* if the relevant modality is epistemic. But something stronger seems in the offing.

Earlier (T 1.4.4) Hume exploited a traditional notion of substance – namely that which may exist by itself – in a *reductio*: if we individuate substances by what we may conceive to exist by itself, then it *seems* perceptions are substances, by that definition. Indeed it seems to entail that perceptions *are* substances. Unlike those who draw a sharp separation between ideas *qua* modes of the soul and ideas *qua* contents, Hume's tendency to reify perceptions means that separable ideas *qua contents* are also separable *qua* mental *objects*. Given that conceivability is a guide to metaphysical possibility, and we are dealing with perceptions themselves, our capacity to conceive of them separately entails that they are metaphysically independent items. With that piece of reasoning comes the bundle theory.

This piece of reasoning also undoes what we have said about necessary connection. If any two items are causally connected, they are necessarily connected: knowledge of that necessary connection would entail that we cannot conceive the cause without its effect. Conceivability does not tell against necessary connection because the perceptions are not clear or adequate representations of objects. But when it comes to causal relations among perceptions *qua* mental objects we are not dealing with representations of perceptions: we are dealing with the very objects themselves, and so our capacity to conceive them apart from each other entails that they are not necessarily – and hence *causally* – connected. But Hume's system demands causal connections among perceptions. Realism cannot be right.

But a joker smiles enigmatically in the middle of this pack. Hume in the Appendix finds himself in a labyrinth, which "the seeming evidence of the precedent reasonings" about persons creates. Reviewing them, he concludes

> there are two principles, which I cannot render consistent; nor is it in my power to renounce either of them, viz. *that all our distinct perceptions are distinct existences*, and *that the mind never perceives any real connexion among distinct existences*. Did our perceptions either inhere in something simple and individual, or did the mind perceive some real connexion between them, there wou'd be no difficulty in the case. (T App. 21)

The worry Hume voices here is notoriously fugitive. The realist however has the following explanation of this particular "inconsistency." Suppose Hume's argument that we have no idea of self is merely that: that we have no *idea* of self other than a succession of related experience, not that the self *is* a succession of related experience. The realist will then argue that instead of delivering the conclusion that we have no idea of self, the "seeming evidence" of his modal reasonings delivers something stronger and unacceptable, namely that perceptions *cannot* be causally related in any way. They cannot be connected as modes of an unknowable self or as bundles related by causation. So the unity of the mind is inexplicable on Hume's principles, not because he is ignorant of what unifies perception, but because his reasoning positively *excludes* causation among perceptions. Why? If our distinct perceptions were causally related, then we should perceive some real connection among them. But since we don't, they are not. But that means Hume is robbed of any principles that unite successive perception. This consequence is certainly *wider* than his account of persons but it is his thinking about persons which generates the problem, and so that is where the problem lies.

This no doubt raises more questions than it answers (see Wright 1996; and Kail 2007). But if realism is right, something like this claim about Hume's *Appendix* worries must be right: otherwise realism seems wrong.

See also 5 "Hume on the Relation of Cause and Effect"; 23 "Hume's Naturalism and His Skepticism"

Acknowledgments

Some material in this chapter is adapted from Kail (2003b). The author wishes to thank the editor of the *British Journal for the History of Philosophy* for permission to draw upon this material. Special thanks to John Wright and Ken Winkler for some very useful comments on an earlier draft of this chapter.

References

Anderson, R. (1966). *Hume's First Principles* (Lincoln, NE: University of Nebraska Press).

Ayers, M. (1996). "Natures and Laws from Descartes to Hume," in G. A. J. Rogers and Sylvana Tomaselli (eds.), *The Philosophical Canon in the Seventeenth and Eighteenth Centuries: Essays in Honour of John W. Yolton* (Rochester: University of Rochester Press), pp. 83–101.

Bell, Martin (2000). "Sceptical Doubts concerning Hume's Causal Realism," in Rupert Read and Kenneth A. Richman (eds.), *The New Hume Debate* (London: Routledge), pp. 122–37.

Bennett, Jonathan (1971). *Locke, Berkeley, Hume: Central Themes* (Oxford: Oxford University Press).

Blackburn, Simon (2000). "Hume and Thick Connexions," in Rupert Read and Kenneth A. Richman (eds.), *The New Hume Debate* (London: Routledge), pp. 100–12.

Broughton, Janet (1987). "Hume's Ideas about Necessary Connection," *Hume Studies*, 13, pp. 217–44.

Buckle, Stephen (2001). *Hume's Enlightenment Tract: The Unity and Purpose of "An Enquiry concerning Human Understanding"* (Oxford: Clarendon Press).

Calderwood, Henry (1898). *David Hume* (Edinburgh and London: Anderson and Ferrier).

Clatterbaugh, Kenneth C. (1999). *The Causation Debate in Early Modern Philosophy: 1637–1739* (New York: Routledge).

Costa, M. J. (1989). "Hume and Causal Realism," *Australasian Journal of Philosophy*, 67, pp. 172–90.

Craig, Edward J. (1987). *The Mind of God and the Works of Man* (Oxford: Clarendon Press).

—— (2000). "Hume on Causality: Projectivist *and* Realist?" in Rupert Read and Kenneth A. Richman (eds.), *The New Hume Debate* (London: Routledge), pp. 113–21.

Flage, Daniel (2000). "Relative Ideas Revisited," in Rupert Read and Kenneth A. Richman (eds.), *The New Hume Debate* (London: Routledge), pp. 138–55.

Garrett, Don (1997). *Cognition and Commitment in Hume's Philosophy* (New York: Oxford University Press).

Hume, David (1757/1779). *Dialogues concerning Natural Religion & the Natural History of Religion*, ed. J. C. A. Gaskin (Oxford: Oxford University Press, 1993). (Cited in the text as DNR.)

Kail, P. J. E. (2001). "Projection and Necessity in Hume," *European Journal of Philosophy*, 9, pp. 24–54.

—— (2003a). "Conceivability and Modality in Hume: A Lemma in an Argument in Defence of Sceptical Realism," *Hume Studies*, 29, pp. 43–61.

—— (2003b). "Is Hume a Causal Realist?" *British Journal for the History of Philosophy*, 11, pp. 509–20.

—— (2007). *Projection and Realism in Hume's Philosophy* (Oxford: Oxford University Press).

Kemp Smith, Norman (1941). *The Philosophy of David Hume* (London: Macmillan).

Knight, William (1886). *Hume* (Edinburgh: Blackwood).

Livingston, Donald (1971). "Hume on Ultimate Causation," *American Philosophical Quarterly*, 8, pp. 63–70.

—— (1984). *Hume's Philosophy of Common Life* (Chicago: University of Chicago Press).

Maund, Constance (1937/1972). *Hume's Theory of Knowledge: A Critical Examination* (London: Macmillan, 1937; reprinted New York: Russell & Russell, 1972).

Passmore, John (1952). *Hume's Intentions* (Cambridge: Cambridge University Press).

Read, Rupert and Richman, Kenneth A. (eds.) (2000). *The New Hume Debate* (London: Routledge).

Richman, Kenneth (2000). "Introduction," in Rupert Read and Kenneth A. Richman (eds.), *The New Hume Debate* (London: Routledge), pp. 1–15.

Strawson, Galen (1989). *The Secret Connexion: Causation, Realism and David Hume* (Oxford: Clarendon Press).

—— (2000). "David Hume: Objects and Power," in Rupert Read and Kenneth A. Richman (eds.), *The New Hume Debate* (London: Routledge), pp. 31–51.

Stroud, Barry (1977). *Hume* (London: Routledge & Kegan Paul).

Winkler, Kenneth (2000). "The New Hume," in Rupert Read and Kenneth A. Richman (eds.), *The New Hume Debate* (London: Routledge), pp. 52–87.

Wright, John P. (1983). *The Sceptical Realism of David Hume* (Manchester: Manchester University Press).

—— (1996). "Hume, Descartes and the Materiality of the Soul," in G. A. J. Rogers and Sylvana Tomaselli (eds.), *The Philosophical Canon in the Seventeenth and Eighteenth Centuries: Essays in Honour of John W. Yolton* (Rochester, NY: University of Rochester Press), pp. 175–90.

—— (2000). "Hume's Causal Realism: Recovering a Traditional Interpretation," in Rupert Read and Kenneth A. Richman (eds.), *The New Hume Debate* (London: Routledge), pp. 88–99.

25

Hume's Epistemological Legacy

WILLIAM EDWARD MORRIS

Ask almost anyone what Hume contributed to epistemology, broadly speaking, and they will tell you, correctly: the skeptical problem of induction and the regularity theory of causation. The problem of induction preoccupied many of the leading lights in twentieth-century analytic philosophy, while the regularity theory is still so prominent that it is regularly called "the Humean theory of causation."

There is considerable irony in both attributions. While Hume is arguably the first person to pose what we now call the skeptical problem of induction (Hacking 1975), recent readers have questioned whether his concerns were really "skeptical," and if so, in what sense. And Hume never held the regularity theory.

Further, these lines of influence do not exhaust Hume's epistemological legacy. Having raised his "skeptical doubts," Hume offers a "skeptical solution" to them in an account of belief formation and improvement that has close affinities with contemporary naturalized epistemology. Hume also suggests a solution to what has been a source of constant concern for naturalists: the problem of how a naturalistic epistemology can also be normative. In addition, Hume's project of founding a science of human nature upon experimental methods has much in common with the aims, methods, and results of contemporary cognitive science. But perhaps the deepest, most insufficiently appreciated, aspect of his epistemological legacy is his profoundly unwavering anti-metaphysical stance.

The Problem of Induction: Hume's Problem

Hume posed what we now call the problem of induction as a question about "the nature of that evidence which assures us of any real existence and matter of fact, beyond the present testimony of the senses, or the records of our memory" (EHU 4.3). He asked whether these inferences from experience are "determin'd by reason," whether they have any "just foundation" (T 1.3.6.10). The problem of induction is now so closely identified with its author that it is often simply called "Hume's problem."

Major figures in the philosophical movements of the twentieth century tried their hands at refuting, rebutting, or resolving Hume's problem, although they rarely paid sufficient attention to the details of his arguments. Most of these responses maintain that Hume's argument assumes *deductivism* – that the only reasonable arguments are deductively valid arguments, and that inductive inferences are faulty because they aren't deductive.

The central responses to Hume's problem may be grouped into six major categories: a priori responses, inductive justifications, pragmatic vindications, falsificationist strategies, analytic dissolutions, and reliabilist justifications, although there is considerable difference of detail within each category.

A priori *responses*

Assuming Hume was a deductivist, an obvious response to his problem is to add a premise that converts inductive inferences to deductively valid ones, which will be some form of what Russell (1912) called "the Principle of Induction," amounting to the claim that nature is uniform. Russell followed Kant in maintaining the principle must be synthetic a priori, while Mill relied on dogmatic assertion ("nature *is* uniform"). Bonjour (1986) recently offered a weaker version of this line of argument, but the prospects for a successful a priori response are "widely thought to be clearly and demonstrably hopeless," since attempts to justify these principles fall to Hume's original argument, properly understood.

Stove–Mackie deductivism

A rather different a priori response is due to Stove (1973) and Mackie (1974), who maintained that Hume's deductivism led him to ignore the possibility that there might be "reasonable but probabilistic" arguments. So "inductive probabilism," the view that there are reasonable probable inductive arguments, is unaffected by Hume's argument. Consequently, the belief that Hume refuted inductive probabilism is "an entirely imaginary episode in the history of thought."

Once so prominent that Stroud (1977) called it "the standard interpretation," Stove and Mackie's rendition of Hume's argument is based on numerous mistranslations of his premises into modern terminology (Morris 1988). There is no textual basis for importing deductivism into the argument, so there is no reason to think that Hume's case against there being "just" probabilistic arguments in support of the Uniformity Principle assumes those arguments must be deductively valid. Nothing he says restricts what those "reasonings" might be, and he never attempts to limit what might constitute "an argument from probability." Moreover, if Hume *had* been a deductivist, he could have used the Separability and Conceivability Arguments against any factual inference to the unobserved, saving him the trouble of introducing the Uniformity Principle and raising questions about its support.

Goodman's new riddle of induction

A powerful challenge to any a priori deductivist attempt to resolve Hume's problem is Goodman's (1955) "new riddle of induction": Introduce a predicate "grue," its meaning stipulated as "green if observed before some future time t and blue afterwards." Every emerald observed so far has been green. Given the Uniformity Principle, observations support the hypothesis that all emeralds are green, but equally well support the hypothesis that they are grue. Both hypotheses can't be true. Even if we suppose that events we *haven't* experienced will resemble those we *have*, our supposition doesn't tell us *in what respects* they will resemble them. So adding the Uniformity Principle to make inductive inferences deductive won't solve this "new riddle," which can be regarded as a particularly dramatic way of posing Hume's problem.

Goodman's "new riddle" has generated an enormous literature (see Stalker 1994), and there is no consensus as to how it should be solved. According to Ian Hacking, it combines "precision of statement, generality of application, and difficulty of solution to a degree greater than any other philosophical problem broached in the [twentieth] century" (Hacking 1965: 41–2).

Inductive justifications

Working from a suggestion in Peirce (1931), Braithwaite (1953), Black (1954), and Skyrms (1975) maintain that inductive arguments are not viciously circular in the classical sense of containing the conclusion in the premises, but are circular in that the conclusion asserts the "predictive reliability" of the rule of inference by which it was reached. "Rule circularity" isn't vicious because an inductive inference is about its particular subject matter, while the rule of inference is about arguments of a certain kind.

But simply appealing to the rule either presupposes the Uniformity Principle or begs Hume's original question. The alternative is to maintain that the rule is justified by another rule at a higher level, and that that rule is justified by a rule at a still higher level, ultimately avoiding circularity by postulating an infinite number of autonomous levels. Technically, this doesn't beg the question, but "comes pretty close."

This strategy is problematic for other reasons. The epistemological significance of the distinctions between levels is obscure, and the rules at each level have the same form. While there is plenty of inductive evidence at lower levels, a level will eventually be reached where there aren't enough successful inductive arguments to provide a basis for justification, at which point the chain collapses. Given that the chain is potentially infinite, it is questionable whether it can provide the "foundation" Hume's argument demands.

Pragmatic vindications

The pragmatic approach to Hume's problem, developed by Reichenbach (1938), maintains that induction is a *method* for arriving at *posits* – rules for the practice of induction, and isn't a form of inference at all. Rules are more or less successful or useful, not true or false. Adopting a rule of induction is a choice that can only be assessed by considering the consequences of adopting it. So induction can at best be *vindicated* – justified by determining whether inductive posits are preferable to competing policies.

Induction, Reichenbach argued, is preferable to all other policies, because we can know that *it will work if anything will*. If nature is uniform, inductive posits will work better than non-inductive ones, such as augury or astrology. If nature lacks uniformity to the degree that inductive posits are unsuccessful, then augury and astrology will also fail. If they didn't, their predictive success would constitute a significant regularity that an inductivist could exploit. So if augury and astrology are successful, so is induction. Thus the inductive posit will succeed *if any other method could.*

Reichenbach's preferred inductive posit is the "straight rule," embedded in his "limiting frequency" account of probability, where statements of the form "n per cent of As are Bs" refer, not to the proportion of observed As that are Bs, but to the proportion of As that are Bs as the number of As examined approaches the limit – infinity. The relative frequency of observed As that are Bs is a provisional estimate of the limiting value, subject to revision in light of new information.

Reichenbach ignores "the problem of the reference class" – the question of when it is more relevant that As are, say, Cs rather than Bs. He also leaves open how many observations justify using the straight rule. Although there may be no general answer to this question, without some understanding of when the straight rule can be legitimately applied, it is useless for making realistic probability estimates. More importantly, his account ignores the fact that in science and everyday life, we're interested in short-run predictions, where limiting frequencies are of dubious relevance.

But there is, further, a long run problem. Even if this method will find laws if they are to be found, no one will ever know it, since we never reach the limit. As Keynes quipped, "In the long run, we'll all be dead."

Popper's falsificationism

Popper (1972) accepts that Hume showed that there are no valid inductive inferences, but maintains that induction plays no role in science, the aim of which is not *inductive verification* but *deductive falsification.* Science proceeds by the method of "conjectures and refutations." Conjectures imply predictions, which permits us to test them. When predictions fail, conjectures are refuted. The mode of inference is deduction; the form of argument, *modus tollens.* The best science aims at producing highly falsifiable conjectures and devising tests designed to falsify – refute – them.

Failure to falsify provides a highly fallibilistic way to provisionally accept conjectures, which Popper calls *corroboration.* He has been widely criticized on the grounds that corroboration isn't really much different from confirmation, and seems to have an inductive inference embedded in it – the inference from the fact that a conjecture has thus far escaped falsification to the (admittedly fallible) conclusion that it will continue to do so.

Since corroboration provides a way to accept conjectures even though their content goes beyond the content of basic statements, it is *ampliative,* and therefore should count as a non-demonstrative form of inference. To the extent that Popper's theory is inductive, it fails to evade Hume's argument.

Analytic dissolutions

Another response to Hume, once popular among analytic philosophers, holds that it is a mistake to demand a justification of induction. Hume's problem can't be solved, but can be *dissolved* through careful attention to the language we use in inductive contexts.

Strawson (1952) offered the most prominent version of this response, arguing that induction and deduction are fundamentally different kinds of inference, each with its own set of standards, so it is illegitimate to demand that induction be justified deductively. But induction can't be justified inductively, since that would presuppose induction. The proper question is whether it is reasonable to rely on induction, where "being reasonable" means "having a degree of belief in a statement which is proportional to the strength of evidence in its favor." We can ask whether it is reasonable to accept this or that statement, but we can no more meaningfully ask whether inductive reasoning is justified in general than we can ask whether the law is legal.

Strawson claims it is an analytic truth that it is reasonable to believe a statement for which there is strong evidence, that it is also analytic that inductive evidence can constitute strong evidence for an inductive conclusion, and that these claims imply that it is analytic that it is reasonable to believe an inductively supported conclusion. However, he also holds that it is an empirical, contingent fact that inductive conclusions will be true in the future, which makes it difficult to see how his claims can really be analytic.

Strawson seems to tie the notions of "strong evidence" and "reasonable belief" to standards a linguistic community accepts and embodies in their inductive practices, avoiding the question whether following these standards makes it likely that we will arrive at the truth. So understood, Strawson's "dissolution" does not really address the issue Hume raised.

Reliabilist approaches to induction

The advent of reliabilist theories of knowledge (Goldman 1986) yielded another response to Hume's problem. Reliabilists also read Hume as a deductivist, and take themselves to have refuted Hume by showing how inductive inferences can be legitimate. But, as we have seen, while Hume is not demanding *deductive* justification for inferences based on "probability," he *is* demanding an argument that establishes a connection between past inductions and future ones.

Papineau (1992) maintains that inductive inferences are "reliable transmitters of truth" on the grounds that "when people have made inductions from true premises in the past . . . their conclusions have turned out to be true." Van Cleve (1984) holds that the connection is made by this rule of inference: "From *Most observed A's have been B's* infer *The majority of all A's are B's.*"

These responses exhibit the same circularity that Hume's original argument highlighted: if we are "engaged by argument to put [this kind of] trust in past experience," then it is reasonable to ask upon what basis we do so, and the only possible basis is past experience itself.

Van Cleve (1984) attempts to avoid this charge by arguing that the circularity is not vicious if knowing that the rule is correct is not a condition of making a legitimate inductive inference. Since reliabilist theories are *externalist*, subjects needn't know the rules they use, or even be aware they are using them. All that is required is that the rules are in fact correct.

But one way of understanding Hume's charge is to read it as asking about the source of support for the rule itself. Since that support must be past experience, reliabilism fails to meet Hume's challenge.

The externalist may reply that he isn't required to support the rule. *If* the process by which he comes to believe is reliable, then his belief is justified. Reliabilism, however, is unable to discharge this conditional. The reliabilist must grant that he will never be in a position to show unconditionally that our beliefs are "determin'd by reason," and thus has only produced a promissory note against Hume's challenge (see Stroud 1994).

Levin (2003), however, embraces this problem. "Reliabilism implies that, if nature is uniform, we do have knowledge." Calling the conditional, "the big catch," he rejects the attempt to make circularity non-vicious: "The catch is important, because it prohibits any self-contained inductive justification of induction. Inductive justifications of induction are inevitably circular, nor does reliabilism say otherwise" (p. 160). But this means that his response doesn't engage with Hume's demand that he show how our inductive inferences could be "determin'd by reason."

Reliabilists see themselves as providing a "solution" to the problem of induction as Hume posed it, and it is far from clear that they have succeeded in providing one. But if their main goal is to provide naturalistic accounts of inductive behavior, then they would be better off to jettison their claims to have successfully responded to Hume's challenge, and recognize that reliabilism has much in common with Hume's "skeptical solution," which accepts that our inductive beliefs aren't "determin'd by reason," and proposes "another principle of equal weight and authority" (EHU 5.2) to account for them. This causal account of causal inference is far closer to the spirit of externalist reliabilism than its proponents are willing to acknowledge.

In the last quarter of the past century, Hume scholars turned from trying to *solve* the problem of induction to the interpretive task of trying to figure out exactly what his arguments were in the passages where he is alleged to have posed the problem. These attempts are discussed in chapter 5, "Hume on the Relation of Cause and Effect," and in chapter 6, "Inductive Inference in Hume's Philosophy."

The Regularity Theory of Causation

Until late in the twentieth century, most of Hume's readers assumed he was a proponent of the regularity theory of causation. Orthodoxy in positivist and post-positivist epistemology, this view is still so prominent that the regularity theory is regularly called "the Humean view of causation."

Hume gave two definitions of cause. Attributing "the Humean view of causation" to him favors, at his second definition's expense, his first:

> We may define a cause to be *an object, followed by another, and where all the objects similar to the first are followed by objects similar to the second.* (EHU 7.29)

Blackwell's *Companion to the Philosophy of Science* summarizes how this definition is usually understood:

> In the world apart from ourselves there is only constant conjunction. There is no causal glue cementing the events of the world together. This is the classic empiricist account of causation. All we can ever experience is constant conjunction. Therefore . . . we can have no legitimate idea of causation that goes beyond that . . . Hume's account . . . remains the source of inspiration for those who seek to demystify causation. (Newton-Smith 2001: 167)

Regularity theorists "demystify causation" by refusing to postulate causal powers, causal properties, or any connection between causes and effects apart from regular succession. For this reason, the theory is considered to be a *reductionist* account of causation.

There are many standard objections to regularity theories, beginning with Reid's and Mill's worries that regular succession, though perhaps *necessary* for causation, is clearly not *sufficient*. As applied to Hume himself, these critiques overlook his positive account of belief, developed in sections 5, 6, 9, and 10 of the first *Enquiry*, and at greater length in Book 1, part 3, of the *Treatise*. Hume's *Treatise* discussion culminates in 1.3.15 with the "Rules by which to judge of causes and effects," which anticipate Mill's Methods, providing him with more resources for responding to these traditional objections than is generally recognized.

Neo-Humean theories

Attempts to avoid these objections, however, have produced a number of neo-Humean theories, inspired by Hume but attempting to go beyond him, so that "the 'Humean' view of causation has taken on a life of its own independently of explicit discussion of Hume" (Strawson 1989: 9). The most notable of these theories, and the most thorough, is Mackie's *The Cement of the Universe*, "the outstanding contribution to the philosophy of causation in the Humean tradition" (Millican 2002: 443). Mackie's account, however, is not without its own problems, especially concerning the direction of causation.

One central difficulty, for both "the Humean view of causation" and Hume himself, is the problem of distinguishing (mere) regularities of succession from genuinely causal sequences, or the problem of distinguishing accidental generalizations and lawlike regularities.

A popular way of addressing this problem is to use subjunctive conditionals in a counterfactual analysis of causation. Genuine causal sequences and lawlike regularities support counterfactuals; regularities of succession and accidental generalizations do not.

Traditional analyses of subjunctive conditionals, however, employ causal notions, so any account of how causal sequences and laws support counterfactuals invites charges of circularity. In addition, those who would explain the difference between accidental and causal sequences in terms of counterfactuals typically appeal to some differences in the objects that make the relevant counterfactuals for lawlike sequences true and the parallel counterfactuals for accidental generalizations false, but these appeals invariably use some version of the notions of causal power and causal necessity that Hume's arguments repudiate.

Lewis's counterfactual account

Although Hume never says what a "law" is, many of his readers take him to be addressing this question in a remark appended to his first *Enquiry* definition of cause:

> Or in other words *where, if the first had not been, the second never had existed.* (EHU 7.29)

This claim is neither obviously equivalent to, nor clearly compatible with, his first definition, as David Lewis noted:

> Hume's "other words" . . . are no mere restatement of his first definition. They propose something altogether different: a counterfactual analysis of causation. (Lewis 1993: 502)

While not everyone agrees that Hume's claim should be read counterfactually (Jacobson 2000: 157, argues that it is merely tensed), Lewis took up what he understood Hume's addendum to propose. He argued that understanding counterfactuals is the key to understanding causation, and developed a theory that defined causation in terms of counterfactual dependence. Accepting Lewis's theory demands accepting his account of the truth conditions for counterfactual conditionals, which many find problematic, if not straightforwardly false (Humphreys 2001: 35). While Lewis has prompted much work on the role of counterfactuals in an account of causation (see Tooley 2003), almost all of it is couched in terms of possible worlds semantics, and has little to do with what *Hume* might have meant.

Heroic Humeanism

One way of addressing the problem of distinguishing accidental generalizations from lawlike ones that doesn't depend upon counterfactual analysis is to argue that Hume's own "Rules by which to judge of causes and effects," given sufficient experience, will suffice to eliminate accidental regularities that have exceptions. If there are any exceptionless accidental regularities, they are no different from genuinely lawlike generalizations. Beauchamp and Rosenberg (1981), who defend this position, call it "heroic Humeanism." In its favor is the important Humean idea that if there *were* something underlying only lawlike sequences, it would have to be a causal power or property that necessarily connects those events, but Hume has shown that there can be no such powers, properties, or necessary connections.

The new Hume

Galen Strawson objects to "the ordinary, Realist form of the Regularity Theory of Causation" because it supposes that "there is no reason in the nature of things for the regularity of the world," which he finds "utterly implausible" (Strawson 1989: 21). In a significant interpretative shift, he rejects the view that Hume held, "the Humean view of causation," joining other scholars (Craig 1987; Wright 1983) who argue that Hume was a *causal realist*. For these "new Humeans" (as Winkler, 1991, called them), Hume "takes it for granted . . . that Causation does exist in reality, although we are entirely ignorant of its ultimate nature" (p. 219). All we can know are the regularities we experience; the real causal connections are "secret" – connections to which we will never have access.

For the new Humeans, reading Hume as a regularity theorist misses what is most important in his philosophy:

> one misses the central aim of Hume's skeptical philosophy unless one recognizes that he consistently maintained . . . that there are real powers and forces in nature which are not directly accessible to our senses. (Wright 1983: 129)

Hume's skepticism, the new Humeans maintain, is best understood as skepticism about our ability to know these "real powers and forces" – these "secret connections." Their "new Hume" is thus a *skeptical realist* about causation.

Quasi-realism

The new Humeans have drawn much critical fire, especially from Simon Blackburn, who argues forcefully that the textual basis for their account is slim. Blackburn maintains that Hume's view is best understood as "a not-so-skepticial anti-realism," which he calls "quasi-realism." Blackburn thinks the new Humeans, in rejecting reductionist readings of Hume, assume the only viable interpretive alternative is skeptical realism. But he urges that

> there is a third option: Hume . . . gives us a story explaining and even justifying our use of the vocabulary of causation, while denying that we represent a real aspect of the world to ourselves as we use it. (p. 103)

His quasi-realist Hume

> celebrates the fact that nature has implanted our fixed propensities to causalizing in us. But these . . . are active mental responses to perceived regularities, rather than passive mental representations of an order of properties and relations that cannot be perceived, and so ones of which we can have no idea. Hence, realism together with anti-realism. (Blackburn 2002: 275)

Skeptical realism, quasi-realism, and Hume

While a full evaluation of the issues between Blackburn and the new Humeans demands detailed discussion of the relevant texts, it is possible to assess it briefly.

This is a controversy in the metaphysics of causation. Regularity theorists, in claiming that all there is to causation "in the objects" is regular succession, are making a metaphysical claim about what there is.

Skeptical realists go beyond the regularists in maintaining that there are real connections in nature over and above what we can experience, and so are also making a metaphysical claim.

Blackburn's "third option" counts "perceived regularities" as "the contributions of the world" about how the world is independently of us, which is the *realism* in quasi-realism. When we project connections between the objects we relate causally, we "are denying that we represent a real aspect of the world," which is the *anti-realist* element in his theory. These two "aspects" of causation give us "realism together with anti-realism." Blackburn thus has two metaphysical commitments: realism about the regularities we perceive; anti-realism about the connections we project.

Hume's interests are very different from those of the parties to this debate. He does not share their interest in metaphysics, and actively avoids commitment to any metaphysical stance in his account of causation, as a look at his *Enquiry* definitions of cause reveals.

Hume believes that "the chief obstacle . . . to our improvement in the moral or metaphysical sciences" is "the obscurity of the ideas, and ambiguity of the terms" (EHU 7.2). Hume thinks he has found a mechanism that permits us to make progress – his theory of definition. He describes it as "a new microscope or species of optics" (EHU 7.4), predicting that it will produce as dramatic results in the moral and metaphysical sciences as its hardware counterparts have produced in natural philosophy.

Hume uses a simple series of tests to determine cognitive content. Begin with a term. Ask what idea is annexed to it. If there is no such idea, then the term has no cognitive content, however prominently it figures in philosophy or theology. If there is an idea annexed to the term, and it is complex, break it up into the simple ideas that compose it. Then trace each component simple idea back to the impressions that spawned it. If the process fails at any point, the idea in question lacks cognitive content. When carried through successfully, however, the theory yields "a just definition" – a precise account of the content of the troublesome idea or term.

To get clear about a contentious idea like causation, Hume directs us to "look for it in all the sources, from which it may be derived" (EHU 7.5), either impressions from "the outward senses" or impressions of "inward sentiment." He finds relevant impressions in both sources: the *external impressions* are "the number of similar instances which occur of the constant conjunction of these events," which we call cause and effect, and the *internal impression* is the feeling of the "transition of the imagination from one object to its usual attendant" (EHU 7.28).

Hume's *Enquiry* definitions of cause sum up these impressions. His first definition:

> an object, followed by another, and where all the objects similar to the first are followed by objects similar to the second. (EHU 7.29)

summarizes the *external* impressions, while his second summarizes the *internal* impressions:

> an object followed by another, and whose appearance always conveys the thought to the other. (EHU 7.29)

Both elements, "the constant union and the inference of the mind," are necessary; to think otherwise is to ignore impressions that are part of the idea's cognitive content. So Hume's "just and precise" definition must be the *conjunction* of the two definitions.

Hume's definitions define *our idea of cause*. Unlike the regularity theorist, the skeptical realist, and the quasi-realist, they make no commitments about the nature of ultimate reality, about the world as it is independently of us.

In claiming that regularity is all there is to causation, the reductive regularist not only ignores Hume's second definition of cause, he also reads the first definition as applying to "causation, as it is in the objects," thus making a metaphysical claim that Hume abstains from making.

In reacting to the regularist's reductive definition of cause, the skeptical realist is also committed to a metaphysical claim: that there are real causal connections in nature to which we don't have access, ignoring Hume's insistence that beyond "these two lights" – his two definitions – "we have no idea" of causation.

Finally, Blackburn's quasi-realism is constituted by two metaphysical claims, one about "the contributions of the world" – "perceived regularities," and the other about our projections of causality onto objects, where we "deny that we represent a real aspect of the world" in projecting. Both claims go beyond Hume's studied agnosticism. In engaging with the metaphysical positions he rejects, the quasi-realist is also doing metaphysics.

It is an irony worthy of Hume himself that "the Humean theory of causation" describes a position he never held. But it is an even greater irony that two prominent contemporary interpretative alternatives to the regularity theory, both of which claim to represent Hume's true position, are also committed to metaphysical stances that it was Hume's genius to avoid altogether.

Hume and Cognitive Science

In the heyday of analytic philosophy, it was not uncommon to criticize Hume for "confounding" philosophy and psychology. Coupled with the long-standing reading of Hume as a purely negative skeptic, it is not surprising that Hume's own sense of his project – "to introduce the experimental method of reasoning into moral subjects" in order to develop a science of human nature – was largely forgotten or ignored.

Now the situation is reversed. Hume is generally viewed as having a positive, naturalistic program that has close affinities to contemporary work in naturalized epistemology, cognitive psychology, and especially, cognitive science. Although Kemp Smith (1941) emphasized Hume's naturalistic stance, the trend toward reading Hume as a naturalist who was well aware of the continuities between philosophy and the sciences is due primarily to Stroud's *Hume*. Hume scholarship has followed suit, so much so that an important recent account (Garrett 1997) treats Hume as working largely within cognitive psychology.

While Hume's concern with the nature of cognition certainly makes it reasonable to see his project as having much in common with research in cognitive psychology, his work is perhaps even more relevant to the aims of the broader research program of contemporary cognitive science.

One of the most exciting intellectual developments of the past century, cognitive science is a multidisciplinary investigation of human, animal, and machine cognition involving philosophy, psychology, the neurosciences, linguistics, and computer science. Hume scholars, as well as researchers in cognitive science, are gradually realizing significant similarities of project and purpose between cognitive science and Hume's "mental geography," or the "delineation of the distinct parts and powers of the mind." Not only did Hume anticipate a number of recent results in cognitive science, but a great deal of research in cognitive science either sheds light on interpretive issues in Hume scholarship or provides confirming evidence for several of Hume's views that have been contested or refuted by developments in twentieth-century analytic philosophy.

The first explicit efforts to link Hume with cognitive science were articles by Kenneth Bower (1984) and John Biro (1986). Experimental work in the late 1970s revived an old debate about mental imagery in memory, which Bower used as a springboard for developing an internal information-processing model of memory imagery that arguably vindicated Hume's Copy Principle as well as providing substantive, plausible construals of Hume's views on resemblance and causality.

Biro's discussion concerned the relation between Hume and the then-dominant theory of cognition, the Representational Theory of Mind (RTM), of which Jerry Fodor (1975) was (and is) the most vocal champion. Biro maintained that a Humean perspective yielded insights into three central problems for RTM. He argued that the problem of providing an acceptable account of meaning and content is better served by adopting Hume's "conventional-cum-historical" account of meaning, as opposed to the Gricean views RTM favored. The problem of qualia can be addressed by interpreting Hume's Copy Principle along the lines sketched by Bower. Finally, RTM's alleged commitment to undischarged homunculi could be resolved by adopting Hume's strategy of keeping personal and sub-personal levels distinct, so that intentional behavior at the personal level can be explained by referring to processes at the sub-personal level without threat of circularity or regress.

Fodor: Hume Variations

There is considerable irony in Biro's efforts to demonstrate Hume's relevance to problems faced by RTM, since Fodor (1987) explicitly contrasts his project with Hume's. Compounding the irony is the fact that Fodor has very recently seemed to change his tune. In *Hume Variations* (2003), Fodor claims that

> Hume's *Treatise* is the foundational document of cognitive science: it made explicit, for the first time, the project of constructing an empirical psychology on the basis of a representational theory of mind; in effect, on the basis of the Theory of Ideas. (p. 134)

The Theory of Ideas, as Fodor sees it, is an essentially Cartesian picture of concepts. "A main reason for being interested in Hume's theory is that it begins to show how a Cartesian account of concepts might be developed into a naturalistic and empirically plausible psychology of cognition" (pp. 16–17), whereby "typical mental processes are constituted by causal interactions among mental representations" (pp. 134–5). Hume "foresaw, with considerable accuracy, what the general structure of a 'representational' theory of mind would have to be" (pp. 7–8).

While Fodor applauds Hume for his insight into the nature of our cognitive architecture, he is more than willing to reject both his empiricism and his epistemology as wrong-headed and dispensable. He is especially disdainful of Hume's associationism, despite the fact that Hume thought it was his use of the association of ideas that staked his claim to being an "inventor" in the science of human nature. For Fodor, however, associationism "makes a mess of intentional content" (p. 115), ultimately "making trouble for [Hume's] whole theory" (p. 113). In the end, though, Fodor holds that Hume "isn't really an associationist when push comes to shove" (p. 115), because he invokes the imagination to do or finish what association isn't capable of doing or finishing by itself. Imagination, however, is a "blank check" that Hume can't cash. Fodor concludes: "Dead end. So be it" (p. 122). He then proceeds to dump both the principles of association and the faculty of imagination. What remains is the Theory of Ideas, shorn of Hume's epistemology, empiricist semantics, and anti-nativism: RTM, in other words.

After gerrymandering Hume's theory by jettisoning most of its distinctive features, there is a serious question as to how much *Hume* is left in Fodor's *Variations*. But it is hardly surprising that Fodor rejects associationism; in some form or other, it has been one of his constant targets, and in *connectionism*, its most prominent current form, it constitutes his most serious rival. Whatever relation Hume may or may not have to RTM, he is generally considered, *because* of his associationism, as a forerunner, if not the father, of connectionism.

Connectionism

Sometimes called Parallel Distributed Processing, or the theory of Neural Networks, *connectionism* is a series of models of cognitive activity based on the premise that complex cognitive operations can be effectively accomplished by large networks of simple, neuron-like units. Intelligent performance is derived from the pattern of connection strengths between units.

Connectionist research expanded dramatically in the late 1980s, and connectionists maintain that their models account for the nature of mental representation as well or better than does RTM. While there are currently several distinct types of connectionist models that attempt to account for the structure of mental representation, all are clearly associationist.

Connectionist models that represent *concepts* by activating an ensemble of distinct units, each of which encodes a certain prototypical property or microfeature that is constitutive of that concept, promise to resolve what Fodor himself regards as the critical issue in the debate between empiricism and nativism – the extent to which lexical concepts have internal structure:

> The empiricist bets that there will prove to be lots of interesting reductions of prima facie un-complex concepts; whereas the nativist bets that . . . we are not going to be able to display the internal structure of most concepts because, simply, most concepts do not have any internal structure. (Fodor 1981: 283)

William Ramsey, a leading interpreter of the philosophical implications of connectionism, maintains that if these models "turn out to be the right story of concept structure, then . . . the empiricist has won hands down." For this kind of network, he notes, "if we represent our concepts this way – by activating constituent atoms which denote lower-level features – empiricists like Hume . . . could hardly ask for a better model to capture their views (Ramsey 1992: 265).

Ramsey adds that versions of this kind of model

> Whose atomic units are linked through some form of learning may provide further insight into the actual nature of empiricist concept acquisition. By providing us with new principles of concept construction, these models may replace or justify assumptions made by past empiricists . . . For example, if the connections are adjusted in accordance with rules of a Hebbian sort, then Hume's principles of association will be closer to the mark than many have assumed. (pp. 265–6)

For models that represent *propositions*, the situation is less clear, but models of this type, Ramsey maintains, "have important implications for traditional work in . . . philosophy of mind" because "they provide associationism with the potential means for avoiding criticism regarding its inability to capture syntactic regularities in thought" (p. 271). In particular, using this kind of model to develop an associationist account based on similarity clustering in vector space would be an especially Humean solution to the problem of capturing syntactic regularities.

Recent work on connectionist learning strongly suggests that networks seem to develop new classifications and abstractions that emerge without the recombination of pre-existing representations. Research by Munakata and his colleagues (1997) gives reason to think that connectionist learning gives rise to new primitive concepts that are developed entirely in response to the system's training input. This arguably captures the essence of empiricist learning and signals a new direction for conceptual change (Ramsey 1999: 187).

Damasio: Descartes' Error

In *Descartes' Error* (1995), a very Humean study of cognition and the role of emotion and feeling in it, Antonio Damasio rejects "the false intuition . . . that what is together in the mind is at one place in the brain" (p. 94). Noting that no area of the brain is equipped to process representations from all sensory modalities simultaneously, and that there is no single area where all these representations could be projected, Damasio concludes that the mind couldn't be a "Cartesian theater," with its audience of a homunculus isolated in a central module. Far from there being a Cartesian separation of mind and body, mind cannot exist or operate at all without body. Failure to see this is Descartes' error.

Instead of depending on a single brain center, Damasio argues that our reasoning and decision-making abilities utilize several brain systems working together across many levels of neuronal organization. Older systems of biological regulation intertwine with "more modern and plastic" systems through a large number of feedback loops. "Nature," he maintains, "built the apparatus of rationality not just *on top of* the apparatus of biological regulation, but also *from* it and *with* it" (p. 128).

The lower levels in this "neural edifice of reason" regulate processing of emotions and feelings as well as the bodily functions necessary for survival. They are directly and mutually related to virtually every bodily organ, putting the body within the chain of operations that "generate the highest reaches of reasoning." Thus "emotion, feeling, and biological regulation all play a role in human reason" (p. xiii).

But "having a mind" requires that the "organism forms neural representations which can become images, be manipulated in a process called thought, and eventually influence behavior." The "center of neurobiology," for Damasio, is "the process whereby neural representations, which consist of biological modifications created by learning in a neuronal circuit, become images [that] we each experience as belonging *to us*" (p. 90).

The organism's functional needs shaped many of these neural circuits, which contain basic representations of it, and continually monitor it as it is perturbed by environmental stimuli and acts in response to its environment. Past representations become part of the organism's dispositional memory, along with other items of its autobiography.

These neural representations become images. Explicitly invoking Hume, Damasio maintains that images of present representations are forceful and vivid; recalled images less so. In doing so, he rejects both the possibility of imageless thought and that of rule-governed manipulation of "pure propositions."

Many of these representations have "somatic markers" attached – feelings registering emotional assessments of past experience relevant to present decisions, which direct attention toward certain representations and away from others, serving both as "alarm bells" and as "beacons of incentive."

Somatic markers are indispensable for reasoning, as indicators of the value of what is represented, as "boosters" for continued working memory and attention, and as a source of *order* for images through their expression of cumulative preferences we have inherited and acquire through experience. They "energize" the reasoning process in terms of the individual's preferences and goals.

But this picture omits a crucial feature of mind, the idea that these images are *our* images. This point of view or perspective – Damasio calls it "subjectivity" – is essential for our idea of the self.

"Subjectivity" emerges when the brain produces, in addition to images of an object and those of an organism's responses to it, "a third kind of image, that of an organism in the act of perceiving and responding to an object" (p. 242). These images result from "third-party ensembles" of neural circuits reciprocally connected with representations of the object and the organism. When "correlated" with the first two sets, we have a relatively stable, "perpetually re-created neurobiological state," which constitutes the neural basis for the self. The source of the stability is the predominantly invariant structure and operation of the organism, and the slowly evolving elements of autobiographical data (p. 238). Damasio believes this explains why "our experiences tend to have a consistent perspective, as if there were an owner and knower."

The "endless reactivation of updated images" – our representations of our bodies, emotions, memories, present experiences, and expectations – constitute the basis for our ideas of ourselves. Current bodily states are constantly incorporated into these pictures, so that at every moment the self is constructed, although so seamlessly *re*constructed that we never realize we're being remade unless something goes wrong with the process.

The central elements of Damasio's account – the prominent role of imagery, the denial of "pure thought," the centrality of the emotions in cognition, and the rejection of a substantial self – bring many of Hume's fundamental views into an exciting, plausible, and – ultimately – testable account of human cognition.

Other developments

On a less global level, there has been extensive experimental research into human reasoning under uncertainty, which has had profound influence on research not only in psychology, but also in the law, medicine, economics, political science, statistics, and philosophy. Research in the heuristics and biases tradition by Tversky and Kahneman and their associates (1982), as well as by Nisbett and Ross (1980), has identified a number of "judgment heuristics," which guide judgment. Like the perceptual cues we use to make judgments about the world, these "natural assessments," which depend on availability, similarity, representativeness, and ease of retrieval from memory, generally serve the individual well, but can also be the source of systematic error.

Almost all of these heuristics were identified and discussed by Hume in part 3 of Book 1 of the *Treatise*, especially in the chapter on "unphilosophical probabilities" (T 1.3.15). Like the researchers in the heuristics and biases tradition, Hume was well aware that our tendency to overgeneralize was rooted in an instinct that had survival value, both for the individual and the species, but could result in prejudice and bias in particular circumstances, unless tempered by reflection on the "general rules" that produced them.

Hume's views have also recently resurfaced in an attempt to connect Hume's naturalism with developments in contemporary learning theory (Wilson, O'Donohue, and Hayes 2001).

Damasio's claim that experimental evidence shows that memories are less vivid than present perceptions has received support from work on olfactory memory, and some of this work also suggests that images in imagination are also less vivid than those of either memory or present perception.

Finally, research in the neuroscience of behavior seems to support Hume's view that regarding the will as an "internal impression we feel and are conscious of, when we knowingly give rise to any new motion of our body" does not warrant the conclusion that we directly perceive the will as a force that moves our bodies, but only that there is a conjunction between the internal impression and the movement of our body. According to Wegner (2002), neural events or processes that cause behavior are under way before consciousness of willing these behaviors is present. The experience of conscious will arises when we infer that our conscious intention has caused our voluntary action, although both intention and action are themselves caused by mental processes that do not feel willed.

Although cognitive science is still in its infancy, the directions prominent research is taking indicate that future results will continue to cement the affinities between some of the most interesting and controversial facets of Hume's work and what cognitive scientists are discovering about the mind.

Hume and Naturalized Epistemology

Although Hume was read as a purely negative skeptic until relatively recently, he is now recognized as having a positive, naturalistic theory of belief formation and improvement that has close affinities with recent developments in contemporary epistemology: "Hume . . . anticipated the best epistemic ideas of the late twentieth century" (Solomon 2001: 52).

Hume's views not only resonate in naturalized epistemology (Quine 1969; Kornblith 1994), but are also prominent in feminist (Baier 2000) and social epistemologies (Solomon 2001; Schmitt 1994). And a very Humean attempt to redirect epistemology by emphasizing work in cognitive psychology, especially research in the heuristics and biases tradition, has just appeared (Bishop and Trout 2005). It has also been suggested that Hume's positive approach to problems about reasonable belief, if developed in detail, provides an effective counter to the fruitless emphasis, in analytic epistemology, on providing conditions for knowing.

Hume's work might also provide the key to solving a central problem in naturalized epistemology: the question of whether a naturalized theory can accommodate the normativity arguably essential to epistemology (Kim 1994), although recent readers differ both on the textual sources for normativity in his theory (Baier 1991; Garrett 1997; Loeb 2002; Morris 2005) and whether it can pass his own test for normativity (Korsgaard 1996).

When Hume develops and refines his theory of belief, he argues that since "any thing may produce any thing," the only way we can determine whether something is "really" a cause or an effect is through experience. Our collective experience also shows which inferences are successful and which are not, giving Hume a means within his naturalism for endorsing certain ways of forming beliefs and rejecting others. He offers "rules by which to judge of causes and effects" as "general rules, by which we *ought* to regulate our judgment," and then goes one step further, recommending that we endorse them as well.

But there is still a question as to whether Hume's account is genuinely normative. Is he *correct* in thinking that we too should place our confidence in these rules and regulate our judgment in accordance with them?

To decide the issue, we must appeal to some normative perspective from which we assess the norms for causal reasoning and endorse or reject them. But since we have no access to the world except through the process of causal reasoning, there is no transcendent point of view from which we can assess them. The only point of view from which we can assess the norms of causal reasoning is that of causal reasoning itself. Hume, believes that applying reflective causal reasoning to our reflection-produced standards for causal reasoning will increase, and not undermine, our confidence in them. In this sense, his account of the norms of causal reasoning is genuinely normative.

Hume as anti-metaphysician

As we saw above, a current debate about Hume's views on causation concerns whether he was a realist, a skeptical realist, or a quasi-realist. We determined that he holds none of the views. Claiming that he does commits him to a metaphysical position he takes care to avoid. This is not the only issue where even Hume's most sympathetic readers have taken him to be adopting a metaphysical stance: similar attributions can be found in recent discussions of "projectivism," "compatibilism," personal identity, and the ideas of space and time. Careful attention to Hume's arguments, however, reveal that he uses his theory of definition, not only as a powerful critical tool to determine whether philosophical terms have genuine cognitive content, but also that he is careful both to ensure that the ideas he uses have cognitive content and that he ends his enquiries before he reaches the bounds of sense. This makes Hume a deeper and more profoundly anti-metaphysical philosopher than is generally acknowledged.

Many of Hume's readers miss what is so distinctive about his approach to philosophy because they are interested in metaphysical questions and take him to be interested in these questions in the way they are. In doing so, they fail to see that part of Hume's attack on traditional approaches to philosophical questions consists in shifting the ground of discussion from what he regards as incoherent metaphysics to the only area where he believes we can have a fruitful discussion – where we have a clear understanding of the cognitive contents of the central ideas involved. Hume's resolute refusal to engage in metaphysics is what is both radically innovative and distinctively modern about his approach to philosophy. To neglect or ignore this is to miss what makes Hume worthy of our serious consideration today.

See also 2 "Hume's Theory of Ideas"; 5 "Hume on the Relation of Cause and Effect"; 6 "Inductive Inference in Hume's Philosophy"; 23 "Hume's Naturalism and His Skepticism"; 24 "Is Hume a Realist or an Anti-realist?"

Acknowledgments

My work on this chapter was made possible by an NEH Summer Stipend and an Artistic and Scholarly Development Grant from Illinois Wesleyan University.

References

Baier, Annette C. (1991). *A Progress of Sentiments: Reflections on Hume's "Treatise"* (Cambridge, MA: Harvard University Press).

—— (2000). "Hume: The Reflective Woman's Epistemologist?" in Anne Jaap Jacobson (ed.), *Feminist Interpretations of David Hume* (State College, PA: Penn State University Press), pp. 19–38.

Biro, John I. (1985). "Hume and Cognitive Science," *History of Philosophy Quarterly*, 2, pp. 257–74.

Bishop, Michael A. and Trout, J. D. (2005). *Epistemology and the Psychology of Human Judgment* (New York: Oxford University Press).

Black, Max (1954). "Inductive Support of Inductive Rules," in *Problems of Analysis: Philosophical Essays* (Ithaca: Cornell University Press), pp. 191–208.

Blackburn, Simon (1993). "Hume and Thick Connexions," in *Essays in Quasi-realism* (New York: Oxford University Press), pp. 94–107.

—— (2002). "Postscript," in Peter Millican (ed.), *Reading Hume on Human Understanding* (Oxford: Clarendon Press), pp. 273–6.

Bonjour, Lawrence (1986). "A Reconsideration of the Problem of Induction," *Philosophical Topics*, 14, pp. 93–124.

Bower, Kenneth (1984). "Imagery: from Hume to Cognitive Science," *Canadian Journal of Philosophy*, 15, pp. 217–34.

Braithwaite, R. B. (1953). *Scientific Explanation* (Cambridge: Cambridge University Press).

Craig, E. J. (1987). *The Mind of God and the Works of Man* (Oxford: Clarendon Press).

Damasio, Antonio R. (1994). *Descartes' Error: Emotion, Reason, and the Human Brain* (New York: G. P. Putnam's Sons).

Fodor, Jerry (1975). *The Language of Thought* (Cambridge, MA: Harvard University Press).

—— (1981). *Representations* (Cambridge MA: MIT Press).

—— (1987). "Mental Representation: An Introduction," in Nicholas Rescher (ed.), *Scientific Inquiry in Philosophical Perspective* (Lanham, MD: University Press of America), pp. 35–74.

—— (2003). *Hume Variations* (Oxford: Clarendon Press).

Garrett, Don (1997). *Cognition and Commitment in Hume's Philosophy* (New York: Oxford University Press).

Goldman, Alvin I. (1986). *Epistemology and Cognition* (Cambridge, MA: Harvard University Press).

Goodman, Nelson (1955). *Fact, Fiction, and Forecast* (Cambridge, MA: Harvard University Press).

Hacking, Ian (1975). *The Emergence of Probability* (London: Cambridge University Press).

—— (1965). *Logic of Statistical Inference* (Cambridge: Cambridge University Press).

Humphreys, Paul (2001). "Causation," in W. H. Newton-Smith (ed.), *A Companion to the Philosophy of Science* (Oxford: Blackwell), pp. 31–40.

Jacobson, Anne Jaap (2000). "From Cognitive Science to a Post-Cartesian Text," in Rupert Read and Kenneth A. Richman (eds.), *The New Hume Debate* (London and New York: Routledge), pp. 156–66.

Kahneman, Daniel, Slovic, Paul, and Tversky, Amos (eds.) (1982). *Judgment under Uncertainty: Heuristics and Biases* (Cambridge: Cambridge University Press).

Kemp Smith, Norman (1941). *The Philosophy of David Hume* (London: Macmillan).

Kim, Jaegwon (1994). "What Is 'Naturalized Epistemology'?" in Hilary Kornblith (ed.). *Naturalizing Epistemology* (Cambridge, MA: MIT Press).

Kornblith, Hilary (ed.) (1994). *Naturalizing Epistemology*, 2nd edn. (Cambridge, MA: MIT Press).

Korsgaard, Christine M. (1996). *The Sources of Normativity* (Cambridge: Cambridge University Press).

Levin, Michael (2003). "Reliabilism and Induction," in Charles Landesman and Roblin Meeks (eds.), *Philosophical Skepticism* (Oxford: Blackwell), pp. 158–68.

Lewis, David (1993). "Causes and Counterfactuals," in Ernest Sosa and Michael Tooley (eds.), *Causation* (Oxford: Oxford University Press), pp. 205–7.

Loeb, Louis E. (2002). *Stability and Justification in Hume's "Treatise"* (New York: Oxford University Press).

Mackie, J. L. (1974). *The Cement of the Universe* (Oxford: Clarendon Press).

Millican, Peter (ed.) (2002). *Reading Hume on Human Understanding* (Oxford: Clarendon Press).

Morris, William E. (1988). "Hume's Refutation of Inductive Probabilism," in James Fetzer (ed.), *Probability and Causality* (Dordrecht: D. Reidel), pp. 43–77.

—— (2005). "Belief, Probability, Normativity," in Saul Traiger (ed.), *The Blackwell Guide to Hume's "Treatise"* (Oxford: Blackwell), pp. 77–94.

Munakata, Yuko, McClelland, James L., Johnson, James L., Siegler, Mark, and Siegler, Robert (1997). "Rethinking Infant Knowledge: Toward an Adaptive Process Account of Successes and Failures in Object Permanence Tasks," *Psychological Review*, 104, pp. 686–713.

Newton-Smith, W. H. (2001). "Hume," in W. H. Newton-Smith (ed.), *A Companion to the Philosophy of Science* (Oxford: Blackwell), pp. 165–8.

Nisbett, Richard and Ross, Lee (1980). *Human Inference: Strategies and Shortcomings of Social Judgment* (Englewood Cliffs, NJ: Prentice-Hall).

Papineau, David (1992). "Reliabilism, Induction, and Skepticism," *Philosophical Quarterly*, 42, pp. 1–20.

Peirce, Charles S. (1931–58). *Collected Papers of Charles Sanders Peirce* (Cambridge, MA: Harvard University Press).

Popper, Karl (1972). *Objective Knowledge* (Oxford: Clarendon Press).

Quine, W. V. O. (1969). *Ontological Relativity and Other Essays* (New York: Columbia University Press).

Ramsey, William (1992). "Connectionism and the Philosophy of Mental Representation," in Steven Davis (ed.), *Connectionism: Theory and Practice* (New York: Oxford University Press), pp. 247–76.

Ramsey, William (1999). "Connectionism, Philosophical Issues," in Robert A. Wilson and Frank C. Keil (eds.), *The MIT Encyclopedia of the Cognitive Sciences* (Cambridge, MA: MIT Press), pp. 186–7.

Reichenbach, Hans (1935). *Experience and Prediction* (Chicago: University of Chicago Press).

Russell, Bertrand (1912). *The Problems of Philosophy* (London: Oxford University Press).

Schmitt, Frederick F. (1994). *Socializing Epistemology: The Social Dimensions of Knowledge* (Lanham, MD: Rowman and Littlefield).

Skyrms, Brian (1975). *Choice and Chance: An Introduction to Inductive Logic* (Encino: Dickenson).

Solomon, Miriam (2001). *Social Empiricism* (Cambridge, MA: MIT Press).

Stalker, Douglas (ed.) (1994). *Grue: The New Riddle of Induction* (Chicago: Open Court).

Stove, David C. (1972). *Probability and Hume's Inductive Scepticism* (Oxford: Clarendon Press).

Strawson, Galen (1989). *The Secret Connexion* (Oxford: Clarendon Press).

Strawson, P. F. (1952). *Introduction to Logical Theory* (London: Methuen).

Stroud, Barry (1977). *Hume* (London: Routledge and Kegan Paul).

—— (1994). "Scepticism, 'Externalism', and the Goal of Epistemology," in *Understanding Human Knowledge* (Oxford: Clarendon Press, 2000), pp. 139–54.

Tooley, Michael (2003). "Causation and Supervenience," in Michael J. Loux and Dean W. Zimmerman (eds.), *The Oxford Handbook of Metaphysics* (New York: Oxford University Press), pp. 386–434.

Van Cleve, James (1984). "Reliability, Justification, and the Problem of Induction," *Midwest Studies in Philosophy*, 9, pp. 555–67.

Wilson, Kelly G, O'Donohue, William T., and Hayes, Steven C. (2001). "Hume's Psychology, Contemporary Learning Theory, and the Problem of Knowledge Amplification," *New Ideas in Psychology*, 19, pp. 1–25.

Winkler, Kenneth P. (1991). "The New Hume," *Philosophical Review*, 100, pp. 541–79.

Wright, John P. (1983). *The Sceptical Realism of David Hume* (Manchester: University of Manchester Press).

Further Reading

Bechtel, William and Abrahamson, Adele (1990). *Cognition and the Mind* (Oxford: Blackwell).

Bechtel, William and Graham, George (eds.) (1998). *A Companion to Cognitive Science* (Oxford: Blackwell).

Collier, Mark (1999). "Filling the Gaps: Hume and Connectionism on the Continued Existence of Unperceived Objects," *Hume Studies*, 25, pp. 155–70.

Howson, Colin (2001). *Hume's Problem: Induction and the Justification of Belief* (Oxford: Oxford University Press).

Kosslyn, Stephen M., and Koenig, O. (1992). *Wet Mind: The New Cognitive Neuroscience* (New York: The Free Press).

Rumelhart, David E. and McClelland, James L. (eds.) (1987). *Parallel Distributed Processing: Explorations in the Microstructure of Cognition*, 2 vols. (Cambridge, MA: MIT Press).

Swinburne, Richard (ed.) (1974). *The Justification of Induction* (Oxford: Oxford University Press).

26

The Humean Theory of Motivation and Its Critics

ELIZABETH S. RADCLIFFE

The Humean Theory of Motivation is one of the prominent theories in current philosophical psychology. It is not the same as Hume's theory of motivation, although it is derived from Hume's celebrated arguments in "Of the influencing motives of the will," a section in Book 2 of *A Treatise of Human Nature*. The Humean Theory of Motivation (hereafter, "HTM") is a contemporary theory concerning what is necessary for an agent to have a motive to action. According to the HTM, action always originates with a desire that furnishes the actor with a goal; that desire, when paired with a belief about how best to pursue the goal, comprises a motive. It follows on this view that neither a desire nor a belief by itself is sufficient to having a motive. Without an aim, or without a belief about how to achieve the aim I have, I cannot act, since my movement must be directed in some way by my psychological states in order to count as my action.

It is common in contemporary philosophy to see the HTM as a theory of *reasons* for action, when reasons are taken to be the motives or causes of action. Philosophers contrast "justifying" or "normative" reasons as considerations that purportedly show why an act is the best one or the right one by some rational standard, with "motivating" reasons, as reasons that can move us, but do not necessarily justify. The HTM as a theory of motivating reasons claims that the reasons for an act, the consideration(s) that explain why one does an act, or might do it, require a desire in addition to a belief.

Hume's own theory of motivation differs in small, but significant, ways from the HTM. On Hume's view, passions or emotions, which include desires, but are not restricted to them, are motives because they give us goals and initiate the impulse to act. That is, Hume did not think of motives as composed of beliefs plus desires. Hume saw various passions as able to set our ends: fear, joy, benevolence, anger, desire, for instance (T 2.3.9). On the current HTM, desire is taken to be the one passion that plays this role, perhaps on the assumption that the other passions can be defined in terms of it, and because desires have particular objects one is motivated to seek. Furthermore, on Hume's view, the beliefs that direct the passions to their goals are not reasons strictly speaking, even though they are necessary to produce the resulting behavior.

Hume never treats the beliefs that play a role in our acting as reasons, since his theory, which will be described in some detail shortly, implies that actions are not subject to rational assessment. However, he recognizes that we call actions rational or irrational in an informal or improper sense, depending on whether the beliefs on which they in part depend are true or false (T 2.3.3.6). Nonetheless, the HTM is distinctively derived from Hume in its insistence on the notion that having two distinct, irreducible mental states, belief and desire (belief and passion, for Hume), is necessary to produce action.

Opposition to both Hume's theory and the HTM comes from contemporary motivational rationalists who argue that Hume and Humeans have the wrong conception of reason and that, on a proper conception of it, we can understand that it is capable of motivating action. Some rationalists have argued that reasons can serve the functions of belief and desire at the same time. In the following, I plan to detail Hume's arguments about motivation, from which the HTM is derived. Then I offer an overview of the contemporary anti-Humean critique, to which I propose some brief replies. Ultimately I suggest that some of the differences between Hume and contemporary Humeans might save him from some of the current critique. No matter what, it will be clear that Hume's views on the passions, reason, and motivation have had an enduring impact on these discussions in philosophical psychology and related debates in moral philosophy.

The Defense of the Humean Theory of Motivation in Hume

What we call the Humean Theory of Motivation may be found as far back as Aristotle; it was anticipated quite explicitly in Hume's immediate predecessor, Francis Hutcheson (1742: 217–20), but the powerful arguments that have made us regard the view as distinctively from Hume come from *Treatise* 2.3.3. There Hume responds to a common, but, he thinks, mistaken notion that human reason and feelings can conflict with each over the determination of what one will or ought to do. For instance, my appetites prompt me to eat whatever appeals to me, while reason prompts me to eat more selectively for the sake of my health. Many believe that in cases of such conflict, the "commands" from reason determine what one ought to do. The issue from where morality derives and the issue over what motivates persons are separate topics, but Hume and many philosophers (some his contemporaries and some ours) argue that they are closely connected. Their view, moral internalism, is the view that to make a moral judgment or to accept one is to have a motive to behave according to it.

To the widespread view that feeling and reason can clash over "the direction of the will" (T 2.3.3.1), Hume replies by arguing for two theses: (1) that reason cannot by itself motivate us to action and (2) that reason and passion (feeling) can never be opposed to each other in directing our actions.

(1) When Hume argues that reason cannot motivate on its own, he begins with an analysis of reason. He describes reason as the power to discover truth and falsity, and maintains that it functions in two ways: to deduce necessary truths (the process of demonstration) and to discover facts about the world based on experience (the process of induction) (T 2.3.3.2–4). In the former case, reason discerns relations between

ideas or concepts, such as is done in deducing geometrical and mathematical relationships. Initiating action has to do with changing the world, and knowledge of conceptual relationships can do this only when applied to the world by people with goals or purposes, as they are in engineering. Then Hume considers induction: Does it have the power to motivate? Inductive reasoning, or reasoning from the particulars of experience, gives us beliefs about matters of fact; in other words, inductive reasoning is the inferring of causal connections that lead to belief in facts about the way the world is. But knowledge of these facts by itself cannot move us either. Writes Hume,

> 'Tis from the prospect of pleasure or pain that the aversion or propensity arises toward any object: And these emotions extend themselves to the causes and effects of that object, as they are pointed out to us by reason and experience. It can never in the least concern us to know, that such objects are causes, and such others effects, if both the causes and effects be indifferent to us. (T 2.3.3.3)

So, reason cannot initiate the impetus to action; we use it to discover what features things have and to what other things they are connected. But unless an emotion of attraction to or aversion from an object exists already (based on its pleasure- or pain-producing features), knowledge of the causes or effects of something will not influence behavior.

There has been some discussion among commentators about the import of Hume's notion just above that we are motivated by the prospect of pleasure and pain, since it sounds as though we develop a motive or passion upon the belief that an object will be pleasurable or painful – for instance, an aversion to medicine we believe tastes bitter. Since Hume indicates that beliefs come from reason, this seems to imply that reason does, after all, give us motives – e.g., motives to do what we believe will result in pleasure. One response is to argue that Hume never meant to say that *all* beliefs are derived from reason; rather, he thinks that some beliefs are non-inferential. Among them are beliefs about pleasurable and painful objects, which are acquired immediately upon a single experience with the object (Sturgeon forthcoming; Cohon 1997). However, I think there are several reasons to doubt this line (see Radcliffe 1999), the most compelling among them being that for Hume, there simply *are* no non-inferential beliefs about what exists in the world. For there to be a non-inferential belief in a matter of fact, the two objects of perception and the relation between them would have to be present in a single experience. Even simple perceptual beliefs go beyond what is immediately given in sense perception; in belief formation, our mind posits the world of objects, using inference to get there. Consequently, I think Hume's remarks about our being moved by considerations of pleasure and pain need to be understood in some other way than that motives are created by *beliefs* about pleasurable and painful objects. These beliefs certainly play a role in what we do, but the issue here is about the genesis of the passions that motivate.

(2) Hume defends his second thesis, that reason and passion cannot oppose each other, by explaining that since reason cannot give rise to an impulse to action, it surely cannot stand in opposition to such an impulse; only a passion can push against passion. Another way to approach the issue is to explain that reason yields representative states of mind; they represent or depict the world to us in certain ways and can do so truly

479

or falsely. Passions, Hume argues, are not representations; anger, for instance, is a feeling and is neither true nor false: "When I am angry, I am actually possest with the passion, and in that emotion have no more reference to any other object, than when I am thirsty, or sick, or more than five foot high" (T 2.3.3.5). Annette Baier, for one, has objected to such a characterization of the passions because contrary to what Hume seems to say here, they do have objects that I cognize: I am angry *at someone* for *doing something* (Baier 1991: 161–2). However, I actually think Hume makes a crucial point here, one on which the HTM turns. It is helpful to know that passions are what Hume calls "impressions of reflection." Impressions are the vivid and forceful experiences we have when we see, hear, taste, smell, or touch (impressions of sensation) or when we feel passions such as love, pride, envy, or desire (impressions of reflection). Ideas, on the other hand, are the less vivid and less lively mental states we have when we think about the original ones; ideas copy the impressions. The passions are vivid and forceful experiences that arise when we think about something that has felt pleasurable or painful (T 1.1.2.1). For instance, if I regularly feel pleasure in someone's company and reflect on aspects of my friend's personality and character that I enjoy, I acquire a feeling of admiration toward a good friend of mine. Passions then are not ideas, even though they occur after reflection. They are separate from the *thought* of the pleasure or the pain, which is an idea. The direct (as opposed to indirect) passions are those that arise immediately from reflection on pleasures and pains, without the need to call upon other perceptions. These are the ones that Hume seems to indicate are motives.

Given this, I think Hume's point in describing passions as non-representative is to say that impressions of reflection are not *copies* of anything, including the sources of the pleasures and pains upon which I reflect before I experience the passions. In other words, he sees representation as a function of something's copying a mental content. When I desire a glass of wine, my desire directs me toward the object, but the desire itself does not copy the impressions of the glass of wine, any more than my anger at a person copies my impressions of that person. Rather the feeling is a response to the ideas or representation of the qualities of the object, and the mental state that contains the reference to the object of my passion is actually the idea upon which the passion arises. My idea of the cup of Starbucks coffee I can get across the street is an idea of a source of pleasure that produces a desire for the coffee (not on its own, but given that I like strong, deep coffee), and in turn a desire to walk across the street. The reference to the coffee is contained in the idea of the pleasurable object, rather than in the desire itself.

Now, Hume says that we do sometimes call passions "unreasonable" in two senses, although the passion is never properly speaking unreasonable: First, when the emotion is founded on a false belief about objects; secondly, when we mistakenly choose insufficient means to the ends of our passion (T 2.3.3.7). Readers sometimes summarize Hume's views on these matters with his striking sentence: "Reason is, and ought to be the slave of the passions, and can never pretend to any other office than to serve and obey them" (T 2.3.3.4). But the idea here is not that reason is unimportant where action is concerned. Reason is as necessary as passion is to produce action. Hume in fact calls belief "requisite to exciting our passions":

As belief is almost absolutely requisite to the exciting our passions, so the passions, in their turn, are very favourable to belief; and not only such facts as convey agreeable emotions, but very often such as give pain, do upon that account become more readily the objects of faith and opinion. A coward, whose fears are easily awaken'd, readily assents to every account of danger he meets with; as a person of a sorrowful and melancholy disposition is very credulous of every thing, that nourishes his prevailing passion. (T 1.3.10.4)

There is a causal interaction between passions and beliefs, with the passionate nature, or dispositions, of a person providing a background for the production of each. It is in this sense that the passions take the lead and are master to reason. The passionate nature of a person will influence what that person believes, since those dispositions that constitute one's temperament also contribute causally to the resulting beliefs. A person of a cynical temperament more easily believes that his friends may lie to him than a sanguine person believes the same of hers. At the same time, specific beliefs about the world, which are acquired by reason, excite or awaken our passions by providing particular objects for our general dispositions. So, my appetite for sweets, along with the belief that the neighborhood bakery has sweets, would give me a motive to turn into the bakery on my way to work in the morning. The belief provokes an occurrent desire to act based on background dispositions, which are non-cognitive or non-representational states. It would thus be inaccurate to describe such cases as cases of beliefs producing motives; the beliefs are not productive of motives on their own, since the general, background passions exist prior to the belief states, and these are necessary as well.

In discussions of practical reasoning, Hume's view that reason gives us only factual beliefs that help us figure out how to get the objects of our passions is called an "instrumentalist" theory of practical reasoning. Theories of practical reasoning concern how we reason about what we ought to do, and some rationalist philosophers would say that classifying instrumentalism as a theory of "practical" reasoning at all is inaccurate (Korsgaard 1996). Philosophers who believe that reason is practical in a more robust sense reject Hume's division of reason into demonstration and causal reasoning. Instead, they look at it this way: "Theoretical" reason gives us beliefs about conceptual relations and beliefs about the world (Hume's two categories), and "practical" reason gives us conclusions about what we ought to do. When rationalists contend that practical reason tells us what we ought to do, they mean it tells us what ends to pursue, and not merely the means to the ends set by the passions. But on Hume's view, reason never gives me a belief of the form, "I ought to pursue A"; rather, it gives us beliefs of the form, "X causes Y." If this information is useful in procuring the object of a passion, I may utilize it, but whether or not I do has nothing to do with rationality.

Hume's opponents are committed to evaluating actions by two standards they see as derived from reason: the moral and the prudential. Hume treats morality in a separate discussion. But his theory of motivation has something to say about prudence. Everyone agrees that prudence is that trait which makes one look after one's long-term self-interest. So, it is prudent to do some things that I really don't like in this moment – getting a root canal or doing my exercises – because I am better off in the long run for doing them. We take for granted that doing what is in one's long-term self-interest, being prudent, is rational, and acting contrary to long-term self-interest is not. After all, long-term, or enlightened, self-interest conduces to survival with a certain quality of life, which is a natural goal of living things. So, practical rationality, on this view, is designed (in part) to tell us what we ought to do to fulfill our enlightened self-interest. (It is also supposedly designed to tell us what we ought to do, morally-speaking.) But Hume's reply is this:

> 'Tis not contrary to reason to prefer the destruction of the whole world to the scratching of my finger. 'Tis not contrary to reason for me to chuse my total ruin, to prevent the least uneasiness of an *Indian* or person wholly unknown to me. 'Tis as little contrary to reason to prefer even my own acknowledg'd lesser good to my greater. (T 2.3.3.6)

Why does Hume make these remarkable claims? His response here to his opponents follows consistently from the conclusion he has already defended: preferences (passions) are never contrary to reason, no matter what preferences they are, and neither are the actions we do in light of them. This is not to say that preferring the destruction of the world over getting a scratch on my finger is not evil, but it is not the sort of thing that can be evaluated by reason, which means that whether something is good or evil is not set by reason either. Although one might subscribe to the HTM without subscribing to Hume's theory of justification, it is important to bear in mind that for Hume, justification of desire lies in the shared sentiments of approval or disapproval we feel under the proper conditions toward the passions (desires) causing the action. The proper conditions are those in which we divest ourselves of particular prejudices that influence our feelings, and consider an agent's motivations from a perspective we share with others, from a general point of view (T 3.3.1.14–18). We generally approve of the philanthropist's desire to help the poor; we normally disapprove of the hoodlum's desire to steal a coat from the homeless person on the street.

Challenges to the Humean Theory of Motivation

Defenders of the HTM (among them Michael Smith, Simon Blackburn, and Bernard Williams) are persuaded that two distinct mental states, a cognitive one, belief, and a conative one, desire, are each necessary to motivation. One variation on the HTM, as I have mentioned, is to present it as a theory of reasons for action by seeing the beliefs that accompany our desires as reasons for the actions we do because of them. The opposition to the HTM is constituted by various rationalist theories of motivation that deny the necessity or the distinctness of the cognitive and conative states. In contemporary discussions, such theories typically have their roots in the work of Immanuel Kant (1786), but the view can be found as far back as Plato, and Hume himself formulated his views in reply to rationalists contemporary to him. Although theories of motivation and theories of justification are distinct, motivational rationalism is invariably bound to moral rationalism, since the judgments derived from reason that rationalists claim have motivating force are claims about morality.

Contemporary normative and motivational rationalism

There are three ways the motivational rationalist might try to defeat the Humean, each of which is defended in contemporary philosophy: (1) by arguing that practical reasons are not always dependent on our desires and that some of these reasons (those about morality at least) are sufficient for motivation (Korsgaard 1989); (2) by arguing that desires are ultimately produced by reason (Nagel 1970; Searle 2000); or (3) by arguing that one psychological state serves as both belief and desire (McDowell 1978; van Roojen 1995). The crucial point common to these views is that reason or cognition is in a critical respect antecedent to or independent of desire and thus the ultimate determinant of action, regardless of the practical import of desire.

(1) Christine Korsgaard, a defender of the neo-Kantian line, maintains that moral reasons motivate us. To understand that an action is required by morality, a function of reason, is to have a motive to do it under "normal" circumstances – i.e., insofar as the person is not suffering from weakness of will, regarded as a form of irrationality (Korsgaard 1989: 162–7). Because rational agents have freedom, their actions, *when* they are acting rationally, could never be caused by desires. Desires play a role in motivation only if we choose to make the fact of our having them practical reasons for us. Our desires determine attractions for us that Kant calls incentives; respect for the moral law is likewise an incentive. Every instance of action reflects a rational commitment to a maxim or principle of acting, and we make these rational commitments based on the incentives that are presented to us in deliberation. When we do our duty out of respect for the moral law, we have chosen to act on the maxim of doing what morality requires and of acting on desire only if it does not conflict with moral duty (p. 165). However, since we also have desires for certain ends, we might adopt a maxim or principle of action to get the things that we desire, even when it conflicts with moral duty. This is adoption of "the maxim of self-love" (pp. 163–5). Furthermore, Korsgaard argues that when one chooses the maxim of self-love, one has put one's will in the service of desire, thus restricting its freedom. Consequently, only when we choose the maxim of morality are we allowing ourselves to act freely (pp. 166–7).

Only on such a Kantian scenario, Korsgaard argues, can we derive a theory of practical reasoning. The Humean view rules out the possibility that reason chooses the goals or ends of action insofar as it begins with the notion that our ends are determined by our desires, which are not produced by reason. As I noted earlier, the notion that we can reason only about the means to our ends, the instrumentalist line, does not really qualify as an account of practical reasoning. According to Korsgaard, if such a line of reasoning only tells us what we will do, given a certain desire, then it cannot tell us what we ought to do. It makes no sense to see instrumental reasoning as giving us even contingent "oughts" ("you ought to go to the dentist if you want to get rid of your toothache"), since on this view, actions are a causal outcome of desires and beliefs. It is nonsense to tell a person that she ought to do what she cannot help but do (Korsgaard 1986: 311–14, 318–21). On Korsgaard's account of practical rationality, the maxims I choose set my ends and are subject to rational assessment. Her view implies that I can be irrational in one of two ways: I can choose the wrong maxim or, out of weakness of will, I may choose no maxim of action at all, even though

I know that I ought to choose the maxim of morality. Either way, I fail to do what I ought to do. Thus, according to the Korsgaardian/Kantian approach, the HTM presents the wrong picture of the scope and function of reason with regard to action.

(2) Thomas Nagel distinguishes what he calls motivated and unmotivated desires and claims that the Humean view involves a confusion of the two. Some desires, the unmotivated ones, simply come on us without prior thought. Hunger and thirst are among these. The motivated desires, on the other hand, are based upon reasons. For instance, I want to eat dinner because it will appease my hunger; I want the neighbors to turn down their stereo because I need peace and quiet to write. Nagel says:

> The claim that a desire underlies every act is true only if desires are taken to include motivated as well as unmotivated desires, and it is only true in the sense that *whatever* may be the motivation for someone's intentional pursuit of a goal, it becomes in virtue of his pursuit *ipso facto* appropriate to ascribe to him a desire for that goal. But if the desire is a motivated one, the explanation of it will be the same as the explanation of his pursuit, and it is by no means obvious that a desire must enter into this further explanation. (Nagel 1970: 29)

John Searle argues for a view closely aligned with Nagel's: There are some desire-independent reasons for action that, in giving rise to secondary desires, serve as motives (Searle 2001: 168–213). Rational action, however, is never *caused* by these reasons, since, he says, we are always free to act contrary to our current reasons. His view in general is that we create desire-independent reasons for ourselves by the commitments we make in acts, including speech-acts. Simply uttering "it is raining," with the intention to make the assertion that it is raining creates a reason "for accepting the logical consequences of one's assertion, for not denying what he has said, for being able to provide evidence for what he has said" (2001: 173). He then goes on to argue that these reasons are also motives because they may give rise to a secondary desire in the agent; they also serve as reasons for wanting to do that to which one is committed (pp. 176–7). Still, they are desire-independent because they require no pre-existing desire in one's motivational repertoire in order to count as reasons and serve as motives. When I order a beer at a bar, I have a reason to pay for it in virtue of my intending my behavior to place me under an obligation to pay for it; I needn't have a desire to pay for the beer, independent of this fact (p. 186). "[B]y freely undertaking to create a reason for myself, I have already manifested a desire that such and such be a reason for me" (p. 189). Citing Williams and Davidson, who include among desires or pro-attitudes such states as "dispositions of evaluation," "personal loyalties," "various projects" (Williams 1980: 105), and attitudes of holding something dear or thinking it dutiful or obligatory (Davidson 1963: 685–6), Searle charges defenders of the HTM with wanting to assimilate desire-independent reasons to desires.

> And the way they do this is to suggest that if we construe the set that includes beliefs and desires broadly enough, then a person's commitments, obligations, etc., are really members of that same set as desires. (Searle 2001: 170)

But this is mistaken, he argues; while my desire to eat chocolate may constitute a reason for my eating chocolate ice cream, the desire to fulfill my obligation is *derived from* a reason, the recognized obligation.

(3) Discussions of the HTM have also focused on ways to defend or attack the distinction between belief and desire. Michael Smith, a proponent of the HTM, defends the distinction between belief and desire in a crucial argument: For any person and that person's evaluation of (belief about) appropriate ends, it is possible that the person lacks the corresponding desire to take the proper means to those ends. This, Smith argues, is the case with weakness of will or depression, which are instances of irrationality where the agent knows what he should do but feels no motivation to do it (Smith 1994: 119–21). I will later refer to this argument as *"the belief-desire separability principle."* Smith also elaborates the difference between belief and desire in terms of "direction of fit," a characterization originally offered by Elizabeth Anscombe (Anscombe 1957: 256–7). Beliefs aim to fit the world and are true when they do; false beliefs are defective because they fail in this regard. Desires aim to have the world conform to them, and it is not a failing of a desire when the world does not change to fit it. Smith writes,

> The Humean says that we understand what it is for someone to have a motivating reason at a time by thinking of her as, *inter alia*, having a goal at that time (*"alia"* here includes having a conception of the means to attain that goal). That is, having a motivating reason just is, *inter alia*, having a goal. But what kind of state is the having of a goal? Which direction of fit does this state have? Clearly, the having of a goal is a state with which the world must fit, rather than vice versa. Thus having a goal is being in a state with the direction of fit of a desire. But since all that there is to being a desire is being a state with the appropriate direction of fit, it follows that having a goal is just desiring. (Smith 1994: 116)

So, Smith maintains that goal-directed explanations of behavior require making reference to states of mind distinct from belief – that is, different from ones that describe the world. To adopt a goal is not simply to believe, but to *what?* – To desire. He elaborates the distinction in terms of the functional roles of belief and desire, emphasizing that a belief that p tends to go out of existence in the presence of a perception with the content not-p, but a desire that p has the propensity to endure and disposes the subject to bring it about that p (p. 115). (Smith's account of the justification of desire is unlike Hume's, however, since Smith has a theory whereby desires are subject to rational assessment; see Smith: ch. 5. Whether one can consistently be a Humean about motivation and a non-Humean about justification is an interesting matter I have no room to pursue.)

I should note that not everyone is convinced that the belief/desire distinction is best articulated in terms of direction of fit. David Sobel and David Copp question the helpfulness of these concepts in distinguishing beliefs and desires and argue that there are some belief states that do not tend to go out of existence under the circumstances in which we would, according to Smith's distinction, expect them to; and there are some desires that do not endure where Smith's account alleges they would (Sobel and Copp 2001: 47–8). Obstinate beliefs, such as someone's belief in God, may not be affected when one acknowledges evidence to the contrary, such as the problem of evil. And a desire for a state of affairs might actually be diminished when the absence of that state of affairs persists. "Sue says that she desires that the 49'ers do well. But their not doing well tends to drive out of existence this desire" (p. 48). Furthermore, Sobel and Copp argue that direction of fit cannot be distinctive of belief and desire, since the functional test is not definitive. On the functional test, if an acquired psychological state with the content not-p drives a background psychological state with the content p out of existence, then the latter state is a belief. However, they argue, other psychological states exhibit this same relationship, and they are not beliefs. For instance, a new desire that not-p can drive out an intention to p; a desire to stay home for my summer vacation can drive out the intention to make a plane reservation (p. 50). This line of criticism does not entail that there is no distinction between belief and desire, but that perhaps it needs to be made in a different way.

However, the "direction of fit" paradigm has dominated recent discussions. Thus, some anti-Humeans argue that a single mental state can have both directions of fit and serve as belief and desire at the same time. The so-called "besire" view is attributed, for instance, to John McDowell by Michael Smith. McDowell's notion of the virtuous person has it that she conceives situations in such a way that disposes her to act in the appropriate way; so, for example, the virtuous person's conception of someone as sensitive and shy (a cognition) disposes that person to behave in certain ways toward the shy person, such as trying to make that person feel comfortable in public settings (McDowell 1978: 18–22). Thus, in moral argument, we try to change another's view and motivate the person at the same time, encouraging the proper besires. Mark van Roojen holds out for the possibility of one psychological state with two directions of fit, since he rejects the belief-desire separability principle (from Smith) this way:

> For the Humean's objection from weakness of will [the separability principle] . . . to work, the tendencies that constitute the functional role of mental states have to be exception-less laws. But such a requirement is too strong . . . The tendencies relied upon . . . are generalizations meant to cover the normal case. (van Roojen 1995: 47)

He thinks that it is reasonable, rather, to adopt the view that all things being equal, we are committed to ascribing a desire for the means when the agent has a positive evaluative belief about the end, arguing that evaluative beliefs are perhaps only different in degree from desires (p. 49).

Defenders of the HTM are by no means without resources to reply to their rationalist critics. The rationalist challenges are, in one form or another, attacks on the belief/desire distinction. The basic argument for their separability, that for any belief state (about good), we can conceive of one who is in that state, but lacks the relevant desire, really is logically compelling. I think van Roojen's objection to it mistakes a logical point for an empirical one. When the issue is the identity of a psychological state – whether normative beliefs just are besires, or one state with two directions of fit – then admitting it possible that there be an instance of a normative belief that is not a besire undermines that identity. All parties to the dispute admit that the concepts of belief and desire are not the same, but a defender of the besires view is contending that under certain conditions one state serves two functions. The problem with this proposal is that neither as introspectors of our mental states, nor as observers of the mental states of others, can we tell what it would be like to find a belief functioning as a desire (or a motive) on its own. We can identify a belief-state only by its role in our mental life, its role of representing the world to us in a certain way, and a desire-state only by its role of providing an impetus to change the world in a certain respect. So it looks as though there is no way to identify besires, since we cannot know, when we find our mind in a motivating state, that it is in that state just in virtue of a cognition. Or consider the following: If I find myself with a belief about my good – for instance, that eating chocolate is good for me – and I also find myself with the corresponding desire – in this case, the desire to eat chocolate – on what experiential basis can I claim that the belief and the desire are the same? My criterion of identity requires me to recognize them separately, and it would feel no differently to me if the belief and desire had the same referent than if they were two different states occurring to me simultaneously. In other words, empirical evidence cannot help here.

So is there instead a logical argument for the notion that some beliefs about goods or beliefs about duty and rightness are motives on their own? The line typically held by a motivational rationalist is that among persons' mental states, we find at least these three: (1) desires, often thought of as inclinations, which are non-rational impetuses to action; (2) non-motivating beliefs, which are beliefs without value content; and (3) motivating beliefs, which are beliefs with value content – about goods, right, or duty. On this view, my inclination for wine at dinner, an appetite, is a non-rational impulse or desire; my belief that the sun is the source of heat is a (non-motivating) belief; and my belief that I ought to tell the truth is a motivating belief or a besire. What distinguishes motivating beliefs from non-motivating beliefs on this view has to be just the content of the respective beliefs; a content concerning morality or prudence makes the cognition a besire. But none of this amounts to an *argument* that some beliefs motivate, that there are besires. Hume and many Humeans agree with the rationalist presumption that "morality" motivates us, but Humeans don't take this fact to justify the conclusion that beliefs about morality motivate. Hume himself also took this fact instead to justify the conclusion that morality must not be derived from reason, which many Humeans translate into the claim that moral judging is not a matter of belief formation alone. The proponents of the besire view could claim a stand-off here, maintaining that Hume's argument leaves it open that morality, which is not a matter of belief also, is a matter of besire. So far, the proposal that there are besires looks to be speculative, with no logical argument compelling us to accept it, while the empirical argument that psychological states must be discerned by function allows us to posit beliefs and desires, but not besires.

Another consideration is relevant to this debate. An adequate motivational psychology should offer an explanation of how we come to act on one motive rather than another. Recall that on Korsgaard's account of how we come to act on the motive that we do, we choose between the maxim of morality and the maxim of self-love. If we choose the latter, we have bound ourselves to be controlled by our desires or inclinations. We turn a desire into a motive when we make it a maxim to act on that particular desire. It follows on Korsgaard's view that there is no competition among motives, since after we have made a desire or respect for the moral law into a motive, we act on it, or at least we attempt to. This is because motives are not causes of action (as they are on the Humean view), but reasons on which action is (somehow) based. Consequently, weakness of will, when one does not do what one thinks to be right, is not due to a gap between motive and action, as it is on the Humean view; it is lack of motivation altogether (as it is in Smith's theory). Korsgaard's account does not violate Hume's "no opposition between reason and passion" thesis, but it leaves something crucial unexplained: Just how we come to choose what incentive we will make into a motive. This choice is described as free, uncaused, and made by reason, but on a theory where the only reasonable choice is the moral one, it is impossible to say anything about why one would ever choose to act on desire, or at least on a desire opposed to moral duty.

On a different rationalist view where value judgments are besires, it is possible to conceive of competition among motives; but then we need an explanation of how we end up choosing to act upon one rather than another. The explanation has to be offered in terms of either the content of the effective besires, or the strength with which the besire is held, since these are the only two relevant dimensions along which a belief can vary. Consider these two possibilities and where they lead.

The only explanation in terms of content that makes sense of our actions is that we always pursue what we believe at the time to be the greatest good, or the highest duty. This is the only possible explanation for our choices in terms of content, because motivating beliefs (besires) are distinct from non-motivating beliefs on the very grounds that the former concern goods or duties; so the good or duty that is effective in action at a certain time must be thought of as the highest in the moment. This view denies, however, that there can be any such thing as weakness of will, since weakness of will is doing something one believes to be wrong or something one believes to be less than the best (or on a view like Korsgaard's, lacking a motive to do what one thinks is the right or the best). This is problematic, since many motivational rationalists (of a Kantian type, not a Socratic type) admit the possibility of moral weakness.

Alternately, if the dimension in which we conceive competition between motives is that of strength, then the only plausible explanation of action on the view that beliefs are motives is that we act on our strongest evaluative belief (besire). For example, my choosing to go out to a movie instead of working on my article is explained by my believing more strongly at the time that seeing the movie is good than that continuing to work on the article is good. This means that if I hold the belief about the goodness of seeing a movie with greater *conviction* than alternative beliefs, it is the one which motivates me, even if I believe that my writing is a *greater* good in the moment than going to a movie is. On this view, strength of evaluative belief, rather than content, is determining my motivations. But this position also seems to deny weakness of will in the end. For when I do the action I do *not* consider best, I do it because I'm more *strongly convinced* of its goodness than I am of the alternative action's goodness. If I neglect to act on my belief about the highest good because I have doubts or lack conviction concerning it, then it seems I am not really suffering from any *motivational* weakness at all. I am actually following my strongest convictions about the relative goodness of my alternatives.

So on either explanation – in terms of content of belief or in terms of strength of belief – the view that some beliefs are motives (besires) leads to a denial of weakness of will. But the only way to account for the phenomenon of weakness is to distinguish beliefs from motives such that it makes sense to say that we can have a belief about the highest good or the highest duty or a most strongly held belief about morality that we don't act on.

Contemporary anti-psychologism

The anti-psychologists present a wider challenge to all standard theories of motivation, including rationalist ones, which depict reasons for action as psychological states. Jonathan Dancy's thesis is that reasons consist in states of affairs: My reason for grabbing an umbrella before I go out is *that* it is raining; your reason for eating a sandwich is *that* you are hungry. He argues, first, that reasons are independent of desires (Dancy 2000: ch. 2). He holds, as others have, that desires, excepting urges and inclinations, are grounded in reasons; what we want, we want for a reason. And ungrounded desires do not provide a reason to take the means to the end desired:

> Desires are held for reasons, which they can transmit, but to which they cannot add. Therefore, a desire for which there is no reason cannot create a reason to do what would subserve it. (p. 39)

Dancy argues that reasons are independent of beliefs (ch. 3). Duties are duties for (moral) reasons. They are objective, that is, dependent on the way things are, rather than subjective, that is, contingent on individual beliefs. I don't do anything wrong while in my car by going through a red light even if I mistakenly thought the light was green.

So, supposing that normative reasons are states of affairs, Dancy's next move is to show that all reasons for actions are actually normative reasons. His argument goes this way. All of us, including those who distinguish motivating from normative reasons, accept two constraints. (1) The "explanatory constraint" says that normative reasons must be able to explain motivating reasons. This is because there are cases where our motives are formed by reference to the considerations that make an action right. (2) The "normative constraint" says that motivating reasons must be capable of being among the reasons in favor of acting (in other words, we must be able to perform an action from the reasons that make it right). Dancy contends that his opponents cannot fulfill the normative constraint, since on their view, normative reasons are a different kind of thing from motivating reasons, with the latter being psychological states and the former being considerations that include normative facts about the world. The only way to fulfill the normative constraint is to see all reasons as one kind of thing, as states of affairs in the world (ch. 5). Even if the agent perceives the world to be other than the way it is, then the explanation of his action is still not in terms of his *beliefs*, but in terms of the *considerations* in light of which he acted, even though they are "non-factive" considerations.

Humeans would of course challenge the anti-psychologist's notion that all desires are had for a reason (that all are so-called "motivated" desires). I may want a coat due to its being cold, but if I didn't mind being cold, I wouldn't want the coat. So, my aversion to cold is also part of the reason I want a coat. My aversion to cold is of course rooted in my nature, which is itself part of the way the world is, but when Dancy says that all desires are reason-based and all reasons are states of affairs, he surely doesn't mean to reduce reasons to facts about human physiology and psychology. Dancy raises large questions about the nature of reasons, and his position can be challenged on grounds having to do with the complexities of the connection between belief and the circumstances that lead to belief, all of which are beyond the scope of this chapter.

489

Hume's Legacy

The debate over the motivating force of belief, whether there exist "besires," is a dispute in which Hume continues to be a player. His original arguments against motivational rationalism are still among the strongest threats to the theory, I think, because he recognizes (ironically) that this is a dispute that has to take place on logical grounds, not empirical ones. Empiricism can only do its work when some logical, conceptual, or functional parameters are set. If we are unable to identify beliefs apart from desires functionally, philosophers of mind are unable to say anything about them one way or the other.

Hume has resources, however, to rise above the debate between the psychologists and the anti-psychologists (or at least to fly under the radar of this dispute). Hume is a psychologist: To be sure he thinks motives are mental states. However, on Hume's theory, motivation is provided by passions of various kinds. Not all of them can be reduced to occurrent desires. So, he does not try, as some of the contemporary Humeans do, to explain how our motives are also reasons. He does not see passions as reasons for action, but as causes of action. It was part of his project to explain our actions causally, as all events are explained. Hence, he is not susceptible to the anti-psychologist arguments aiming to undermine the use of motivating reasons in explanations, since he does not appeal to motivating reasons. However, some argue that Hume's disengagement from this dispute is at a cost. If we are not moved by reasons, then our actions are not the result of choices, but of passions that we seem unable to control. He fails to account for freedom in the sense that rationalists think we have it. I think there are resources in Hume to argue that we can develop our passions, desires, and dispositions when we have them, but offering these arguments would require another discussion of great length. No matter what one's reaction to Hume and the HTM, it represents the naturalistic, empirical perspective on human motivation and has a permanent place in moral and motivational psychology.

See also 10 "Hume on the Direct Passions and Motivation"; 11 "Hume on Liberty and Necessity"; 12 "Hume on Moral Rationalism, Sentimentalism, and Sympathy"; 13 "Sympathy and Hume's Spectator-centered Theory of Virtue"

References

Anscombe, G. E. M. (1957). *Intention* (Oxford: Basil Blackwell).

Baier, Annette C. (1991). *A Progress of Sentiments: Reflections on Hume's "Treatise"* (Cambridge, MA: Harvard University Press).

Cohon, Rachel (1997). "Is Hume a Noncognitivist in the Motivation Argument?" *Philosophical Studies*, 85, pp. 251–66.

Dancy, Jonathan (2000). *Practical Reality* (Oxford: Oxford University Press).

Davidson, Donald (1963). "Actions, Reasons, Causes," *Journal of Philosophy*, 60, pp. 685–700; repr. in Donald Davidson, *Essays on Actions and Events* (Oxford: Clarendon Press, 1980, 2001).

Hutcheson, Francis (1742). *Illustrations on the Moral Sense*, in *Essay on the Nature and Conduct of the Passions and Affections, with Illustrations on the Moral Sense*, ed. Paul McReynolds (Gainesville, FL: Scholars' Facsimiles and Reprints, 1969).

Kant, Immanuel (1786). *Groundwork of the Metaphysics of Morals*, trans. Mary Gregor (Cambridge: Cambridge University Press, 1998).

Korsgaard, Christine M. (1986). "Skepticism about Practical Reason," in C. Korsgaard, *Creating the Kingdom of Ends* (Cambridge: Cambridge University Press, 1996).

—— (1989). "Morality as Freedom," in C. Korsgaard, *Creating the Kingdom of Ends* (Cambridge: Cambridge University Press, 1996).

McDowell, John (1978). "Are Moral Requirements Hypothetical Imperatives?" *Proceedings of Aristotelian Society*, supplement 52, pp. 13–29.

Nagel, Thomas (1970). *The Possibility of Altruism* (Princeton, NJ: Princeton University Press).

Radcliffe, Elizabeth S. (1999). "Hume on the Generation of Motives: Why Beliefs Alone Never Motivate," *Hume Studies*, 25, pp. 101–22.

Searle, John (2001). *Rationality in Action* (Cambridge, MA: MIT Press).

Smith, Michael (1994). *The Moral Problem* (Oxford: Blackwell Publishing).

Sobel, David, and Copp, David (2001). "Against Direction of Fit Accounts of Belief and Desire," *Analysis*, 61, pp. 44–53.

Sturgeon, Nicholas (forthcoming). "Hume on Reason and Passion," in Donald Ainslie (ed.), *Critical Essays on Hume's "Treatise"* (Cambridge: Cambridge University Press).

van Roojen, Mark (1995). "Humean Motivation and Humean Rationality," *Philosophical Studies*, 79, pp. 37–57.

Williams, Bernard (1980). "Internal and External Reasons," in B. Williams, *Moral Luck* (Cambridge: Cambridge University Press, 1981).

Further Reading

Audi, Robert (2001). *The Architecture of Reason: The Structure and Substance of Rationality* (Oxford: Oxford University Press).

—— (2002). "Prospects for a Naturalization of Practical Reason: Humean Instrumentalism and the Normative Authority of Desire," *International Journal of Philosophical Studies*, 10, pp. 235–63.

Blackburn, Simon (1998). *Ruling Passions* (Oxford: Clarendon Press).

—— (2000). "Kant versus Hume on Practical Reasoning," in D. P. Chattopadhyaya (ed.), *Realism: Responses and Reactions (Essays in Honour of Pranab Kumar Sen)* (New Delhi: Indian Council of Philosophical Research), pp. 462–80.

Cohon, Rachel and Owen, David (1997). "Hume on Representation, Reason and Motivation," *Manuscrito*, 20, pp. 47–76.

Cullity, Garrett and Gaut, Berys (eds.) (1997). *Ethics and Practical Reason* (Oxford: Oxford University Press).

Dancy, Jonathan (1993). *Moral Reasons* (Oxford: Blackwell).

Hubin, Donald (1999). "What's Special about Humeanism," *Noûs*, 33, pp. 30–45.

Karlsson, Mikael (2005). "Reason, Passion and the Influencing Motives of the Will," in Saul Traiger (ed.), *The Blackwell Guide to Hume's "Treatise"* (Oxford: Blackwell Publishing).

—— (2000). "Rational Ends: Humean and Non-Humean Considerations," *Sats-Nordic Journal of Philosophy*, 1, pp. 15–47.

—— (2001). "Cognition, Desire and Motivation: 'Humean' and 'Non-Humean' Considerations," *Sats-Nordic Journal of Philosophy*, 2, pp. 30–58.

Radcliffe, Elizabeth (1997). "Kantian Tunes on a Humean Instrument: Why Hume Is Not *Really* a Skeptic about Practical Reasoning," *Canadian Journal of Philosophy*, 27, pp. 247–69.

—— (2006). "Moral Internalism and Moral Cognitivism in Hume's Metaethics," *Synthese*.

Railton, Peter (2006). "Humean Theory of Practical Rationality," in David Copp (ed.), *The Oxford Handbook of Ethical Theory* (New York: Oxford University Press), pp. 265–81.

Sayre-McCord, Geoffrey (1997). "The Metaethical Problem," *Ethics*, 108, pp. 55–83.

Smith, Michael (2004). "Humean Rationality," in Alfred R. Mele and Piers Rawling (eds.), *The Oxford Handbook of Rationality* (Oxford: Oxford University Press), pp. 75–92.

Stampe, Dennis (1987). "The Authority of Desire," *Philosophical Review*, 96, pp. 335–81.

Wallace, R. Jay (1990). "How to Argue about Practical Reason," *Mind*, 99, pp. 355–85.

27

The Sources of Normativity in Hume's Moral Theory

TOM L. BEAUCHAMP

David Hume is almost universally placed in the canon of major moral philosophers, yet disagreement persists regarding even the fundamentals of his theory. The titles and arguments in his *Treatise* (T) and second *Enquiry* (EPM) concentrate on virtue and vice, and EPM is said by Hume to be primarily a book about personal merit and virtue (EPM 1.10). Beyond these elementary facts, Hume's moral theory has engendered numerous competing interpretations.

Several commentators have asserted that the theory is not normative (Glathe 1950: 99, 153; Kemp 1970: 51–2; Penelhum 1975: 131; Mackie 1980: 5–6; Fogelin 1985: 139–45; Hampton 1995: 66ff.; Schneewind 1998: 361). Although most comment-ators ignore this question, I regard it as pivotal: On the one hand, Hume's arguments spread into the normative territory of the *justification* and *correction* of moral beliefs. On the other hand, Hume never explicitly states that he defends a normative theory and at times seems intentionally to back away from the task.

One fortunate point of scholarly agreement on these issues is that Hume's theory of morals must be rendered consistent with his project of an experimental science of human nature. Some commentators hold that Hume is a naturalist who maps and explains reason, passion, instinct, moral sentiment, and that any apparent normativity can be reduced to this naturalistic framework. This interpretation of Hume's moral philo-sophy has many attractions (see Darwall 1995: 318). It is particularly attractive as an interpretation of the *Treatise*, by contrast to the second *Enquiry*, which is motivated by the goal of a theory of personal merit. In the case of both works, however, a natural-istic interpretation must be able to explain the role and status of normative discourse in Hume's writings.

I will argue that Hume relies upon and recommends normative standards both in his epistemology and in his moral philosophy. In my interpretation, Hume finds the core of morality in virtues of character that are universal and authoritative. This uni-versalism is not the sort found in rationalism: Morality, for Hume, is contingent on human nature, which alone is the source of moral universality. Whether Hume attempts to *justify* the proposition that morality is universally authoritative is a separate question, and one that I will not address.

I begin with the norms and normativity in Hume's science of human nature and in epistemology. Only afterwards do I discuss his moral philosophy.

Normativity in the Science of Human Nature

By a *norm* I mean a rule or standard having the authority to judge or direct human reasoning, behavior, or belief. A norm guides, commands, orders, requires, constrains, or commends. Norms state what ought to be done. Failure to comply with norms warrants censure, criticism, condemnation, disapproval, or some related form of negative appraisal. There are norms of linguistic usage, scientific method, epistemology, moral conduct, law, professional practice, etiquette, etc. By *normative* I mean the adjectival form of norm. There are normative guidelines, statements, commands, judgments, beliefs, rules, and the like. Epistemic justification of belief occurs if the relevant norms governing what ought to be believed are satisfied.

Hume's criteria for the formation, correction, and justification of inferences and beliefs are the sources of his normativity. Beliefs that stand in need of correction arise from limited information, biased hypothesis, superstition, prejudice, overconfidence in human testimony, speculative metaphysics, improper methodology, rash causal inference, and certain fictions of the mind.

The authority of experience as a source of normativity

The authority of experience

Hume's foundational normative category is *experience*. Experience is authoritative: "none but a fool or madman will ever pretend to dispute the authority of experience, or to reject that great guide of human life" (EHU 4.20). "Experience and observation" provide "the only solid foundation" of science and matters of fact (T Intro. 7).

Because inference-drawing is often rash and unjustified by broader experience (T 1.3.9.12), Hume "promises to draw no conclusions but where . . . authorized by experience" and says that he will speak "with contempt of hypotheses" (*Abstract*, para. 2). The word "authorized" is here normative, and experience is recommended as authoritative. At times Hume is bluntly normative: "'tis still certain we cannot go beyond experience; and any hypothesis, that pretends to discover the ultimate original qualities of human nature, ought at first to be rejected as presumptuous and chimerical" (T Intro. 8–9). Experience authorizes decisively negative evaluations; less decisively, it warrants positive conclusions.

The lack of authority in education

In contrast to this endorsement of experience is Hume's disdain for *education*, which he regards as doctrinal schooling lacking in authority and justification. It "commands our assent beyond what experience will justify" (T 1.3.9.12). Being "frequently contrary to reason" (i.e., contrary to evidence collected through experience), it is "never upon that account recogniz'd by philosophers" (T 1.3.9.19). Experience is its proper corrective.

The authority of the learned and the wise

In many passages Hume appeals to the "wise," the "learned," "those of success" in inquiry, what is "receiv'd by philosophy," "the man of the best sense and longest experience," and the like. These characterizations serve as tacit models of the standards that we *ought* to use in reasoning and belief-formation (T 1.3.13.12; 1.4.1.5; 1.4.4.1).

Norms of evidence and general rules

Despite experience's authority, Hume notes that even many beliefs derived from experience need correction and refinement: "Though experience be our only guide, ... this guide is not altogether infallible, but in some cases is apt to lead us into errors ... [A man could even] reason justly, and conformably to experience; but ... find himself mistaken" (EHU 10.3). Hume therefore discusses how judgments from experience should be tested and corrected. He advances norms of belief-formation and belief-correction and attempts to distinguish beliefs that should be accepted from those that should be rejected.

Building on a distinction of Locke's, Hume marks "the several degrees of evidence" that "distinguish human reason into three kinds, viz. *that from knowledge, from proofs, and from probabilities.*" All three kinds of reason incorporate a normative viewpoint (T 1.3.11.2; cf. EHU, note at section 6 title). Proofs are based on well-documented evidence of unexceptionable regularities. Proofs provide the model and highest standard for science because they provide the best evidence, leaving no room for warranted doubt. Probabilities form the remaining class of arguments from experience.

Whereas demonstrative reasoning must, to be authoritative, conform to the norms of demonstrative reasoning (e.g., as found in geometry, algebra, and arithmetic: EHU 4.1), proofs and probabilities are authoritative when they conform to the norms of inductive reasoning, proofs being distinguished from probabilities by "a superior kind of evidence" (T 1.3.11.2). In "Rules by which to judge of causes and effects" (T 1.3.15), Hume attempts to "fix some general rules ... by which we *ought* to regulate our judgments concerning causes and effects" (T 1.3.13.11; italics added). They contain the "logic" that should guide reasoning about matters of fact (T 1.3.15.11).

Having recommended these rules as authoritative for science and all factual reasoning, Hume issues a warning about the uncritical use of general rules. Not all rules derived from induction deserve the status of norms. In his section on "unphilosophical probability" (which treats of *improper* influences on belief), Hume notes that some rules are formed rashly. These rules may express prejudice:

> A *fourth* unphilosophical species of probability is that deriv'd from *general rules*, which we rashly form to ourselves, and which are the source of what we properly call PREJUDICE. An *Irishman* cannot have wit, and a *Frenchman* cannot have solidity; ... they must be dunces or fops in spite of sense and reason. Human nature is very subject to errors of this kind. (T 1.3.13.7)

Hume is asserting that we sometimes unreflectively transfer customary associations formed from experience to objects that are not sufficiently of the same type (T 1.3.13.8, 2.2.5.12–13, 3.2.9.3). "The imagination naturally carries us to a lively conception of the usual effect, tho' the object be different in the most material and most efficacious circumstances from that cause." Such inference is the result of what Hume calls a "first influence" of general rules. This first influence, he argues, should be countered or augmented by "a second influence of general rules" in which "the more general and authentic operations of the understanding" and "the most establish'd principles of reasoning" prevail (T 1.3.13.12, 2.2.8.5). In this way, rules of first influence, themselves derived from experience, are corrected by the broader norms "by which we ought to regulate our judgment." "Wise men" follow the second influence, which "implies a condemnation" of the first influence (T 1.3.13.11–12). Hume is here expounding a norm of how we ought to reason in science and philosophy. (Cf. Martin 1993: 250–1; Lyons 2001: 252–4.)

Normativity in Epistemology

I will now attempt to fill out Hume's normative landscape in epistemology. I call the features in this landscape *norms* because they state the conditions of right reasoning (how we ought to reason) and determine the authoritativeness of judgments, inferences, beliefs, and rules. A good example of these norms appears in Hume's introduction to the subject of miracles:

> I flatter myself, that I have discovered an argument . . . which, if just, will, with the wise and learned, be an everlasting *check to all kinds of superstitious delusion* . . .
>
> A wise man . . . proportions his belief to the evidence. In such conclusions as are founded on an infallible experience, he . . . regards his past experience as a *full proof* of the future existence of that event. In other cases, he proceeds with more caution: He weighs the *opposite experiments*: He considers which side is supported by the *greater number* of experiments: To that side he inclines, with doubt and hesitation; and when at last he fixes his judgment, the evidence exceeds not what we properly call *probability*. (EHU 10.2, 10.4; italics added)

Hume here moves, in the course of two sentences, from the model of *full proof* to *opposite experiments* and on to "which side is supported by the *greater number* of experiments." I begin with the notion of "greater number" and then return to the other two.

The quantity norm

"Greater number" refers to extensive experience (multiple experiences). This quantitative consideration of inductive support is, in specifiable circumstances, authoritative for belief: "[W]hen we transfer the past to the future, the known to the unknown, every past experiment has the same weight, and . . . 'tis only a superior number of them, which can throw the ballance on any side" (T 1.3.12.15). The authority of inductive conclusions and general rules increases as the supporting experiences increase. Even in the class of proofs, those proofs that rest on more extensive acquaintance are "superior" to others. I will call this norm that beliefs should be formulated on the basis of multiple experiences the *quantity norm*. (Cf. Lyons 2001: 258–65.)

The uniformity norm

"Uniform" and "infallible" join other terms in Hume's vocabulary, such as "constant" and "regular," to point to the authority of uniformity: "Where . . . experience is not entirely uniform on any side, it is attended with an unavoidable contrariety in our judgments" (EHU 10.6), but "a uniform experience amounts to a proof" (EHU 10.12). The forms of uniformity found in probabilities can be evidential, but they are deficient by comparison to the greater uniformity found in proofs. Hume's norm that the authority of beliefs increases with uniformity I will call the *uniformity norm*.

The experiment norm

Hume links *uniformity* to *experimentation*: "It is only after a long course of uniform experiments in any kind, that we attain a firm reliance and security" (EHU 4.20). "Experiments" and "experimental" often mean nothing more for Hume than based on experience or observation, but he also uses "experimental," more precisely, to refer to the controlled "observation of those particular effects, which result from . . . different circumstances and situations" (T Intro. 8). Hume admires the experimental methods used in natural philosophy, while recognizing their limits: "our progress in natural philosophy is chiefly retarded by the want of proper experiments and phænomena" (EHU 7.2; cf. T 1.3.15.11). Hume subscribes to progressive experimental inquiry: "in order to arrive at the decisive point, we must carefully separate whatever is superfluous, and enquire by new experiments, if every particular circumstance of the first experiment was essential to it" (T 1.3.15.11). I will refer to this norm that the authority of beliefs increases as sound experimental methods are used as the *experiment norm*.

The reliable-principles norm

Hume distinguishes between reliable and unreliable principles of the mind:

> I must distinguish in the imagination betwixt the principles which are permanent, irresistible, and universal; such as the customary transition from causes to effects, and from effects to causes: And the principles, which are changeable, weak, and irregular. . . . The former are the foundation of all our thoughts and actions . . . The latter . . . take place in weak minds . . . [T]he former are receiv'd by philosophy, and the latter rejected. (T 1.4.4.1)

The "universal," "permanent," "constant," "established," and "stable" principles of human nature are those of *reasoning*. These principles stand in contrast to unstable and untrustworthy principles. Stable principles supply norms that are reliable and authoritative for belief. General rules formed on the basis of these permanent principles function to correct the judgments deriving from weak, irregular principles. Inductive rules descend from these permanent features of mind (T 1.3.13.11–12). A steady application of these rules lends authority to judgments. I will call this standard that permanent and universal principles of the human frame are (or yield rules that are) reliable and authoritative for belief the *reliable-principles norm*.

The impartiality norm

In the passage from his treatment of miracles Hume submits that we should follow the wise and learned and avoid delusion. In related passages, he observes that we should avoid the effects of limited information, education, prejudice, bias, bigotry, and the like by preserving what he calls "a proper impartiality in our judgments. We should "wean our mind from all those prejudices, which we may have imbibed from education or rash opinion" (EHU 12.4). I will call Hume's standard that belief-formation and belief-correction should occur by taking an impartial point of view the *impartiality norm*.

To conclude now this discussion of Hume's epistemology, he proposes that the norms I have identified should guide all scientific inquiry. The authority of beliefs, judgments, and rules increases as these norms are followed, and decreases as they are not satisfied. Epistemic justification of belief occurs if these norms have been satisfied. I have not considered whether Hume offers a justification of these norms in terms of, say, utility or stability; nor have I considered whether Hume is entitled to or is consistent in the appeal to these norms (Loeb 2002: 22ff.; Lyons 2001: 259, 274–7; Strawson 1985: 19). I have only attempted to show that Hume's science of human nature commits him to them and that he embraces them. With this thesis in hand, I move now to questions of normativity in Hume's account of morals.

Normativity in Moral Philosophy

That Hume's normativity carries over to his moral philosophy is unsurprising inasmuch as his epistemology and moral philosophy are component parts of the larger program of a philosophy of human nature. His philosophy is constructed, from its foundations, on a theory of authoritative experience that has both normative and nonnormative components, as I argued earlier. The moral philosophy shows this dual commitment in its use of the term "experience" and in notions such as "impartiality."

However, there is not a perfect transfer of normativity from epistemology to moral philosophy. To see why, I start, as before, with the attractions of a naturalistic interpretation.

Naturalism and the foundations of morals in sentiment

Hume says that virtue and vice, indeed all moral good and evil, are "distinguish'd by our *sentiments*, not by *reason*" (T 3.3.1.22). Morality

> consists not in any *matter of fact*, which can be discover'd by the understanding . . . [M]oral-ity is not an object of reason. But can there be any difficulty in providing, that vice and virtue are not matters of fact, whose existence we can infer by reason? Take any action allow'd to be vicious: Wilful murder, for instance. Examine it in all lights, and see if you can find that matter of fact, or real existence, which you call *vice*. In which-ever way you take it, you find only certain passions, motives, volitions, and thoughts. There is no other matter of fact in the case. The vice entirely escapes you, as long as you consider the object. You never can find it, till you turn your reflection into your own breast, and find a sentiment of disapprobation, which arises in you, towards this action. *Here is a matter of fact; but 'tis the object of feeling, not of reason.* It lies in yourself, not in the object. Vice and virtue, therefore, may be compar'd to sounds, colours, heat and cold, which, according to modern philosophy, are not qualities in objects, but perceptions in the mind. (T 3.1.1.26; italics added)

This passage asserts that vice and virtue are *not matters of fact gleaned from reason* (or the understanding) by observing objects; they are *matters of fact gleaned from sentiment* (or feeling) directed toward objects. If we focus only on the physical or psychological properties of an object (e.g., the physical properties of an act of killing or the motive to kill), we will not detect virtue and vice, because they require an internal sentiment of approbation or disapprobation of observers directed at the object.

Hume compares virtues and vices to secondary qualities such as sounds and colors. Modern philosophy, in his interpretation, regards secondary qualities as perceptions in the mind, not as (primary) qualities in objects. Primary qualities are in objects, whereas secondary qualities are not in objects, though the latter are caused to appear to us by the objects. Secondary qualities are vulgarly attributed to external objects (red is thought to be in the rose), just as virtues are vulgarly attributed to persons (benevolence is thought to be in the person). In short, Hume holds that both virtues and secondary qualities of objects require subjective contributions for their existence. (For confirmation of this view as Hume's, see his letter of March 16, 1740, to Hutcheson, in Greig 1932: 1, 39–40. This letter repeats the words of the *Treatise* above and shows that the comparison to secondary properties is central to Hume's thinking. See also Hume's explicit statements in "The Sceptic," in Miller, ed., 1987: 166n.)

When we judge certain mental qualities of persons to be *virtues or vices*, we add a perception comparable in status to a secondary quality. This moral perception is directed at some existing mental quality in the person, which Hume likens to a primary quality. A motive or character trait of helping others is an example of a real quality, whereas a sentiment of approval of this quality that is *projected* as a property of the object (being in fact a creation of the mind) is an example of an added quality:

> [T]he distinct boundaries and offices of *reason* and of *taste* are easily ascertained. The former conveys the knowledge of truth and falsehood: The latter gives the sentiment of beauty and deformity, vice and virtue. The one discovers objects, as they really stand in nature, without addition or diminution: The other has a productive faculty, and gilding or staining all natural objects with the colours, borrowed from internal sentiment, raises, in a manner, a new creation. (EPM App. 1.21)

In asserting that the faculty of taste "gilds" objects, Hume does not deny that we gild qualities that the objects actually possess. Of course they possess these qualities. A truthful person objectively has the quality or trait of truthfulness. The truthful person is gilded with the *virtue* of truthfulness by adding the projected sentiment of approbation. The virtue of truthfulness requires a universality of impartial public approbation, whereas the objective property of being truthful does not. Many qualities or traits of persons are *not* gilded by sentiment and therefore are not virtues. For example, combativeness and shyness are not virtues, though in principle they could be virtues if human nature led us to respond with approbation to these mental qualities in the way we do to truthfulness.

We *correctly* attribute virtue to a person only if the person in fact possesses the properties (the mental qualities, principles, or motives) that cause, universally, the subjective response of approbation. In this respect, a person can be virtuous whether or not particular individuals notice or feel that the person is virtuous (T 3.3.1.19). This theory of the apprehension and status of moral qualities is analogous to Hume's theory of the apprehension and status of the metaphysical quality of necessary connection: Objective regularities (i.e., constantly conjoined relata) underlie judgments of causal connection; these causal judgments gild the regularities by the projection of feelings of necessary connection. We attribute causation to objects or events through causal inference, but we *correctly* attribute causal connections only if universal regularities in fact exist. In this respect causal regularities exist whether or not persons make causal inferences.

Hume says that both the real quality and the added quality are matters of fact. This thesis seems the correct interpretation of Hume, yet it is puzzling for two reasons. First, he appears to say that evaluative statements (*ought* statements) cannot be derived from factual statements (*is* statements) (T 3.1.1.27). Second, he appears to say that matters of taste are not matters of truth (cf. EPM 1.5). These textual puzzles cannot be adequately addressed here, but it is worth noting that Hume does have one ready answer. Hume thinks of an object of reason and truth in terms of the real qualities of objects, by contrast to the qualities that we add to them through subjective experience. Even a full and comprehensive knowledge of all of the real properties of objects would not disclose vice or virtue, because they emerge only when we add properties. Therefore evaluative statements cannot be merely statements *about the objects*.

Statements about sentiments are *factual* statements; they simply are not statements *about the objects* at which sentiments are directed. Facts of morals derive from facts about sentiments as these sentiments are directed at objects (the objects being mental qualities). So interpreted, Hume seems to be a naturalist in moral theory. Nicholas Sturgeon has set out in commendable detail such a reductive naturalistic interpretation, and I will not directly challenge it. That is, I will not attempt to refute the thesis that Hume's theory of normativity in morals is a *reductive* naturalism; nor will I attempt to determine whether moral beliefs are true or false in Hume's theory. However, I will attempt to show that Hume's moral theory is not a *subjective* naturalism.

A subjective interpretation of Hume's moral theory has been championed by numerous Hume scholars (perhaps most impressively and influentially by Mackie, 1980, pp. 64–73). Sturgeon himself is inclined to subjectivism in contending that virtue and vice are entirely matters of feeling for Hume (Sturgeon 2001: 6–7, 19), but reductivism does not seem to me to require subjectivism. In any event, and whatever Sturgeon's precise position, I will now argue that Hume insists on *objectivity* in morals, in particular the objectivity of judgments about virtue. (For more robust objectivist interpretations than my own, see Norton 1982: 109–20, 135, 141–5; Norton 1985; and Baier 1991: 193–5; for a weaker objectivist interpretation, see Korsgaard 1996: 55–63.)

The definition of virtue

Hume's definition of "virtue" provides commanding evidence that he is no pure subjectivist: "It is the nature, and, indeed, the definition of virtue, that it is *a quality of the mind agreeable to or approved of by every one, who considers or contemplates it*" (EPM 8, note to title, and cf. App. 1.10). A virtue for Hume is a fusion of two components: (1) an objective mental quality in the person contemplated (the person judged to have a virtue), and (2) a subjective feeling of approbation by all who (impartially) contemplate (judge) the person. The latter feeling is not that of a single individual (hence "every one" in the definition). It is a human perception that all impartial persons experience. Neither component (1) nor component (2) by itself qualifies as a virtue. A mental quality is a virtue if and only if it evokes universal commendation in impartial persons; a mental quality is a vice if and only if the quality evokes universal condemnation in impartial persons.

The sense of virtue and the entitlements of the virtues

Even if Hume's interests in morals are primarily naturalistic (matter of fact, empirical, psychological, and the like), his theory of the value of the virtues also acknowledges their moral authority and presents them as models of proper conduct (and motive). Here is a typical passage.

> IT may be esteemed, perhaps, a superfluous task to prove, that the benevolent or softer affections are ESTIMABLE . . . The epithets *sociable, good-natured, humane, merciful, grateful, friendly, generous, beneficent*, or their equivalents, are known in all languages, and universally express the highest merit, which *human nature* is capable of attaining. (EPM 2.1)

It may be esteemed a *superfluous task* to prove that these affections are estimable because every unbiased person ("universally") knows that they are estimable. Hume thinks it is a "reasonable presumption" that anyone who disagrees with this normative appraisal is following a perverted system or hypothesis (EPM 9.1–13). To say that the affections listed are *estimable* is to say that they are worthy and deserving of esteem and respect. These properties "express the highest merit." Hume often represents the virtues as estimable, agreeable, amiable, and the like. He does not in these passages say merely that these qualities are *regarded as* estimable or that he can *explain* why they are judged estimable (though he does assert this). He says that these qualities *are* estimable, desirable, amiable, agreeable, and the like (T 3.2.1.6, 3.3.1.9, 3.3.4.2; EPM 1.10, 2.1, 2.3, 3.48, 5.4).

Hume sometimes lavishly praises the virtues, only to realize that too much commendation has crept into his philosophy. He then pulls back:

> But I forget, that it is not my present business to recommend generosity and benevolence, or to paint, in their true colours, all the genuine charms of the social virtues. These, indeed, sufficiently engage every heart, on the first apprehension of them; and it is difficult to abstain from some sally of panegyric, as often as they occur in discourse or reasoning. But our object here being more the speculative, than the practical part of morals, it will suffice to remark, (what will readily, I believe, be allowed) that no qualities are more *entitled* to the general good-will and approbation of mankind, than beneficence and humanity, friendship and gratitude, natural affection and public spirit. (EPM 2.5; italics added. I return to the theme of painting and why Hume avoids it in the final section below.)

501

Even in backing away from the tasks of commending and painting, Hume here displays a normative commitment: "no qualities are more *entitled* to the general good-will and approbation of mankind."

Some of Hume's passages suggest that *common life* is the ultimate source of authority in his virtue ethics (EPM 9.3), but the deepest explanation of the authority of morals for Hume is *human nature*, which contains "a sense of morals [that] is a principle inherent in the soul." "All lovers of virtue (and such we all are in speculation, however we may degenerate in practice)" appreciate that "moral distinctions [are] deriv'd from so noble a source" (T 3.3.6.3). The moral sense has a second-order capacity to reflectively look at and approve its own first-order moral judgments. In this way the moral sense comes to see its own force and authority, as well as that of the principles of human nature from which it is derived. Here is Hume's statement in the "Conclusion" to Book 3 of the *Treatise*:

> [T]his sense must certainly acquire new force, when reflecting on itself, it approves of those principles, from whence it is deriv'd, and finds nothing but what is great and good in its rise and origin . . . According to [my] system, not only virtue must be approv'd of, but also the sense of virtue: And not only that sense, but also the principles, from whence it is deriv'd. So that nothing is presented on any side, but what is laudable and good. (T 3.3.6.3. Contrast the interpretation of this passage in Korsgaard, 1996, pp. 62–5.)

No deeper appeal to the authority of morals is available to Hume, because there is no source or sanction of moral good or virtue outside of the sense of morals itself. Ultimately we can judge the authority of morals only from the moral point of view, circular as this claim may seem. While we could, of course, attempt to evaluate or warrant moral judgments and the sense of morals from some perspective outside of morals, such as self-interest, the authority of morals – as Hume understands morals – does not derive from a nonmoral point of view. Any point of view external to morals, even if itself normative, will fail to justify morality or determine whether a judgment or sense is *morally* good or virtuous. Naturalism may be able to explain our moral constitution, but it cannot account for the authority of morality.

Universal sentiment, reliable principles, and impartiality

To appreciate the spread of Hume's normative moral commitments, I return now to two of the norms outlined earlier in discussing his epistemology; later a third will be considered.

The reliable-principles norm and the impartiality norm in moral theory

Morality is derived from sentiment, but how and with what authority? What is required of us in order to effect the proper sentiment? In a famous passage, Hume says:

> The *notion of morals* implies some *sentiment common to all mankind*, which recommends the same object to general approbation, and makes *every man, or most men, agree* in the same opinion or decision concerning it. It also implies some sentiment, so *universal and comprehensive* as to extend to all mankind . . . Whatever conduct gains my approbation,

by touching my humanity, procures also the applause of all mankind, by affecting the same principle in them: But what serves my avarice or ambition pleases these passions in me alone . . . [Moral sentiments are] universal sentiments of censure or approbation, which arise from humanity, or from views of general usefulness and its contrary. VIRTUE and VICE become then known: Morals are recognized. (EPM 9.5, 9.8; italics added)

Many beliefs and sentiments held by individuals are particular to them or their cultures – e.g., the beliefs that meat-eating is a vice or that living by the creeds of a particular religion is virtuous. These beliefs and sentiments are not authoritative or reliable beyond the norms accepted by the individual or the local community in which they are resident. However, some judgments and beliefs derive from universally shared, morally-authoritative sentiments of humanity. The notion of morals and all moral notions have their normative foundation in these reliable sentiments.

In speaking of universally shared opinion, "universally" does not for Hume refer to all persons who have opinions. He is referring exclusively to *impartial* persons who take the moral point of view. His theses about universality do not apply to madmen, fiends, knaves, hate-saturated warriors, malicious ideologues, those "in a fever," those misinformed about relevant objects, the extremely selfish, the indoctrinated, the depraved, religious zealots, and all whose faculties of judgment are not in a "sound state." They are hardened against the humanity in their person; prejudice blocks, distorts, or destroys moral sentiment as well as moral motivation (EPM 9.6–8, App. 1.12; "Of the Standard of Taste," paras. 12–13, in Miller, ed., 1987).

Hume's appeals to impartial sentiment in morals (moral judgment) are analogous to his appeals to impartial inductive inference (factual judgment) in science. In each instance he relies upon both the reliable-principles norm and the impartiality norm. Like impartial and extensive inductive inference, impartial and informed moral judgment is a reliable source of belief about the mental qualities that constitute personal merit (the virtues). Just as impartial inductive inference determines what ought to be believed in science, so impartial and informed moral sensibility that yields "the proper sentiment" determines what is morally authoritative. (A condition of obtaining the proper sentiment is "a proper discernment of its object" [EPM 1.9] – a related theory, but not one we need explore here.)

Hume more assumes than argues that we ought to remain impartial in reaching moral conclusions, but impartiality plainly functions for him as a normative standard. The moral point of view itself requires impartiality. The following passage deserves more notice than it has received:

'Tis seldom men heartily love what lies at a distance from them, and what no way redounds to their particular benefit; as 'tis no less rare to meet with persons, who can pardon another any opposition he makes to their interest, however justifiable that opposition may be by the general rules of morality. Here we are contented with saying, that reason requires such an impartial conduct, but that 'tis seldom we can bring ourselves to it, and that our passions do not readily follow the determination of our judgment . . . When we form our judgments of persons, merely from the tendency of their characters to our own benefit, or to that of our friends, we find so many contradictions to our sentiments in society and conversation . . . that we seek some other standard of merit and demerit. (T 3.3.1.18)

Hume here, and in related passages (T 3.1.2.4, 3.3.1.14–16), asserts that morally astute persons accept the impartiality standard as having moral authority. Only this impartiality fosters the proper distance from self-interest, enabling us to reach the same judgments that other impartial persons reach.

Hume's most celebrated passage on universality and impartiality in morals appears in EPM:

> When a man . . . bestows on any man the epithets of *vicious* or *odious* or *depraved*, he . . . expresses sentiments, in which, he expects, all his audience are to concur with him. *He must here, therefore, depart from his private and particular situation, and must choose a point of view, common to him with others*: He must move some universal principle of the human frame . . . The humanity of one man is the humanity of every one; and the same object touches this passion in all human creatures. (EPM 9.6; some italics added)

Hume is distinguishing individual from universal responses, and limiting the scope of the universal to disinterested persons. The following passages from the *Treatise* add perspective:

> [E]very particular person's pleasure and interest being different, 'tis impossible men cou'd ever agree in their sentiments and judgments, unless they chose some common point of view, from which they might survey their object, and which might cause it to appear the same to all of them. (T 3.3.1.30)
>
> In order, therefore, to . . . arrive at a more *stable* judgment of things, we fix on some *steady* and *general* points of view; and always, in our thoughts, place ourselves in them, whatever may be our present situation. (T 3.3.1.15)

We should take the impartial point of view in making moral judgments in order to correct our limited or biased opinions, thereby taking the moral point of view. Similarly, we should take the impartial point of view in making scientific judgments in order to correct our assumptions and hypotheses, thereby taking the scientific point of view. A person who fails to adopt an impartial point of view loses moral authority in judgment, whereas the person who judges impartially gains moral authority. A "judicious spectator" (T 3.3.1.14), then, ought to retreat from his or her "private and particular situation" – avoiding the effects of education, prejudice, bias, hate, bigotry, rashness, temporal or relational remoteness, and the like – to find the impartial perspective. Only then are we able to "correct the momentary appearances of things [and] overlook our present situation" of partiality (T 3.3.1.16), and judge morally (T 3.1.2.4).

Hume is not centering his theory around our actual feelings of approbation or disapprobation on any given occasion, but rather around those feelings of approbation and disapprobation that we ought to have, which are those feelings that all persons would have if they were to adopt the morally correct, impartial point of view. Hume recognizes that we often judge persons close to us more favorably than we judge persons remote from us, even though their actions or character are relevantly similar. This reaction is understandable, but from the moral point of view such judgments need correction (T 3.3.1.15, 3.3.3.2; EPM 5.42). These judgments are based on a bias of proximity to which we are all subject, but which can be corrected.

Finally, it is worth noting that Hume never asserts that *disinterested* judgment is solely sufficient to justify belief. Moral judgment must also be properly *informed* in order to be suitable:

> But in order to pave the way for such a sentiment, and give a proper discernment of its object, it is often necessary, we find, that much reasoning should precede, that nice distinctions be made, just conclusions drawn, distant comparisons formed, complicated relations examined, and general facts fixed and ascertained . . . [I]n many orders of beauty . . . it is requisite to employ much reasoning, in order to feel the proper sentiment; and a false relish [a preference developed from an inadequate understanding] may frequently be corrected by argument and reflection. There are just grounds to conclude, that moral beauty partakes much of this latter species, and demands the assistance of our intellectual faculties, in order to give it a suitable influence on the human mind. (EPM 1.9)

To summarize, I have argued in this section that Hume uses both the reliable-principles norm and the impartiality norm to reach the conclusion that we should correct for partiality and adopt a steady, disinterested, and informed point of view.

Discovering and cataloguing the virtues and vices

The experiment norm in moral theory

Hume also utilizes the experiment norm in an attempt to identify the framework for and the catalogue of the virtues and vices. His ambition is to distinguish the virtuous from the nonvirtuous and then to identify the common qualities that make virtues virtues and vices vices.

> We shall analyze . . . what, in common life, we call PERSONAL MERIT: We shall consider *every attribute of the mind*, which renders a man an object either of esteem and affection, or of hatred and contempt . . . The . . . universal [capacity for moral judgments found] among mankind, gives a philosopher sufficient assurance, that he can never be considerably mistaken in *framing the catalogue* [of the virtues and vices] . . . The only object of reasoning is to discover the circumstances on both sides, which are common to these qualities; to observe that particular in which the estimable qualities agree on the one hand, and the blameable on the other; and thence to reach the foundation of ethics, and find those universal principles, from which all censure or approbation is ultimately derived. As this is a question of fact, not of abstract science, we can only expect success, by following *the experimental method*, and deducing general maxims from a comparison of particular instances. (EPM 1.10; italics added)

The experimental method is required to discover the circumstances common to all virtuous qualities (and likewise all vicious qualities), separating them from whatever is superfluous (cf. Shaver 1995: 322). Hume's investigation reaches the conclusion that virtue and personal merit consist "altogether in the possession of mental qualities, *useful* or *agreeable* to the *person himself* or to *others*" (EPM 9.1). This conclusion states the relevant universal principles of human nature as well as the analytical framework of his catalogue of the virtues.

505

The catalogue of the virtues

But why is Hume's catalogue of the virtues (and vices) *normative*, rather than psychological, or perhaps lexicographical? Consider a passage near the end of EPM in which he reflects back on what he has written in this work:

> I . . . proposed simply to collect on the one hand, a *list* of those mental qualities which are the object of love or esteem, and form a part of personal merit, and on the other hand, a *catalogue* of those qualities, which are the object of censure or reproach, and which detract from the character of the person, possessed of them. (EPM, App. 4.1; italics added)

I take Hume's normative language literally. His catalogue of virtues and vices lists qualities that render persons meritorious and, in the case of vices, qualities that warrant censure. Vices *detract* from character; virtues *ornament* character. The latter deserve praise, the former reproach.

Cataloguing the virtues and vices had a long history in moral philosophy (possibly dating from Aristotle's *Nicomachean Ethics*, in and around the passages cited by Hume at EPM App. 4.12). Hume situates himself in this tradition and commends Cicero's catalogue, in particular. In a letter to Francis Hutcheson of September 17, 1739 (Greig 1932: 1, 34), Hume said, "Upon the whole, I desire to take my Catalogue of Virtues from *Cicero's Offices* [*De officiis*], not from the *Whole Duty of Man*. I had, indeed, the former Book in my Eye in all my Reasonings." The latter was a widely circulated book on Christian ethical and religious duty that, according to James Boswell, Hume studied as a boy (Boswell 1970: 11). Unlike Cicero, *Whole Duty* gives a Christian analysis of the virtues, incorporating virtues such as meekness and humility. (See, on this theme, T 3.3.2.13–14. There is no straightforward catalogue in Cicero, but Hume says only that he desires to "take" his catalogue from Cicero.)

Hume's downgrading of the catalogue of virtues in *Whole Duty* is consistent with the negative, and unquestionably normative, view that he presents of the virtues that have often been extolled in certain traditions of religious ethics:

> And as every quality, which is useful or agreeable to ourselves or others, is, in common life, allowed to be a part of personal merit; so no other will ever be received, where men judge of things by their natural, unprejudiced reason, without the delusive glosses of superstition and false religion. Celibacy, fasting, penance, mortification, self-denial, humility, silence, solitude, and the whole train of monkish virtues; for what reason are they every where rejected by men of sense, but because they serve to no manner of purpose . . . They cross all these desirable ends; stupify the understanding and harden the heart, obscure the fancy and sour the temper. We justly, therefore, transfer them to the opposite column, and place them in the catalogue of vices . . . A gloomy, hair-brained enthusiast, after his death, may have a place in the calendar [the calendar, or registry, of the saints]; but will scarcely ever be admitted, when alive, into intimacy and society, except by those who are as delirious and dismal as himself. (EPM 9.3)

This passage bristles with normativity. A *hair-brained enthusiast* is a giddy-headed zealot. The *monkish virtues* do not, Hume says, render a person "a more valuable member of society"; "they cross all these desirable ends." The monkish fail to understand what is useful and how morality turns on the useful. Their virtues (Hume places them in the column of vices) had been defended not only in monkish traditions, but by Blaise Pascal and to some extent by Diogenes the Cynic; Hume comments very negatively on both philosophers at the end of "A Dialogue" (EPM A Dialogue 54), mentioning also Saint Dominic and Saint Ignatius of Loyola. Hume states, or at least implies using the dialogue form, that they live extravagant and artificial lives and persist under "illusions of religious superstition or philosophical enthusiasm." Their "virtues" incorporate a moral aberration that impartial persons reject.

It is a tortured reading of such passages to say that Hume is merely *explaining why* we place certain qualities in the catalogue of vices. His often profoundly negative conclusions involve him in evaluating, judging, recommending, correcting, and proposing moral standards. He is stating what persons of good sense believe, where "good sense" functions as a term of evaluation and commendation.

The analytical framework of the catalogue

When Hume uses the language of *framing the catalogue* (see quotation above from EPM 1.10), he suggests that his goal is a *systematically structured classification scheme*. EPM presents an analytical framework of qualities that comprise personal merit – and, in the case of vice, demerit (cf. *Treatise* 3.3.1.27–30). Hume advances a fourfold categorization or classification scheme (see Vodraska 1981, for a detailed analysis):

1 qualities useful to others;
2 qualities useful to ourselves;
3 qualities immediately agreeable to ourselves;
4 qualities immediately agreeable to others.

The virtues listed under each category all serve the indicated function – for example, as in (1), furthering the interests of others in society. Hume's table of contents and section headings in EPM display his last three categories (2–4) – the titles of sections 6–8. The first category (1) does not appear as a title in the table of contents, but only because sections 2–5 all include content that falls under this central moral category.

The mental qualities that Hume catalogues (not all of which are *moral* virtues) include the following:

1 *Qualities useful to others* (see EPM, sections 2–5; summary at 9.12; T 3.3.3.3): benevolence, sociability, being good-natured, humanity, mercifulness, generosity, compassion, gratitude, friendliness (or friendship), truthfulness, justice, fidelity, disinterestedness, liberality, honor, allegiance, chastity, charity, affability, lenity, mercy, and moderation.
2 *Qualities useful to ourselves* (see EPM 6; T 3.3.1.24, 3.3.4.7): discretion, industry, frugality, caution, strength of mind, wisdom, memory, enterprise, assiduity, frugality, economy, resolution, good sense, prudence, discernment, temperance, dexterity, sobriety, patience, constancy, perseverance, vigilance, judgment, forethought,

507

considerateness, secrecy, order, insinuation, address, presence of mind, quickness of conception, and facility of expression.

3 *Qualities immediately agreeable to ourselves* (see EPM 7; T 3.3.1.28, 3.3.2.8–16, 3.3.3.4): cheerfulness, greatness of mind, courage, intrepidity, restrained self-esteem/pride, dignity, tranquility, poetic talent, serenity, love, love of glory, good humor, and delicacy of taste.

4 *Qualities immediately agreeable to others* (see EPM 8; T 3.3.1.27–30, 3.3.4.8–10): good manners, wit, ingenuity, eloquence, affability, genius, modesty, decency, politeness, genteelness, and cleanliness.

Hume says that the "whole class of virtues" would occupy "many pages" (EPM 9.12). Although he does not regard his list of the virtues as complete, he does regard his fourfold classification scheme as complete. Here is his condensed statement: "PERSONAL MERIT consists altogether in the possession of mental qualities, *useful* or *agreeable* to the *person himself* or to *others*." This theory, "so simple and obvious," is what he found "it requisite to prove" (EPM 9.1; cf. T 3.3.1.30, 3.3.2.1, 3.3.2.16, 3.3.5.1).

Conclusion

I have argued that Hume's moral philosophy includes a normative virtue theory according to which personal merit consists in the possession of the mental qualities in the correct catalogue of the virtues. Hume seems to think – though this would involve more interpretation than I have provided – that the justification of moral beliefs, including acceptance of his catalogue, occurs if the relevant norms governing what one ought to believe in morals have been satisfied. These norms, I have proposed, overlap with his epistemic norms. In particular, the impartiality norm, the reliable-principles norm, and the experiment norm play vital roles in his virtue theory.

When Hume's moral philosophy is so interpreted, it is not difficult to appreciate the normative point in passages such as the following:

> [W]e may easily account for that merit, which is commonly ascrib'd to *generosity, humanity, compassion, gratitude, friendship, fidelity, zeal, disinterestedness, liberality*, and all those other qualities, which form the character of good and benevolent. A propensity to the tender passions makes a man agreeable and useful in all the parts of life . . . Courage and ambition, when not regulated by benevolence, are fit only to make a tyrant and public robber. (T 3.3.3.3)

Hume's theory of the passions is here joined with his theory of the virtues to introduce a more finely delineated theory of good and benevolent character and just direction in the moral life than I have been able to develop. Elements of normativity in his ethics that I have not been able to address include the nature and grounding of obligation, the nature and basis of rules of justice, how right action differs from good character, and the theory of moral motivation according to which "*no action can be virtuous, or morally good, unless there be in human nature some motive to produce it, distinct from the sense of its morality*" (T 3.2.1.7). To interpret these notions would be to spell out the *particulars* of the normative theory whose *general* normative features I have interpreted as a virtue theory. (See partial attempts to work out a few of the particulars by Abramson 2002; Baier 1991: 152–219.)

Ask What Virtue Is and Ask for a Model of the Honorable Man

When Hume published the third book of the *Treatise*, he prefixed to its title page an injunction from Lucan's *Civil Wars* (9.562–3): "ask what virtue is and ask for a model of the honorable man." Is this model what Hume pursues in the third book of the *Treatise*? Did he postpone such an undertaking until he wrote EPM (where he speaks of the character Cleanthes as "a model of perfect virtue," at 9.2).

In 1739 Hume engaged in correspondence with Francis Hutcheson about his goals and commitments in moral philosophy. Hume sent comments on his soon-to-be published manuscript of the third book. Although Hutcheson's commentary has been lost, Hume's reply suggests its content. Hume says, "What affected me most in your Remarks is your observing, that there wants a certain Warmth in the Cause of Virtue, which, you think, all good Men wou'd relish, & cou'd not displease amidst abstract Enquirys" (September 17, 1739, to Francis Hutcheson, in Greig 1932: 1, 32–3). Evidently, Hutcheson judged that Hume's empirical, metaphysically engaged moral philosophy failed to warmly champion virtue. Hume responded:

> There are different ways of examining the Mind as well as the Body. One may consider it either as an Anatomist or as a Painter; either to discover its most secret Springs & Principles or to describe the Grace & Beauty of its Actions. I imagine it impossible to conjoin these two Views . . . An Anatomist, however, can give very good Advice to a Painter or Statuary: And in like manner, I am perswaded, that a Metaphysician may be very helpful to a Moralist; tho' I cannot easily conceive these two Characters united in the same Work. Any warm Sentiment of Morals, I am afraid, wou'd have the Air of Declamation amidst abstract Reasonings, & wou'd be esteem'd contrary to good Taste. And tho' I am much more ambitious of being esteem'd a Friend to Virtue, than a Writer of Taste; yet I must always carry the latter in my Eye, otherwise I must despair of ever being servic[e]able to Virtue. I hope these Reasons will satisfy you; tho at the same time, I intend to make a new Tryal, if it be possible to make the Moralist & Metaphysician agree a little better. (September 17, 1739, to Hutcheson, Greig 1932: 1, 32–3)

In a 1740 letter to Hutcheson, Hume indicates that he made revisions based on Hutcheson's comments on the manuscript (March 4, 1740, Greig 1932: 1, 36–8). The final paragraph of the *Treatise* returns to these ideas in the letter and reiterates that "an anatomist . . . is admirably fitted to give advice to a painter," though "the anatomist ought never to emulate the painter" (T 3.3.6.6).

Three observations about the distinction between anatomy and painting are in order. First, Hume likens himself to an anatomist (one who states in fundamental detail what is the case) rather than a painter (or one who makes something beautiful and engaging) and identifies his work as that of a metaphysician rather than moralist. (T 1.4.6.23; 2.1.12.2; Abstract 2; and EHU 1.8. EHU 1 is a useful but difficult resource for interpreting these metaphors.) Second, he says that the objectives of the metaphysician and the moralist are very different and cannot suitably be combined in the same work.

Third, he seeks to avoid an air of declamation in his work. When these comments are linked to his avowed intention to write a science of human nature, it is evident that Hume envisioned the *Treatise* as unconnected to painting.

However, Hume's comments do not preclude or discourage a normative moral philosophy. Painting and declamation are not the only ways to be normative, and the anatomist-painter distinction does not suggest that an anatomist cannot be normative. An anatomist could state what virtue is and frame the catalogue of the virtues, and a painter could use panegyric to present virtue and personal merit in their most engaging colors.

Hume's concluding sentence in the letter to Hutcheson leaves open the possibility that morals and metaphysics can be brought into closer agreement, and he states that he intends to "make a new Tryal" to achieve this objective. Nowhere does Hume explain this "new Tryal." His comments may only reflect his thoughts about revisions to his manuscript prior to publication – or, perhaps, thoughts about a second edition. As there was neither a second edition nor an intervening moral treatise, one hypothesis is that EPM is the work in which Hume attempted this trial. The first section of EHU, Hume's initial recasting of parts of the *Treatise*, strongly suggests that combining the functions of anatomist and moralist was on his mind (EHU 1.1–3, 8), and section 9 of EPM praises virtuous conduct in acclamatory terms (cf. Abramson 2000: 64–80).

It would be unwarranted to assert, on the tenuous basis of Hume's correspondence with Hutcheson, that EPM, in contrast to the *Treatise*, was written to present virtue with greater warmth or to increase Hume's commitment to normative ethics (i.e., what, in the concluding paragraph of the *Treatise*, is called "practical morality"; T 3.3.6.6; cf. T 3.1.1.5). However, EPM is a very different work from the *Treatise* and one in which there is less of a focus on the science of human nature and an evident concentration on a theory of personal merit and the catalogue of the virtues. If EPM is Hume's new trial, he may there be assuming more of the mantle of a moralist, or at least of an aid to the moralist.

See also 16 *"Enquiry concerning the Principles of Morals*: Incomparably the Best?"

References

Abramson, K. (2002). "Two Portraits of the Humean Moral Agent," *Pacific Philosophical Quarterly*, 83, pp. 301–34.
—— (2000). "Sympathy and the Project of Hume's *Second Enquiry*," *Archiv für Geschichte der Philosophie*, 83, pp. 45–80.
Baier, A. (1991). *A Progress of Sentiments* (Cambridge, MA: Harvard University Press).
Boswell, J. (1970). *Boswell in Extremes, 1776–1778*, ed. Charles McC. Weis and Frederick A. Pottle (New York: McGraw-Hill).
Cicero, Marcus Tullius (1921). *De officiis*, trans. Walter Miller (Cambridge, MA: Harvard University Press, Loeb Library).
Cohen, Mendel F. (1990). "Obligation and Human Nature in Hume's Philosophy," *Philosophical Quarterly*, 40, pp. 316–41.
Darwall, S. (1995). *The British Moralists and the Internal "Ought": 1640–1740* (Cambridge: Cambridge University Press).

Fogelin, R. J. (1985). *Hume's Skepticism in the "Treatise of Human Nature"* (London: Routledge and Kegan Paul).

Glathe, A. B. (1950). *Hume's Theory of the Passions and of Morals: A Study of Books II and III of the "Treatise"* (Berkeley: University of California Press).

Greig, J. Y. T. (ed.) (1932). *The Letters of David Hume*, 2 vols. (Oxford: Clarendon Press).

Hampton, J. (1995). "Does Hume Have an Instrumental Conception of Practical Reason?" *Hume Studies*, 21, pp. 57–74.

Hume, David (1741–77). *Essays, Moral, Political and Literary*, ed. Eugene F. Miller (Indianapolis, IN: Liberty Fund, 1987).

Kemp, J. (1970). *Ethical Naturalism: Hobbes and Hume* (London: Macmillan and Co.).

Korsgaard, C. (1996). *The Sources of Normativity* (Cambridge: Cambridge University Press).

Loeb, L. E. (2002). *Stability and Justification in Hume's "Treatise"* (New York: Oxford University Press).

Lyons, J. C. (2001). "General Rules and the Justification of Probable Belief in Hume's *Treatise*," *Hume Studies*, 27, pp. 247–77.

Mackie, J. (1980). *Hume's Moral Theory* (London: Routledge and Kegan Paul).

Martin, M. A. (1993). "The Rational Warrant for Hume's General Rules," *Journal of the History of Philosophy*, 31, pp. 245–57.

Millican, P. (ed.) (2002). *Reading Hume on Human Understanding* (Oxford: Clarendon Press).

Norton, D. F. (1982). *David Hume: Common-sense Moralist, Sceptical Metaphysician* (Princeton, NJ: Princeton University Press).

—— (1985). "Hume's Moral Ontology," *Hume Studies*, 10th Anniversary edn., pp. 189–214.

Penelhum, T. (1975). *Hume* (New York: St. Martin's Press).

Schneewind, J. (1998). *The Invention of Autonomy* (Cambridge: Cambridge University Press).

Shaver, R. (1995). "Hume's Moral Theory?" *History of Philosophy Quarterly*, 12, pp. 317–31.

Strawson, P. F. (1985). *Skepticism and Naturalism* (New York: Columbia University Press).

Sturgeon, N. L. (2001). "Moral Skepticism and Moral Naturalism in Hume's *Treatise*," *Hume Studies*, 27, pp. 3–83.

Vodraska, S. (1981). "Hume's Moral Enquiry: An Analysis of Its Catalogue," *Philosophical Topics*, 2, pp. 79–108.

The Whole Duty of Man (1658). Published anonymously, authorship now generally attributed to Richard Allestree. Originally published under the title *The Practice of Christian Graces, or, the Whole Duty of Man*.

Further Reading

Árdal, P. S. (1966). *Passion and Value in Hume's "Treatise"* (Edinburgh: Edinburgh University Press).

Baxter, D. L. M. (1990). "Hume on Virtue, Beauty, Composites, and Secondary Qualities," *Pacific Philosophical Quarterly*, 71, pp. 103–18.

Buckle, S. (1991). *Natural Law and the Theory of Property: Grotius to Hume* (Oxford: Clarendon Press).

Falkenstein, L. (1997). "Naturalism, Normativity, and Scepticism in Hume's Account of Belief," *Hume Studies*, 23, pp. 29–72.

Garrett, D. (1997). *Cognition and Commitment in Hume's Philosophy* (New York: Oxford University Press).

Hearn, T. K. (1976). "General Rules and the Moral Sentiments in Hume's *Treatise*," *Review of Metaphysics*, 30, pp. 57–72.

Owen, D. (1999). *Hume's Reason* (New York: Oxford University Press), ch. 9.

Pitson, A. E. (1989). "Projectionism, Realism, and Hume's Moral Sense Theory," *Hume Studies*, 15, pp. 61–92.

Radcliffe, E. S. (1999). "Hume on the Generation of Motives: Why Beliefs Alone Never Motivate," *Hume Studies*, 25, pp. 101–22.

Shaver, R. (1992). "Hume and the Duties of Humanity," *Journal of the History of Philosophy*, 30, pp. 545–56.

Smith, N. K. (1905). "The Naturalism of Hume," *Mind*, 14, pp. 149–73, 335–47.

Spector, J. (2003). "Value in Fact: Naturalism and Normativity in Hume's Moral Psychology," *Journal of the History of Philosophy*, 41, pp. 145–63.

28

Hume's Metaethics: Is Hume a Moral Noncognitivist?

NICHOLAS L. STURGEON

To the question whether Hume is a noncognitivist about moral judgments, an unqualified "yes" or "no" answer would invite a charge of anachronism and would surely oversimplify. Noncognitivism is a theory that has been clearly defined only in debates since the 1930s, and Hume's discussions of moral judgments are in any case complex: even those interpreters who have emphasized what they see as strong noncognitivist strands in his writing allow that these need to be disentangled from conflicting lines of thought that are also present. However, in the neighborhood of this too-simple question with its too-simple answers are subtler questions precisely about how to untangle these various threads, and it is these questions that I shall explore. At an abstract level, my conclusion will be similar to that of many others who have written on Hume on these topics: that Hume is not entirely consistent, that some of his remarks tend to noncognitivism, and there may be no definitive answer to the question of just how to weigh those remarks against ones that point in a different direction. But I find that I disagree with many of these other writers about important details. I think that Hume is frequently more consistent than his interpreters have supposed, that not every remark that has been thought to support noncognitivism actually does so, and that many complications in his views on these topics have been widely overlooked.

If Hume's thought is complex, the issue of how to define noncognitivism, at least for our purposes, is less so. I am going to assume a fairly simple and historically standard version, the central tenet of which is that holding a moral view is not a matter of having a belief about the world that might be either true or false. What it is said to involve instead will then vary with different versions of noncognitivism; with an eye on Hume, I am going to take it that this will be the having a favorable or unfavorable attitude or sentiment of some kind. Thus, according to noncognitivism as I will understand it, to think an action virtuous or vicious – Hume's most central and most common example of a moral judgment – will not be a matter of having a belief about the action, but instead of feeling a sentiment of approval or disapproval of it. In the development of noncognitivist views, other complexities have emerged. For example, some noncognitivists have thought that holding a moral view need not involve feeling a sentiment, but might involve instead having some other kind of noncognitive attitude, such as an intention. (The original view, proposed by A. J. Ayer and Charles Stevenson, is usually called emotivism; an example of the latter sort of view would be R. M. Hare's prescriptivism [Ayer 1952: 102–14; Stevenson 1944; Hare 1952].) And more recently, having discovered minimalist accounts of truth, some noncognitivists have attempted to distance their view from what I am here taking as its central thesis, that moral views are neither true nor false. (See, e.g., Blackburn 1996; an early version of this position is in Stevenson 1963: 214–20.) In an independent discussion of noncognitivism these further issues would matter, but in a discussion of whether Hume is a noncognitivist they do not matter. For the passages in Hume that invite a noncognitivist reading are precisely the ones that seem to identify having a moral view with having a feeling of some kind (as in: "To have the sense of virtue, is nothing but to *feel* a satisfaction of a particular kind from the contemplation of a character" [T 3.1.2.3]), and that seem to deny that it involves discerning a truth of any kind (as in: "Morality . . . is more properly felt than judg'd of; tho' this feeling or sentiment is commonly so soft and gentle, that we are apt to confound it with an idea" [T 3.1.2.1]). If Hume is any kind of noncognitivist, he is the old-fashioned kind, an emotivist who denies that there is any truth to be found in morals.

What complicates the interpretation of Hume's view about moral judgments, despite the existence of these and some other passages we shall examine, is the existence, both in his *Treatise of Human Nature* and in the *Enquiry concerning the Principles of Morals*, of passages that look like definitive assertions of a different sort of view that is not noncognitivist at all. It is, to be sure, a view that gives our moral sentiments a central role in moral assessments, but that role is to be the topic of those assessments, what they are about; and it allows these assessments to be true or false. According to this sort of subjectivist view, as I shall call it, to think an action virtuous is to think, about some person or persons, that they feel (or would feel) approval toward the action; and to think an action vicious is to think, in a corresponding way, that what they feel (or would feel) is disapproval. I have had to hedge this general statement of the view because there are variations in Hume's account of exactly whose feelings matter; but none of these variations make questions of virtue and vice any less questions of fact. Introducing this sort of view in the *Treatise*, he makes a speaker's own, current feelings the dispositive ones:

> So that when you pronounce any action or character to be vicious, you mean nothing, but that from the constitution of your nature you have a feeling or sentiment of blame from the contemplation of it. (T 3.1.1.26)

Later in the *Treatise*, however, he modifies this view to make the truth of one's ascription of virtue or vice depend, not on one's actual feelings, but on the feelings one would have under the right conditions, whether or not one now is (or even could be) in those conditions. Thus we take "*Marcus Brutus*, as represented in history," to be more virtuous than our faithful servant, because we know

> that were we to approach equally near to that renown'd patriot, he wou'd command a much higher degree of affection and admiration. (T 3.3.1.16)

Here Hume seems to mean by "nearness" just familiarity; he seems also to have in mind that moral judgments are about our feelings as they would be if corrected for the influence of self-interest.[1] (For what looks like the same suggestion, see T 3.3.3.2 and EPM 5.41–2.) And then there is a similar line in an oft-cited passage from the *Enquiry concerning Morals*. Hume writes that

> the hypothesis which we embrace is plain. It defines virtue to be *whatever mental action or quality gives to a spectator the pleasing sentiment of approbation*; and vice the contrary. We then proceed to examine a plain matter of fact, to wit, what actions have this influence. (EPM App. 1.10)

And there are a number of other passages in a similar vein (at least T 2.1.7.5, 2.1.8.3–6, 3.2.8.8, 3.3.1.3 and 3.3.5.1; also EPM, pp. 215–16 [note to 1.10]).

The passages conflict about details, but they nevertheless have a common theme, that moral views are views about someone or other's feelings. With their talk of what "you mean" and of "defining" virtue and vice, moreover, they seem to embrace one twentieth-century philosophical stereotype of what is called ethical naturalism, holding not just that moral facts are facts about the natural world (in this case, about someone's feelings) but that this can be shown just by examination of the meanings of moral terms, their definition.

It is no doubt because of the centrality of these passages that the idea that Hume might be read even partly as a noncognitivist is, by the standards of philosophical discussion, quite a recent one. This is perhaps not so surprising for interpretations that pre-dated the formulation of noncognitivism as a distinct philosophical position. More striking, however, is the fact that in none of the seminal works by the major founding figures of noncognitivism is Hume cited as a close, distinctive confederate. A. J. Ayer, despite crediting Hume's empiricism as an inspiration for the general philosophical program of *Language, Truth and Logic*, cites Hume not at all in his chapter on ethics (Ayer 1952: 31, 102–14). Charles Stevenson discusses Hume along with such figures as John Dewey and Ralph Barton Perry, as a writer whose views bear some resemblance to his own – since they all connect morality somehow with "interests" or sentiments – but are not, in Stevenson's view, noncognitivist (Stevenson 1944: 273–6).[2] R. M. Hare is perhaps a minor exception, since he credits Hume with a noncognitivist insight in maintaining that no *ought* can be derived from an *is*. But Hare does this in a passage that attributes the same insight to Aristotle, Kant, Moore, and Prichard, and which in no way suggests that Hume is any more of a noncognitivist than any of these other philosophers (Hare 1952: 29–31). It is only in the early to mid-1960s, almost three decades after Ayer's proclamation of the doctrine, that one begins to find writers noticing the ways in which Hume might be read as an inspiration to noncognitivists. (See, for example, Flew 1963; Foot 1963; Hudson 1964.) This reading has since become much more common; even commentators who do not fully endorse it now standardly list it as one possibility that has to be taken seriously (for example, Mackie 1970: 64–75; Harrison 1976: 110–25; and Stroud 1977: 180–92). So we need to examine its basis.

It should be clear that anyone who wants to portray Hume as, in some measure, a noncognitivist, must do more than point out that, for Hume, moral assessments have some intimate connection with sentiments. For every version of subjectivism easily accommodates that point. The situation is much the same, it seems to me, with

515

some other considerations sometimes mentioned by writers who see Hume as a non-cognitivist: for example, his speaking of our taste having "a productive faculty," so that, "gilding and staining all natural objects with the colours, borrowed from internal sentiment [it] raises, in a manner, a new creation" (EPM App. 1.21; Blackburn 1981: 163). Gilding and staining objects does, after all, produce a change in the facts about them, though a change that is more superficial than an incautious observer might suspect; just as a change in our feelings about some act or character produces a change in what is true about that character, though a change that is more superficial (because, in this case, extrinsic and relational) than most people are inclined to think that a change in a moral characteristic must be. So there is nothing here to dislodge a subjectivist reading. What proponents of a noncognitivist reading need, instead, are claims Hume makes or arguments he gives that (1) seem inconsistent with subjectivism, and (2) are consistent with – or, even better, fit integrally with – a proposed non-cognitivist reading. I will examine a number of considerations that have been taken to suggest or require a noncognitivist interpretation, beginning with ones that seem to me the easiest to respond to and proceeding to ones that need to be taken more seriously.

Morality Not a Matter of Fact?

There are passages in both the *Treatise* and the second *Enquiry* that have been read as asserting that morality – that is, the moral status of a character or an action – does not consist of any sort of matter of fact. This, of course, would be inconsistent with subjectivism, which makes the moral status of a character or an action consist in a fact about someone's sentiments, but would fit well with noncognitivism: if there are no moral truths, then there should be no moral facts, either (Harrison 1976: 118). The passages in question sit in close proximity, however, to others in which Hume says that morality *does* consist in a matter of fact. (One of these I quoted above: "We proceed to examine a plain matter of fact" [EPM App. 1.10].) But I do not believe that Hume is inconsistent on this point. It is a mistake, in my view, to read him as denying that morality consists in a matter of fact.

Begin with the *Treatise*. Hume concludes section 3.1.1 with a connected argument to show that morality is not discovered by "thought and understanding" or, as he also puts it, that morality is not an "object of reason" (T 3.1.1.18, 26). He sees two pos-sibilities to eliminate here: if morality were an object of reason, it would have to consist either in some demonstrable "relations of objects" or else in "a matter of fact, which is discovered by our reasoning" (T 3.1.1.18). After a detailed argument against the first possibility, he then devotes a single paragraph to rebutting the second, reiter-ating, twice, what it is that he proposes to show.

> Nor does this reasoning only prove, that morality consists not in any relations, that are the object of science; but if examin'd, will prove with equal certainty, that it consists not in any *matter of fact*, which can be discover'd by the understanding.

And again: "But can there be any difficulty in proving, that vice and virtue are not matters of fact, whose existence we can infer by reason?" (T 3.1.1.26).

The place to start, in order to see that Hume is not here denying that morality consists in a matter of fact, is less with his philosophy than with his punctuation. In contemporary English, relative clauses set off with commas are read as non-restrictive. But Hume punctuates far more heavily than is now standard, and frequently sets off with commas what are clearly restrictive clauses. (For example, about the nature of belief: "We may make use of words, that express something near it" [T 1.3.7.7]. Or, in the paragraph following the one I am here discussing: "In every system of morality, which I have hitherto met with" [T 3.1.1.27].) So, I suggest, Hume's relative clauses in the passages I have just quoted, though set off with commas, are to be read as restrictive. He is thus not denying that morality consists in a matter of fact, but only that it consists in a certain sort of matter of fact, the sort discoverable by the understanding, through reasoning or inference. This reading has the distinct advantage, not only of saving him from contradiction, but of also of allowing us to see him as elaborating the same point, when he continues, about the example of an act of willful murder:

> Examine it in all lights, and see if you can find that matter of fact, or real existence, which you call *vice* . . . The vice entirely escapes you, as long as you consider the object. You can never find it, till you turn your reflection into your own breast, and find a sentiment of disapprobation, which arises in you, towards this action. Here is a matter of fact; but 'tis the object of feeling, not of reason. It lies in yourself, not in the object. So that when you pronounce any action or character to be vicious, you mean nothing, but that from the constitution of your nature you have a feeling or sentiment of blame from the contemplation of it.

Thus, in Hume's view, morality does consist in a matter of fact, but not in one that is an object of reason. (He also says that the matter of fact it consists in is an "object of feeling"; we shall come back to this.)

Similar passages in the second *Enquiry* invite a similar reading. To be sure, when Hume says there that the "crime" (meaning criminality) "of ingratitude is not any particular individual fact" (EPM App. 1.6), there is no relative clause, however punctuated. But since the structure of this passage closely parallels the one we have just examined in the *Treatise* – it is part of an argument that reason does not discover moral distinctions, and is followed shortly by what appears to be the identification of virtue and vice with a "plain matter of fact" about our sentiments (EPM App. 1.10) – it seems reasonable to save him from contradiction by supplying the express qualification from his earlier exposition. The relative clause reappears, in any case, when Hume returns to the point a few pages later: we must acknowledge, he says, "that the crime or immorality is no particular fact or relation, *which can be the object of the understanding*" (EPM App. 1.16, my emphasis). We may read this as a restrictive clause, just as we may read the similar clauses in the *Treatise*.

No Ought from an Is

In a famous passage Hume appears to deny the possibility of inferring an *ought* from an *is* (T 3.1.1.27). Many readers, taking *is*'s to be about matters of fact and *ought*'s to

517

be moral claims, have understood this passage to say that no moral conclusion can be inferred solely from premises about matters of fact. If that is what the passage means, then it is relevant to our question in two ways. For, first, this doctrine, of a logical gap between facts and moral values, though not exclusive to noncognitivists, is certainly a characteristic noncognitivist doctrine. Second, it is a doctrine that seems to conflict with Hume's naturalistic subjectivism. For if all you mean in calling an action vicious is, as Hume suggests in the immediately preceding paragraph, that it gives rise to a feeling of disapprobation in you, then it looks as if there is a safe inference you may make, from a premise about a matter of fact (that you have the feeling toward the action) to a moral conclusion (that the action is vicious). And a similar problem will arise on Hume's other versions of subjectivism. If, for example, it is as Hume says a "plain matter of fact" that a certain action gives rise to approbation in "a spectator," and if we follow him in defining virtue as whatever gives rise to that feeling, then we can infer from a matter of fact that the action in question is virtuous. So Hume has here looked to many to be of two minds about an important issue, with one strand of his thought clearly opposed to noncognitivism but another, conflicting one much more hospitable to it.

There are two strategies for resisting this line of interpretation.

(1) The first takes advantage of the fact that Hume does not say, outright, that no *ought* can be inferred from an *is*. What he says about this transition is that

> as this *ought*, or *ought not*, expresses some new relation or affirmation, 'tis necessary that it shou'd be observ'd and explain'd; and at the same time that a reason shou'd be given, for what seems altogether inconceivable, how this new relation can be a deduction from others, which are entirely different from it. (T 3.1.1.27)

Many readers have taken "seems altogether inconceivable" as ironic understatement, and have thus understood Hume to be denying that an *ought* can be a "deduction" from an *is*. But of course one might read him more literally. In that case he would be remarking only on the apparent impossibility, but not necessarily the real impossibility, of deriving an *ought* from an *is* (Macintyre 1959; Baier 1991: 176–7). Indeed, on this reading, he could be understood as presenting his own subjectivism, with its insistence on the connection between sentiments and moral characteristics, as precisely the insight that explains how the inference can be justified. In that case, of course, there is no conflict between this passage and any of Hume's affirmations of subjectivism, nor is there anything that might lead us to read him as a noncognitivist.

(2) A second option is to grant that Hume is indeed maintaining that no *ought* can be derived from an *is*, but to reject the assumption that all statements about matters of fact count as *is*'s. Hume introduces the terms "*is*" and "*ought*" in this paragraph with little explanation, and his brief suggestion that wording is the key to the distinction has to be dismissed by any reader who thinks (as almost all have) that "Willful murder is vicious" falls on the *ought* side of the divide, even though it contains the word "is" and not the word "ought."[3] What appears to justify readers in doing this is a fact about the context of the discussion. This is that it comes at the end of a sustained

argument that moral distinctions are not objects of reason; it would thus seem quite surprising if Hume did not mean to count as an *ought* any claim about moral distinctions, however worded. But the same consideration suggests that *is*'s, the other side of the contrast, are not intended to include all matters of fact, but only those that are objects of reason – that is, the sort of facts we can discover by reasoning or inference. And, as I noted above, Hume has spent the previous paragraph insisting that not all matters of fact are of this sort and, in particular, that the facts about our feelings with which his subjectivism identifies moral facts are not. So, on this reading, there is no conflict between his subjectivist views and his remarks about *is* and *ought* (and, so far, no hint of noncognitivism). The subjectivism does equate moral assessments with certain factual claims about our feelings, but this is not the equation of an *ought* with an *is* (Sturgeon 2001: 8–13).

Of course, this reading leaves some questions. It has Hume putting the logical gap between *is* and *ought* between two sorts of matters of fact – those that are "in the object" and are discoverable by inference, and those that are in us and, he appears to claim, not discoverable by inference – and one may ask why he would put a skeptical line precisely there. I shall return to this question.

Of these readings, the two that have Hume affirming a logical gap between *is* and *ought* – the reading just described and the noncognitivist one – appear to have one advantage over the reading that does not, just because the paragraph comes at the end of an entire section arguing that morality is not discoverable by reason. That moral conclusions cannot be derived from some class of knowable premises is a thesis that fits that theme well; it is more surprising to think that Hume would conclude this section by adding that moral conclusions can after all be discovered by reasoning, if only we are careful to do it properly. Still, the important point is that there is reasonable controversy about how to read Hume's remarks about *is* and *ought*. They can certainly be fitted into a noncognitivist reading, but there are other possible readings which do not conflict with Hume's apparent subjectivism, and which do not require noncognitivism.

Morality an Object of Feeling

As I have noted, Hume not only says that morality is not an object of reason, but says that it is instead an object of feeling. Of course, morality is in some sense an "object of feeling" on either a subjectivist or a noncognitivist interpretation. But some of Hume's remarks in this vein have struck some readers as calling out for a noncognitivist reading. The most prominent example is his statement that "Morality . . . is more properly felt than judg'd of." (Mackie 1980: 70, says that this remark "seems explicitly emotivist"; cf. Stroud 1977: 233–4; Harrison 1976: 120.) That is presumably because the remark appears to suggest that precisely where we might have thought there was a moral judgment, capable of truth or falsity, there is, instead, only a feeling: just what one would expect a noncognitivist, rather than a subjectivist, to say.

However, once again, that is not the only plausible reading of this passage. First, it is important to note that Hume elsewhere speaks of "feeling" as a source of factual knowledge, the noninferential knowledge we have of the "perceptions" in our own minds (T 1.4.2.7). So it is quite possible that that is what he means here: that it is by feeling (that is, without reasoning or inference) that you know exactly what he has just said that you need to know in order to know that willful murder is vicious, namely that "from the constitution of your nature you have a feeling or sentiment of blame from the contemplation of it." What, though, of morality's not being "judg'd of"? Here it helps to note that Hume normally reserves the term "judgment" for the judgments of the understanding, all of which (at least if they are about matters of fact) are arrived at by inference. (That is, he does not count our knowledge, obtained without inference, of matters of fact about our own mind, as involving "judgment.") On a plausible reading, therefore, what this passage says is merely that moral knowledge, since it is just knowledge of our own feelings, is more properly obtained without inference than by inference. This is a position that Hume surely sees as compatible with the version of subjectivism that he has just endorsed, and it does not appear to push him towards noncognitivism.

A similar comment applies to another passage from this same discussion, sometimes cited to illustrate Hume's noncognitivist leanings. He writes:

> To have the sense of virtue, is nothing but to *feel* a satisfaction of a particular kind from the contemplation of a character. The very *feeling* constitutes our praise or admiration.

One can certainly see how a noncognitivist might say this sort of thing. But, as Hume immediately elaborates this point, what he says is that

> we do not infer a character to be virtuous, because it pleases: But in feeling that it pleases after such a particular manner, we in effect feel that it is virtuous. (T 3.1.2.3)

So once again, it turns out, feeling is a source of knowledge of a matter of fact, non-inferential knowledge *that* the character pleases and so equally, it appears, knowledge that the character is virtuous. That appears to support a subjectivist rather than a non-cognitivist reading.

A Problem

So the details of Hume's talk of morality as an object of feeling appear not to require the noncognitivist reading that some have supposed they do. At the same time, I should point out a problem for Hume in this last reply on behalf of a subjectivist reading. This Problem (as I shall call it for easy reference) comes in two versions, the second deeper than the first. Its bearing on the question whether to read Hume as a noncognitivist or a subjectivist is complex, and will become apparent in stages. The simple version arises from the observation that the plausibility of Hume's view that moral knowledge could be obtained by "feeling" varies sharply with the version of his sub-jectivism that we are considering. The passages just mentioned all come shortly after his equation of one's claim that an act is vicious with a claim about one's own cur-rent feelings. And there is at least some plausibility to the idea that one could know one's own current feelings noninferentially, by "feeling." But as I have explained, some of Hume's formulations of a subjectivist position make other feelings the relevant ones (T 3.3.1.16, 3.3.3.2 and EPM 5.41–2). In these passages, an ascription of virtue or vice becomes a judgment about the feelings one *would* have under improved conditions; and there is no plausibility (nor would Hume see any plausibility) in the idea that we have noninferential knowledge of counterfactual judgments about what we would feel under such circumstances. The same is probably true about the second *Enquiry*'s imprecise standard of what "a spectator" would feel.[4]

The deeper version of the Problem is that, for Hume, this same difficulty surely arises even where I have said his view might be plausible: that is, for the version of subject-ivism that makes your pronouncements about virtue and vice into statements about your own current feelings. For what Hume has you saying about your feelings, recall, is that "*from* the constitution of your nature you have a sentiment of disapprobation *from* the contemplation" of an action (emphasis added). But Hume clearly under-stands both of these occurrences of "from" as causal. And while there have been philosophers who thought that some knowledge of causal relations might be non-inferential, Hume is certainly not among them (see chapter 5 here). So, by his own standards, "feeling" seems unable to provide the right kind of knowledge even of one's own current feelings.

I see no explicit evidence that Hume is aware of either version of the Problem. The difficulty that either version creates is to force Hume, if he wishes to be consistent, to make some choices that he appears to have thought that he could avoid. As we have seen, he is quite emphatic in his skepticism about the power of reason to discover moral conclusions. But, at least in all the passages that appear to assert any version of subjectivism, he does not mean to deny that we have moral knowledge: this know-ledge concerns a "plain matter of fact" (EPM App. 1.10) that we are supposed to be able to know. However, if "feeling," involving noninferential knowledge of matters of fact, is the only alternative to reason, and the relevant facts are ones that cannot be known that way, then Hume will either have to be more generous about the powers of reason to discover these facts, or else will have to give up on the existence of moral knowledge.

Though this is certainly a difficulty for Hume's subjectivism, one might think it a point that produced no pressure toward a noncognitivist reading. For suppose that Hume were to take the skeptical alternative. His subjectivism would then fail to account, as he hoped it would, for our moral knowledge. But noncognitivism will surely do no better on that count, since it is a version of moral skepticism, and so also denies the existence of moral knowledge. However, the situation will be more complicated if there is some other feature of Hume's view that noncognitivism would secure while a subjectivist reading would not. Defenders of a noncognitivist interpretation have maintained that this is so; we need now to examine their reasons.

Morality an Active Principle

Hume describes morality as an "active principle," in contrast to reason, which, he has argued, is not (T 3.1.1.5, 2.3.3). This contrast underlies one of his most prominent arguments that reason does not discover moral distinctions, an argument that can appear to commit him directly to noncognitivism. That morality is active means, crucially, that agents' moral views play a distinctive role in motivation, in that they "produce or prevent actions" in a way that reason alone never does. People are, for example, "deter'd from some actions by the opinion of injustice, and impell'd to others by that of obligation," whereas, Hume insists, "reason of itself is utterly impotent in this particular" (T 3.1.1.6). It has been standard to take Hume to mean, by the claim that reason alone never does these things, that beliefs alone never do them: that beliefs contribute to motivation, of course, but only when they are accompanied by appropriately related passions or sentiments. If all moral "opinions" have this special motivating power that beliefs alone lack, however, then it must be a mistake to identify moral opinions with beliefs of any sort, even beliefs about our own sentiments. Here, then, is what appears to be an argument that requires a noncognitivist reading. With only a little elaboration, moreover – Hume's own elaboration – it appears to provide a rationale for Hume's is–ought gap, understood as falling between all statements of fact on the one side and moral judgments on the other: namely that "an active principle can never be founded on an inactive" (T 3.1.1.7).

These arguments are very similar to ones on which noncognitivists relied since the mid-twentieth century (Stevenson 1944; Hare 1952; but contrast Ayer 1952, in which there is no such argument). So it is not surprising that Hume has come, even if somewhat belatedly, to be seen as a predecessor of such views. And, indeed, this is likely where we find the strongest case for reading Hume, in one portion of his not-fully-consistent views, as a noncognitivist. Even here, however, there are complications that need to be taken into account before we can reach a balanced assessment. I shall mention three.

(1) There are reasons, which for reasons of space I shall not explore here, for doubting that Hume is as committed as he sounds in these passages to the crucial claims about motivation on which this argument relies. He allows that there is an "improper sense" in which reason may after all motivate (T 2.3.3.4, 8–10), and some interpreters have thought that he treats that sense more seriously than this dismissive characterization would suggest, especially if one looks at more of the *Treatise* than just 2.3.3 and 3.1.1. (Baier 1991: 157–74; Sturgeon, forthcoming.) It has also been noted in recent discussion that it is unclear, from Hume's account of our moral sentiments, how he can ascribe to them a power to motivate "of themselves"; the passage I have just quoted certainly suggests that he wants to claim this for them, but the details of his moral psychology appear to block his way (Brown 1988).

(2) Even if we put these doubts to one side, there is a plausible case that Hume did not *believe* that his denial of a special motivating power to reason meant that moral beliefs, understood as beliefs about our own sentiments, would lack this power. When Hume says that reason does not motivate, I suggest, he is plausibly read as denying special motivating power, not to all beliefs, but only to beliefs about objects of reason.[5] If that is right, he has not denied that beliefs about objects of feeling – the beliefs with which he contrasts beliefs about objects of reason, and with which he several times identifies our moral beliefs – can motivate. How, though, might he think that they could do this? His answer, on the reading I am proposing, is that our noninferential belief about one of our sentiments can motivate just as the sentiment itself

can, because the belief and the sentiment are not distinct states of mind. Hume is led to this view, I believe, because (a) his account of our sentiments treats them simply as a special sort of impression, and because (b) his account of the distinction between impressions and ideas, combined with his account of belief, requires him to regard any impression as a belief. Beliefs, according to Hume, differ from other ideas simply in being more forceful and vivacious, but impressions differ from ideas only in being more forceful and vivacious still. So every impression must be a belief, a non-inferential belief, as it turns out according to Hume, in its own occurrence. Thus, the noninferential belief that one is having a certain sentiment can motivate just as the sentiment itself would, and as no belief in an object of reason could, because the belief just *is* the sentiment.[6] (Notice that although this position identifies our moral opinions with sentiments, it is *not* noncognitivism. The central tenet of noncognitivism is that what we call our moral opinions are not beliefs that are capable of truth or falsity; the sort of noncognitivist we are considering then adds that they are senti-ments instead. This position holds, by contrast, that our moral opinions are beliefs about our sentiments – but that these noninferential, self-referential beliefs are in fact identical with the sentiments themselves.)

The reader may have noticed, however, that this account of how moral beliefs might motivate in a way that reason never does, requires not just that moral beliefs be beliefs about our sentiments but that they be *noninferential* beliefs about our senti-ments. For it is only noninferential beliefs in the existence our sentiments that Hume is prepared, on my suggestion, to identify with the sentiments themselves. But this means that the Problem that I explained above is relevant again. To be consistent with his own views, Hume cannot regard any of the beliefs about our own sentiments with which he identifies moral beliefs as noninferential. And this means he does not have a consistent account of how those beliefs, though genuinely about matters of fact, can motivate in a way that reason cannot. But, as I have suggested above and again here, he does not see the Problem, and so *believes* that he has such an account. The result, again, is that a reader looking for a consistent Hume will have to make some choices that Hume thought he could avoid. A defender of a noncognitivist reading may argue that since Hume emphatically affirms the special motivational role of moral opinions, and since he cannot consistently fit this view with his subjectivism, the best interpre-tation will abandon the subjectivism. A defender of the subjectivist reading may argue in reply that Hume would not have affirmed such a special motivational role for moral opinions unless he thought (as I have suggested that he did) that this view was consistent with his subjectivism; so, since it turns out not to be consistent with the subjectivism, the best interpretation, overall, will preserve the subjectivism and downplay the remarks on moral motivation. It is unlikely that any single detail of Hume's text will settle a debate like this; the appeal will have to be to the plausibility of an overall interpretation. (At the same time, the consideration mentioned under (1), above – that the remarks on moral motivation in 2.3.3 and 3.1.1 look in the light of other passages in the *Treatise* like oversimplifications of Hume's view – presumably lends some weight to the second option.)

(3) It is controversial, as we have seen, whether Hume really means that no *ought* can be inferred from an *is*. If we assume that he does mean this, he still does not say that the impossibility derives from the motivating power of moral opinions. Even if that

is supposed to be one source of the difficulty, moreover, a plausible argument can be made that it is not, in his view, the only one. It is clear from a passage in the second *Enquiry* that Hume thinks there is a problem in reason's inferring moral conclusions that depends, not on the motivational impact of these conclusions, but rather on their being exactly what his subjectivist account says they are, claims about what feelings we will or would have about various kinds of characters or actions. Among the arguments he calls "solid and satisfactory" (EPM 1.9) to show that "it is impossible for reason ever to draw conclusions of this nature," is this one:

> To virtue . . . it belongs to be *amiable*, and vice *odious*. This forms their very nature or essence. But can reason or argumentation distribute these different epithets to any subjects, and pronounce before-hand, that this must produce love, and that hatred? Or what other reason can we ever assign for these affections, but the original fabric and formation of the human mind, which is naturally adapted to receive them? (EPM 1.6)

There is no hint in this passage as to why reason is blocked from making these particular predictions. But in the *Treatise*, just after he has identified moral facts with facts about our moral feelings, and just before he says that no *ought* can be deduced from an *is*, Hume draws an interesting comparison: "Vice and virtue, therefore, may be compar'd to sounds, colours, heat and cold, which, according to modern philosophy, are not qualities in objects, but perceptions in the mind" (T 3.1.1.26). Hume is here alluding to the distinction, drawn by several seventeenth-century philosophers, between what John Locke called primary qualities (such as bulk, figure, and motion or rest) which were said to be real qualities of bodies, and what Locke called secondary qualities (such as sounds, colors, heat, and cold), which were most often said to be nothing but powers of bodies to produce certain sensations in perceivers, but were also sometimes said, as the quotation from Hume would have it, to be nothing but those sensations or "perceptions" themselves. Locke's very influential discussion of this distinction is permeated by a deep skepticism about the ability of our reason to predict or understand anything about the occurrence of these secondary-quality sensations. So one possibility is that Hume thinks that the analogy, which he here affirms, between secondary qualities and moral qualities – and, especially, between secondary quality sensations and moral sentiments – is close enough to explain why reason is unable to "pronounce beforehand" about either. (This would then be his reason for putting the *is–ought* gap between two kinds of matters of fact, those "in the object" and those concerning our feelings that are "in us." For a discussion pushing this idea about as far as it can be taken, see Sturgeon, 2001.)

It is a complex question whether this interpretation of the *is–ought* passage, and more generally of Hume's denial that moral distinctions can be discovered by reason, would strengthen or weaken the case for a subjectivist over a noncognitivist reading. In one way it could help the case for a subjectivist reading. That is because someone might easily think that, whereas a noncognitivist reading of Hume must of course incur certain costs, it would also have some distinctive advantages over a subjectivist reading. It would have to give up on Hume's claims that moral assessments are about our sentiments and express claims that we can know to be true. But it would preserve Hume's thesis about the special motivational role of moral assessments and, in consequence, it would provide a rationale for the *is–ought* gap. What we have just seen, however, is that Hume may have another rationale for believing in an *is–ought* gap, one that depends only on his subjectivist construal of moral claims: so the noncognitivist reading would have no advantage here after all. (And, of course, we have seen that there can be debate about the importance of the motivational claims.)

On the other hand, this understanding of the *is–ought* gap also creates a problem for a subjectivist reading. It creates a problem because, as we noted above, if Hume cannot maintain that our moral knowledge is noninferential (and obtained by "feeling"), and if he also maintains for the reasons we have just examined that reason cannot obtain this knowledge either, then a subjectivist reading will have him denying the existence of moral knowledge every bit as much as a noncognitivist reading does. Thus, a defender of a noncognitivist interpretation could argue that a subjectivist reading fails either way: it must either allow that reason can discover moral truths or else embrace moral skepticism. A noncognitivist reading will also make Hume a skeptic, of course, but at least has the advantage of preserving his apparent views about moral motivation, as subjectivism cannot. This is probably the best basis available for a noncognitivist reading. Any reply on behalf of subjectivism will undoubtedly have to address, in more detail than I have space to do here, exactly what Hume means to be denying when he says that reason cannot discover moral truths. It is hard to see how he can maintain, in a discussion in which reason is understood to be able to predict, on the basis of past experience, the distant consequences of actions (EPM 1.9, App. 1.2), that reason cannot in *any* way predict, on similar grounds, the sentiments we will feel about various actions. One suspects that he must have in mind that, even if there is some broad notion of reason on which it can do this, there is a narrower and more interesting one on which it cannot. But any exploration of this possibility would take us far from anything that is explicit in Hume's texts.[7]

Conclusion

What we have seen, then, is that any discussion of the question whether Hume is, in any measure, a noncognitivist needs to note several points. First, a number of Hume's most definitive-looking pronouncements about the nature of morality and moral judgment are explicitly subjectivist rather than noncognitivist. Second, several passages that have struck some readers as distinctly noncognitivist in flavor, can in fact be given a plausible subjectivist reading: on close attention to Hume, it can be shown that they either fit with some version of his subjectivism or, at least, that Hume would have thought that they did. Third – a point anticipated by the qualification I have had to make to the second conclusion – Hume makes a mistake about how much of what he says is consistent with his professed subjectivism. This is the difficulty I called the Problem: that Hume thinks that his subjectivism will allow our moral knowledge to consist just in noninferential knowledge of our own sentiments, whereas in fact, and by his own standards, no version of his subjectivism will allow this. As a result, there are inconsistencies in his views, and different choices a reader can make trying to extract a consistent doctrine from his remarks. It is here that a serious case can be made for seeing Hume, from one angle, as a noncognitivist, highlighting his emphasis on the distinctive motivational role of moral assessments. But one can easily, and equally, make a case for seeing him as primarily a subjectivist. As I have indicated, the debate about which of these is the more plausible reconstruction will turn partly on large issues that I have only had space to mention here: how much weight to give to Hume's remarks on the distinctiveness of moral motivation, whether there is some way for his subjectivism to preserve the possibility of moral knowledge even while incorporating some version of his denial that reason can provide that knowledge. It should not be too surprising that the only way to pursue these issues beyond the introduction I have supplied here is to plunge even deeper into Hume's text and into the philosophical issues.

See also 27 "The Sources of Normativity in Hume's Moral Theory"

Notes

1 It is worth noting that Hume is here not merely endorsing a theory inconsistent with noncognitivism but actually pointing out a serious difficulty with the doctrine, at least on a natural elaboration of it. If "thinking" a person virtuous is merely a matter of feeling approval of them, then it seems natural to add that thinking one person more virtuous than another is just a matter of feeling stronger approval of the former than of the latter. But, as Hume points out, this is surely false: even if we feel approval of all those we think virtuous, we do not always experience stronger feelings of approval of those we think more virtuous; because of our particular relations to people, the reverse is often true. For an attempt to deal with a near relative of this difficulty, on behalf of one of those more complex versions of noncognitivism that I have here put aside, see Gibbard (1990: 126–7).

2 Stevenson bases his reading primarily on the second *Enquiry*; he does say in a note that in the *Treatise* Hume "seems very close to acknowledging the quasi-imperative [that is, action-guiding] effect of moral judgments, but he veers off." His interpretation of Hume as a subjectivist, he adds, "seems most consonant with the body of Hume's work" (Stevenson 1944: 274n.).

3 If "Willful murder is vicious" does not count as an *ought*, for purposes of Hume's discussion, then of course the inference from "I disapprove of willful murder" to "Willful murder is vicious" does not after all cross the *is–ought* divide, and the apparent conflict in Hume's remarks disappears; but almost no readers have thought that the solution could be that simple.

4 It is certainly true of a formulation that Hume included in two editions of the second *Enquiry*, according to which "we shall call *every Quality or Action of the Mind*, virtuous, *which is attended with the general Approbation of Mankind*. And we shall denominate vicious, *every Quality, which is the Object of general Blame or Censure*" (EPM, p. 216 [note to 1.10]). But one should note that Hume omitted this passage from the last edition.

5 This is what one would expect from Hume's emphasis, in 3.1.1.26, on the distinction between objects of reason and objects of feeling. It is further confirmed by his argument in 2.3.3, his section on "the influencing motives of the will," that reason alone does not motivate. For what he maintains there is merely that *reasoning* does not motivate. (That is, he does not say, about beliefs arrived at without reasoning, that they are incapable of motivating by themselves.)

6 This thesis, that Hume treats all impressions, including sentiments, as noninferential beliefs in their own occurrence, needs more defense than I provide here; for some of the needed defense,

see Sturgeon (2001: 17–18) and attached note. Hume's account of impressions is at T 1.1.1.1, and his account of sentiments as impressions is at T 1.1.2.1 and 2.1.1. His official account of belief is at T 1.3.7; further relevant passages are at T 1.3.10.3, App.1–9 and Abstract 20–2. To anticipate just one objection: because this account has Hume treating impressions, including sentiments, as entirely self-referential beliefs, beliefs in their own occurrence, it is consistent with Hume's emphatic assertion that "a passion is an original existence . . . and contains not any representative quality, which renders it a copy of *any other* existence or modification" (T 2.3.3.5, emphasis added).

7   There is one possible solution to this difficulty that deserves to be mentioned, even though I do not find it plausible on balance. In most of Hume's extended discussions of whether reason can motivate, or can establish moral conclusions, he carefully takes reason to include both the comparing of ideas (or, he sometimes says, of objects) that is involved in demonstration, and the inferring of matters of fact from the evidence of our experience (T 2.3.3.2–3, 3.1.1.18–26); also EPM App. 1.6–10). But there are nevertheless a surprising number of passages in the *Treatise* in which, denying that reason can discover moral conclusions, he paraphrases his denial by saying only that these conclusions cannot be reached by comparison of ideas – that is, by demonstration (T 3.1.1.4, 3.1.1.27, 3.1.2.1, 3.2.2.20, 3.2.5.4n, 3.3.1.15). Although these passages may represent nothing more than careless abbreviation, it is also possible to wonder whether Hume is here wavering about how much he means to deny. And if, in proclaiming that reason cannot "pronounce before-hand" which actions will arouse love, which hatred, he meant only that reason cannot demonstrate these things a priori, that would of course be compatible with his acknowledging that there is a broader notion of reason – one that includes inference from experience, and is acknowledged in the first set of passages cited above – on which reason can discover these things after all.

The problem with this proposed solution is that although EPM 1 does not explicitly distinguish reasoning about matters of fact from engaging in demonstration, it does nevertheless appear to be working throughout with a generous notion of reason, for it is by its means, Hume says, that nice distinctions are made, "just conclusions drawn, distant comparisons formed, complicated relations examined, and general facts fixed and ascertained" (EPM 1.9). The establishing of general facts, in particular, is a task that Hume would assign only to reasoning from experience. So, when he denies, only three paragraphs earlier, that reason can "pronounce before-hand" about the objects of love and hatred, it is presumably the broader account of reason that he has in mind. The problem therefore remains. (For a consideration of a different possible solution, see Sturgeon 2001: 44–58.)

References

Ayer, Alfred Jules (1952). *Language, Truth and Logic*, 2nd edn. (New York: Dover).
Baier, Annette C. (1991). *A Progress of Sentiments: Reflections on Hume's "Treatise"* (Cambridge, MA: Harvard University Press).
Blackburn, Simon (1996). "Securing the Nots: Moral Epistemology for the Quasi-realist," in Walter Sinnott-Armstrong and Mark Timmons (eds.), *Moral Knowledge* (New York: Oxford University Press), pp. 82–100.
—— (1981). "Reply: Rule-following and Moral Realism," in Stephen Holtzman and Christopher Leich (eds.), *Wittgenstein: To Follow a Rule* (London: Routledge and Kegan Paul), pp. 163–87.
Brown, Charlotte (1988). "Is Hume an Internalist?" *Journal of the History of Philosophy*, 26, pp. 69–87.
Flew, A. G. N. (1963). "On the Interpretation of Hume," *Philosophy*, 38, pp. 178–82.

Foot, Philippa (1963). "Hume on Moral Judgement," in D. F. Pears (ed.), *David Hume: A Symposium* (London: Macmillan), pp. 67–76.

Gibbard, Allan (1990). *Wise Choices, Apt Feelings* (Cambridge, MA: Harvard University Press).

Hare, R. M. (1952). *The Language of Morals* (Oxford: Clarendon Press).

Harrison, Jonathan (1976). *Hume's Moral Epistemology* (Oxford: Clarendon Press).

Hudson, W. D. (1964). "Hume on *Is* and *Ought*," *Philosophical Quarterly*, 14, pp. 246–52.

MacIntyre, A. C. (1959). "Hume on 'Is' and 'Ought'," *Philosophical Review*, 68, pp. 451–68.

Mackie, J. L. (1980). *Hume's Moral Theory* (London: Routledge and Kegan Paul).

Stevenson, Charles (1944). *Ethics and Language* (New Haven, CT: Yale University Press).

—— (1963). *Facts and Values: Studies in Ethical Analysis* (New Haven, CT: Yale University Press).

Stroud, Barry (1977). *Hume* (London: Routledge and Kegan Paul).

Sturgeon, Nicholas L. (2001). "Moral Skepticism and Moral Naturalism in Hume's *Treatise*," *Hume Studies*, 27, pp. 3–83.

—— (forthcoming). "Hume on Reason and Passion," in Donald Ainslie (ed.), *Hume's Treatise: A Critical Guide* (Cambridge: Cambridge University Press).

Bibliography

Abramson, Kate (1999). "Correcting *Our* Sentiments about Hume's Moral Point of View," *Southern Journal of Philosophy*, 37, pp. 333–61.

—— (2000). "Sympathy and the Project of Hume's *Second Enquiry*," *Archiv für Geschichte der Philosophie*, 83, pp. 45–80.

—— (2002). "Two Portraits of the Humean Moral Agent," *Pacific Philosophical Quarterly*, 83, pp. 301–34.

—— (forthcoming). "What's So 'Natural' about the Natural Virtues?" in Donald Ainslie (ed.), *Critical Essays on Hume's "Treatise"* (Cambridge: Cambridge University Press).

Adams, R. M. (1992). "Miracles, Laws of Nature and Causation – II," *The Aristotelian Society*, supplementary vol. 60, pp. 207–24.

Ahern, Dennis (1975). "Hume on the Evidential Impossibility of Miracles," in Nicholas Rescher (ed.), *Studies in Epistemology* (Oxford: Blackwell), pp. 1–32.

Ainslie, D. C. (1999). "Scepticism about Persons in Book II of Hume's *Treatise*," *Journal of the History of Philosophy*, 37, pp. 469–92.

—— (2001). "Hume's Reflections on the Identity and Simplicity of Mind," *Philosophy and Phenomenological Research*, 62, pp. 557–78.

—— (2003). "Hume, a Scottish Socrates?" *Canadian Journal of Philosophy*, 33, pp. 133–54.

Alanen, Lilli (2006). "The Powers and Mechanisms of the Passions," in Saul Traiger (ed.), *The Blackwell Guide to Hume's "Treatise"* (Malden, MA: Blackwell), pp. 179–98.

Allan, James (1998). *A Sceptical Theory of Morality and Law* (New York: Peter Lang).

Allen, John (1825). "Review of John Lingard's *A History of England*," repr. in James Fieser (ed.), *Early Responses to Hume's History of England*, 2 vols. (Bristol: Thoemmes, 2002).

Allestree, Richard (1658/1677). *The Whole Duty of Man*. Published anonymously, authorship now generally attributed to Richard Allestree. Originally published under the title *The Practice of Christian Graces, or, the Whole Duty of Man*.

Alston, William P. (1991). *Perceiving God: The Epistemology of Religious Experience* (Ithaca, NY: Cornell University Press).

Anderson, James (1790). "Review of Sir John Sinclair's *History of the Public Revenue*," *Monthly Review*, 2nd series, 3, pp. 93–4.

Anderson, R. (1966). *Hume's First Principles* (Lincoln, NE: University of Nebraska Press).

Anon. (1684). *The Whole Duty of Man* (London: R. Norton for Robert Pawley, at the Sign of the Bible in Chancery Lane, near Fleet Street).

Anscombe, G. E. M. (1957). *Intention* (Oxford: Basil Blackwell).

Árdal, Páll S. (1966). *Passion and Value in Hume's "Treatise"* (Edinburgh: Edinburgh University Press, 1989).

—— (1977). "Another Look at Hume's Account of Moral Evaluation," *Journal of the History of Philosophy*, 15, pp. 405–21.

Armstrong, Benjamin F. (1995). "Hume's Actual Argument against Belief in Miracles," *History of Philosophy Quarterly*, 12, pp. 65–76.

Arnauld, Antoine and Nicole, Pierre (1662). *The Art of Thinking*, ed. James Dickoff and Patricia James (Indianapolis, IN: Bobbs-Merrill, 1964).

Arnold, N. Scott (1983). "Hume's Skepticism about Inductive Inference," *Journal of the History of Philosophy*, 21, pp. 31–55.

Audi, Robert (2001). *The Architecture of Reason: The Structure and Substance of Rationality* (Oxford: Oxford University Press).

—— (2002). "Prospects for a Naturalization of Practical Reason: Humean Instrumentalism and the Normative Authority of Desire," *International Journal of Philosophical Studies*, 10, pp. 235–63.

Ayer, A. J. (1936/1952). *Language, Truth and Logic* (London: Gollancz; 2nd edn. New York: Dover).

—— (1954). *Philosophical Essays* (New York: St. Martin's Press).

—— (1980). *Hume* (New York: Hill and Wang).

Ayers, Michael (1996). "Natures and Laws from Descartes to Hume," in G. A. J. Rogers and Sylvana Tomaselli (eds.), *The Philosophical Canon in the Seventeenth and Eighteenth Centuries: Essays in Honour of John W. Yolton* (Rochester, NY: University of Rochester Press), pp. 83–101.

Ayers, Michael (ed.) (1993). *Philosophical Works: Including the Works on Vision / George Berkeley* (London: J. M. Dent).

Bagger, Matthew C. (1997). "Hume and Miracles," *Journal of the History of Philosophy*, 35, pp. 237–51.

Baier, Annette C. (1978). "Hume's Analysis of Pride," *Journal of Philosophy*, 75, pp. 27–40.

—— (1991). *A Progress of Sentiments: Reflections on Hume's "Treatise"* (Cambridge, MA: Harvard University Press).

—— (1994). *Moral Prejudices, Essays on Ethics* (Cambridge, MA: Harvard University Press).

—— (1998). "Hume, David (1711–76)," in Edward Craig (ed.), *Routledge Encyclopedia of Philosophy*, vol. 4 (London: Routledge), pp. 543–62.

—— (2000). "Hume: The Reflective Woman's Epistemologist?" in Anne Jaap Jacobson (ed.), *Feminist Interpretations of David Hume* (State College, PA: Penn State University Press), pp. 19–38.

—— (2001). "Hume, David (1711–1776)," in Lawrence C. Becker and Charlotte B. Becker (eds.), *Encyclopedia of Ethics*, vol. 2 (New York: Routledge), pp. 803–15.

Baillie, James (2000). *Hume on Morality* (London: Routledge).

Balfour, James (1753). *A Delineation of the Nature and Obligation of Morality* (Edinburgh: Hamilton, Balfour and Neill; repr. Bristol: Thoemmes Antiquarian Books Ltd., 1989).

Baron, Marcia (1988). "Morality as a Back-up System: Hume's View?" *Hume Studies*, 14, pp. 25–53.

Basinger, David (1986). *Philosophy and Miracle: The Contemporary Debate* (New York: Mellen Press).

Baxter, Donald L. M. (1990). "Hume on Virtue, Beauty, Composites, and Secondary Qualities," *Pacific Philosophical Quarterly*, 71, pp. 103–18.

—— (1998). "Hume's Labyrinth concerning the Idea of Personal Identity," *Hume Studies*, 24, pp. 203–34.

Bayle, Pierre (1682). *Various Thoughts on the Occasion of a Comet*, trans. Robert C. Bartlett (Albany, NY: State University of New York Press, 2000).

—— (1697). *Historical and Critical Dictionary*, trans. Richard H. Popkin (Indianapolis, IN: Bobbs-Merrill, 1965).

Bayles, M. (1976). "Hume on Blame and Excuse," *Hume Studies*, 2, pp. 17–35.

Beattie, James (1770). *An Essay on the Nature and Immutablity of Truth, in Opposition to Sophistry and Scepticism*, 10th edn. (London: Lackington, Allen and Co., 1810).

Beauchamp, Tom L. (1979). "Self Inconsistency or Mere Self Perplexity," *Hume Studies*, 5, pp. 37–44.

Beauchamp, Tom L. and Mappes, Thomas A. (1975). "Is Hume Really a Sceptic about Induction?" *American Philosophical Quarterly*, 12, pp. 119–29.

Beauchamp, Tom L. and Rosenberg, Alexander (1981). *Hume and the Problem of Causation* (New York: Oxford University Press).

Bechtel, William and Abrahamson, Adele (1990). *Cognition and the Mind* (Oxford: Blackwell).

Bechtel, William and Graham, George (eds.) (1998). *A Companion to Cognitive Science* (Oxford: Blackwell).

Beckwith, Francis J. (1989). *David Hume's Argument against Miracles: A Critical Analysis* (Lanham, MD: University Press of America).

Beebee, Helen (2006). *Hume on Causation* (London: Routledge).

Bell, Martin (2000). "Sceptical Doubts concerning Hume's Causal Realism," in Rupert Read and Kenneth A. Richman (eds.), *The New Hume Debate* (London: Routledge), pp. 122–37.

Bell, Martin and McGinn, Marie (1990). "Naturalism and Scepticism," *Philosophy*, 65, pp. 399–418.

Bennett, Jonathan (1971). *Locke, Berkeley, Hume: Central Themes* (Oxford: Clarendon Press).

—— (2001). *Learning from Six Philosophers: Descartes, Spinoza, Leibniz, Locke, Berkeley, Hume*, vol. 2 (Oxford: Clarendon Press).

Berkeley, George (1732). *Alciphron, or, the Minute Philosopher in Focus / George Berkeley*, ed. David Berman (London: Routledge, 1993).

—— (1732). *An Essay towards a New Theory of Vision*, from Michael R. Ayers (ed.), *Philosophical Works, Including the Works on Vision / George Berkeley* (London: J. M. Dent, 1975).

Biro, John I. (1985). "Hume and Cognitive Science," *History of Philosophy Quarterly*, 2, pp. 257–74.

Bishop, Michael A. and Trout, J. D. (2005). *Epistemology and the Psychology of Human Judgment* (New York: Oxford University Press).

Black, Max (1954). "Inductive Support of Inductive Rules," in *Problems of Analysis: Philosophical Essays* (Ithaca: Cornell University Press), pp. 191–208.

Blackburn, Simon (1981). "Reply: Rule-following and Moral Realism," in Stephen Holtzman and Christopher Leich (eds.), *Wittgenstein: To Follow a Rule* (London: Routledge and Kegan Paul), pp. 163–87.

—— (1984). *Spreading the World* (New York: Oxford University Press).

—— (1993). *Essays in Quasi-realism* (New York: Oxford University Press).

—— (1993). "Hume on the Mezzanine Level," *Hume Studies*, 19, pp. 273–88.

—— (1996). "Securing the Nots: Moral Epistemology for the Quasi-realist," in Walter Sinnott-Armstrong and Mark Timmons (eds.), *Moral Knowledge* (New York: Oxford University Press), pp. 82–100.

—— (1998). *Ruling Passions* (Oxford: Clarendon Press).

—— (1999). "Playing Hume's Hand," in D. Z. Phillips and Timothy Tessin (eds.), *Religion and Hume's Legacy* (Basingstoke and New York: Macmillan and St. Martin's Press).

—— (2000). "Kant versus Hume on Practical Reasoning," in D. P. Chattopadhyaya (ed.), *Realism: Responses and Reactions* (*Essays in Honour of Pranab Kumar Sen*) (New Delhi: Indian Council of Philosophical Research), pp. 462–80.

—— (2002). "Postscript," in Peter Millican (ed.), *Reading Hume on Human Understanding* (Oxford: Clarendon Press), pp. 273–6.

—— (2002). "Hume and Thick Connexions," in Peter Millican (ed.), *Reading Hume on Human Understanding* (New York: Oxford University Press), pp. 259–76.

—— (2005). *Truth: A Guide* (Oxford: Oxford University Press).

Blair, Hugh (1825). *Sermons*, 2 vols. (Edinburgh: T. and W. Nelson).

—— (1965). *Lectures on Rhetoric*, 2 vols., ed. Harold F. Harding (Carbondale, IL: Southern Illinois University Press).

Blaug, M. (ed.) (1995). *The Quantity Theory of Money: From Locke to Keynes and Friedman* (Aldershot: Elgar).

Bongie, Laurence (1965). *David Hume: Prophet of the Counter Revolution* (Oxford: Clarendon Press).

Bonjour, Lawrence (1986). "A Reconsideration of the Problem of Induction," *Philosophical Topics*, 14, pp. 93–124.

Boswell, James (1928–34). *Private Papers of James Boswell from Malahide Castle*, ed. G. Scott and F. A. Pottle, 18 vols. (New York).

—— (1970). *Boswell in Extremes, 1776–1778*, ed. Charles McC. Weis and Frederick A. Pottle (New York: McGraw-Hill).

Botterill, George (2002). "Hume on Liberty and Necessity," in Peter Millican (ed.), *Reading Hume on Human Understanding* (Oxford: Clarendon Press), pp. 277–300.

Bower, Kenneth (1984). "Imagery: from Hume to Cognitive Science," *Canadian Journal of Philosophy*, 15, pp. 217–34.

Box, M. A. (1990). *The Suasive Art of David Hume* (Princeton, NJ: Princeton University Press).

Braithwaite, R. B. (1953). *Scientific Explanation* (Cambridge: Cambridge University Press).

Braudy, Leo (1970). *Narrative Form in History and Fiction: Hume, Fielding, Gibbon* (Princeton, NJ: Princeton University Press).

Bricke, John (1980). *Hume's Philosophy of Mind* (Princeton, NJ: Princeton University Press).

—— (1988). "Hume, Freedom to Act, and Personal Evaluation," *History of Philosophy Quarterly*, 5, pp. 141–56.

—— (1996). *Mind and Morality: An Examination of Hume's Moral Psychology* (Oxford: Clarendon Press).

Broad, C. D. (1944). *Five Types of Ethical Theory* (London: Kegan Paul, Trench, Trubner and Co.).

Broadie, A. (ed.) (2003). *The Cambridge Companion to the Scottish Enlightenment* (Cambridge: Cambridge University Press).

Broughton, Janet (1983). "Hume's Skepticism about Causal Inferences," *Pacific Philosophical Quarterly*, 64, pp. 3–18.

—— (1987). "Hume's Ideas about Necessary Connection," *Hume Studies*, 13, pp. 217–44.

—— (1992). "What Does the Scientist of Man Observe?" *Hume Studies*, 28, pp. 155–68.

—— (2004). "Hume's Naturalism about Cognitive Norms," *Philosophical Topics*, 31, pp. 1–19.

—— (2004). "The Inquiry in the *Treatise*," *Philosophical Review*, 113, pp. 537–56.

—— (2006). "Impressions and Ideas," in Saul Traiger (ed.), *The Blackwell Guide to Hume's "Treatise"* (Malden, MA: Blackwell Publishers), pp. 43–58.

Brown, Charlotte (1988). "Is Hume an Internalist?" *Journal of the History of Philosophy*, 26, pp. 69–82.

—— (1994). "From Spectator to Agent: Hume's Theory of Obligation," *Hume Studies*, 20, pp. 19–35.

Buckle, Stephen (1991). *Natural Law and the Theory of Property: Grotius to Hume* (Oxford: Clarendon Press).

—— (2001). *Hume's Enlightenment Tract: The Unity and Purpose of "An Enquiry concerning Human Understanding"* (Oxford: Clarendon Press).

—— (2001). "Marvels, Miracles, and Mundane Order: Hume's Critique of Religion in *An Enquiry concerning Human Understanding*," *Australasian Journal of Philosophy*, 79, pp. 1–31.

Burns, R. M. (1981). *The Great Debate on Miracles: From Joseph Glanvill to David Hume* (Lewisburg, PA: Bucknell University Press).

Burnyeat, Myles (ed.) (1983). *The Skeptical Tradition* (Berkeley: University of California Press).

Butler, Joseph (1736). *The Analogy of Religion to the Constitution and Course of Nature: Also Fifteen Sermons* (London: Religious Tract Society, 1881).

—— (1736). *The Works of Bishop Butler*, 2 vols., ed. J. H. Bernard (London: Macmillan, 1900).

Butler, R. J. (1960). "Natural Belief and the Enigma of Hume," *Archiv für Geschichte der Philosophie*, 42, pp. 73–100.

Caffentzis, C. G. (2001). "Hume, Money, and Civilization; Or, Why Was Hume a Metalist?" *Hume Studies*, 27, pp. 301–35.

Calderwood, Henry (1898). *David Hume* (Edinburgh and London: Anderson and Ferrier).

Calvin, John (1536). *Institutes of the Christian Religion*, ed. John T. McNeill, trans. Ford Lewis Battles (Philadelphia: Westminster Press, 1960).

Campbell, George (1762). *A Dissertation on Miracles* (New York: Garland Publishing, 1983).

Capaldi, Nicholas (1975). *David Hume: The Newtonian Philosopher* (Boston: Twayne).

—— (1989). *Hume's Place in Moral Philosophy* (New York: Peter Lang).

Capaldi, Nicholas and Livingston, Donald (1990). *Liberty in Hume's History of England* (Dordrecht: Kluwer).

Chambers, E. (1728). *Cyclopaedia: Or, An Universal Dictionary of Arts and Sciences* (London: James and John Knapton, John Darby, Daniel Midwinter, Arthur Bettesworth, John Senex [and 13 others]).

Charron, William C. (1980). "Conventions, Games of Strategy, and Hume's Philosophy of Law and Government," *American Philosophical Quarterly*, 17, pp. 327–34.

Chisholm, Roderick (2003). "Human Freedom and the Self," in Gary Watson (ed.), *Free Will* (Oxford: Oxford University Press), pp. 26–37.

Cicero, Marcus Tullius (1921). *De officiis*, trans. Walter Miller (Cambridge, MA: Harvard University Press, Loeb Library).

—— (1972). *The Nature of the Gods*, trans. Horace C. P. McGregor (Harmondsworth: Penguin).

Clarke, Samuel (1705). *A Discourse concerning the Unchangeable Obligations of Natural Religion, and the Truth and Certainty of the Christian Revelation* (The Boyle Lectures), excerpted in D. D. Raphael (ed.), *British Moralists 1650–1800*, vol. 1 (Indianapolis: Hackett Publishing Co., 1991).

—— (1738). *Works*, vol. 2: *A Demonstration of the Being and Attributes of God* (New York: Garland Publishing Inc., 1978).

Clarke, Steve (1999). "Hume's Definition of Miracles Revised," *American Philosophical Quarterly*, 36, pp. 49–57.

Clatterbaugh, Kenneth C. (1999). *The Causation Debate in Early Modern Philosophy: 1637–1739* (New York: Routledge).

Cohen, Mendel F. (1990). "Obligation and Human Nature in Hume's Philosophy," *Philosophical Quarterly*, 40, pp. 316–41.

Cohon, Rachel (1994). "On an Unorthodox Account of Hume's Moral Psychology," *Hume Studies*, 20, pp. 179–94.

—— (1997). "The Common Point of View in Hume's Ethics," *Philosophy and Phenomenological Research*, 57, pp. 827–50.

—— (1997). "Is Hume a Noncognitivist in the Motivation Argument?" *Philosophical Studies*, 85, pp. 251–66.

Cohon, Rachel and Owen, David (1997). "Hume on Representation, Reason and Motivation," *Manuscrito*, 20, pp. 47–76.

Collier, Mark (1999). "Filling the Gaps: Hume and Connectionism on the Continued Existence of Unperceived Objects," *Hume Studies*, 25, pp. 155–70.

Collingwood, R. G. (1993). *The Idea of History*, ed. J. van der Dussen (Oxford: Clarendon Press).

Connon, R. W. (1976). "The Naturalism of Hume Revisited," in David Fate Norton, Nicholas Capaldi, and Wade L. Robison (eds.), *McGill Hume Studies*, vol. 1: *Studies in Hume and Scottish Philosophy* (San Diego, CA: Austin Hill Press), pp. 121–45.

Cook, J. W. (1968/1995). "Hume's Scepticism with Regard to the Senses," *American Philosophical Quarterly*, 5, from Stanley Tweyman (ed.), *David Hume: Critical Assessments*, vol. 3 (London: Routledge), pp. 567–96.

Cooper, Anthony Ashley, Third Earl of Shaftesbury (1711). *Characteristics of Men, Manners, Opinions, Times*, 3 vols., ed. Lawrence E. Klein (Cambridge: Cambridge University Press, 1999).

Costa, J. L. (1988/1995). "Hume and the Existence of an External World," *Philosophical Studies* (1988–90), from Stanley Tweyman (ed.), *David Hume: Critical Assessments*, vol. 3 (London: Routledge, 1995), pp. 555–66.

Costa, M. (1981). "Hume and Justified Belief," *Canadian Journal of Philosophy*, 11, pp. 219–28.

—— (1989). "Hume and Causal Realism," *Australasian Journal of Philosophy*, 67, pp. 172–90.

—— (1990). "Hume, Strict Identity, and Time's Vacuum," *Hume Studies*, 16, pp. 1–16.

—— (1998). "Hume on the Very Idea of a Relation," *Hume Studies*, 24, pp. 71–94.

Costelloe, Timothy M. (2004). "Hume's Aesthetics: The Literature and Directions for Research," *Hume Studies*, 30, pp. 87–126.

Craig, E. J. (1987). *The Mind of God and the Works of Man* (Oxford: Clarendon Press).

—— (2000). "Hume on Causality: Projectivist *and* Realist?" in Rupert Read and Kenneth A. Richman (eds.), *The New Hume Debate* (London: Routledge), pp. 113–21.

—— (2002). "The Idea of Necessary Connexion," in Peter Millican (ed.), *Reading Hume on Human Understanding* (New York: Oxford University Press), pp. 211–29.

Crane, Tim (1998). "Intentionality," in E. Craig (ed.), *Routledge Encyclopedia of Philosophy* (London: Routledge), retrieved June 20, 2007, from http://www.rep.routledge.com/article/V019SECT2.

Cullity, Garrett and Gaut, Berys (eds.) (1997). *Ethics and Practical Reason* (Oxford: Oxford University Press).

d'Alembert, J. Le R. (1751). *Preliminary Discourse to the Encyclopedia of Diderot*, trans. R. N. Schwab (Chicago: University of Chicago Press, 1995).

Damasio, Antonio R. (1994). *Descartes' Error: Emotion, Reason, and the Human Brain* (New York: G. P. Putnam's Sons).

Dancy, Jonathan (1993). *Moral Reasons* (Oxford: Blackwell).

—— (2000). *Practical Reality* (Oxford: Oxford University Press).

Darwall, Stephen (1995). *The British Moralists and the Internal "Ought": 1640–1740* (Cambridge: Cambridge University Press).

—— (1998). "Empathy, Sympathy, Care," *Philosophical Studies*, 89, pp. 261–82.

—— (1999). "Sympathetic Liberalism," *Philosophy and Public Affairs*, 28, pp. 139–64.

—— (2002). *Welfare and Rational Care* (Princeton, NJ: Princeton University Press).

Dauer, Francis W. (1975). "Towards a Copernican Reading of Hume," *Noûs*, 9, pp. 269–93.

—— (1980). "Hume's Skeptical Solution and the Causal Theory of Knowledge," *Philosophical Review*, 89, pp. 357–78.

David, Philip and Gillies, Donald (1989). "A Bayesian Analysis of Hume's Argument concerning Miracles," *Philosophical Quarterly*, 39, pp. 57–65.

Davidson, Donald (1963/1980/2001). "Actions, Reasons, Causes," *Journal of Philosophy*, 60, pp. 685–700; repr. in Donald Davidson, *Essays on Actions and Events* (Oxford: Clarendon Press, 1980, 2001).

—— (1976). "Hume's Cognitive Theory of Pride," *Journal of Philosophy*, 73, pp. 744–56.

—— (2001). "Freedom to Act," in Donald Davidson, *Essays on Actions and Events* (Oxford: Clarendon Press), pp. 63–81.

—— (2001). "Mental Events," in Donald Davidson, *Essays on Actions and Events* (Oxford: Clarendon Press), pp. 207–25.

Dees, Richard H. (1997). "Hume on the Characters of Virtue," *Journal of the History of Philosophy*, 35, pp. 45–64.

Dennett, Daniel (1984). *Elbow Room: The Varieties of Free Will Worth Wanting* (Cambridge, MA: MIT Press).

Descartes, René (1641). *Meditations on First Philosophy*, in *The Philosophical Writings of Descartes*, trans. J. Cottingham, R. Stoothoff, and D. Murdoch (Cambridge: Cambridge University Press, 1985).

—— (1649). *The Passions of the Soul*, trans. Robert Stoothoff, in *The Philosophical Writings of Descartes*, vol. 1, trans. J. Cottingham, R. Stoothoff, and D. Murdoch (New York: Cambridge University Press, 1985).

Dicker, Georges (1998). *Hume's Epistemology and Metaphysics: An Introduction* (London: Routledge and Kegan Paul).

Diderot, D. (1754). *Thoughts on the Interpretation of Nature and Other Philosophical Works*, ed. D. Adams (Manchester: Clinamen Press, 1999).

Dostoevsky, Fyodor (1964). "Rebellion" (from *The Brothers Karamazov*), in Nelson Pike (ed.), *God and Evil: Readings on the Theological Problem of Evil* (Englewood Cliffs, NJ: Prentice-Hall), pp. 6–16.

Dretske, Fred I. (1991/2000). "Two Conceptions of Knowledge: Rational vs. Reliable," *Grazer Philosophische Studien*, 4, pp. 15–30, repr. in Fred I. Dretske, *Perception, Knowledge, and Belief: Selected Essays* (Cambridge: Cambridge University Press, 2000), pp. 80–93.

Earman, John (1993). "Bayes, Hume, and Miracles," *Faith and Philosophy*, 10, pp. 293–310.

—— (2000). *Hume's Abject Failure: The Argument against Miracles* (New York: Oxford University Press).

Ellin, Joseph S. (1993). "Again: Hume on Miracles," *Hume Studies*, 19, pp. 203–12.

Emerson, Roger L. (1990). "Science and Moral Philosophy in the Scottish Enlightenment," in M. A. Stewart (ed.), *Studies in the Philosophy of the Scottish Enlightenment* (Oxford: Clarendon Press).

—— (1995). "The 'Affair' at Edinburgh and the 'Project' at Glasgow: The Politics of Hume's Attempts to Become a Professor," in M. A. Stewart and John P. Wright (eds.), *Hume and Hume's Connexions* (University Park, PA: Pennsylvania State University Press), pp. 1–22.

Falkenstein, Lorne (1997). "Naturalism, Normativity, and Scepticism in Hume's Account of Belief," *Hume Studies*, 23, pp. 29–72.

Ferreira, M. Jamie (1986). *Scepticism and Reasonable Doubt: The British Naturalist Tradition in Wilkins, Hume, Reid and Newman* (Oxford: Clarendon Press).

Fieser, James (1992). "Hume's Classification of the Passions and Its Precursors," *Hume Studies*, 18(1), pp. 1–17.

—— (1995). "Introduction to the Essays on Suicide and the Immortality of the Soul" (1783 edn.), in James Fieser (ed.), *The Writings of David Hume* (internet publication).

—— (2002). *Early Responses to Hume's "History of England,"* 2 vols. (Bristol: Thoemmes).

—— (2003). *A Bibliography of Hume's Writings and Early Responses* (Bristol, England: Thoemmes Press, internet publication).

Fischer, John Martin (ed.) (1993). *The Metaphysics of Death* (Stanford, CA: Stanford University Press).

Flage, Daniel (1985). "Hume on Memory and Causation," *Hume Studies*, 10th anniversary issue, pp. 168–88.

—— (1990). *David Hume's Theory of Mind* (London: Routledge).

—— (2000). "Relative Ideas Revisited," in Rupert Read and Kenneth A. Richman (eds.), *The New Hume Debate* (London: Routledge), pp. 138–55.

Flew, Antony (1961). *Hume's Philosophy of Belief: A Study of His First Inquiry* (London: Routledge and Kegan Paul).

—— (1963). "On the Interpretation of Hume," *Philosophy*, 38, pp. 178–82.

—— (1967). "Miracles," *Encyclopedia of Philosophy*, vol. 5 (New York: Macmillan and Free Press), pp. 346–53.

—— (1986). *David Hume, Philosopher of Moral Science* (Oxford: Basil Blackwell).

Flew, Antony, Hare, R. M., and Mitchell, Basil (1955). "Theology and Falsification," in Antony Flew and Alasdair MacIntyre (eds.), *New Essays in Philosophical Theology* (London: SCM Press), pp. 66–105.

Fodor, Jerry (1975). *The Language of Thought* (Cambridge, MA: Harvard University Press).

—— (1981). *Representations* (Cambridge, MA: MIT Press).

—— (1987). "Mental Representation: An Introduction," in Nicholas Rescher (ed.), *Scientific Inquiry in Philosophical Perspective* (Lanham, MD: University Press of America), pp. 35–74.

—— (2003). *Hume Variations* (Oxford: Clarendon Press).

Fogelin, Robert J. (1984). "Hume and the Missing Shade of Blue," *Philosophy and Phenomenological Research*, 45, pp. 263–72.

—— (1985). *Hume's Skepticism in the "Treatise of Human Nature"* (London: Routledge and Kegan Paul).

—— (1993). "Hume's Scepticism," in David Fate Norton (ed.), *The Cambridge Companion to Hume* (Cambridge: Cambridge University Press), pp. 90–116.

—— (2003). *A Defense of Hume on Miracles* (Princeton, NJ: Princeton University Press).

Foot, Philippa (1963). "Hume on Moral Judgement," in D. F. Pears (ed.), *David Hume: A Symposium* (London: Macmillan), pp. 67–76.

—— (1978). *Virtues and Vices* (Oxford: Basil Blackwell).

Forbes, Duncan (1975). *Hume's Philosophical Politics* (Cambridge: Cambridge University Press).

Force, J. E. (1987). "Hume's Interest in Newton and Science," *Hume Studies*, 13, pp. 166–216.

Frankfurt, Harry G. (1971). "Freedom of the Will and the Concept of a Person," *Journal of Philosophy*, 68, pp. 5–20.

—— (2004). *The Reasons of Love* (Princeton, NJ: Princeton University Press).

Frasca-Spada, Marina (1998). *Space and the Self in Hume's* Treatise (Cambridge: Cambridge University Press).

Gardiner, P. L. (1963). "Hume's Theory of the Passions," in D. F. Pears (ed.), *David Hume: A Symposium* (London: Macmillan), pp. 31–42.

Garrett, Don (1981). "Hume's Self-doubts about Personal Identity," *Philosophical Review*, 90, pp. 337–58.

—— (1997). *Cognition and Commitment in Hume's Philosophy* (New York: Oxford University Press).

—— (2004). " 'A Small Tincture of Pyrrhonism': Skepticism and Naturalism in Hume's Science of Man," in Walter Sinnott-Armstrong (ed.), *Pyrrhonian Skepticism* (Oxford: Oxford University Press), pp. 68–98.

—— (2006). "Hume's Naturalistic Theory of Representation," *Synthese*, 152.

Gaskin, J. (1974). "God, Hume and Natural Belief," *Philosophy*, 49, pp. 281–94.

—— (1978). *Hume's Philosophy of Religion* (London: Macmillan, 1988).

—— (1993). "Hume on Religion," in David Fate Norton (ed.), *The Cambridge Companion to Hume* (Cambridge: Cambridge University Press), pp. 331–44.

—— (2002). "Religion: The Useless Hypothesis," in Peter Millican (ed.), *Reading Hume on Human Understanding* (Oxford: Oxford University Press), pp. 349–69.

—— (ed.) (1998). *Principal Writings on Religion: Including "Dialogues concerning Natural Religion" and "The Natural History of Religion"* (Oxford: Oxford University Press).

Gauthier, David (1990). *Moral Dealing: Contract, Ethics, and Reason* (Ithaca, NY: Cornell University Press).

Giarizzo, Giuseppe (1962). *David Hume, politico e storico* (*David Hume, Political Theorist and Historian*) (Turin: Einaudi).

—— (1971). "Ancora su Hume storico," *Rivista storica italiana*, 83, pp. 429–49.

Gibbard, Allan (1990). *Wise Choices, Apt Feelings* (Cambridge, MA: Harvard University Press).

Glathe, A. B. (1950). *Hume's Theory of the Passions and of Morals: A Study of Books II and III of the "Treatise"* (Berkeley: University of California Press).

Goldman, Alvin (1975). "Innate Knowledge," in Stephen Stich (ed.), *Innate Ideas* (Berkeley, CA: University of California Press), pp. 111–20.

—— (1986). *Epistemology and Cognition* (Cambridge, MA: Harvard University Press).

Goodman, Nelson (1955). *Fact, Fiction, and Forecast* (Cambridge, MA: Harvard University Press).

Govier, Trudy (1972). "Variations on Force and Vivacity in Hume," *Philosophical Quarterly*, 86, pp. 44–52.

Gower, Barry (1990). "David Hume and the Probability of Miracles," *Hume Studies*, 16, pp. 17–31.

Greig, J. Y. T. (1931). *David Hume* (Oxford: Oxford University Press).

Greig, J. Y. T. (ed.) (1932). *The Letters of David Hume*, 2 vols. (Oxford: Clarendon Press).

Gunn, J. A. W. (1983). *Beyond Liberty and Property* (Kingston: McGill Queens University Press).

Haakonssen, Knud (1981). *The Science of a Legislator: The Natural Jurisprudence of David Hume and Adam Smith* (Cambridge: Cambridge University Press).

—— (1993). "The Structure of Hume's Political Theory," in David Fate Norton (ed.), *The Cambridge Companion to Hume* (Cambridge: Cambridge University Press), pp. 182–221.

Habermas, J. (1987). *The Philosophical Discourse of Modernity*, trans. F. G. Lawrence (Cambridge, MA: MIT Press).

Hacking, Ian (1965) *Logic of Statistical Inference* (Cambridge: Cambridge University Press).

—— (1975). *The Emergence of Probability: A Philosophical Study of Early Ideas about Probability, Induction, and Statistical Inference* (Cambridge: Cambridge University Press).

Haji, Ishtiyaque (2002). *Deontic Morality and Control* (Cambridge: Cambridge University Press).

Haldane, John J. and Smart, Jack J. C. (1996). *Atheism and Theism* (Oxford: Blackwell).

Hampton, Jean (1986). *Hobbes and the Social Contract Tradition* (Cambridge: Cambridge University Press).

—— (1995). "Does Hume Have an Instrumental Conception of Practical Reason?" *Hume Studies*, 21, pp. 57–74.

—— (1997). "The Hobbesian Side of Hume," in Herman, Korsgaard, and Reath (eds.), *Reclaiming the History of Ethics* (Cambridge: Cambridge University Press).

Hansen, Stacey J. (1988). "Hume's Impressions of Belief," *Hume Studies*, 14, pp. 277–304.

Hare, R. M. (1952). *The Language of Morals* (Oxford: Clarendon Press).

Harman, Gilbert (1965). "Inference to the Best Explanation," *Philosophical Review*, 74, pp. 88–95.

—— (1986). *Moral Agent and Impartial Spectator*, The Lindley Lecture.

Harris, James A. (2005). *Of Liberty and Necessity: The Free Will Debate in Eighteenth-century British Philosophy* (Oxford: Clarendon Press).

Harrison, Jonathan (1976). *Hume's Moral Epistemology* (Oxford: Clarendon Press).

—— (1981). *Hume's Theory of Justice* (Oxford: Clarendon Press).

Hatfield, Gary (1995). "Remaking the Science of Mind: Psychology as Natural Science," in Christopher Fox, Roy Porter, and Robert Wokler (eds.), *Inventing Human Science: Eighteenth-century Domains* (Berkeley, Los Angeles, and London: University of California Press).

Haugeland, John (1998). *Having Thought: Essays in the Metaphysics of Mind* (Cambridge, MA: Harvard University Press).

Hayek, Friedrich August von (1963/1966). *The Legal and Political Philosophy of David Hume. Il Politico*, 28, from V. C. Chappell (ed.), *Hume: A Collection of Critical Essays* (Garden City, NY: Anchor Books, 1966), pp. 335–60.

Hearn, T. K. (1973). "Árdal on the Moral Sentiments in Hume's *Treatise*," *Philosophy*, 48, pp. 288–92.

537

—— (1976). "General Rules and the Moral Sentiments in Hume's *Treatise*," *Review of Metaphysics*, 30, pp. 57–72.

Helm, P. (1967). "Hume on Exculpation," *Philosophy*, 42, pp. 265–71.

Hendel, Charles (1963). *Studies in the Philosophy of David Hume* (Indianapolis, IN: Bobbs-Merrill).

Henry, Robert (1823). *The History of Great Britain, from the First Invasion of It by the Romans . . . Written on a New Plan*, 6th edn. (London: T. and J. Allman), 12 vols.

Herdt, Jennifer A. (1997). *Religion and Faction in Hume's Moral Philosophy* (Cambridge: Cambridge University Press).

Herman, Barbara (1993). *The Practice of Moral Judgment* (Cambridge: Harvard University Press).

Hicks, Philip (1996). *Neoclassical History and English Culture* (New York: St. Martin's Press).

Hilson, J. C. (1978). "Hume: The Historian as Man of Feeling," in J. C. Hilson, M. M. B. Jones, and J. R. Watson (eds.), *Augustan Worlds: New Essays in Eighteenth-century Literature* (Leicester: Leicester University Press).

Hobbes, Thomas (1650). *Human Nature*, excerpted in D. D. Raphael (ed.), *British Moralists 1650–1800*, vol. 1 (Indianapolis: Hackett Publishing Co., 1991).

—— (1651). *Leviathan*, ed. Richard Tuck (Cambridge: Cambridge University Press, 1996, repr. 1999).

—— (1668). *Leviathan*, ed. Edwin Curley (Indianapolis, IN: Hackett Publishing Co., 1994).

Holden, Thomas (2002). "Infinite Divisibility and Actual Parts in Hume's *Treatise*," *Hume Studies*, 28, pp. 3–26.

Honderich, T. (1993). *How Free Are You? The Determinism Problem* (Oxford: Oxford University Press).

Honderich, T. (ed.) (1973). *Essays on Freedom of Action* (London: Routledge and Kegan Paul).

Hont, I. and Ignatieff, M. (eds.) (1983). *Wealth and Virtue: The Shaping of Political Economy in the Scottish Enlightenment* (Cambridge: Cambridge University Press).

Houston, J. (1994). *Reported Miracles: A Critique of Hume* (New York: Cambridge University Press).

Howson, Colin (2000). *Hume's Problem: Induction and the Justification of Belief* (Oxford: Clarendon Press).

Hubin, Donald (1999). "What's Special about Humeanism," *Noûs*, 33, pp. 30–45.

Hudson, W. D. (1964). "Hume on *Is* and *Ought*," *Philosophical Quarterly*, 14, pp. 246–52.

Hume, David (1739–40). *A Treatise of Human Nature*, ed. David Fate Norton and Mary J. Norton (New York: Oxford University Press, 2000).

—— (1741). *An Abstract of a Book Lately Published: Entituled "A Treatise of Human Nature"* (London: C. Corbet).

—— (1741–77). *Essays Moral, Political and Literary*, ed. Eugene F. Miller (Indianapolis, IN: Liberty Fund, 1987).

—— (1745) *A Letter from a Gentleman to His Friend in Edinburgh containing Some Observations on a Specimen of the Principles concerning Religion and Morality, said to be Maintain'd in a Book Lately Publish'd Intituled "A Treatise of Human Nature,"* ed. Ernest Campbell Mossner and J. V. Price (Edinburgh: Edinburgh University Press, 1967).

—— (1748). *An Essay concerning Human Understanding*, ed. Tom Beauchamp (Oxford: Clarendon Press, 2000).

—— (1751). *An Essay concerning the Principles of Morals*, ed. Tom Beauchamp (Oxford: Clarendon Press, 1998).

—— (1752). "Political Discourses," in Eugene F. Miller (ed.), *Essays, Moral, Political and Literary* (Indianapolis, IN: Liberty Fund, 1987).

—— (1754–78). *The History of England* (Indianapolis, IN: Liberty Fund, 1983).

—— (1757). *Dissertation on the Passions*, in *Four Dissertations and Essays on Suicide and the Immortality of the Soul* (South Bend, IN: St. Augustine's Press, 1992, 1995).

—— (1757). *The Natural History of Religion*, ed. H. E. Root (Stanford, CA: Stanford University Press, 1957).

—— (1757/1779). *Dialogues concerning Natural Religion & the Natural History of Religion*, ed. J. C. A. Gaskin (Oxford: Oxford University Press, 1993).

—— (1776). "My Own Life," in Eugene F. Miller (ed.), *Essays, Moral, Political and Literary* (Indianapolis, IN: Liberty Fund, 1987).

—— (1779). *Dialogues concerning Natural Religion*, ed. N. Kemp Smith (Indianapolis: Bobbs-Merrill, 1947).

—— (1783). "Of the Immortality of the Soul," in Paul Edwards (ed.), *Immortality* (Amherst, NY: Prometheus Books), pp. 134–40.

—— (1783). *Essays on Suicide and the Immortality of the Soul* (Bristol: Thoemmes Press, 1992).

—— (1932, 1969). *The Letters of David Hume*, 2 vols., ed. J. Y. T. Greig (Oxford: Clarendon Press).

Humphreys, Paul (2001). "Causation," in W. H. Newton-Smith (ed.), *A Companion to the Philosophy of Science* (Oxford: Blackwell), pp. 31–40.

Hunter, Graeme (1996). "Arnauld's Defence of Miracles and Its Context," in Elmar J. Kremer (ed.), *Interpreting Arnauld* (Toronto: University of Toronto Press).

Hurlbutt, Robert H., III (1965). *Hume, Newton, and the Design Argument* (Lincoln, NE: University of Nebraska Press).

Hursthouse, Rosalind (1999). *On Virtue Ethics* (Oxford: Oxford University Press).

—— (1999). "Virtue Ethics and Human Nature," *Hume Studies*, 25, pp. 67–82.

Hutcheson, Francis (1725/1738). *An Enquiry concerning the Original of Our Ideas of Virtue or Moral Good* (repr. from 4th edn., 1738), in R. S. Downie (ed.), *Philosophical Writings*, Everyman Library (London: Orion Publishing Group; Rutland, VT: Charles E. Tuttle Co., Inc., 1994).

—— (1725). *An Inquiry into Our Ideas of Beauty and Virtue in Two Treatises*, ed. Wolfgang Leidhold (Indianapolis, IN: Liberty Fund, 2004).

—— (1728). *An Essay on the Nature and Conduct of the Passions and Affections, with Illustrations upon the Moral Sense*, ed. Aaron Garrett (Indianapolis, IN: Liberty Fund, 2002).

—— (1742). *Illustrations on the Moral Sense*, in *Essay on the Nature and Conduct of the Passions and Affections, with Illustrations on the Moral Sense*, ed. Paul McReynolds (Gainesville, FL: Scholars' Facsimiles and Reprints, 1969).

Huxley, T. H. (1894). *Hume: With Helps to the Study of Berkeley, Essays* (New York: D. Appleton and Company).

—— (1909). *Hume* (London: Macmillan).

Inoue, Haruko (2003). "The Origin of the Indirect Passions in the *Treatise*: An Analogy between Books 1 and 2," *Hume Studies*, 29 (Nov.), pp. 205–21.

Jacobson, Anne Jaap (2000). "From Cognitive Science to a Post-Cartesian Text," in Rupert Read and Kenneth A. Richman (eds.), *The New Hume Debate* (London and New York: Routledge), pp. 156–66.

Jacquette, Dale (2001). *David Hume's Critique of Infinity* (Leiden: Brill Academic Publishers).

Jessop, T. E. (1952/1966). "Some Misunderstandings of Hume," *Revue Internationale de Philosophie*, 20, pp. 155–67, repr. in Vere Chappell (ed.), *Hume: A Collection of Critical Essays* (Garden City, NY: Doubleday, 1966), pp. 35–52.

Johnson, Oliver (1987). " 'Lively' Memory and 'Past' Memory," *Hume Studies*, 13, pp. 343–59.

—— (1995). *The Mind of David Hume: A Companion to Book I of "A Treatise of Human Nature"* (Urbana, IL: University of Illinois Press).

Jones, Peter (1982). *Hume's Sentiments: Their Ciceronian and French Context* (Edinburgh: Edinburgh University Press).

Jones, Peter (ed.) (2005). *The Reception of David Hume in Europe* (London and New York: Continuum).

Kahneman, Daniel, Slovic, Paul, and Tversky, Amos (eds.) (1982). *Judgment under Uncertainty: Heuristics and Biases* (Cambridge: Cambridge University Press).

Kail, P. J. E. (2001). "Projection and Necessity in Hume," *European Journal of Philosophy*, 9, pp. 24–54.

—— (2003). "Conceivability and Modality in Hume: A Lemma in an Argument in Defence of Sceptical Realism," *Hume Studies*, 29, pp. 43–61.

—— (2003). "Is Hume a Causal Realist?" *British Journal for the History of Philosophy*, 11, pp. 509–20.

—— (2007). *Projection and Realism in Hume's Philosophy* (Oxford: Oxford University Press).

Kane, Robert (1998). *The Significance of Free Will* (Oxford: Oxford University Press).

—— (2002). "Free Will: Ancient Dispute, New Themes," in Joel Feinberg and Russ Shafer-Landau (eds.), *Reason and Responsibility: Readings in Some Basic Problems of Philosophy* (Belmont, CA: Wadsworth), pp. 499–512.

Kant, Immanuel (1785). *Groundwork of the Metaphysics of Morals*, ed. Mary Gregor (Cambridge: Cambridge University Press, 1997).

Karlsson, Mikael (2000). "Rational Ends: Humean and Non-Humean Considerations," *Sats-Nordic Journal of Philosophy*, 1, pp. 15–47.

—— (2001). "Cognition, Desire and Motivation: 'Humean' and 'Non-Humean' Considerations," *Sats-Nordic Journal of Philosophy*, 2, pp. 30–58.

—— (2005). "Reason, Passion and the Influencing Motives of the Will," in Saul Traiger (ed.), *The Blackwell Guide to Hume's "Treatise"* (Oxford: Blackwell Publishing).

Kemp, J. (1970). *Ethical Naturalism: Hobbes and Hume* (London: Macmillan).

Kemp Smith, Norman (1905). "The Naturalism of Hume (I)," *Mind*, 14, pp. 149–73.

—— (1941). *The Philosophy of David Hume* (London and New York: Macmillan and St. Martin's Press).

Kemp Smith, Norman (ed.) (1947). *Hume's Dialogues concerning Natural Religion* (Edinburgh: Thomas Nelson).

Kidd, Colin (1993). *Subverting Scotland's Past* (Cambridge: Cambridge University Press).

Kim, Jaegwon (1994). "What Is 'Naturalized Epistemology'?" in Hilary Kornblith (ed.), *Naturalizing Epistemology* (Cambridge MA: MIT Press).

King, James T. (1976). "The Place of the Language of Morals in Hume's Second *Enquiry*," in Donald W. Livingston and James T. King (eds.), *Hume: A Re-evaluation* (New York: Fordham University Press).

Knight, William (1886). *Hume* (Edinburgh: Blackwood).

Kornblith, Hilary (2002). *Knowledge and Its Place in Nature* (Oxford: Clarendon Press).

Kornblith, Hilary (ed.) (1994). *Naturalizing Epistemology*, 2nd edn. (Cambridge, MA: MIT Press).

Korsgaard, Christine M. (1986). "Skepticism about Practical Reason," *Journal of Philosophy*, 83, pp. 5–25.

—— (1989). "Morality as Freedom," in C. Korsgaard, *Creating the Kingdom of Ends* (Cambridge: Cambridge University Press, 1996).

—— (1996). *The Sources of Normativity*, ed. Onora O'Neill (Cambridge: Cambridge University Press).

—— (1999). "The General Point of View: Love and Moral Approval in Hume's Ethics," *Hume Studies*, 25, pp. 3–42.

Korsmeyer, Carolyn W. (1976). "Hume and the Foundations of Taste," *Journal of Aesthetics and Art Criticism*, 35, pp. 201–15.

Kosslyn, Stephen M., and Koenig, O. (1992). *Wet Mind: The New Cognitive Neuroscience* (New York: The Free Press).

Kydd, Rachel (1946). *Reason and Conduct in Hume's "Treatise"* (London: Oxford University Press).

Labrousse, Elisabeth (1983). *Bayle* (Oxford and New York: Oxford University Press).

Laird, John (1932). *Hume's Philosophy of Human Nature* (London: Methuen).

Langtry, Bruce (1990). "Hume, Probability, Lotteries and Miracles," *Hume Studies*, 16, pp. 67–74.

Lecaldano, Eugenio (1991). *Hume e la nascita dell'etica contemporanea* (*Hume and the Birth of Contemporary Ethics*) (Roma-Bari: Laterza).

—— (2002). "The Passions, Character, and the Self in Hume," *Hume Studies*, 28, pp. 175–93.

Leibniz, G. W. (1704). *New Essays on Human Understanding*, ed. P. Remnant and J. Bennett (Cambridge: Cambridge University Press, 1996).

—— (1714). *Monadology*, in *Philosophical Texts*, trans. R. Francks and R. S. Woolhouse (Oxford: Oxford University Press, 1998).

Lenz, John W. (1958/1966). "Hume's Defense of Causal Inference," *Journal of the History of Ideas*, 19, pp. 559–67, repr. in Vere Chappell (ed.), *Hume: A Collection of Critical Essays* (Garden City, NY: Doubleday, 1966), pp. 169–86.

Levin, Michael (2003). "Reliabilism and Induction," in Charles Landesman and Roblin Meeks (eds.), *Philosophical Skepticism* (Oxford: Blackwell), pp. 158–68.

Levine, Joseph (1987). *Humanism and History: Origins of Modern Historiography* (Ithaca, NY: Cornell University Press).

Levine, Michael P. (1984). "Hume's Analysis of Causation in Relation to His Analysis of Miracles," *History of Philosophy Quarterly*, 1, pp. 195–202.

—— (1987). "What Does Death Have to Do with the Meaning of Life?" *Religious Studies*, 23, pp. 457–65.

—— (1988). "Belief in Miracles: Tillotson's Argument against Transubstantiation as a Model for Hume," *International Journal for Philosophy of Religion*, 23, pp. 125–60.

—— (1988). "Camus, Hare, and the Meaning of Life," *Sophia*, 27, pp. 13–30.

—— (1988). "Hume on Miracles: The Coalescence of the a priori with the a posteriori Arguments against Justified Belief," in Venant Cauchy (ed.), *Philosophy and Culture*, vol. 3 (Montreal: Ed-Montmorency), pp. 340–4.

—— (1989). *Hume and the Problem of Miracles: A Solution* (Dordrecht: Kluwer Publishers).

—— (1993). "Swinburne's Heaven: One Hell of a Place," *Religious Studies*, 29, pp. 519–31.

—— (1996). "Miracles," in E. Zalta (ed.), *Stanford Encyclopedia of Philosophy*, http://plato.stanford.edu.

—— (1998). "Bayesian Analyses of Hume's Argument concerning Miracles," *Philosophy and Theology*, 10, pp. 101–6.

—— (2000). "Contemporary Christian Analytic Philosophy of Religion: Biblical Fundamentalism, Terrible Solutions to a Horrible Problem, and Hearing God," *International Journal for Philosophy of Religion*, 48, pp. 89–119.

—— (2002). "Review of John Earman, *Hume's Abject Failure: The Argument against Miracles*," *Hume Studies*, 28, pp. 161–7.

Lewis, David (1989). "Dispositional Theories of Value," *Aristotelian Society Supplement*, 63, pp. 113–37.

—— (1993). "Causes and Counterfactuals," in Ernest Sosa and Michael Tooley (eds.), *Causation* (Oxford: Oxford University Press), pp. 205–7.

Livingston, Donald (1971). "Hume on Ultimate Causation," *American Philosophical Quarterly*, 8, pp. 63–70.

—— (1984). *Hume's Philosophy of Common Life* (Chicago: University of Chicago Press).

—— (1998). *Philosophical Melancholy and Delirium: Hume's Pathology of Philosophy* (Chicago: University of Chicago Press).

Lloyd Thomas, D. A. (1990). "Hume and Intrinsic Value," *Philosophy*, 65, pp. 419–37.

Locke, John (1689). *Two Treatises of Government*, ed. Peter Laslett (Cambridge: Cambridge University Press, 1960).

—— (1690, 1694). *An Essay concerning Human Understanding*, ed. Peter H. Nidditch (Oxford: Clarendon Press, 1975).

—— (1706). *A Discourse on Miracles*, ed. I. T. Ramsey (London: A. and C. Black, 1958).

Loeb, Louis E. (1977). "Hume's Moral Sentiments and the Structure of the *Treatise*," *Journal of the History of Philosophy*, 4, pp. 395–403.

—— (2001). "Integrating Hume's Accounts of Belief and Justification," *Philosophy and Phenomenological Research*, 63, pp. 279–303.

—— (2002). *Stability and Justification in Hume's "Treatise"* (New York: Oxford University Press).

—— (2006). "Psychology, Epistemology, and Skepticism in Hume's Argument about Induction," *Synthese*, 152, pp. 221–38.

Lovelace, Richard (1649). *Lucasta: On Going to Wars* (Scholar Press, Facs edn., 1972).

Lucas, Jr., R. E. (1996). "Nobel Lecture: Monetary Neutrality," *Journal of Political Economy*, 104, pp. 661–82.

Lyons, J. C. (2001). "General Rules and the Justification of Probable Belief in Hume's *Treatise*," *Hume Studies*, 27, pp. 247–77.

MacIntyre, A. C. (1959). "Hume on 'Is' and 'Ought'," *Philosophical Review*, 68, pp. 451–68.

Mackay, D. S. (1945). "The Illusion of Memory," *Philosophical Review*, 54, pp. 297–320.

Mackie, J. L. (1974). *The Cement of the Universe: A Study of Causation* (Oxford: Clarendon Press).

—— (1980). *Hume's Moral Theory* (London: Routledge and Kegan Paul).

—— (1982). *The Miracle of Theism: Arguments for and against the Existence of God* (Oxford: Oxford University Press).

Mackintosh, Sir James (1853). *Memoirs of the Life and Writings*, ed. R. Mackintosh (Boston: Little, Brown), 2 vols.

MacNabb, D. G. C. (1951/1966). *David Hume: His Theory of Knowledge and Morality* (Oxford: Basil Blackwell).

Magri, Tito (1994). *Contratto e convenzione: razionalità, obbligo e imparzialità in Hobbes e Hume* (*Contract and Convention: Rationality, Obligation and Impartiality in Hobbes and Hume*) (Milan: Feltrinelli).

—— (1996). "Natural Obligation and Normative Motivation in Hume's *Treatise*," *Hume Studies*, 22, pp. 231–54.

—— (forthcoming). "Hume's Justice," in Donald Ainslie (ed.), *Critical Essays on Hume's "Treatise"* (Cambridge: Cambridge University Press).

Malebranche, N. (1674–5). *The Search after Truth*, ed. T. M. Lennon and P. J. Olscamp (Cambridge: Cambridge University Press, 1997).

Malherbe, Michel (2002). "David Hume: système sceptique et autres systèmes" (*Traité* I, 4) [David Hume: "Of the Sceptical and Other Systems" (*Treatise* I, 4)] (Paris: le Seuil).

Mandelbaum, Maurice (1974). "The Distinguishable and the Separable: A Note on Hume and Causation," *Journal of the History of Philosophy*, 12, pp. 242–7.

Manuel, Frank E. (1959). *The Eighteenth Century Confronts the Gods* (Cambridge, MA: Harvard University Press).

Martin, C. B. and Deutscher, Max (1966). "Remembering," *Philosophical Review*, 75, pp. 161–96.

Martin, M. (1992). "Hume on Human Excellence," *Hume Studies*, 18, pp. 383–400.

—— (1993). "The Rational Warrant for Hume's General Rules," *Journal of the History of Philosophy*, 31, pp. 245–57.

Mason, Michelle (2001). "Moral Prejudice and Aesthetic Deformity: Rereading Hume's 'Of the Standard of Taste'," *Journal of Aesthetics and Art Criticism*, 59, pp. 59–71.

Maund, Constance (1937/1972). *Hume's Theory of Knowledge: A Critical Examination* (London: Macmillan, 1937; repr. New York: Russell & Russell, 1972).

Mazza, E. (2005). "Cannibals in 'A Dialogue' (in Search of a Standard of Morals)," in E. Mazza and E. Ronchetti (eds.), *"Instruction and Amusement": Le ragioni dell'illuminismo britannico* (Padua: Il Polygrato).

Mazza, Emilio and Ronchetti, Emanuele (eds.) (2007). *New Essays on David Hume* (Milan: FrancoAngeli).

McDonough, Jeffrey K. (2002). "Hume's Account of Memory," *British Journal for the History of Philosophy*, 10, pp. 71–87.

McDowell, John (1978). "Are Moral Requirements Hypothetical Imperatives?" *Proceedings of Aristotelian Society*, supplement 52, pp. 13–29.

McIntyre, Jane L. (1979). "Is Hume's Self Consistent?" in D. Fate Norton, N. Capaldi, and W. L. Robison (eds.), *McGill Hume Studies* (San Diego: Austin Hill), pp. 79–88.

—— (1979). "Further Remarks on the Consistency of Hume's Account of the Self," *Hume Studies*, 5, pp. 55–61.

—— (1989). "Personal Identity and the Passions," *Journal of the History of Philosophy*, 27, pp. 545–57.

—— (1990). "Character: A Humean Account," *History of Philosophy Quarterly*, 7, pp. 193–206.

—— (2000). "Hume's Passions: Direct and Indirect," *Hume Studies*, 26, pp. 77–86.

—— (2006). "Hume's 'New and Extraordinary' Account of the Passions," in Saul Traiger (ed.), *The Blackwell Guide to Hume's "Treatise"* (Malden, MA: Blackwell), pp. 199–215.

Mill, John Stuart (1865). "Mr Mansel on the Limits of Religious Thought," in Nelson Pike (ed.), *God and Evil: Readings on the Theological Problem of Evil* (Englewood Cliffs, NJ: Prentice-Hall, 1964), pp. 37–45.

—— (1874). *Three Essays on Religion* (London: Longman).

Miller, David (1981). *Philosophy and Ideology in Hume's Political Thought* (Oxford: Clarendon Press).

Miller, Eugene (1990). "Hume on Liberty in Successive English Constitutions," in N. Capaldi and D. Livingston (eds.), *Liberty in Hume's History of England* (Dordrecht: Kluwer Academic Publishing), pp. 53–103.

Millgram, Elijah (1995). "Was Hume a Humean?" *Hume Studies*, 21, pp. 75–93.

—— (1997). "Hume on Practical Reasoning," *Iyyun: The Jerusalem Philosophical Quarterly*, 46, pp. 235–65.

Millican, Peter (1993). "Hume's Theorem concerning Miracles," *Philosophical Quarterly*, 43, pp. 489–95.

—— (2002). "The Context, Aims, and Structure of Hume's First *Enquiry*," in Peter Millican (ed.), *Reading Hume on Human Understanding* (Oxford: Oxford University Press), pp. 27–65.

—— (2002). "Hume's Sceptical Doubts concerning Induction," in Peter Millican (ed.), *Reading Hume on Human Understanding* (Oxford: Oxford University Press), pp. 107–73.

Millican, Peter (ed.) (2002). *Reading Hume on Human Understanding* (Oxford: Clarendon Press).

Milton, J. R. (1987). "Induction before Hume," *British Journal for the Philosophy of Science*, 38, pp. 49–74.

Monteiro, J. P. (1976). "Hume, Induction, and Natural Selection," in David Fate Norton, Nicholas Capaldi, and Wade L. Robison (eds.), *McGill Hume Studies*, vol. 1: *Studies in Hume and Scottish Philosophy* (San Diego, CA: Austin Hill Press), pp. 291–308.

Montesquieu, Baron de (Charles-Louis de Secondat) (1721). *Persian Letters*, ed. George R. Healy (Indianapolis, IN: Bobbs-Merrill, 1964).

Moore, G. E. (1909). "Hume's Philosophy," *New Quarterly*, 2, pp. 545–65, from G. E. Moore (New York: Harcourt, Brace, 1922), pp. 147–67.

Moore, James (2000). "Hutcheson's Theodicy: The Argument and the Contexts of *A System of Moral Philosophy*," in Paul Wood (ed.), *The Scottish Enlightenment: Essays in Reinterpretation* (Rochester, NY: University of Rochester Press), pp. 239–66.

—— (2002). "Utility and Humanity: The Quest for the *honestum* in Cicero, Hutcheson, and Hume," *Utilitas*, 14, pp. 356–86.

Morris, William E. (1988). "Hume's Refutation of Inductive Probabilism," in James Fetzer (ed.), *Probability and Causality* (Dordrecht: D. Reidel), pp. 43–77.

—— (2005). "Belief, Probability, Normativity," in Saul Traiger (ed.), *The Blackwell Guide to Hume's "Treatise"* (Oxford: Blackwell), pp. 77–94.

543

Mossner, Ernest C. (1980). *The Life of David Hume*, 2nd edn. (Oxford: Clarendon Press).

Mothersill, Mary (1984). *Beauty Restored* (Oxford: Oxford University Press).

Mounce, H. O. (1999). *Hume's Naturalism* (New York: Routledge).

Munakata, Yuko, McClelland, James L., Johnson, James L., Siegler, Mark, and Siegler, Robert (1997). "Rethinking Infant Knowledge: Toward an Adaptive Process Account of Successes and Failures in Object Permanence Tasks," *Psychological Review*, 104, pp. 686–713.

Nagel, Thomas (1970). *The Possibility of Altruism* (Princeton, NJ: Princeton University Press).

Newton, I. (1687). *Sir Isaac Newton's Mathematical Principles of Natural Philosophy and His System of the World*, trans. A. Motte and F. Cajori (Berkeley, CA: University of California Press, 1934).

—— (1730). *Opticks, or a Treatise of the Reflections, Refractions, Inflections, & Colours of Light*, 4th edn. (New York: Dover, 1979).

Newton-Smith, W. H. (2001). "Hume," in W. H. Newton-Smith (ed.), *A Companion to the Philosophy of Science* (Oxford: Blackwell), pp. 165–8.

Nisbett, Richard and Ross, Lee (1980). *Human Inference: Strategies and Shortcomings of Social Judgment* (Englewood Cliffs, NJ: Prentice-Hall).

Noonan, Harold W. (1999). *Hume on Knowledge* (London: Routledge).

Norton, David Fate (1965). "History and Philosophy in Hume's Thought," in David Fate Norton and R. Popkin (eds.), *David Hume: Philosophical Historian* (Indianapolis, IN: Bobbs-Merrill).

—— (1982). *David Hume: Common-sense Moralist, Sceptical Metaphysician* (Princeton, NJ: Princeton University Press).

—— (1985). "Hume's Moral Ontology," *Hume Studies*, 10th anniversary edn., pp. 189–214.

Norton, David Fate and Taylor, Jacqueline (eds.) (forthcoming 2008). *Cambridge Companion to Hume*, 2nd edn. (New York: Cambridge University Press).

Noxon, James (1973). *Hume's Philosophical Development: A Study of His Methods* (Oxford: Clarendon Press).

—— (1976). "Hume's Concern with Religion," in K. R. Merrill and R. S. Shahan (eds.), *David Hume: Many-sided Genius* (Norman, OK: University of Oklahoma Press).

—— (1976). "Remembering and Imagining the Past," in Donald W. Livingston and James T. King (eds.), *David Hume: A Re-evaluation* (New York: Fordham University Press).

O'Brien, Karen (1997). *Narratives of Enlightenment: Cosmopolitan History from Voltaire to Gibbon* (Cambridge: Cambridge University Press).

O'Connor, D. (1981). "Hume's Scepticism with Regard to the Senses," *Philosophical Studies*, 28, from Stanley Tweyman (ed.), *David Hume: Critical Assessments*, vol. 3 (London: Routledge, 1995), pp. 597–612.

—— (2001). *Hume on Religion* (London: Routledge).

Okie, Laird (1991). *Augustan Historical Writing: Histories of England in the Enlightenment* (Lanham, MD: University Press of America).

Oppy, Graham (1996). "Hume and the Argument for Biological Design," *Biology and Philosophy*, 11, pp. 519–34.

O'Shea, James (1996). "Hume's Reflective Return to the Vulgar," *British Journal for the History of Philosophy*, 4, pp. 285–315.

Owen, David (1999). *Hume's Reason* (Oxford: Clarendon Press).

Owen, David (ed.) (2000). *Hume: General Philosophy* (Aldershot and Burlington, VT: Ashgate).

Owen, David and Cohon, Rachel (1997). "Representation, Reason, and Motivation," *Manuscrito*, 20, pp. 47–76.

Paley, William (1794). *The Works of William Paley*, vol. 2: *The Evidences of Christianity* (London: Longman, 1838), 4 vols.

Papineau, David (1992). "Reliabilism, Induction, and Skepticism," *Philosophical Quarterly*, 42, pp. 1–20.

Parfit, Derek (1984). *Reasons and Persons* (Oxford: Clarendon Press).

Passmore, John A. (1952). *Hume's Intentions* (London: Gerald Duckworth, 1968, 1980).

Patten, S. C. (1976). "Hume's Bundles, Self-consciousness, and Kant," *Hume Studies*, 2, pp. 59–75.

Pears, David (1990). *Hume's System: An Examination of the First Book of his "Treatise"* (Oxford: Oxford University Press).

Peirce, Charles S. (1931–58). *Collected Papers of Charles Sanders Peirce* (Cambridge, MA: Harvard University Press).

Penelhum, Terence (1971). *Religion and Rationality* (New York: Harper and Row).

—— (1975). *Hume* (London: Macmillan).

—— (1979). "Hume's Scepticism and the *Dialogues*," in David Fate Norton, Wade Robison, and Nicholas Capaldi (eds.), *McGill Hume Studies* (San Diego, CA: Austin Hill Press).

—— (1983). "Natural Belief and Religious Belief in Hume's Philosophy," *Philosophical Quarterly*, 33, pp. 266–82.

—— (1983). *God and Skepticism* (Dordrecht: Reidel).

—— (1985). *Butler* (London: Routledge).

—— (1992). *David Hume: An Introduction to His Philosophical System* (West Lafayette, IN: Purdue University Press).

—— (1993). "Hume's Moral Psychology," in David Fate Norton (ed.), *The Cambridge Companion to Hume* (Cambridge: Cambridge University Press), pp. 117–47.

—— (2000). *Themes in Hume: The Self, the Will, Religion* (Oxford: Clarendon Press).

Phillips, Mark Salber (1997). "Adam Smith and the History of Private Life; Social and Sentimental Narratives in Eighteenth-century Historiography," in D. R. Kelley and D. H. Sacks (eds.), *The Historical Imagination in Early Modern Britain* (Cambridge: Cambridge University Press).

—— (2000). *Society and Sentiment: Genres of Historical Thought, 1740–1820* (Princeton, NJ: Princeton University Press).

—— (2003). "Relocating Inwardness: Historical Distance and the Transition from Enlightenment to Romantic Historiography," *Publications of the Modern Languages Association*, 118, pp. 436–49.

—— (2005). "Adam Smith, Belletrist," in K. Haakonssen (ed.), *Cambridge Companion to Adam Smith* (Cambridge: Cambridge University Press).

Phillips, Mark Salber and Smith, Dale R. (2005). "Canonization and Critique: Hume's Reputation as a Historian," in Peter Jones (ed.), *The Reception of Hume in Europe* (London: Continuum).

Phillipson, Nicholas (1989). *Hume* (London: Weidenfeld and Nicholson).

Pike, Nelson (ed.) (1970). *Dialogues concerning Natural Religion* (Indianapolis, IN: Bobbs-Merrill).

Pitson, A. E. (1989). "Projectionism, Realism, and Hume's Moral Sense Theory," *Hume Studies*, 15, pp. 61–92.

—— (2002). *Hume's Philosophy of the Self* (London: Routledge).

Plantinga, Alvin (1967). *God and Other Minds* (Ithaca, NY: Cornell University Press).

—— (1983). "Reason and Belief in God," in Alvin Plantinga and Nicholas Wolterstorff (eds.), *Faith and Rationality* (Notre Dame, IN: University of Notre Dame Press).

Pocock, J. (1985). *Virtue, Commerce and History* (Cambridge: Cambridge University Press).

—— (1999). *Barbarism and Civilization* (Cambridge: Cambridge University Press).

Pompa, Leon (1990). *Human Nature and Historical Knowledge: Hume, Hegel, and Vico* (Cambridge: Cambridge University Press).

Pope, A. (1966). *Poetical Works*, ed. H. Davis (Oxford: Oxford University Press).

Popkin, Richard (1951/1966). "David Hume: His Pyrrhonism and His Critique of Pyrrhonism," in Vere Chappell (ed.), *Hume: A Collection of Critical Essays* (Garden City, NY: Doubleday, 1966), pp. 53–98.

—— (1976). "Hume: Philosophical versus Prophetic Historian," in K. Merill and R. W. Shahan (eds.), *David Hume, Many-sided Genius* (Norman, OK: University of Oklahoma Press).

—— (1979). *The History of Skepticism from Erasmus to Spinoza* (Berkeley: University of California Press).

Popper, Karl (1972). *Objective Knowledge* (Oxford: Clarendon Press).

Porter, R. (2000). *Enlightenment: Britain and the Creation of the Modern World* (Harmondsworth: Penguin).

Price, H. H. (1940). *Hume's Theory of the External World* (Oxford: Clarendon Press).

—— (1940/1965). "The Permanent Significance of Hume's Philosophy," *Philosophy*, 15, pp. 7–37, repr. in Alexander Sesonske and Noel Fleming (eds.), *Human Understanding: Studies in the Philosophy of David Hume* (Belmont, CA: Wadsworth, 1965), pp. 5–33.

—— (1969). *Belief* (London: George Allen & Unwin).

Price, John Valdimir (1969/1990). *David Hume* (Boston: Twayne Publishers).

Purviance, Susan M. (1997). "The Moral Self and the Indirect Passions," *Hume Studies*, 23, pp. 195–212.

Quine, W. V. (1969). *Ontological Relativity and Other Essays* (New York: Columbia University Press).

—— (1992). *Pursuit of Truth* (Cambridge, MA: Harvard University Press).

Radcliffe, Elizabeth S. (1994). "Hume on Motivating Sentiments, the General Point of View, and the Inculcation of Morality," *Hume Studies*, 20, pp. 37–58.

—— (1996). "How Does the Humean Sense of Duty Motivate?" *Journal of the History of Philosophy*, 34, pp. 383–407.

—— (1997). "Kantian Tunes on a Humean Instrument: Why Hume Is Not *Really* a Skeptic about Practical Reasoning," *Canadian Journal of Philosophy*, 27, pp. 247–69.

—— (1999). "Hume on the Generation of Motives: Why Beliefs Alone Never Motivate," *Hume Studies*, 25, pp. 101–22.

—— (2004). "Love and Benevolence in Hutcheson's and Hume's Theories of the Passions," *British Journal for the History of Philosophy*, 12, pp. 631–53.

—— (2006). "Moral Internalism and Moral Cognitivism in Hume's Metaethics," *Synthese*, 152, pp. 353–70.

—— (2007). "Representation and Motivation: Hume and His Predecessors," presented at New Philosophical Perspectives on Hume conference, University of San Francisco, San Francisco, CA.

Railton, Peter (2006). "Humean Theory of Practical Rationality," in David Copp (ed.), *The Oxford Handbook of Ethical Theory* (New York: Oxford University Press), pp. 265–81.

Ramsey, William (1992). "Connectionism and the Philosophy of Mental Representation," in Steven Davis (ed.), *Connectionism: Theory and Practice* (New York: Oxford University Press), pp. 247–76.

—— (1999). "Connectionism, Philosophical Issues," in Robert A. Wilson and Frank C. Keil (eds.), *The MIT Encyclopedia of the Cognitive Sciences* (Cambridge, MA: MIT Press), pp. 186–7.

Raphael, David Daiches (2001). *Concepts of Justice* (Oxford: Clarendon Press).

Rawls, John (1971). *A Theory of Justice* (Cambridge, MA: Harvard University Press, 1999).

—— (2000). *Lectures on the History of Moral Philosophy*, ed. Barbara Herman (Cambridge, MA: Harvard University Press).

Read, Rupert and Richman, Kenneth A. (eds.) (2000). *The New Hume Debate* (London: Routledge).

Redman, D. A. (1997). *The Rise of Political Economy as a Science* (Cambridge, MA: MIT Press).

Reichenbach, Hans (1935). *Experience and Prediction* (Chicago: University of Chicago Press).

Reid, Thomas (1764). *An Inquiry into the Human Mind on the Principles of Common Sense*, ed. Derek Brookes (Edinburgh: Edinburgh University Press, 1997).

—— (1785). *Essays on the Intellectual Powers of Man*, ed. B. A. Broady (Cambridge, MA: MIT Press, 1969).

—— (1788). *Essays on the Active Powers of Man*, in D. D. Raphael (ed.), *British Moralists: 1650–1800*, 2 vols. (Indianapolis, IN: Hackett, 1991).

—— (1788). *Essays on the Active Powers of the Human Mind*, ed. B. A. Broady (Cambridge, MA: MIT Press, 1969).

—— (1849). *The Works of Thomas Reid*, ed. William Hamilton (Edinburgh: Maclachlan, Stewart, and Co.).

Richman, Kenneth (2000). "Introduction," in Rupert Read and Kenneth A. Richman (eds.), *The New Hume Debate* (London: Routledge), pp. 1–15.

Rivers, Isabel (1993). " 'Galen's Muscles': Wilkins, Hume, and the Educational Use of the Argument from Design," *Historical Journal*, 36, pp. 577–98.

—— (2000). *Reason, Grace and Sentiment: A Study of the Language of Religion and Ethics in England, 1660–1780*, 2 vols. (Cambridge: Cambridge University Press).

Robertson, John (1989–90). "Hume on Practical Reason," *Proceedings of the Aristotelian Society*, 90, pp. 267–82.

Robinson, J. A. (1962). "Hume's Two Definitions of 'Cause'," *Philosophical Quarterly*, 12, pp. 162–71.

Robison, Wade (1974). "Hume on Personal Identity," *Journal of the History of Philosophy*, 12, pp. 181–93.

—— (1982). "One Consequence of Hume's Nominalism," *Hume Studies*, 8, pp. 102–18.

Rorty, Amelie O. (1990). "Pride Produces the Idea of the Self: Hume on Moral Agency," *Australasian Journal of Philosophy*, 68, pp. 255–69.

Rosen, Frederick (2003). *Classical Utilitarianism from Hume to Mill* (London: Routledge).

Ross, Ian (2000). "The Natural Theology of Lord Kames," in Paul Wood (ed.), *The Scottish Enlightenment: Essays in Reinterpretation* (Rochester, NY: University of Rochester Press).

Rostow, W. W. (1990). *Theorists of Economic Growth from David Hume to the Present* (New York: Oxford University Press).

Rotwein, E. (1970). "Introduction," in E. Rotwein (ed.), *David Hume: Writings on Economics* (Madison: University of Wisconsin Press).

Rumelhart, David E. and McClelland, James L. (eds.) (1987). *Parallel Distributed Processing: Explorations in the Microstructure of Cognition*, 2 vols. (Cambridge, MA: MIT Press).

Russell, B. (1912). *The Problems of Philosophy* (London: Oxford University Press).

—— (1995). *History of Western Philosophy* (London: Routledge).

Russell, Paul (1985). "Hume's *Treatise* and Hobbes's *The Elements of Law*," *Journal of the History of Ideas*, 46, pp. 51–64.

—— (1995). *Freedom and Moral Sentiment: Hume's Way of Naturalizing Responsibility* (New York: Oxford University Press).

Russow, Lilly-Marlene (1980). "Simple Ideas and Resemblance," *The Philosophical Quarterly*, 30, pp. 342–50.

Sakamoto, T. (2003). "Hume's Political Economy as a System of Manners," in T. Sakamoto and H. Tanaka (eds.), *The Rise of Political Economy in the Scottish Enlightenment* (London: Routledge), pp. 86–102.

Sayre-McCord, Geoffrey (1994). "Why Hume's General Point of View Isn't Ideal – and Shouldn't Be," *Social Philosophy and Policy*, 11, pp. 202–28.

—— (1995). "Hume and the Bauhaus Theory of Ethics," *Midwest Studies in Philosophy*, 20, pp. 280–98.

—— (1997). "The Metaethical Problem," *Ethics*, 108, pp. 55–83.

Schabas, Margaret (2001). "David Hume on Experimental Natural Philosophy, Money and Fluids," *History of Political Economy*, 33, pp. 411–35.

Schmidt, Claudia (2003). *David Hume: Reason in History* (University Park, PA: Pennsylvania State University Press).

Schmitt, Frederick F. (1992). *Knowledge and Belief* (London: Routledge & Kegan Paul).

547

—— (1994). *Socializing Epistemology: The Social Dimensions of Knowledge* (Lanham, MN: Rowman and Littlefield).

Schmitter, Amy (2006). "17th and 18th Century Theories of Emotions," in Edward N. Zalta (ed.), *Stanford Encyclopedia of Philosophy* (summer 2006 edn.), http://plato.stanford.edu/archives/sum2006/entries/emotions-17th18th/.

Schneewind, J. B. (1983). "Introduction," in David Hume, *Enquiry concerning the Principles of Morals*, ed. J. B. Schneewind (Indianapolis, IN: Hackett Publishing).

—— (1998). *The Invention of Autonomy* (Cambridge: Cambridge University Press).

—— (2003). "The Misfortunes of Virtue," *Ethics*, 101, pp. 42–63.

Schoen, Edward L. (1991). "David Hume and the Mysterious Shroud of Turin," *Religious Studies*, 27, pp. 209–22.

Searle, John (2001). *Rationality in Action* (Cambridge, MA: MIT Press).

Selby-Bigge, L. A. (1894). "Editor's Introduction," in David Hume, *Enquiries concerning Human Understanding and concerning the Principles of Morals*, 3rd edn., ed. P. H. Nidditch (Oxford: Oxford University Press, 1975).

Sessions, William Lad (2002). *Reading Hume's Dialogues: A Veneration for True Religion* (Bloomington, IN: Indiana University Press).

Sextus Empiricus (1933). *Outlines of Pyrrhonism*, trans. R. G. Bury (Cambridge, MA, and London: Harvard University Press).

—— (1976). *Sextus Empiricus*, trans. Robert Gregg Bury, Loeb Classical Library (Cambridge, MA: Harvard University Press), 4 vols.

Shaftesbury (Anthony Ashley Cooper) (1699/1711). *An Inquiry concerning Virtue or Merit*, in *Characteristics of Men, Manners, Opinions, Times*, Shaftesbury (1711), ed. Lawrence Klein (Cambridge: Cambridge University Press, 1999).

—— (1709/1711). *The Moralists: A Philosophical Rhapsody*, in *Characteristics of Men, Manners, Opinions, Times*, Shaftesbury (1711), ed. Lawrence Klein (Cambridge: Cambridge University Press, 1999).

Shaver, R. (1992). "Hume and the Duties of Humanity," *Journal of the History of Philosophy*, 30, pp. 545–56.

—— (1995). "Hume's Moral Theory?" *History of Philosophy Quarterly*, 12, pp. 317–31.

Sher, Richard B. (1985). *Church and University in the Scottish Enlightenment* (Edinburgh: Edinburgh University Press).

—— (1990). "Professors of Virtue: The Social History of the Edinburgh Moral Philosophy Chair in the Eighteenth Century," in M. A. Stewart (ed.), *Studies in the Philosophy of the Scottish Enlightenment* (Oxford: Clarendon Press).

Sidgwick, Henry (1902). *Outline of the History of Ethics, for English Readers* (London: Macmillan).

Singer, Ira (1995). "Hume's Extreme Skepticism in *Treatise* I IV 7," *Canadian Journal of Philosophy*, 25, pp. 595–622.

Skyrms, Brian (1975). *Choice and Chance: An Introduction to Inductive Logic* (Encino: Dickenson).

—— (1986). *Choice and Chance: An Introduction to Inductive Logic* (Belmont, CA: Wadsworth Publishing).

Slupik, Chris (1995). "A New Interpretation of Hume's 'Of Miracles'," *Religious Studies*, 31, pp. 517–36.

Smart, Ninian (1964). *Philosophers and Religious Truth* (London: SCM Press).

Smith, Adam (1759). *The Theory of Moral Sentiments*, ed. D. D. Raphael and A. L. Macfie (Oxford: Clarendon Press, 1976).

—— (1759). *The Theory of Moral Sentiments*, ed. Knud Haakonssen (Cambridge: Cambridge University Press, 2002).

—— (1762). *Lectures on Rhetoric and "Belles Lettres,"* ed. J. C. Bryce (Indianapolis, IN: Liberty Fund, 1985).

—— (1776). *An Inquiry into the Nature and Causes of the Wealth of Nations*, ed. R. H. Campbell, A. S. Skinner, and W. B. Todd (Oxford: Clarendon Press, 1976).

Smith, Michael (1987). "The Humean Theory of Motivation," *Mind*, 96, pp. 36–61.

—— (1994). *The Moral Problem* (Oxford: Blackwell Publishing).

—— (2004). "Humean Rationality," in Alfred R. Mele and Piers Rawling (eds.), *The Oxford Handbook of Rationality* (Oxford: Oxford University Press), pp. 75–92.

Smith, N. K. (1905). "The Naturalism of Hume," *Mind*, 14, pp. 149–73, 335–47.

Smith, R. J. (1987). *The Gothic Bequest: Medieval Institutions in British Thought, 1688–1863* (Cambridge: Cambridge University Press).

Snare, Francis (1975). "The Argument from Motivation," *Mind*, 84, pp. 1–9.

—— (1991). *Morals, Motivation and Convention: Hume's Influential Doctrines* (Cambridge: Cambridge University Press).

Sobel, David and Copp, David (2001). "Against Direction of Fit Accounts of Belief and Desire," *Analysis*, 61, pp. 44–53.

Solomon, Miriam (2001). *Social Empiricism* (Cambridge, MA: MIT Press).

Spector, J. (2003). "Value in Fact: Naturalism and Normativity in Hume's Moral Psychology," *Journal of the History of Philosophy*, 41, pp. 145–63.

Spinoza, Baruch (1677). "Ethics," in *Ethics, Treatise on the Emendation of the Intellect, and Selected Letters* (Indianapolis: Hackett, 1992).

Stalker, Douglas (ed.) (1994). *Grue: The New Riddle of Induction* (Chicago: Open Court).

Stalley, R. F. (1986). "The Will in Hume's *Treatise*," *Journal of the History of Philosophy*, 24, pp. 41–53.

Stampe, Dennis (1987). "The Authority of Desire," *Philosophical Review*, 96, pp. 335–81.

Stevenson, Charles (1944). *Ethics and Language* (New Haven, CT: Yale University Press).

—— (1963). *Facts and Values: Studies in Ethical Analysis* (New Haven, CT: Yale University Press).

Stewart, Dugald (1818). *Outlines of Moral Philosophy, for the Use of Students at Edinburgh University* (Edinburgh: Archibald Constable and Co., Fairbairn and Anderson, successors to Mr. Creech).

Stewart, John B. (1963). *The Moral and Political Philosophy of David Hume* (New York: Columbia University Press).

—— (1992). *Opinion and Reform in Hume's Political Philosophy* (Princeton, NJ: Princeton University Press).

Stewart, M. A. (1995). "Hume's Historical View of Miracles," in M. A. Stewart (ed.), *Hume and Hume's Connexions* (University Park, PA: Pennsylvania State University Press), pp. 171–200.

—— (2000). "The Dating of Hume's Manuscripts," in Paul Wood (ed.), *The Scottish Enlightenment: Essays in Reinterpretation* (Rochester, NY: University of Rochester Press), pp. 267–314.

—— (2002). "Two Species of Philosophy: The Historical Significance of the First *Enquiry*," in Peter Millican (ed.), *Reading Hume on Human Understanding: Essays on the First Enquiry* (Oxford: Clarendon Press), pp. 67–95.

—— (2005). "Hume's Intellectual Development," in M. Frasca-Spada and P. J. E. Kail (eds.), *Impressions of Hume* (Oxford: Oxford University Press), pp. 11–58.

Stewart, M. A. (ed.) (1990). *Studies in the Philosophy of the Scottish Enlightenment* (Oxford: Clarendon Press).

Stewart, M. A. and Wright, John P. (eds.) (1994). *Hume and Hume's Connexions* (Edinburgh: Edinburgh University Press).

Stove, D. C. (1965/1966). "Hume, Probability, and Induction," *Philosophical Review*, 74, pp. 160–77, repr. in Vere Chappell (ed.), *Hume: A Collection of Critical Essays* (Garden City, NY: Doubleday, 1966), pp. 187–212.

—— (1973). *Probability and Hume's Inductive Scepticism* (Oxford: Clarendon Press).

Strawson, Galen (1989). *The Secret Connexion: Causation, Realism and David Hume* (Oxford: Clarendon Press).

—— (2000). "David Hume: Objects and Power," in Rupert Read and Kenneth A. Richman (eds.), *The New Hume Debate* (London: Routledge), pp. 31–51.

Strawson, P. F. (1952). *Introduction to Logical Theory* (London: Methuen).

—— (1958). "On Justifying Induction," *Philosophical Studies*, 9, pp. 20–1.

—— (1982). "Freedom and Resentment," in Gary Watson (ed.), *Free Will* (Oxford: Oxford University Press).

—— (1985). *Skepticism and Naturalism: Some Varieties* (New York: Columbia University Press).

Streminger, Gerhard (1994). *David Hume: Sein Leben und sein Werk* (*David Hume: His Life and Work*) (Paderborn, Munich, Vienna, Zurich: Ferdinand Schoeningh).

Stroud, Barry (1977). *Hume* (London: Routledge and Kegan Paul).

—— (1991). "Hume's Scepticism: Natural Instincts and Philosophical Reflection," in Margaret Atherton (ed.), *The Empiricists: Critical Essays on Locke, Berkeley, and Hume* (Lanham, MD: Rowman & Littlefield), pp. 229–52.

—— (1993). "'Gilding or Staining' the World with 'Sentiments' and 'Phantasms'," *Hume Studies*, 19, pp. 253–72.

—— (1994). "Scepticism, 'Externalism', and the Goal of Epistemology," in *Understanding Human Knowledge* (Oxford: Clarendon Press, 2000), pp. 139–54.

—— (1997). *Hume* (London: Routledge and Kegan Paul).

Sturgeon, Nicholas (2001). "Moral Skepticism and Moral Naturalism in Hume's *Treatise*," *Hume Studies*, 27, pp. 3–84.

—— (forthcoming). "Hume on Reason and Passion," in Donald Ainslie (ed.), *Hume's "Treatise": A Critical Guide* (Cambridge: Cambridge University Press).

Swain, Corliss (1991). "Being Sure of Oneself: Hume on Personal Identity," *Hume Studies*, 17, pp. 107–24.

Swinburne, Richard (1970). *The Concept of Miracle* (London: Macmillan).

—— (1974). *The Justification of Induction* (London: Oxford University Press).

—— (1979). *The Existence of God* (Oxford: Clarendon Press, 1991).

—— (1995). "Theodicy, Our Well-being, and God's Rights," *International Journal for the Philosophy of Religion*, 38, pp. 75–91.

Taylor, Gabriele (1985). *Pride, Shame and Guilt* (Oxford: Clarendon Press).

Taylor, Jacqueline (1998). "Justice and the Foundations of Social Morality," *Hume Studies*, 24, pp. 5–30.

—— (2002). "Hume on the Standard of Virtue," *Journal of Ethics*, 6, pp. 43–62.

—— (forthcoming). "Hume's Later Moral Philosophy," in David Fate Norton and Jacqueline Taylor (eds.), *The Cambridge Companion to Hume*, 2nd edn. (Cambridge: Cambridge University Press).

Teichgraeber, R. F. (1986). *"Free Trade" and Moral Philosophy: Rethinking the Sources of Adam Smith's "Wealth of Nations"* (Durham: Duke University Press).

Tindal, Matthew (1730). *Christianity as Old as the Creation* (New York: Garland Publishers, 1978).

Toland, John (1696). *Christianity Not Mysterious*, ed. Gunther Gawlick (Stutttgart-Bad Cannstatt: Friedrich Frommann, 1964).

Tooley, Michael (2003). "Causation and Supervenience," in Michael J. Loux and Dean W. Zimmerman (eds.), *The Oxford Handbook of Metaphysics* (New York: Oxford University Press), pp. 386–434.

Townsend, Dabney (2001). *Hume's Aesthetic Theory: Taste and Sentiment* (New York: Routledge).

Traiger, Saul (1985). "Flage on Hume's Account of Memory," *Hume Studies*, 12, pp. 166–72.

—— (1994). "Beyond Our Senses: Recasting Book I, Part III of Hume's *Treatise*," *Hume Studies*, 20, pp. 241–59.

Tweyman, Stanley (1991). "Introduction," in Stanley Tweyman (ed.), *David Hume: Dialogues concerning Natural Religion in Focus* (London and New York: Routledge).

Tweyman, Stanley (ed.) (1995). *David Hume: Critical Assessments*, vol. 3 (London: Routledge).

—— (1996). *Hume on Miracles* (Bristol: Thoemmes Press).

Urmson, John (1967). "Memory and Imagination," *Mind*, 76, pp. 83–91.

Van Cleve, James (1984). "Reliability, Justification, and the Problem of Induction," *Midwest Studies in Philosophy*, 9, pp. 555–67.

Van Inwagen, Peter (1995). *God, Knowledge and Mystery: Essays in Philosophical Theology* (Ithaca, NY: Cornell University Press).

Van Roojen, Mark (1995). "Humean Motivation and Humean Rationality," *Philosophical Studies*, 79, pp. 37–57.

Vodraska, S. (1981). "Hume's Moral Enquiry: An Analysis of Its Catalogue," *Philosophical Topics*, 2, pp. 79–108.

Voltaire, F.-M. A. (1733). *Letters on England*, trans. L. Tancock (Harmondsworth: Penguin, 1980).

Wallace, R. J. (1990). "How to Argue about Practical Reason," *Mind*, 99, pp. 355–85.

—— (1996). *Responsibility and the Moral Sentiments* (Cambridge: Harvard University Press).

Watson, Gary (1990). "On the Primacy of Character," in Flanagan and Rorty (eds.), *Identity, Character, and Morality: Essays in Moral Psychology* (Cambridge: MIT Press).

Watson, Gary (ed.) (2003). *Free Will* (Oxford: Oxford University Press).

Waxman, Wayne (1992). "Hume's Quandary concerning Personal Identity," *Hume Studies*, 18, pp. 233–54.

—— (1994). *Hume's Theory of Consciousness* (Cambridge: Cambridge University Press).

—— (1996). "The Psychologistic Foundations of Hume's Critique of Mathematics," *Hume Studies*, 22, pp. 123–69.

—— (2004). *Kant and the Empiricists: Understanding Understanding* (New York: Oxford University Press).

Weller, Cass (2002). "The Myth of Original Existence," *Hume Studies*, 28, pp. 195–230.

Wennerlind, C. (2005). "David Hume's Monetary Theory Revisited: Was He Really a Quantity Theorist and an Inflationist?" *Journal of Political Economy*, 113, pp. 223–37.

Wexler, Victor G. (1979). *David Hume and the History of England* (Philadelphia: American Philosophical Society).

Whelan, Frederick (1985). *Order and Artifice in Hume's Political Philosophy* (Princeton, NJ: Princeton University Press).

Williams, Bernard (1978). *Descartes: The Project of Pure Enquiry* (Harmondsworth: Penguin).

—— (1980). "Internal and External Reasons," in B. Williams, *Moral Luck* (Cambridge: Cambridge University Press).

—— (2002). *Truth and Truthfulness: An Essay on Genealogy* (Princeton, NJ: Princeton University Press).

Williams, Michael (1977). *Groundless Belief: An Essay on the Possibility of Epistemology* (New Haven, CT: Yale University Press).

Wilson, Fred (1989). "The Logic of Probabilities in Hume's Argument against Miracles," *Hume Studies*, 15, pp. 255–75.

—— (1997). *Hume's Defence of Causal Inference* (Toronto: University of Toronto Press).

Wilson, Kelly G., O'Donohue, William T., and Hayes, Steven C. (2001). "Hume's Psychology, Contemporary Learning Theory, and the Problem of Knowledge Amplification," *New Ideas in Psychology*, 19, pp. 1–25.

Winkler, Kenneth (1991). "The New Hume," *Philosophical Review*, 100, pp. 541–79.

—— (1999). "Hume's Inductive Skepticism," in Margaret Atherton (ed.), *The Empiricists: Critical Essays on Locke, Berkeley, and Hume* (Lanham, MD: Rowman & Littlefield), pp. 183–212.

551

—— (2000). "The New Hume," in Rupert Read and Kenneth A. Richman (eds.), *The New Hume Debate* (London: Routledge), pp. 52–87.

Winters, Barbara (1979). "Hume on Reason," *Hume Studies*, 5, pp. 20–35.

Wittgenstein, Ludwig (1958). *Philosophical Investigations*, trans. G. E. M. Anscombe (Oxford: Basil Blackwell).

Wollaston, William (1724). *The Religion of Nature Delineated* (London: S. Palmer; repr. New York: Garland Publishing, 1978).

Wolterstorff, Nicholas (1995). *Divine Discourse* (Cambridge: Cambridge University Press).

—— (1996). *John Locke and the Ethics of Belief* (Cambridge: Cambridge University Press).

Wood, P. B. (1989). "The Natural History of Man in the Scottish Enlightenment," *History of Science*, 27, pp. 89–123.

Woolhouse, R. S. (1988). *The Empiricists* (Oxford: Oxford University Press).

Wootton, David (1990). "Hume's 'Of Miracles'," in M. A. Stewart (ed.), *Studies in the Philosophy of the Scottish Enlightenment* (Oxford: Oxford University Press).

—— (1993). "David Hume, 'the Historian'," in D. F. Norton (ed.), *Cambridge Companion to Hume* (Cambridge: Cambridge University Press), pp. 281–312.

Wright, John P. (1983). *The Sceptical Realism of David Hume* (Manchester: Manchester University Press).

—— (1996). "Hume, Descartes and the Materiality of the Soul," in G. A. J. Rogers and Sylvana Tomaselli (eds.), *The Philosophical Canon in the Seventeenth and Eighteenth Centuries: Essays in Honour of John W. Yolton* (Rochester, NY: University of Rochester Press), pp. 175–90.

—— (2000). "Hume's Causal Realism: Recovering a Traditional Interpretation," in Rupert Read and Kenneth A. Richman (eds.), *The New Hume Debate* (London: Routledge), pp. 88–99.

Yandell, Keith E. (1990). *Hume's "Inexplicable Mystery": His Views on Religion* (Philadelphia: Temple University Press).

Yeats, William Butler (1930). "For Anne Gregory," in Oscar Williams (ed.), *The Mentor Book of Major British Poets* (New York: New American Library, 1963).

Yolton, J. (1983). *Thinking Matter: Materialism in Eighteenth-century Britain* (Oxford: Basil Blackwell).

—— (1991). *Locke and French Materialism* (Oxford: Clarendon Press).

Index

Note: "n." after a page number indicates the number of a note on that page.